Croatia

written and researched by

Jonathan Bousfield

ROUGH GUIDES

www.roughguides.com

Introduction to

Croatia

With nearly 2000km of rocky, indented shore and more than 1000 islands, many blanketed in luxuriant Mediterranean vegetation, Croatia boasts one of the most dramatic stretches of coastline that Europe has to offer. Despite the region's popularity as a package destination for over four decades, exploitation of the coastal settlements has been kept in check, and there are still enough off-the-beaten-track islands, quiet coves and stone-built fishing villages to make you feel as if you're visiting one of southern Europe's most unspoilt areas. As a bonus, many of Croatia's coastal towns and cities are living museums of Mediterranean culture, generously sprinkled with historical remains from Roman times onwards. The rest of the country isn't devoid of interest either: inland, a varied profusion of mountains, lakes and bird-inhabited wetlands provide plenty of interest for the nature lover.

The country has come a long way since the early 1990s, when within the space of half a decade – almost uniquely in contemporary Europe – it experienced the collapse of communism, a war of national survival and the securing of **independence**. Croatia is now once again an optimistic, welcoming and safe

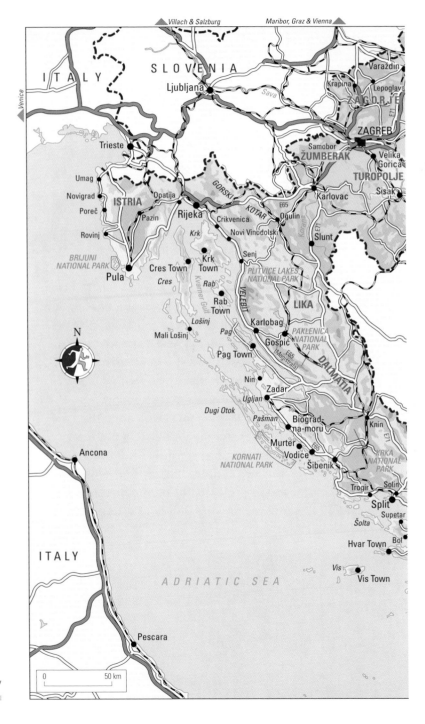

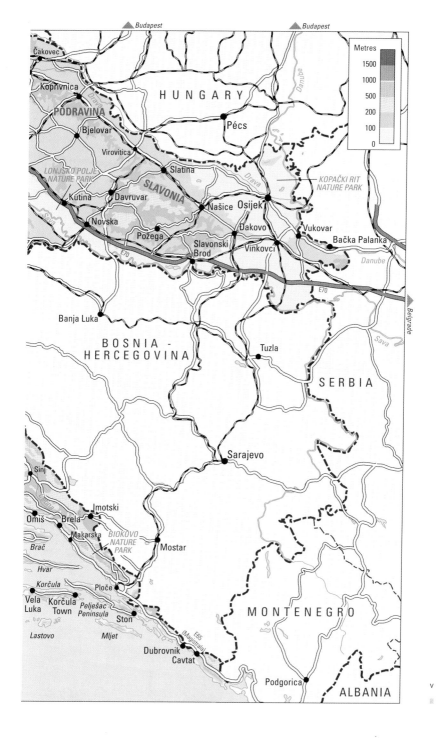

Fact file

● Croatia (**Hrvatska** in Croatian) is a crescent-shaped country of 4.5 million people. Roughly 85 percent of the population are **Croats**, who speak a Slavic language akin to Serbian and Bosnian, and practise the **Catholic Christian** faith. There is also a sizeable **Serbian** population (about thirteen percent of the total), who belong to the **Orthodox Church** and are concentrated along Croatia's borders with Bosnia-Hercegovina and Serbia.

● Croatia is a **parliamentary democracy** with a directly elected – though nowadays largely ceremonial – president as head of state. The Croatian parliament, the **Sabor**, comprises two houses – the 151-member Zastupnički dom (House of Representatives), from which the prime minister and most of his cabinet are usually chosen; and the 68-member Županijski dom (House of Regional Representatives).

● **Tourism** is Croatia's most important industry, and is increasingly seen as the cash cow which will support all other branches of the economy. The prime exports are textiles, pharmaceuticals and agricultural products. Croatia's heavy industries have not found the transition from state ownership to a market economy easy – most notably shipbuilding, which was one of Croatia's prime earners in the 1970s and 1980s, and almost totally collapsed in the 1990s.

destination, and visitors will be struck by the tangible sense of pride that independent statehood has brought, and the feeling of togetherness and unity that the experience of war has engendered. National culture is a far from one-dimensional affair, however, and much of Croatia's individuality is due to its geographical position straddling the point at which the sober central European virtues of hard work and order collide with the spontaneity, vivacity and taste for the good things in life that characterizes the countries of southern Europe – a cultural blend of Mitteleuropa and Mediterranean which gives Croatia its particular flavour. Not only that, but the country also stands on one of the great faultlines of European civilization, the point at which the Catholicism of Central Europe meets the Islam and Orthodox Christianity of the East. Though Croats traditionally see themselves as a Western people, distinct from the other South Slavs who made up the former state of Yugoslavia, many of the hallmarks

The most attractive sweeps of pebble beach are at Bol, on the island of Brač

of **Balkan culture** – patriarchal families, hospitality towards strangers, and a fondness for grilled food – are as common in Croatia as in any other part of southeastern Europe, suggesting that the country's relationship with its neighbours is more complex than many Croats will admit.

National sensitivity about such matters has its roots in Croatia's troubled relationship with the **Serbs**, who arrived in southeastern Europe at around the same time, some fifteen hundred years ago, and whose language is almost identical to Croatian. Historical circumstances later drove the two groups psychologically and culturally apart, even though they often continued to live together – the fact that so many areas of Croatia and Bosnia-Hercegovina were ethnically mixed is one reason why the break-up of Yugoslavia was such a tragically messy affair. Despite the events of recent years, however, the destinies of Croats and Serbs look set to remain intertwined: there's still a sizeable Serb minority within Croatia, and Serbs who fled the country in the wake of the Croatian army's campaigns in 1995 are (officially, at least) being encouraged to return.

Bringing life back to war-damaged areas and resettling both Croatian and Serbian refugees is just one of the problems faced by a country which continues to suffer many of the ills experienced by post-communist societies in general: the collapse of outdated industries, high unemployment, low wages for the majority, and the rise of a new entrepreneurial class which is often flamboyantly

Island hopping

The main feature of Croatia's coastline is its string of islands, linked to the mainland and with one another by regular ferries. It's here that the country's laid-back Mediterranean character reveals itself to the full: even on popular islands like Rab, Hvar and Korčula you'll find the pace of life more relaxed, the countryside more unspoilt, and the cicadas more vociferous than on the mainland. Many of the bigger islands boast modern hotels and a fully developed tourist industry, although package-oriented culture tends to fade into the distance the further out to sea you get – Vis and Lastovo are particularly favoured by independent travellers. Offering a more or less total escape from urban life are the many smaller islands which have no hotels at all – although there are plenty of eager landladies offering private rooms – and precious little infrastructure: car-free Silba and Veli Drvenik are easily accessible from the mainland, yet exude a half-abandoned, end-of-the-world appeal once you arrive. For true connoisseurs of desert-island idylls, the middle-of-nowhere cottages available for rent on the Kornati islands offer the perfect getaway – although you'll have to book well in advance.

corrupt. Tourism was always Croatia's biggest source of income before the war, and the return of holiday-makers to the Adriatic coast has been eagerly welcomed by the Croats. Unlike many of her Eastern European neighbours, however, Croatia was initially slow to receive aid and investment from the West, until elections in January 2000 removed a nationalist, anti-Western government from office. Since then, the country has applied for **EU membership**, and its international standing has improved immeasurably.

Where to go

Croatia's underrated capital **Zagreb** is a typical Central European metropolis, combining elegant nineteenth-century buildings with plenty of cultural diversions and a vibrant café life. It's also a good base for trips to the undulating hills and charming villages of the rural **Zagorje** and **Žumberak** regions to the north and west, and to the well-preserved Baroque town of **Varaždin** to the northeast.

The rest of **inland Croatia** provides plenty of opportunities for relaxed exploring. Stretching east from Zagreb, the plains of **Slavonia** form the richest agricultural parts of Croatia, with seemingly endless corn and sunflower fields fanning out from handsome, Habsburg-era provincial towns such as **Osijek** and **Vukovar** – although the latter was almost totally destroyed in a

Pršut

Croatia's foremost culinary delicacy is *pršut*, the home-cured ham made in inland Istria and Dalmatia, where it's common for families to own a handful of pigs. The ham you'll find served up in restaurants usually comes from these suppliers – the industrially produced, vacuum-packed stuff sold in supermarkets can't really compare for succulence.

The pigs are slaughtered in late autumn, and the hind legs from which *pršut* is made are meticulously washed and salted. The meat is then flattened under rocks or in a wooden press to encourage any remaining blood to seep out, and may be repeatedly removed, cleaned, salted and flattened until all traces of red juices have disappeared. It is then hung outside the house to be dried out by the Bura, a cold, dry wind which sweeps down to the coast from inland Croatia. After that, the ham is hung indoors to mature, ready to be eaten the following summer. *Pršut* from Dalmatia is usually smoked at some stage during the maturing period, while that from Istria is left as it is – producing a significant difference in flavour between the two regions' produce.

notoriously bitter siege during the 1991–95 war and will take time to rebuild. Inland Croatia also offers numerous **hiking** opportunities: **Mount Medvednica**, just above Zagreb, or the **Samoborsko gorje** just to the west of the capital are good for gentle rambling, while the mountains of the **Gorski kotar** between Zagreb and the sea offer more scope for strenuous hikes. Also lying between Zagreb and the coast, and easily visited from either, are the deservedly hyped **Plitvice Lakes**, an enchanting sequence of forest-fringed turquoise pools linked by miniature waterfalls.

Croatia's lengthy stretch of coastline, together with its islands, is big enough to swallow up any number of tourists. At the northern end, the peninsula of **Istria** contains many of the country's most developed resorts, along with old Venetian towns like **Poreč** and

Religious feast days

As befits a devoutly Catholic
country, the Croatian year is
peppered with religious feasts and
holidays. The pre-Lenten carnival
(*karneval*, often known as *fašnik* in
inland Croatia, *pust* on the Adriatic)
reaches a climax on Shrove
Tuesday or the weekend immediately preceding it, when there are
processions and masked revelry in
towns all over Croatia. Easter week
is characterized by solemn processions in many places, especially
Hvar and Korčula. More important
still is the Assumption (Aug 15),
when churches throughout the
country hold special services and
large pilgrimages are made to
Marian shrines such as Marija
Bistrica near Zagreb, Sinj in the
Dalmatian hinterland, and Trsat
near Rijeka. The Birth of the Virgin
(Sept 8) is only slightly less
important in the Catholic calendar,
and is celebrated in similar
fashion.

Rovinj, rubbing shoulders with the
raffish port of **Pula**, home to some
impressive Roman remains. Inland
Istria is characterized by sleepy hilltop
villages, often dramatically situated,
such as **Motovun**, **Grožnjan**, **Roč**
and **Hum** – each mixing medieval
architecture with rustic tranquillity.

The island-scattered **Kvarner Gulf**,
immediately south of Istria, is presided
over by the city of **Rijeka**, a hard-
edged industrial centre and the
Adriatic's most important transport
hub. Close by are a clutch of resorts
that were chic high-society hangouts
in the late nineteenth century and
retain a smattering of belle-époque
charm: quaint, diminutive **Lovran**, and
the larger, more developed **Opatija**
and **Crikvenica**. Not far offshore, the
Kvarner islands of **Cres**, **Lošinj** and
Krk have long been colonized by the
package-holiday crowds, although
each has retained its fair share of quiet

seaside villages and tranquil coves, while the capital of **Rab**, south of Krk, is arguably the best-preserved medieval town in the northern Adriatic.

Beyond the Kvarner Gulf lies **Dalmatia**, a dramatic, mountain-fringed stretch of coastline studded with islands. It's a stark, arid region where fishing villages and historic towns cling to a narrow coastal strip rich in figs, olives and subtropical vegetation. Northern Dalmatia's main city is **Zadar**, whose busy central alleys are crammed with medieval churches. From here, ferries serve a chain of laid-back islands such as **Silba**, **Ugljan**, **Pašman** and the ruggedly beautiful **Dugi otok** – none of them sees many

> A clutch of resorts were chic high-society hangouts in the late nineteenth century and retain a smattering of belle-époque charm

package tourists, and they're enticingly relaxing as a result. Despite being the site of an unmissable Renaissance cathedral, middle Dalmatia's main town, **Šibenik**, is the least compelling of the region's urban centres, but makes a good staging post en route to the waterfalls of the **River Krka** just inland, and the awesome, bare islands of the **Kornati archipelago**.

Croatia's second city, **Split**, is southern Dalmatia's main town, a vibrant and chaotic port with an ancient centre moulded around the palace of the Roman emperor, Diocletian. It's also the obvious jumping-off point for

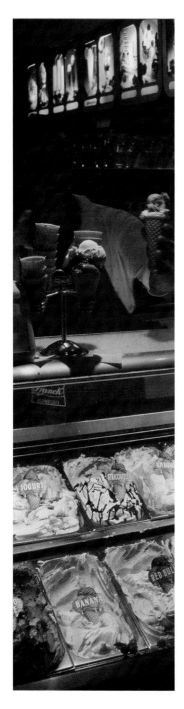

some of the most enchanting of Croatia's islands. The closest of these to the city is **Brač**, where you'll find lively fishing villages and some excellent beaches, while nearby **Hvar** and **Korčula** feature smallish towns brimming with Venetian architecture and numerous beaches. Slightly further afield, the islands of **Vis** and **Lastovo**, which were closed to tourists until the late 1980s, remain particularly pristine.

South of Split lies the walled medieval city of **Dubrovnik**, site of an important arts festival in the summer and a magical place to be whatever the season. Much of the damage inflicted on the town during the 1991–95 war has been repaired, and tourists have been quick to return. Just offshore lie the sparsely populated islands of **Koločep**, **Lopud** and **Šipan** – oases of rural calm only a short ferry ride away from Dubrovnik's tourist bustle. Also reachable from Dubrovnik is one of the Adriatic's most beautiful islands, the densely forested and relaxingly serene **Mljet**.

Most Adriatic **beaches** are pebbly or rocky affairs, and on some parts of the coast man-made concrete bathing platforms make up for the lack of a proper strand. The most attractive sweeps of pebble beach are at **Bol**, on the island of Brač, and at the towns lining the **Makarska Riviera** south of Split. Sandy beaches are rare, though glorious examples can be found at **Baška** on the island of Krk, the **Lopar peninsula** on Rab, or **Lumbarda** on Korčula.

When to go

Croatia's climate follows two patterns: **Mediterranean** on the coast, with warm summers and mild winters, and **continental** inland – slightly hotter during the summer, and extremely cold in winter, with average daily temperatures barely scraping freezing from December to February. **July and August** constitute the peak season on the Adriatic, and this is definitely the time to visit if busy beaches and lively café life are what you're looking for. Many Croats make their way to the coast at this time, and social and cultural activity in the inland cities tends to dry up as a result. Peak-season daytime temperatures can be roasting, both on the coast and inland, and dawn-to-dusk sightseeing can be a gruelling experience at the height of summer. Hotel accommodation soon fills up in the peak season, and it may be more relaxing to travel in **June and September**, when there is significantly less pressure on facilities. From October to May the coast can be very quiet

Average temperatures (°C)

	Jan	Feb	March	April	May	June	July	Aug	Sept	Oct	Nov	Dec
Dubrovnik												
	8.3	9.1	11.2	13.9	17.8	22.2	25.6	25.0	22.3	17.8	12.9	10.2
Split												
	7.5	8.5	11.5	12.8	18.9	23.9	26.7	26.1	22.8	16.7	12.5	9.5
Zagreb												
	0	1.2	5.5	11	16	18.7	22.3	21.8	15.6	12.3	5.4	2.3

indeed, and many hotels and tourist attractions may well shut up shop for the winter. **Autumn** is a good time to enjoy inland Istria and national-park areas like the Plitvice Lakes and the River Krka, when the woodland colours produced by the mixture of deciduous and evergreen trees are at their best. Given the innocuous winters on the Adriatic coast, urban sightseeing in historic centres such as Zadar, Split and Dubrovnik can be enjoyable at any time of year. It's also worth bearing in mind that hotel prices on the Adriatic may be up to fifty percent cheaper in winter than they are in peak season. Winters in inland Croatia are a different kettle of fish entirely: snow is common here over this period, and can be a picturesque backdrop to sightseeing, although transport in highland areas is frequently disrupted as a result. **Spring** is well into its stride by mid-March, and in southern Dalmatia the sea might be warm enough to swim in by mid- to late May.

things not to miss

It's not possible to see everything that Croatia has to offer in one trip – and we don't suggest you try. What follows is a selective and subjective taste of the country's highlights, from Baroque palaces to belly-filling bean soup. They're arranged in five colour-coded categories to help you find the very best things to see, do and experience. All entries have a page reference to take you straight into the guide, where you can find out more.

01 **The Zagorje** Page **99** • In Zagreb's rural hinterland, hilltop castles such as Veliki Tabor and Trakošćan perch decoratively above vineyards, cornfields and turkey-filled farmyards.

03 Rovinj Page **167** • Riviera-town chic collides with fishing-port charm in the most Italianate of Istria's coastal resorts.

02 Vis Page **333** • The most unspoiled of the major islands, with wild mountainous scenery, secluded coves and a brace of picturesque fishing ports.

04 Café society Page **37** • Pavement cafés play a key social role in this nation of gregarious coffee-gluttons.

05 **Scuba diving** Page **46** • Fast becoming the number-one activity on the coast, offering the perfect opportunity to get up close to Croatia's colourful undersea world.

07 **The Dominican monastery, Dubrovnik**
Page **383** • The quiet cloister provides a perfect home for a small but superb collection of Renaissance paintings.

06 **Trsteno** Page **392** • Once the favoured hangout of Dubrovnik's Renaissance nobles, the clifftop gardens of Trsteno are still a premier horticultural attraction.

xvii

08 **Čigoč** Page **120** • This bucolic timber-built village in the Lonjsko polje wetlands is the famed nesting ground of white storks.

10 **Istrian hill towns** Page **180** The weather-beaten, brown-stone settlements of Motovun, Oprtalj and Grožnjan provide the perfect vantage points from which to survey the lush landscape of central Istria.

09 **Holidays on the farm** Page **33** • "Agricultural tourism" is the new buzz-phrase in Istria and northern Croatia, with an increasing number of rural families offering cosy farmhouse-style accommodation and home-made food and drink.

11 **Zagreb Folk Festival** Page **88** • The most important folklore gathering in the country, when ensembles from all over Croatia gather for three days of instrument-twanging excitement.

12 **Telašćica bay** Page **270** • Compact natural wonderland comprising rugged coastline, dramatic sea cliffs and a tangle of offshore islands.

13 **Zadar** Page **255** • Vibrant peninsula town packed with Roman ruins, Romanesque churches and café-crowded alleyways.

14 **Hvar** Page **324** • The swankiest resort on the Adriatic is also one of the most evocative, offering a welter of Renaissance palaces and churches.

15 **Walking Dubrovnik's walls** Page 376 • The briefest of trots round the battlements will serve as a breathtaking introduction to this ancient city.

16 **Grah** Page 37 • Liberally laden with paprika and pork, this tasty bean stew is Croatia's favourite stomach-filler.

17 **Diocletian's palace, Split** Page 300 • Taken over by the townsfolk centuries ago, the Roman emperor's pied-à-terre now forms the chaotic heart of the modern city.

18 **Windsurfing** Page **46** Launch your board into wind-rippled waters at surfer-friendly resorts like Bol and Viganj.

19 **Varaždin** Page **108** • A postcard-perfect Baroque town, complete with crumbling palaces, ornate churches and a unique garden cemetery.

20 **Paklenica National Park** Page **229** • A hiker's paradise, combining craggy limestone gorges, dense pine forests and meadow-carpeted alpine uplands.

21 **Sailing** Page **10** • With its richly indented coastline and tangle of offshore islands, Croatia is one of the best places in Europe for messing arond on boats.

22 **Trogir cathedral** Page **285**
The west portal of this venerable monument to medieval Christianity bears the most spectacular stone carvings in the country.

23 **Gradec, Zagreb** Page **71**
Stately ensemble of historic buildings, terracotta tiles and leafy backstreets squatting unobtrusively above the noise and bustle of the capital's modern centre.

24 **Amphitheatre, Pula** Page **156** • Imperial Rome's greatest gift to the eastern Adriatic, this awesome arena still serves as the venue for pack-em-in summertime concerts.

25 **Boat trips to the Kornati islands** Page **272** • These stark, sparsely populated islands, now a national park, form the target of spectacular boat excursions from the mainland.

26 **Truffle Days, Istria** Page **183** The start of the truffle-hunting season is marked by festivities throughout Istria in September – especially in Buzet, where the world's largest truffle omelette is eagerly scoffed by an army of celebrants.

27 **Splashing around at Skradinski buk** Page **282** • Head for the Krka National Park to admire this stunning series of waterfalls.

28 **Dubrovnik Summer Festival** Page 390 • Croatia's most important arts festival – and an invigorating time to hang out in the city whether you've got tickets for the performances or not.

29 **Plitvice Lakes** Page 144 • A bewitching sequence of foaming waterfalls and turquoise lakes, hemmed in by forest-clad hills.

30 **Grilled fish** Page 35 • The rich waters of the Adriatic produce enough varieties of fish to fill an aquatic encyclopedia; expertly grilled, they're the perfect centrepiece to any meal.

Contents

Using this Rough Guide

We've tried to make this Rough Guide a good read and easy to use. The book is divided into six main sections, and you should be able to find whatever you want in one of them.

Colour section

The front colour section offers a quick tour of Croatia. The **introduction** aims to give you a feel for the place, with suggestions on where to go. We also tell you what the weather is like and include a basic country fact file. Next, our author rounds up his favourite aspects of Croatia in the **things not to miss** section – whether it's fortified hill towns, folk festivals or fish suppers. Right after this comes a full **Contents** list.

Basics

You've decided to go and the Basics section covers all the **pre-departure** nitty-gritty to help you plan your trip. This is where to find out which airlines fly to your destination, what paperwork you'll need, what to do about money and insurance, about Internet access, food, security, public transport, car rental – in fact just about every piece of **general practical information** you might need.

Guide

This is the heart of the Rough Guide, divided into user-friendly chapters, each of which covers a specific region. Every chapter starts with a list of **highlights** and an **introduction** that helps you to decide where to go, depending on your time and budget. Likewise, introductions to the various towns and smaller regions within each chapter should help you plan your itinerary. We start most town accounts with information on arrival and accommodation, followed by a tour of the sights, and finally reviews of places to eat and drink, and details of nightlife. Longer accounts also have a directory of practical listings. Each chapter concludes with **public transport** details for that region.

Contexts

Read Contexts to get a deeper understanding of how Croatia ticks. We include a brief **history**, a primer on Croatian **folk music**, and a detailed further reading section that reviews **books** relating to the country.

Language

The **language** section gives useful guidance for speaking Croatian and pulls together all the vocabulary you might need on your trip, including a comprehensive menu reader. Here, you'll also find a **glossary** of words and terms that are peculiar to the country.

Index + small print

Apart from a **full index**, which includes maps as well as places, this section covers publishing information, credits and acknowledgements, and also has our contact details in case you want to send in updates and corrections to the book – or suggestions as to how we might improve it.

Chapter list and map

○ Colour section

● Contents

🅑 Basics

❶ Zagreb

❷ Inland Croatia

❸ Istria

❹ The Kvarner Gulf

❺ Dalmatia

❻ Dubrovnik and around

🅖 Contexts

🅛 Language

🅘 Index

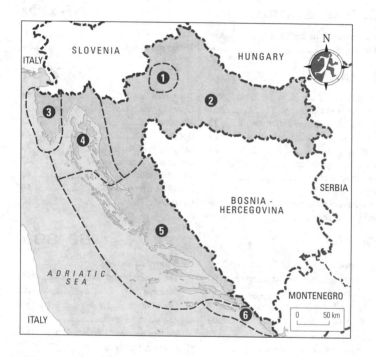

Contents

Colour section   i–xxiv

Colour map of the country ....iv–v
Where to go viii
When to go xiii
Things not to miss xv

Basics   7–51

Getting there 9
Visas and red tape 21
Information, websites and maps 22
Insurance 24
Health......................................25
Costs, money and banks 25
Getting around 27
Accommodation 31
Eating and drinking 34
Communications 38
The media 39
Opening hours, public holidays and
  festivals.................................40
Sport 44
Outdoor pursuits 45
Crime and personal safety..................47
Work and study 48
Travellers with disabilities 49
Directory 50

Guide   53–399

❶ **Zagreb** 53–93
  Arrival, information and transport 60
  Accommodation...........................64
  Trg bana Jelačića and around 67
  Kaptol..................................69
  Gradec 71
  Donji grad..............................75
  From Mažuranićev trg to the
    Botanical Gardens.....................78
  The suburbs 80
  Mount Medvednica 82
  Eating..................................83
  Drinking 85
  Nightlife and entertainment 87
  Shopping 91
  Travel details 93

❷ **Inland Croatia** 95–147
  The Zagorje 99
  Varaždin 108
  Čakovec................................112
  Koprivnica and Hlebine 114
  The Turopolje and Lonjsko polje 116
  Slavonia 123
  Samobor 135
  Zagreb to Karlovac.....................137
  West of Karlovac: the Gorski kotar....142
  South of Karlovac:
    the Plitvice Lakes 144
  Travel details 147

❸ **Istria** 149–190
  Pula 154
  The Brijuni Islands 163
  Vodnjan and Bale.......................165
  Rovinj.................................167
  The Limski kanal and Vrsar 171
  Poreč..................................172
  Novigrad, Umag and Savudrija 175
  Pazin and Beram 177
  Dvigrad and Svetvinčenat 179
  Gračišće and around 179

Motovun and Oprtalj 180
Grožnjan..181
Buzet, Roč, Hum and around 182
Labin and around 187
Travel details 189

❹ **The Kvarner Gulf** 191–242
Rijeka 194
The Opatija Riviera.........................202
Cres and Lošinj 208
Krk 216
Crikvenica and Novi Vinodolski 226
Senj 226
The Paklenica National Park 229
Rab...231
Pag...239
Travel details 242

❺ **Dalmatia** 243–363
Nin 253
Zadar 255
Silba 265
Ugljan and Pašman 265
Iž...268
Dugi otok 268
Pakoštane and Lake Vrana 271
Murter and the Kornati
    archipelago 271
Vodice 273
Šibenik and around 274
The Krka National Park 281
Trogir and around...........................285
Split 292

Salona 312
Klis 313
Šolta...316
Brač 316
Hvar 322
Vis 333
Korčula...339
Lastovo 347
The Pelješac peninsula 349
Omiš...353
The Makarska Riviera.....................356
Travel details 362

❻ **Dubrovnik and around** ..365–399
Arrival, information and
    accommodation 371
The city walls 376
Along Stradun 376
Luža Square 379
The Rector's Palace 380
The cathedral and St John's
    Fortress 381
The Dominican monastery and
    museum 383
Lokrum...386
Mount Srđ 387
Eating, drinking and nightlife 388
Trsteno 392
Cavtat...392
Čilipi 394
The Elaphite Islands.......................394
Mljet 397
Travel details 398

Contexts   401–438

A brief history of Croatia 403
Croatian folk music 429

Books...435

Language   439–452

Croatian 441
Useful words and phrases 442

Food and drink 445
Glossary...450

Index + small print   453–462

Full index 455
Twenty years of Rough Guides 459
Rough Guide credits 460
Publishing information 460

Help us update 460
Acknowledgements 461
Readers' letters 461
Photo credits 462

5

Map symbols

maps are listed in the full index using coloured text

┅┅	International boundary	♛	Fortress
---	Chapter boundary	♜	Castle
▬▬	Motorway	♟	Church (regional maps)
▬ ▬	Motorway under construction	♟	Monastery
═══	Major road	⛺	Campsite
═══	Minor road	◉	Hotel
�	Steps	◼	Eating
}=====(	Tunnel	✡	Synagogue
═══	Railway	☉	Statue
▪▪▪▪▪	Funicular	ⓘ	Information office
•‑‑‑•	Cable car	⊠	Post office
‑‑‑‑‑	Footpath	@	Internet access
▪▪▪▪	Wall	⊞	Hospital
———	River	▣	Parking
— —	Ferry route	★	Bus stop
♦	Place of interest	⌬	Swimming pool
✕	Airport	▬	Building
▲	Mountain peak	⊞	Church (town maps)
⋀⋀	Mountain range	☐	Market
⌒	Cave	◯	Stadium
⚲	Waterfall	▦	Park
⩊	Marsh	▦	Beach
⌣	Bridge	⊞	Cemetery

Basics

Basics

Getting there 9

Visas and red tape 21

Information, websites and maps 22

Insurance..24

Health...25

Costs, money and banks..25

Getting around 27

Accommodation...31

Eating and drinking 34

Communications 38

The media 39

Opening hours, public holidays and festivals............40

Sport 44

Outdoor pursuits 45

Crime and personal safety...47

Work and study...48

Travellers with disabilities 49

Directory...50

Getting there

The easiest way to get to Croatia is by air, though fares from outside Europe can be expensive; a cheaper option may be to pick up a flight to a city outside Croatia (such as Trieste or Venice in Italy, Salzburg or Graz in Austria), and continue by train or bus.

Travelling **overland from Britain** is a moderately long haul, and you'll save little, if anything, by taking the train, although with an InterRail pass you can take in Croatia as part of a wider European trip. **Driving** there from Britain will involve a journey of at least 1400km, best covered over two days.

Airfares always depend on the **season**, with the highest fares in July and August, when the weather is best; you'll get the best prices during the low season, October to April (excluding Christmas and New Year when prices are hiked up and seats are at a premium). Note also that flying on weekends may add a small premium to the round-trip fare; price ranges quoted below assume midweek travel.

The cheapest ticket is usually an **Apex return**, generally valid for a trip of up to three months. It may be a good idea to note the conditions attached to these tickets: you may have to pay a penalty if you change your schedule, and the ticket may have to be booked no later than a specified number of days prior to your trip; ask your travel agent for details. It's best to book early to travel in high season, as Apex tickets for this period can sell out some time in advance.

You can often cut costs by going through a **specialist flight agent** – either a consolidator, who buys up blocks of tickets from the airlines and sells them at a discount, or a **discount agent**, who in addition to dealing with discounted flights may also offer special student and youth fares and a range of other travel-related services such as travel insurance, rail passes, car rentals, tours and the like.

You may even find it cheaper to pick up a bargain **package deal** from one of the tour operators listed below. The main advantage of package holidays is that hotel accommodation is much cheaper than if you arrange

things independently, bringing mid-range hotels well within reach and making stays in even quite snazzy establishments a fraction of the price paid by walk-in guests. The season for Adriatic packages runs from April to October; city breaks in Zagreb and Dubrovnik are available all the year round. Croatia is also the venue for an increasing number of **maritime** packages – ranging from sailing courses for beginners to boat charter for the experienced (see p.13).

If Croatia is only one stop on a longer journey, you might want to consider buying a **Round-the-World (RTW)** ticket. Some travel agents can sell you an "off-the-shelf" RTW ticket that will have you touching down in about half a dozen cities (Zagreb is rarely included on these itineraries, but another city in a nearby country may well feature); others will have to assemble one for you, which can be tailored to your needs but is apt to be more expensive. Figure on £1000/$1500 for a RTW ticket including Croatia.

Many airlines and discount travel websites offer you the opportunity to book your tickets **online**, cutting out the costs of agents and middlemen. Good deals can often be found through discount or auction sites, as well as through the airlines' own websites.

Online booking agents

ⓦ**www.flyaow.com** Online air travel info and reservations site.

ⓦ**www.cheaptickets.com** US discount flight specialists.

ⓦ**www.lastminute.com** UK site offering good last-minute holiday package and flight-only deals.

ⓦ**www.expedia.com** Discount airfares, all-airline search engine and daily deals.

ⓦ**www.travelocity.com** Destination guides, hot Web fares and best deals for car hire, accommodation and lodging as well as fares.

Sailing and yachting packages

Croatia's island-scattered littoral is the perfect place for sailing and yachting, the season usually lasting from early May to early October. The most basic form of **sailing holiday**, involving no previous nautical experience, is a cruise in a **motorsailer** – basically a large, engine-powered yacht with simple bunk accommodation and a crew to do the work. Those who already know the ropes might consider **flotilla sailing**, in which a group of yachts with an expertly crewed lead boat embarks on a set seven- or fourteen-day itinerary. Flotilla yachts usually range from two-berth to eight-berth, so per-person prices decrease according to the size of your group. At least one of your party will have to have sailing experience – exactly how much differs from one travel company to the next.

Yacht charter can either be "bareboat" (meaning you have to sail it yourself) or "skippered" (which means you pay for the services of a local captain). Prices are subject to many variables, the most important being the model of yacht and the number of berths. For bareboat charter, at least one member of the party has to have about two years' sailing experience – again, precise requirements differ from company to company. To find out more, you can contact a specialist agency in your home country – see the relevant listings in this section – or go to ⓦ www.planetadria.com, which has information on yacht charter and accommodation in yacht-friendly resorts, with an online booking facility.

ⓦ **www.hotwire.com** Bookings from the US only. Last-minute savings of up to forty percent on regular published fares.

ⓦ **www.priceline.com** and ⓦ **www.priceline.co.uk** Name-your-own-price website that has deals at around forty percent off standard fares. You cannot specify flight times (although you do specify dates) and the tickets are non-refundable, non-transferable and non-changeable.

ⓦ **www.skyauction.com** Bookings from the US only. Auctions tickets and travel packages. The best strategy is to bid the maximum you're willing to pay, since the winner is required to pay only just enough to beat the runner-up.

ⓦ **www.travelshop.com.au** Australian website offering discounted flights, packages and insurance.

Flights from the UK and Ireland

The only year-round, direct scheduled flights **from the UK** to Croatia are with British Airways (London Gatwick to Zagreb), and Croatia Airlines (London Heathrow to Zagreb and to Split). In addition, Croatia Airlines operate seasonal routes from May to October inclusive, with flights from London Gatwick to Dubrovnik, Split and Pula; London Heathrow to Rijeka; and Manchester to Dubrovnik and Split. It takes just over two hours to fly direct from London

to Zagreb or Split, about half-an-hour longer to Dubrovnik. Flying to Croatia from a British city other than London or Manchester, or **from Ireland**, which has no direct flights to Croatia, will involve a change of plane in London or another European hub city.

An Apex ticket from London to Zagreb costs around £180 in low season, rising to about £240–260 at peak times. Flights to Split and Dubrovnik – whether direct or changing at Zagreb – tend to work out £30–40 more expensive. Airlines based in Europe are especially worth considering if you're looking for a good fare to the Adriatic coast: many of them have year-round or seasonal flights from a major European hub to Dubrovnik or Split, and connecting flights from regional UK and Irish airports ensure that you don't have to go via London.

Most package-tour operators use scheduled flights to Croatia, so there are only rarely discounted tickets on **charter flights**; that said, cheap seats on planes from Manchester and London to Pula, Split and Dubrovnik are occasionally advertised in the press or in the windows of travel agents.

If it's difficult to find a ticket to Croatia at an affordable price, consider flying to a **nearby country** and continuing your journey overland or by ferry. The budget airlines easyJet and Ryanair both fly from London Stansted to **Venice** for £60–70 return; Ryanair also flies to **Trieste**, **Ancona**, **Klagenfurt**, **Graz** and **Salzburg**, with fares on these routes coming in at between £70 and £140. The relative convenience of the above destinations largely depends on which part of Croatia you're aiming for: Venice, Trieste, Klagenfurt, Graz and Salzburg all have direct train connections with Zagreb; Trieste also enjoys daily bus connections with Istria and the Dalmatian coast. If it's Dalmatia you're aiming for, bear in mind that Ancona has numerous ferry links with Split and Zadar (see box on p.20 for details). You could also fly with the Slovene airline Adria from London Gatwick to **Ljubljana**, from where there are rail connections to Zagreb.

Airlines

Adria UK ☎020/7734 4630, www.adria.si. The Slovene national carrier flies daily from London Gatwick to Ljubljana, from where Zagreb is 2hr 30min away by train.

Aer Lingus UK ☎0845/973 7747, Republic of Ireland ☎01/705 3333 or 844 4777, ⊛www.aerlingus.ie. Flights from Cork, Dublin and Shannon to UK and European destinations, with connections to Croatia with one of Aer Lingus's partner airlines.

Air France UK ☎0845/0845 111, Republic of Ireland ☎01/605 0383, ⊛www.airfrance.co.uk. Paris–Zagreb flights, with connections from London and other major British cities, and from Dublin.

Alitalia UK ☎08705/448259, Republic of Ireland ☎01/677 5171, ⊛www.alitalia.it. Dublin to Zagreb via Milan.

Austrian Airlines UK ☎0845/601 0948, ⊛www.aua.com. Flights to Zagreb via Vienna.

British Airways ☎0845/773 3377, Republic of Ireland ☎0141/222 2345, ⊛www.britishairways.com. Daily London Heathrow–Zagreb flights; connections available from other UK airports.

British Midland UK ☎0870/607 0555, Republic of Ireland ☎01/283 8833, ⊛www.flybmi.com. Flights from Dublin and Belfast to London where they'll connect you with another airline for the trip to Croatia.

Croatian Airlines ☎020/8563 0022, ⊛www.croatiaairlines.hr. London Heathrow to Zagreb daily, and once a week to Split. Additional flights May–Oct: London Gatwick to Dubrovnik (3 weekly), Split (3 weekly), Pula (1 weekly); London Heathrow to Rijeka (1 weekly); Manchester to Dubrovnik (2 weekly) and Split (1 weekly).

CSA Czech Airlines UK ☎0870/444 3747,

Republic of Ireland ☎01/814 4626, ⊛www.csa.cz/en. To Zagreb and Split from London, Birmingham, Edinburgh and Manchester, via Prague.

easyJet UK ☎0870/600 0000, ⊛www.easyjet.com. Budget flights from London Stansted to Venice Marco Polo airport.

KLM UK ☎08705/074074, ⊛www.klm.com. Flights to Zagreb from Dublin and from UK regional airports, via Amsterdam.

Lauda Air UK ☎020/7630 5924, ⊛www.laudaair.co.uk. Flights to Zagreb from London via Vienna.

Lufthansa UK ☎0845/773 7747, Republic of Ireland ☎01/844 5544, ⊛www.lufthansa.com. To Zagreb from various UK airports, via Frankfurt.

Malev Hungarian Airlines ☎020/7439 0577, ⊛www.malev.hu. Flights from London, Manchester and Dublin to Zagreb, via Budapest.

Ryanair UK ☎0870/156 9569, Republic of Ireland ☎01/609 7800, ⊛www.ryanair.com. Budget flights from London Stansted to Venice Treviso, Trieste, Ancona, Klagenfurt, Graz and Salzburg.

Swiss UK ☎0845/601 0956, Republic of Ireland ☎1890 200 515, ⊛www.swiss.com. To Zagreb from London, Manchester, Birmingham and Dublin, via Zürich.

Turkish Airlines ☎020/7766 9300, ⊛www.turkishairlines.com. Flights to Zagreb from Istanbul, with connections from London and Manchester.

Flight and travel agents

UK

Bridge the World ☎0870/444 7474, ⊛www.bridgetheworld.com. Specializing in RTW tickets, with good deals aimed at the backpacker market.

Co-op Travel Care ☎0870/112 0099, ⊛www.travelcareonline.com. Flights and holidays around the world.

Destination Group ☎020/7400 7045, ⊛www.destination-group.com. Good discount airfares.

Flightbookers ☎0870/010 7000, ⊛www.ebookers.com. Low fares on an extensive selection of scheduled flights.

North South Travel ☎ & ☎01245/608291, ⊛www.northsouthtravel.co.uk. Offers discounted fares worldwide; profits are used to support projects in the developing world.

Premier Travel ☎028/7126 3333, ⊛www.premiertravel.uk.com. Discount flight specialists.

Rosetta Travel ☎ 028/9064 4996, ⊛ www
.rosettatravel.com. Flight and holiday agent.
STA Travel ☎ 0870/160 0599,
⊛ www.statravel.co.uk. Low-cost flights and tours
for students and under-26s, though other
customers welcome.
Trailfinders UK ☎ 020/7628 7628,
⊛ www.trailfinders.co.uk. Resourceful travel agent
geared up for independent travellers.
Travel Cuts UK ☎ 020/7255 2082 or 7255 1944,
⊛ www.travelcuts.co.uk. Canadian company
specializing in budget, student and youth travel
and RTW tickets.

Republic of Ireland

Aran Travel International ☎ 091/562 595,
⊛ homepages.iol.ie/~arantvl/aranmain.htm. Good-
value flights to all parts of the world.
CIE Tours International ☎ 01/703 1888,
⊛ www.cietours.ie. General flight and tour agent.
Joe Walsh Tours ☎ 01/676 0991,
⊛ www.joewalshtours.ie. General budget fares
agent.
Lee Travel ☎ 021/277 111, ⊛ www.leetravel.ie.
Flights and holidays worldwide.
McCarthy's Travel ☎ 021/427 0127,
⊛ www.mccarthystravel.ie. General flight agent.
Student & Group Travel Republic of Ireland
☎ 01/677 7834. Student and group specialists,
mostly to Europe.
Trailfinders ☎ 01/677 7888,
⊛ www.trailfinders.ie. Efficient agent for
independent travellers.
usit NOW ☎ 01/602 1600, ⊛ www.usitnow.ie.
Student and youth specialists for flights and trains.

Package deals

The **resorts** most frequently offered by British
companies are in Istria (Poreč and Rovinj),
Dalmatia (Hvar, Korčula and Makarska) and
Dubrovnik (either in Dubrovnik itself or in the
Mlini-Cavtat area just to the south). Some of
the hotels in Poreč and Dubrovnik are a bus
ride away from their respective towns (check
before you commit yourself to a particular
holiday), but almost everywhere else your
accommodation will be within walking distance of an attractive town or fishing port of
some sort, while the frequency of public
transport makes it easy to explore further.
The widest range of resorts is offered by
Croatia specialists such as Bond Tours,
Holiday Options and Europa Skylines, who
can put together customized flight-plus-
accommodation deals. Low-season (April,

May, late Sept & Oct) prices begin at about
£330 for seven days, rising to £420–450 for
two weeks. In high season (July & Aug)
expect to pay from around £450 for a week,
and from £650 for two weeks. As for **city
breaks**, a three-day stay in Zagreb or
Dubrovnik will cost £330–450 per person
depending on which grade of hotel you
choose. **Coach holidays** to Croatia work out
slightly cheaper than those involving flights –
see p.20 for details. A few specialist operators offer **naturist** holidays in the self-contained mega-resorts of Istria.

Motorsailer cruises in Dalmatia start at
around £500 for seven days. To learn the
rudiments of sailing, you can arrange a one-
week **beginner's course** – prices start at
about £550 per person. The cheapest
seven-day holiday in an eight-berth yacht is
typically around £450–500 per person (rising
to £600–700 in a two-berth yacht), depending on which part of the season you go in.
Prices rise steeply for fancier yachts. You
won't be able to charter a smallish three- to
four-berth bareboat yacht for much under
£480 per week, while prices for larger craft
can run into thousands; a skipper will cost
upwards of £60 a day extra.

Tour operators and agents

Abercrombie & Kent ☎ 0845/070 0610,
⊛ www.abercrombiekent.co.uk. Tours of Dalmatia
including Split and Dubrovnik.
Balkan Holidays ☎ 020/7543 5555,
⊛ www.balkanholidays.co.uk. Packages in Istria,
Hvar, Dubrovnik and on the Makarska Riviera; city
breaks in Zagreb.
Bond Tours ☎ 01372/745300,
⊛ www.bondtours.com. Package operator
specializing in the Dalmatian coast and islands,
with accommodation ranging from private
apartments to smart hotels. Also offer holidays in
Kornati island cottages and city breaks in Zagreb.
Bosmere Travel ☎ 01473/831518. Small family-
run hotels outside the major resorts. Also scuba
diving, painting and walking holidays.
Captivating Croatia ☎ 0870/887 0121,
⊛ www.captivating-croatia.co.uk. Makarska
Riviera, the southern Dalmatian islands, and
Dubrovnik.
Club Med ☎ 0700/258 2932,
⊛ www.clubmed.com. Operates a luxury holiday
village at Pakoštane in northern Dalmatia.
Croatian Villas ☎ 020/8368 9978,
⊛ www.croatianvillas.com. Tasteful apartments

throughout Dalmatia and the Kvarner region, with a particularly good choice of properties in Lovran and on the island of Veli Brijun.
Dalmatian and Istrian Travel ⓣ020/8749 5255. Tailor-made package deals throughout Croatia, plus Jadrolinija ferry reservations.
Europa Skylines ⓣ020/7226 4460, ⓦwww.croatiafortravellers.co.uk. Tailor-made packages using a wide choice of hotel and apartment accommodation along the Adriatic coast and to Zagreb and the Plitvice Lakes. Can also arrange "Robinson Crusoe" holidays in Kornati island cottages, fly-drive deals, and Adriatic cruises in motorsailers.
Exodus ⓣ020/8675 5550, ⓦwww.exodus.co.uk. Adventure tour operators taking small groups to Plitvice, Brač and other destinations.
Golden Sun Holidays ⓣ0870/708 5444, ⓦwww.goldensun.co.uk. Dubrovnik and Cavtat.
Holiday Options ⓣ0870/013 0450, ⓦwww.holidayoptions.co.uk. Packages to a big range of destinations in Dalmatia and the islands – from the obvious (Dubrovnik) to the not so obvious (Orebić) – plus a choice of two-centre holidays, including Croatia/Slovenia combinations, and seven-day Dalmatian cruises in motorsailers.
Inghams ⓣ020/8780 4433, ⓦwww.inghams.com. Istria and Dubrovnik.
Mercian Travel ⓣ0870/036 8372, ⓦwww.merciantravel.co.uk. Bridge-playing holidays near Dubrovnik.
Page & Moy ⓣ0870/010 6373, ⓦwww.page-moy.co.uk. Dubrovnik.
Palmair ⓣ01202/200700. Packages to Dubrovnik, Cavtat and Korčula, and two-centre holidays combining Dubrovnik and Korčula. Direct flights from Bournemouth.
Saga ⓣ0800/300 500, ⓦholidays.saga.co.uk. Holidays for the older traveller in Istria, Dubrovnik and the Makarska Riviera.
Simply Travel ⓣ020/8541 2280, ⓦwww.simply-travel.com. Upmarket tour company specializing in charming villas and hotels in the less-touristy parts of Croatia.
Solo's Holidays ⓣ020/8951 2800, ⓦwww.solosholidays.co.uk. Singles packages in Opatija.
Thomson ⓣ0870/165 0079, ⓦwww.thomson-holidays.com. Packages in Rovinj and Poreč.
Transun ⓣ0870/444 4747, ⓦwww.transun.co.uk. Packages in Istria, Dalmatia and Dubrovnik.
Travelscene ⓣ0870/777 9987, ⓦwww.travelscene.co.uk. City breaks in Zagreb.
Voyages Jules Verne ⓣ020/7616 1000. Dubrovnik.

Naturist holidays

Dune Leisure ⓣ0115/931 4110, ⓦwww.duneleisure.co.uk. Packages in the big Istrian resorts of Monsena (Rovinj), Koversada (Vrsar) and Solaris (Poreč).
Peng Travel ⓣ0870/751 8866. Packages in Istria.
Sunlovers Emsdale ⓣ01708/472715. Istria.

Sailing holidays and yacht charter

Activity-Sunvil ⓣ01932/867418, ⓦwww.activity-holidays.co.uk. One-week sailing courses, one- and two-week flotilla sailing, and bareboat and skippered charter.
Cosmos Yachting ⓣ020/8547 3577, ⓦwww.cosmosyachting.com. Individual yacht charter or skippered charter out of Zadar, Pula, Split, Dubrovnik and other ports.
Crestar Yachting ⓣ020/7730 2299. Luxury charter specialists with top-of-the-range crewed yachts and motor yachts.
Holiday Options ⓣ0870/013 0450, ⓦwww.holidayoptions.co.uk. Seven-day Dalmatian cruises in motorsailers, though note that these require you to book a week's holiday in a resort as well.
Nautilus Yachting ⓣ01732/867445, ⓦwww.nautilus-yachting.co.uk. Learn-to-sail packages based in Murter, plus bareboat yacht and motor-yacht charter from various Dalmatian ports.
Neilson ⓣ0870/333 3356, ⓦwww.neilson.com. Flotilla sailing in Dalmatia.
Sailing Holidays ⓣ020/8459 8787, ⓦwww.sailingholidays.com. Two-week flotilla sailing holidays in the central Dalmatia, Kornati and Dubrovnik areas.
Seafarer ⓣ01732/229900, ⓦwww.seafarercruises.com. Bareboat and skippered yacht charters based in Dalmatia.
Setsail Holidays ⓣ01737/764443, ⓦwww.setsail.co.uk. Yacht and motor-yacht charter out of Sukošan and Primošten; two-week flotilla sailing in Dalmatia.
Sunsail ⓣ023/9222 2222, ⓦwww.sunsail.com. One- and two-week flotilla sailing trips, and bareboat charter, out of Pula, Dubrovnik and Rogoznica (near the Kornati).
Templecraft Yacht Charters ⓣ01273/695074, ⓦwww.templecraft.com. Individual yacht charter out of Pula, Zadar and Split.
Tenrag ⓣ01227/721874, ⓦwww.tenrag.com. Yacht charter out of Pula, Zadar and Split.
Top Yacht Charter ⓣ01243/520950,

ⓦwww.top-yacht.com. Individual yacht charter out of Pula, Zadar and Split.

Flights from the US and Canada

There are currently no direct flights from North America to Croatia, though most major airlines offer one- or two-stop flights via major European cities, often in conjunction with Croatia Airlines, the national carrier. **From the US**, a midweek round-trip fare to Zagreb in low season starts at $600 from New York ($800 from US West Coast cities), rising to $1100 ($1300 from the West Coast) during high season. **From Canada**, Apex round-trip fares start at Can$1200 from Toronto and Can$1600 from Vancouver during the low season, rising to Can$1600 and Can$1900 respectively during high season.

The major Croatian travel agencies – in particular Atlas Travel Agency and TravelTime – offer an extensive selection of **packages** including fully guided tours (from US$800 for 8 days); Adriatic cruises (from US$600 for 1 week); flotilla-sailing packages (around US$650 for 1 week); cycling tours (US$950 for 8 days); canoeing and rafting tours (US$850 for 8 days) and sea-kayaking (US$1000 for 8 days). There are several other North American tour operators offering escorted and independent tours to Croatia – a number of which also include Slovenia in their itinerary.

If you just want to book accommodation and transport within Croatia, contact Atlas Travel Agency, TravelTime or the Croatian National Tourist Board. If you want to visit Croatia as part of a wider trip across Europe, you may want to get the cheapest trans-Atlantic flight you can find, and continue your journey overland – in which case it's worth considering a **Eurail pass** for train travel; see p.17 for details.

Airlines

Aeroflot US ☏1-888/340-6400, Canada ☏416/642-1653, ⓦwww.aeroflot.com. Flights from New York, Washington, Seattle, San Fransisco and Los Angeles to Zagreb via Moscow.
Air Canada ☏1-888/247-2262, ⓦwww.aircanada.ca. Flights to numerous European cities, with connections to Croatia on partner airlines.

Air France US ☏1-800/237-2747, ⓦwww.airfrance.com; Canada ☏1-800/667-2747, ⓦwww.airfrance.ca. Flights from New York, San Francisco, Montreal and Toronto to Zagreb via Paris.
Alitalia US ☏1-800/223-5730, Canada ☏1-800/361-8336, ⓦwww.alitalia.com. Flights from most major US airports to Zagreb, Dubrovnik and Split via Rome and/or Milan.
American Airlines ☏1-800/433-7300, ⓦwww.aa.com. Useful for flights from the US to major European cities (London, Frankfurt, Zürich), from where you can make your own way to Croatia.
Austrian Airlines ☏1-800/843-0002, ⓦwww.aua.com. Flights from New York and Washington to Zagreb via Vienna.
British Airways ☏1-800/247-9297, ⓦwww.british-airways.com. Flights from numerous North American airports to Zagreb via London.
CSA Czech Airlines US ☏1-877/359-6629 or 212/765-6022, Canada ☏416/363-3174, ⓦwww.czechairlines.com. Flights from New York to Zagreb and Split, via Prague.
Lufthansa US ☏1-800/645-3880, Canada ☏1-800/563-5954, ⓦwww.lufthansa-usa.com. From New York and Chicago to Zagreb, via Frankfurt or Munich.
Malev Hungarian Airlines ☏1-800/223-6884 or 212/566-9944, ⓦwww.hungarianairlines.com. New York JFK and Toronto to Zagreb via Budapest.
Swiss ☏1-800/221-4750, ⓦwww.swiss.com. Flights from Boston, Chicago, Los Angeles, Miami, Montreal, New York and Washington to Zagreb, via Zürich.
Turkish Airlines ☏1-800/874-8875 or 212/339-9650, ⓦwww.thy.com. Flights from Denver, Houston, Las Vegas, Los Angeles, Miami, Orlando and Washington to Zagreb, via Istanbul.
United Airlines Domestic ☏1-800/241-6522, international ☏1-800/538-2929, ⓦwww.ual.com. Flights from all over the US to a major European hub (such as Frankfurt), with connecting flights to Zagreb furnished by partner airlines (such as Lufthansa).
Virgin Atlantic Airways ☏1-800/862-8621, ⓦwww.virgin-atlantic.com. Flights from Los Angeles, Miami, New York and Washington to London, followed by a Croatia Airlines connection to Zagreb.

Discount travel companies

Air Brokers International ☏1-800/883-3273, ⓦwww.airbrokers.com. Consolidator and specialist in RTW tickets.

Airtech ☎212/219-7000, ✆www.airtech.com. Standby seat broker; also deals in consolidator fares.

Council Travel ☎1-800/2COUNCIL, ✆www.counciltravel.com. Nationwide organization that mostly specializes in student/budget travel. Flights from the US only.

Educational Travel Center ☎1-800/747-5551 or 608/256-5551, ✆www.edtrav.com. Student/youth discount agent.

SkyLink US ☎1-800/AIR-ONLY or 212/573-8980, Canada ☎1-800/SKY-LINK, ✆www.skylinkus.com. Consolidator.

STA Travel US ☎1-800/781-4040, Canada 1-888/427-5639, ✆www.sta-travel.com. Worldwide specialists in independent travel; also student IDs, travel insurance, car rental, rail passes, etc.

Student Flights ☎1-800/255-8000 or 480/951-1177, ✆www.isecard.com. Student/youth fares, student IDs.

TFI Tours ☎1-800/745-8000 or 212/736-1140, ✆www.lowestairprice.com. Consolidator.

Travac ☎1-800/TRAV-800, ✆www.thetravelsite.com. Consolidator and charter broker with offices in New York City and Orlando.

Travel Avenue ☎1-800/333-3335, ✆www.travelavenue.com. Full-service travel agent that offers discounts in the form of rebates.

Travel Cuts Canada ☎1-800/667-2887, US ☎1-866/246-9762, ✆www.travelcuts.com. Canadian student-travel organization.

Travelers Advantage ☎1-877/259-2691, ✆www.travelersadvantage.com. Discount travel club; annual membership fee required.

Worldtek Travel ☎1-800/243-1723, ✆www.worldtek.com. Discount travel agency for worldwide travel.

Tour operators

Abercrombie & Kent ☎1-800/323-7308 or ☎630/954-2944, ✆www.abercrombiekent.com. Upmarket tours to Dubrovnik.

Adriatic Travel ☎310/548-1446, ✆www.adriatic1.com. Adriatic cruises.

Adventure Center ☎1-800/228-8747 or ☎510/654-1879, ✆www.adventure-center.com. Dubrovnik and Dalmatia tours and cruises.

Adventures Abroad ☎1-800/665-3998 or 360/775-9926, ✆www.adventures-abroad.com. Eighteen-day guided tours of Croatia and Slovenia; departures from most major North American cities.

American Express Vacations ☎1-800/241-1700, ✆www.americanexpress.com/travel. Range of Dalmatian packages.

Atlas Travel Agency ☎1-800/442 222, ✆www.atlas-croatia.com. Croatian firm with a wide range of holidays including coach tours, sailing holidays, adventure tours (such as canoeing, rafting and sea-kayaking) and programmes for senior citizens.

Elderhostel ☎1-877/426-8056, ✆www.elderhostel.org. Specialists in educational and activity programmes, cruises and homestays for senior travellers, including several Croatia-based options.

Fugazy International ☎1-800/342-3444. Tours to Dubrovnik, Opatija and other Croatian destinations. Also a good source of discounted plane tickets to Croatia.

Globus and Cosmos ✆www.globusandcosmos.com. Dalmatia-based packages.

Insight International Tours ☎1-800/582-8380, ✆www.inusa.insightvacations.com. Tours worldwide, including the fifteen-day "Country roads of Dalmatia and the Adriatic Riviera".

International Market Place ☎1-800/641-3456, ✆www.imp-world-tours.com. Tours or one-centre holidays on the Adriatic.

Interpac Yachts ☎888/99-YACHT or 619/222-0327, ✆www.interpacyachts.com. Yacht-charter specialists.

Kompas ☎1-800/233-6422, ✆www.kompas.net. Various packages including city breaks in Dubrovnik, Split and Zagreb and customized tours.

Saga Holidays ☎1-800/343-0273, ✆www.sagaholidays.com. Vacations for the older traveller in Dubrovnik and the Makarska Riviera.

TravelTime ☎1-800/354-8728 or 718/721-1132, ✆www.traveltimeny.com. One of the main Croatian specialist operators, with a wide range of packages including guided tours, city breaks, wine-tasting and culinary tours, and programmes for senior citizens.

Wilderness Travel ☎1-800/368-2794, ✆www.wildernesstravel.com. Tours focusing on culture or hiking, including a cruise from Dubrovnik to Venice.

Flights from Australia and New Zealand

The cheapest flights to Zagreb from Australia and New Zealand usually involve a combination of two airlines and two stops en route. For example, a common combination **from Australia** would get you to Zagreb via first Singapore, then Frankfurt or Zürich. Fares on these routes range from Aus$1450 in low season to Aus$2100 in high season. You can restrict your journey to one change of plane by opting for a slightly more expensive combination – flying Sydney to Zagreb via Vienna, Frankfurt or even London will add another Aus$100–200. Flights **from New Zealand** will involve at least two stops and cost NZ$2100 in low season, rising to NZ$2500 in high season. Alternatively, you might be able to save a little money by flying to, say, Vienna and continuing overland to Croatia; if you want to see the country as part of a wider trip across Europe, it might be worth your while to consider a European rail pass (see opposite).

RTW travellers can include Zagreb as one of the stops on a Qantas/British Airways "One World" ticket (from Aus$2500/NZ$3000 depending on season and mileage) or on the RTW ticket from the Star Alliance group of airlines (ⓦwww.star-alliance.com; from Aus$2700/NZ$3300), among them Air New Zealand and Lufthansa.

There's a small number of **package-tour operators** offering holidays in Croatia from Australia and New Zealand, including accommodation, cruises along the Dalmatian coast, sightseeing packages and rail passes.

Airlines

Aeroflot Australia ⓣ02/9262 2233, ⓦwww.aeroflot.com.au. Flights from Auckland, Sydney and Wellington to Zagreb via Singapore and Moscow, involving at least one other airline.

Air New Zealand Australia ⓣ13 24 76, ⓦwww.airnz.com.au; New Zealand ⓣ0800/737 000, ⓦwww.airnz.co.nz. Two-stop flights to Croatia in conjunction with at least one other airline.

British Airways Australia ⓣ02/8904 8800, New Zealand ⓣ09/356 8690, ⓦwww.british -airways.com. Flights from Sydney to Zagreb via London.

Lauda Air Australia ⓣ1800/642 438 or 02/9251 6155, New Zealand ⓣ09/522 5948, ⓦwww.aua.com. From Sidney and Melbourne to Zagreb, via Vienna.

Lufthansa Australia ⓣ1300/655 727, ⓦwww.lufthansa-australia.com; New Zealand ⓣ09/303 1529, ⓦwww.lufthansa.com. Two-stop flights from Australia to Zagreb in partnership with at least one other airline.

Malaysia Airlines Australia ⓣ13 26 27, ⓦwww.malaysiaairlines.com.au; New Zealand ⓣ0800/777 747, ⓦwww.malaysiaairlines.co.nz. Two-stop flights from Auckland and several Australian cities to Zagreb, in partnership with at least one other airline.

Qantas Australia ⓣ13 13 13, ⓦwww.qantas.com.au; New Zealand ⓣ0800/808 767, ⓦwww.qantas.co.nz. One-stop flights from Australia to Zagreb via a major European hub, in partnership with one of several European airlines. Two-stop flights to Zagreb from New Zealand via Sydney and a European hub.

Singapore Airlines Australia ⓣ13 10 11, New Zealand ⓣ0800/808 909, ⓦwww.singaporeair.com. Two-stop flights from Sydney and Melbourne to Zagreb via Singapore and a European city, involving at least one other airline.

Travel agents

Flight Centres Australia ⓣ13 31 33 or 02/9235 3522, ⓦwww.flightcentre.com.au; New Zealand ⓣ0800 243 544 or 09/358 4310, ⓦwww.flightcentre.co.nz.

Holiday Shoppe New Zealand ⓣ0800/808 480, ⓦwww.holidayshoppe.co.nz.

Northern Gateway Australia ⓣ1800/174 800, ⓦwww.northerngateway.com.au.

STA Travel Australia ⓣ1300/733 035, ⓦwww.statravel.com.au; New Zealand ⓣ0508/782 872, ⓦwww.statravel.co.nz.

Student Uni Travel Australia ⓣ02/9232 8444, ⓦwww.sut.com.au; New Zealand ⓣ09/379 4224, ⓦwww.sut.co.nz.

Trailfinders Australia ⓣ02/9247 7666, ⓦwww.trailfinders.com.au.

Tour operators and agents

Adriatic Adventures ⓣ02/9709 8033, ⓦwww.adriatictours.com.au. Croatian travel specialists offering packages to Adriatic resorts such as Bol, Brela and Dubrovnik.

Danube Travel Australia ⓣ03/9530 0888. Adriatic cruises and specialist tours.

Eastern Eurotours Australia ⓣ07/5591 0326 or ⓣ1800/242 353, ⓦwww.easterneurotours.com. Holidays in Dubrovnik, Split and Zagreb, and multi-centre Adriatic tours and sea cruises.

Sydney International Travel Centre ⓣ02/9299 8000, ⓦwww.sydneytravel.com.au. Among their offerings is a nine-day Dalmatia tour, including Dubrovnik and Zagreb, priced at Aus$1800 excluding flights.

By rail

Travelling to Croatia **by train** from the UK is unlikely to save money compared with flying, but can be a leisurely way of getting to the country if you plan to stop off in other parts of Europe on the way. It's certainly simpler and more cost-effective to buy a rail pass, invest in an international rail timetable (see p.18) and plan your own itinerary than to try and purchase a rail return ticket to Croatia: most ticket agents deal exclusively with super-fast, deluxe services to well-known destinations such as Venice, Salzburg and Vienna, and fares usually work out significantly more expensive than flying – a London–Venice return will set you back something in the region of £350–400. The high cost is at least partly explained by the fact that almost all through tickets from London to European destinations now use Eurostar trains, which go through the Channel Tunnel, rather than the (traditionally cheaper) ferries. It's still possible to travel by rail from London to the continent via ferry, but (unless you have a rail pass) you'll probably have to buy individual tickets for each stage of the journey.

There are two main **London–Zagreb** rail itineraries: the first is via Paris, Lausanne, Milan, Venice and Ljubljana; the second via Brussels, Cologne, Salzburg and Ljubljana. The total journey time on either route is around thirty hours, depending on connections – considerably longer if you cross the Channel by ferry rather than taking the Eurostar. If you're making a beeline for Dalmatia, consider heading for Ancona in Italy (16hr from Paris), the departure point for ferries to Zadar, Split and Dubrovnik.

Rail passes

If you're travelling across Europe by train, it's worth considering the huge array of **rail passes** available, covering regions as well as individual countries. Some have to be bought before leaving home while some can only be bought in the country for which they're valid.

Inter-Rail passes are only available to European residents, and you'll be asked to provide proof of residency before being allowed to purchase one. They come in over-26 and (cheaper) under-26 versions, and cover 28 European countries (including Turkey and Morocco) grouped together in zones:

  A Republic of Ireland/Britain
  B Norway, Sweden, Finland
  C Germany, Austria, Switzerland, Denmark
  D Czech & Slovak Republics, Poland, Hungary, Croatia
  E France, Belgium, Netherlands, Luxembourg
  F Spain, Portugal, Morocco
  G Italy, Greece, Turkey, Slovenia plus some ferry services between Italy and Greece
  H Bulgaria, Romania, Yugoslavia, Macedonia

The passes are available for 12 or 22 days (one zone only) or 1 month, and you can purchase up to three zones or a global pass covering all zones. As Croatia is in zone D, you'll need an all-zone pass (£355; £249 for under-26s) to get there from Britain or Ireland. Inter-Rail passes do not include travel between Britain and the continent, although Inter-Rail Pass holders are eligible for discounts on rail travel in the UK and cross-Channel ferries, free travel on the Brindisi–Patras ferry between Italy and Greece, plus discounts on other shipping services around the Mediterranean. The Inter-Rail Pass also gives a discount on the London–Paris Eurostar service.

Eurail passes

Non-European residents qualify for the **Eurail Pass**, which must be purchased before arrival in Europe (or from RailEurope in London by non-residents who were unable to get it at home). The Pass allows unlimited free first-class train travel in sixteen European countries, but not in Croatia or neighbouring Slovenia – so you'll have to buy a regular ticket to cover the last leg of the journey. The Pass is available in increments of 15 days, 21 days, 1 month, 2 months and 3 months. If you're under 26, you can save money with a **Eurail Youthpass**, which is valid for second-class travel or, if you're travelling with up to four other companions, a joint **Eurail Saverpass**, both of which are available in the same increments as the Eurail Pass. You stand a better chance of getting your money's worth out of a **Eurail Flexipass**, which is good for 10 or 15 days' travel within a 2-month period. This, too, comes in first-class, under-26/second-class.

Useful rail publications

The red-covered *Thomas Cook European Timetables* details schedules of over 50,000 trains in Europe, as well as timings of over 200 ferry routes and rail-connecting bus services. It's updated and issued every month; main changes are in the June edition (published end of May), which has details of the summer European schedules, and the October one (published end of Sept), which includes winter schedules; some have advance summer/winter timings also. The book can be purchased online (which gets you a ten percent discount) at ⓦ www.thomascookpublishing.com or from branches of Thomas Cook (see ⓦ www.thomascook.co.uk for your nearest branch), and costs £9.50. Their useful *Rail Map of Europe* can be purchased online for £6.95.

Further details of these passes and other Eurail permutations, and prices, can be found on ⓦ www.raileurope.com, and the passes can be purchased from one of the agents listed below.

Euro Domino passes

Only available to European residents, these are individual country passes which provide unlimited travel in 28 European and North African countries. The passes are available for between three and eight days' travel within a one-month period; prices vary depending on the country, but include most high-speed train supplements. There is a discounted youth price for those under 26, and a half-price child (age 4–11) fare. A Eurodomino pass covering Croatia itself costs around £34 for three days, £57 for eight days.

Rail contacts

UK and Ireland

Eurostar UK ☎ 0870/160 6600, ⓦ www.eurostar.com. Passenger train which goes from Waterloo International in London to Paris (3hr) or Brussels (2hr 40min). You can get through tickets – including the tube journey to Waterloo International – from Eurostar itself, from most travel agents or from mainline train stations in Britain. Inter-Rail passes give discounts on the Eurostar service.
Iarnród Éireann Dublin ☎ 01/8366 6222, ⓦ www.irishrail.ie. Inter-rail tickets.
International Rail ☎ 0870/120 1606, ⓦ www.international-rail.com. Rail passes.
Northern Ireland Railways ☎ 028/9089 9411, ⓦ www.nirailways.co.uk. Inter-rail passes.
Rail Europe UK ☎ 0870/584 8848, ⓦ www.raileurope.co.uk. Discounted fares for under-26s on a variety of European routes; also agents for Inter-Rail, Eurostar and individual European rail passes.

US & Canada

CIT Rail US ☎ 1-800/CIT-RAIL or 212/730-2400, Canada ☎ 1-800/361-7799, ⓦ www.cit-rail.com. Eurail, Europass and other rail passes.
DER Travel US ☎ 1-888/337-7350, ⓦ www.dertravel.com/rail. Eurail, Europass and many individual country passes.
Europrail International Canada ☎ 1-888/667-9734, ⓦ www.europrail.net. European rail passes.
Rail Europe US ☎ 1-877/257-2887, Canada ☎ 1-800/361-RAIL, ⓦ www.raileurope.com. Eurail agent; also sells Europass, multinational passes and most single-country passes.

Australia and New Zealand

CIT World Travel Australia ☎ 02/9267 1255 or 03/9650 5510, ⓦ www.cittravel.com.au. Eurail, Europass and Italian rail passes.
Rail Plus Australia ☎ 1300/555 003 or 03/9642 8644, ⓦ www.railplus.com.au. European rail passes.
Trailfinders Australia ☎ 02/9247 7666, ⓦ www.trailfinder.com.au. All Europe passes.

Mainline Europe

Belgian Railways ⓦ www.b-rail.be.
German Rail ⓦ www.bahn.de.

By car from the UK

Driving to Croatia is straightforward. The most direct route from the UK is to follow motorways from the Belgian coast via Brussels, Cologne, Frankfurt, Stuttgart, Munich, Salzburg and Villach as far as the Slovene capital Ljubljana, from where you can continue by ordinary road south to Rijeka on the Adriatic coast or southeast to Zagreb. An alternative approach is through France, Switzerland and Italy as far as **Ancona** on Italy's Adriatic coast, from where there are ferries to various points on the Dalmatian coast. Further down towards the heel of Italy there are ferries from **Bari** to Dubrovnik.

Note that if you're driving through Austria you'll have to buy a **vignette** (a windscreen sticker available at border crossings and petrol stations) to use the motorway system. The cheapest vignette is valid for ten days and costs €5 (£3.50/$5).

UK and Irish ferry operators

Brittany Ferries UK ☎0870/901 2400, Republic of Ireland ☎021/42 77801, ⊛www.brittanyferries.co.uk. Poole to Cherbourg; Portsmouth to Caen and St Malo; Plymouth to Roscoff and to Santander (March–Nov/Dec); Cork to Roscoff (March–Oct only).

DFDS UK ☎0870/533 3000, ⊛www.dfdsseaways.co.uk. Harwich to Hamburg; Newcastle to Amsterdam.

Hoverspeed UK ☎0870/240 8070, ⊛www.hoverspeed.co.uk. Twenty-four daily departures. Dover to Calais and Ostend; Newhaven to Dieppe.

Irish Ferries UK ☎0870/517 1717, Republic of Ireland ☎1890/313 131, ⊛www.irishferries.com. Dublin to Holyhead; Rosslare to Pembroke, Cherbourg and Roscoff. Continental services March to end Sept.

NorseMerchant Ferries UK ☎0870/600 4321, Republic of Ireland ☎01/819 2999, ⊛www.norsemerchant.com. Belfast and Dublin to Liverpool.

P&O Irish Sea UK ☎0870/242 4777, Republic of Ireland ☎1800/409 049, ⊛www.poirishsea.com. Larne to Cairnryan and to Fleetwood; Dublin to Liverpool.

P&O North Sea Ferries UK ☎01482/377 177, ⊛www.ponsf.com. Hull to Rotterdam and Zeebrugge.

P&O Portsmouth UK ☎0870/242 4999, ⊛www.poportsmouth.com. Portsmouth to Cherbourg, Le Havre and Bilbao.

P&O Stena Line UK ☎0870/600 0600, ⊛www.posl.com. Dover to Calais.

Sea Cat UK ☎0870/5523 523, Republic of Ireland ☎1800/805 055, ⊛www.seacat.co.uk. Belfast to Stranraer, to Heysham, to Troon, and to Isle of Man; Dublin to Liverpool and to Isle of Man.

Sea France UK ☎0870/571 1711, ⊛www.seafrance.com. Dover to Calais.

Stena Line UK ☎0870/570 7070, Republic of Ireland ☎01/204 7777, ⊛www.stenaline.co.uk. Harwich to the Hook of Holland; Fishguard to Rosslare; Holyhead to Dun Laoghaire and Dublin; Stranraer to Belfast.

Swansea Cork Ferries UK ☎01792/456 116, Republic of Ireland ☎021/427 1166, ⊛www.swansea-cork.ie. Cork to Swansea (no sailings Nov 7 to March 11).

Italy–Croatia ferries

Ferry services from Ancona and Bari in Italy to Croatia are run by three companies: **Jadrolinija**, **SMC** and **Adriatica Navigazione**. Foot passengers can usually buy tickets on arrival in Ancona or Bari, either from the Stazione Marittima or from travel agents around town, but if you're travelling with a vehicle it's wise to book in advance, especially in July and August. Simple deck passage between the Italian and Croatian ports costs about £32/$48 (payable in local currency), but as most crossings are overnight, consider investing an additional £10/$15 for a bed in a basic cabin. Bikes cost about £15/$22, cars £35/$50. Return tickets are usually twenty percent cheaper than two singles. Jadrolinija run a couple of weeked catamaran services in summer, charging about £35/$52 each way.

Adriatica Navigazione Zattere, 1411 Venezia ☎+39 41.781.611, ⊕+39 41.781.894, ✉adn@maritime.it; c/o Agenzia Sri, Via XXIX Settembre 10; Ancona ☎+39 71.204.915, ⊕+39 71.202.296; c/o Jadroagent, Gat Sv. Duje, Split ☎+385 21/338-335, ⊕338-334, ⊛www.jadroagent.com; in the UK, c/o Serena Holidays ☎020/7373 6548.

Jadrolinija Riva 16, Rijeka ☎+385 51/666-111, ⊕213-116, ⊛www.jadrolinija.tel.hr; Stazione Marittima Ancona ☎+39 71.204.305, ⊕+39 71.200.211; c/o P. Lorusso & Co, Via Piccini; Bari ☎+39 80.521.2840, ⊕39 80.521.8229; in the UK, c/o Dalmatian and Istrian Travel ☎020/8749 5255 or Viamare ☎020/7431 4560.

SMC Gat Sv. Duje, Split ☎+385 21/338-292, ⊕338-291, ⊛www.sem.hr; c/o Agenzia Mauro, Via Loggia 6, Ancona ☎+39 71.204.090, ⊕+39 71.202.618.

Italy–Croatia ferry timetables

Adriatica Navigazione

Ferries   Ancona–Split (2 weekly rising to 4 weekly in July & Aug).
                   Bari–Dubrovnik (1 weekly).

Jadrolinija

Ferries   Ancona–Vis–Split–Korčula (1 weekly early July to mid-Sept).
                   Ancona–Split–Hvar Stari Grad (1 weekly June–Sept rising to 4
                       weekly July & Aug).
                   Ancona–Šibenik (2 weekly June–Sept rising to 3 weekly July & Aug).
                   Ancona–Split (3 weekly).
                   Ancona–Zadar (3 weekly June–Sept rising to 5 weekly July & Aug).
                   Bari–Dubrovnik (1 weekly rising to 4 weekly in July & Aug).

Catamarans   Ancona–Božava–Zadar (1 weekly mid-June–mid-Sept).
                   Ancona–Mali Lošinj (1 weekly July & Aug)

SMC

Ferries   Ancona–Split (July–Aug: daily; April–June & Sept–Oct: 6 weekly;
                       Jan–Oct: 4 weekly).
                   Ancona–Hvar Stari Grad (2 weekly mid-July to late Aug).
                   Ancona–Vis (2 weekly mid-July to Aug).

By bus from the UK

If you really don't want to fly, the cheapest –
though hardly the most convenient – way of
getting to Croatia from the UK is by bus.
From London, a return ticket with Eurolines
costs £133 to Zagreb, £158 to Split, with a
five percent reduction for under-26s and
seniors.

Eurolines offers a **pass** for Europe-wide
travel, valid for either 15, 30 or 60 days,
between 46 European cities – no Croatian
destination is featured among these, but you
could get as far as Vienna on this pass and
pay for an additional bus or train ticket to
Zagreb once you get there.

It may be worth considering a **coach
package trip** to Croatia, although note that
only Istrian resorts are offered. The length of
the journey can be a disadvantage – out of

a nine-day holiday, you only get to spend
seven nights in Croatia.

Bus and coach-tour operators

Alfa Travel ☏ 0845/130 5666. Coach holidays to
Lovran.
Eurolines UK ☏ 0870/514 3219, Republic of
Ireland ☏ 01/836 6111, ⊛ www.eurolines.co.uk.
Daily services, via Frankfurt, from London to
Zagreb (35hr) and to Split (38hr); both journeys
require two nights on the road.
Leger ☏ 0845/130 7007, ⊛ www.leger.co.uk.
Coach tours to Poreč.
Shearings ☏ 01942/824824. Coach holidays to
Opatija.
Siesta Holidays ☏ 01642/227711. Coach
holidays to Poreč.
Skills Travel ☏ 08456/665544. Coach tours to
Poreč in Istria.

Visas and red tape

Citizens of EU countries, the US, Canada, Australia and New Zealand are allowed to enter Croatia without a visa for stays of up to ninety days. If you want to stay longer, it's easier to leave the country and re-enter than to go through the hassle of applying for an extension at the local police station.

Visitors to Croatia are required by law to **register** with the local police within 24 hours of arrival. If you're staying in a hotel, hostel or campsite, or if you've booked a private room through a recognized agency, the job of registration will be done for you. If you're staying with friends or in a room arranged privately, your hosts are supposed to register you. In practice however, they very rarely do so. This only becomes a problem if the police have reason to question you about where you're staying, which in well-touristed areas is very rare. Even if they do, official attitudes to registration are flexible: the police often turn a blind eye to tourists and hosts alike if you're merely enjoying a short holiday on the coast, but can throw you out of the country if you've been staying in Croatia unregistered for a long period of time.

There are no **customs** restrictions on the kind of personal belongings that you need for your holiday, although you are limited to 200 cigarettes, one litre of spirits and 500g of coffee. It's a good idea to declare major items – laptop computers, boats, televisions and other electronic equipment – to ensure that you can take them out of the country when you leave. Pets are allowed in providing you have a recent vaccination certificate. You can only take 2000Kn of currency with you when leaving.

Croatian embassies and consulates

Australia 14 Jindalee Crescent, O'Malley, Canberra ACT 2606 ☎ 02/6286 6988, ℻ 6286 3544, ✉ croemb@bigpond.com. Consulates: Level 4, 379 Kent St, Sydney NSW 2001 ☎ 02/6286 6988; and in Melbourne and Perth.

Canada 229 Chapel Street, Ottawa, ON K1N 7Y6 ☎ 613/562-7820, ℻ 562-7821, ⊕ www.croatiaemb.net.

Ireland Adelaide Chambers, Peter St, Dublin 8 ☎ 01/498 3018, ✉ croatianembassy@eircom.net.

New Zealand 291 Lincoln Rd, Edmonton, Auckland ☎ 09/836 5581, ℻ 836 5481, ✉ cro-consulate@xtra.co.nz.

UK 21 Conway St, London W1P 5HL ☎ 020/7387 2022, ✉ consular-dept@croatianembassy.co.uk.

US 2343 Massachusetts Ave NW, Washington, DC 20008 ☎ 202/588-5899, ℻ 588-8936, ⊕ www.croatiaemb.org. Also consulates in New York, Chicago and Los Angeles.

Information, websites and maps

The best source of general information on Croatia is the Croatian National Tourist Office, but note that most of their offices abroad prefer to deal with the public by telephone rather than admit personal callers – ring ahead and check before trying to visit them in person. The staff are generally very helpful and can usually supply brochures, accommodation details and maps of specific towns and resorts. There are no Croatian tourism offices in Ireland, Canada, Australia or New Zealand – here, either contact the Croatian embassy or consulate (see p.21) or the tourist offices in London or Washington. Bear in mind too that an increasing amount of practical information is available from the tourism-related websites maintained by Croatian towns and tourist destinations – we've mentioned these where relevant throughout the guide.

All towns and regions within Croatia have a **tourist association** (*turistička zajednica*) whose job it is to promote local tourism. Many of these maintain tourist offices (*turistički ured* or *turistički informativni centar*), although they vary a great deal in the services they offer. All offer advice on private rooms, but only some of them (usually in areas lacking a recognized accommodation agency) will book a room on your behalf. English is widely spoken, and staff in coastal resorts invariably speak German and Italian as well. Opening times vary according to the amount of tourist traffic. In July and August they might be open daily from 8am to 8pm or later, while in May, June and September, hours might be reduced to include an afternoon break or earlier closing times at weekends. Out of season, tourist offices on the coast tend to observe normal office hours (Mon–Fri 8am–3pm) or close altogether – although there's usually someone on hand to respond to faxes or email messages.

Croatian tourist information offices abroad

UK Croatian National Tourist Office, 2 The Lanchesters, 162–164 Fulham Palace Rd, London W6 9ER ☎020/8563 7979, ☏8563 2616, ⓦwww.croatia.hr.
US Croatian National Tourist Office, 350 Fifth Avenue, Suite 4003, New York, NY 10118 ☎212/279-8672, ☏279-8683, ⓦwww.croatia.hr.

Recommended websites

ⓦ**www.adriatica.net**. General info about the Adriatic resorts, and an online booking service with wide range of apartments, villas and hotels.
ⓦ**www.croatia.hr**. Official site of the Croatian National Tourist Board, offering a wealth of general information on Croatia as well as specific coverage of all the main resorts. Numerous links to regional tourist boards and more detailed sites dealing with history and culture.
ⓦ**www.croatia.net**. A wealth of information on history and culture, with lots of useful links.
ⓦ**www.croatianwriting.com**. Admirable project promoting the best in contemporay Croatian literature, with well-chosen English-language extracts online.
ⓦ**www.dalmacija.net**. Useful guide to the southern Adriatic – you can also book hotels and private rooms here online.
ⓦ**dubrovnik.laus.hr**. Most informative of the sites covering Dubrovnik and the surrounding region.
ⓦ**www.hina.hr**. Daily Croatian news reports in English, in dry style.
ⓦ**www.hns-cff.hr**. The Croatian Football Federation's site, with results, league tables and news of the national team.
ⓦ**www.istra.com**. Best of the regional tourist authority websites. Full details of accommodation throughout Istria and a useful calendar of events.
ⓦ**www.kvarner.hr**. Run by the regional tourist association covering the Kvarner Gulf and its islands, packed with useful information.
ⓦ**www.mvp.hr**. The Croatian foreign ministry site, with links to all Croatian embassies and consulates abroad.

ⓦ **www.slavophilia.net**. Wide-ranging resource covering all aspects of history, culture and language in the Slav countries of Europe – including plenty on Croatia.

ⓦ **www.thebambimolesters.com**. Legendary surf-punks the Bambi Molesters are (so far) the only Croatia-based rock band to succesfully release an album in western Europe.

ⓦ **www.tzzz.hr**. One of the better regional sites, run by the tourist association of Zagreb county (comprising Samobor, Turopolje and parts of the Žumberak)

Maps

The best maps of Croatia are by Freytag & Berndt, who produce a 1:600,000 map of Slovenia, Croatia and Bosnia-Hercegovina, a 1:300,000 map of Croatia, a 1:250,000 map of Istria and northern Croatia and a 1:000,000 regional maps of the Adriatic coast. Generalkarte also do a useful 1:200,000 map of the Adriatic coast.

City and town plans are more difficult to come by, although tourist offices often give away (or sell quite cheaply) serviceable maps of their town or island. In addition, Freytag & Berndt publish city plans of Zadar, Split and Dubrovnik. The best map of **Zagreb** is the 1:20,000 plan prepared by the Geodetski zavod Slovenije (Slovene Geodesic Institute), available in three versions: one published by a local firm in Zagreb, a second published by the Hungarian firm Cartographia and the third by Freytag & Berndt. All the above are available from shops in Croatia as well as the specialist map stockists listed below.

Map outlets

UK and Ireland

Blackwell's Map and Travel Shop 50 Broad St, Oxford OX1 3BQ ☎01865/793 550, ⓦ maps.blackwell.co.uk.
Easons Bookshop 40 O'Connell St, Dublin 1 ☎01/858 3881, ⓦ www.eason.ie.
Heffers Map and Travel 20 Trinity St, Cambridge CB2 1TJ ☎01865/333 536, ⓦ www.heffers.co.uk.
Hodges Figgis Bookshop 56–58 Dawson St, Dublin 2 ☎01/677 4754.
The Map Shop 30a Belvoir St, Leicester LE1 6QH

☎0116/247 1400, ⓦ www.mapshopleicester.co.uk.
National Map Centre 22–24 Caxton St, London SW1H 0QU ☎020/7222 2466, ⓦ www.mapsnmc.co.uk.
Newcastle Map Centre 55 Grey St, Newcastle-upon-Tyne NE1 6EF ☎0191/261 5622.
Stanfords 12–14 Long Acre, London WC2E 9LP ☎020/7836 1321, ⓦ www.stanfords.co.uk.
The Travel Bookshop, 13–15 Blenheim Crescent, London W11 2EE ☎020/7229 5260, ⓦ www.thetravelbookshop.co.uk.

US and Canada

Adventurous Traveler Bookstore ☎1-800/282-3963, ⓦ www.AdventurousTraveler.com.
Elliot Bay Book Company, 101 S Main St, Seattle, WA 98104 ☎1-800/962-5311, ⓦ www.elliotbaybook.com.
Globe Corner Bookstore 28 Church St, Cambridge, MA 02138 ☎1-800/358-6013, ⓦ www.globercorner.com.
Map Link 30 S La Patera Lane, Unit 5, Santa Barbara, CA 93117 ☎1-800/962-1394, ⓦ www.maplink.com.
Rand McNally Around thirty stores across the US; call ☎1-800/333-0136 ext 2111 or check ⓦ www.randmcnally.com for the nearest store.
Travel Books & Language Center 4437 Wisconsin Ave, Washington, DC 20016 ☎1-800/220-2665, ⓦ www.bookweb.org/bookstore/travellers.
The Travel Bug Bookstore 2667 West Broadway, Vancouver V6K 2G2 ☎604/737-1122, ⓦ www.swifty.com/tbug.
World of Maps 1235 Wellington St, Ottawa, Ontario K1Y 3A3 ☎1-800/214-8524, ⓦ www.worldofmaps.com.

Australia and New Zealand

Mapland 372 Little Bourke St, Melbourne, Victoria 3000 ☎03/9670 4383, ⓦ www.mapland.com.au.
MapWorld 173 Gloucester St, Christchurch ☎0800/627 967 or 03/374 5399, ⓦ www.mapworld.co.nz.
The Map Shop 6–10 Peel St, Adelaide, SA 5000 ☎08/8231 2033, ⓦ www.mapshop.net.au.
Perth Map Centre 900 Hay St, Perth, WA 6000 ☎08/9322 5733, ⓦ www.perthmap.com.au.
Specialty Maps 46 Albert St, Auckland 1001 ☎09/307 2217, ⓦ www.specialtymaps.co.nz.

Insurance

You'd do well to take out an insurance policy before travelling to cover against theft, loss and illness or injury. Before paying for a new policy, however, it's worth checking whether you are already covered: some all-risks home insurance policies may cover your possessions when overseas; many private medical schemes include cover when abroad; and Croatia has a reciprocal health care agreement with most EU countries (the UK and Ireland included; see opposite). In Canada, provincial health plans usually provide partial cover for medical mishaps overseas, while holders of official student/teacher/youth cards in Canada and the US are entitled to meagre accident coverage and hospital in-patient benefits. Students will often find that their student health coverage extends during the vacations and for one term beyond the date of last enrolment.

After exhausting the possibilities above, you might want to contact a specialist travel insurance company. A typical travel insurance policy usually provides **cover** for the loss of baggage, tickets and – up to a certain limit – cash or cheques, as well as cancellation or curtailment of your journey. Most of them exclude so-called **dangerous sports** unless an extra premium is paid: in Croatia this can mean scuba-diving, whitewater rafting, windsurfing and trekking, though probably not kayaking or jeep safaris. Many policies can be chopped and changed to exclude coverage you don't need – for example, sickness and accident benefits can often be excluded or included at will. If you do take medical coverage, ascertain whether benefits will be paid as treatment proceeds or only after return home, and whether there is a 24-hour medical emergency number. When securing baggage cover, make sure that the per-article limit – typically under £500 – will cover your most valuable possession. If you need to make a claim, you should keep receipts for medicines and medical treatment, and in the event you have anything stolen, you must obtain an official statement from the police.

Rough Guides travel insurance

Rough Guides offers its own travel insurance, customized for our readers by a leading UK broker and backed by a Lloyd's underwriter. It's available for anyone, of any nationality and any age, travelling anywhere in the world.

There are two main Rough Guide insurance plans: **Essential**, for basic, no-frills cover; and **Premier** – with more generous and extensive benefits. Alternatively, you can take out **annual multi-trip insurance**, which covers you for any number of trips throughout the year (with a maximum of 60 days for any one trip). Unlike many policies, the Rough Guides schemes are calculated by the day, so if you're travelling for 27 days rather than a month, that's all you pay for. If you intend to be away for the whole year, the Adventurer policy will cover you for 365 days. Each plan can be supplemented with a "Hazardous Activities Premium" if you plan to indulge in sports considered dangerous, such as skiing, scuba-diving or trekking.

For a policy quote, call the Rough Guide Insurance Line on UK freefone ☏0800/015 0906, US toll-free ☏1-866/220 5588, or ☏+44 1243/621 046 if you're calling from elsewhere. Alternatively, get an online quote or buy online at ⊛www.roughguidesinsurance.com.

Health

No inoculations are required for travel to Croatia. Standards of public health are good, and tap water is safe everywhere. However, anyone planning to spend time walking in the mountains should consider being inoculated against tick-borne encephalitis.

Minor complaints can be treated at a **pharmacy** (*ljekarna*); in cities, many of the staff will speak some English, while even in places where the staff speak only Croatian, it should be easy enough to obtain repeat prescriptions if you bring along the empty pill container. A rota system ensures that there will be one pharmacy open at night-time and weekends – details are posted in the window of each pharmacy.

For serious complaints, head for the nearest **hospital** (*bolnica* or *klinički centar*), or call an ambulance (☎94). Hospital treatment is free to citizens of most EU countries, including the UK and Ireland, on production of a valid passport; nationals of other countries should check whether their government has a reciprocal health agreement, or ensure they have adequate insurance cover. Conditions in Croatian hospitals are generally good, although expensive Western drugs are sometimes in short supply, and you might have to buy your own.

Costs, money and banks

Croatia isn't the bargain destination it was in the 1970s and 1980s, but the cost of accommodation, eating and drinking is reasonably competitive compared to Western Europe. Prices in shops are another matter, however, with food and other goods often slightly more expensive than those in EU countries.

Croatia's unit of currency is the **kuna** (Kn; the word *kuna*, meaning "marten", recalls the days in medieval Croatia when taxes were paid for in marten pelts), which is divided into 100 **lipa**. Coins come in denominations of 1, 5, 10, 20 and 50 lipa, and 1, 2 and 5 kuna; notes come in denominations of 5, 10, 20, 50, 100, 500 and 1000 kuna. At the time of writing, the **exchange rate** was reasonably stable at 12Kn to £1 or 8Kn to US$1.

Costs

Accommodation will be your biggest single expense, with the cheapest private room weighing in at around £10/$15 for a double, rising to £20/$30 in fashionable places like Dubrovnik. The cheapest doubles in hotels hover around the 350–450Kn mark.

As for **transport**, short journeys by ferry and bus (say from Split to one of the nearby islands) cost in the region of £1.70/$2.50, while moving up and down the country will naturally be more expensive (a Zagreb–Split bus ticket, for instance, costs upwards of £12/$18).

About £9/$13 per person day will suffice for **food and drink** if you're shopping in markets for picnic ingredients, maybe eating out in inexpensive grill-houses and pizzerias once a day, and limiting yourself to a couple of drinks in cafés; £20/$30 a day will be sufficient for breakfast in a café, a sit-down lunch and a decent restaurant

Youth and student discounts

Various official and quasi-official **youth/student ID cards** soon pay for themselves in savings. Full-time students are eligible for the International Student ID Card (ISIC; ⊛www.isicard.com), which entitles the bearer to special air fares and discounts at museums and other attractions in Croatia. For Americans there's also a health benefit, providing up to $3000 in emergency medical coverage and $100 a day for 60 days in the hospital, plus a 24-hour hotline to call in the event of a medical, legal or financial emergency. The card costs $22 for Americans; Can$16 for Canadians; Aus$16.50 for Australians; NZ$21 for New Zealanders; and £6 in the UK. You can get ISIC cards in Croatia through the Croatian Youth Hostel Association (Hrvatski ferijalni i hostelski savez – HFHS), Dežmanova 9, 10 000 Zagreb (☎01/484-7474, ⊛www.hfhs.hr).

dinner followed by a couple of night-time drinks. The prices of accommodation, ferry tickets, international bus tickets and tourist excursions are often quoted in euros, although you can pay in kuna.

Banks and exchange

The kuna isn't a fully convertible currency, so you can't buy it from your bank prior to leaving home. It's also hard to get rid of once you've left Croatia, although exchange offices in neighbouring countries such as Slovenia and Hungary often accept it. The best advice is to spend up, or change the leftovers back to hard currency before you quit the country (some banks may ask to see your exchange **receipts** before doing this, so keep them safe).

The best place to **change money** is at a bank (*banka*) – Zagrebačka Banka, Zagrebačka Privredna Banka and Splitska Banka are some of the main firms, although each region of Croatia has its own (perfectly respectable) banking outfit – or exchange bureau (*mjenjačnica*). **Banks** are generally open Monday to Friday 8am to 5pm, and Saturday 8am to 11am or noon, although summer opening hours often come into effect in the Adriatic, when an afternoon break is introduced and hours are lengthened to 8pm or even 10pm in the evenings to compensate. In smaller places banks normally close for lunch on weekdays year round, and aren't open at all on Saturdays. Exchange bureaux are often found inside travel agencies (*putničke agencije*) and have more flexible hours, remaining open until 9 or 10pm seven days a week in summer if there are enough tourists around to justify it. The larger **post offices** also have exchange facil-

ities, offering rates similar to those in banks (for post office opening times, see p.38). Exchange rates in hotels usually represent extremely poor value for money.

Traveller's cheques are the safest way to carry money, and can be exchanged in almost all banks and exchange bureaux in Croatia for a one to two percent commission. The cheques can be in US dollars, pounds sterling or euros – all are accepted with equal enthusiasm. American Express cheques can also be exchanged at any office of the Atlas Travel Agency.

Credit cards are accepted in most hotels and in the more expensive restaurants and shops, and can be used to get cash advances in banks (note that these can incur high rates of interest). You can use credit and debit cards to withdraw cash from ATMs, found in all Croatian town centres and at most points of arrival in the country, though note that many of the less touristed islands do not yet have ATMs. Another way of carrying funds is **Visa Travel Money**, a disposable debit card prepaid with funds which you can access from Visa ATMs; for more details see ⊛www.visa.com.

Wiring money

Having money wired from home using one of the companies listed below is never convenient or cheap, and should be considered a last resort. It's also possible to have money wired directly from a bank in your home country to a bank in Croatia, although this is somewhat less reliable because it involves two separate institutions. If you go down this route, your home bank will need the address of the bank where you want to pick up the money and the address and telex number of the Zagreb head office, which will act as the clearing house; money wired this way normally takes two working days to arrive, and costs around £25/$40 per transaction.

Money-wiring companies

Thomas Cook Britain ☎01733/318 922, Northern Ireland ☎028/9055 0030, Republic of Ireland ☎01/677 1721, US ☎1-800/287-7362, Canada ☎1-888/823-4732, ⊛www.thomascook.com.

Travelers Express MoneyGram UK ☎0800/018 0104, Republic of Ireland ☎1850/205 800, US ☎1-800/955-7777, Canada ☎1-800/933-3278, Australia ☎1800/230 100, New Zealand ☎0800/262 263, ⊛www.moneygram.com.
Western Union UK ☎0800/833 833, Republic of Ireland ☎1800/395 395, US and Canada ☎1-800/325-6000, Australia ☎1800/501 500, New Zealand ☎0800/270 000, ⊛www.westernunion.com.

Getting around

Croatia's train system covers the north and east pretty well, but is little use on the coast, where the country's extensive and reliable bus network comes into its own. As well as offering the only route to the islands, ferries offer a leisurely way of getting up and down the coast, and travelling the length of the Adriatic by boat is one of the most memorable journeys Croatia has to offer.

Trains

Croatian Railways (Hrvatske željeznice; ⊛www.hznet.hr) run a smooth and efficient service which is slightly cheaper than using buses in those areas where routes overlap. Around Zagreb and in the north the network is pretty dense, and you can use trains to visit most places of interest in inland Croatia. Trains also run from Zagreb to Pula, Rijeka and Split on the Adriatic, but there are no rail lines running up and down the coast. The **InterRail** pass is valid for Croatia (which is in zone D along with the Czech and Slovak republics, Poland and Hungary; see p.17), but **Eurail** isn't. If you're resident in Europe, you could buy a **Euro Domino pass** for Croatia itself, but this is hardly worth it unless you're in constant transit from one end of the country to the other.

There are two types of train (*vlak*, plural *vlakovi*): **putnički** (slow ones which stop at every halt) and **IC** (inter-city trains which are faster and more expensive). **Tickets** (*karte*) are brought from the ticket counter at the station (*kolodvor*) before travel; those bought from the conductor on the train are subject to a surcharge unless you've joined the train at an insignificant halt which doesn't have a

ticket counter. On some inter-city routes, buying a return ticket (*povratna karta*) is cheaper than buying a single ticket (*karta u jednom pravcu*) twice, although it often makes no difference. Seat reservations (*rezervacije*) are obligatory on some inter-city services. The only journey on which sleeping car (*spalnica*) or couchette (*kušet*) accommodation is available is the overnight service between Zagreb and Split.

Timetables (*vozni red* or *red vožnje*) are usually displayed on boards in station departure halls – *polazci* or *odlasci* are departures, *dolasci* are arrivals. The timetable for the whole network is available in a compact paperback from most larger train stations (30Kn), although it sells out fast. Timetable information is theoretically available on Croatian Railways' website, although you might need a degree in Croatian to understand it.

Buses

Croatia's **bus** network is run by a confusing array of local companies, but services are well integrated and bus stations are generally well organized, with clearly listed departure times and efficient booking facilities.

Buses (*autobusi*) operating inter-city services are usually modern air-conditioned coaches, and travelling large distances is rarely uncomfortable – stops of ten minutes or more are made every ninety minutes or so. The buses operating shorter routes on the islands or in the provinces are more likely to be ageing and uncomfortable vehicles which can get unbearably stuffy in summer – but you're unlikely to be spending a long time in them.

There are few places in the country that you can't get to by bus, and there are usually hourly departures on the principal routes (Zagreb to the coast, and routes up and down the coast). Rural areas, however, may only be served by one or two departures a day, and maybe none at all at weekends. Out in the sticks, the bus timetable is much more likely to correspond to the needs of the locals: there'll be a flurry of departures in the early morning to get people to work, school or market, and a flurry of departures in mid-afternoon to bring them back again, but nothing in between.

If you're at a big city bus station, **tickets** must be obtained from ticket windows before boarding the bus, and will bear the departure time (*vrijeme polaska*), platform number (*peron*) and a seat number (*sjedalo*). Your ticket will also carry the name of the bus company you're travelling with: two different companies might be running services to the same place at around the same time. If you're not getting on at the start of the route, tickets might not go on sale until the bus actually arrives. If there's nowhere to buy a ticket, sit on the bus and wait for the conductor to sell you one. It's a good idea to buy tickets well **in advance** in summer if you can, especially for any services between Zagreb and the coast – though bear in mind that you can only buy advance tickets from the city where the bus originates rather than some point along the route.

Fares are a little cheaper than in Western Europe, although costs differ slightly according to which company you're riding with and what part of the country you're in. Generally speaking, you get more kilometres for your money in inland Croatia than you do on the coast. Long inter-city trips like Rijeka–Zadar or Split–Dubrovnik weigh in at around 90Kn one-way; Split–Zagreb will cost around 140Kn. **Return tickets** are sporadically offered by some companies on a selection of their inter-city routes – if you do see them advertised, they'll work out slightly cheaper then buying two one-way fares. On bus journeys that involve a **ferry crossing** (such as Rijeka–Lošinj or Rijeka–Rab), the cost of the ferry will be included in the price. You'll be charged extra (5–6Kn for each item) for rucksacks and suitcases.

Tickets for **municipal buses** in towns and cities should usually be bought in advance from kiosks, and then cancelled by punching them in the machine on board. You can buy tickets from the driver as well in most cases, although this might be slightly more expensive and you may have to provide the correct change.

Ferries

A multitude of ferry services link the Croatian mainland with the Adriatic islands, most of which are run by **Jadrolinija** (see p.19), the main state ferry firm, although a few private operators are beginning to offer competition.

Short hops to islands **close to the mainland** – such as Brestova to Porozina on Cres, Jablanac to Mišnjak on Rab, or Orebić to Dominče on Korčula – are handled by simple roll-on-roll-off ferries which either operate a shuttle service or run every half-hour or so. Prices for foot passengers on such routes rarely exceed 10Kn (this will usually be incorporated into your fare if you're crossing by bus). A car will cost about 70Kn; a motorbike, 25Kn.

Departures to destinations slightly **further offshore** run to a more precise timetable. The ports which offer access to the most important groups of islands are Zadar (Ugljan, Dugi otok), Split (Šolta, Brač, Hvar, Vis and Lastovo) and Dubrovnik (Koločep, Lopud, Šipan and Mljet). Fares for foot passengers are low: approximate prices are Zadar–Sali (Dugi otok) 14Kn, Split–Hvar 26Kn, Split–Lastovo 35Kn, Split–Supetar (Brač) 18Kn, Split–Vis 28Kn, Dubrovnik–Mljet 30Kn. On these routes you'll pay 170–280Kn for a car, 50–80Kn for a motorbike. If you're travelling without a vehicle, look out for summer-only **hydrofoils** and **catamarans** linking Split with destinations on Šolta, Brač, Hvar and Vis. Although slightly more expensive than ferries, they'll be twice as fast.

Jadrolinija also operate a **coastal service** from Rijeka to Dubrovnik, calling at Zadar,

Split, Stari Grad (Hvar) and Korčula on the way, and sometimes continuing to Bari in Italy and Igoumenitsa in Greece in the summer. This runs at least once a day in both directions in summer, twice a week in winter. Travelling from Rijeka to Dubrovnik takes twenty hours and always involves one night on the boat. Prices (often quoted in euros but payable in kuna) vary greatly according to the level of comfort you require. The cheapest Rijeka–Dubrovnik fare (which involves spending the journey either on the open deck or in smoky bar areas) is 200Kn, while you'll pay double that for a couchette-style bunk bed, three times as much for a bed in a well-appointed cabin. Taking a car on the same journey will cost an extra 600Kn, a motorbike 180Kn; bicycles can be taken free of charge. Return tickets are twenty percent cheaper than the price of two singles, and prices fall by up to twenty percent in winter. **Tickets** are sold at offices or kiosks near the departure dock. For longer journeys, book in advance wherever possible; Jadrolinija addresses and phone numbers are given in the text where relevant.

All ferries apart from simple shuttle services will have a **buffet** where you can buy a full range of drinks, although food may consist of crisps and unappetizing sandwiches, so it's best to bring your own. The main coastal ferry has a restaurant with a full range of reasonably priced food; breakfast is included if you book a cabin.

Flights

The obvious attraction of flying is the time it saves: the plane journey from Zagreb to Dubrovnik takes an hour, compared to a whole day to get there overland. **Croatia Airlines** (ⓦwww.croatianairlines.com) operate domestic services between Zagreb and Pula (1 daily), Split (summer 4 daily; winter 3 daily), Zadar (summer 2 daily; winter 1 daily) and Dubrovnik (summer 3 daily; winter 2 daily). Between May and October there are flights (weekends only) to Bol on the island of Brač. A Zagreb–Dubrovnik return costs about 700Kn. There's not normally any point in booking internal flights from Croatia Airlines offices in your home country – they invariably work out twice as expensive as buying them in Croatia, unless they're bought in conjunction with an international flight to Croatia.

By car

Croatia's **road system** is comprehensive, but not always of good quality once you get beyond the main highways. There are currently five stretches of motorway (*autocesta*) in Croatia: Zagreb to Slavonski Brod, Zagreb to Novi Marof (on the way to Varaždin), Varaždin to Goričan on the Hungarian border, Zagreb to Krapina, and Zagreb to Karlovac. All are subject to tolls – take a ticket as you come on and pay as you exit – though few extend far enough for you to amass significant tolls: Zagreb to Karlovac, for example, is 12Kn for a car or motorbike, Zagreb to Slavonski Brod is 44Kn. Elsewhere, the main routes (especially the main road down the Adriatic coast, the Magistrala) are single carriageway and tend to be clogged with traffic – especially in summer, when movement up and down the coast can be time-consuming. The much-vaunted motorway extension from Karlovac to Zadar and Split, due to open in 2004, will significantly ease traffic congestion between Zagreb and the coast. Note that everywhere in Croatia, roads in off-the-beaten-track areas can be badly maintained.

To drive in Croatia, you'll need a driving licence, registration documents and a Green Card. **Speed limits** are 50kph in built-up areas, 80kph on normal roads, 130kph on motorways. If you **break down**, the Croatian Automobile Club (HAK) has a 24-hour emergency service (☎987). **Petrol stations** (*ben-zinska stanica*) are usually open daily 7am–7pm, although there are 24-hour stations in larger towns and along major international routes. If there's anything wrong with your vehicle, petrol stations are probably the best places to ask where you can find a mechanic (*automehaničar* or *majstor*) or a shop selling spare parts (*rezervni dijelovi*). A tyre repair shop is a *vulkanizer*.

Finding **parking** spaces in big cities can be a nightmare, and illegally parked vehicles will be swiftly removed by tow-truck (known locally as the *pauk*, or "spider") and impounded until payment of a 500Kn fine. Most cities have garages where you can leave your car for a small fee.

Car rental in Croatia is pricey, at around £50/$75 a day and £220/$380 a week for a small hatchback with unlimited mileage, depending on the season. The major rental chains have offices in all the larger cities and at Zagreb airport; addresses are detailed in the "Listings" sections at the end of city accounts throughout the Guide. Most travel agents in Croatia will organize car rental through one of the big international firms or a local operator. It's usually cheaper if you arrange rental in advance, either through one of the agents listed below or with specialist tour operators like Europa Skylines or Holiday Options (see p.13).

Car rental agencies

UK

Avis ℡0870/606 0100, ℗www.avis.co.uk.
Budget ℡0800/181181,
℗www.budget.co.uk.
Europcar ℡0845/722 2525,
℗www.europcar.co.uk.
Hertz ℡0870/844 8844, ℗www.hertz.co.uk.
Holiday Autos ℡0870/400 0099,
℗www.holidayautos.co.uk.
National ℡0870/536 5365,
℗www.nationalcar.co.uk.

Republic of Ireland

Avis ℡01/605 7500, ℗www.avis.ie.
Budget ℡0903/27 711, ℗www.budget.ie.
Europcar ℡01/614 2888, ℗www.europcar.ie.
Hertz ℡01/676 7476, ℗www.hertz.ie.
Holiday Autos ℡01/872 9366,
℗www.holidayautos.ie.

US and Canada

Alamo US ℡1-800/522-9696,
℗www.alamo.com.
Avis US ℡1-800/331-1084, Canada ℡1-800/272-5871, ℗www.avis.com.
Budget US ℡1-800/527-0700,
℗www.budgetrentacar.com.
Hertz US ℡1-800/654-3001, Canada ℡1-800/263-0600, ℗www.hertz.com.

Holiday Autos US ℡1-800/422-7737,
℗www.holidayautos.com.
National ℡1-800/227-7368,
℗www.nationalcar.com.

Australia

Avis ℡13 63 33 or 02/9353 9000,
℗www.avis.com.au.
Budget ℡1300/362 848, ℗www.budget.com.au.
Hertz ℡13 30 39 or 03/9698 2555,
℗www.hertz.com.au.
National ℡13 10 45, ℗www.nationalcar.com.au.

New Zealand

Avis ℡09/526 2847 or 0800/655 111,
℗www.avis.co.nz.
Budget ℡09/976 2222, ℗www.budget.co.nz.
Hertz ℡0800/654 321, ℗www.hertz.co.nz.
National ℡0800/800 115,
℗www.nationalcar.co.nz.

Motoring organizations

UK and Ireland

AA UK ℡0870/600 0371, ℗www.theaa.com.
AA Ireland Dublin ℡01/617 9988,
℗www.aaireland.ie.
RAC UK ℡0800/550 055, ℗www.rac.co.uk.

US and Canada

AAA ℡1-800/AAA-HELP, ℗www.aaa.com. Each state has its own club – check the phone book for local address and phone number.
CAA ℡613/247-0117, ℗www.caa.ca. Each region has its own club – check the phone book for local address and phone number.

Australia and New Zealand

AAA Australia ℡02/6247 7311,
℗www.aaa.asn.au.
New Zealand AA New Zealand ℡09/377 4660,
℗www.nzaa.co.nz.

Accommodation

The tourism boom of the 1960s and 1970s gave Croatia an impressive number of large beachside hotels, while small B&Bs and pensions are on the increase. For the moment, though, the inexpensive private rooms and apartments offered by families up and down the coast still represent the country's best-value accommodation. The Adriatic coast is well provided with campsites, but hostels, on the other hand, are a rarity.

Hotels

Most Croatian **hotels** are multistorey affairs providing modern comforts but little atmosphere, although there are a handful of stately, early twentieth-century establishments in major cities and in resorts (such as Opatija) which were originally patronized by the Habsburgs. Most of the hotels used by Western European package holidaymakers have been expensively renovated since the end of the 1991–95 war, bringing them up to contemporary international standards. Hotels which see more in the way of Croatian or East European guests have generally received less investment, and often still sport worn carpets and freakish 1970s wallpaper – although they're perfectly clean and comfortable in all other respects.

Most Croatian hotels have now been classified according to the international **star grading** system, although some of the grades awarded might seem a little generous – some of Croatia's three-star hotels would only qualify for two stars elsewhere. Generally speaking, one-star hotels have rooms with shared WC and bathroom; two-star hotels have rooms with en-suite facilities; three-star hotels have slightly larger en-suite rooms and, most probably, a television; four-star corresponds to comfy business class; and five-star are in the international luxury bracket. There are hardly any one-star places left however: most have been refurbished in order to meet the standards required by international package companies, and those that do exist can't compete, value-wise, with private rooms.

In most places, two-star establishments represent the cheapest option – expect to pay 350–500Kn a double – but it's worth bearing in mind that the better categories of private room offer similar comforts for less money. Three-star hotels are the hardest to predict both quality- and price-wise, and you'll pay anything between 400Kn and 1000Kn depending on whether it's just a glorified two-star with an extra lick of paint, or a genuinely comfortable and well-managed outfit which meets international standards. Any four-star hotel will have plush carpets, bathtubs in the bathroom and a range of other facilities (such as gym or swimming pool) for around 700–1200Kn. There are currently around a dozen five-star hotels in Croatia, most of which are in Zagreb or in and around Dubrovnik (1100Kn a double upwards). Prices in each category vary considerably according to which part of Croatia you're staying in: Dubrovnik and Hvar are currently the most fashionable – and consequently most expensive – parts of

Accommodation price codes

The accommodation in this guide has been graded using the following price codes, based on the cost of each establishment's **least expensive double room** in high season (July & Aug), excluding special offers. Where single rooms exist, they usually cost 60–70 percent of the price of a double.

❶ Less than 200Kn
❷ 200–300Kn
❸ 300–400Kn

❹ 400–500Kn
❺ 500–600Kn
❻ 600–800Kn

❼ 800–1000Kn
❽ 1000–1200Kn
❾ Over 1200Kn

the country, and hotels in areas such as northern and mid-Dalmatia can work out significantly cheaper.

Hotels in inland Croatia charge the same price all year round. On the coast, however, prices drop by ten to twenty percent in the shoulder season (May, June & Sept), and may be as much as fifty percent cheaper in winter. Some hotels in resort areas close between November and April, although most moderate-sized Adriatic towns will have at least one mid-range hotel open all year.

There's a growing number of small **family-run hotels** aiming to conquer the mid-range market, offering the comforts and level of service of a good three-star hotel but in cosy, informal surroundings and at a fraction of the cost. Unfortunately, there's not enough of them in the heavily touristed parts of Croatia to make big inroads into the accommodation scene as yet, but we've recommended them throughout the guide whenever they exist.

Hotel prices almost invariably include **breakfast**. At its most basic, this will feature rolls with butter, jam, and some ham and cheese, although the majority of hotels hosting Western package guests now offer a buffet selection. Many of the hotels on the Adriatic also offer full-board (*pansion*) and half-board (*polupansion*) deals for a few extra kuna, but bear in mind that you'll be eating bland, internationalized food in large, institutional dining rooms.

Private rooms and apartments

Private **rooms** (*privatne sobe*) are available everywhere in Croatia where there are tourists. They're offered by locals eager to rent out unoccupied space in their homes – many Croats on the coast have enlarged or modernized their houses to provide extra rooms. Standards vary widely, but rooms are usually grouped into three categories by the tourist association in each area. **Category I** rooms are simple affairs furnished with a couple of beds, a wardrobe and not much else, and you'll be using your host's bathroom. **Category II** rooms have en-suite bathrooms, and **category III** rooms will probably come with TV and plusher furnishings. Prices start at around 120/150/180Kn for a category I/category II/category III double in a smallish resort, rising to about

240/260/280Kn in relatively expensive cities like Dubrovnik and Zagreb. Prices are subject to a thirty to fifty percent surcharge if you stay for less than three nights. Single travellers usually pay about seventy percent of the price of a double except in July and August, when the full double price might have to be paid to secure a room.

Bookings are administered by local travel agencies; where there's no established travel agency, the local tourist office will handle the job. Agencies usually open daily 8am to 8pm or later in July and August, although they may take a long afternoon break on Sundays. In May, June and September opening hours will include longish afternoon breaks Monday to Friday, and shorter hours (often mornings only) at weekends. When paying for a private room, you'll be charged a fee of about 5Kn for registering you with the police (see p.47), and a residence tax (*boravišna pristojba*) of 5–8Kn each per night, which functions as the local tourist association's main source of funding.

If you can't find a tourist agency or tourist office, it's usually very easy to find a private room by asking around or looking for "sobe" or "Zimmer frei" signs posted up outside local houses. You may also be offered rooms by landladies waiting outside train, bus and ferry stations, especially in Split and Dubrovnik – be sure to establish the location of the room and agree a price before setting off. Rooms obtained in this way sometimes work out slightly cheaper than the agency-approved ones, but equally leave you prone to rip-offs. There's little chance that your hosts will be passing on registration fees or tourist tax to the relevant authorities (they'll charge you for them, then pocket the cash themselves), and they may exploit your naivety by inflating these additional costs, or inventing new ones of their own. However you find a room, it's acceptable to have a look at it before committing yourself.

Apartments

Rented out in the same way as private rooms, **apartments** (*apartmani*) usually consist of a self-contained unit or floor of a house with its own kitchen and bathroom, maybe a small lounge, and possibly a terrace for sitting outside. It's worth bearing in mind that two-person apartments often provide much more convenience, comfort and value for money than a double room in a hotel. Even single travellers – who will have to pay the price of a double – may find apartments favourably priced compared to bland hotel rooms. For those travelling as a family or in a group, apartments offer excellent value, providing that sleeping quarters are not too cramped – check how many beds are crammed into a single bedroom before accepting.

Two-person apartments – for which we've given price codes in the Guide – generally cost around 300–400Kn per night (price code ❸). Where available, four-person apartments cost around 400–600Kn; six-person apartments 500–700Kn. The higher the price, the more likely you are to get a central location, TV and a parking space should you need it. Prices fall by ten to twenty percent in May, June and September.

Rural homestays

In northern Croatia attempts are being made to encourage the development of **rural homestays** under the banner of *agroturizam* or "agricultural tourism". The idea is to encourage people in the countryside to offer farmhouse-style accommodation and locally produced food and drink. This is at its most developed in inland Istria, where the regional tourist association (Turistička zajednica Istarske županije; Forum 3, 52100 Pula, ☎052/452-797, ✆www.istra.com) publishes an annually updated *Agroturizam* booklet detailing all the rural homestay possibilities. The other areas in which the concept has made significant inroads is the Zagorje, north of Zagreb; the region around the Plitvice National Park; and the Slavonian village of Bilje near the Kopački Rit nature park.

Room quality varies from place to place, although most village homestays offer neat little en suites, often with a rustic feel to the furnishings. Prices are roughly equivalent to those in private rooms and apartments, and usually include breakfast; half- or full-board arrangements featuring tasty home-cooked food are often available for an extra cost.

Hostels and student halls

HI-affiliated **youth hostels** run by the Croatian Hostelling Association (Hrvatski ferijalni i hostelski savez; Dežmanova 9, 10000 Zagreb; ☎01/48-47-474, ✆www.hfhs.hr) are thin on the ground, although those that do exist (in Zagreb, Pula, Zadar, Dubrovnik, Krk and Punat) are clean and well run. Prices vary according to season: around 70–90Kn for a bed in winter, rising to 90–120Kn in July and August. Breakfast costs 20–30Kn. Half-board and full-board deals are also offered at very reasonable prices, although the food may not be particularly special. Most hostels close during the day, and you're expected to check in either in the morning (around 8–9am) or in the evening (typically 5–10pm). If you're doing a lot of hostelling, it's worth joining the hostelling organization of your home country to qualify for the member's rate, about fifteen percent cheaper.

In Zagreb, rooms in **student halls of residence** are rented out to travellers during the summer vacation – usually mid-July to the end of August. Rates include breakfast, with doubles costing 320–400Kn per night depending on whether facilities are en suite or shared.

Youth hostel associations

UK and Ireland

Hostelling International Northern Ireland ☎028/9032 4733, ✆www.hini.org.uk.
Irish Youth Hostel Association ☎01/830 4555, ✆www.irelandyha.org.
Scottish Youth Hostel Association ☎0870/155 3255, ✆www.syha.org.uk.
YHA England & Wales ☎0870/770 8868, ✆www.yha.org.uk.

US and Canada

Hostelling International-American Youth Hostels ☎202/783-6161, ✆www.hiayh.org.
Hostelling International Canada ☎1-800/663-5777 or 613/237-7884, ✆www.hostellingintl.ca.

Australia and New Zealand

Australia Youth Hostels Association ☎02/9261 1111, ✆www.yha.com.au.
Youth Hostelling Association New Zealand ☎0800/278 299 or 03/379 9970, ✆www.yha.co.nz.

Campsites

Campsites (*autokamp*) abound on the Adriatic coast, ranging from large-scale affairs with plentiful facilities, restaurants and shops to small family-run sites squeezed into private gardens or olive groves. Some major centres – notably Split and Dubrovnik – are currently without campsites, but almost everywhere else is catered for. Sites are generally open from May to September and charge 30–55Kn per person, plus 15–40Kn per pitch and 20–40Kn per vehicle. Electricity in the bigger sites costs a few extra kuna. Bear in mind that the stony ground of the Adriatic coast often makes it difficult to hammer in tent pegs – spare rope comes in handy to fasten your canvas home to nearby rocks and trees. Camping rough is illegal, and the rocky or pebbly nature of most Croatian beaches makes them uncomfortable to sleep on anyway.

Naturist campsites are a common feature of the northern Adriatic resorts, with big, self-contained complexes outside Rovinj, Poreč and Vrsar in Istria, and Krk, Baška and Punat on the island of Krk.

Eating and drinking

There's a varied and distinctive range of food on offer in Croatia, largely because the country straddles two culinary cultures: the seafood-dominated cuisine of the Mediterranean and the filling schnitzel-and-strudel fare of central Europe. Drinking revolves around a solid cross-section of wines and some charterful, fiery spirits.

Main meals are eaten in a **restoran** (restaurant, sometimes also called a *restauracija*) or a **konoba** (tavern) – the latter is more likely to have folksy decor but essentially serves the same range of food. A **gostiona** (inn) is a more rough-and-ready version of a *restoran*. For Croatians the most important meal of the day is lunch (*ručak*) rather than dinner (*večera*), although restaurants are accustomed to foreigners who eat lightly at lunchtime and more expansively in the evening, and offer a full range of food throughout the day. Throughout the Guide, we've given **phone numbers** for those restaurants where it may be worth booking in advance.

Because many Croatians eat lunch relatively late in the afternoon, restaurants frequently offer a list of brunch-snacks (called *marende* on the coast, *gableci* inland) between 10.30am and noon. These are usually no different from main meat and fish dishes, but come in slightly smaller portions, making an excellent low-cost midday meal. Details are often chalked up on a board outside rather than written on a menu.

No Croatian town is without at least one **pizzeria**, where the price of a filling meal will be significantly cheaper than in a standard meat-and-fish Croatian restaurant. Most of these establishments serve Italian-style, thin-crust pizzas made to reasonably authentic recipes, and seafood pizzas are quite a feature on the coast. Pizzerias tend to serve larger and more imaginative salads than the standard Croatian restaurant, and are often the best places to eat pasta dishes, although there are a growing number of spaghetterias which specialize in pasta and nothing else. Again, Croatian pasta dishes are normally authentic, cheap and filling. Look out also for **slastičarnice** (patisseries), the traditional place for buying eat-in or take-away cakes, pastries and ice cream.

What to eat

Any list of **starters** should begin with *pršut*, a home-cured ham from Istria and Dalmatia which, at its best, is a real melt-in-the-mouth delicacy (see box on p.ix). It's often served on a platter together with cheese: *Paški sir*

For a comprehensive list of Croatian food and drink terms, see pp.445–448.

from the island of Pag is the most famous, a hard, piquant cheese tasting somewhere between parmesan and mature cheddar; *sir sa vrhnjem* (cream cheese) is a milder alternative. *Kulen*, a spicy, paprika-laced sausage from Slavonia, is also worth trying. Soups (*juha*) are usually clear and light and are served with spindly noodles, unless you opt for the thicker *krem-juha* (cream soup).

One starter which is stodgy enough to serve as a main course is *štrukli*, a pastry-and-cheese dish which is common to Zagreb and the Zagorje hills to the north. It comes in two forms: *kuhani* (boiled) *štrukli* are enormous ravioli-like pockets of dough filled with cottage cheese; while for *pečeni* (baked) *štrukli* the dough and cheese are baked in an earthenware dish, resulting in a cross between cheese soufflé and lasagne.

Meat dishes

Main meat dishes normally consist of a grilled or pan-fried *kotlet* (chop) or *odrezak* (fillet or escalope). These are usually either **pork** or **veal**, and can be prepared in a variety of ways: a *kotlet* or *odrezak* cooked *na žaru* will be a simple grill, *bečki odrezak* (Wiener schnitzel) comes fried in breadcrumbs, *pariški odrezak* (Pariser schnitzel) is fried in batter, and *zagrebački odrezak* (Zagreb schnitzel) is stuffed with cheese and ham. *Mješano meso* (mixed grill) appears on all menus and will usually consist of a pork or veal *kotlet*, a few *ćevapi* (rissoles of minced beef, pork or lamb), a *pljeskavica* (a hamburger-like mixture of the same meats) and maybe a spicy *kobasica* (sausage), served alongside a bright red aubergine and pepper relish known as *ajvar*.

Lamb is usually prepared as a spit-roast. In sheep-growing regions (Cres, Rab, the hinterland of Zadar and Split) it's quite common to see roadside restaurants where a whole sheep is being roasted over an open fire in the carpark to tempt travellers inside. One way of preparing diced lamb that's typical of Istria and the Adriatic islands is to cook it *ispod peke* – when it's placed under a metal lid which is then covered with hot embers, and slowly baked. Stewed meats are less common than grilled or baked ones, although goulash (*gulaš*) is frequently employed as a sauce served with pasta. A main course associated with Dalmatia

(where it's traditionally considered a special-occasion food eaten on the big holy days, although it's perfectly common in restaurants) is *pašticada* (beef and bacon cooked in vinegar, wine and sometimes prunes). The most common **poultry** dish is *purica z mlincima* (turkey with baked pasta slivers), which is indigenous to Zagreb and the Zagorje. Other meaty main courses include *punjene paprike* (peppers stuffed with rice and meat) and *sarma* (cabbage leaves filled with a similar mixture). *Arambašica*, a version of *sarma* found in the Dalmatian hinterland, contains more meat and less rice.

Seafood dishes

On the coast you'll be regaled with every kind of **seafood**. Starters include *salata od hobotnice* (octopus salad), and the slightly more expensive *salata od jastoga* (nibble-size portions of lobster flesh seasoned with olive oil and herbs). **Fish** can come either *na žaru* (grilled), *u pećnici* (baked) or *lešo* (boiled). Grilling is by far the most common way of preparing freshly caught fish, which is sold by weight (the best fish starts at about 200Kn per kilo in cheap and mid-range restaurants, 300Kn per kilo in top-class establishments). Waiting staff will tell you what fish they have in stock, or will show you a tray of fish from which to choose. A decent-sized fish for one person usually weighs somewhere between a third and half a kilo, although you can always order a big fish and share it between two people.

The tastiest white meat is said to come from the *kovač* (John Dory), *list* (sole), *orada* (gilthead seabream) and *škrpina* (scorpion fish), although the range of fish caught in Adriatic waters is almost limitless. *Oslić* (hake) is slightly cheaper than the others, and is often served sliced and pan-fried in batter or breadcrumbs rather than grilled – when it will be priced per portion rather than by weight. Cheaper still is so-called *plava riba* (literally "blue fish"), a category which includes anchovies and mackerel. Another budget choice is *girice*, tiny fish similar to whitebait which are deep fried and eaten whole. Inexpensive main courses which crop up almost everywhere on the coast are *brodet* (boiled fish accompanied by a hot peppery sauce), *lignje na žaru* (grilled squid) and *crni rižot* (squid risotto).

The more expensive or specialist establishments will have delicacies such as crab, oysters, mussels and lobster. *Scampi* usually comes as whole prawns which must be cracked open with the fingers, rather than the sanitized, breadcrumbed variety found in northwestern Europe. They're often served with a *buzara* sauce, made from garlic and white wine.

Salads, accompaniments and desserts

You'll usually be offered a choice of what your main course is served with: boiled potatoes, chips, rice and gnocchi are the most common accompaniments. Indigenous forms of pasta include *fuži* in Istria, *šurlice* on the island of Krk, and *mlinci* in Zagreb and the Zagorje – the latter are lasagne-thin scraps of dough which are boiled, then baked. Additional vegetables can be ordered as items from the menu. Croatians eat an enormous amount of bread, and you'll be expected to scoff a couple of large slices with your meal regardless of whatever else you order.

The most common **salads** are *zelena salata* (green salad) and *mješana salata* (mixed salad). Other common side-dishes are gherkins (*krastavci*) and pickled peppers (*paprike*). Fish dishes are usually accompanied by *blitva* (mangelwurzel), a spinach-like plant indigenous to Dalmatia which is served with boiled potatoes and garlic.

Typical restaurant **desserts** include *sladoled* (ice cream), *torta* (cake) and *palačinke* (pancakes), which are usually served *sa marmeladom* (with marmalade), *s čokoladom* (with chocolate sauce) or *s oresima* (with walnuts). In Dubrovnik, try *rožata*, the locally produced version of creme caramel. A *slastičarnica* is another place to find ice cream, cakes and pastries, including *baklava*, the syrup-coated pastry indigenous to the Balkans and Middle East.

Breakfast and snacks

Unless you're staying in a private room or a campsite, **breakfast** will almost always be included in the cost of your accommodation. At its simplest it will include a couple of bread rolls, a few slices of cheese and/or salami, and some butter and jam. Mid- and top-range hotels will offer a buffet breakfast, complete with a range of cereals, scrambled eggs and bacon. Few Croatian cafés serve breakfast of any kind, although few of them mind if you bring along bread buns or pastries brought from a nearby bakery and consume them alongside your coffee.

Basic **self-catering** and **picnic** ingredients like cheese, vegetables and fruit can be bought at a supermarket (*samoposluga*) or an open-air **market** (*tržnica*). Markets often open early (about 6am) and begin to pack up in the early afternoon, though in well-touristed areas they sometimes keep going

Vegetarians in Croatia

Vegetarianism hasn't really caught on in Croatia, and the choice of dishes on restaurant menus is correspondingly meagre; many items which look like good vegetarian choices – the various bean soups and the ratatouille-style *duveč* – are invariably made with meat stock. Even in well-meaning restaurants, it's not uncommon to find dishes advertised as "vegetarian" which turn out to have ham or chicken in them. One traditional meat-free dish is *štrukli*, although this is a north Croatian speciality which can rarely be found on the coast.

Most vegetarians will be reduced to making a meal out of vegetable side dishes, or picking from the small number of meatless starters: *omlet sa gljivama* (mushroom omelette) and *pohani sir* (cheese fried in breadcrumbs) are safe choices. Italian-influenced pizzerias and spaghetteries are perhaps the best bet: most pizzerias offer a *pizza vegeterianska* featuring a selection of seasonal vegetables, and there's usually a choice of meatless pasta dishes including, if you're lucky, a vegetarian lasagne.

Ja sam vegeterijanac (*vegeterijanka* is the female form of the noun) means "I am a vegetarian." To ask "Have you got anything which doesn't contain meat?", say *Imate li nešto bez mesa?*

until late evening. Bread can be bought from either a supermarket or a **pekarnica** (bakery). Small outlets may offer a simple white loaf and little else, although you'll usually be offered a wide choice of breads, ranging from French sticks through wholemeal loaves to pumpernickel-style black breads. You'll have to point at what you want though: names of different loaves differ from one place to the next. A *pekarnica* may often sell sandwiches filled, most commonly, with ham, cheese or *pršut*, Croatia's excellent home-cured ham.

For **snacks**, look out for *slastičarnice* selling *burek*, a flaky pastry filled with cheese; it's delicious when fresh, although it can be stodgy and greasy if left standing for too long. For a more substantial snack, try the traditional southeast European repertoire of grilled meats: *ćevapi*, *ražnjići* (shish kebab) or *pljeskavica*, all of which are often served in a *somun* – a flat bread bun which is rather larger than a standard Western-style burger bun. Although these basic grill snacks will be on the menu of all but the grandest restaurants, they're at their best in the unpretentious fast-food places you'll find clustered around markets and bus stations. For an excellent light lunch, look out for the traditional working-man's food of inland Croatia, **grah** (or *fažol* in Dalmatia), a delicious soup of paprika-spiced haricot beans (*grah* literally means "beans") with bits of sausage or *pljeskavica* added. While in Istria, look out for *maneštra*, a rich bean-and-vegetable soup which often includes sweetcorn.

Drinking

Drinking takes place in a **kavana** (café) – usually a roomy and comfortable place with plenty of outdoor seating and serving the full range of alcoholic and non-alcoholic drinks, as well as pastries and ice creams – or in a **kafić** (café-bar), essentially a smaller version of the same thing, although usually catering to a younger clientele. The word **pub** is frequently adopted by café-bars attempting to imitate British, or more often Irish, styles; these places will probably have Guinness adverts on the walls and a familiar range of Irish brews on tap. Both cafés and café-bars open extraordinarily early (sometimes as early as 6am) in order to serve the first espresso to those going to work, although alcohol isn't served until 9am. Closing time is

usually 11pm, although regulations are often relaxed in summer, when café-bars stay open much later. You can also find coffee and soft drinks in a *slastičarnica* (often also the best place to find freshly made lemonade), although they're often less atmospheric than a *kavana* or a *kafić* and may close earlier in the evening. Slastičarnice aside, few Croatian cafés of any kind serve substantial food except from the odd sandwich.

Most Croatian **beer** is of the light lager variety. Karlovačko and Ožujsko are two good brands to look out for; Favorit, from Buzet in Istria, is widely considered to be the worst. Domestic dark beers include Tomislav from Zagreb and the less widespread Osiječko Crno from Osijek. Certain foreign brands – Stella Artois, Tuborg and Laško (from Slovenia) – are made in Croatia under licence. Of the foreign beers you're likely to find served on tap in café-bars and pubs, Guinness and Kilkenny are the most common. Whether you're drinking beer in bottles or on tap, a *malo pivo* (small beer) usually means 30cl and costs 6–10Kn, a *veliko pivo* (large beer) means a half-litre and will set you back 10–15Kn. Bottled beers are slightly more expensive.

Croatia produces an impressive range of red and white **wines**, few of which find their way onto Western supermarket shelves. Among the dry and medium-dry **whites**, look out for Vrbnička Žlahtina from Vrbnik on Krk; Vugava from Vis; Semion and Malvazija from Istria; and Kaštelet, Grk and Pošip from Korčula. Of the **reds**, the dark heady Dingač from the Pelješac peninsula has the best reputation and is the most expensive, although Babić from Primošten and Viški plavac from Vis are frequently as good, as is Teran, a fresh, light red from Istria. In shops and supermarkets table wine sells for about 15–25Kn per litre bottle, while a decent Dingač will set you back about 80Kn. Popular wine-derived drinks include *bevanda* (white or red wine mixed with plain water), *gemišt* (white wine and fizzy mineral water), *špricer* (white wine and soda water) and the eternally popular summer tipple *bambus* (red wine mixed with cola).

Local **spirits** (*žestoka pića*) are commonly consumed as an aperitif before meals and are usually produced from grapes (in which case they're called *loza* or *lozovača*) or from other fruits – the most common of these being plum brandy (*šljivovica*) and pear brandy (*viljamovka*). Grape-based spirits are often given additional flavours and have health-giving properties, notably as *travarica* (herb brandy), *medovina* (honey brandy) or *orahovača* (walnut brandy). *Pelinkovac* is a juniper-based spirit similar to Jägermeister, *vinjak* is locally produced cognac, and *maraskino* is a cherry liqueur from Zadar in Dalmatia. *Biska* is a mistletoe-flavoured aperitif from inland Istria. Foreign brandies and whiskies are available pretty much everywhere.

Apart from the vast urns of overstewed brown liquid served up by hotels at breakfast time, **coffee** is usually of a high quality. It is served as a strong black espresso unless specified otherwise – *kava sa mlijekom*

comes with a drop of milk, *kava sa šlagom* comes with cream, and *bijela kava* (white coffee) is usually like a good caffe latte. Cappucino is also fairly ubiquitous. Tea is usually of the herbal variety; ask for *indijski čaj* (Indian tea) if you want the English-style brew. *Čaj sa limunom* is with a slice of lemon, *sa mlijekom* comes with milk.

In the best cafés coffee is served with an accompanying glass of water; otherwise feel free to ask for one. Mineral water and other **soft drinks** are often served in multiples of 10cl or *dec* (pronounced "dets"). If you want 20cl of mineral water ask for *dva deca*, 30cl is *tri deca*. If you want fruit juice, note that the word *đus* ("juice") usually means orange juice.

Communications

Phone and mail services in Croatia are, on the whole, well organized and problem-free. Internet cafés are well established in Croatia's cities, and are increasingly common in the Adriatic resorts as well. Prices are generally reasonable: expect to pay around 20–30Kn per hour online. Some Internet cafés require customers to register as members (usually free of charge) before letting them loose on the computers – so keep a passport or other form of ID handy.

Mail

Most **post offices** (*pošta* or *HPT*) are open Monday to Friday from 7 or 8am to 7 or 8pm, and Saturday 8am to 1 or 2pm. In villages and on islands, Monday to Friday 8am to 2pm is more common, though in big towns and resorts some offices open daily, sometimes staying open until 10pm.

Airmail (*zrakoplovom*) takes about three days to reach Britain, and eight to ten to reach North America; surface mail takes at least twice as long. Stamps (*marke*) can be bought either at the post office or at newsstands. If you're sending parcels home, don't seal the package until the post office staff have had a look at what's inside: customs duty is charged on the export of most things, although newsprint and books are exempt. **Post restante** services are available at the main post office (*glavna pošta*) in every sizeable town – mail should be

addressed to Poste Restante, followed by the name of the town. Mail sent to poste restante in Zagreb (the official address is Poste Restante, 10 000 Zagreb) is held at the post office next to the train station, which is open round the clock. American Express customers can use the mailing addresses of any branch of the Atlas travel agency – they represent American Express in Croatia and will hold your mail for two months.

Telephones

Croatian **phone booths** use magnetic cards (*telekarta*), which you can pick up from post offices or newspaper kiosks. They're sold in denominations of 25, 50, 100, 200 and 500 units (*impulsa*). Generally speaking, a single unit will be enough for a local call, and the 25-unit card (costing around 13Kn) will be sufficient for making a

Useful dialling codes

To **call Croatia from abroad**, dial your international dialling prefix, then 385 for Croatia, followed by the number you want, omitting the initial zero. To **call abroad from Croatia**, dial the following, then the number you want, omitting the initial zero:

Australia ℡00 61
Ireland ℡00 353
New Zealand ℡00 64
UK ℡00 44
US and Canada ℡00 1

few longer-distance calls within the country or a short international call. For **international calls** of longer duration, invest in a higher-value card, or head for the post office, where you're assigned a cabin from which to phone and given the bill afterwards – either way, rates are cheapest Monday to Saturday 10pm to 7am, and all day Sunday. Avoid making international calls from your hotel room: charges are extortionate, and seem to rise in proportion to the star-rating of the hotel.

Mobile phones

The network for GSM phones in Croatia covers the whole country apart from a few blackspots in mountain areas. Before leaving home, you should contact your service provider to ensure that your **international roaming** facility is switched on (often entailing the payment of a hefty deposit); travellers from North America will also need to ensure they have a triband phone. Bear in mind that you are likely to be charged extra for incoming calls when abroad. If you want to retrieve messages while you're away, you'll have to ask your provider for a new access code, as your home one is unlikely to work abroad.

Both of Croatia's mobile phone operators, Cronet and VIP, operate schemes whereby it's possible to buy a local **SIM card** that you can use in your GSM phone, allowing you to make calls within the country at local rates, and to be called within Croatia without the caller incurring international charges. It may cost you as much as 300Kn to get on the scheme (although a certain amount of this fee is in the form of pre-payment for your future calls), after which you can purchase pre-payment top-ups in increments of 30Kn and upwards – so it's worth doing a few sums to see whether it's going to be worthwhile signing up.

The media

Having enjoyed a lively media scene in the 1980s and 1990s, when political and social changes reflected themselves in a startling array of opinionated and often subversive newspapers and magazines, Croatia has settled down to something approaching central European sobriety.

The most prestigious national **daily newspaper**, *Vjesnik* (ⓦwww.vjesnik.com), has a reputation for stodgy reporting and obsequiousness to whichever government happens to be in power. In comparison, the other national daily, *Jutarnji List*, is breezy and populist, contains much more showbiz gossip, and is more independent politically. Closest to Western tabloids in style is the evening paper *Večernji List*, which nevertheless includes good cultural coverage buried among the human interest stories.

The most influential of the **weeklies** is *Globus*, a glossy news magazine that reflects the broadly pro-Western, pro-liberal attitudes of Zagreb's emerging business class. However it fails to inspire the love and respect enjoyed by Split's **Feral Tribune** (ⓦwww.feral.hr), an irreverent cross between serious news magazine and counter-cultural youth rag, which began life as a humorous and satirical supplement of *Slobodna*

Dalmacija (Dalmatia's leading regional newspaper) in the late 1980s. *Feral* was an important source of opposition to the HDZ during the 1990s, offering a vibrant alternative to the stuffy and uninspiring political analysis offered by other papers and frequently ridiculing Franjo Tuđman. Tuđman took it personally and attempted a number of ruses to have *Feral* shut down – having it classified as a pornographic publication in order to qualify it for a higher tax rate, taking its editor to court for defaming the office of the president, and threatening its staff with military call-up being just three. Now that Tuđman's party is no longer in power, *Feral* has lost much of its bite, but remains the main anti-establishment voice in the country.

An increasing range of **foreign-language newspapers** is available from news kiosks in Zagreb and on the coast. Many of the most well-known English, German and Italian dailies are easy to come by, alongside all kinds of international fashion, lifestyle and computer magazines. There have been various attempts at publishing locally produced, English-language magazines about Croatia in recent years, almost always with turgid, uninformative results. If you can read Italian, you could always try *La Voce del Popolo*, the daily newspaper of Croatia's Italian minority – although the editorial offices are based in Rijeka, it's now published by Trieste's *Il Piccolo* and comes as a supplement of the latter.

TV and radio

Like some of Croatia's newspapers, the three national **television** channels, all run by state-owned HRT (Hrvatski radio i televizija), have a history of deference to successive governments, although they're now far from being the blatant propaganda tools they were under the Communists and then the HDZ. Current output tends towards the didactic, with plenty of plodding documentaries about Croatian history and culture, although HRT1 produces plenty of lavish shows featuring Croatian pop stars, especially in the summer when outdoor concerts are screened. HRT3 concentrates exclusively on sport. **Croatia Radio** (92.1Mhz), as well as numerous local stations on the coast, has news in English at regular intervals in summer.

With a shortwave radio, you can pick up the broadcasts of the BBC World Service (ⓦwww.bbc.co.uk/worldservice), Voice of America (ⓦwww.voa.gov) and Radio Canada (ⓦwww.rcinet.ca) among others; check their respective websites for frequencies and schedules.

Opening hours, public holidays and festivals

Shops in Croatia are usually open Monday to Friday from 8am to 8pm, and on Saturdays from 8am to 2 or 3pm. City supermarkets often stay open until about 6pm on Saturdays, and open on Sunday mornings as well. On the coast, during summer, shops introduce a long afternoon break and stay open later in the evenings to compensate. Office hours are generally Monday to Friday 8am to 3 or 4pm.

Tourist offices, travel agents and tourist attractions often change their opening times as the year progresses, generally remaining open for longer during the summer season (usually June–Sept). Note, though, that summer opening times don't necessarily come into force at the beginning of June: most places change over from summer to winter times according to how many tourists are around, rather than according to a fixed schedule. For this reason, we've occasionally listed "summer" and "winter" opening times in the guide rather than trying to give specific months.

On the coast, **museums and galleries** are often open all day every day (sometimes with a long break in the afternoon) in July and August, and closed altogether in the

Public holidays

All shops and banks are closed on the following public holidays:

January 1 New Year	**June 24** Day of Croatian Statehood
January 6 Epiphany	**August 5** National Thanksgiving Day
March or April Easter Monday	**August 15** Assumption
May 1 Labour Day	**October 8** Independence Day
May Corpus Christi	**November 1** All Saints Day
June 22 Day of the 1941 Anti-Fascist Uprising	**December 25 & 26** Christmas

depths of winter. At other times, things can be unpredictable, with attractions opening their doors when tourist traffic seems to justify it. In big cities and inland areas, museums and galleries are more likely to have regular opening times year round, and are often closed on Mondays.

Churches in city centres and well-touristed areas usually stay open daily between 7am and 7pm or later, but many in smaller towns and villages only open their doors around mass times. Churches or chapels which are known for being architecturally unique or which contain valuable frescoes may have set opening times (in which case we've mentioned them in the guide); otherwise you'll have to ask around to establish which of the locals has been nominated as holder of the key (*ključ*).

Monasteries are often open from dawn to dusk to those who want to stroll around the cloister, although churches or art collections belonging to the monasteries conform to the opening patterns for museums and churches outlined above. Accessibility often depends on the number of monks in residence and the regulations governing the monastic order itself – Benedictines, for example, have strict rules governing how much of the day should be set aside for prayer, and Benedictine nuns traditionally shun contact with the outside world, thereby limiting opportunities for members of the public to visit.

Traditional festivals

As befits a devoutly Catholic country, the Croatian year is peppered with **feast days** and **religious holidays**, featuring church processions and celebratory masses. In addition, each town or village has its own patron saint, whose feast day becomes the excuse for a communal knees-up – a selection is included on p.42.

The church calendar frequently dovetails with an older pagan one, corresponding to the changing seasons and the agricultural cycle. The most important event in the early part of the year is the pre-Lenten **carnival** (*karneval*; often known as *fašnik* in inland Croatia, *pust* on the Adriatic), which actually begins before Christmas but does not reach a climax until Shrove Tuesday or the weekend immediately preceding it, when there are processions and masked revelry in towns all over Croatia. A lot of places organize parades with floats, the participants donning disguises which frequently satirize local politicians or comment on the events of the past year. Rijeka, Samobor and Velika Gorica (just south of Zagreb) host the biggest events. The amount of post-parade hedonism differs from place to place, although the recently revived carnival in Split has already earned a reputation for its relaxed party atmosphere. Carnival processions are repeated in summer in some Adriatic resorts – a fun fancy-dress affair aimed at children and tourists. In smaller places carnival practices are still linked to pre-Christian fertility rites: in the villages near Rijeka groups of men (called *zvončari* or "ringers") don sheepskins and ring bells to drive away evil spirits, while in many areas a doll known as *pust* (or *poklad* in Lastovo) is ritually burned in order to cleanse the coming agricultural year of bad luck.

The next big event is **Easter week**, characterized by solemn processions in many towns, especially Hvar, Korčula and Vodice. Traditionally, the beginning of the summer agricultural cycle was marked by **St George's Day** (April 23), when a villager clad in branches and known as Zeleni Juraj (Green George) went from house to house accompanied by local children performing songs and dances. He received a gift from each household and in return presented

41

them with a fertility charm in the form of a twig. Unfortunately you'll see references to Jurjevo in ethnographic museums more often than in real life, although it's still celebrated in the villages of the Stubica valley north of Zagreb, and at Donja Lomnica, Gradići, Hrašće, Lukavac and Mala Mlaka just south of Zagreb (the Zagreb county tourist office will have details of many of these; ●www.tzzz.hr).

Another celebration with distinct pagan undertones is **St John's Day** (June 24), when local youths jump over bonfires (Ivanjski krijes) in a typical summer-solstice celebration. It's still practised in many places, especially in Karlovac. High summer is characterized by a sequence of important Christian holidays. **Our Lady of the Snows** (Aug 5) is celebrated with processions to churches associated with "miraculous" summer snowfalls, most famously at Kukljica on the island of Ugljan, where the procession takes the form of a flotilla of small boats. More important still is the **Assumption** (Aug 15), when churches throughout the country hold special services and large pilgrimages are made to Marian shrines such as Marija Bistrica near Zagreb, Krasno near Senj, Ludbreg between Varaždin and Koprivnica, Sinj in the Dalmatian hinterland, and Trsat near Rijeka. The **Birth of the Virgin** (Sept 8) is only slightly less important in the Catholic calendar, and is celebrated in similar fashion.

All Saints' Day (Nov 1) is one of the most important Catholic feasts of the autumn, when families visit graveyards to pay their respects to the departed. By the evening, many big-city cemeteries are transformed into a sea of candles. **St Martin's Day** (Nov 11) is traditionally the day when the year's wine is first tasted, and is often used as an excuse for revelry in wine-producing areas. In accordance with a widespread central European tradition, St Martin's Day is also marked by the slaughter and roasting of a goose. A slaughter of a more widespread kind takes place at the end of November, when many rural families (especially in Slavonia and the Dalmatian hinterland) set aside a weekend in order to carry out the annual **pig slaughter** (svinokolja or kolinja), and begin preparation of the sausages and hams which will be consumed over the next year.

On **St Nicholas's Day** (Dec 6) children leave out stockings and are rewarded with small presents if they're good. They also receive a gold- or silver-painted twig (šiba) – a symbol of the beating they will receive should they misbehave. Children are also threatened by visits from the monster Krampus, a kind of St Nicholas in reverse, who takes away bad children in his bag. **Christmas** itself is much the same as anywhere else in Europe, with presents laid out under the family Christmas tree. The main family meal is eaten on Christmas Eve (Badnja večer), and traditionally consists of fish (often carp), after which everyone attends midnight mass.

The country's main **folk festival** is the International Folklore Festival, held in Zagreb on the last weekend of July and traditionally the best place to see songs and dances from all over the country. The tradition of the Dalmatian klapa (male-voice choir) is preserved in numerous festivals up and down the coast, the biggest being the one held in Omiš in July. The remaining big folk events are all in Slavonia and have a more regional character, although the Brodsko Kolo Festival in Slavonski Brod (mid-June), Vinkovci Autumn (late Sept) and Đakovo Folk Festival (end Sept) are all worthwhile shindigs. Guests in Adriatic hotels will be treated to folklore shows, often over dinner, throughout the summer season. Local songs and dances are performed outside the church in Čilipi, near Dubrovnik, every Sunday morning.

Feast days and folkloric events

Feb 2 Kumpanjija Sword Dance, Korčula.
Feb 3 Feast of St Blaise, Dubrovnik.
Sunday before Shrove Tuesday Carnival Procession, Rijeka.
Shrove Tuesday Carnival Procession, Split.
Good Friday Procession of the Religious Brotherhoods, Korčula.
April 23 St George's Day (Jurjevo).
May 7 Feast of St Domnius, Split.
May 8 Birthday of Cardinal Stepinac, Krašić.
Second weekend in May Roč Accordion Festival.
June Festival of Međimurje songs (Međimurske popevke), Nedelišće, midway between Varaždin and Čakovec.
Mid-June Brodsko Kolo Folklore Festival, Slavonski Brod.
June 24 St John's Day (Ivanje).
July Krk Folklore Festival.
July Klapa Festival, Omiš.
Mid-July Summer Carnival, Novi Vinodolski.

July 25 **Feast of St James**. Performances of the Kumpanjija Sword Dance, Korčula.

July 27 **St Christopher's Day**. Crossbow Tournament, Rab.

July 29 **Feast of St Theodore**. Performance of the Moreška Sword Dance, Korčula.

Late July **Carnival**, Iž.

Late July **International Folklore Festival**, Zagreb.

Early Aug **Fešta od srdela** (Anchovy Festival). Food and folklore, Fažana.

Early Aug **Sinjska Alka**, Sinj.

Early Aug **Saljske užance**. Folk festival and town carnival, Sali.

Aug 5 **Feast of Our Lady of the Snows** (Madona od snijega/sniga). Boat procession on Ugljan, and performance of the Kumpanjija Sword Dance, Korčula.

Aug 8 **Feast of St Lawrence**.

Mid-Aug **Tilting at the Ring** (Trka na prstenac), Barban. Competition in which horsemen attempt to spear a ring on the end of a lance.

Aug 15 **Assumption** (Velika Gospa). Large gatherings at Marija Bistrica, Trsat, Sinj and Aljmaš.

Aug 16 **Feast of St Rock**. Performance of the Moštra Sword Dance at Postrana and the Kumpanjija Sword Dance at Korčula.

Late Aug **Susret sopaca** (Meeting of Sopila Players). Folk Music Festival, Pinezići, Krk.

Aug 27–29 **Feast of St Pelagius**, Novigrad.

Mid-Sept **Vinkovačka Jesen** (Vinkovci Autumn), Vinkovci. Folklore Festival.

Early Sept **Kaj su jeli naši stari** (What our forefathers ate), Vrbovec, just east of Zagreb. Traditional food and folklore festival.

Sept 8 **Birth of the Virgin** (Mala Gospa).

Last weekend in Sept **Đakovački vezovi** (Đakovo Embroidery), Đakovo.

Last weekend in Sept **Grape Harvest Festival**, Pregrada, Zagorje.

Oct 8 **Feast of St Simeon**, Zadar. Religious procession and opening of St Simeon's coffin.

Nov 1 **All Saints' Day** (Svi sveti).

Nov 11 **Feast of St Martin** (Martinje). Celebrations at Dugo Selo, Tar, Vrsar and Buzet.

Dec 6 **Feast of St Nicholas** (Sveti Nikola). Presents are given to children and a fishing boat is burnt outside the Benedictine monastery at Komiža, Vis.

Dec 25 **Christmas** (Božić).

Cultural festivals

Every Adriatic town organizes cultural events of some sort over the summer, usu-ally featuring outdoor concerts of pop, classical music or folk. The most important of these is the **Dubrovnik Summer Festival**, six weeks of classical music and drama beginning in early July, much of which is performed in the squares and courtyards of the old town. The Dubrovnik Festival's only real rival in the high-culture stakes is the **Split Summer**, which offers a varied diet of top-notch music and theatre. Historical buildings also form the backdrop for a number of other classical music events, including the Osor Music Evenings on the island of Cres; summer concerts in the half-abandoned hill village of Lubenice, also on Cres; the Musical Summer in the Istrian hill town of Grožnjan; summer recitals in St Donat's Church in Zadar; and the Varaždin Festival of Baroque Music, which uses many of the city's fine churches.

Zagreb has a full roster of festival events, the most prestigious being the Biennale of New Music, a festival of cutting-edge contemporary classical work held in odd-numbered years, although challenging new work also crops up at the Contemporary Dance Week in early June; Eurokaz European Theatre Festival in late June; and PIF international puppet festival in late August.

Avant-garde traditions elsewhere in the country are showcased at the Požega Festival of One-Minute Films, the Zadar Dreams festival of new theatre, the Split Festival of Creative Disorder, and Split's Festival of New Film and Video.

Outdoor rock concerts and dance events take place all over the Adriatic coast in summer. The Valkana Beach Festival near Pula in August is one of the better established rave and techno extravaganzas, although new ones are emerging all the time.

Croation arts festivals

Late April **Biennale of New Music**, Zagreb (odd-numbered years only).

May **Festival of One-Minute Films**, Požega.

Early June **Contemporary Dance Week** (Tjedan suvremenog plesa), Zagreb.

Late June **Eurokaz Festival of Contemporary Theatre**, Zagreb.

Early July **Split Jazz Festival**.

Early July to late Aug **Dubrovnik Summer Festival** (Dubrovačke ljetne igre).

Mid-July **Naive Art Fair** (Sajam naive), Koprivnica.

July Osor Music Evenings (Osorske večeri), Osor, Cres. International chamber-music festival.

July Istria Ethno Jazz, Pula, Pazin and Svetvinčenat.

Mid- to late July Festival of Dance and Non-verbal Theatre (Festival plesa i neverbalnog kazališta), Svetvinčenat.

Mid-July to mid-Aug Zadar Theatrical Summer (Zadarsko kazališno ljeto).

Late July to early Aug Grožnjan Jazz Festival.

July to early Aug Concerts in the Church of St Donat, Zadar.

Mid-July to mid-Aug Split Summer (Splitsko ljeto), Split. Music and drama, staged in what was once Diocletian's Palace.

Early Aug Valkana Beach Festival, Pula. DJs and club culture.

Aug Etho Ambient Live, Salona, near Split. World music.

Aug Croatian Film Festival, Pula.

Aug International Film Festival, Motovun.

Aug Zadar Dreams (Zadar snova). Festival of alternative drama and performance art.

Aug Festival of Creative Disorder (Festival kreativnog nereda), Split. Alternative art, music and performance.

Aug Kamplin Jazz Festival, Krk.

Aug Musical Summer (Glazbeno ljeto), Grožnjan.

Late Aug Pontes Literature Festival, Krk.

Late Aug to early Sept PIF International Festival of Puppet Theatre, Zagreb.

Late Sept to early Oct International Festival of New Film (Međunarodni festival novog filma), Split. Shorts, documentaries and art-house films.

Late Sept to early Oct Varaždin Festival of Baroque Music. Performances in Varaždin cathedral and other city churches.

Oct Nebo World Music Festival, Zagreb.

Sport

Sport in Croatia occupies an important position in society, not least because sporting successes have proved consistently important in enhancing national prestige abroad – something of which former Wimbledon champion Goran Ivanišević (whose face you'll see on billboards advertising everything from bank accounts to beer) is an outstanding individual example. Participation in group activities carries a high value in a society in which solidarity and togetherness are prized, sometimes at the expense of individual self-expression. Male team sports have always been encouraged, and recent years have seen an explosion in the number of majorettes and marching bands – as if to provide girls with a parallel sphere of activity.

Football (*nogomet*) has come a long way in Croatia since it was introduced to the country in 1893 by the crew of a British frigate who took on a team of locals just outside Trogir's main town gate. Croatian footballers formed an important part of the Yugoslav sides of the 1960s and 1970s, whose reputation for skill and audacity earned them the tag of "the Brazilians of Europe", although few imagined the impression the Croats would make on the international scene in the 1990s. Resting on a backbone of talented individuals including Robert Prosinečki, Davor Šuker, Alen Bokšić, Slaven Bilić and Igor Štimac, the Croatian team finished third in the 1998 World Cup, beating Germany 3–0 in the quarter-finals before narrowly succumbing in the semis to host nation France. However, Croatia failed to qualify for the European Championships in 2000 and performed poorly in the 2002 World Cup, leading many to believe that the golden age of Croatian football was over.

The domestic league is hampered by a lack of real competition. The big teams **Dinamo Zagreb** and **Hajduk Split** have more or less monopolized domestic honours since 1991, occasionally challenged by the likes of NK Zagreb, Rijeka and Osijek. Both Hajduk and Dinamo (under their previous name of Croatia Zagreb) have performed creditably in the UEFA Champions' League, although both teams are hamstrung by the fact that their best players invariably leave to play abroad as soon as they've made a name for themselves. Matches between the big two can attract big crowds, but otherwise attendances are all too often in the low thousands, with most fans content to follow the game on the HRT3 television channel.

The football season lasts from mid-August to late May, with a two-month winter break in January and February. Matches usually take place on Saturdays or Sundays, with extra games scheduled for Wednesday evenings as the season draws to a climax in April–May. The cheapest seats rarely cost more than 30Kn. Tickets for all but the biggest matches can be bought at the ground before the game. For international matches (usually played at Dinamo Zagreb's Maksimir stadium) or European ties, purchase tickets from the stadium box office as far in advance as possible.

After football, the most popular sport is **basketball** (*košarka*), with teams like Split, Zadar and Cibona Zagreb enjoying large followings and a Europe-wide reputation. It's

another sport in which Croatia exports its best players, with performers like Tony Kukoč, Dino Rađa and the late Dražen Petrović (see p.79) finding big-time success in the NBL. **Handball** (*rukomet*), **volleyball** (*odbojka*) and **waterpolo** (*vaterpolo*) all get a good deal of newspaper and television coverage. One sport which is definitely not televised – although you'll see a lot of it in Dalmatia and Istria – is a form of **bowls** known as *bočanje* (derived from the Italian *boccie*), which is played in villages on a sandy outdoor rectangle by local men on summer evenings. Finally, no discussion of Croatian sport would be complete without mention of skiing phenomenon and all-round national treasure **Janica Kostelić**, who returned from the 2002 Winter Olympics with a three gold medals, sending the nation into paroxysms of jubilation as a result.

You can **bet** on all kinds of sports in one of the betting shops (*sportska kladionica*) which have sprung up all over Croatia in recent years – nowadays there's hardly a single high street without one. The emergence of these establishments owes a great deal to the Croatian football stars who spent a large part of their careers playing for clubs in England, observed betting shops at work, and decided to invest in them once they returned home.

Outdoor pursuits

Croatia is not well known as a destination for adventure tourism, but there are numerous outdoor activities on offer, whether hiking in the hills of the interior or scuba-diving in the Adriatic. Sailing is best organized before you arrive (see p.10).

Hiking

Hiking was first popularized in Croatia in the late nineteenth century, when the exploration of the great Croatian outdoors was considered a patriotic duty as well as a form of exercise. It's still a popular weekend activity, especially in spring and early summer, before the searing Mediterranean heat sends people scurrying for the beaches.

Easy rambling territory in inland Croatia is provided by wooded **Mount Medvednica** and the **Samobor Hills** (Samoborsko gorje), both close to Zagreb and crisscrossed by well-used trails. Higher altitudes and longer walks can be found in the **Gorski Kotar** region, between Karlovac and the coast: the main targets here are Risnjak in the north of the range, best reached from Rijeka, and Klek and Bijele stijene in the south. On the

Adriatic coast, **Učka**, immediately above Opatija and Lovran, is one of the most easily accessible mountains, and can be safely bagged by the moderately fit hiker. Further south, the more challenging **Velebit** range stretches for some 100km along the eastern shore of the Kvarner Gulf; its main hiking areas are around the Zavižan summit near Senj, and the Paklenica National Park at Velebit's southern end. In Dalmatia, the principal peaks are **Kozjak** and **Mosor** (immediately west and east of Split respectively) and, most challenging of all the Adriatic mountains, **Biokovo**, above the Makarska Riviera.

Ranges such as Gorski Kotar and Velebit seem to invite extended expeditions, but unfortunately hut-to-hut walking in Croatia is still in its infancy, and no local travel agencies organize it. Mountain refuges (*planinarski dom*) run by local hiking associations do exist, but they're usually only open at the weekend, making anything longer than a 36-hour trek unfeasible.

Detailed hiking **maps** are published by the Croatian Hiking Association, Kozarčeva 22, Zagreb (Hrvatski planinarski savez; Mon–Fri 9am–3pm; ☎01/445-79-11, ◉hps.inet.hr), although they're only sporadically available in bookshops and you'll have to visit the association in person to inspect the full range. Tourist offices sometimes sell hiking maps of their own area (for instance the tourist information centre in Zagreb sells maps of Mount Medvednica), but don't bank on it.

Rafting

An increasing range of **whitewater rafting** trips are being organized by the bigger travel agents. GeneralTurist, Praška 5, Zagreb (☎01/48-10-033, ℻48-10-420, ◉www.generalturist.com), run weekend trips to the Kupa, Dobra and Mrežnica rivers near Zagreb from early July until late October. On the coast, tourist agencies organize trips down the River Cetina southeast of Split, and the River Zrmanja just east of Zadar; you'll find contact details in the relevant sections of the Guide. The rafting season here usually runs from May to September, although trips on the Zrmanja may be suspended in July owing to low water levels. Prices vary according to the duration of the trip – expect to pay 220–350Kn per person for a day's excursion.

Diving

Thanks to the crystal-clear waters of the Adriatic and the diversity of the local marine life, Croatia has become one of the most popular **scuba-diving** venues in the Mediterranean over the last few years. There's a growing number of diving centres along the Adriatic coast offering lessons, guided expeditions and equipment rental. Most resorts will have somewhere offering one-day introductory courses for 200–300Kn, as well as a range of other courses for all abilities. If you already hold a diving certificate, you need to pay a registration fee (100Kn), available from registered diving centres or from the local harbourmaster's office (*lučka kapetanija*), before being allowed to dive in Croatia.

One of the most rewarding areas for diving, with clear waters and rich marine life, is the **Kornati islands** in mid-Dalmatia. Its national-park status means that diving here can only be arranged through officially sanctioned operators like Neptun in Vodice (☎022/331-444,◉www.neptun-sub.hr) and Aquanaut in Murter (☎022/434-988). For general information, contact the Croatian Diving Federation at Pro Diving Croatia, Dalmatinska 12, 10 000 Zagreb (☎01/48-48-765, ℻48-49-119, ◉www.diving.hr).

Windsurfing

There are only really two places to go in Croatia for serious windsurfers. The best is **Bol** on the island of Brač, which stands on the northern side of the narrow channel dividing Brač from Hvar, providing calm waters and channelling the right kind of winds. Second-best is the **Kućište-Viganj** area just west of Orebić, which occupies a similar position on the Pelješac channel dividing the mainland from Korčula. Bol is a fully developed package resort with all the accommodation and nightlife opportunities one would expect; Kućište and Viganj on the other hand are unspoiled villages equipped with a few private rooms and campsites. Whichever you choose, you'll find plenty of people renting out gear (boards 200–250Kn per day) and offering courses (8hr tuition costs about 600Kn).

Skiing

Croatia has two main skiing areas: **Sljeme** on Mount Medvednica just outside Zagreb, and

Bjelolasica in the Gorski kotar between Zagreb and Rijeka. Although both are fun venues for occasional skiing if you're already visiting Croatia, neither is worth planning a holiday around. Altitudes (1035m and 1533m respectively) are too low to guarantee long periods of adequate snow cover, and most Croats treat skiing trips as spur-of-the-moment events if the weather is right. You can rent gear and sign up for lessons at either place.

Crime and personal safety

The crime rate in Croatia is low by European standards. Your main defence against petty theft is to exercise common sense and refrain from flaunting luxury items. Take out an insurance policy before you leave home (see p.24) and always carry a photocopy of the crucial information-bearing pages of your passport with you – this will enable your consulate to issue you swiftly with new travel documents in the event of your passport being stolen.

Croatian police (*policija*) are generally helpful and polite when dealing with foreigners, but rarely speak English. Routine police checks on identity cards are common in Croatia: always carry your passport or driving licence. If you get into trouble with the authorities, wait until you can explain matters to someone in English if at all possible. The police are not allowed to search your car or place of abode without a warrant.

Should you be arrested, you can be held in a police station for 24 hours without charge. They will automatically notify your consulate of your arrest – this will usually take place within the first 24 hours.

Emergency numbers

Police ☎92
Ambulance ☎94
Fire ☎93
Sea rescue and diving alert ☎9155

Sexual harassment

Croatia is a patriarchal society in which many women find themselves holding down a full-time job while simultaneously managing the household on behalf of their menfolk. However, there are few specific situations in which female travellers might feel uncomfortable, and no real no-go areas, although some of the more down-at-heel café-bars can feel like male-only preserves. By Western standards, Croatia's streets are relatively safe at night, even in the cities.

Croatian men like to regard the annual deluge of foreign female tourists as fair game, but any display of Mediterranean machismo tends to be leavened by genuine attempts at gallantry and charm. A suitably firm response should be enough to cope with unwanted attentions. Alternatively, try to imitate the repertoire of stony silences and withering looks employed by the local women.

The aftermath of war

Almost a third of Croatia was occupied by Serb forces between 1991 and 1995, and although you shouldn't have any qualms about visiting these areas now, a few precautions should be borne in mind. Almost all frontline areas were heavily **mined** during the war, and few of these minefields have been fully cleared. Most are well marked with signs bearing the skull-and-bones symbol and the word "mine", although it would be unwise to trust this marking system 100 percent – some mined areas may not be as well labelled as others. Basically, any abandoned village or stretch of agricultural land which looks as if it has been left uncultivated since 1995 is potentially dangerous. If you're travelling to eastern Slavonia (Beli Manastir, Vukovar, Ilok), western Slavonia (Jasenovac, Novska, Pakrac), the area between Karlovac and Split (Slunj to Knin) and the Zadar hinterland, stick to roads and pavements and don't go wandering off into the countryside unsupervised.

Travellers exploring the above itineraries are likely to see **war damage** in the shape of shelled buildings and burned-out houses, but also a great deal of energetic building and reconstruction. Both Croats and Serbs are returning to areas where they once lived side by side, and outbreaks of inter-communal violence are now few and far between. However, the casual visitor will probably miss the nuances of Croat–Serb relations: tension still exists, many refugees continue to occupy houses claimed by others, and each community tends to stick to its own cafés and bars. Exercise discretion therefore before embarking on historical or political discussions with the locals.

Work and study

High levels of unemployment in Croatia ensure that work is not that easy to find, and local wages are in any case pretty low – anything above £400/$600 a month is generous indeed. All foreigners need a work permit in order to be employed in Croatia: few employers actually enjoy this kind of paperwork and are even less likely to take you on as a result.

The easiest way to find **voluntary work** in Croatia is by enrolling in one of the organized programmes run by the state or various charitable organizations. The US-based Volunteers for Peace (☏802/259-2759, ⊛www.vfp.org) is a non-profit organization with links to a huge international network of workcamps, some in Croatia, offering two- to four-week programs that bring volunteers together from many countries to carry out needed community projects. Voluntary work helping to protect the **griffon vultures** on the island of Cres (see p.211) can be arranged through **ECCIB** (Eco-centre Caput Insulae in Beli, Beli 4, Cres (☏051/840-525, ⊛www.caput-insulae.com). The **Croatian Heritage Foundation** (Hrvatska Matica Iseljenika) occasionally organizes "task forces" of young people – often of Croatian descent – who help in war reconstruction and participate in various archeological and ecological programmes; for details, contact them at Odjel za školstvo, Trg Stjepana Radića 3, 10 000 Zagreb (☏01/611-5116, ⊛www.matis.hr).

If you speak some Croatian, you could approach **Suncokret**, Avenija Dubrovnik 10, 10 000 Zagreb (☏01/655-1705, ⊛www.suncokret.hr), a non-governmental organization which provides help for socially needy Croatians and organizes programmes working with people traumatized by the recent war. They run a couple of summer camps around the country, at which you're expected to pay for your own food and accommodation.

Teaching English has traditionally been the main opportunity for work in Croatia, though this sort of work, too, is not easy to come by: the standard of local English teaching is reasonably high and few schools specifically seek out native English speakers. Vacancies are unlikely to be advertised anywhere; most people find work through personal contacts rather than official channels. If you're determined to get a teaching job, consider getting a **CELTA** (Certificate in English Language Teaching to Adults) qualification before you leave home. Strictly speaking, you don't need a degree to do the course, but you'll certainly find it easier to get a job with the degree/certificate combination. The **British Council** in the UK (☏020/7930 8466, ⊛www.britishcouncil.org) recruits TEFL teachers for posts worldwide and occasionally has placements in Croatia; check the website for a current list of vacancies.

Courses

The **Croatian Heritage Foundation** (Hrvatska Matica Iseljenika; see opposite) organizes summer courses on various aspects of Croatian culture and language, including folk-music workshops. They also organize academic courses at the University of Zagreb in conjunction with American and Canadian universities. Full details from Hrvatska Matica Iseljenika, Odjel za školst-vo, Trg Stjepana Radića 3, 10 000 Zagreb (℡01/611-5116, ⊛www.matis.hr). For students from the USA, another resource to investigate is ⊛www.studyabroad.com, which carries listings of study and work programmes worldwide, including some in Croatia.

Travellers with disabilities

More attention has been paid to Croatians with disabilities since the 1991–95 war, in view of the large number of wounded and disabled veterans it created. Many public places in Croatia are wheelchair accessible, especially in larger cities, though in general, access to public transport and tourist sites still leaves a lot to be desired.

There's a growing number of wheelchair-accessible hotels, though these tend to be in the more expensive price brackets. Some areas of the country seem slower to adapt than others – at the last visit, the fashionable town of Hvar didn't have a single hotel with wheelchair access.

Tourist offices throughout Croatia will usually find out whether there are any suitable accommodation facilities in their region if you ring in advance, but be sure to double-check the information they give you – some tourist office listings optimistically state that a place has disabled facilities, when in fact it doesn't.

Planning a holiday

There are organized tours and holidays specifically for people with disabilities – the contacts in the box below will be able to help with latest information. If you want to be more independent, it's important to become an authority on where you must be self-reliant and where you may expect help, especially regarding transport and accommodation. It's also vital to be honest – with travel agencies, insurance companies and travel companions. Know your limitations and make sure others know them. If you don't use a wheelchair all the time but your walking capabilities are limited, remember that you are likely to need to cover greater distances while travelling (often over rougher terrain and in hotter temperatures) than you are used to. If you use a wheelchair, have it serviced before you go and carry a repair kit.

Read your travel insurance small print carefully to make sure that people with a pre-existing medical condition are not excluded, and use your travel agent to make your journey simpler: airline or bus companies can cope better if they are expecting you, with a wheelchair provided at airports and staff primed to help. A medical certificate of your fitness to travel, provided by your doctor, is also extremely useful; some airlines or insurance companies may insist on it. Make sure that you have extra supplies of drugs – carried with you if you fly – and a prescription including the generic name in case of emergency. Carry spares of any clothing or equipment that might be hard to find; if there's an association representing people with your disability, contact them early in the planning process.

Contacts for travellers with disabilities

UK and Ireland

Irish Wheelchair Association Blackheath Drive, Clontarf, Dublin 3 ℡01/818 6400, ⊛www.iwa.ie. Useful information provided about travelling abroad with a wheelchair.
Tripscope Alexandra House, Albany Rd, Brentford, Middlesex TW8 0NE ℡0845/758 5641, ⊛www.tripscope.org.uk. This registered charity provides a telephone information service offering

free advice on transport for those with a mobility problem.

US and Canada

Access-Able www.access-able.com. Online resource for travellers with disabilities.
Society for the Advancement of Travelers with Handicaps (SATH) 347 5th Ave, New York, NY 10016 ☏212/447-7284, www.sath.org. Non-profit educational organization, with some useful online information.
Wheels Up! ☏1-888/38-WHEELS, www.wheelsup.com. Provides discounted airfare, tour and cruise prices for disabled travellers.

Australia and New Zealand

ACROD (Australian Council for Rehabilitation of the Disabled) PO Box 60, Curtin ACT 2605 ☏02/6282 4333, TTY ☏02/6282 4333,
www.acrod.org.au. Provides lists of travel agencies and tour operators for people with disabilities.
Disabled Persons Assembly 4/173–175 Victoria St, Wellington, New Zealand ☏04/801 9100, www.dpa.org.nz. Resource centre with details of travel agencies for people with disabilities.

Croatia

Association of Organizations of Disabled People in Croatia (Savez Organizacija Invalida Hrvatske) Savska cesta 3, 10 000 Zagreb ☏ & ℗01/48-29-394. Publishes informative guides – though only in Croatian – for disabled travellers to Zagreb, Pula, Split, Varaždin and Rijeka.
ZET Balokoviceva bb, Zagreb ☏01/66-00-443, ℗685-179. The Zagreb Electric Tram Company organizes free transport for disabled people anywhere in and around Zagreb in a specially adapted vehicle.

Directory

Addresses The Croatian word for street, *ulica*, is either abbreviated to *ul.* or omitted altogether if the meaning is clear enough without it. The street name always comes before the number; in some cases you'll come across the name of a street followed by "bb", which simply means *bez broja*, or "without a number" – this often refers to a newly constructed building which hasn't been fitted into the street's numbering system. In Adriatic cities, the main seafront boulevard – whatever its official name – is usually known simply as the Riva, and is often denoted as such in addresses.

Cigarettes Croatia produces major international brands of cigarettes under licence, as well as its own makes, which are not nearly as bad as their ersatz names (such as Ronhill and Walter Wolf) suggest. Cigarettes are sold in kiosks marked with the word *duhan* (tobacco), supermarkets, bars and restaurants and cost about 15Kn a packet for domestic brands, 20Kn a packet for international brands. *Zabranjeno pušenje* means "no smoking", an injunction that applies to cinemas, all buses, trams and Croatian Airlines flights. There are few no-smoking areas in Croatia's cafés and restaurants unless you go to a *slastičarnica*

(patisserie), where smoking is very rare.
Cinema Most towns of any size will have a cinema (*kino*), although many of these amount to little more than a ticket booth and the auditorium itself – if you want drinks or popcorn, buy them before you arrive. Ticket prices rarely exceed 20–30Kn, and films are shown in their original language with Croatian subtitles. The cinema repertoire consists almost entirely of Hollywood films, with new releases arriving in the country a month or two after opening in Western Europe.
Electricity 220 volts. Round, two-pin plugs are used – if you need an adaptor, equip yourself with one before you leave home.
Film Major brands of colour print film are widely available in Croatia, as well as instant developing facilities. Film for black-and-white prints or colour transparencies is harder to get hold of outside major resorts, and you won't be offered the range you're used to at home – best to stock up before you leave.
Gay and lesbian Although homosexuality has been legal in Croatia since 1977, it remains something of an underground phenomenon, and public displays of affection between members of the same sex may provoke hostility, especially

outside big cities. The younger generation is more liberal in its attitudes to homosexuality, and though there are few recognized gay hangouts, some of the more alternative clubs in Zagreb have a reputation for attracting a tolerant, mixed crowd. For the most part, however, life for gay men in Croatia still consists of cruising public parks and running the risk of being beaten up by skinheads. Zagreb has a small gay and lesbian community, with organizations such as Because Press, a lesbian activist group founded in 1977 (info at ⓔsuncana@zamir.net), and Kontra, another lesbian group, with a help line for women. For more information, visit ⓦwww.gay-croatia.com.

Laundry Self-service launderettes are hard to come by in Croatia, although most towns have a laundry (*praonica*) where you can leave a service wash.

Left luggage Most train stations have a left-luggage office (*garderoba*), which has a daily charge (calculated on the size of your bags – roughly 5–10Kn) for each item deposited. Keep all the scrappy little receipts, or you'll never get your gear back. A few large stations have coin-operated luggage lockers which can store your baggage for up to 24 hours.

Naturism Naturism (denoted locally by the German acronym "FKK") has a long history on the Adriatic coast. There are self-contained naturist holiday villages in Istria (the biggest are just outside Poreč, Rovinj and Vrsar), and naturist campsites in Istria and the island of Krk. Throughout Croatia, you'll find isolated coves or stretches of beach which have been set aside for naturists, at a discreet distance from the main family-oriented sections. Topless bathing is acceptable almost anywhere, but entering cafés or buses in your beachwear is strongly disapproved of.

Taxes Prices often include a sales tax, known locally as PDV, of up to 22 percent. Foreign visitors can claim a PDV tax refund at the Croatian Customs Service for goods over 500Kn (around $63), as long as they have kept all original invoices, though your refund can take up to a year to arrive.

Time Croatia is always one hour ahead of GMT (except for one week at the end of September when the time is the same), six hours ahead of US Eastern Standard Time, nine hours ahead of Pacific Standard Time, ten hours behind Australian Eastern Standard Time, and twelve hours behind New Zealand.

Tipping Tipping is not obligatory, but it's polite to round the bill up to a convenient figure, although waiting staff won't expect this if you've only had a cup of coffee – tipping is only really expected when you've had a round of drinks or a meal.

Toilets Public toilets (*zahod* or *WC*) are rare outside bus and train stations, although every restaurant, café or bar will have one.

Guide

Guide

1 Zagreb 55–93

2 Inland Croatia 95–147

3 Istria 149–190

4 The Kvarner Gulf 191–242

5 Dalmatia 243–363

6 Dubrovnik 365–400

Zagreb

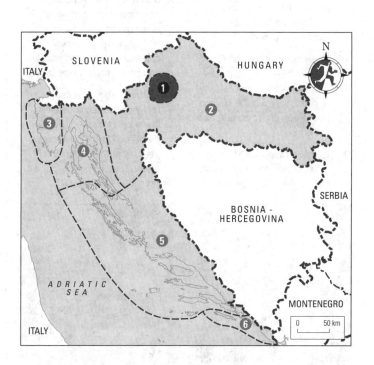

CHAPTER 1

Highlights

✱ **Tkalčićeva ulica** This pedestrianized strip of cafés and bars is the perfect venue for night-time promenading, people-watching or just posing. **See p.69**

✱ **Gradec** Relaxing Baroque quarter, nestling unobtrusively in the heart of the modern city. **See p.71**

✱ **Museum of Arts and Crafts** Labyrinthine collection harbouring every form of applied art, from the classic to the downright quirky. **See p.77**

✱ **Mimara Museum** You can lose yourself for hours in this vast collection of painting and sculpture from all over the world. **See p.77**

✱ **Mount Medvednica** The mountain ridge on Zagreb's doorstep is a paradise for woodland walkers. **See p.82**

✱ **Saturday morning coffee** The most important social event of the week for locals, who pack the pavement cafés to overdose on caffeine and conversation. **See p.86**

✱ **Licitarska srca** Garish, tacky and totally inedible, these heart-shaped, peppercorn-flavoured biscuits are the only authentic souvenir of the Zagreb region you're likely to find. **See p.91**

Zagreb

Although it has been the capital of an independent nation for little more than a decade, **ZAGREB** has served as the cultural and political focus of Croatia since the Middle Ages. Now home to almost a quarter of the country's population, the city grew out of the medieval communities of Kaptol and Gradec, which began life as separate fortified settlements but gradually grew to identify themselves as a single city. However, the present-day appearance of Zagreb owes most to the rapid growth of the nineteenth century, and many of the city's buildings are grand, peach-coloured monuments to the self-esteem of the Austro-Hungarian Empire. Outwardly, at least, Zagreb still shares the refined urban culture of Mitteleuropa – public transport is well organized, the streets are clean, the parks impeccably manicured – but behind the city's genteel facade teems a complex blend of central European, Mediterranean and Balkan cultures. The city's high-rise suburbs, built to accommodate families drawn to the capital by the rapid industrialization which followed World War II, continue to function as collection points for Croatia's diverse population.

In recent years the city's population has nudged beyond the million mark. Fighting in the south and east of the country produced an influx of migrants – especially Croats from Hercegovina, who enjoyed a disproportionate amount of influence in the city due to their links with the right-of-centre HDZ, the political party of Tuđman. They're still referred to (only half-jokingly) as "white socks" due to their supposed lack of sartorial sophistication, while those families which have been resident here for a few generations are proud to call themselves *purgeri*, a term which comes from the same Germanic root as the English word "burgher" and harks back directly to the city's Habsburg past. True purgerism in all its heel-clicking, hand-kissing extravagance may have died out, but the name lives on as an important badge of Zagreb identity and, inevitably, is used pejoratively by outsiders to describe the snobbish urban pretensions of the capital.

With most travellers to Croatia heading straight for the coast, Zagreb is rarely overrun by foreign tourists, encouraging visitors to adapt to the unhurried rhythms of local life rather than trawling from one tourist trap to another. Sightseeing is a low-key affair – museums are occasionally absorbing but rarely spectacular – and a couple of days will be enough to give you a good taste of what the city offers, unless you get sucked in by the city's burgeoning nightlife, in which case a somewhat longer sojourn may well be in order. By day, Zagreb functions best as an outdoor city. The alleyways of the Baroque **Kaptol** and **Gradec** districts are an atmospheric place for a wander whatever the season, and in spring and summer downtown streets which can seem oppressively sombre during the winter suddenly become clogged with café tables as soon

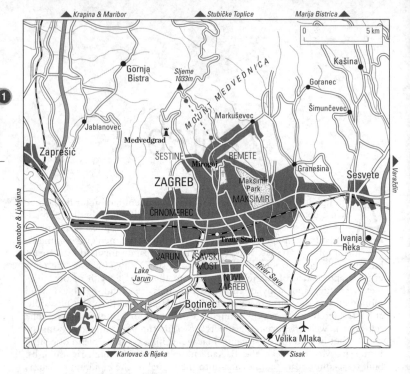

as the weather improves, while popular strolling areas such as **Tkalčićeva** and **Preradovićev trg** take on a languorous Mediterranean glamour.

Leaving aside urban attractions, you shouldn't leave Zagreb without exploring at least some of the city's attractive rural hinterland. To the north, the ridge of **Mount Medvednica** and its peak, **Sljeme**, provide the city with a year-round recreation area, and much of inland Croatia (see chapter 2) is within day-trip range.

Some history

Despite evidence of Iron Age settlements on top of Gradec hill, the history of Zagreb doesn't really start until 1094, when Ladislas I of Hungary established a bishopric here in order to bring the northern Croatian lands under tighter Hungarian control. A large ecclesiastical community grew up around the cathedral and its girdle of episcopal buildings on **Kaptol** (which roughly translates as "cathedral chapter"), while the Hungarian crown retained a garrison opposite on **Gradec**. Both were significantly damaged during the Mongol incursions of 1240–42, prompting King Bela IV of Hungary to rebuild the settlement on Gradec and accord it the status of a royal free town in order to attract settlers and regenerate urban life. The settlements prospered from their position on the trade routes linking Hungary to the Adriatic, despite the growing Ottoman threat that began to emerge in the fifteenth century.

By the sixteenth century the name **Zagreb** (meaning, literally, "behind the hill" – a reference to the town's position at the foot of Mount Medvednica) was being used to describe both Kaptol and Gradec, although the two communities rarely got on – control of the watermills on the river dividing them was a constant source of enmity. The biggest outbreak of intercommunal fighting occurred in 1527, when the throne of Croatia was disputed by the Habsburg emperor Ferdinand II (supported by Gradec) and the Hungarian noble Ivan Zapolyai (supported by Kaptol), a conflict which culminated in the sacking of Kaptol by Habsburg troops. With the Turks in control of much of Slavonia and the Adriatic hinterland, and the Venetians pre-eminent on the coast, by the late 1500s the Croatian lands had been reduced to a northern enclave with Zagreb at its centre. Because of Zagreb's growing importance as a centre of political power, the separate identities of Kaptol and Gradec began to disappear. The Croatian parliament, the Sabor, usually met here from the sixteenth century onwards, and Croatia's governor, the Ban, resided here more or less permanently after 1621.

Much of what remained of Croatia was reorganized as the **Military Frontier** – a belt of territory running around the Habsburg Empire's border with Ottoman-controlled Bosnia – and taken away from the Sabor's control; with real political power concentrated in Vienna and Budapest, Zagreb increasingly became a provincial outpost of the Habsburg Empire. The Sabor was moved to Varaždin in the mid-eighteenth century, and Zagreb may well have lost its pre-eminence in Croatian affairs permanently had Varaždin not been almost totally destroyed by fire in 1776. It wasn't until the mid-nineteenth century that the growth of a Croatian national consciousness confirmed Zagreb's status as guardian of national culture. The establishment of an academy of arts and sciences (1866), a philharmonic orchestra (1871), a university (1874) and a national theatre (1890) gave Zagreb a growing sense of cultural identity, although ironically it was an Austrian, the architect Hermann Bollé (1845–1926), creator of the School of Arts and Crafts, Mirogoj Cemetery and Zagreb Cathedral, who contributed most to the city's new profile.

With the creation of **Yugoslavia** in 1918, political power shifted from Vienna to Belgrade – a city which most Croats considered an underdeveloped Balkan backwater. Things improved marginally after World War II, when Croatia was given the status of a socialist republic and Zagreb became the seat of its government, but the city still resented the extent to which it was overshadowed by Belgrade. A major period of architectural change came in the 1950s and 1960s, when visionary mayor Večeslav Holjevac presided over the city's southward expansion, and the vast concrete residential complexes of **Novi Zagreb** were born.

Zagreb survived the collapse of Yugoslavia relatively unscathed – despite the rocket attack on President Franjo Tuđman's offices on Gradec in October 1991 – although there's little doubt that the long-term effects of war, economic stagnation and post-communist corruption have left their mark. Politically, Zagreb entered the 1990s as a stronghold of the HDZ, but drifted towards the opposition (as did most of urban Croatia) as the decade wore on. A coalition of anti-Tuđman parties thought that they'd won city elections in 1997, only for Tuđman to block the appointment of a mayor until sufficient numbers of city councillors could be cajoled into voting for the HDZ candidate. With the city deprived of a convincing political life during the Tuđman era, symbols of civic pride tended to lie outside the realms of "official" culture. Prime among these were the **Bad Blue Boys**, the supporters of football team Dinamo Zagreb (see box on p.90); having boycotted their team's matches after the politically motivated decision to change the club's name to "Croatia Zagreb", these fans still enjoy the respect of people who have never followed the sport in their lives. Much the same could be said of popular local radio station **Radio 101**, whose brash style and anti-establishment stance made it a thorn in the side of successive regimes. Radio 101's moment of glory came in November 1996 when, in a clumsy attempt to extend government control over the media, they were denied a licence to broadcast. Ten thousand people staged an impromptu protest in central Zagreb that very night, and the following evening saw a 120,000-strong rally of support. The government backed down and gave Radio 101 a new lease of life, eventually awarding it another franchise in November 1997.

Since the death of President Tuđman in December 1999, political passions have become far less important in shaping the city's identity. With Croatia speedily rebuilding its commercial links with the rest of Europe, the capital's citizens are more interested in business than ideology, and have clearly benefited from economic change more than anyone else in the country – a fact which has given Zagreb a stylish, prosperous and optimistic sheen.

Arrival, information and city transport

Zagreb is a disarmingly easy place to find your way around, with almost everything of importance revolving around the city's central square and main reference point, **Trg bana Jelačića**. Most attractions are within walking distance of here, although many of the cheaper accommodation options, along with a selection of outlying museums, restaurants, bars and clubs, are in inner-city areas within 2–3km (a short tram ride) of the square. Zagreb north of the main square is an attractively hilly place, merging with the slopes of **Mt Medvednica**; elsewhere the terrain is unremittingly flat, with grid-plan suburbs stretching south to the broad **River Sava** 3km from the square, with the concrete-and-steel settlement of **Novi Zagreb** on the opposite bank.

Zagreb's **airport**, situated about 10km southeast of the city, is connected with the bus station by half-hourly Croatia Airways buses (25Kn) between 7.30am and 8pm; after that time buses run only to connect with specific flights. A taxi from the airport to the centre costs about 200–250Kn. Zagreb's central **train station** is on Tomislavov trg, on the southern edge of the city centre, ten minutes' walk from the **main square**, Trg bana Jelačića. The main **bus station** is about ten minutes' walk east of the train station at the junction of Branimirova and Držićeva. Tram #6 (destination Černomerec) runs from here to Trg bana Jelačića, passing the train station on the way.

There are two main **tourist information centres** (*turistički informativni centar*; TIC) in central Zagreb, one at Trg bana Jelačića 11 (summer Mon–Fri 8am–8pm, Sat & Sun 9am–6pm; winter Mon–Fri 8.30am–8pm, Sat 10am–5pm, Sun 10am–2pm; ☎01/48-14-051 or 48-14-052, ⍟www.zagreb -touristinfo.hr), and another a few hundred metres to the south at Zrinjevac 14 (summer Mon–Fri 8am–8pm, Sat & Sun 9am–6pm; winter Mon, Wed & Fri 9am–5pm, Tues & Thurs 9am–6pm; ☎01/49-21-645). Both offices have free city maps and can recommend accommodation options, although neither will book rooms. Free **booklets** available from the tourist offices include *Events and Performances* (providing monthly concert listings) and *Zagreb A–Z* (yellow-pages-style information covering hotels, restaurants and other services). However, neither compares in terms of detail or readability with *Zagreb in Your Pocket* (available from news kiosks for 20Kn, or see ⍟www.inyourpocket .com), a city guide covering accommodation, food and nightlife, updated every two months.

Both tourist offices sell the **Zagreb Card** (60Kn for 72hr), which entitles the bearer to free public transport, free use of the Sljeme cable car (see p.82), a fifty percent reduction on museum and gallery fees, and reductions in some theatres, discos and restaurants; it's just about worth having for the transport and cable car alone.

City transport

Zagreb has an efficient and comprehensive network of trams and buses run by **ZET**, the municipal transport authority (Ⓦ www.zet.hr), with Trg bana Jelačića and the train station as the main **hubs** of the system. Maps of the system are displayed at each tram stop. The network is divided into three concentric **zones**; all Zagreb's **tram routes** operate entirely within the central zone, so you'll only enter the outer two zones if making an out-of-town excursion by suburban bus.

Regular bus and tram services run from about 4.30am to 11.20pm, after which **night trams** come into operation. Night services operate different routes from their daytime counterparts (although they use the same stops), and run at irregular intervals (usually every 40–50min), so knowing when and where to wait for them is very much a local art form.

Zagreb street names

The flexible nature of Croatian grammar means that there are often two ways of saying a **street name**, and the version you hear in the spoken language may not be the same one you see on street signs. Maps tend to feature the versions of names used in the spoken language, although be prepared for inconsistencies on this score. Thus "Nikola Tesla Street" in the centre of Zagreb can be rendered as either ulica Nikole Tesle ("street of Nikola Tesla") or Teslina ulica ("Tesla's street"). The latter is more common in everyday speech and on maps, although the word ulica ("street") is usually dropped. Similarly, ulica Pavla Radića becomes Radićeva, and ulica Ivana Tkalčića becomes Tkalčićeva.

To complicate matters further, a couple of Zagreb's best-known squares have **colloquial names** which differ from their official ones. Trg Nikole šubića Zrinskog usually goes under the name of Zrinjevac; and Trg Petra Preradovića is almost universally referred to as Cvjetni trg ("Flower Square"), because it used to be the venue of a large florists' market.

Version seen on street signs	Version used in spoken language and on maps
Trg svetog Marka	Markov trg
Trg Marka Marulića	Marulićev trg
Trg brace Mažuranića	Mažuranićev trg
Trg Petra Preradovića	Preradovićev trg/Cvjetni trg
Trg Josipa Jurja Strossmayera	Strossmayerov trg
Trg kralja Tomislava	Tomislavov trg
Trg Nikole Šubića Zrinskog	Zrinjevac
Ulica kneza Branimira	Branimirova
Ulica Ljudevita Gaja	Gajeva
Ulica Janka Draškovića	Draškovićeva
Ulica Andrije Hebranga	Hebrangova
Ulica Junije Palmotića	Palmotićeva
Ulica Pavla Radića	Radićeva
Ulica Augusta Šenoe	Šenoina
Ulica Nikole Tesle	Teslina
Ulica Ivana Tkalčića	Tkalčićeva

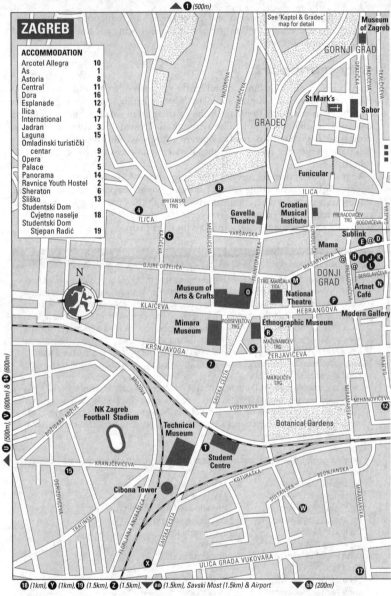

ZAGREB

ACCOMMODATION

Arcotel Allegra	10
As	1
Astoria	8
Central	11
Dora	16
Esplanade	12
Ilica	4
International	17
Jadran	3
Laguna	15
Omladinski turistički centar	9
Opera	5
Palace	14
Panorama	2
Ravnice Youth Hostel	2
Sheraton	6
Sliško	13
Studentski Dom Cvjetno naselje	18
Studentski Dom Stjepan Radić	19

Tickets are brought from ZET kiosks at major tram stops and terminuses, tobacco (*duhan*) kiosks, some newspaper kiosks or from the driver. There's a flat fare per journey: single-zone tickets are 6.50Kn from kiosks, 8Kn from the driver; two-zone tickets are 12/14Kn; three-zone tickets, 17/18Kn. All kiosks also sell day tickets (*dnevne karte*; 18Kn), which can be used for unlimited travel within a single zone and are valid until 4am the following morning. All tickets are validated by punching them in the machines once on board.

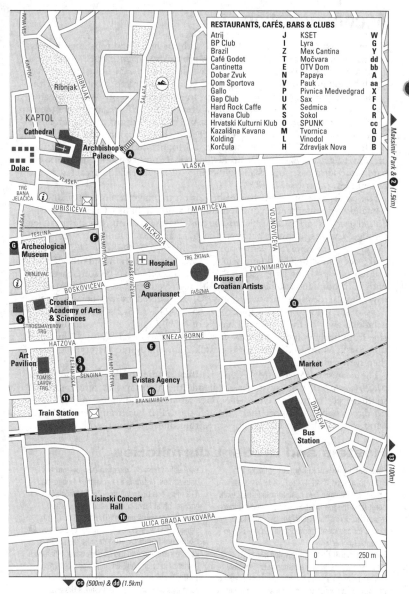

RESTAURANTS, CAFÉS, BARS & CLUBS

Atrij	J	KSET	W
BP Club	I	Lyra	G
Brazil	Z	Mex Cantina	Y
Café Godot	T	Močvara	dd
Cantinetta	E	OTV Dom	bb
Dobar Zvuk	N	Papaya	A
Dom Sportova	V	Pauk	aa
Gallo	P	Pivnica Medvedgrad	X
Gap Club	U	Sax	F
Hard Rock Caffe	K	Sedmica	C
Havana Club	S	Sokol	R
Hrvatski Kulturni Klub	O	SPUNK	cc
Kazališna Kavana	M	Tvornica	Q
Kolding	L	Vinodol	D
Korčula	H	Zdravljak Nova	B

For **taxis**, there's an initial charge of around 10Kn, after which it's 10Kn per kilometre, prices rising by about thirty percent after midnight. Taxis are most easily found on Trg maršala Tita, at the northern end of Gajeva, and at the bottom of Bakačeva between Trg bana Jelačića and Kaptol. There's nowhere to rent **bicycles** in central Zagreb, although open-air stalls beside Lake Jarun (see p.81) rent out bikes during the summer to cycle round the lake.

Accommodation

While Zagreb is reasonably well served with medium- and top-range **hotels**, budget choices are relatively thin on the ground, so advance reservations are a good idea. Always try and ring a few days in advance – 24 hours' notice may not be enough to secure a bed. Unless you can afford to splash out on the handful of places which measure up to international five-star standards, Zagreb's downtown hotels don't offer a great deal of choice: rooms are pretty much the same wherever you go, and few places have a distinct character. There are better deals in the suburbs, although the cheapest rooms are over 20km north of town near the Sljeme summit of Mount Medvednica (for directions on how to get there, see p.82), an idyllic spot if you like woodland walks, but hardly the ideal base for urban sightseeing. All hotels include breakfast in the price unless otherwise stated.

The city's stock of **youth hostel** beds is on the increase, and between mid-July and late September accommodation in **student halls of residence** (*studentski dom*) is made available to tourists. Private **rooms** can be arranged through **Evistas**, midway between the train and bus stations at Šenoina 28 (Mon–Fri 9am–8pm, Sat 9am–5pm; ☎01/48-39-546, ℻48-39-543; ❷), who will place you with a local family in the town centre or in the suburbs of Novi Zagreb (see p.81) or Jarun (see p.81). They also offer two-person apartments with bathroom and kitchenette (❸), although you have to stay at least three days. Similar deals on private rooms (❷) are offered by the helpful **Lacio**, Trnsko 15e (Mon–Fri 9am–4pm; ☎01/65-52-047, ℻65-21-523). Their office is hidden away in the residential blocks of Novi Zagreb, a thirty-minute tram ride from likely points of arrival – from the bus station, take tram #7 (destination Savski Most) to the Trnsko stop, walk 200m south into the housing estate, then turn right.

The nearest **campsite** (May–Sept) is 10km southeast of town at the *Plitvice Motel* (see p.66), a grassy spot right beside the highway that runs round the southern side of the city, with self-service restaurants and shops on site. There's no direct public transport there, though the #112 bus from Zagreb's Savski Most to the village of **Lučko** goes to within fifteen minutes' walk of the site.

Hostels and student dormitories

Omladinski turistički centar Petrinjska 77 ☎01/48-41-261 & 48-47-267, ℻48-41-269. Grotty two-hundred-bed hostel five minutes' walk north from the train station, offering beds in four- or six-bed dorms for 120Kn per person. May closed for complete renovation in 2004 – ring in advance to check.
Ravnice Youth Hostel 1. Ravnice 38d ☎01/233-2325, ⊛www.ravnice-youth-hostel.hr. Privately owned, easy-going and friendly hostel 4km east of the centre, in a large modern house just behind Croatia's biggest confectionery factory – which produces a pleasant chocolatey aroma here whenever the wind's in the right direction. Bright, sunny bunk-bed rooms, and a couple of doubles. There's no breakfast, but you get free use of a kitchen and there are plenty of neighbourhood shops. You can get your washing done here for a nominal fee.

Take either tram #4 (direction Dubec) from the train station, or trams #11 (direction Dubec) and #12 (direction Dubrava) from Trg bana Jelačića, and get off at Ravnice (the second stop after Maksimir soccer stadium). The hostel is a well-signed 5min walk down 1. Ravnice. Beds 99kn, ❶
Studentski Dom Cvjetno naselje Odranska 8. Beds booked through the student travel office here (Turistisički ured; Mon–Fri 9am–4pm; ☎01/619-1240). There are single and double rooms with en-suite facilities, and the rate includes breakfast. Tram #14 (direction Zapruđe) or #17 (direction Prečko) from Trg bana Jelačića or tram #4 (direction Savski most) from the train station to Vjesnikov neboder (the office block where the *Vjesnik* newspaper is produced); Odranska is round the back of the block. ❸
Studentski Dom Stjepan Radić Jarunska 2

(booked through the student travel office at Cvjetno naselje; see above). Doubles only, with facilities in the hallway. Breakfast included in the rate. Tram #17 (direction Prečko) from Trg bana Jelačića to Stjepan Radić. ❸

Hotels

Note that accommodation in the immediate vicinity of the main square and within the Kaptol and Gradec areas to the north is marked on the map on p.68.

Central Zagreb

Arcotel Allegra Branimirova 29 ☎01/46-96-000, ⊛www.arcotel.at. Austrian-owned business hotel, handy for the train station and a 15min walk from the main square. En-suite rooms with TV offer a mixture of warm colours and minimalist chic. ❻

Astoria Petrinjska 71 ☎01/48-41-222, ⓕ48-41-212, ⓔhotel-astoria@zg.tel.hr. Compact en-suite rooms with TV and phone. The furnishings are ageing fast, but rooms are generally clean. Convenient for the train and bus stations. Some triples. ❺

Central Branimirova 3 ☎01/48-41-122, ⊛www.hotel-central.hr. Small rooms with en-suite facilities and TV, diagonally opposite the train station. Rooms are smart and comfortable, if a little cramped. ❺

Dubrovnik Gajeva 1 ☎01/48-73-555, ⓕ48-18-447, ⊛www.tel.hr/hotel-dubrovnik. Modern glass-and-steel palace just off Trg bana Jelačića; some rooms in the older wing overlook the square. Recently renovated to international standards, offering smart en-suite rooms (doubles have baths, singles come with showers) with TV and telephone. ❼

Esplanade Mihanovićeva 1 ☎01/45-66-666, ⓕ45-77-907, ⊛www.esplanade.tel.hr. Luxurious outpost of Mitteleuropa next to the train station, with marble-clad Art Deco interior and opulent café and function rooms. Fully refurbished in 2002, it's a bit over the top for some tastes, but still the most characterful of Zagreb's hotels. Doubles from 1600Kn. ❾

Ilica Ilica 102 ☎01/37-77-522, ⊛www.hotel-ilica.hr. Friendly family-run hotel featuring small-ish but smart en-suite rooms with TV and phone. Enormously popular – reserve well in advance and, if possible, ring to reconfirm the day before your arrival. It's in the courtyard of a low-rise office block 1500m west of Trg bana Jelačića. Take tram #6 from the bus or train station (destination Černomerec) until you see the hotel on your right. ❹

Jadran Vlaška 50 ☎01/45-53-777, ⓕ46-12-151, ⊛www.hup-zagreb.hr. Medium-rise hotel just east of the city centre and a 15min walk from the train station. Dingy from the outside, it's quite pleasant inside and has modest en-suite rooms with TV and phone. Take tram #4 (destination Dubrava) from the train station or tram #8 (destination Mihaljevac) from the bus station to Draškovićeva, after which it's a short walk east along Vlaška. ❹

Opera Kršnjavoga 1 ☎01/48-92-000, ⓕ48-92-001, ⊛www.opera-zagreb.com. Modern luxury hotel handily located close to the theatres and museums around Trg maršala Tita; it also boasts an indoor swimming pool. Doubles from 1800Kn. ❾

Palace Strossmayerov trg 10 ☎01/48-14-611, ⓕ48-11-358, ⊛www.palace.hr. Attractive turn-of-the-century pile between the train station and Trg bana Jelačića, with comfortable a/c rooms, all with bath. ❽

Pension Jägerhorn Ilica 14 ☎01/48-33-877, ⓕ48-33-573. In a courtyard just off the main shopping street, and only 500m from Trg bana Jelačića. Comfortable, central and soon fills up. Take tram #6 (destination Černomerec) from the bus or train station to Trg bana Jelačića, then walk west. ❻

Sheraton Kneza Borne 2 ☎01/45-53-535, ⓕ45-53-035, ⊛www.sheraton.com/zagreb. Pretty much without equal in the comfort stakes, although it's in an uninspiring grid of streets ten minutes' walk east of the centre. The atmosphere in the lobby area's cafés and restaurants is rather sterile, but the hotel does boast a gym and indoor pool. Doubles from 1600Kn. ❾

The suburbs

As Zelengaj 2a ☎01/46-09-111, ⓕ46-09-303. Four-star comforts 2km northwest of the centre in the leafy suburb of Zelengaj, in a curvy-roofed contemporary building that blends rather well with its woodland surroundings. The roomy doubles offer classy nineteenth-century-style furnishings, TV, minibar, and big bathtubs. There's a formal, top-notch restaurant on site. You can walk down into the city through a belt of suburban forest – the perfect way to clear your head before that all-important business meeting. ❼

Dora Trnjanska 11e ☎01/631-1900, ⊛www.zeljeznicko-ugostiteljstvo.hr. Railway-owned former worker's hostel, transformed into an unpretentious but comfy medium-sized hotel, offering simple but neat en-suite rooms without TV. Somewhat unromantically situated beside a busy multi-lane highway, but handily placed for both bus and train stations, and the city centre is only a 20min walk away. Very popular with both tourists and businessmen on a budget, so ring in advance. ⑤

International Miramarska 24 ☎01/610-8800, ⓦwww.hotel-international.hr. Bland ten-storey building offering Eighties-era beige-brown rooms with TV and bathtub. It's in a modern area of government offices and grey residential blocks, a 10min walk south of the train station. On the characterless side, but perfectly comfortable and well run. ⑤

Laguna Kranjčevićeva 29 ☎01/38-20-222, ⓦwww.hotel-laguna.hr. Five-storey concrete affair opposite the NK Zagreb football stadium and a stone's throw from the Dražen Petrović basketball centre – which probably explains why it's so popular with visiting sports teams. Rooms are on the small side, but come with TV, bathtub and standard-issue socialist-era furniture. ⑤

Lido Jarun ☎01/38-32-839. Small hotel at the eastern end of Lake Jarun, 4km southwest of the centre, featuring attractive loft rooms with en-suite facilities. Take tram #17 (destination Jarun) from Trg bana Jelačića to the Srednjaci stop, after which it's a 10min walk down Hrgovići to the lake. ⑥

Motel Plitvice Lučko ☎01/65-30-444, ⓕ65-30-445, ⓔmotel@motel-plitvice.hr. Modern architect's idea of a rustic hut, sitting beside the motorway 10km southeast of town – useful if you just want a place to rest up before heading for the coast. The rooms are functional en-suite affairs with TV, grouped around an indoor courtyard stuffed with potted plants. There's a self-service canteen on site, as well as a full-blown restaurant serving up roast meats. Also the site of Zagreb's only campsite (see above). ❸

Panorama Trg sportova 9 ☎01/36-37-333, ⓕ30-92-657, ⓦwww.hup-zagreb.hr. High-rise hotel 2km east of the centre, recently renovated to provide four-star levels of comfort. North-facing rooms on the higher floors come with great views of the city. Take tram #9 (destination Ljubljanica) from the train station to Trešnjevački trg, then turn right onto Trakošćanska and you'll see the hotel looming up on your left after 5min. ⑥

Sliško Supilova 13 ☎01/618-4777, ⓦwww.slisko.hr. Medium-sized hotel in a residential street 20m away from the bus station. Some of the rooms are a tight squeeze, but they all come with modern furnishings, TV and air conditioning. Ask about cash discounts. ⑤

Zagreb Bundek bb, Novi Zagreb ☎01/66-37-333, ⓕ66-37-229, ⓦwww.hup-zagreb.hr. Characterless though acceptable concrete box 3km south of the centre in the modern suburb of Novi Zagreb, offering small, minimally furnished and careworn rooms with showers. A good place from which to explore the mysterious, tree-shrouded Lake Bundek (see p.82). There's plenty of parking on site, but if you're heading there by public transport, you'll need to take tram #6 from the train or bus station to the Sopot terminus, then walk 600m north. ❸

Mount Medvednica

Janica Sljemenska cesta bb ☎01/45-80-397, ⓕ45-52-185, ⓦwww.hunjka.hr. Medium-sized hotel on the eastern shoulder of Mount Medvednica, offering simple but smart en-suite rooms with pine floors and furnishings, plus on-site restaurant. It's sited in a lovely meadow encircled by forest about 23km out of Zagreb on the road to Donja Stubica; the nearest public transport is the top station of the Sljeme cable car, a 40min walk away. ❷

Tomislavov Dom Sljeme ☎01/45-55-833, ⓕ45-55-834, ⓦwww.sljeme.hr. Large mountaintop hotel surrounded by woodland, with café, restaurant and neat en-suite rooms featuring TV and telephone. There's an indoor swimming pool too. Just below the summit of Sljeme, a 5min walk from the cable-car station, or 21km from the centre of Zagreb by road. ❸

The City

Central Zagreb divides into three distinct areas, joined by the main square, **Trg bana Jelačića**. Occupying the high ground north of the square are the two oldest parts of the city, **Kaptol** and **Gradec**, the former the site of the cathedral, the latter a peaceful district of ancient mansions and quiet squares. Beneath them spreads the nineteenth- and twentieth-century **Donji grad**, or "Lower Town", a bustling area of prestigious public buildings and nineteenth-century apartment blocks.

Beyond the centre, there's not much of interest among the broad boulevards and bland modern buildings which extend south to the River Sava and, beyond that, to the suburb of Novi Zagreb. Aside from the artificial lake at Jarun, southwest of the city, and the leafy park of Maksimir to the east, the most obvious target is the ramblers' paradise of nearby Mount Medvednica, served by cable car from suburban Zagreb and an easy trip out from the centre.

Trg bana Jelačića and around

A broad, flagstoned expanse flanked by cafés and hectic with the whizz of trams and hurrying pedestrians, **Trg bana Jelačića** ("Governor Jelačić Square") is as good a place as any to start exploring the city, and is within easy walking distance of more or less everything you're likely to want to see. It's also the biggest tram stop in the city, standing at the intersection of seven cross-town routes, and the place where half the city seems to meet in the evening – either beneath the tall clock on the western side of the square, or at the Znanje bookshop (colloquially known as "Krleža" after Croatia's greatest twentieth-century writer, Miroslav Krleža) on the corner of the square and Gajeva. In recent years the square has occasionally provided the venue for mass outbreaks of Croatian solidarity, most notably on February 25, 2002, when thousands assembled here to greet downhill skiing phenomenon Janica Kostelić, who had returned from the Winter Olympics at Salt Lake City with a record haul of medals – three gold and one silver – to her credit.

Originally a vast open space known as "Harmica" due to its use as a collection point for local taxes (after the Hungarian word *harmincad*, meaning a thirtieth), Trg bana Jelačića was laid out as the city's main square in the 1850s and has been Zagreb's focal point ever since. The elegant pastel blues and pinks of its surrounding buildings provide a suitable backdrop for the attention-hogging equestrian statue of the nineteenth-century Ban of Croatia, **Josip Jelačić** (see p.410), completed in 1866 by the Viennese sculptor Fernkorn just as the Habsburg authorities were beginning to erode the semi-autonomy which Jelačić had won for the nation. The square was renamed Trg republike in 1945 and the statue – considered a potential rallying point for Croatian nationalism – was concealed behind a wooden shell covered with communist propaganda slogans. Party agitators finally dismantled the statue on the night of July 25, 1947, although its constituent parts were saved from destruction by a local museum curator, who stored them in a basement of the Yugoslav (now Croatian) Academy of Arts and Sciences. In 1990 the square was renamed Trg bana Jelačića and Jelačić restored to his rightful place, although his statue now faces a different way. In the 1860s it was positioned with Jelačić's drawn sabre pointing eastwards, indicating the direction in which Croatia's then enemies – the Hungarians – were to be found. Now it points southwards, as if to emphasize the historic rupture between Croatia and her Balkan neighbours. On the eastern side of the statue is the **Manduševac**, a small, stepped depression – named after a stream which used to run through the area – concealing a modest fountain, built in 1987, when the whole square was repaved in preparation for Zagreb's hosting of the World Student Games.

West of Trg bana Jelačića, trams rumble along **Ilica**, the city's main shopping street, which runs below Gradec hill. South of the square is the popular modern pedestrianized area around **Gajeva**, where the glass facade of the *Dubrovnik* hotel serves as a futuristic backdrop for passing shoppers or the drinkers seated outside *Charlie Brown's*, the café where most of the city's political elite seem to gather for conspiratorial chin-wagging on Saturday and Sunday lunchtimes – even in winter, Zagreb's movers and shakers would rather freeze to death

ZAGREB:
KAPTOL & GRADEC

Museum
of Zagreb

Natural
History
Museum

Meštrović
Atelier

DEMETROVA

Sabor

St Mark's
Church

MARKOV
TRG

Historical
Museum
of Croatia

Kamenita
Vrata

Komedija
Theatre

Ribnjak

KAPTOL

Gallery of Naive Art

Museum of
Modern
Art

Kula
Lotršćak

JEZUITSKI
TRG

KATARININ
TRG

Klovićevi
Dvori

Archbishop's
Palace

Cathedral

St Catherine's
Church

Funicular

Dolac

GRADEC

N

ILICA

TRG BANA
JELAČIĆA

Serbian
Orthodox
Church

PRERADOVIĆEV
TRG

BOGOVIĆEVA

JURIŠIĆEVA

0   100m

TESLINA

ACCOMMODATION
Dubrovnik   2
Pension Jägerhorn   1

RESTAURANTS, CAFÉS, BARS & CLUBS

Baltazar	C	Jabuka	A	Maharadža	J	Pod Gričkim Topom	O
Boban	U	K. u. K	S	Melin	H	Rubelj	Q
Bulldog	T	Kerempuh	N	Nokturno	M	Saloon	F
Dubravkin Put	D	Lapidarij	I	Oliver Twist	G	Stari Fijaker	P
Fellini	R	Londoner Pub	B	Pizzeria Dvojka	E	Tolkien	K
Hemingway	L						

drinking coffee outside *Charlie's* than risk not being seen. A sharp right here leads into **Bogovićeva**, a promenading area full of cafés and shops which culminates in **Preradovićev trg**, a lively square known for its cinemas and pavement cafés. It's still referred to by most locals as Cvjetni trg ("Flower Square") after the flower market which used to be held here until the area was cleaned up in the 1980s – a few sanitized florists' pavilions still survive. Watching over the scene is Ivan Rendić's 1895 statue of **Petar Preradović** (1818–72), an ethnic Serb from Bjelovar in eastern Croatia who served as a general in the Austro-Hungarian army and wrote romantic poetry which, although it's no longer widely read, contributed to the development of an evolving Croatian literary language. Behind the statue rises the grey form of the **Serbian Orthodox Church** (Pravoslavna crkva), an unassuming nineteenth-century building whose icon-filled interior, rich with candles and the smell of incense, is worth a quick peek.

Dolac and Tkalčićeva

Occupying a large terrace overlooking Trg bana Jelačića to the north is **Dolac**, the city's main market. This feast of fruit, vegetables and meat is held every morning, but is at its liveliest on Friday mornings, when fresh fish arrives from the coast. Curving uphill immediately to the left of Dolac is **Tkalčićeva**, formerly known as Potok ("Stream") due to its position on the dried-up water-course that once separated Kaptol from Gradec. Probably the prettiest single street in the city, Tkalčićeva preserves a neat ensemble of the one- and two-storey, steep-roofed nineteenth-century houses that have largely disappeared elsewhere. There's a smattering of boutiques and art galleries tucked into the street's low-ceilinged mansions, although most of these are now occupied by the youthful café-bars which have transformed Tkalčićeva into the city's prime area for drinking on warm summer evenings. The whole area used to have a somewhat darker reputation in the years before World War I, when Kožarska, the alleyway which runs parallel to Tkalčićeva to the west, served as the city's red-light district, "reeking of debauchery, adultery, crime, drunkenness, and promiscuity", in the words of diarist and novelist Miroslav Krleža. Also leading off to the west of Tkalčićeva is **Krvavi most** ("Bloody Bridge" – a reminder of the often violent disputes between Gradec and Kaptol), a street which links up with Radićeva, offering a short cut up to Gradec.

Kaptol

Northeast of Trg bana Jelačića, the filigree spires of Zagreb's cathedral mark the edge of the district known as **KAPTOL**, home to the city's Catholic institutions and still patrolled by pious citizens and nuns of various orders. The area consists of little more than one long street – initially called Kaptol, later becoming Nova ves in its northern reaches – and the **cathedral** itself, at its southern end, is the district's only arresting feature. Ringed by the ivy-cloaked turrets of the eighteenth-century **Archbishop's Palace** ("a southern Kremlin", fancied the archeologist Arthur Evans), the cathedral is almost wholly neo-Gothic, having been rebuilt by Viennese architects Friedrich von Schmidt and Hermann Bollé after a catastrophic earthquake in 1880. Most of the money and creative endeavour was invested in the two spires – the big architectural statement it was felt a growing city like Zagreb needed. The interior is high and bare – only four Renaissance choir stalls from the early sixteenth century and the faded remains of some medieval frescoes survive from before the earthquake. The modest main altar, bearing a copy of the statue of the Madonna and Child in the church at Maria Bistrica, stands in front of a glass casket holding an effigy of Archbishop Alojzije Stepinac (see box on p.70), head of the Croatian Church during World War II and imprisoned by the communists immediately afterwards. Stepinac's grave, near the altar on the north wall of the church, is marked by a touching relief by Ivan Meštrović in which the archbishop kneels humbly before Christ. There's another statue by Fernkorn in front of the cathedral of a richly gilded Madonna surrounded by four angels, which provides a beckoning sparkle as you approach Kaptol from the south.

Descending east from the cathedral to Vlaška and turning left brings you to **Ribnjak**, a small, shady park situated on the site of a former fishpond, and overshadowed on one side by the crumbling remains of Kaptol's erstwhile fortifications. One of the city's most charming open spaces, the park was reserved for Kaptol's priests until 1947, when the railings surrounding it were demolished by the same communist activists who put paid to the statue of Jelačić on Trg bana Jelačića.

Archbishop Alojzije Stepinac

For many, **Alojzije Stepinac** (1898–1960) personifies the link between the Croatian nation and the Catholic Church. Branded a quisling by the communists, but regarded by most ordinary Croats as a martyr and patriot, he has assumed immense symbolic importance since his death in 1960. It's a development which has been broadly encouraged by the Vatican: Stepinac was beatified by Pope John Paul II on his visit to Croatia in October 1998.

Born into a relatively prosperous peasant family in the village of Krašić (see p.141), 50km southwest of Zagreb, Stepinac was initially dissuaded from entering the priesthood by parents eager for him to manage the family farm. During World War I he served with the Yugoslav Legion, a body assembled by the Allies to fight for a united South Slav state. After the war he briefly studied agronomy in Zagreb, but soon returned to Krašić, dismayed by the immoral lifestyles of his fellow students. Settling back into village life he got engaged to girl-next-door Marija Horvat, who addressed him as "my dear ice-cold betrothed" and eventually broke off the relationship, realizing that his mind was focused on more spiritual matters.

Having finally opted for the Church, Stepinac ascended through the priestly ranks at great speed, becoming **Archbishop of Zagreb** in 1937. Stepinac's rise was promoted by the government in Belgrade, which still viewed him as pro-Yugoslav – although Stepinac, like many Croats, had by this stage lost his faith in South Slav unity. Stepinac had little enthusiasm for Nazism, but his response to the German-imposed NDH, the "Independent State of Croatia" proclaimed in April 1941, was at best contradictory. He initially instructed Croatian priests to support the new regime, naively regarding the Nazi puppet Ante Pavelić as a patriot who would keep Croatia free from the great Catholic bugbears: communism and freemasonry. Once the true nature of the NDH became apparent, however, he began to change tack. By June 1941 he was already protesting to Pavelić about the inhuman treatment of Serbian deportees, though he initially thought the crimes committed in the name of the NDH were the work of individual hotheads rather than the regime itself – according to the memoirs of the sculptor Ivan Meštrović, the archbishop burst out crying when he finally realized that Pavelić himself was giving the orders. Stepinac consequently stepped up his criticism of the regime as the war went on, and also used his personal authority to save many individuals who would otherwise have faced execution.

As the war neared its end, Stepinac's profound hostility to the Partisans prevented him from reaching an understanding with Croatia's new masters. Eager to demoralize the anti-communist opposition, Yugoslavia's new strongman Josip Broz Tito (see box on p.104–105) decided to make an example of the archbishop, and had him **arrested** in May 1945. After a preposterous trial in which the Catholic hierarchy was accused of working in tandem with foreign intelligence services, Stepinac was found guilty of "anti-national activities" in December 1946 and sentenced to sixteen years' imprisonment.

Stepinac spent five years in **Lepoglava jail** (see p.107) before being allowed home to Krašić, where he occupied a modest two-room apartment in the house of the local priest. Stepinac's release was presented to the world media as an example of the communist regime's leniency, although he was effectively under house arrest until his death. Foreign journalists who tried to see the archbishop were told that a constant police guard was needed to protect Stepinac from the wrath of the working class. Made a **cardinal** by the pope in 1952, Stepinac was the subject of quiet admiration to those Croats who remained unconvinced by government propaganda, and his grave in Zagreb cathedral became an unofficial shrine long before the collapse of communism in 1990.

Gradec

Uphill to the northwest of Trg bana Jelačića, **GRADEC** (known colloquially as "Grič") is the most ancient and atmospheric part of Zagreb, a leafy, tranquil backwater of tiny streets, small squares and Baroque palaces, whose mottled brown roofs peek out from the hill. The most leisurely approach is to take the **funicular** (*uspinjača*; daily 6.30am–9pm every 10min; 2.50Kn each way), which ascends from Ilica, about 200m west of Trg bana Jelačića; alternatively, wander up the gentle gradient of Radićeva towards the **Kamenita vrata**, or "stone gate", which originally formed the main eastern entrance to the town. Inside Kamenita vrata – actually more of a long curving tunnel than a gate – lies one of Zagreb's most popular shrines, a simple sixteenth-century statue of the Virgin in a grille-covered niche. Miraculous powers have been attributed to the statue, largely on account of its surviving a fire in 1731 – a couple of benches inside the gate accommodate passing city folk eager to offer a quick prayer.

Katarinin trg and around

Just to the south of Kamenita vrata, Jezuitski trg is flanked on the east side by **Klovićevi dvori**, a seventeenth-century former Jesuit monastery now used for temporary art exhibitions (Tues–Sun 11am–7pm; the admission price varies according to what's on display; ⓦwww.galerijaklovic.hr), and housing a small café and courtyard that hosts concerts during the Zagreb Summer Festival (see box on p.88). Beyond here, where Jezuitski trg opens out onto the next square, **Katarinin trg**, is **St Catherine's Church** (Crkva svete Katerine; daily 10am–1pm), built by the Jesuits in the 1620s and containing one of the most delightful Baroque interiors in Croatia, with its lacework pattern of pink and white stucco whorls executed by Antonio Quadrio in the 1720s. Francesco Robba's delicate portrayal of the Jesuit order's founder, St Ignatius of Loyola, to the right of the main altar, is the outstanding piece of statuary, portraying the saint in a typically Baroque swoon of spiritual ecstasy.

On the north side of the square, the **Museum of Modern Art** (Muzej suvremene umjetnosti; Tues–Sat 11am–7pm, Sun 10am–1pm; prices depend on what's on; ⓦwww.mdc.hr/msu) mounts imaginative temporary shows from Croatia and abroad – its large collection of contemporary work is currently in storage, awaiting the construction of a new museum south of the centre in Novi Zagreb. On the south side of the square, Dverce leads down to the top station of the funicular down to Ilica and to **Kula lotrščak**, or "Burglars' Tower" (May–Oct Tues–Sun 11am–8pm; 5Kn), another remnant of the upper town's fortifications, from which a bell was once sounded every evening before the city gates were closed (to keep out burglars, hence the name). An energetic tramp up a tightly-wound spiral staircase brings you out onto a wooden terrace, with superb views of Zagreb's red-tiled roofs below. On the way up you'll pass the window through which a small cannon is fired every day at noon, a practice begun in 1877 to coordinate the city's bell-ringers. A story linking the firing of a cannon on this spot with the defeat of a fifteenth-century attack by the Turks is regularly trotted out by the tourist guides, but is most likely a nineteenth-century invention: Ottoman armies once succeeded in sacking Remete (now a suburb of Zagreb; see p.81) to the northeast, but never mounted a serious assault on the city itself. On either side of the tower stretches **Strossmayerovo šetalište**, a promenade which follows the line of Gradec's former south-facing fortifications. Again, the views over the city and plains beyond are terrific.

The Gallery of Naive Art

About fifty metres north of Katarinin trg, the **Gallery of Naive Art** (Galerija naivne umjetnosti; Tues–Fri 10am–6pm, Sat & Sun 10am–1pm; 20Kn; ⓦwww.hmnu.org) at Ćirilometodska 3 provides an excellent introduction to the work of Croatia's village painters. The development of a school of painting inspired by peasant craft traditions was largely the work of an academically trained outsider, **Krsto Hegedušić**, who had been impressed by the work of untutored painters like "Le Douanier" Rousseau while studying in Paris. Visiting family in the Slavonian village of Hlebine (see p.115) in the 1930s, Hegedušić discovered that the paintings of local lads Ivan Generalić and Franjo Mraz displayed much of the style and verve he had seen in the work of other European non-academic artists, and took them under his wing, encouraging them to exhibit more widely. The work of Generalić dominates the first of the gallery's six rooms, with his early watercolours of Croatian village life reflecting a Brueghelesque fascination with rural festivities. His pictures soon developed a more fairy-tale, symbolic style, however – his numerous pictures of stags in forests resemble the illustrations in medieval manuscripts. Subsequent rooms deal with later generations of naive painters from across Croatia, with highlights including Ivan Lacković-Croata's scenes of villages in winter, crowded with spindly, stylized trees and snow-laden houses; Emerik Feješ's kaleidoscopic cityscapes; and Ivan Rabuzin's meditative, almost abstract visions of rural harmony. The final room concentrates on Josip Generalić (son of Ivan), who painted like a comic-strip artist on acid, deserting rural themes in favour of subjects like war, actresses, and the mass suicides of cult members. His 1973 portrait of Sophia Loren is one of the most garish in the collection (note the ugly cat, which allegedly represents Loren's husband, Carlo Ponti).

Markov trg and around

It's a short walk north up Ćirilometodska to the heart of Gradec, **Markov trg**, a restrained square of golden-brown buildings which serves as the symbolic heart of Croatia. Though it's not obvious from their modest facades, the buildings on the western side of the square house the Croatian cabinet offices, while those on the east include the **Sabor** (national parliament) and the so-called **Banski dvor** (Ban's Palace), originally the seat of the Habsburg-appointed governor and now used by the Croatian president for formal receptions. Markov trg has always been an important focus of government ceremonial: rulers of Croatia were sworn in here from the mid-sixteenth century onwards, a tradition renewed by President Tuđman in the 1990s, while in 1573 peasant leader Matija Gubec (see p.100) was executed here in a parody of such ceremonies by being seated on a throne and "crowned" with a band of white-hot steel. Nowadays, however, you're unlikely to come across any signs of political activity aside from the occasional purr of a ministerial Mercedes or the furtive glances of sharp-suited security men.

The main focus of the square is the squat **St Mark's Church** (Crkva svetog Marka), a much-renovated structure whose multicoloured tiled roof displays the coats of arms of Zagreb and Croatia to the sky – and, it would seem from opening any book on Zagreb, dozens of photographers. The emblems adorning the Croatian coat of arms (the one on the left as you face it) symbolize the three areas which originally made up the medieval kingdom: north-central Croatia is represented by the red-and-white chequerboard known as the *šahovnica* – a state symbol since the Middle Ages; Dalmatia by three lions' heads; and Slavonia by a running beast (the *kuna*, or marten, Croatia's national animal) framed by two rivers – the Sava and Drava. The church itself is a homely

△ Funicular railway, Ilica

Gothic building, originally constructed in the fourteenth century but ravaged since by earthquake, fire and nineteenth-century restorers – though some parts, including the south portal, are original. The Baroque bell tower was added in the seventeenth century, while the interior decorations, by the painter Jozo Kljaković and the sculptor Ivan Meštrović, date from the 1930s. Kljaković's frescoes are imposing but rigid, portraying huge, muscle-bound Croatian kings caught in dramatic mid-gesture; Meštrović's *Crucifixion* is more sensitive, merging sympathetically with the rest of the church.

Slightly downhill to the west of Markov trg at Matoševa 9, the **Croatian Historical Museum** (Hrvatski povijesni muzej; Mon–Fri 10am–5pm, Sat & Sun 10am–1pm; 10Kn; ⊛www.hismus.hr), in one of the more crumbly of Gradec's Baroque mansions, houses prestigious temporary exhibitions relating to Croatian history. A few steps to the north at Demetrova 1, the **Natural History Museum** (Hrvatski prirodoslovni muzej; Tues–Fri 10am–5pm, Sat & Sun 10am–1pm; 15Kn; ⊛www.hpm.hr) is remarkable as much for the style of the display as for the exhibits themselves, with objects laid out in a succession of old-fashioned cabinets that haven't been significantly reorganized in over half a century. The history of the world's fauna on the second floor is particularly atmospheric, with visitors proceeding through a narrow corridor lined with corals, skeletons and creatures in bottles. There's an impressive range of stuffed mammals at the end – although pride of place goes to the eight-metre-long basking shark caught in the north Adriatic in 1934.

The Meštrović Atelier and the Museum of Zagreb

Just north of Markov trg, at Mletačka 8, the **Meštrović Atelier** (Tues–Fri 9am–2pm, Sat 10am–6pm; 10Kn) occupies the house where Croatia's foremost twentieth-century sculptor, Ivan Meštrović, lived between 1924 and 1942. This is a delightful museum – one which you don't have to be a Meštrović fan to enjoy – with an intimacy that's lacking in the artist's other former home and museum, in Split (see p.307). On display are sketches, photographs and small-scale studies for creations such as the giant *Grgur Ninski* in Split and the *Crucifixion* in St Mark's Church, along with some lovely female statuettes in the small atrium.

Beyond the Atelier, Mletačka leads into Demetrova and thence to Opatička. Turn left here to the **Museum of Zagreb** at no. 20 (Muzej grada Zagreba; Tues–Fri 10am–6pm, Sat & Sun 10am–1pm; 20Kn; ⊛www.mdc.hr/mgz), undoubtedly the city's best, telling the tale of Zagreb's development from medieval times to the present day, with the help of snazzy presentations and English-language texts. Approached through the courtyard of the former Convent of the Poor Clares, the museum occupies a complex of buildings tacked on to the thirteenth-century **Popov toranj** (Priests' Tower), which was built to provide the clerics of poorly defended Kaptol with a refuge in case of attack. Inside the museum, models of Zagreb through the ages reveal the changing face of the city, and there's a modest but well-chosen selection of weaponry, furnishings and costumes. Sacral art taken from local churches includes an expressive seventeenth-century sculptural ensemble depicting Jesus flanked by the apostles, which originally stood above the portal of Zagreb cathedral. Upstairs, political posters, photographs of political leaders and ideological slogans help to breathe life into the turbulent history of the twentieth century; one of the final rooms contains an unintentionally surreal display of the furniture destroyed by the JNA (Yugoslav People's Army) rocket attack on Gradec in October 1991, with smashed crockery and splintered furniture arranged as if part of some contemporary art exhibit.

Donji grad

South of Gradec, the modern **Donji grad** ("Lower Town") sprawls out in all its grey, grid-patterned glory. Breaking the urban uniformity is the series of interconnected garden squares, laid out from the 1870s onwards, which give the downtown area an unbroken, U-shaped succession of promenading areas and parks. Known as **Lenuci's Horseshoe** (Lenucijeva podkova) after Milan Lenuci, the city engineer responsible for its layout, this was a deliberate attempt to give Zagreb a distinctive urban identity, providing it with public spaces bordered by the set-piece institutions – galleries, museums, academies and theatres – that it was thought every modern city should have. The horseshoe was never entirely finished, though, and it's unlikely you'll walk round the full U-shaped itinerary intended by Lenuci. The first of the horseshoe's two main series of squares starts with Trg Nikole Šubića Zrinskog – usually referred to as **Zrinjevac** – which begins a block south of Trg bana Jelačića; to the west of Zrinjevac is the second line of squares, culminating with **Trg maršala Tita**. To the south are the **Botanical Gardens**, which were intended to provide the final green link between the two arms of the horseshoe, but don't quite manage it: several characterless downtown blocks stand in the way. The set-piece buildings on and around both Zrinjevac and Trg maršala Tita wouldn't look out of place in such bastions of Mitteleuropa as Graz or Linz, giving this part of Zagreb a prosperous, dignified air, although Donji grad's other buildings are mostly offices, ministry buildings or apartments, and there's not much in the way of shopping or café life in this part of town.

Zrinjevac

South of Trg bana Jelačića, the first section of Lenuci's Horseshoe, **Zrinjevac**, is a typical late nineteenth-century city park, featuring shady walks, a bandstand, and a fountain designed by the ubiquitous Herman Bollé, which looks a bit like a cake-stand topped by a mushroom. Until 1873, when the square was first laid out, Zrinjevac marked the southern boundary of the city, the muddy site of fairs and markets where peasants from the surrounding countryside gathered to trade cows and horses. Today's Zrinjevac is a pleasing ensemble of nineteenth-century office blocks and apartment buildings, flanked to the west by the **Archeological Museum** (Arheološki muzej; Tues–Fri 10am–5pm, Sat & Sun 10am–1pm; 20Kn; ⊛ www.amz.hr), with three floors of exhibits ranging from the Neolithic to the Roman eras. Things get off to a colourful start with a collection of Greek vases amassed by nineteenth-century Habsburg army officer Laval Nugent, before moving on to pottery and inscriptions recalling the Greek settlements on the Adriatic coast. Presiding over a room of Roman-period heads and torsos is a third-century relief of the Goddess Nemesis, portrayed here as a frowny-faced woman dismounting from her chariot. Among the most striking of the museum's exhibits is the collection of ancient pottery decorated with zigzags and chequer patterns produced by the Vučedol culture, an upsurge in crafts and agriculture from the fourth millennium BC that takes its name from the Bronze Age settlement at Vučedol near Vukovar. The star exhibit here is the famous **Vučedol Pigeon** (Vučedolska golubica), the three-legged zoomorphic pouring vessel pictured on the 20Kn banknote. There are also two rooms of Egyptian mummies, mostly dating from the Ptolemaic period, one of which has a climate-controlled chamber all to itself. This last was found wrapped in a linen shroud (now displayed on the wall beside it) bearing ancient Etruscan writing – the longest known text in this as yet untranslated language.

Strossmayerov trg to the train station

Back on the horseshoe just south of Zrinjevac lies **Strossmayerov trg**, and the Croatian Academy of Arts and Sciences, founded as the Yugoslav Academy of Arts and Sciences by **Bishop Juraj Strossmayer** in 1866. Based in the cathedral town of Đakovo (see p.131) in eastern Slavonia, Strossmayer was a leading figure in the current of nineteenth-century Croatian nationalism that regarded Yugoslavism – the drawing together of all southern Slavs – as the best way of offering resistance to Croatia's traditional enemies – Hungarians, Austrians and Italians. He's still a respected figure, regardless of what may have happened in the intervening hundred years. A statue of Strossmayer by Ivan Meštrović sits among the trees in front of the building, a curiously gangling piece of sculpture that makes the Bishop look more like a hyperactive conjurer than a dignified cultural leader. In the academy itself, the **Strossmayer Gallery of Old Masters** (Strossmayerova galerija starih majstora; Tues–Sun 9am–5pm; 20Kn; ⓦ www.mdc.hr/strossmayer) includes pieces by prominent Venetians, including Veronese and Tintoretto, together with a small *Mary Magdalene* by El Greco, some early Flemish canvases by Joos van Cleve and the anonymous Master of the Virgin among the Virgins, and French paintings by the likes of Fragonard and Boucher. Crouched in the lobby of the building is the **Baška Tablet** (Bašćanska ploča), an eleventh-century inscription from the island of Krk which bears the oldest-known example of Glagolitic (see p.222), the archaic script used by the medieval Croatian church.

Across the street from the Strossmayer Gallery is the **Modern Gallery** (Moderna galerija; Tues–Sun 10am–1pm & 5–8pm; 20Kn), a vast collection of Croatian art from 1850 to World War II. Quality is largely sacrificed for quantity here, and highlights are relatively easy to pick out: Vlaho Bukovac heads the list of pre-World War I painters with his monumental *Krist na odru* ("Christ on the funeral bier") of 1905, in which ghostly angels play around the catafalque. Krsto Hegedušić (see p.115) is represented by three canvases depicting life in the village of Hlebine in the 1930s, while contemporaneous Dalmatian painters Ignjat Job and Petar Dobrović contribute animated and colourful representations of Adriatic life. Just round the corner from the Modern Gallery, the Croatian Academy's **Graphic Art Gallery** (Kabinet grafike; Mon–Sat 11am–7pm; admission prices vary depending on what's on display) hosts temporary exhibitions.

At the far end of Strossmayerov trg, the early twentieth-century **Art Pavilion** (Umjetnički paviljon; Mon–Sat 11am–7pm, Sun 10am–1pm; 10Kn; ⓦ www.umjetnicki-paviljon.hr), resplendent in the bright yellow paint job beloved of Habsburg-era architects, hosts regular temporary art exhibitions in its gilded stucco and mock-marble interior. Beyond lie the immaculate lawns and flowerbeds of **Tomislavov trg**, its name taken from the tenth-century Croatian king, Tomislav, whose equestrian statue stands at the square's southern end, greeting travellers emerging from the Neoclassical portals of Zagreb's main train station.

Trg hrvatskih velikana

East of Zrinjevac and Strossmayerov trg, all roads seem ultimately to lead to **Trg žrtava fašizma** (Victims of Fascism Square), a large traffic roundabout which was renamed Trg hrvatskih velikana (Square of Great Croatians) in 1990 – until anti-fascist groups complained vociferously enough to have the old name returned. The square is dominated by the **House of Croatian Artists** (Dom hrvatskih likovnih umjetnika; Mon 2–7pm, Tues–Sun 11am–7pm; prices depend on what's on), an arresting circular pavilion designed as an art gallery by Meštrović in the 1930s, but converted into a mosque in August 1944 by the NDH in an attempt to cultivate Bosnian Muslim support for their pro-Nazi regime. It's still colloquially referred to as the *džamija* (mosque), though its three minarets were demolished in 1947, after which it was press-ganged into use as a museum of the socialist revolution. The long, curving galleries inside are now an atmospheric venue for changing displays of contemporary painting and sculpture.

Trg maršala Tita

Heading westward from Zrinjevac along either Teslina or Hebrangova, it's a five-minute walk to **Trg maršala Tita** (Marshal Tito Square), a grandiose open space dominated by the solid, peach-coloured pile of the **Croatian National Theatre**. Opened by Emperor Franz Josef in 1890 and boasting a Neoclassical portal topped by a trumpet-blowing muse, it's an ostentatious statement of late nineteenth-century Croatia's growing cultural self-confidence. In front of the theatre, in a circular concrete pit, is yet another work by Meštrović, the tenderly erotic *Well of Life* (1905), while in the southwestern corner of the square, somewhat overshadowed by a trio of pines, is a sculpture by Fernkorn, showing St George on a rearing horse laying into a snarling dragon.

On the western side of the square, a long gabled building houses the **Museum of Arts and Crafts** (Muzej za umjetnost i obrt; Tues–Fri 10am–6pm, Sat & Sun 10am–1pm; 20Kn; ⓦ www.muo.hr), a rewarding collection of furniture, ceramics, clothes and textiles from the Renaissance to the present day. The interior is impressive in itself, with gilt lion heads gazing down from cast-iron balustrades above the central atrium. The first floor kicks off with a fifteenth-century Virgin and Child altarpiece of Tyrolean origin, continues with a parade of furniture and porcelain through the ages, and culminates in a hall of religious art with restored wooden altarpieces from churches all over northern Croatia. Most striking is the seventeenth-century altar of St Mary from the village of Remetinec, northeast of Zagreb, showing a central Madonna and Child flanked by smaller panels in which a whole panoply of saints bend in a stylized swoon of spiritual grace. There's a fine selection of seventeenth-century paintings in the first-floor ambulatory, notably Charles Lebrun's fleshily sensuous *Bacchanal*, and Guido Reni's *Aeneas and Dido*, in which the love-struck pair fix each other with puppy-like gazes. Objects on the second floor reflect Zagreb's status at the turn of the twentieth century as a prosperous outpost of Mitteleuropa, with locally produced ceramics from the Arts and Crafts School (Zagreb's school of applied art, opened in 1882), as well as imported furnishings – notably Tiffany and Gallé glassware, and a plant-pot stand by doyen of the Viennese arts-and-crafts scene prior to World War I, Josef Hoffmann. The stairs leading up to the third floor are lined with examples of 1960s poster art, including several geometric designs produced by the Croatian abstract art pioneer Ivan Picelj. At the top lie an array of clocks from throughout the ages, a lot of silverware, and a collection of early twentieth-century stained glass produced by local firm Koch & Marinković. Among the last, look out for Vilko Gecan's *Life of the Woodcutter* (*Život drvosječe*) from 1924, five idealized panels illustrating the life cycle of the Croatian peasant, depicted here with the kind of reverence one would normally expect from a church altarpiece.

The Mimara Museum

Lying just southwest of Trg maršala Tita on Rooseveltov trg is the most prestigious – and controversial – museum in the area, the **Mimara Museum** (Muzej Mimara; Tues, Wed, Fri & Sat 10am–7pm, Thurs 10am–2pm; 25Kn;

ⓦwww.mimara.hr). Housed in an elegant neo-Renaissance former high school, the museum is made up of the bequest of **Ante Topić Mimara** (1899–1987), a native of Dalmatia who grew rich abroad and presented his vast art collection to the nation. No one really knows how he amassed his wealth, how he came by so many prized objects, or indeed whether he was even the real Ante Topić Mimara – some maintain that he was an impostor who, in the chaos of a World War I battlefield, stole the identity tags of a fallen comrade. What's more, doubts have been raised about the attributions given to some of the paintings in Mimara's collection – many are labelled "workshop of . . ." or "school of . . ." in order to keep the art historians happy.

Whatever the truth, Mimara's tastes were nothing if not eclectic. There's a bit of everything here, and the collection can easily take up a couple of hours' viewing time. On the **ground floor** are exhibits of ancient glassware from Egypt, Greece, Syria and the Roman Empire, together with later examples of glass from Venice and the rest of Europe. Close by are Persian carpets from the seventeenth to the nineteenth centuries. Among the far-eastern artefacts are Ming vases decorated with bendy-bodied dragons, and a monumental bronze Head of Buddha clad in the kind of exotic pimpled headgear that would send most twenty-first century trendsetters racing for the fashion boutiques. The **first floor** gets under way with a collection of European applied art, containing Carolingian reliquary boxes, an extraordinary thirteenth-century enamelled crucifix from Limoges bearing a skinny, bulbous-headed Jesus (room 16), and an exquisitely carved ivory English hunting horn from the 1300s (room 17). Next come several rooms of religious sculpture – among the finer pieces is a fifteenth-century Flemish Archangel Gabriel with beautifully rendered wing feathers (room 20). The **second floor** presents a chronological trot through the history of European painting, beginning with Byzantine icons and several outstanding renaissance altarpieces, most arresting of which is Bicci di Lorenzo's *Virgin and Child* (room 31), in which a rosy-cheeked infant enthusiastically sucks away at an aubergine-shaped breast. A lavishly decorated ceremonial hall (room 35) provides a suitable home for many of the collection's larger-format canvases – Rubens' *Virgin with the Innocents* is a riot of pink puppy fat, while the sitter for Rembrandt's *Portrait of a Lady* appears in the process of being suffocated by her enormous ruff. Among the nineteenth-century French paintings in the final room (no. 40), you'll find an effortlessly light *Bather* by Renoir, and a brace of small-format still lifes by Manet.

From Mažuranićev trg to the Botanical Gardens

South of Trg maršala Tita, the horseshoe continues with Trg braće Mažuranića, an unspectacular quadrangle of administrative buildings, including the **Ethnographic Museum** (Etnografski muzej; Tues–Thurs 10am–6pm, Fri–Sun 10am–1pm; 10Kn; ⓦwww.etnografski-muzej.hr), a dimly lit and seemingly little visited place. Its collection of costumes from every corner of Croatia is as complete as you'll get, displaying numerous examples of the embroidered aprons and tunics that are found throughout the country. Downstairs lies an engaging jumble of artefacts brought back from the South Pacific, Asia and Africa by intrepid Croatian explorers. Foremost among these were the brothers Mirko and Stjepan Seljan, who served King Menelik II of Ethiopia as provincial governors, studied indigenous cultures in Brazil and Paraguay, and built roads in Peru – where Mirko disappeared in 1912. Stjepan went on to become a mine-owner in Brazil, where he died in 1936.

Marulićev trg, the next square to the south, is named after – and boasts a statue of – the Renaissance writer and father of Croatian literature **Marko Marulić** (1450–1524), author of *Judita*, the first narrative poem in the Croatian language. A reworking of the biblical tale of Judith, who killed the Assyrian general Holofernes, Marulić's poem was taken to be an allegory of Croatia's struggles agtainst the Turks. The square was controversially – some say tastelessly – modernized in the late 1990s, when the lawn was lowered and the statue surrounded by what look like rows of airport landing lights, illuminating the bard in a manner not entirely in keeping with the restrained nineteenth-century apartment houses on either side. The bottom end of Marulićev trg is occupied by the former **University Library** (Sveučilišna knjižnica), opened with much pomp in 1913 and now home to the state archives. Arguably Zagreb's finest Secession-era building, it mixes a staid Neoclassical facade with eccentric ornamental details, such as the globes held aloft by owls which adorn each corner of the flattened, tent-like cupola.

On the far side of the library, just across Mihanovićeva beside the railtracks, are the city's tranquil **Botanical Gardens** (Botanički vrt; Tues–Sun 9am–7pm; free), with well-tended but modest plant collections fading into wilder areas of long grass and overgrown pathways. The novelist Miroslav Krleža, who used to sit here to write his diary during World War I, compared the gardens to a "boring second-rate cemetery" – it's nowhere near that bad, of course, although it's more a place for quiet relaxation than for botanical inspiration.

The Technical Museum and beyond

South of the Mimara Museum, **Savska cesta** heads southwest towards the concrete-and-steel confections of twentieth-century Zagreb, passing the **Technical Museum** (Tehnički muzej; Tues–Fri 9am–5pm, Sat & Sun 9am–1pm; 20Kn; ⓦ www.mdc.hr/tehnicki), one of the city's more entertaining collections, at no. 18. The displays begin with a set of historic fire engines, followed by a jumble of wooden watermills and steam turbines designed to illustrate the harnessing of natural power sources. Steam- and diesel-powered machinery comes next: the line-up of disembodied plane engines (including a Rolls-Royce Merlin II from 1938, used to power the Spitfire aircraft) has the abstract dignity of a sculpture gallery. A central hall holds buses, cars, trams and aeroplanes, as well as a World War II Italian submarine captured by the Partisans in 1943 and drafted into the Yugoslav navy under the name *Mališan* ("The Nipper"). Other attractions include a small planetarium with regular showings (Tues–Fri 4pm, Sat noon; 10Kn); a reconstruction of a mine shaft (entrance by guided tour only: Tues–Fri 3pm, Sat 11am; 10Kn); and the reconstructed laboratory of physicist **Nikola Tesla** (entrance by guided tour only: Tues–Fri 3.30pm, Sat 11.30am; 10Kn), who pioneered the use of alternating current and developed dynamos, transformers and lighting systems for the Westinghouse company in the USA. Perhaps it's because Tesla was a Serb from the ethnically mixed province of Lika that today's Croatian establishment seems unsure whether or not to enshrine him as their greatest ever scientist.

Over the road lies the **Student Centre** (Studentski centar), where a theatre and cinema occupy the pavilions of the former Zagreb Fair. Further south along Savska, trams rattle on towards the River Sava, passing an important symbol of Zagreb en route: the cylindrical **Cibona Tower**, a 1980s office block whose highly reflective surface exudes a silvery, futuristic haughtiness. Zagreb's main basketball team (also called Cibona) play immediately next door in a similarly circular structure, named the **Dražen Petrović Basketball Centre** after the player whose career was cut short by a fatal car crash in 1993. The best

European player of his generation, Petrović led Cibona to the European championships in 1985 and 1986, and went on to play for Real Madrid, Portland and the New Jersey Nets – before posthumously making it into the NBA's Hall of Fame in 2002. There are plans for a Dražen Petrović museum here in the future; in the meantime, head for the next-door *Amadeus* café, which is stuffed with photographs of the man in action.

The suburbs

Zagreb's sightseeing potential is largely exhausted once you've covered the compact centre, although there are a few worthwhile trips into the suburbs – all of which are easily accessible by tram or bus. **Maksimir**, **Lake Jarun** and **Mirogoj Cemetery** are the park-like expanses to aim for if you want a break from the downtown streets, while the peaceful village-suburb of **Remete** provides the setting for a celebrated pilgrimage church.

Western Zagreb is particularly devoid of interest, although those travelling along Ilica en route to the Černomerec tram terminal will pass one of Zagreb's more poignant sights, the **Zid boli** (Wall of Pain). Running along the pavement outside the (now empty) United Nations compound 3km west of the centre, this is a low, ad hoc structure, each brick of which is inscribed with the name of a casualty from the siege of Vukovar in 1991. Largely the work of refugees from Vukovar and their relatives (many of whom still come here to lay flowers or light candles), the wall is intended to act as both a memorial to the victims and a reminder of the international community's failure to take decisive action at the time. There's currently much discussion on whether to leave the Zid boli here or move it to a new location – it's likely that a small section of it will be preserved *in situ* whatever happens to the rest.

Mirogoj

Ranged across a hillside just over 2km northeast of the centre, the main city cemetery of **Mirogoj** was laid out by Hermann Bollé in 1876. The main (western) entrance to the graveyard is in many ways his most impressive work: an ivy-covered, fortress-like wall topped by a row of greening cupolas. The cemetery serves all Zagreb's citizens regardless of faith, so alongside the Catholic gravestones you'll find Orthodox memorials bearing Cyrillic script, Muslim graves adorned with the crescent of Islam, and socialist-era tombstones boasting the *petokraka*, or five-pointed star. The most evocative parts of this vast necropolis are the arcades running either side of the main entrance, containing work by some of Croatia's best late-nineteenth-century sculptors, with rows of elegantly rendered memorials overlooked by spindly cast-iron lanterns. If you head right from the entrance, it's difficult to miss Ivan Rendić's grieving female figures atop the graves of Petar Preradović and Emanuel Priester; while, slightly further on, Robert Frangeš Mihanović's extraordinary bleak relief of stooping bearded figures decorates the tomb of the Mayer family. Head left from the entrance to find the Miletić tomb, where Rudolf Valdec's fine *Angel of Death* is framed on either side by outstretched sculpted hands into which descendants of the family still place roses.

Bus #106 heads up to Mirogoj from Kaptol every fifteen minutes or so; otherwise, take tram #14 (direction Mihaljevac) from Trg bana Jelačića to Gupčeva Zvijezda, then walk for ten minutes up to the cemetery via Mirogojska cesta.

Maksimir

Three kilometres east of the centre is Zagreb's largest and lushest open space, **Maksimir**, reached by tram #11 or #12 (direction Dubrava) from Trg bana

Jelačića. Named after Archbishop Maximilian Vrhovac, who in 1774 established a small public garden in the southwestern corner of today's park, Maksimir owes much to his successors Aleksandar Alagović and Juraj Haulik, who imported the idea of the landscaped country park from England. It's perfect for aimless strolling, with the straight-as-an-arrow, tree-lined avenues at its southwestern end giving way to more densely forested areas in its northern reaches. As well as five lakes, the park is dotted with follies, including a mock Swiss chalet (Švicarska kuća), and a recently spruced-up belvedere (*vidikovac*), now housing a café which gets mobbed on fine Sunday afternoons. The eastern end of the park holds the city's **zoo** (daily 9am–5pm; 20Kn; ⓦwww.zoo.hr), shaded by trees and partly situated on a small island; it's a pleasant place to stroll whether or not you're taken with the animals. On the opposite side of the road to the park stands the **Maksimir football stadium**, home to both Dinamo Zagreb and the national side (see p.91).

Remete

From the western side of Maksimir park, Bukovačka cesta threads its way uphill through increasingly affluent hillside residential districts before arriving at **Remete**, a village suburb some 6km north of the city centre. Crouched in a grassy vale below Mt Medvednica, the village was chosen by Pauline monks as the site of a monastery in the thirteenth century, and, despite the dissolution of the order in the 1790s, the monastery's **Church of St Mary** (Crkva svete Marije) remains an important focus for pilgrims on Marian feast days – especially August 15 (Assumption) and September 8 (Birth of the Virgin). Essentially a gothic structure with a tacked-on Baroque facade, the church maintains its popularity with the faithful thanks to the presence on the high altar of a tender fifteenth-century wooden statue of the Madonna, to which miracle-working properties are ascribed. More powerful still are the the richly coloured Baroque frescoes which swirl around the ceiling, the likely work of **Ivan Ranger**, the widely travelled painter-monk from Lepoglava (see p.107). Outside stands a pillar topped with a suitably ascetic-looking statue of Simeon the Stylite, a fifth-century saint who spent 36 years living on top of a pole in the Syrian desert. You can get to Remete on bus #226 from either Kaptol or Bukovačka cesta.

Jarun

On sunny days, city folk head out to **Jarun**, a two-kilometre-long artificial lake encircled by footpaths and cycling tracks 4km southwest of the city centre. Created to coincide with Zagreb's hosting of the 1987 World Student Games, it's an important venue for rowing competitions, with a large spectator stand at the western end, although most people come here simply to stroll or sunbathe. The best spot for the latter is **Malo jarunsko jezero** at Jarun's eastern end, a bay sheltered from the rest of the lake by a long thin island. Here you'll find a shingle beach, several outdoor cafés (which remain open well into the night), and grassy, partly shaded areas of park. This is a good place from which to clamber up onto the dyke which runs along the banks of the **River Sava**, providing a good vantage point from which to survey the cityscape of Novi Zagreb beyond.

The best way of getting to the lake is to catch tram #17 from Trg bana Jelačića (direction Prečko) to the Staglišće or Jarun stops, either of which is a five-minute walk north of the water's edge.

Novi Zagreb

Spread over the plain on the southern side of the River Sava, **Novi Zagreb** (New Zagreb) is a vast grid-iron of housing projects and multi-lane highways that nowadays looks much less attractive than its utopian planners intended. Thrown up in the 1960s in order to accommodate the stream of migrants drawn by the booming economy of the big city, it's a true melting pot of Croatia's population. The central part of Novi Zagreb is not that bad a place to live: swaths of park help to break up the architectural monotony, and each residential block has a clutch of bars and pizzerias in which to hang out. Outlying areas have far fewer facilities, however, and possess the aura of half-forgotten dormitory settlements on which the rest of Zagreb has turned its back.

Those drawn to the aesthetics of high-rise buildings and graffiti will find the area strangely compelling, but otherwise there's little to do here except visit the **Zagreb Fair Grounds** (Zagrebački velesajam) on Avenija Dubrovnik, where major trade exhibitions take place throughout the year – the Zagreb tourist office will have details of what's on. To get there from Trg bana Jelačića, take tram #14 (destination Zapruđe) until you see the main entrance building on your left.

The only other reason to venture into this part of town is to stroll around the **Bundek**, an incongruously swampy, kidney-shaped lake surrounded by thick woods and untended meadows. Located on the northern fringes of Novi Zagreb near the banks of the Sava, it's popular with picnickers and dog-walkers eager to escape from the concrete wastelands nearby. Paths lead towards the Bundek from opposite the *Zagreb* hotel (see p.66 for directions).

Mount Medvednica

The wooded slopes of **Mount Medvednica**, or "Bear Mountain" (also known as the Zagrebačka Gora, or "Zagreb uplands"), offer the easiest escape from the city, with the range's highest peak, **Sljeme** (1033m), accessible by cable car and easily seen on a half-day trip. The mountain slopes are densely forested and the views from the top are not as impressive as you might expect, but the walking is good and there's a limited amount of skiing in winter, when you can rent gear from shacks near the summit. Driving, you can reach Sljeme by heading north out of central Zagreb along Ribnjak, and taking a well-signed right turn after about 3km. On public transport, take tram #14 from Trg bana Jelačića to the Mihaljevac terminus, followed by #15 to the Dolje terminus, from where it's a ten-minute walk via pedestrian tunnel and woodland path to the cable-car station (*žičara*; daily 8am–8pm; departures on the hour; 10Kn one way, 15Kn return). From here it's a stately twenty-minute journey to the top, with expansive views of greater Zagreb opening up as you ascend. If the cable car isn't running due to maintenance work or bad weather, a small yellow sign reading *žičara ne vozi* is posted at the Mihaljevac tram terminus.

At the top, a flight of steps leads straight ahead past a couple of refreshment huts to the summit, capped by a TV transmission tower, completed in 1980. The tower's top floor originally housed a restaurant and viewing terrace, but the lifts broke down after three months and it's been closed to the public ever since. Views of the low hills of the Zagorje to the north occasionally reveal themselves through gaps in the surrounding trees, a rippling green landscape broken by red-roofed villages. A left turn out of the cable-car station brings you to the *Tomislavov Dom* hotel (see p.66), home to a couple of cafés and a restaurant, below which you can pick up a trail to the medieval fortress of Medvedgrad (2hr; see below). A right turn from the cable-car station leads after ten minutes to **Činovnička livada**, a sloping meadow popular with picnickers. The path carries on over the meadow towards the **Chapel of Our Lady of Sljeme** (Majke Božje Sljemenske; Thurs, Sat & Sun 10am–6pm), built in 1932 to commemorate the one-thousandth anniversary of Croatia's conversion to Christianity. Ostensibly inspired by Croatian medieval architecture, it's actually a highly idiosyncratic modern building, featuring elegantly sloping buttresses and an obliquely angled bell tower. Paths continue east along the ridge, emerging after about twenty minutes at the **Puntijarka** mountain refuge, a popular refreshment stop whose cafeteria serves excellent *grah* (bean soup) and grilled meats. Another twenty minutes along the ridge brings you to the *Janica* hotel (see p.66), where there's another small restaurant and several more trails leading off into the woods which cover Medvednica's eastern flanks.

Medvedgrad

Commanding a spur of the mountain 4km southwest of Sljeme, the fortress of **Medvedgrad** was built in the mid-thirteenth century at the instigation of Pope Innocent IV in the wake of Tatar attacks, although its defensive capabilities were never really tested, and it was abandoned in 1571. Then, in the 1990s, it was decided to rebuild the fortress as a monument to the Croatian nation. Walls and towers were swiftly reconstructed, and an **Altar of the Homeland** (Altar domovine) – an eternal flame surrounded by stone blocks and glass sculptures in the form of tears – was placed at the fortress's eastern rim. Conservationists were dismayed by the altar's failure to blend in with its historic surroundings, but it has quickly assumed an important role in state ceremonial, with the president of the republic and other dignitaries laying wreaths here on national holidays. You can roam the castle's south-facing ramparts, enjoying panoramic views of Zagreb and the plain beyond, and there's a restaurant in a subterranean hall serving traditional north-Croatian favourites like *grah*, *štrukli* and *štrudl*.

Unless you're walking here from Sljeme via the marked paths which slant down from the *Tomislavov Dom* hotel, Medvedgrad is best approached from the suburb of **Šestine**, 5km northwest of central Zagreb, which can be reached by bus #102 from Mihaljevac or Britanski trg (400m west of Trg bana Jelačića along Ilica). Get off when you see the bright yellow Šestine church 4km out of the centre and walk north past the church towards the *Šestinski Lagvić* restaurant (see p.85) 1km uphill. About 80m beyond the restaurant, a path – initially difficult to spot – darts into the woods on the left; look out for the red-and-white waymarkings painted onto a nearby tree. From here it's a straightforward forty-minute ascent through oak forest to the fortress.

Eating

Whatever your budget, there's no shortage of places to eat in Zagreb, although the range of food on offer is pretty much the same wherever you go. The majority of **restaurants** concentrate on the pork- and veal-based central European dishes indigenous to northern Croatia, and there are several excellent fish restaurants which are as good as anything you'll find on the coast. The number of ethnic restaurants in Zagreb is still quite modest, but decent Italian pasta is widely available, and there's a surfeit of pizzerias around Trg bana Jelačića and Tkalčićeva. Some of the best restaurants for traditional food are to be found in the **northern suburbs** – worth the trek out if you want to observe the local bigwigs at play. Naturally, prices vary according to what you're eating: pizzas, pasta and grills are cheapest, fresh fish the most expensive, with standard Croatian meat dishes falling somewhere in between.

For **snacks**, the best place to find *burek* or cheap grills is the area around Dolac market, just above Trg bana Jelačića. *Mimice*, Jurišićeva 21, is a stand-up buffet serving inexpensive portions of whitebait (*ribice*), squid (*lignje*) and other fishy snacks. A good sandwich bar is *Pingvin*, open until 2am; it's inside the courtyard at Teslina 7. There are also a few 24-hour **bakeries** in the city centre: *Pekarnica Dora*, at Strossmayerov trg 8; *Pekarna Grič*, Vlaška 7; and *Pekarnica Radićeva*, Radićeva 10. Picnic supplies can be purchased from the stalls of Dolac market or from the **supermarkets** in the subterranean Importanne shopping centre in front of the train station; in the Importanne Galerija on Vlaška; or in Kaptol Centar on Nova Ves. **Ice cream** is enormously popular whatever the time of year; best of the ice-cream parlours are *Slastičarna Vincek*, Ilica 18, and *Central*, Jurišićeva 24.

Restaurants

We've graded the restaurants below according to the following ranges: **inexpensive** (30–60Kn), **moderate** (60–100Kn), and **expensive** (100–150Kn), based on the average cost of a basic meal (main course, salad and a drink). Indulging in aperitifs, bottles of wine and desserts will, of course, push the bill up considerably. Restaurants are usually open daily from around 11am until 11pm or midnight unless stated otherwise. If it's advisable to book a table in advance, we've included a telephone number.

Central Zagreb

Croatian cuisine

Baltazar Nova ves 4. A 5min walk north of the cathedral along Kaptol, this is one of the best venues in the city for the standard north-Croatian repertoire of veal cutlets and pork fillets, all expertly grilled. There's a pleasant courtyard and service is attentive. Closed Sun. Moderate to expensive.

Dubravkin Put Dubravkin Put 2 ☎01/48-34-970. Pricey place in the leafy Tuškanac district (head west from Trg bana Jelačića along Ilica, turn right up Dežmanova and carry straight on for 5min), with excellent fish and shellfish, delicious roasted meats and plenty of outdoor seating. Expensive.

Hrvatski Kulturni Klub Trg maršala Tita 10 ☎01/48-28-084. Comfy, old-fashioned restaurant in the basement of the Arts and Crafts Museum (see p.77), garnering a loyal clientele of writers, older-generation arty types and other would-be pillars of the cultural establishment. The kitchen sticks to a tried-and-trusted veal and pork repertoire, although it also grills a decent fish. Moderate to expensive.

Kerempuh Dolac bb. Often overlooked because it's hidden away behind the main fruit-and-veg market, this is one of the best places in town to fill up on traditional Croatian pork-based favourites. The cheap lunchtime dishes draw a regular of local office workers. Inexpensive to moderate.

Korčula Teslina 17. Smallish, centrally located Dalmatian restaurant serving excellent grilled fish, shellfish and seafood risottos in unpretentious surroundings. Moderate to expensive.

Pod Gričkim Topom Zakmardijeve stube 5 ☎01/48-33-607. Good Croatian food in a cosy restaurant on the steps leading down from Strossmayerovo Šetalište to Trg bana Jelačića. There's a nice garden terrace overlooking the lower town too. Moderate.

Rubelj Dolac Market. Cheapest place in the centre for simple but tasty grilled-meat standards such as *čevapi*, *ražnjići* and *pljeskavica*. Excellent value for a quick feed, but not the kind of place to linger over a meal. There are a couple more good grill places right next door. Inexpensive.

Stari Fijaker Mesnička 6, about 300m west along Ilica from Trg bana Jelačića. Charmingly old-fashioned downtown restaurant with a pretty good line in standard Croatian meat dishes. Good place for a slap-up evening meal, although inexpensive standbys such as *punjene paprike* (stuffed peppers) are also available. Moderate to expensive.

Vinodol Teslina 10. Handily placed a block away from the central square, with tables ranged across an enormous covered courtyard. Famous for its spit-roast lamb, but most other central-European meat dishes are available too. Moderate.

Other cuisines

Asia Ground floor of the *Astoria* hotel, Petrinjska 71. Best of the city's modest handful of Chinese restaurants, offering authentic fare and formal service. A place in which to savour a relaxing evening meal rather than wolf down a budget feed. Moderate to expensive.

Boban Gajeva 9. Owned by the family of football star Zvonimir Boban, this popular and central pasta restaurant with breezy service is located in the vaulted cellar of the café of the same name. Inexpensive to moderate.

Cantinetta Teslina 14. Good-quality Croatian, Italian and modern European food, conveniently located just south of Trg bana Jelačića. A stylish place with warm decor and a few snazzy interior design touches, but not too formal. Moderate to expensive.

Fellini Jurišićeva 1. Cosy trattoria located on the first floor of the labyrinthine Evropski dom (European House), just round the corner from the main square. Great place for tasty lunchtime pastas and salads, or more extravagant evening feasts. Inexpensive to moderate.

Gallo Hebrangova 34 ☎01/48-14-014. Meaty European dishes with an Italian twist, and a sizeable international wine list. Smart but chic with it, this is popular with businessmen and the expat community. Expensive.

Havana Club Perkovčeva 2. Grilled meats done in spicy Cuban style, in a swanky place with cigar shapes predominating in the decor. Handy for the Mimara Museum. Moderate to expensive.

Maharadža Opatovina 19. A familiar range of satisfyingly spiced curries, served up in a relaxing ambience. Handily placed just round the corner from Tkalčićeva, the city's main bar-crawling area. Also serves pizzas to the unadventurous. Moderate.

Nokturno Skalinska 4. In a side street just off Tkalčićeva, offering serviceable pizzas, a varied choice of lasagnes, simple pasta dishes, good salads and a small outdoor terrace. Inexpensive.

Pizzeria Dvojka Nova ves 2. A 5min walk north of the cathedral, this bright, functional pizzeria has a solid range of pasta and pizzas, including mammoth *obiteljska* ("family-size") servings. Inexpensive.

Zdravljak Nova Ilica 72. A friendly, unfussy vegetarian restaurant in a cramped but cosy upstairs room, sharing the same building as Zagreb's premier health food shop. Daily lunchtime specials. Inexpensive.

South of the centre

Mex Cantina Savska cesta 154. Of several Mexican joints in Zagreb, this is the longest established, the most authentic food-wise, and the most fun, with surprisingly decent Mariachi music several nights a week. Located near the Stjepan Radić student dorms 3km southwest of the centre, but worth the trip: take tram #17 (destination Prečko) from Trg bana Jelačića or tram #4 (destination Savski most) from the train station. Moderate.

Pivnica Medvedgrad Savska 56. Large beer hall slightly off the beaten track, 1500m southwest of the centre – take tram #17 (destination Prečko) from Trg bana Jelačića or tram #4 (destination Savski most) from the train station. Large portions of traditional Croatian meat dishes are served here, and the beer – brewed on the premises – is excellent. Moderate.

The northern suburbs

Gušti Markuševačka cesta 22, Markuševac ☎01/46-76-000. Traditional home cooking and frequent live tamburica (traditional Slavonian) music in a cosy interior decked out with rustic implements and folksy fabrics. Good for either an intimate meal or a celebratory banquet. It's 8km from the centre in the northeastern suburb of Markuševac: take tram #14 to the Mihaljevac terminus, followed by tram #5 to the Dolje terminus, then a 10min walk northeast along Gračanska (subsequently Markuševačka) cesta.

Okrugljak Mlinovi 28 ☎01/46-74-112. Traditional Croatian food in rustic surroundings, with wood-panelled separés indoors, plenty of seating outdoors, and regular live music – popular tunes from classical to folk – on violin and piano. It's a popular venue for family celebrations. Take tram #14 to the Mihaljevac terminus, from where it's a 10min walk north on the road to Šestine. Expensive.

Šestinski Lagvić Šestinska cesta bb ☎01/426-486. Just above the village of Šestine on a shoulder of Mount Medvednica, this is a convenient stop-off en route to Medvedgrad with an (often crowded) terrace looking back down towards the city. Known for its *štrukli* and other north-Croatian favourites. Take tram #14 to the Mihaljevac terminus, then bus #102 to Šestine. Get off at the church and walk a little way uphill. Moderate to expensive.

Zrinski Remete. Traditional restaurant in the northeastern suburbs, handy if you've been visiting Remete church (see p.81 for directions). Croatian pork and veal dishes predominate, although there are a few pasta alternatives and some decent salads. The outdoor terrace has great views of central Zagreb if you crane your neck. Moderate.

Drinking

There's a wealth of **café-bars** with outdoor seating in central Zagreb, especially in the pedestrianized area around Bogovićeva and Preradovićev trg. The other main strolling area is Tkalčićeva, just north of Trg bana Jelačića, which, with a watering hole every few metres, looks like one vast outdoor bar. In these central areas, there's often little difference between individual establishments when it comes to the kind of music they play or the range of drinks on offer: it's really just a question of finding a free table from which to watch the world go by. Saturday morning is the traditional time for meeting friends and lingering over a coffee, although downtown areas remain busy day and night, seven days a week, if the weather is good enough for alfresco imbibing. Things quieten down as soon as the weather gets cold, although the more characterful café-bars retain their clientele through the winter.

The cafés and bars listed below are open daily from early in the morning until 11pm or midnight unless stated otherwise. Larger cafés may offer a range of pastries, ice creams and sandwiches, but there are no hard-and-fast rules about this. Late-night drinking takes place in clubs (see p.88) or in the rather unatmospheric café-bars of the Importanne shopping centre in front of the train station. The latter are open round the clock and function as useful pre-dawn bolt holes if you can't face waiting for Zagreb's elusive night trams.

The number of **cybercafés** in Zagreb is on the increase. Most insist on registering you as a member before letting you loose on the computers, so bring your passport. Membership is usually free; expect to pay 20–30Kn per hour online.

Cafés and bars

Atrij Teslina 7. One of several café-bars in a courtyard one block south of Trg bana Jelačića, heaving with bright young things day and night.

Boban Gajeva 9. Perpetually busy café-bar in prime city-centre position, with a roomy, vaulted interior, low-key lighting, and loungey corners equipped with sofas – the kind of place where drinkers of all descriptions feel at home.

Brazil North bank of the River Sava, near Savski most. Small but characterful bar in a (now landlocked) boat, with an interior decorated in the style of an Amazonian thatched hut. Proximity to student dorms ensures that it's lively at weekends during term time, when it's usually open past midnight. Take tram #4 from the train station to the Savski most terminus and head east along the dyke above the river. *Brazil* is the second structure down to the right.

Bulldog – Belgian Beer Café Bogovićeva 6. Elegant split-level bar and pavement café, and one of the most popular meeting places in town, especially on Saturday mornings, when the whole of Zagreb seems to insist on sipping coffee here.

Café Godot Savska 23. Cosy and relaxing place somewhere between a European café and an Irish pub in feel. Convenient place for a drink after visiting the Technical Museum.

Dobar Zvuk Gajeva 18. Popular café-bar with a slightly bohemian clientele, restrained music and adverts for Irish beer on the wall. No outdoor seating.

Dubrovnik Trg bana Jelačića. Roomy, rather posh café attached to the hotel of the same name, occupying a classic position by the square. Good range of cakes and ice cream.

Hard Rock Caffe Gajeva 10. Not part of the international chain, but with a similarly raucous, memorabilia-crowded ambience. In summer the *Caffe* sets out tables in the garden of the Archeological Museum just across the road – an excellent place to enjoy a coffee amid Roman gravestones.

Hemingway Dežmanova. Funky cocktail bar west of the main square and off Ilica. Popular with Zagreb's trend-setting smart set, it's littered with memorabilia related to some bearded old scribbler. On the expensive side.

Kazališna Kavana Trg maršala Tita. Zagreb's only surviving Viennese-style coffee house, though it's been modernized many times over the years, and the literary and artistic set who used to hang out here have moved on. A good place to recharge your batteries after a visit to the Mimara Museum.

Kolding Berislavićeva 8, three blocks south of Trg bana Jelačića. A civilized cellar bar with vaguely turn-of-the-century furnishings, *Kolding* is elegant but easy-going with it. Nice place for an intimate drink, and there's plenty of outdoor seating in the courtyard.

K. u. K Jurišićeva. Small, cosy city-centre café on two levels, decked out with pictures of Zagreb old and new. Closed Sun.

Londoner Pub Kaptol Centar, Nova Ves 11. Nothing like a pub and on the other side of the moon to London, this roomy basement bar is a mecca for cool Croatian drinkers. The youthful and the trendy pack themselves in at weekends to generate a raucous party atmosphere. Occasional live music. Open until 4am.

Lyra Teslina 3. Hidden away in an initially rather unpromising courtyard, this turns out to be one of the cosiest places for a coffee break that central Zagreb has to offer – a couple of chintzy rooms stuffed with bric-a-brac, with plenty of photos of Zagreb old and new on the walls.

Melin Tkalčićeva. For years the Melin has been attracting a wide-ranging crowd with inexpensive drinks, post-industrial grunge decor, and an eclectic range of sounds. About the only bar in Zagreb in which you are ever likely to hear a Captain Beefheart record, this is a terrific alternative to some of the posier establishments nearby.

Oliver Twist Tkalčićeva 36. One of the prime places to see and be seen in a street that's full of bars, serving up a generous selection of local and imported beers in a wood-panelled interior on two levels, and a big outdoor terrace. Open until 2am or later.

Papaya Schlosserove stube 2. Kitted out to look like a tropical island, this place is hidden away beside the steps that lead up towards the Šalata

sports complex. Expect a generous choice of cocktails, and a snazzily dressed, show-off crowd. Open until 2am or later.

Pivnica Medvedgrad Savska 56. Cavernous, if not particularly atmospheric, beer hall serving ales brewed on the premises and an extensive range of traditional Croatian food (see "Restaurants", p.85).

Sedmica Kačićeva 7. Laid-back, mildly arty hangout hidden inside the hallway of an apartment block about 1km west of Trg bana Jelačića, just beyond Britanski trg. Serves good Viški plavac red wine from the island of Vis.

SPUNK Hrvatske bratske zajednice bb. An inconvenient 2km south of the centre, this memorably-monikered bar (inspired by a 1970s comic-strip character, apparently) is in the same building as the National University Library, and fills up with students eager to listen to loud offbeat music and the occasional live band. Handy for a pre-club drink if you're on the way to Močvara (see p.89).

Tolkien Vraničanijeva 5. Comfortable café-bar in Gradec equally good for either a civilized daytime drink or a more animated evening boozing session. Pleasant leafy courtyard outside, Middle Earth-inspired memorabilia inside.

Cybercafés

Aquarius.net Držislavova 4, just west of Trg hrvatskih velikana ☎01/46-18-873, @www.aquariusnet.hr. Small, dark and functional. Enter via the *Plava Ptica* café next door.

Art.net café Preradovićeva 25 ☎01/45-58-471, @www.haa.hr. Roomy, very plush and rather formal in atmosphere, with occasional live music and literary evenings. Closed Sun.

Mama Preradovićeva 18 ☎01/48-56-400, @www.mama.mi2.hr. Alternative cultural centre where you can hang out, drink coffee and listen to chill-out beats as well as send emails.

Sublink In the courtyard of Teslina 12 ☎01/48-11-329, @www.sublink.hr. Croatia's first cybercafé and still a cult Zagreb meeting-point, it's friendly and relaxed, if cramped at times.

Nightlife and entertainment

It's not difficult to go out partying most nights of the week in Zagreb, and the capital also offers the rich and varied diet of entertainment that you would expect from a metropolis of a million people, although the combined effects of war and financial belt-tightening mean that the city is still struggling to recapture the vibrancy it enjoyed in the 1980s. The events of the last decade have produced a measure of artistic isolation: international performers rarely tour here unless lured by high-profile festivals, and cultural events also tend to thin out in August, when many of Zagreb's culture fiends head for the coast.

Extensive entertainment **listings** appear in the free monthly English-language pamphlet *Events and Performances*, available from the Zagreb tourist office (or on their website, @www.zagreb-touristinfo.hr). There's also daily listings information in the back pages of Croatian-language newspapers like *Jutarnji List*, *Novi List* and *Vjesnik*, the last of which has cinema and theatre schedules on its website at @www.vjesnik.hr.

Zagreb festivals

The most accessible of Zagreb's annual events is the **International Folklore Festival** (Međunarodna smotra folklora), usually held over the last weekend in July, with performances of ethnic music and dance from all over Croatia, plus a range of international guests. Performances take place on the central Trg bana Jelačića and in venues throughout the town. Advance information can be obtained from Concert Direction Zagreb, Kneza Mislava 18 (Koncertna Direkcija Zagreb; ☎01/46-11-797, ℻46-11-807, ⓦwww.msf.hr). Taken chronologically, the city's other important festivals are the **Music Biennale** (Musičko biennale; April), a festival of resolutely modern music held every odd-numbered year; the **Contemporary Dance Week** (Tjedan suvremenog plesa; early June); the **Eurokaz Theatre Festival** (late June), which features challenging avant-garde drama; and the **Zagreb Summer Festival** (Zagrebački ljetni festival; mid-July to mid-Aug) of orchestral and chamber music, which brings together many of the international performers appearing at the Dubrovnik festival the same year. **Nebo** (which means both "sky" and "heaven" in Croatian; ⓦwww.nebofestzagreb.com) is a world-music festival of relatively recent vintage, attracting local and international names in October. Advance information on all these events can be obtained from the Zagreb tourist office.

Clubs

Despite a lean period during the war years, the emergence of a vibrant rave, techno and house scene in the mid-1990s revived the city's fortunes, and today Zagreb nightlife centres around a growing contingent of characterful and informal discos and clubs, many of which present the only real opportunities for catching live **rock** and **jazz**. The student year (which roughly runs from late September to late June) is the period which sees most activity in the clubs. Conversely, things quieten down significantly in July and August – some clubs may close up completely for a few weeks over the summer. Venues tend to be open from about 10pm to 4 or 5am unless stated otherwise. Admission charges for clubs and gigs range between 30 and 60Kn – more for big, one-off events. To find out about forthcoming gigs, check the posters plastered liberally around the city centre or pick up flyers from record shops (see "Shopping", p.92).

Aquarius Jarun. This waterfront pavilion at the eastern end of Lake Jarun, 4km southwest of the centre, is the city's main venue for electronic dance music – most of the big American house DJs have played here at least once over the last ten years. Expect commercial-ish house and techno at weekends, more experimental stuff on Thursdays and Sundays. Big name Croatian pop-rock stars perform on the outdoor terrace in summer. Check the current programme at ⓦwww.aquarius.hr.

The Best Mladost Sports Centre. Run-of-the-mill disco offering mainstream techno and themed party nights; attracts a youngish crowd looking for uncomplicated hedonistic fun. Tram #17 (destination Jarun) from Trg bana Jelačića to the Stjepan Radić stop, then a short walk down Jarunska.

BP Club Teslina 7. Basement bar and jazz club featuring frequent live music, owned by godfather of the Croatian jazz scene, vibe-player Boško

Petrović. A convivial late-night drinking haunt with waiter-served tables for the smart set, and a long, thin, standing-only bar area for the hoi polloi. Gets crowded on gig nights, but well worth the squeeze.

Dom Sportova Metalčeva. Cavernous sports-hall-type venue for major gigs, with poor acoustics and long lines for beer, though the enthusiasm of a big Zagreb crowd usually makes up for any inherent lack of atmosphere. Most touring Western rock bands end up here. Take tram #3, #9 or #12 (direction Ljubljanica) to Trešnjevački trg, then turn right up Trakošćanska.

Gap Club Florijana Andrašeca 14. Newish club with three separate dance floors and a play-hard party-animal crowd. They play mainly commercial dance music, with a few offbeat DJs thrown in. Tram #3, #9 or #12 (direction Ljubljanica) to Tehnički muzej.

Jabuka Jabukovac 28. Cult alternative club which

had its heyday in the 1980s and seems to be enjoying a new lease of life, playing predominantly retro sounds to a coterie of ageing goths and new-wavers. Housed in the building that once served as Nazi puppet Ante Pavelić's private bowling alley in the 1940s. In the Tuškanac suburb, a 20min walk northwest of the centre.

KSET Unska 3, ⓦ www.kset.org. Small, intimate, student-run club and concert venue, concentrating on rock, jazz and experimental music – an impressive number of alternative acts from Europe and the US have guested here in recent years. Notoriously difficult to find: from Savska head east along Koturaška, turn right into Unska, then go straight over the crossroads and take the first dingy alley on the left. Open until midnight, Sept–June only.

Lapidarij Habdelićeva 1. Attractive cellar-like space in Gradec, with programmes ranging from indie rock to cutting-edge dance music.

Močvara Jedinstvo factory, Trnjanski nasip bb, ⓦ www.urk.hr. Mecca for non-mainstream musical tastes run by independent art cooperative URK in an old factory on the northern banks of the River Sava. Live gigs (by established foreign performers as well as Croatian indie bands) at least twice weekly, art-house film shows, theatre and club nights (anything from world music to Seventies funk) on other evenings. Cheap drinks and friendly atmosphere. About 3km south of the centre: take tram #13 (destination Žitnjak) from Trg bana Jelačića to the Lisinski stop, head south along Hrvatske bratske zajednice to Freedom Bridge (Most slobode), and turn right onto the riverbank. Closed at least one night a week, and most of July and August.

OTV Dom Vukovarska 68. Sparsely decorated, roomy club in the HQ of one of Zagreb's private television networks, a 10min walk south of the train station. Themed DJ nights aiming at the cooler end of dance culture.

Pauk Savska cesta bb. Spaceship-sized auditorium (a brief glance at the ribbed ceiling will tell you why it's called *pauk*, or "spider"), located amid the dorms of the Stjepan Radić student village. Gigs and themed DJ nights on weekends from October through to June. Tram #17 (direction Prečko) from Trg bana Jelačića to the Stjepan Radić stop.

Saloon Tuškanac 1a. Legendary Zagreb meeting-place in a leafy corner of town 500m west of the centre, with a warren of stylish, wood-panelled rooms inside and a large terrace outside. A moderately dressy clientele includes a sprinkling of beautiful people and showbiz personalities, but it's not dishearteningly exclusive by any means. The music is an enjoyable mishmash of commercial disco, except on Tuesdays, when you'll hear pop-rock nostalgia for 30-, 40- and even older-somethings.

Sax Palmotićeva 22. Large, comfortable basement club, two blocks east of Zrinjevac, with live music (with a jazz bias) most nights. Plenty of seating, Western beers on tap and a range of cocktails.

Sokol Trg maršala Tita 6 (entrance opposite the Ethnographic Museum). Big disco with commercial dance music, domestic pop and themed party nights.

Tvornica Šubićeva 1, ⓦ tvornica.corner.hr. Former ballroom just north of the bus station currently serving as venue for live rock, club nights and theatre. Doesn't open every night of the week, so check listings info or posters before setting out.

Classical music, drama and ballet

Theatre and concert tickets are usually easy to come by, and tend to be about half the price of those in Western Europe. Drama and opera are almost invariably in Croatian, unless you happen to be in town during one of the major festivals, when international groups are invited.

Croatian Musical Institute (Hrvatski glazbeni zavod) Gundulićeva 6 ☏ 01/48-30-822. Main city venue for chamber music, just west of the main square. Mon–Fri 11am–1pm, and 1hr prior to performance.

Croatian National Theatre (Hrvatsko narodno kazalište; HNK) Trg maršala Tita 15 ☏ 01/48-28-532, ⓦ ww.hnk.hr. Zagreb's cultural flagship, this sumptuous Neoclassical building provides the city's main venue for prestige classical drama, as well as opera and ballet. Box office Mon–Fri 10am–1pm & 5–7.30pm, Sat 10am–1pm & 1hr 30min before performances; Sun 30min before each performance.

Gavella West of the main square, at Frankopanska 8 ☏ 01/48-48-552, ⓦ www.gavella.hr. Second only to the Croatian National Theatre in terms of prestige, this is an elegant, medium-sized auditorium hosting leading local and foreign theatre companies, plus occasional concerts. Box office 10am–1pm & 2hr prior to performances.

Kerempuh Ilica 31 ☏ 01/48-33-347. Offers a mixture of serious theatre, satire and comedy, with frequent late-night performances beginning at 11pm. Box office Tues–Sun 10am–8pm.

Komedija Kaptol 9 ☏ 01/48-14-566, ⓦ www.komedija.hr. Musicals, operettas and occasional heavyweight drama. Box office opens 1hr 30min prior to performances.

Off Theatre Bagatelle Bednjanska 13 ☏01/61-70-423. Fringe productions, theatre workshops and cabaret. Box office opens 4hr prior to performances.

Scena Vidra Draškovićeva 80 ☏01/48-10-111. Small studio theatre housed in a former cinema. Functional auditorium, funky pre-show bar. Box office Tues–Sun 10am–3pm & 2hr before performances.

Student Cultural Centre Savska 25 ☏01/48-43-492, ⊛www.sczg.hr. Home to leading contemporary theatre company &TD, with repertoire ranging

from the populist to the experimental. Box office Mon–Sat 11am–1pm & 2hr prior to performance.

Vatroslav Lisinski Concert Hall (Koncertna dvorana Vatroslav Lisinski) Trg Stjepana Radića 4 ☏01/61-21-166, ⊛www.lisinski.hr. South of the train station, this modern complex with two auditoriums is a favoured venue for orchestral concerts and prestige drama events. Box office Mon–Fri 9am–8pm, Sat 9am–2pm.

Zagreb Youth Theatre (ZeKaeM) Teslina 5 ☏01/48-11-955, ⊛www.zekaem. Top-quality work by leading youth-theatre groups, in a modern mid-size auditorium. Mon–Fri 10am–8pm, Sat 5–8pm, Sun 1hr prior to performances.

Cinemas

Zagreb's cinemas show a wide range of recently released Western films, which are shown in the original language with Croatian subtitles. The country's largest film distributor carries details of screenings on its website (⊛www.kinematografi.hr) under the heading *raspored projekcija*. The best of the big city-centre cinemas are

---

Dinamo Zagreb and the Bad Blue Boys

From 1990 until the turn of the century, many **Bad Blue Boys** – as the supporters of Dinamo Zagreb call themselves – claimed to be the true defenders of the honour of Zagreb. Modelling themselves on the fans of the English club Chelsea, the Bad Blue Boys were a sporting subculture of negligable social significance until May 13, 1990, when a Dinamo home match against Red Star Belgrade ended in chaos, an event which for many symbolized the disintegration of the Yugoslav federation. The trouble started when Red Star fans began ripping up seats and throwing them on the pitch. The police (at this time widely believed to be under Serbian influence) failed to take action, and so Dinamo fans decided to invade the pitch. The police set about truncheoning the trespassers, enraging the Dinamo players, who were still on the field. Zvonimir Boban, the youngest-ever Dinamo captain and a byword for coolness under pressure, was so incensed that he kicked a pair of policemen – TV pictures of which were beamed around Europe the same night. The events of the day were soon mythologized, with the Bad Blue Boys exaggeratedly claiming that they had been the first to stand up to Greater Serbian chauvinism before the outbreak of all-out war the following year.

The Bad Blue Boys therefore enjoyed considerable kudos when, in 1992, the club decided to drop the "Dinamo" from the club's name on the basis that it was too reminiscent of communist ideology. The team was renamed Croatia Zagreb, in the hope that it would serve as an advertisement for the country in prestige European competitions, but the Bad Blue Boys saw it as a betrayal of club tradition, and started a campaign to restore the team's original name. This earned the Bad Blue Boys considerable Croatia-wide respect as the 1990s progressed: with Croatia Zagreb increasingly identified with government structures (the team's honorary president, Franjo Tuđman, also happened to be president of the country), the team's truculent supporters came to be regarded as an unofficial opposition to the HDZ regime.

With Tuđman's death in December 1999, and his party's defeat in the parliamentary elections of 2000, the way was clear for an immediate return to the club's original name. Since then the Bad Blue Boys have lost much of the symbolic importance they once enjoyed, although they remain a vociferous presence on the terraces.

the **Zagreb**, Preradovićev trg 4, and the nearby, old-world **Europa**, Varšavska 3. Slightly further afield, **Broadway Tkalča**, just north of the Cathedral at Nova ves 14, is a plush modern cinema with excellent sound. **Kinoteka**, Kordunska 1, is the main venue for art-house movies and cinema classics, while **Croatia**, Katančićeva, is a tiny, fifty-seater cinema with a uniquely intimate feel, showing mainstream movies or matinée cartoon features made by the local Croatia Film studio.

Spectator sports

Football remains the city's principal sporting preoccupation, with the big teams playing matches on Sunday afternoons between August and May (with a mid-season break in Jan & Feb). Tickets rarely exceed 30Kn for league matches, when they can be bought from kiosks near the turnstiles. Prices go up for European matches or internationals, when tickets are best bought in advance from the relevant stadium. **Dinamo Zagreb** (and the Croatian national team) play at the Stadion Maksimir, Maksimirska 128 (tram #1 or #17 from Trg bana Jelačića or #9 from the train station to the Borongaj terminus). The rather basic stadium at Kranjčevićeva 4 is home to the city's other major team, **NK Zagreb**. Take tram #3, #9 or #12 (direction Ljubljanica) to the Cibona Tower, then head straight on under the railway bridge. Few other spectator sports attract sizeable crowds save **basketball**, with Zagreb's top team, Cibona, playing at the Dražen Petrović Basketball centre, Savska 30 (☎01/48-43-333) – matches take place on Saturdays from September to late April.

Shopping

Retail culture has made big strides in Zagreb over the past five years or so, with a plethora of fashion shops, mobile-phone showrooms and interior-design stores sprouting up along the main thoroughfares. The principal high-street shopping areas are relatively easy to pinpoint, however, and you should be able to find most of the consumer items you're ever likely to want along **Ilica**, the long, sinuous street running west from the main square; in **Importanne Galleria**, a multistorey mall just east of the main square on Vlaška; or at **Kaptol Centar**, a smart shopping centre complete with cafés, a cinema and at least one pub, north of the cathedral at Nova ves 17. **Radićeva**, running uphill from the main square, harbours a growing number of kooky designer-label fashion boutiques and antique shops. There are some tacky **souvenir** outlets near the cathedral, but there's little in the way of locally made products that you would actually want to take home with you – unless you seek out some of the speciality stores we've listed below.

Gifts and souvenirs

Bakina škrinja Petrinjska 20. Hidden away in the courtyard, "Grannie's Cupboard" offers a small but imaginative selection of locally made ceramics and nick-nacks. Funky rather than folkloric.

Franja Vlaška 62. Coffee shop which also sells the kind of fancy food products that make perfect presents – Croatian wine, *rakija*, olive oil and fig jam included.

Mahmet Opatovina 15. Specialists in traditional north-Croatian nibbles like *medenjaci* (honey biscuits) and *licitarska srca*, the vividly decorated (but rock hard) gingerbread hearts which are meant to be hung on the wall rather than eaten.

Pršut Galerija Vlaška 7. Lots of lovely *pršut* (Croatia's delectable home-cured ham; see p.ix), sold by the gram or by the leg.

Books

Algoritam Gajeva 1, next to the *Hotel Dubrovnik*. Large, up-to-date selection of foreign-language publications, including lots in English. International magazines are sold on the ground floor; books in the basement below.

Jesenski and Turk Branches at Gajeva 1 (in the arcade behind Algoritam), Vukotinovićeva 4, and Preradovićeva 5. Browser-friendly secondhand bookseller with a small selection of foreign-language paperbacks and plenty of large-format international art books.

Moderna vremena Teslina 16. A smattering of English-language titles, and a secondhand department upstairs. If you can read Croatian, this is a good place to come for contemporary literature – and friendly advice on what to buy.

Records and CDs

Aquarius Vlaška 48 and corner of Varšavska and Gundulićeva. Retail offshoot of the club of the same name (see p.88), specializing in dance music but carrying a good selection of everything else as well.

Croatia Records Bogovićeva bb. Biggest of the high-street CD stores, run by Croatia's biggest record label – best place for commercial rock-pop.

Dancing Bear Gundulićeva 7. Wide range of both domestic and international releases in all genres.

Dinaton Preradovićeva 12. Specialists in jazz and classical CDs.

Dobar Zvuk Preradovićeva 24. Secondhand store hidden away in a courtyard. A mecca for vinyl junkies.

Listings

Airlines Adria, Praška 9 ☎01/48-10-011; Aeroflot, Varšavska 13 ☎01/48-72-055; Air Canada, Hotel Esplanade, Mihanovićeva 1 ☎01/45-77-924; Air France, Hotel Opera, Kršnjavoga 1 ☎01/48-37-100; Austrian Airlines, at the airport ☎01/62-65-900; Bosna Air, airport ☎01/45-62-672; British Airways, Sheraton Hotel, Kneza Borne 2 ☎01/45-53-336; Croatia Airlines, Zrinjevac 17 ☎01/48-19-633; CSA, Zrinjevac 17 ☎01/48-73-301; KLM, *Hotel Esplanade*, Mihanovićeva 1 ☎01/45-73-133; LOT, Trg bana Jelačića 2/I ☎01/48-37-500; Lufthansa, GeneralTurist, Zrinjevac 18 ☎01/48-73-123; Swissair, Zrinjevac 6 ☎01/48-14-144.

Airport Enquiries ☎01/62-65-222.

ATMs There are usefully located ATMs on the eastern side of Trg bana Jelačića; outside Zagrebačka banka on Praška; and outside Varaždinska banka on Draškovićeva.

Bus station Enquiries on ☎060/313-333, or check ⊕www.akz.hr.

Car rental Avis, *Hotel Opera*, Kršnjavoga 1 ☎01/48-36-006; Budget, Praška 5 ☎01/48-05-687, ⊕www.budget.hr; Hertz, Vukotinovićeva 4 ☎01/48-46-777, ⊕www.hertz.hr; Sixt, Rooseveltov trg 4 ☎01/48-28-385, ⊕www.e-sixt.com.

Embassies and consulates Australia, 3rd floor, Kaptol Centar, Nova Ves 11 ☎01/48-91-200, ⊕www.auembassy.hr; Bosnia-Hercegovina, Pavla Hatza 3 ☎01/48-19-420); Canada, Prilaz Gjure Deželića 4 ☎01/48-81-200; Czech Republic, Savska cesta 41/8 ☎01/61-77-246; Netherlands, Medveščak 56 ☎01/48-19-533; UK, Ivana Lučića 4 ☎01/60-09-100; US, Hebrangova 2 ☎01/66-

12-200, ⊕www.usembassy.hr; Yugoslavia, Mesićeva 19 ☎01/46-80-552. Citizens of Ireland or New Zealand should ring one of the English-speaking embassies to find out who is curently representing their interests.

Exchange There are exchange counters (*mjenjačnica*) at all banks, travel agents and post offices. Outside regular office hours, try the exchange counter at the bus station (24hr), or at the post office next to the train station at Branimirova 4 (24hr except midnight Sat to 1pm Sun).

Ferry bookings Jadrolinija, Zrinjevac 20 ☎01/48-73-307.

Hospital The main casualty department is at Draškovićeva 19.

Laundry Service washes and dry cleaning at Petecin, Kaptol 11 (Mon–Fri 8am–8pm, Sat 8am–3pm) and Predom, Draškovićeva 31 (Mon–Fri 7am–7pm, Sat 8am–noon).

Left luggage At the bus station (daily 6am–10pm) and train station (24hr).

Libraries British Council, Ilica 12 (Mon, Tues & Thurs 10am–4.30pm, Wed 1.30–6.30pm, Fri 10am–1.30pm; ☎01/48-13-700); French Cultural Institute, Preradovićeva 40 (Mon–Fri 9am–5pm; ☎01/48-55-222); Goethe Institute, Ulica grada Vukovara 64 (Mon–Thur 8.30am–5pm, Fri 8.30am–4.30pm; ☎01/61-95-000); Italian Cultural Institute, Preobraženska 4 (Mon–Thurs noon–3pm, Fri noon–2pm; ☎01/48-30-208).

Pharmacy Ilica 43 (24hr).

Photographic supplies Foto Studio Zagreb, Praška 2.

Post offices Jurišićeva 13 (Mon–Fri 7am–9pm,

Sat 7am–7pm, Sun 8am–2pm); Branimirova 4 (24hr except Sat midnight to Sun 1pm).

Sporting equipment Elan, Draškovićeva 25, sells equipment for all manner of winter sports; for snowboarding gear specifically, you can also try Extreme Sport, Mesnička 3.

Swimming The best of the city's indoor pools have confusingly similar names: SP Mladost, Jarunska 5 (directions as for Lake Jarun, see p.81; Mon–Fri 11am–3pm & 6–8pm, Sat 1–5pm, Sun 10am–2pm) and Zimsko Plivalište Mladost, Trg sportova 10 (directions as for *Hotel Panorama*, see p.66; Tues & Thur 1–4pm, Sun 4pm–7pm). For an outdoor swim, you can choose between the beach at Jarun or the more central outdoor pool at Šalata, ten minutes' walk northeast from Trg bana

Jelačića at the top end of the Schlosserove stube steps (June–Sept Mon–Fri 1.30–6pm, Sat & Sun 11am–7pm).

Taxis There are taxi ranks on Trg maršala Tita and on the corner of Teslina and Gajeva. To book, call ☎970, 66-82-505 or 66-82-558.

Telephones National and international calls can be made from the metered booths at the post offices on Jurišićeva or Branimirova.

Train enquiries Information on ☎9830 (domestic services), ☎01/45-73-238 (international).

Travel agents Atlas, Zrinjevac 17 ☎01/48-73-064, ✆www.atlas-croatia.com; Croatia Express, Teslina 4 ☎01/48-11-842; GeneralTurist, Praška 5 ☎01/48-05-555, ✆www.generalturist.com; Kvarner Express, Praška 4 ☎01/48-10-522.

Travel details

Trains

Zagreb to: Berlin (1 daily; 17hr); Budapest (2 daily; 7hr); Čakovec (6 daily; 2hr 30min); Geneva (1 daily; 16hr); Ljubljana (2 daily; 2hr 20min); Milan (1 daily; 11hr); Munich (2 daily; 9hr); Osijek (4 daily; 5hr); Rijeka (5 daily; 4–5hr); Salzburg (2 daily; 7hr); Split (2 daily; 9hr); Trieste (3 daily; 5hr 40min); Varaždin (9 daily; 2hr 30min); Venice (2 daily; 7hr 30min); Vienna (1 daily; 6hr 30min).

Buses

Zagreb to: Belgrade (1 daily; 10hr); Ćakovec (10 daily; 2hr 30min); Cres (2 daily; 6hr 30min); Dubrovnik (4 daily; 11hr); Karlovac (every 30min;

50min); Korčula Town (1 daily; 13hr); Osijek (6 daily; 5hr 30min); Pag Town (5 daily; 5hr); Plitvice (hourly; 2hr 30min); Poreč (6 daily; 6hr 30min); Pula (10 daily; 5hr–6hr 30min); Rijeka (20 daily; 3–4hr); Rovinj (6 daily; 5hr 40min); Split (8 daily; 9hr); Varaždin (12 daily; 2hr); Zadar (hourly; 5hr).

Domestic flights

Zagreb to: Bol (April–Sept 1 or 2 weekly; 50min); Dubrovnik (April–Sept 3 daily; Oct–March 2 daily; 50min); Pula (1 daily; 50min); Split (April–Sept 4 daily; Oct–March 3 daily; 45min); Zadar (April–Sept 2 daily; Oct–March 1 daily; 30min).

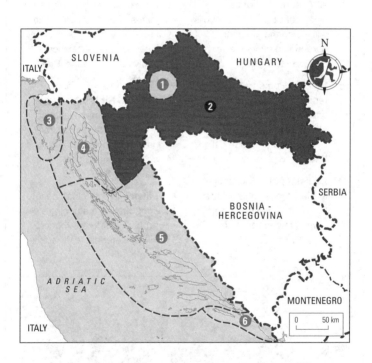

Inland Croatia

CHAPTER 2

Highlights

✱ **Kumrovec** Beautifully preserved Zagorje village which is also the birthplace of Croatia's most famous son – Josip Broz Tito. **See p.102**

✱ **Varaždin cemetery** The lovingly tended shrubs and hedgerows of this nineteenth-century necropolis will excite the amateur gardener in everyone. **See p.111**

✱ **Hlebine** Home to a world-renowned colony of self-taught painters, whose effervescent canvases can be seen in the village gallery. **See p.115**

✱ **Lonjsko polje** Enchantingly archaic timber-built villages, frequented by storks, wild horses and spotty-hided pigs. **See p.117**

✱ **Jasenovac** Site of a notorious World War II concentration camp and now home to a dignified and thought-provoking memorial park. **See p.120**

✱ **Slavonian food** Slavonians will eat anything as long as it tastes of paprika. Join them in the fiery *fiš paprikaš* (fish stew), or its meat-based equivalent, *čobanac*. **See p.124**

✱ **Kopački Rit** One of central Europe's premier wetland areas, providing a natural habitat for herons, cormorants and bird-watchers. **See p.129**

✱ **Plitvice** Breathtaking beauty spot offering a stunning profusion of forest-fringed lakes, waterfalls and rapids. **See p.144**

Inland Croatia

The jumble of geographical regions which make up **inland Croatia** seem, on the face of it, to have little in common with one another. Historically, however, the Croats of the interior were united by a set of cultural influences very different from those which prevailed on the coast. After the collapse of the medieval Croatian kingdom in the early twelfth century, inland Croatia fell under the sway of first Hungary, then the Habsburg Empire, increasingly adopting the culture and architecture of central Europe. All this has left its mark: sturdy, pastel-coloured farmhouses dot the countryside, while churches sport onion domes and Gothic spires, providing a sharp contrast with the pale stone houses and Venetian-inspired campaniles of the coast.

The main appeal of inland Croatia lies in its generous selection of contrasting landscapes. It's here that the mountain chains which run from the Alps down to the Adriatic meet the Pannonian plain, which stretches all the way from Zagreb to eastern Hungary. The **Zagorje** region, just north of Zagreb, resembles southern Austria with its mixture of knobbly hills, vineyards and compact, busy villages, while southwest of Zagreb are the slightly wilder uplands of the **Žumberak** and the smoother, pastoral hills of the **Lika**. Nestling among the latter are the **Plitvice Lakes**, a sequence of pools linked by picturesque mini-waterfalls – Croatia's most captivating, and most visited, natural attraction. Much less touristed but equally rewarding are the misty, marshy flatlands immediately south of the capital, with the **Turopolje** and **Lonjsko polje** offering a mixture of archaic timber-built villages and bird-watching opportunities. The eastern provinces of **Podravina** and **Slavonia**, watered by the rivers Drava and Sava respectively, are classic corn-growing territory: broad expanses of flat, chequered farmland only partially broken up by low green hills.

There are worthwhile urban centres here too, with well-preserved Baroque towns in which something of the elegance of provincial Habsburg life has survived. The most attractive of these is **Varaždin**, northeast of Zagreb, although **Karlovac**, to the southwest, and **Požega**, to the southeast, are also worth a look. There's little in the way of big-city thrills except in **Osijek**, inland Croatia's main urban centre after Zagreb, and the most convenient place from which to explore eastern Slavonia.

The obvious starting point for travel in the region is Zagreb, from where road and rail routes fan out in all directions: north through the Zagorje towards Slovenia, northeast via Varaždin to Hungary, and east across the Slavonian plain towards the nowadays little-used border with Serbia. Busiest of all is the route southwest towards the coast, which runs through Karlovac before splitting two

Vienna
Lake Balaton & Budapest
Budapest
0
50 km
N
Ljubljana & Salzburg
Ljubljana & Salzburg
Rijeka
Zadar, Split & Dubrovnik
Sarajevo
Banja Luka
Tuzla
Novi Sad
Novi Sad
Belgrade
SLOVENIA
HUNGARY
SERBIA
BOSNIA-
HERCEGOVINA
Maribor
Ptuj
MEĐIMURJE
Čakovec
Nagykanisza
Celje
Varaždin
Trakošćan
Lepoglava
Pregrada
Krapina
Krapsinke
Topice
ZAGORJE
Koprivnica
Hlebine
Drava
Kumrovec
Zabok
Marija Bistrica
Gornja Stubica
Križevci
PODRAVINA
Pécs
Mohács
Danube
ZAGREB
Bjelovar
Bregana
Samobor
Japetić
879m
Dugo Selo
Virovitica
Drava
Beli
Manastir
ŽUMBERAK
Ivanić Grad
Slatina
Donji
Miholjac
BARANJA
KOPAČKI RIT
NATURE PARK
Bilje
Kopačevo
Krašić
Velika
Gorica
Jastrebarsko
Crna Mlaka
TUROPOLJE
LONJSKO POLJE
NATURE
PARK
Papuk
953m
RISNJAK
NATIONAL
PARK
Ozalj
Karlovac
Donja
Kupčina
Kupa
Petrinja
Sisak
Daruvar
SLAVONIA
Jelisavac
Osijek
Kutina
Velika
Kutjevo
Našice
Gorski Kotar
Duga Resa
Čigoč
Lonja
Pakrac
Požega
Kula
Vukovar
Delnice
Glina
Mužilovčica
Novska
Đakovo
Danube
Šarengrad
Klek
1187m
Ogulin
Krapje
Nova Gradiška
Slavonski
Brod
Vinkovci
Bjelolasica
Jasenovac
Bapska
Ilok
Josipdol
Šid
Novi Vinodolski
Slunj
Sava
Oštarski Stanovi
Županja
Senj
Rakovica
Sava
LIKA
Grabovac
Korana
Prijedor
PLITVICE
NATIONAL PARK
Bihać
E71
E59
E661
E73
E70

ways – straight on across the Gorski kotar hills towards Rijeka, or south across the Lika towards Zadar and Split, passing the Plitvice Lakes on the way. Travellers making forays south or east of Zagreb will almost certainly cross parts of former war zones, and visitors to war-affected areas will see evidence of the recent conflict in the shape of burned-out houses and large signs warning of uncleared minefields. There's no reason to be wary of travelling in the region, however: life has returned to the towns, public transport runs smoothly, and a reasonable amount of accommodation is back in business.

The Zagorje

Spread out between Zagreb and the Slovene border, the **Zagorje** is an area of chocolate-box enchantment: miniature wooded hills are crowned with the castles they seem designed for, and streams tumble through lush vineyards, almost all of which feature a *klet*, a small, steep-roofed structure traditionally used for storing wine, though nowadays they're more often put to use as weekend cottages. Although the area is covered with a dense patchwork of villages, human beings seem outnumbered by the chickens, geese and turkeys that scavenge between the cornfields and vegetable plots. The museum-village of **Kumrovec**, the pilgrimage church at **Marija Bistrica** and the castles at **Veliki Tabor** and **Trakošćan** are the main targets for visitors, although there's any number of Baroque churches and attractive rural villages awiting the attentions of those who wish to explore further. If you have a car, it's feasible to visit three or four of these attractions in the course of a single day-trip from Zagreb; for those dependent on public transport, however, one Zagorje destination a day seems more realistic.

Denizens of the Zagorje speak **kajkavski**, a dialect named after the distinctive local word for "what?" ("*kaj?*"), and whose grammatical idiosyncrasies fall somewhere between modern Croatian and Slovene. Local delicacies include *štrukli* (pockets of dough filled with cottage cheese) and the ubiquitous *purica z mlincima*, or turkey served with *mlinci* (pasta noodles which look like scraggy bits of pastry). Look out too for *licitari*, the pepper-flavoured biscuits covered in icing which often take the form of a big red heart (*licitarsko srce*) and can sometimes assume enormous proportions – they're supposed to be presented to a loved one and preserved as an ornament rather than eaten.

Most towns in the Zagorje have direct **bus** links with Zagreb, but you'll need your own transport if you want to explore the region in depth. The **road** from Zagreb via Krapina to Maribor in Slovenia is the most direct route into the region, although all the interesting touring itineraries lie on the minor roads to either side. **Trains** offer a dependable, if slow, way of getting to Kumrovec, Krapina, Stubičke Toplice and Gornja Stubica.

Gornja Stubica and around

The part of the Zagorje most easily accessible from Zagreb is the gently undulating Stubica valley, spread out below the northern slopes of Mount Medvednica, which provides a lush agricultural backdrop for the long, straggling settlement of Stubica – really three villages, Stubičke Toplice, Donja Stubica and Gornja Stubica. Coming by public transport from the capital, you'll have to endure the notoriously slow Zagreb–Varaždin train to **Zabok**, where you change for the train to Gornja Stubica. By car, the most impressive approach is along the road over Mount Medvednica via Sljeme (see p.82): the views from the northern flanks of the mountain are breathtaking.

Emerging from a rustic patchwork of greens, the small spa resort of **STUBIČKE TOPLICE** is a relaxing place, although there's nothing much here apart from a cluster of sanatoriums and an open-air swimming pool complex (*kupalište*; summer daily 7am–7pm; 20Kn) behind a screen of trees in the centre. There's a **tourist office** on the main street at Viktora Šipeka 24 (Mon–Fri 8am–3pm, Sat 10am–3pm; ☏049/282-727, ℱ283-404), which can provide addresses of local private **rooms** (❷); and a **hotel**, the *Matija Gubec*, close by at Viktora Šipeka 27 (☏049/282-501, ℱ282-403, ✉hmg@kr.tel.hr; ❹), which has bland, modern en-suite rooms and a large indoor swimming pool.

Six kilometres east of Stubičke Toplice, beyond the undistinguished settlement of Donja Stubica, lies **GORNJA STUBICA**, a village famous for its role as the launching place of the **Peasants' Revolt of 1573**. The inhabitants of the sixteenth-century Zagorje were overloaded with feudal obligations, while their proximity to the Habsburg–Ottoman front line landed them with the additional burden of supplying the war effort with food and manpower. To make matters worse, the Protestant leanings of local landowners offended the staunchly Catholic sensibilities of an already disgruntled peasantry. Ironically, it was the big Catholic magnates of Croatia who put the rebellion down, with the Bishop of Zagreb, Juraj Drašković, routing a badly armed peasant army at the Battle of Stubičko Polje on February 9, 1573. Drašković deliberately spread rumours that peasant leader **Matija Gubec** had been elected "king" by his co-conspirators, an accusation which served both to discredit the rebels and to provide the excuse for a fiendishly appropriate punishment – Gubec was

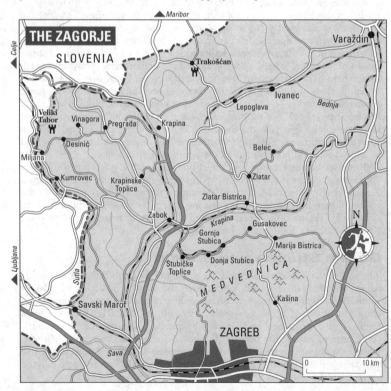

executed in Zagreb by being "crowned" with a red-hot ring of iron.

The stirringly named **Museum of Peasant Uprisings** (Muzej seljačkih buna; daily April–Sept 9am–7pm, Oct–March 9am–5pm; 20Kn), in the creakily floored confines of the Orsić Palace, 2km north of the village (and behind Antun Augustinčić's vast hilltop statue of Gubec), has a few period weapons, but otherwise relies heavily on a didactic words-and-pictures display to tell the story of the revolt. A smaller hillock just southwest of the village is crowned by the stout lime tree known as **Gubčeva Lipa**, where the peasants supposedly met to launch the insurrection. The adjacent *Birtija Pod Lipom*, decked out with rustic furnishings and embroidered tablecloths, is a good place for a **drink**, while the *Puntar* **restaurant**, just downhill from here on the village's triangular main square, doles out *grah* and other filling standards. The nearest places to **stay** are either back in Stubičke Toplice or in the Marija Bistrica area to the east.

Marija Bistrica and around

Located below the northeastern spur of Mount Medvednica, some 37km from Zagreb and 11km east of Gornja Stubica, the town of **MARIJA BISTRICA** is home to the most important Marian shrine in Croatia. It's a popular destination for pilgrims year round, though things can get particularly crowded on August 15 (Assumption) and on the Sunday preceding St Margaret's Day (July 20), when the shrine is traditionally reserved for the city folk of Zagreb.

The town itself is a small, rustic place onto which modern coach-party tourism has been rather unceremoniously grafted. It's dominated totally by the **Pilgrimage Church of St Mary of Bistrica** (Hodočasnička crkva Marije Bistričke), which perches on a hillock in the centre of town, and has been rebuilt on numerous occasions to accommodate ever-growing numbers of visitors. The current structure, put together by the architect of Zagreb cathedral, Hermann Bollé, between 1880 and 1884, is a remarkably eclectic and playful building (unlike the comparatively stern cathedral) – a jumble of Baroque and Neoclassical detail crowned by a hulking black-and-red chevroned steeple flanked by castellated red-brick turrets.

The principal object of popular veneration is the **Black Madonna**, a fifteenth-century statue of the Virgin set into the main altar. According to tradition, the statue was bricked into a church wall in 1650 to prevent it from falling into the hands of marauding Turks, and here it remained for 34 years until (it is said) a miraculous beam of light revealed its hiding place. News of the Madonna was spread by the then Bishop of Zagreb, Martin Borković, who was eager to promote Marija Bistrica as a spiritual centre at a time when pilgrimages in general were being encouraged throughout the Habsburg lands – popular religion was seen as a useful way of getting the masses behind the Catholic regime. The Madonna subsequently survived a fire in 1880 that destroyed almost everything else in the church, thereby adding to its aura.

The vast outdoor amphitheatre at the back of the church was built for the pope's visit here in October 1998, an occasion marked by the beatification of Archbishop Alojzije Stepinac (see box on p.70). Behind the amphitheatre, paths lead up the Calvary Hill (Kalvarija) past sculptures of the Stations of the Cross, culminating in a fine view back towards the town.

Practicalities

Marija Bistrica is served by numerous buses from Stubičke Toplice to the west and Zagreb to the south – the latter route following a scenic road which crawls over the eastern shoulder of Medvednica by way of the villages of Kašina and

Las. Buses stop on the main street immediately below the church, from where the pedestrianized Zagrebačka leads up to the **tourist office** at no. 66 (Tues–Fri 7am–2pm, Sat & Sun 8am–2pm; ☎ & ℻049/468-380, ⓦwww.marija -bistrica.hr), which can provide the addresses of a handful of local families offering private **rooms** (❷). Otherwise, accommodation in town is limited to the *Kaj* **hotel** just down the hill (☎049/469-026; ❸), with acceptable but charmless en-suite rooms in a modern two-storey building. Far preferable if you have your own transport is *Lojzekova hiža* (☎049/469-325; ❷), near the village of **Gusakovec**, a well-signposted six-kilometre drive west of town – from Marija Bistrica, follow signs to Stubičke Toplice and look for a right turn after 5km. This traditional farmhouse offers tiny but cosy en-suite attic rooms (including some with bunks for children) in a delightful spot bordered by woods on one side and livestock-filled meadows on the other. The other out-of-town place worth considering is *Purga*, a small family-run place 6km north of Marija Bistrica on the eastern outskirts of **Zlatar Bistrica**, at Grančarska 45b (☎049/462-232, ⓔpurga@kr.hinet.hr; ❷). There are three bright rooms here with sloping attic ceilings, a folksy restaurant, and an attatched stable offering horse-riding for 50Kn per hour.

Lojzekova hiža and *Purga* are also the best places locally to **eat and drink**, although there are numerous cafés and bistros close by Marija Bistrica's church offering the usual refreshments and snacks. *Grozd*, just outside the church entrance, serves up exemplary *štrukli* and has the customary range of Croatian meat dishes. On big pilgrimage days, several establishments along the main street offer grills and spit-roasts cooked on outdoor barbecues.

North of Marija Bistrica

The road heading north out of Marija Bistrica descends towards the broad Krapina valley before rising again into the foothills of the next ridge to the north, wooded Mount Ivanščica. After 12km you hit the small market town of **ZLATAR**, unremarkable in itself, but a useful jumping-off point for the near-by village of **BELEC**, accessible by a minor road which runs northeast out of Zlatar. Standing beside Belec's main street is the **Church of Our Lady of the Snow** (Svete Marije Snježne; Sun 8–11am), deceptively ordinary from the out-side, but containing a fantastic riot of frothy Baroque furniture and ornament within. Countess Elisabeth Keglević-Erdödy had the church built in 1675 after hearing that a miraculous apparition of the Virgin Mary had occurred in near-by Kostanjek. It soon became a popular pilgrimage site, especially among the Croatian nobility, who stumped up the cash for a thorough redecoration in the 1740s. Resplendent in pinks, eau de nil greens and luxurious gilt, the resulting ensemble of altars and wall-paintings (the latter executed by Ivan Ranger, a Pauline monk who worked all over northern Croatia, and also decorated the monastery church at Lepoglava) is designed to be viewed as a single work of art, although several individual details stand out. The most important of these is the wooden pulpit from which statuettes of prophets seem poised to leap, above a relief of revellers dancing around the golden calf. It was carved by Josip Schokotnigg of Graz, who was also responsible for the altars of St Barbara and St Joseph, which stand on either side of the main altar of the Holy Trinity, a swirling mass of cherubs and gesticulating saints.

Kumrovec and around

About 30km northwest of Zagreb, close to the border with Slovenia, the vil-lage of **KUMROVEC** is renowned both as the best of Croatia's museum-villages and as the birthplace of the father of communist Yugoslavia, **Josip Broz Tito**. The simple peasant house in which Tito was born was turned into a museum during his own lifetime, while the surrounding properties were rebuilt and restored in the ensuing decades to provide an example of what an early-twentieth-century Zagorje village must have looked like. Those who remember Tito with affection still collect here every year on May 4, the anniversary of his death.

The **"Old Village" Museum** (Muzej "staro selo"; daily: April–Sept 9am–7pm; Oct–March 9am–4pm; 20Kn; ⊛ www.mdc.hr/kumrovec) is about twenty minutes' walk east of Kumrovec's train station, set back from the main road behind a large car park, with a range of pastel-coloured houses and farmsteads ranged alongside a gurgling brook. Tito's birthplace is easy enough to spot: it's got a statue of the Marshal (caught in pensive mid-stride by Antun Augustinčić) in the garden. Inside, life-like re-creations of the 1890s rooms contain a restrained collection of photos and mementoes, including the uniform worn by Tito while leading the Partisan struggle from the island of Vis in 1944. The other buildings are each devoted to a particular rural craft, with displays of blacksmithing, weaving and toy-making – the latter featuring dainty, brightly painted wood-carved horses and other animals. One house is given over to a series of tableaux illustrating a traditional wedding feast, with rooms crowded with costumed mannequins and tables decked with imitation food.

A couple of **buses** run to Kumrovec from Zagreb daily, although **trains** (usually involving a change at Savski Marof) are more frequent. There's no accommodation in Kumrovec, but a couple of **cafés** near the museum entrance offer drinks and snacks. For something more substantial, *Zagorska klet*, within the museum complex, has local staples like cheese, sausage and *štrukli*, while *Stara Vura*, 100m east of the museum complex in the new part of the village, has a wider choice of dishes.

Miljana and beyond

Nine kilometres beyond Kumrovec, the village of **MILJANA** is overlooked by the best-preserved Renaissance palace in the Zagorje, built some time in the early 1600s by the Rafkay family and painstakingly restored by Croatian pharmaceutical magnate Franjo Kajfež in the 1970s. The palace isn't open to the public, but you're free to admire the ochre facade, and may be allowed to peek inside the asymmetrical arcaded courtyard.

The hills rearing up behind Miljana harbour one of the few local sources of accommodation in the shape of the *Masnec family*, Luka Poljanska 41 (☎049/552-133; ❷), a modern farmhouse with prim balconied en suites offering views over the vineyards; home-produced wine is on offer in the ground-floor restaurant. It's reached by driving towards the Slovene border and making a right turn 50m before the frontier post – from here the *Masnec* is a well-signed three-kilometre drive through hilltop villages. Once settled in, you can hike to Veliki Tabor along farm tracks, or walk down into the Slovenian spa town of **Atomske Toplice** (keep your passport handy), which spreads over the opposite bank of the Sutla river.

Veliki Tabor

It's only 6km on from Miljana to the most impressive of the Zagorje castles, **Veliki Tabor** (daily: April–Sept 10am–5pm, Oct–March 10am–3pm; 20Kn), whose imposing bastions look down on the road from a grassy hilltop. Built in the twelfth century to guard the lands of the counts of Celje (a Slovenian town

Josip Broz Tito (1892–1980)

Josip Broz was born on May 7, 1892, the seventh son of peasant smallholder Franjo Broz and his Slovene wife Marija Javeršek. After training as a blacksmith and metalworker, Josip Broz became an officer in the Austrian army in World War I, only to be captured by the Russians in 1915. Fired by the ideals of the Bolshevik Revolution, he joined the Red Army and fought in the Russian Civil War before finally heading for home in 1920. Some believe that the man who came back to Croatia with a discernible Russian accent was a Soviet-trained impostor who had assumed the identity of the original Josip Broz – an appealing but unlikely tale. Whatever the truth, Broz found himself in a turbulent Yugoslav state in which the Communist Party was soon outlawed, and it was his success in reinvigorating demoralized party cells that ensured his rise through the ranks. He spent time in Moscow in the 1930s, somehow surviving Stalin's purges, though whether he merely kept his head down or actively betrayed party colleagues remains the subject of much conjecture.

Broz took the pseudonym **Tito** in 1934 upon entering the central committee of the Yugoslav Communist Party (he became leader in 1937). Nobody really knows why he chose the name: the most frequently touted explanation is that the nickname was bestowed on him by colleagues amused by his bossy manner – "*ti to!*" means "you [do] that!" in Croatian – although it's equally possible that he took it from the eighteenth-century Croat writer Tito Brezovacki.

Tito's finest hour came following the German invasion of Yugoslavia in 1941, when he managed to take control of the anti-fascist uprising, even though it wasn't initially inspired by the communists. Despite repeated (and often very successful) German counteroffensives, he somehow succeeded in keeping the core of his movement alive – through a mixture of luck, bloody-mindedness and sheer charisma rather than military genius. He also possessed a firm grasp of political theatre, promoting himself to the rank of marshal and donning slightly impressive uniforms whenever Allied emissaries were parachuted into Yugoslavia to meet him. The British and Americans lent him their full support from 1943 onwards, thereby condemning all other, non-communist factions in Yugoslavia to certain political extinction after the war.

Emerging as dictator of Yugoslavia in 1945, Tito showed no signs of being anything more than a loyal Stalinist until the Soviet leader tried to get rid of him in 1948. Tito's survival – subsequently presented to the world as "Tito's historic 'no' to Stalin" – rested on his innate ability to inspire loyalty among the tightly knit circle of former Partisans who, by and large, surrounded him until his death. Flushed with the prestige of having survived Soviet pressure, Tito concentrated on affirming Yugoslavia's position on the world stage and increasingly left the nitty-gritty of running the country to others. Forming the **non-aligned movement** with Nehru and Nasser in 1955

50km to the west), it acquired its present shape in the fifteenth and sixteenth centuries, when its characteristic semicircular towers were grafted onto the earlier pentagonal shell. Inside the courtyard, three tiers of galleries contain a warren of exhibition spaces filled with pikes, maces, knightly tombstones and other medieval oddments. A display of photographs and weaponry on the ground floor recalls Veliki Tabor's status as an important centre of resistance activity in World War II, local Partisans having controlled large chunks of the Zagorje between 1943 and 1945.

There are eight **buses** daily from Zagreb to the village of **Desinić** to the east of the castle, from where it's a three-kilometre walk to the castle access road, and a further 2km uphill to the site. About 1km east of the castle, a well-signed turn-off leads up to the *Grešna Gorica* farmhouse **restaurant**, a popular venue for long weekend lunches. With a traditionally furnished dining room and splendid views of Veliki Tabor, it does a full range of Croatian cuisine, including provided a platform which allowed him to travel the world, giving Yugoslavia an international profile which is yet to be reattained by any of its successor republics. In domestic affairs he contrived to present himself as the lofty arbiter who, far from being responsible for the frequent malfunctions of Yugoslav communism, emerged to bang heads together when things got out of control. Thus, his decision to bring an end to the Croatian Spring in 1971 was sold to the public as a Solomonic intervention to ensure social peace rather than the authoritarian exercise it really was.

A vain man who loved to wear fancy uniforms and medals, dyed his hair and used a sun lamp, Tito enthusiastically acquiesced to the **personality cult** constructed around him. May 25 was declared his official birthday and celebrated nationwide as "Dan mladosti" (the "Day of Youth"), enhancing Tito's aura as the kindly father of a grateful people. He was also a bit of a ladies' man, marrying four times and switching partners with a speed that dismayed his more puritanical colleagues. During the war, he negotiated an exchange of prisoners with the Ustaše in order to secure the release of his second wife, Herta Hass, from a concentration camp. On her arrival at Tito's Partisan HQ, Hass was informed by bemused aides that she'd already been supplanted by wireless operator Zdenka Paunović.

Affection for Tito in Yugoslavia was widespread and genuine, if not universal. There's no doubt that Titoist communism was "softer" than its Soviet counterpart after 1948: many areas of society were relatively free from ideological control and, from the 1950s onwards, Yugoslavs were able to travel and work abroad. Indeed, ideological innovation was never Tito's strong point, and the relaunch of Yugoslav communism as "**self-managing socialism**" (in large measure a PR exercise designed to win support at home and ensure financial aid from the West) was largely the work of abler theorists such as Edvard Kardelj and Milovan Đilas.

For most Croats nowadays, Tito's legacy is ambiguous. Tito was fortunate enough to die before Yugoslavia's economy went seriously wrong in the 1980s, and for many he remains a symbol of the good old days when economic growth (paid for by soft Western loans) led to rising living standards and a consumer boom. However, the authority of the party – and Tito's leadership of it – was never to be questioned, and many dissenting voices ended up in prison as a result. Tito is also seen as the man responsible for the **Bleiburg massacre** of 1945 (when thousands of Croatian reservists were put to death by avenging Partisans), the repression of Croatia's Catholic Church, and the crackdown on the Croatian Spring. Despite keeping national aspirations on a tight leash, however, Tito's Yugoslavia ensured Croatian territorial continuity by establishing borders which are still in existence today. For this reason alone, many streets and squares in Croatia continue to bear Tito's name.

Zagorje specialities like *štrukli*, *purica z mlincima* and *srneći gulaš* (venison goulash). There's a small playground and a farmhouse zoo outside.

Masnec apart, the nearest **accommodation** to Veliki Tabor is the delightfully rustic *Seljački Turizam Trsek* ("Village Tourism Trsek"; ℡049/343-464; ❷), 2km beyond Desinić at Trnovec Desinički 23 – to get there, take the main road east out of Desinić and turn left when you see the sign. If you're hankering after cosy en-suite rooms in a hilltop farmstead surrounded by vineyards, then this is the place to be. With tasty traditional meals served up in a dining room hung with rustic nick-nacks, half board is well worth considering.

South to Krapinske Toplice

Around 6km east of Desinić, the arcade-encircled **Pilgrimage Church of St Mary** (Crkva svete Marije) squats picturesquely on a hillock at the top of the village of Vinagora. The church is relatively plain inside, but the view from here, with the rippling greens of the Zagorje hills laid out to the south, is the best in the region.

Some 4km further along the main road, the village of **PREGRADA** (served by Zagreb–Desinić buses) is dwarfed by the twin-towered **Church of the Ascension** (Crkva Uznesenja Marijinog), often called the "Zagorje Cathedral" on account of its incongruously large size. It's now home to a gargantuan organ which was intended for the cathedral in Zagreb, but was rejected on the grounds that it wasn't loud enough. Locals pour into town during the last weekend in September for the **Branje grojzdja** (grape harvest), a rural fair featuring folk songs and dances. An altogether more mysterious folk event takes place at **Kostel**, 5km north of Pregrada, on Easter Sunday, when locals gather at dawn near the church of St Emerik to fire traditional handmade pistols known as *kubure* – a stylized and solemn religious occasion rather than a sporting contest, aiming to honour God by making as loud a noise as possible.

Four kilometres southeast of Pregrada towards Krapinske Toplice, the road passes the top-notch *Dvorec Bežanec* **restaurant** and **hotel** (T049/376-800, Wwww.bezanec.hr; ❽), housed in a Neoclassical palace built for the Keglević family and offering spacious five-star rooms, contemporary artwork in the corridors, and a peaceful parkland setting. The hotel can organize horse-riding (100Kn per hour) and balloon trips (from 900Kn; at least 24hr notice required).

KRAPINSKE TOPLICE itself is a tiny spa town with a renowned medical centre specializing in the treatment of cardiac complaints and serious bone and muscle injuries. It's also a great place for a **swim**, boasting four outdoor pools fed by soothing spring waters in a central park. The **tourist office** (Mon–Fri 7am–3pm, Sat 8am–10.30pm; T & F049/232-106, Etzo-krapinsketoplice@ kr.hinet.hr) in the bus station can direct you towards local private **rooms** (❷); otherwise, the modern and reasonably priced *Toplice* **hotel** in the town centre (T049/232-165, F232-322; ❹) offers en-suite rooms with TV, together with sauna, massage and mud-treatment facilities.

From Krapinske Toplice, you can either head east to rejoin the main road just south of Krapina, or wend your way south back to Zagreb.

Krapina

Squeezed among lumpish, vine-covered hills midway between Zagreb and Maribor in Slovenia, the busy little town of **KRAPINA** is famous for its connections with so-called "Krapina Man" (*krapinski čovjek*), a type of Neanderthal which lived in caves hereabouts some thirty thousand years ago. The bones of several such hominids were discovered by Dragutin Gorjanović Kramberger in 1899 on Hušnjakovo hill, a short walk west of the town centre on the far side of the River Krapinica. The find is now commemorated by a **museum** just below the site (daily: summer 8am–6pm; winter 8am–3pm; 10Kn), which offers a fairly dry line-up of reconstructed skulls, together with artists' impressions of hairy men hunting bears. Outside, a pathway leads up through the woods to the exact spot where Kramberger found the bones, nowadays marked by life-size statues of a Neanderthal family.

The only other real attraction hereabouts is 2km east of town in the hillside suburb of Trški Vrh, where the arcaded **Church of St Mary of Jerusalem** (Crkva svete Marije Jeruzalemske) provides the Zagorje faithful with another important pilgrimage destination. Inside lies an exemplary riot of eighteenth-century religious fervour, although the gilded altarpieces and pink-blue frescoes work better as an integrated whole rather than as individual works of art.

The church is usually closed outside mass times, but a local keyholder (currently the Gumbas family in the small green house opposite the church; otherwise check with the Krapina tourist office) will open up for you.

Krapina's **bus** and **train stations** lie five minutes south of the town centre, where the **tourist office** at Magistratska 11 (Mon–Fri 8am–3pm, Sat 8am–noon; ☎049/371-330, ✉tzg-krapina@kr.tel.hr) can provide advice on accommodation, although there are no private rooms in the immediate vicinity of town. Luckily there's a cosy well-run **pension** in the form of the *Gostionica pod Starim Krovovima*, right on the main square at Trg Ljudevita Gaja 15 (☎049/370-536, ⓕ370-594; ❸), offering a handful of bright, clean en-suite rooms with TV – the most atmospheric of which are the attic rooms with sloping ceilings – and a couple of three- and four-bed rooms for families. On the eastern side of town, the thirteen-room **motel** *Croatia* lies right beside the Maribor–Zagreb road at Antuna Mihanovića 1 (☎049/370-547, ⓕ300-146; ❸), and has simple no-frills en suites and a fast-food canteen. The **restaurant** of the *Gostionica pod Starim Krovovima* is an informal place in which to tuck into a meaty repertoire of north Croatian classics – there seems no limit to the number of different ways you can cut up and fry a pig in the Zagorje. *Pizzeria Picikato*, Magistratska 2, has a limited range of pizzas, but comes with pleasant courtyard seating.

Lepoglava and Trakošćan

Twenty kilometres northeast of Krapina, the bland town of **LEPOGLAVA** is dominated by the dour facade of the country's largest **prison**, occupying the former buildings of a Pauline monastery. The list of those who have passed through its gates reads like a *Who's Who* of twentieth-century Croatian politics. Numerous communists, Josip Broz Tito included, languished here during the 1930s, only to turn Lepoglava to their own uses once they came to power. Archbishop Stepinac was here for five years after World War II, and subsequent internees included many who went on to play a prominent role in post-independence Croatia – President Tuđman, Dražen Budiša (leader of the Social Liberal Party), Vlado Gotovac (leader of the Liberal Party) and Ivan Zvonimir Čičak (founder of the Croatian branch of the Helsinki Committee on Human Rights) among them.

Lepoglava's only other claim to fame is the Gothic chapel of the **monastery church** (Sun 9am–noon), which stands beside the prison entrance on the main street. The lozenge-shaped gaps between the rib-vaulting were filled in with exuberantly colourful frescoes by local monk Ivan Ranger (who also worked at Belec, see p.102) in the sixteenth century, and an imposing Baroque altar was installed around a much older, Byzantine-style painting of the Madonna. There are a couple of daily **buses** to Lepoglava from Zagreb, and more frequent train and bus services from Varaždin (see p.108), 30km to the northeast.

Trakošćan

Of all the Zagorje castles, **Trakošćan**, 11km northwest of Lepoglava, is the most visited. It's actually a bit of a fake – a fanciful nineteenth-century rebuilding of a thirteenth-century original – but the sight of its cod-medieval battlements looming above the artificial lake is one of the Zagorje's most famous. After passing through the hands of several local magnates, Trakošćan fell into the possession of the Habsburg treasury in 1566 when its then owner, Ivan Gyulay, died without heir. Twenty-two years later it was presented to the Drašković family in lieu of payment for their services in subduing the Peasants Revolt (see p.100) and fighting off the Turks. It was Count Juraj Drašković who substantially rebuilt Trakošćan in romantic, neo-Gothic style between 1853 and 1862, when the landscaped park and boating lake were also added.

The **interior** (daily: April–Sept 9am–6pm; Oct–March 9am–3pm; 20Kn) is a tribute to the medievalizing tastes of its nineteenth-century restorers, full of extravagantly pinnacled door frames and elaborate woodcarving. Sundry hunting trophies, suits of armour and Julija Erdödy-Drašković's idealized nineteenth-century paintings of Zagorje peasants all add to the effect. After looking round the castle, you can walk through the forest around the lake or hire pedalos from the waterside café.

There are currently no direct **buses** to Trakošćan from Zagreb, although the ten daily services (six at weekends) from Varaždin (see below) ensure that you can just about tackle the castle as a long day-trip from the capital. The *Coning Trakošćan* **hotel** (☎042/796-224, ⓦwww.hotel.hr/coning; ❹), situated in meadows below the castle, has en-suite rooms with TV, along with a restaurant, bar, sauna, gym and tennis courts.

Varaždin to the Podravina

Northeast of Zagreb, road and rail lines to Budapest cross an outlying spur of the Zagorje hills before descending towards the lush farmlands bordering the River Drava, which for much of its length forms Croatia's border with Hungary. In the midst of this green, agricultural region lies **Varaždin**, mainland Croatia's best-preserved Habsburg-era town, well worth a day-trip from Zagreb. Other settlements in the region are very much in Varaždin's shadow, although **Čakovec**, half an hour to the northeast, is worth a stop-off if you're in the area. It serves as the centre of the **Međimurje**, a rustic frontier province, totally flat and traditionally isolated, which stretches out between the Mura and Drava rivers.

Southeast of Varaždin, roads run parallel to the Drava through prosperous rural **Podravina**, an area whose neat villages, orchards and maize fields exude an air of bucolic plenty. Fringed by gentle hills raked by the occasional vineyard, it's a pretty area to drive through once you get onto the country roads, although specific attractions are thin on the ground save for the village of **Hlebine**, a renowned centre of naive art just outside Podravina's main market town, **Koprivnica**. From Koprivnica, road and rail routes continue southeast through the Podravina towards the Slavonian towns of Našice (see p.125) and Osijek (p.126), passing through the dusty and uninspiring towns of Virovitica and Slatina en route.

Varaždin

Seventy kilometres northeast of Zagreb, **VARAŽDIN** occupied a key position on the medieval Hungarian kingdom's route to the sea and became an important military stronghold for successive Hungarian and Habsburg rulers in their struggle against Ottoman expansion. Varaždin grew fat on the profits of the Austrian–Turkish wars of the late 1600s and early 1700s, encouraging many noble families to build houses here – from 1756 to 1776 it was actually Croatia's capital, until a disastrous fire (allegedly started by a pipe-smoking local youth who fell over while chasing a pig) forced relocation of the capital to Zagreb. Following the fire, life slowly returned to the town's opulent **Baroque palaces**, many of which are resplendent in their original cream, ochre, pink and pale-blue colours following restoration. Most now do duty as apartment blocks, offices and banks, so there's a limit to the number of places you can actually visit, although there's a postcard-perfect **castle**, now home to northeastern Croatia's most worthwhile museum, and a generous sprinkling of churches – many of which survived the fire – all crammed within a compact and still relatively untouristed old town. An additional reason to visit is provided by Varaždin's **graveyard**, famous throughout Croatia for its towering topiary and strollable park-like feel. A large student population ensures that modern Varaždin has a vivacious, youthful edge – the presence of a faculty of information technology has made the town into one of the most prestigious places to study outside the capital. Varaždin's one remaining claim to fame is the extraordinarily high incidence of **bicycle use** among its inhabitants, giving it the air of a prosperous provincial town in the low countries.

Although too far north to be directly affected by the Croat–Serb conflict, Varaždin was the site of one of the war's more unusual episodes when, in September 1991, the regional commander of the Serb-dominated JNA (Yugoslav People's Army), **Vlado Trifunović**, surrendered his garrison to the local authorities in order to avoid fighting between his troops and Croatian forces. On returning to Belgrade, Trifunović was tried for treason and sentenced to twelve years in jail.

The Town

The heart of the old town is largely pedestrianized, with modern boutiques and cafés hidden behind the shuttered windows and carved doorways that embellish the former town houses of the nobility. The sturdy grey-and-yellow tower of the **Church of St Nicholas** (Crkva svetog Nikole), one of the town's few surviving Gothic monuments, presides over the small, triangular **Trg slobode** (Freedom Square) – your likely starting point if arriving from the bus or train stations.

From here, Gundulićeva leads north to **Franjevački trg** (really a broad street rather than a square), which is flanked by the mansions of wealthy merchants, their ostentatious arched portals surmounted by family crests and heavy stone balconies. Grabbing most of the attention is the cream and beige **Patačić Palace** (Palača Patačić) with Rococo mouldings writhing their way across its facade, and a huge oriel window hovering above the corner of Franjevački trg and Gundulićeva. Now occupied by an Austrian bank, the palace was built for Franjo Patačić and his poetess wife, and became the centre of salon society in late eighteenth-century Varaždin. On the square's northern side is the seventeenth-century **Franciscan Church of St John the Baptist** (Crkva svetog Ivana Krstitelja), with soaring belfry and extravagantly gilded main altar. A scaled-down copy of Ivan Meštrović's *Grgur Ninski* statue, the original of which is in Split, stands outside.

A few steps west of the statue, the Neoclassical **Herczer Palace** at Franjevački trg 6 houses the **Entomology Museum** (Entomološki muzej; Tues–Fri 10am–3pm, Sat & Sun 10am–1pm; 10Kn). It features a display of over 4500 insects based on the collection of local biologist Franjo Košćec (whose study is also re-created here), arranged thematically according to habitat – forest, meadow, riverbank and so on. Modern display cases and imaginative lighting lend the collection the character of a contemporary art installation. North of here, Ursulinska leads up to the castle via the **Ursuline church** (Ursulinska crkva), recent recipient of

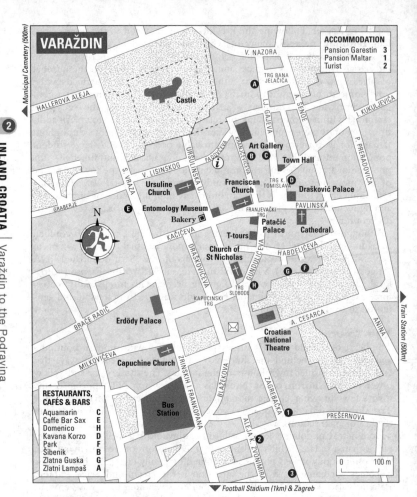

VARAŽDIN

Municipal Cemetery (500m)

HALLEROVA ALEJA

Castle

V. NAZORA

TRG BANA JELAČIĆA

ACCOMMODATION
Pansion Garestin 3
Pansion Maltar 1
Turist 2

LJ. GAJEVA

A. ŠENDE

I. KUKULJEVIĆA

P. PRERADOVIĆA

URSULINSKA U.

PADOVĆEVA

FRANCEVIĆEVA

Art Gallery

Town Hall

S. VRAZA

V. LISINSKOG

Ursuline
Church

Franciscan
Church

TRG K. TOMISLAVA

Drašković Palace

GRABERJE

N

Entomology Museum

Bakery

FRANJEVAČKI TRG

PAVLINSKA

Patačić
Palace

Cathedral

KAČIĆEVA

DRAŠKOVIĆEVA

GUNDULIĆEVA

T-tours

Church of
St Nicholas

HABDELIĆEVA

TRG
SLOBODE

KAPUCINSKI
TRG

BRAĆE RADIĆ

Erdödy Palace

A. CESARCA

ANINA

Train Station (500m)

ZRINSKIH I FRANKOPANA

Croatian
National
Theatre

MILKOVIĆEVA

Capuchine Church

BLAŽEKOVA

ZAGREBAČKA

ALEJA K. ZVONIMIRA

PREŠERNOVA

Bus
Station

0   100 m

RESTAURANTS,
CAFÉS & BARS
Aquamarin   C
Caffe Bar Sax E
Domenico   H
Kavana Korzo   D
Park   F
Šibenik   B
Zlatna Guska   G
Zlatni Lampaš A

Football Stadium (1km) & Zagreb

an attention-grabbing bright pink makeover, whose soaring onion-topped tower is one of the most distinctive features of the Varaždin skyline.

Franjevački trg's eastern end opens out onto **Trg kralja Tomislava**, the main town square, surrounded by balustraded palaces and overlooked by the sky-rocketing clock tower of the sixteenth-century town hall. Hugging the eastern side of the square, the coffee-coloured **Drašković Palace** (Palača Drašković) was where the Ban of Croatia Franjo Nadasdy took up residence in 1756, in the process turning Varaždin into the de facto capital of Croatia. Just off the main square to the east, the **Church of the Ascension** (Crkva Marijinog Uznesenja) was originally built by the Jesuits in the 1640s. Now the town's cathedral, it stands on the cusp of the Baroque and Rococo eras, most of the interior decorations, including the main altar, having been added in the 1730s. The plain, whitewashed interior provides the perfect setting for a no-holds-barred display of gilded statuary on the high altar and in the side chapels. A block north of Trg kralja Tomislava, the bright orange exterior of the seventeenth-century Palača Šermage conceals the town's **art gallery** (Galerija starih i novih majstora; Tues–Fri 10am–3pm, Sat & Sun 10am–1pm; 10Kn), which holds a few old Dutch and French paintings by lesser masters, as well as a fair amount of obscure Croatian work.

The castle and cemetery

Immediately opposite the art gallery, a wooden drawbridge and gatehouse marks the entrance to the **Castle** (*stari grad*), an irregular rectangle surrounded by two concentric moats divided by grassy earthworks. Dating from the mid-1500s, when Varaždin was in the front line against the advancing Turks, it was eventually transformed into a stately residence by the powerful Erdödy family, who lorded it over the region for several centuries. The courtyard, with its three tiers of balustrades, has been beautifully restored; the **museum** within (Tues–Fri 10am–3pm, Sat & Sun 10am–1pm; 20Kn) contains an engrossing display of weaponry, local crafts and furniture throughout the ages, much of it accompanied by English-language captions. It's easy to miss the first-floor **Chapel of St Lawrence** (Kapelica svetog Lovre), built by Toma Bakač Erdödy in thanks for his victory over the Ottomans at Sisak in 1593, and the adjoining circular sacristy, squeezed into a defensive tower.

About 400m west of the castle, down Hallerova aleja, Varaždin's **Municipal Cemetery** (*gradsko groblje*) is a minor horticultural masterpiece. Laid out in 1905 by chief cemetery-keeper Hermann Haller, it's as much a public park as a graveyard, with row upon row of conifers carefully sculpted into tall hedges and pillars, stately green monoliths which seem to swallow up the graves themselves.

The Erdödy Palace and Capuchine Church

Returning from the castle or cemetery to the bus station via Stanka Vraza, you'll pass the **Erdödy Palace** (Palača Erdödy) at no. 8, another creamy-coloured testament to Varaždin's dominant architectural style. Built by the Erdödys to provide themselves with a cosy downtown alternative to the draughty medieval rooms they had to put up with at the castle, it's now the seat of the city's prestigious music school (Glazbena škola) and the venue for occasional chamber concerts. A few steps further south, the eighteenth-century **Capuchine Church of the Holy Trinity** (Kapucinska crkva svetog Trojstva) is worth a quick peek for its organ, embellished with delightful figures of angels contentedly twanging away on various instruments.

Practicalities

Varaždin's **bus station** is a five-minute walk west of the town centre, separated from Trg slobode by the modern, flagstoned Kapucinski trg. The **train station** is slightly further out, on the eastern fringes of the town centre at the far end of Kolodvorska. The staff at the **tourist office**, near the castle at Padovčeva 3 (Mon–Fri 7am–9pm, Sat 8am–3pm; ☎042/210-985 and 210-987, ⓦwww.varazdin.hr), can provide friendly advice and a free town map, while T-tours, Gundulićeva 2 (☎042/210-989, ⓕ210-990), handle bookings of private **rooms** (❶–❷) in the town and outlying villages.

The *Turist* at Aleja Kralja Zvonimira bb (☎042/395-395, ⓦwww.hotel -turist.hr; ❹) is a modern, centrally located one-hundred-room **hotel** with comfortable en-suite rooms. Just behind it at Preŝernova 1 is the *Pansion Maltar* (☎042/311-100, ⓕ211-190; ❸), a cosy and informal twelve-room bed-and-breakfast. A few steps to the south, *Pansion Garestin*, Zagrebačka 34 (☎042/214-314, ⓦwww.gastrocom.hr; ❼), provides well-equipped rooms – though not quite as luxurious as the price tag suggests – with private facilities and TV.

Travelling on to Hungary

Crossing Croatia's long border with Hungary is relatively straightforward, with local buses connecting the main settlements on both sides. The main road between Zagreb and Budapest is the **E71**, which passes through Varaždin and Čakovec before crossing the border at **Goričan** (a motorway along this route is currently under construction). There are also road crossings at **Gola** (between Koprivnica and Nagyatad), **Terezino Polje** (between Virovitica and Barcs), **Donji Miholjac** (between Našice and Pécs) and **Kneževo** (between Osijek and Szekszárd).

If you're aiming for Budapest, the most direct form of public transport is the **train**, with two daily expresses – the *Kvarner* (Rijeka–Zagreb–Koprivnica–Budapest) and the *Drava* (Venice–Ljubljana–Čakovec–Budapest) – connecting the Hungarian capital with points in Croatia. The city of Osijek is a useful starting point for heading into southern Hungary **by bus**, with three daily services to Pécs, and one to Mohács.

The best place to **eat** in the centre is *Zlatna Guska* ("Golden Goose"), housed in a seventeenth-century palace at Habdelićeva 4 (reservations advised at weekends; ☎042/213-393), and serving up succulent steaks, freshwater fish, and a handful of vegetarian dishes in a barrel-vaulted cellar. Next door, *Park*, Habdelićeva 6, offers a workmanlike range of veal- and pork-based fare, although the outdoor terrace, jutting out into the town park, is a wonderful place to sit in summer. *Šibenik*, near the castle at Kranjčevićeva 12, specializes in seafood, while *Domenico*, Trg slobode 7, is the classiest of several central pizza outlets, and also offers a choice of pasta dishes. For **snacks**, the *pekarna* (bakery) at Kačićeva 2 serves up a tasty selection of sandwiches and pastries until 10pm.

For **drinking**, *Kavana Korzo*, Trg kralja Tomislava, is a venerable relic of Habsburg times, offering numerous varieties of coffee and a wealth of cakes, and a square side terrace that's the place to be seen on summer evenings. Plenty of youthful bars are scattered around the city centre: *Zlatni Lampaš*, Trg bana Jelačića 3, is a comfortable pub-style bar in a stylish cellar; *Aquamarin*, Gajeva 1, offers two tiers of seating, bluey-green decor and fishy artworks; and *Caffe Bar Sax*, Vraza 15, is a relaxing and comfy corner with a small outdoor terrace.

The tourist office has details of the annual **Festival of Baroque Music** (late Sept to early Oct), which features concerts in many of the town's historic churches. Varaždin also has a first-division **football** team, Varteks (named after the textile company which sponsors them), who play in an all-seater stadium 1km south of town on the Zagreb road.

Čakovec

Northeast of Varaždin, the main road to Hungary crosses the River Drava and traverses the flatlands of the Međimurje before arriving at **ČAKOVEC**, some 15km beyond. A relaxing if unspectacular provincial town, it centres on a largely modern area around Trg kralja Tomislava. The western end of the square features one of the finest Secession-era buildings in Croatia, the so-called **Casino**; designed by Hungarian architect Ödön Horvath in 1908, it's a vivacious red-brick structure whose mushroom-shaped protuberances look like a deliberate affront to its po-faced neighbours.

Čakovec's main draw, however, is its seventeenth-century **Castle**, in a park just west of the centre, the former home of the powerful Zrinski family (see box opposite). Beyond the moat and surviving western wall, the two-storey Baroque palace in the heart of the fortress now houses the **Museum of the Međimurje** (Tues–Fri 10am–3pm, Sat & Sun 10am–1pm; 15Kn). Objects connected with the Zrinskis, including the fine Renaissance tombstone of Nikola Šubić Zrinski, are complemented here by two rooms of Iron Age finds from nearby Goričan, including several big urns decorated with geometric patterns, and an enormous

The Zrinskis

From the sixteenth century onwards, eastern Croatia's status as a borderland disputed between the Habsburg and Ottoman empires led to the rise of a new breed of warrior aristocrats, whose power rested on military prowess on the battlefield and unswerving loyalty to the Habsburg dynasty. One of the most powerful Croatian families of the time was the Zrinskis, four of whom were elected Ban of Croatia between the mid-sixteenth and mid-seventeenth centuries.

The first of these was **Nikola Šubić Zrinski** (1508–66), who was awarded the castle of Čakovec by Habsburg Emperor Ferdinand I in 1546 – an acknowledgement of his financial contribution to the war against the Turks. Nikola Šubić used Čakovec as a base from which to grow rich on the export of Međimurje livestock, although the need to ward off Turkish attacks remained a lifelong preoccupation. When Suleyman the Magnificent advanced into Habsburg territory in 1566, Nikola Šubić led the defence of the fortress of **Szigetvár** in southern Hungary (about 100km southeast of Čakovec). Faced by overwhelmingly superior forces, he led his men on an attempted breakout from the fortress. They perished to the last man, but their heroism weakened the Ottomans sufficiently to stall their advance. Nikola Šubić's exploits were immortalized by his great-grandson, **Nikola VII** (1620–64), whose epic Hungarian-language poem *Szigeti Veszedelem* ("Sziget in Peril") was to become a standard text for Hungarian patriots.

The Zrinskis continued to flourish as long as the Habsburg court valued their role as frontier barons, but the relationship became strained after the **Treaty of Vásvár** in 1664, which many Hungarian and Slavonian aristocrats felt made too many territorial concessions to the Turks. Feeling that loyalty to the Habsburgs had been insufficiently rewarded, a group of Hungarian nobles under **Wesselényi** conspired to establish an independent Hungary with a French or Polish monarch at its head. The conspiracy was enthusiastically supported by Nikola VII Zrinski, but Wesselényi died in 1667 and Nikola was killed by a boar during a hunt, leaving Nikola's brother **Petar Zrinski** (1621–71) and brother-in-law **Fran Krsto Frankopan** to assume leadership of the revolt. A harebrained scheme to kidnap the Emperor Leopold I in November 1667 having failed, Petar opened negotiations with the Turks, promising to make Hungary-Croatia a vassal state of the Ottoman Empire in return for help against the Austrians. Turkish help never materialized – indeed Turkish diplomats are thought to have provided details of the conspiracy to Leopold's court – and after failing miserably to whip up any popular support, Petar and his allies surrendered. They expected to be treated leniently by an emperor keen to rebuild bridges with his unruly aristocratic subjects, but Leopold had both Petar and Frankopan **executed** in Wiener Neustadt on April 30, 1671. Their bodies were returned home to be buried in Zagreb cathedral in 1919, although the fact that they'd originally been thrown into a common grave meant that the bones of innumerable other execution victims had to be collected in order to make sure that Petar Zrinski and Frankopan were among them.

The Zrinskis and Frankopans remain important symbols of Croatia's unfulfilled destiny in central Europe. Neither were ever Croatian patriots in the modern sense: they belonged to a cosmopolitan aristocracy which invested most of its political energies in the defence of family privileges. However, the ending of both the Zrinski and Frankopan dynasties in 1671 dealt Croatian culture a serious blow; both families supported the publishing of Croatian-language books, and Fran Krsto Frankopan was himself an able poet. Once they had been replaced by nobles solidly oriented towards Vienna and Budapest, Croatia was deprived of an upper class with any real enthusiasm for national culture.

drinking vessel whose handle is adorned with pictures of horned beasts. The rest of the collection is a bit of a hotchpotch, featuring nineteenth-century furnishings, a reconstructed town pharmacy, and an old telescope built by the local astronomical society.

The weekend preceding Shrove Tuesday sees the traditional **Međimurje carnival** (Međimurski fašnik) parades here, when villagers from the surrounding area converge on the town sporting – among other things – wild animal masks and imitation storks' heads on sticks; more information about the festivities can be obtained from the tourist office.

Practicalities

Čakovec's **bus station** is a block north of Trg Kralja Tomislava, while the **train station** is slightly further out to the southwest. There's a helpful **tourist office** at Kralja Tomislava 2 (Mon–Fri 8am–4pm, Sat 8am–1pm; ☎040/313-319 or 310-969, ℱ310-991). Čakovec's proximity to the Hungarian border ensures that there's a handful of decent **accommodation** options, although there's nothing much to choose between them price-wise. *Aurora*, behind the bus station at Franje Punčeca 2 (☎040/310-700, ⓦwww.gutex.hr; ❹), has a handful of bright en-suite rooms with TV and sloping attic ceilings. Just north of the castle and a few steps west of the bus station, *Pansion kod Jape* at Zrinsko-Frankopanska bb (☎040/310-238 & 310-243; ❹) offers similarly cosy rooms with private facilities on the top floor of a brand-new office block. *Hotel Park* (☎040/311-255, ⓦwww.union-ck.hr; ❹), a couple of hundred metres further west at Zrinsko-Frankopanska bb, is a 1960s box which conceals comfy and well-appointed en suites. Downtown **eating** options include fish specialities at the *Riblji Restoran*, and cheaper Italian fare at *Pizzeria Pipo*, both occupying different halves of the same building on Ulica kralja Tomislava 2. *Gradska kavana*, just off Ulica kralja Tomislava at Matice Hrvatska 2, is a good place to enjoy a daytime **drink** and slice of cake; *Arcus*, down from the tourist office at Strossmayerova 8, is an elegant café-bar with a youngish clientele.

Koprivnica and Hlebine

Southeast of Varaždin and Čakovec stretches the **Podravina**, a ribbon of maize- and sunflower-covered flatlands running between the River Drava to the northeast and the Bilogora highlands to the south. Most routes pass through the agribusiness centre of **KOPRIVNICA**, where the rail lines from Zagreb to Osijek and Budapest part company. It's a neat and prosperous provincial town, laid out around an attractive central square with an adjoining grassy park, but there are few specific attractions; its main use to the traveller is as a jumping-off point for the village of **Hlebine** and the nearby Hungarian border.

The **bus** and **train** stations lie next to each other, ten minutes' walk west of the main square, Florijanski trg, where the **tourist office** at no. 3 (Mon–Fri 8am–4pm, Sat 8am–noon; ☎048/621-433, ℱ623-178, ℮tzg-koprivnica@kc.tel.hr) can help with local information. The only accommodation is at the *Podravina* **hotel**, a couple of blocks south of the tourist office at Hrvatske državnosti 9 (☎048/621-026, ℱ621-178; ❻). For **eating**, the *Pivnica Kraluš* on the main square offers the standard Croatian culinary repertoire in beer-cellar-like surroundings.

One annual festival worth looking out for is the **Naive Art Fair** (Sajam naïve; usually the second weekend of July), when there's a big display of local arts and crafts together with folkloric performances on the main square.

Hlebine

Sixteen kilometres southeast of Koprivnica, **HLEBINE** has been associated with naive art since the 1930s, and is home to an estimated two hundred self-taught painters and sculptors. The **Galerija Hlebine** (Mon–Sat 10am–4pm; 10Kn), a modern pavilion on your left as you enter the village from the Koprivnica direction, documents the work of the Hlebine School, with changing exhibitions chosen from their extensive archive collection. There's a special room devoted to Ivan Generalić, whose personal brand of magical realism had an enormous impact on successive generations, and helped make Hlebine painters so popular with the buying public. Generalić's rather jolly, bucolic vision of peasant life is showcased here with portraits of local characters, fanciful visions (as in *Eiffel Tower in Hlebine*), and examples of one of his favourite

Naive art in Croatia

The emergence of a group of untutored painters in rural Croatia owes a great deal to the academically trained artist **Krsto Hegedušić** (1901–75) who, while studying in Paris, became an admirer of "naive" artists such as Henri "Le Douanier" Rousseau and the Georgian painter of Tbilisi streetlife, Pirosmani. Returning to Hlebine, Hegedušić was amazed to find that village youths such as **Ivan Generalić** (1914–92) and **Franjo Mraz** (1910–81) seemed to possess the same talent for rendering the world around them in a fresh and vivid style. Hegedušić was heavily influenced by the work of great Flemish painters like Pieter Bruegel the Elder, and probably saw Generalić and Mraz as an opportunity to reinvent Bruegel in a contemporary Croatian setting. He was also a left-leaning intellectual who believed that rural life should be depicted in a non-idealized way to show people how the Croatian peasant really lived. Hegedušić invited Generalić and Mraz to exhibit with Zemlja ("Earth"), a group of socialist artists from Zagreb, giving naive painting a respectability which has endured ever since. He also encouraged the young artists to adopt the traditional craft of painting in oil or tempera on glass, a technique which gave their colourful scenes of village life an added luminescence.

The early works of Generalić and Mraz were grittily documentary in conception, although for gutsy realism even they couldn't compare with the images of peasant toil being produced by **Mirko Virius** (1889–1943), a self-taught painter from Đelekovec, north of Koprivnica, who sought to present a true picture of rural poverty to the urban public. However Croatian naive art became less politically engaged as the years went on: Zemlja was outlawed in 1935, Virius was killed in a World War II Ustaše concentration camp, and the social concerns of the original Hlebine painters fell into the background. Ivan Generalić entered his magic-realist phase, and the second generation of Croatian village painters, such as **Ivan Rabuzin** (b. 1921) and **Josip Generalić** (son of Ivan; b. 1936), increasingly used the naive style to paint the world inside their heads rather than the world outside the garden gate.

After World War II the tradition of village painting was encouraged all over Yugoslavia by a new regime eager to promote a type of people's art free of Western "decadence", and in both in communist Yugoslavia and post-independence Croatia, naive art has been hailed as an authentic expression of indigenous peasant culture. Nowadays it's rather self-consciously promoted under the label "the miracle of the Croatian naive" (*Čudo hrvatske naive*). Miracle or not, most of the work produced by today's naive artists tends towards the decorative and the kitsch – largely because there's such a big market for homely rustic themes. Hlebine remains the only village in Croatia where naive art is regarded as a legitimate local craft passed from one generation to the next; if you don't make it here, the best place to view the works of Croatia's rural painters is the **Gallery of Naive Art** in Zagreb (see p.72).

subjects, the crucified rooster (*raspeti petao*) – not the mock-religious image you might imagine, but the artist's revenge on the beast that used to wake him up every morning when he was a child. Ten minutes' walk further down the village's main street, the **Galerija Josip Generalić** (prearranged group visits only; ☎048/836-430, ⓦwww.generalic.com) occupies the former studio of both Ivan Generalić and his son Josip, and holds examples of their work, alongside paintings by Ivan's grandson Goran Generalić.

Hlebine is served by six daily **buses** from Koprivnica on weekdays, but services are few and far between at weekends, when you'll need your own transport to visit. The only **accommodation** in the village is the lovely two-person apartment in the garden of the Galerija Josip Generalić (☎048/836-430; ❷). Opposite the main art gallery are a **café** and a small store where you can buy food.

The Turopolje and Lonjsko polje

The area **southeast of Zagreb** is characterized by unbroken green flatlands watered by the Sava and its tributaries. To begin with, the region is dotted with modern villages that serve as dormitory suburbs of the capital, but the further south you go, the more examples of ancient timber houses and rustic lifestyles you'll come across. **Sisak** is the rather characterless main town in the region, and is really a staging point on the way to more enticing rural destinations: the **Turopolje**, between Zagreb and Sisak, contains some excellent examples of peasant architecture; although it can't compete in terms of mystique or beauty with the **Lonjsko polje**, south of Sisak, a wetland area justly famous for its bucolic villages and birdlife. The southern extremity of the Lonjsko polje is marked by the town of **Jasenovac**, site of a notorious concentration camp in World War II and now home to a dignified – and deeply rewarding – memorial centre.

Zagreb is the best base from which to explore the region, with roads (and bus routes) traversing the Turopolje towards Sisak and beyond. If you're in a hurry to get to the Lonjsko polje, or if you're approaching from Slavonia, then you'll probably use the Autocesta (the Zagreb–Belgrade highway; see p.124) which skirts the region to the east.

The Turopolje

Immediately south of Zagreb, the **Turopolje** (supposedly named after the *tur*, a now-extinct breed of wild ox which once roamed the area) extends for some 20–30km before coming up against the low hills of the Vukomeričke Gorice. It's not an outstandingly interesting area, but if traditional village architecture is your thing, it merits a brief trip. Several villages harbour surviving pockets of wooden Turopolje houses, characterized by the covered staircases which run up the outside of the building, usually finishing at a upstairs veranda, while several timber churches add a quaintly Ruritanian atmosphere to what is otherwise a rapidly urbanizing region.

The main road from Zagreb to Sisak passes through – or near – the main points of interest. Zagreb–Sisak commuter **trains** serve Velika Gorica and Mraclin, while **buses** from the main Zagreb bus station to Sisak go through Buševec. In addition, bus #268 from Zagreb train station (the bus stands are reached by passing under the tracks through the subterranean Importanne shopping centre) runs to Velika Gorica, the Turopolje's main town.

Velika Mlaka, Velika Gorica and around

Barely 5km beyond the southern boundaries of Novi Zagreb, the main road (served by the #268 Velika Gorica bus) passes **VELIKA MLAKA**, a former village but nowadays a prosperous dormitory suburb of Zagreb. Here, about ten minutes' walk north of the main road, an enclosure shaded by pine trees provides the setting for **St Barbara's Church** (Crkva svete Barbare), a timber construction covered in small wooden shingles and topped by a jaunty spire. Founded in 1642, it was substantially rebuilt in 1912, when the porch – decorated with sun symbols and squiggle patterns – was added. A few oblong wooden houses and barns still survive in the surrounding streets, although most have been demolished to make way for the kind of sturdy family houses that wouldn't look out of place anywhere between here and Hamburg.

Bus #268 finishes up in **VELIKA GORICA**, a plain, residential town situated a few kilometres beyond Zagreb airport. Velika Gorica's bus terminal is just off the main street, where the fetchingly pink-and-orange former town hall contains the **Museum of the Turopolje** (Tues–Fri 10am–6pm, Sat & Sun 10am–1pm; closed Aug; 10Kn), a small but thoughtfully presented collection of local crafts. The most striking exhibits are the traditional costumes – white, pleated skirts with vivacious crimson embroidery for the women; extravagantly wide pantaloons and black-brimmed hats for the men. Velika Gorica's only other sight is the dainty wooden **Chapel of Jesus in Wounds** (Kapela ranjenog Isusa), located in a field 3km north of the centre, a couple of hundred metres from the airport entrance. Originally raised by the widow of local nobleman Ladislav Plepelić in 1758, the chapel was substantially rebuilt in the nineteenth century and, though rarely open (Sunday mass is your best bet), it remains an impressive clump of blackened timbers, dramatically floodlit at night. The #268 bus passes the airport access road on entering and leaving the town; get off here, then head towards the airport until you see the chapel on your right.

Six kilometres south of Velika Gorica and just west of the main Zagreb–Sisak road, the sleepy village of **Mraclin** (reached by bus #304 from Velika Gorica or by commuter train from Zagreb) boasts a sufficiently large number of traditional Turopolje houses to make a brief stroll through the centre worthwhile, although it won't detain you for long. Much the same might be said of **Buševec**, 5km further south, which has a small wooden church with a cone-like steeple at the southern end of the village, and several timber farmsteads nearby. Buševec is on the main Zagreb–Sisak highway, so Sisak-bound buses pass through here. Further on along the main Sisak road, **Dužica** boasts a fair proportion of traditional houses – if you're driving, it's the kind of place you may well want to park up and take a few photographs.

The Lonjsko polje and Jasenovac

Southeast of the Turopolje lies the **Lonsko polje**, an area of wetland just east of the River Sava famous for its wooden village architecture and nesting storks. The oak forests and pastures of the *polje* (field) are also home to the Posavlje horse (Posavski konj), a stocky, semi-wild breed which wanders the area, and the spotty-hided Turopolje pig (Turopoljska svinja), which lives off acorns. The other main characteristic of the *polje* are the swamplands and riverine forest which appear in spring and autumn, when the tributaries of the River Sava habitually break their banks and the area is colonized by spoonbills, herons and storks. The area between Sisak and Jasenovac was declared a **nature park** (*park prirode*) in 1990, although the development of tourism in the area is still in its infancy – there's nowhere to stay in the Lonjsko polje, and few places to eat. Public transport is meagre, so it's best to come by car if you can.

Croatia's long border with Bosnia and Serbia has long been ethnically mixed, a legacy of the population movements caused by Ottoman advances into the central Balkans. Christians of various creeds who had been displaced from their homes by the Turks were settled here by the Habsburgs to man the so-called **Military Frontier**, a wedge of land along the border with Ottoman-controlled territory, which was placed under direct rule from Austria and organized along military lines. Established in the sixteenth century as a belt of territories running through the north of present-day Croatia, the Military Frontier gradually moved southwards as Austrian armies threw the Ottomans back, until by the early 1700s it had stabilized into the wish-bone-shaped frontier with Ottoman-controlled Bosnia which is still reflected in the modern-day border. Many of the people settled here were migrants from the southern Balkans, a mixture of Slavs and Vlach shepherds who – owing to the fact that they were Orthodox Christians, and therefore subject to the Serbian patriarchate – developed a Serbian national consciousness as the centuries passed. The waning of Ottoman power in the 1700s meant that the Military Frontier lost its use as a defensive cordon, although the Habsburgs kept it as a way of maintaining a permanently armed and drilled population for use in the empire's wars in other parts of Europe. This provided the Serbs and Croats of the region with powerful national myths: both communities came to consider themselves the most war-like, noble and masculine expressions of their respective peoples, and by the early twentieth century many Serbs regarded the Military Frontier region – or simply **Krajina** ("border land"), as they now called it – as the heartland of martial Serb values.

The Military Frontier was abolished in 1881, but the region's ethnically mixed character remained. After the creation of Yugoslavia in 1918, the continuing presence of a large Serbian minority in Croatia was used by successive regimes to keep Croatian aspirations for self-government under control. The so-called **Independent State of Croatia** (NDH), created by Nazi Germany after the fall of Yugoslavia in 1941, tried to "cleanse" Croatia of its Serbian population by violent means – hundreds of thousands of Croatian Serbs in the border regions were either driven from their homes, forcibly converted to Catholicism, or killed. Memories of the NDH period had a profound effect on Serbian attitudes in the years leading up to the collapse of communist Yugoslavia, and with the victory of the pro-independence HDZ in the Croatian elections of April 1990, Serbian propagandists in Belgrade deliberately played on the fears of Serbs living in Croatia by suggesting that the dark days of the NDH were about to return. In an atmosphere of inter-ethnic mistrust generated in large part by the Belgrade media, Serbs living in the border regions of Croatia launched a **rebellion** from the town of Knin (northwest of Split; see p.283) in September 1990, which later developed into all-out war following Croatia's declaration of independence in June 1991. Supported by the Yugoslav People's Army, Serbian insurgents took control of a swathe of territory stretching from Slavonia in the east to the Knin region in

Sisak

The obvious northern gateway to the region is **SISAK**, a dreary, medium-sized town 22km west of the Popovača exit of the Autocesta. Sisak is also connected to the capital by bus and train (the buses come here via the single-lane highway which crosses the Turopolje). The **bus** and **train stations** stand next to each other on Trg republike, 500m north of the **tourist office**, on the western fringe of the town centre in a seventeenth-century riverside granary known as the Mali Kaptol, Rimska bb (Mon–Fri 8am–3pm; ☎044/522-622, ℗521-615). If you need to use Sisak as a base for exploring the Lonjsko polje, uninspiring but perfectly palatable en-suite rooms are available at the *Panonija* **hotel**, a concrete structure right in the centre at I. K. Sakcinskog 21 (☎044/515-600 & 515-601, ⓔhotel-panonija@hi.hinet.hr; ❸); and you can the west, which they planned to detach from the nascent Croatian state. Croat settlements within these Serb-controlled areas were ethnically cleansed, while the east Slavonian town of **Vukovar**, one of the places that stood in the way of the Serbian land grab, was almost totally destroyed in the autumn of 1991. Other inland towns such as Osijek, Vinkovci, Slavonski Brod and Karlovac found themselves at the heart of Croat resistance to further Serbian expansion and, although all were subjected to heavily shelling, they remained in Croatian hands.

By the end of 1991 large chunks of inland Croatia were under the control of the Serbs, who proceeded to organize the breakaway territory as the **Serbian Republic of the Krajina** – a nominally independent state which was in practice heavily dependent on Belgrade. The deployment of UN peacekeepers to the front line after March 1992 temporarily brought the conflict to an end, but only seemed to confirm Serb gains. Aware that international diplomacy was unlikely to secure a return of the Serb-occupied territories, the Croatian government re-equipped its armed forces and prepared to take them back by force. In May 1995 the **Blijesak** ("Flash") offensive cleared Serbian forces from western Slavonia, a pocket of land midway between Zagreb and Slavonski Brod. In August of the same year **Oluja** ("Storm") resulted in the collapse of Krajina forces around Knin. Flushed with military success, the Croats were able to negotiate a peaceful transfer of power in the one remaining area of Croatia under Serb control, eastern Slavonia. Local Serbs opted to surrender the territory without a struggle: according to the terms of the 1995 **Erdut Agreement**, eastern Slavonia was to be governed by the UN for two years before returning to Croatian sovereignty in January 1998. The changeover took place relatively peacefully, and despite an initial exodus of local Serbs, most chose to stay and accept the new administration.

Croats who had been forced out of Serb-controlled areas in 1991 were now free to return, although war damage and the lack of a functioning economy meant that many stayed away. The situation was complicated by the position of the local Serb population, who had fled in their thousands in the wake of Blijesak and Oluja – the right of all refugees, regardless of ethnicity, to return to their prewar homes was one of the key elements of the 1995 **Dayton Accord**, which was designed to bring a definitive end to the conflicts in Croatia and Bosnia. As a result, both Croatian and Serbian returnees are competing for an insufficient number of homes and jobs, and tensions between the two communities remain. Returning Croats are understandably suspicious of Serbian neighbours against whom they were fighting a few years before, while those Serbs who have chosen to stay feel they are being made to bear a collective guilt for the actions of a few. The question of **war crimes** remains ever-present: the graves of Croats who disappeared in 1991 are still being uncovered, while a true picture of the excesses committed by Croatian irregulars in the wake of Blijesak and Oluja is yet to be established.

get hearty local food at the *Mali Kaptol* **restaurant**, in the same building as the tourist office.

Sited near the junction of the Sava, Odra and Kupa rivers, Sisak has served successive rulers as a strategic strongpoint, beginning with the Romans, who named it Siscia and used it as a base for their river fleet. A few waist-high stretches of Roman **wall** are preserved just behind the tourist office, near the bridge across the river Kupa, but there's little else of captivating interest in town save for the sixteenth-century **castle** 3km to the south. Watching over the confluence of the Sava and Kupa, it's a splendid triangular structure protected by a barrel-shaped bastion at each corner. Inside the galleried courtyard is a small museum (Mon–Fri 8am–3pm; 10Kn) displaying pottery and weapons through the ages, and telling the story of the Battle of Sisak in 1593, when Habsburg forces (with a lot of Croats and Slovenes in their ranks) defeated a powerful Ottoman army – thereby saving central Europe from Turkish invasion for another century. There are two ways of getting to the fortress from central Sisak: either follow the Popovača road heading southeast out of the centre and turn right onto Obala T. Bakača just before the bridge over the Sava, or walk south from the tourist office along the banks of the Kupa.

Sisak to Krapje

From Sisak you can catch one of the four daily buses to the Lonjsko polje village of Čigoć (of which two carry on to the village of Lonja, calling at Mužilovčica on the way), 28km from Sisak. These follow the old Sisak–Jasenovac road which winds along the northeast bank of the River Sava, passing through a sequence of single-street villages renowned for their chicken-choked yards and for the kind of tumbledown, timber-built houses that seem to have jumped straight out of an illustated book of fairy stories.

The most famous of these villages is **ČIGOĆ**, not least because of its importance to the local stork population, which descends on the village in ever-increasing numbers every spring (usually arriving late March/early April) ready to feast on the Lonsko Polje's abundant supply of insects, fish and frogs. You stand a good chance of seeing baby storks during the hatching season, which falls in late April or May. According to tradition, the storks leave Čigoć for the wintering grounds of southern Africa (an eight- to twelve-week journey) on St Bartholomew's Day (August 24), although a handful of creatures stay in the village all year, their migratory instincts weakened by food handouts by soft-hearted locals. Most of the houses in Čigoć are traditional two-storey structures placed end-on to the road, with thatched roofs, overhanging eaves, and a main entrance on the first floor reached by a covered outside staircase known as a *ganjak*; many also have elaborately carved porches or balconies. One of these structures midway through the village houses a **park information point** (May–Sept daily 8am–4pm; ☎044/715-115), which can provide a map of the area and advise on trails leading east from Čigoć and the other villages out into the countryside, parts of which might be under water depending on the time of year. Towards the eastern end of the village, the *Stara hiža* **restaurant** offers drinks, snacks and possibly more substantial dishes, depending on what they have in stock.

Beyond lie a succession of villages similar to Čigoć but without as many storks: first is **MUŽILOVČICA**, where you'll find a small, private ethnographic **museum** at *Seoski turizam Mužilovčica* ("Rural tourism Mužilovčica"), the beautifully preserved timber house of Jakša and Zlata Ravlić at no. 72 on the village's only street. The Ravlićes serve up excellent home-cooked **food**, ranging from tasty cold cuts to more filling meat and fish main courses (give them advance warning if you can; ☎044/710-151).

Six kilometres further on lies **Lonja**, another long, tumbledown village, followed after another 12km by **Krapje**, whose rather better-preserved wooden houses sit in a neat row, spaced at regular intervals – the orderly result of strict regulations introduced by the Habsburgs to control house-building in the settlements of the Military Frontier.

Jasenovac

Fifteen kilometres beyond Krapje and 10km south of the Novska exit of the Autocesta is **JASENOVAC**, the site of a notorious World War II concentration camp. Established in autumn 1941, this was the largest in an archipelago of

△ War damage, Vukovar

camps stretching from Krapje in the north to Stara Gradiška in the south. The inmates were used as a slave labour force to produce bricks and metal chains – indeed the industrial aspect of Jasenovac was seized upon by propagandists for the NDH (the Croatian acronym for the so-called "Independent State of Croatia", run by the Croatian Ustaše on behalf of their German masters), who distributed photographs (now on display here) of happy prisoners beavering away in camp workshops in an attempt to convince the public that no one here was being tortured or killed. In reality, the liquidation of unproductive or unwanted prisoners was a regular fact of life in Jasenovac from its inception – an unknown number of Serbs, Jews, gypsies and Croatian anti-fascists were killed here – while overwork, malnourishment and a succession of cold winters reduced numbers even further. Jasenovac was finally wound up in April 1945, the Ustaše attempting to murder the remaining inmates, 600 of whom staged a mass breakout – a total of 91 got away.

Jasenovac and its legacy

Alojzije Stepinac, the archbishop of Croatia during World War II, was so shamed by the concentration camp at Jasenovac that he likened it to the mark of Cain, to be worn by the nation for ever. Since then, the failure of first Yugoslav, then Croatian, officialdom to come to terms with what really happened at Jasenovac has only served to prove the wisdom of Stepinac's words. Initially, there was a tendency among postwar Yugoslav historians to inflate the numbers of the camp's victims, and an estimate of 700,000 to 1,000,000 dead came to be officially accepted, despite the lack of research to back it up. Croatian historians, led by **Franjo Tuđman**, felt that the circulation of such high figures was exploited by official circles in Yugoslavia to blacken the reputation of the whole Croatian nation and render feelings of Croatian patriotism impossible for future generations. Developed over several decades, Tuđman's point of view, originally aired in the 1970s, was eventually published in his lengthy theoretical work *The Impasses of Historical Reality* in 1989, together with his assertion that the death toll at Jasenovac could not have exceeded 30,000–40,000. The lack of unbiased research makes all figures questionable, although outside observers nowadays consider 85,000–90,000 to be a fair estimate – the majority of the victims are likely to have been Serbs. With Tuđman's controversial writings fuelling the debate, Jasenovac became a political football during the dying days of Yugoslavia, the Serbian media whipping up anti-Croatian feeling by harking back to the crimes of World War II, the Croats minimizing the importance of Jasenovac in an attempt to sweep the excesses of the Nazi period under the carpet.

Even after Croatian independence, Jasenovac lost none of its power to divide opinion. Faced with the question of what to do with the site once it was returned to Croatian control, President Tuđman suggested turning Jasenovac into a memorial to all the victims of World War II by burying the remains of casualties from both sides in one **common grave**. The idea that bones of the Ustaše might be mixed together with their victims shocked liberal opinion, as well as outraging Jewish organizations worldwide and souring Croatia's relations with Israel. Not surprisingly, the idea was swiftly dropped. Jasenovac was in the news again in May 1998, with the extradition from Argentina of one of the camp's former commanders, **Dinko Šakić**. The decision to charge Šakić with "crimes against humanity", but not with full-blown genocide, merely led to further accusations that the trial was another attempt to lessen the significance of Jasenovac rather than recognize the horrors that took place there. Šakić was found guilty and given a twenty-year sentence in October 1999.

Situated beside the road into town from Novska, the camp was razed in 1945 and turned into a **memorial park** (*spomen-park*) two decades later. The park is centred on a striking modern sculpture resembling a giant concrete orchid, the work of Serbian architect, sculptor and politician Bogdan Bogdanović (who, as the "liberal" mayor of Belgrade in the 1980s, was purged by Slobodan Milošević's hardliners). At the park entrance is a concrete pavilion holding a **museum** (Mon–Fri 7am–3pm; free; Ⓦ www.ushmm.org/jasenovac) with photographs and documents relating to the history of this camp and the others around it, although there's a work-in-progress character to the display; most of the archives and exhibits were removed to Belgrade during the Serbian occupation of Jasenovac in 1991–95 and haven't been returned.

The rest of Jasenovac still bears the scars of a more recent war: the centre of town was cleared of Croats in 1991, and its church dynamited (the Serbs suffered a similar fate when the Croats returned in May 1995). There's little to do in town except call in at the **Lonjsko Polje Nature Park administration office**, housed in local government buildings opposite the (now rebuilt) church on the main square, Trg kralja Petra Svačića (Mon–Fri 8am–3pm; ☎044/672-080, ⒺPP.lonjsko.polje@sk.tel.hr), where you can pick up maps and advice on exploring the park. The **tourist office**, in the municipal library building behind the church (Mon–Fri 7.30am–3.30pm; ☎044/672-587, Ⓔtz_opcine_jasenovac@net.hr), can help you book a room at the *Gostionica kod Ribiča* just up the road (☎044/672-066; ❷), a simple **pension** whose owner doesn't speak English. The *Gostionica*'s **restaurant** serves up filling, paprika-landed stews of fish caught in local rivers.

Slavonia

Stretching from the Lonjsko polje to the Danube, which forms Croatia's border with Serbia, the rich agricultural plain of **Slavonia** has an unjust reputation as the most scenically tedious region of the country. All most visitors ever see of it is the view from the Autocesta – the highway originally built to link Zagreb with Belgrade, and still the main route into the eastern corner of the country (see box, p.124) – as it forges across unbroken flatlands. The effects of war, Serbian occupation and the painfully slow pace of reconstruction have left their mark, but the region has its attractions, not least a distinctive and often captivating rural landscape, characterized by a seemingly endless carpet of corn and sunflowers, with vineyards on the low hills to the north.

Traffic on the Autocesta thins out as it nears the border with Serbia, 310km east of Zagreb, with most travellers veering north towards eastern Croatia's main urban centre, **Osijek**, a former Austrian fortress town which retains a dash of Habsburg-era elegance. The best of Slavonia's scenery lies around here, a patchwork of greens and yellows dotted with dusty, half-forgotten villages, where latticed wooden sheds groan under the weight of corncobs and strings of red paprikas hang outside to dry in the autumn. Just north of Osijek, the **Kopački Rit nature reserve**, with its abundant birdlife, is Croatia's most intriguing wetland area, while in the far southeast the siege-scarred town of **Vukovar** – though hardly the tourist attraction it once was – is a worthwhile side-trip if you want to see the consequences of the war at first hand. Elsewhere in Slavonia there's a relative dearth of urban sights, save in the pleasant provincial towns of **Požega** and **Đakovo**.

Slavonian **culinary culture** is characterized by a rich variety of fresh fish from the Sava and Drava rivers, notably carp, catfish and pike. A mixture of the above are stewed together to produce *fiš paprikaš*, the spicy, soupy mainstay of most restaurant menus around Osijek and in the southeast. The meat-eater's alternative to this is *čobanac*, a goulash-esque paprika-laden stew which is served up in vast tureens. Many Slavonian families keep a pig or two, traditionally slaughtered towards the end of November in the annual *kolinje*, or pig cull. The main pork-based delicacy is *kulen*, a rich, paprika-flavoured sausage served as a snack or hors d'oeuvre.

Požega

Some 150km east of Zagreb, at the **Nova Gradiška** exit, a minor road heads north from the Autocesta to **POŽEGA**, an appealing market town lying amid the small lumpish hills of the **Babja Gora**. The town was occupied by the Turks between 1536 and 1691, but today the look of the place is overwhelm-ingly Baroque, its main square, Trg svetog Trojstva, surrounded by yellow, arcad-ed, two-storey monuments to provincial contentment.

On the southern side of the square, the Gothic Franciscan **Church of the Holy Spirit** (Crkva svetog Duha) was used as a mosque by the Turks and has been recently spruced up, while the older **St Lawrence's Church** (Crkva sve-tog Lovre) is said to contain some fine Gothic frescoes, though it's currently undergoing restoration and is inaccessible. The **Town Museum** (Gradski muzej; Mon–Fri 10am–noon & 5–7pm; 10Kn), at the east end of the main square, has a limited display of local archeological finds, and a small ethno-graphic section featuring some incandescent hand-woven rugs with vegetal and bird designs. There's also a small display devoted to local-born nineteenth-century adventurer Dragutin Lehrmann, who served the King of Belgium as colonial administrator of the Congo, helped found Požega museum by donat-ing many of the artefacts he brought back with him, and died while prospect-ing for gold in the mountains of Bosnia. A few steps south along Županijska lies the most eye-catching of Požega's nineteenth-century civic buildings, the **County Hall** (Zgrada Županije), its avocado-coloured facade topped by a trio of clock towers.

Down an alleyway at the western end of the square, the attention-hungry lemon-yellow belfry of **St Theresa's Church** (Crkva svete Terezije) overlooks a statue commemorating Luka Ibrišimović Sokol, a fearsome-looking Franciscan friar who won a famous victory over the Turks at nearby Sokolovec, liberating Požega in the process. It's a strikingly militant piece of anti-Ottoman propaganda, portraying the priest with sword unsheathed, trampling on a crescent symbolizing Islam.

Požega is the unlikely setting for one of Croatia's strangest cultural events, the **Festival of One-Minute Films** (Revija jednominutnih filmova), which attracts largely avant-garde work from all over the world every year in May. The other cultural attraction here is the **Golden Strings of Slavonia Festival** (Zlatne žice slavonije; Sept), a celebration of indigenous **tamburica** music (named after the *tambura*, a ferociously strummed lute-like instrument), which has come to dominate the Croatian pop mainstream in the last decade or so. Contact the tourist office for information about both festivals.

Practicalities

Both bus and train stations are at the southern end of town; a ten-minute walk up Stjepana Radića will get you to the centre. Požega's **tourist office**, Trg svetog Trojstva 3 (Mon–Fri 8am–3pm, Sat 8am–1pm; ☎034/274-900, ⊕274-901), can point you in the direction of a couple of **pensions** (❶–❷) in the suburbs. There are a pair of smallish **hotels** in the shape of *Grgin Dol* (☎034/273-222; ❹), just west of the main square at Grgin Dol 20, with poky but smart rooms with their own bathroom and TV; and *Vila Stanišić*, midway between the stations and the main square at Dr Franje Tuđmana 10 (☎034/312-168; ❸), its cosy en-suite rooms above a restaurant. There are loads of **cafés** and simple **restaurants** tucked away in the streets just south of the main square: *Pečenjarnica Kamenita Vrata*, Kamenita Vrata, is a no-frills snack stop offering filling bowls of *čobanac* and *grah* as well as basic grilled-meat dishes; while *Tomislav*, round the corner at Babukićeva 25, offers more in the way of sit-down restaurant fare, with a range of hearty pork and chicken dishes. The **patisserie** at *Vila Stanišić* is perfect for picking up pastry-snacks and cakes.

Northeast from Požega

If you're heading for Đakovo, Vinkovci or Belgrade from Požega, your best option is to rejoin the Autocesta at Slavonski Brod (see p.130) and continue eastwards from there. Travellers bound for Osijek, however, would do best to follow the minor road **northeast from Požega**, which crosses the low-lying limbs of wooded **Papuk** – which at 953m is Slavonia's only "mountain" – before dropping down towards the Drava basin at Našice. The route takes you through some of the best of Slavonia, with lush green tobacco plantations breaking up the more familiar vineyards and cornfields. The villages are quite pretty too: **Kula**, 20km out of town, is a typical example, with a single row of neat little one-storey houses placed end-on to the road.

Despite being very much a town rather than a village, **NAŠICE**, 20km further on, is another typically Slavonian one-street settlement, all its principal buildings laid out in a single strip. Midway along this main street at Pejačevićev trg, the resplendently ochre former mansion of the Pejačević family now houses the **Našice Regional Museum** (Zavičajni muzej Našice; Mon–Fri 8am–1pm; 20Kn) with a collection rich in nineteenth-century furnishings and locally made flax and embroidery. Požega–Osijek **buses** pick up and drop off outside the museum (it's much better to alight here than at the bus station, 2km away on the northeastern side of town), and there's a comfortable if unexciting two-star **hotel**, the *Park*, virtually next door at Pejačevićev trg 4 (☎031/613-822, ⊛www.hotel-park.hr; ❸).

Beyond Našice, the road heads across arable flatlands towards Osijek, passing through a line of villages stocked with narrow nineteenth-century houses with wooden porches. Most attractive of these settlements is probably **Jelisavac**,

7km out of Našice, a predominantly Slovak village which has bilingual street signs – a product of eighteenth-century population movements, when Christian peasants from throughout the Habsburg lands were encouraged to settle in a Slavonia recently won back from the Ottoman Turks.

Osijek

Tucked into the far northeastern corner of Slavonia, 30km from the Hungarian border and just 20km west of the Serbian province of Vojvodina, **OSIJEK** is the undisputed capital of the region. An easy-going, park-filled city hugging the banks of the River Drava, Osijek has a relaxed spaciousness due in large part to its being spread out across three quite separate town centres. The oldest of these, **Tvrđa**, retains the air of a living museum. Originally a Roman strongpoint, it was subsequently fortified by the Ottomans and then finally rebuilt in Baroque style by the Austrians, who kicked the Turks out in 1687. The Austrians were also responsible for the construction of **Gornji grad** (Upper Town – so called because it's upriver from Tvrđa), the nineteenth-century area which still exudes a degree of fin-de-siècle Habsburg refinement and now serves as the administrative heart of the modern city. At the eastern end of town, **Donji grad** (Lower Town) is a residential district of little interest to visitors, which developed at around the same time as Gornji grad in order to accommodate economic migrants from the surrounding plains.

After the fall of Vukovar in November 1991, the Yugoslav People's Army and Serb irregulars laid siege to Osijek and subjected the town to a nine-month bombardment. Osijek survived, but the scars of war are still plain to see. Nowadays there's a palpable sense of isolation, brought about by Osijek's geographical position on the fringes of Croatia, pushed up against the borders of a Yugoslav state with which normal economic and cultural relations are largely frozen; the cosmopolitanism of the pre-1991 city is unlikely to re-emerge for some time.

Osijek's sights won't detain you for more than a day, but it's the obvious place from which to venture into the **Kopački Rit nature reserve** and is a useful jumping-off point **to southern Hungary**, with daily buses to both Pécs (Pečuh in Croatian) and Mohács (Mohač).

Arrival and accommodation

Osijek's **bus** and **train stations** are next to each other on Trg L. Ružička, on the south side of the town centre. From here it's a ten-minute walk – first up Radićeva, then left into Kapucinska – to reach Trg Ante Starčevića, the heart of Gornji grad (alternatively, travel three stops on tram #2). The helpful staff at the **tourist office**, just next to the cathedral at Županijska 2 (Mon–Fri 7am–4pm, Sat 8am–noon; ℡031/23-755, Ⅎ23-947), can provide a free monthly events guide (*gradski vodič*). OK Tours, Trg slobode 7 (℡031/212-815, ⓦwww.ok-tours.hr) have a meagre handful of apartments (❹) in town, although they have much more in the way of private rooms (❷) in the village of **Bilje**, a twenty-minute bus ride to the north (see p.129).

Cheapest of the town's **hotels** is the plain but tolerable *Mursa*, which has sparsely furnished en-suite rooms in a concrete lump that looks like a grain silo; it's a short distance east of the train and bus stations at Bartula Kašića 2a (℡031/207-640; ❸). In the town centre, the *Central*, Trg Ante Starčevića 6 (℡031/126-188; ❹), is a rather more characterful nineteenth-century place with comfortable en-suite rooms. The business-oriented high-rise *Hotel Osijek*, on the waterfront at Šamačka 4 (℡031/201-333, Ⓕ212-135, Ⓔhotel.osijek@ hinet.hr; ❹), is overpriced – unless you can get a room facing the river.

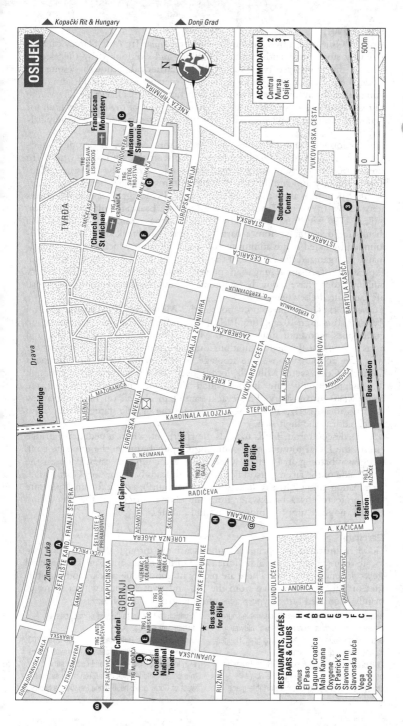

OSIJEK

Kopački Rit & Hungary

Donji Grad

ACCOMMODATION
Central 2
Mursa 3
Osijek 1

Footbridge

Drava

Zimska Luka

TVRĐA

Franciscan Monastery

Museum of Slavonia

Church of St Michael

GORNJI GRAD

Cathedral

Croatian National Theatre

Art Gallery

Market

Studentski Centar

Bus stop for Bilje

Bus station

Train station

RESTAURANTS, CAFÉS, BARS & CLUBS
Bonus   H
El Paso   A
Laguna Croatica B
Mala Kavana   D
Oxygene   E
St Patrick's G
Slavonia Inn J
Slavonia kuća F
Vega   C
Voodoo   I

The Town

Modern Osijek is centred around the neat, triangular Trg Ante Starčevića, bordered by stout nineteenth-century buildings and overlooked by the elegant spire of the town's red-brick, neo-Gothic **Cathedral**, although despite the bustle there's not much else in the way of specific attractions. Heading east along Europska avenija, just beyond the junction with Radićeva, you'll pass the best group of Jugendstil buildings in Croatia, a series of town houses built for rich local German merchants, with caryatid-encrusted facades and spindly balconies.

Two kilometres along Europska avenija lies the complex of Baroque buildings known as **Trvđa** (literally "fortress"; also reachable on tram #1 from Trg Ante Starčevića or by walking along the riverside path by the Drava), a collection of military and administrative buildings thrown up by the Austrians after the destruction of the earlier Ottoman castle. Tvrđa's grid of cobbled streets zeros in on Trg svetog Trojstva, a broad expanse bearing a **plague column**, built in 1729 with funds donated by the local fortress commander's wife to give thanks for deliverance from a particularly nasty outbreak of disease; it's surrounded by faded ochre administration buildings from which Habsburg commanders organized the defence of the southern frontier. Originally built as an expression of Austro-Hungarian power, these arcaded eighteenth-century buildings today have a quietly forgotten air, now that the centre of municipal life has shifted elsewhere.

One of these buildings now houses the **Museum of Slavonia** (Muzej slavonije; Tues–Sun 10am–1pm; 10Kn), which displays sculptural fragments and gravestones recovered from Roman Mursa, Osijek's distant forerunner, and hosts temporary themed exhibitions on local history. Off the square to the west, the double onion-dome frontage of the former Jesuit **St Michael's Church** (Crkva svetog Mihovila) lords it over a knot of narrow alleys, although it's disappointingly bare inside. Much the same might be said of the **Franciscan monastery** (Franjevački samostan) church on Lisinskog a few steps northeast of Trg svetog Trojstva, despite the Gothic statue of the Virgin which adorns the high altar.

Alleys descend from Tvrđa towards the riverfront, where a pedestrian bridge crosses the Drava towards ritzy-sounding **Copacabana** on the opposite bank – a grassy bathing area with a waterslide and a couple of cafés. Back on the Tvrđa side of the river, a broad flagstoned path leads back towards Gornji grad, terminating at the **Zimska luka** ("winter harbour"), a dock for small pleasure craft protected by a breakwater from the strong currents of the Drava, and another popular spot for lounging around in cafés.

Eating

Good **restaurants** are sprinkled rather sparingly through the city. Once you locate them, however, you'll find the range of fish dishes and paprika-flavoured stews generally excellent. There are plenty of good-value snack-food possibilities on the way into town from the bus and train stations, with a string of plainly decorated bistro-type places offering grill-food and pizzas.

Bonus Hrvatske Republike 1. Dependable source of workmanlike meat and fish dishes midway between the train station and Gornji grad. Hedges its bets by offering so-so pizzas.

El Paso Zimska luka. A snazzy glass-fronted pavilion on a barge in front of the *Hotel Osijek*, this is a classy but comfortable place in which to tuck in to decent pizzas, pasta dishes and salads.

Laguna Croatica Dubrovačka 13 ☏031/369-203. The best place in town to sample freshwater fish, with local trout, pike-perch and catfish served up in a smart-looking brick cellar. Ten minutes' walk west of Gornji grad: head along Pejačevića behind the cathedral, and turn left into Dubrovačka after about 5min.

Slavonia Inn Trg L. Ružičke. No-frills restaurant in the train station offering cheap, tasty and filling fare – mostly meaty schnitzels and cutlets with the occasional fish dish thrown in.

Slavonska kuća Firingera 26 ☎031/208-277. Friendly little place in the Tvrđa district with rustic wooden-bench decor, offering vast bowls of fiery *fiš paprikaš* and *čobanac*, accompanied by home-made noodles. Also good foir freshwater fish, either grilled or fried in breadcrumbs.

Drinking and nightlife

The city's key **drinking areas** are the Zimska luka, where there's a string of flashy glass-fronted cafés below the *Hotel Osijek*, and the stretch of Radićeva between Hrvatske republike and Gundulićeva, where there's a packed bar every 20m or so. In Gornji grad, *Mala Kavana*, next to the cathedral on Trg Marina Držića, is ideal for a daytime coffee break, and has an outdoor terrace that remains lively until well into the evening. In Tvrđa, *St Patrick's*, Trg svetog Trojstva, is an Irish-style pub with a terrace facing the best of Osijek's Baroque buildings, and a comfy interior featuring (for some perverse reason) a shrine to Chelsea football club. *Voodoo*, just off Radićeva at Sunčana 6, is a studenty, alternative rock-oriented meeting-place on two floors. There's a **cybercafé** a few doors up from the *Voodoo* café-bar on Sunčana. **Clubs** go in and out of fashion fairly quickly, although you could try *Vega*, at Fakultetska 2 in Tvrđa, which has rave parties and themed DJ nights, or the largely mainstream-techno *Oxygene*, opposite the tourist office at Županijska 7.

The main venue for **classical music** and **theatre** is the Croatian National Theatre (Hrvatsko narodno kazalište), Županijska 9. Osijek has two **cinemas**: the Europa, near the *Hotel Osijek* on Lučki Prilaz, and the Urania, just east at the junction of Europska and Radićeva. There's a dearth of live **rock-pop** music in Osijek, although a programme of gigs is organized during the **Summer of Youth** (Ljeto mladih) in July, with most events taking place at the Studentski centar on Istarska.

Kopački Rit and around

Beyond Osijek, the main road to Hungary forges through the pastel-coloured villages and corn-rich fields of the **Baranja**, a fertile extension of the Slavonian plain filling the triangle formed by the Drava to the west, the Danube to the east, and the low hills of southern Hungary to the north. A border region once known for its mixed population and tolerant ways (the area was 42 percent Croatian and 36 percent Serb in 1981), the Baranja spent the years from 1991 to 1998 under Serbian occupation, then UN control. Most of the Croats fled in 1991, and are only slowly returning, kept away by poor employment prospects, painful memories, and suspicion of those local Serbs who have chosen to remain.

Eight kilometres out of Osijek the road passes through the village of **Bilje**, main gateway to the **Kopački Rit Nature Park** (Park prirode Kopački Rit). The park covers an area of marsh and partly sunken forest just north of the point where the fast-flowing River Drava pours into the Danube, forcing the slower Danube waters to back up and flood the plain. The resulting wetland is most inundated from spring through to early autumn, when fish come here to spawn and wading birds congregate to feed off them. At this time you'll see cormorants, grey herons, and, if you're lucky, black storks, which nest in the oak forests north of Bilje. Many of the fields and country lanes surrounding the park are yet to be cleared of mines – so anyone walking or driving through the area should stick to the roads, and remain on the lookout for local "mine" signs.

Visitors should head first for the park administration office on the eastern fringes of Bilje (Mon–Fri 8am–4pm, plus summer weekends; ☎031/750-855,

ⓟ750–755, ⓔpp-kopacki-rit@os.tel.hr); it's housed in the former hunting lodge of Prince Eugene of Savoy, the dashing Habsburg commander who drove the Ottomans out of Slavonia at the end of the seventeenth century. Here you can pay the 20Kn **entrance fee**, pick up English-language leaflets and a map. There's also an information kiosk at the Lake Sakadaš entrance to the park (May–Sept weekends only). Individual tourists can then drive or walk into the park, although you'll see much more by booking a **jeep tour**, for which 24 hours' notice is required. Led by national park guides, these trips range from two to six hours in length (40–60Kn per person). In summer, it's possible to visit the flood plain by small boat (1hr 30min–2hr; 250Kn per boat).

The main route into the park is along the road which leads east from Bilje to **Kopačevo**, 3km away, a village which hosts a mixed Croatian-Hungarian population. It also contains some of the best traditional architecture in eastern Slavonia, with the kind of houses you'll see all over the Hungarian plain, southeastern Croatia and the Serbian Vojvodina, laid end-on to the road, with long verandas facing in onto secluded courtyards. The **park entrance** is just north of Kopačevo: from here a road runs along a north-leading dyke which separates a series of commercial fishponds on the left-hand side from the magisterial sunken forest of **Lake Sakadaš** on the right, where wading birds stalk their prey among the white willows. North of here, tracks continue through **Tikveš**, an area of oak forest where you stand a good chance of spotting wild pigs and deer. Josip Broz Tito used the fine villa of **Dvorac Tikveš** as a hunting lodge; after suffering neglect during the Serbian occupation, it's currently being transformed into an ecology centre which will offer multimedia displays and upmarket accommodation.

To get to Bilje from Osijek, catch one of the half-hourly buses from either Hrvatske republike or Trg Ljudevita Gaja, or one of the Osijek–Beli–Manastir services from Osijek bus station. Get off in the centre of Bijle and head east along the road to Kneževi Vinogradi to find the park administration office. The turn-off to Kopačevo and Kopački Rit is five minutes' walk further on.

There's a handful of very comfortable **private rooms** (❷) in Bilje itself (ⓦwww.bilje.hr contains details of some of them), which can be booked through the park administration or through OK Tours back in Osijek (see p.126). The *Varge* **restaurant**, at the southern end of Bilje, serves up a superbly spicy *čobanac*; while the *Zelena Žaba* in Kopačevo offers equally enticing local fare in the shape of *fiš paprikaš* and *fiš perkelt* (Hungarian fish casserole).

Slavonski Brod

Fifty kilometres east along the Autocesta from Nova Gradiška, **SLAVONSKI BROD** is a largely modern town whose high-rise suburbs were built to house workers drawn by the local Đuro Đaković engineering works, although a smattering of Habsburg-era buildings in the centre – including an eighteenth-century fortress – may tempt you to take a breather here before pressing on. The town hardly merits an overnight stop unless you're in town for the **Brodsko Kolo Folklore Festival** (mid-June), which features songs, dance and horse-and-trap displays from all over Slavonia. Details are available from the Slavonski Brod tourist association (ⓣ & ⓕ035/447-721, ⓦwww.tzgsb.hr).

The heart of the town, **Trg I. B. Mažuranić**, faces the broad sweep of the Sava, with views of the sister town of Bosanski Brod (in the Serbian-controlled half of Bosnia-Hercegovina) on the opposite bank. From here, Šetalište braće Radić follows the river eastwards to the eighteenth-century **Franciscan monastery** (Franjevački samostan), which features a nice colonnaded courtyard and a church rich in wooden Baroque altarpieces painted in garish green and brown hues to provide a fake marble sheen. Just north of the monastery, a modern pavilion hosting temporary exhibitions is the only currently functioning part of the **Museum of the Brod-Posavlje Region** (Muzej brodskog posavlja; Mon–Fri 9am–3pm; 10Kn), which has been forced to put the bulk of its collection into storage due to war damage. Heading back to the main square and then continuing west, you can't miss the vast earthen ramparts of **Brod Fortress** (Brodska tvrđava), built in 1715 to protect Slavonia from Ottoman-controlled Bosnia on the other side of the river. This once vast complex of barrack-buildings enclosed by star-shaped earthworks is now rather run-down, although you're free to wander round inside and scramble up onto the grassy ramparts.

Both **bus** and **train stations** are ten minutes' walk north of Trg I. B. Mažuranić. Brod Turist, just north of the main square at Trg Pobjede 30 (Mon–Fri 7am–7.30pm, Sat 7am–1pm; ☎035/445-765), acts as an **information point** on behalf of the local tourist association, handing out leaflets and selling town maps. Functional en-suite rooms are available at the *Brod* **hotel**, in a greying modern block just round the corner at Petra Krešimira IV 3 (☎035/440-515; ❸). You may prefer trying your luck at the *Studentski centar*, 500m east of the train and bus stations at Svačićeva bb (☎035/444-265; ❷), which rents out simple, clean rooms to all-comers if there are vacancies.

The best of the **restaurants** is *Slavonski podrum* at A. Štampara 1, serving up substantial cuts of pork and veal in a half-timbered house with wooden beams and benches; *Pizzeria Mamma Mia*, Starčevićeva 3, has a basic range of pizzas and grills. *Kavana Mala*, Trg I. B. Mažuranić, is the best place for a relaxing **drink**, although there are innumerable café-bars along Krešimirova and Starčevićeva, both of which lead east from here.

Đakovo and Vinkovci

Beyond Slavonski Brod, the Autocesta forges ever eastwards towards the frontier with Serbia, some 95km distant. After 35km a secondary route breaks off northwards towards the neat-and-tidy plains town of **ĐAKOVO**, which is served by regular buses from both Slavonski Brod and Osijek, as well as occasional trains on the Vrpolje–Osijek branch line. Whatever your point of arrival, you'll be guided into the centre by the skyline-hogging, 84-metre-high twin towers of Đakovo's neo-Gothic, red-brick **Cathedral** (daily 7am–noon & 3–7pm). This vast building, constructed between 1862 and 1882 by the Viennese Gothic Revival architect Baron Frederick Schmidt, was commissioned by Bishop Josip Juraj Strossmayer (see p.76), who used his Đakovo see as a base from which to promote a Croatian – and indeed South-Slav – cultural renaissance. Despite its initially austere appearance, the cathedral is decorated with a wealth of intriguing detail, from the beehive-like cones which stand guard on either side of the entrance to the pinnacled cupola which rises above the main transept. Inside, walls and ceilings are decorated with uplifting biblical scenes, painted in the style of the Nazarenes (German contemporaries of the Pre-Raphaelites) by the father-and-son team of Alexander and Ljudevit Seitz.

Immediately north of the cathedral, a squat, custard-coloured building houses the **Strossmayer Museum** (Spomen-muzej Biskupa Josipa Jurja Strossmayera; Tues–Fri 8am–7pm, Sat 8am–2pm; 5Kn), with a few of Strossmayer's personal effects and copies of his writings. Beyond lies the café-lined Korzo, a pedestrianized main street at whose far end stands one further curiosity – a dainty **parish church**, occupying the shell of a sixteenth-century mosque. Ten minutes' walk from the centre (follow ul. Matije Gupca eastwards from the cathedral), the **Lippizaner stud farm** on Augusta Šenoe is another legacy of the Strossmayer period, and still enjoys a Europe-wide reputation for rearing and training these famous white horses. It doesn't put on regular tourist shows, but you may well see the horses being put through their paces if you turn up on spec.

Đakovo's **train station** is 1km east of the centre at the far end of Kralja Tomislava, while the **bus station** is a mere five minutes' walk east of the cathedral along Splitska. The **tourist office** at Kralja Tomislava 3 (Mon–Fri 8am–3pm; ☎031/812-319) has free town maps, but you may not find an English speaker. The only place **to stay** in town is *Croatia Turist*, Preradovićeva 25 (☎031/813-391, ☎814-063; ❹), which has smart rooms with TV and bathroom. They're situated above a highly regarded **restaurant** offering a range of classic continental pork and veal dishes (including *šumski odrezak*, a rolled pork fillet stuffed with mushrooms), washed down with local wines. *Gradski podrum*, on the Korzo, offers a slightly cheaper range of grills and does a satisfying *čobanac*.

Đakovo is the scene of one of Croatia's most important **festivals** of authentic folk culture, **Đakovački vezovi** (literally "Đakovo embroidery"; last weekend in Sept), featuring a weekend-long series of song-and-dance performances by folkloric societies from throughout eastern Croatia, and providing the excuse for a grand open-air party, with each evening culminating in gigs by Croatian pop bands.

Vinkovci

Thirty kilometres due east of Đakovo, **VINKOVCI** was once the most important rail junction in the region, standing at the crossroads of lines linking Zagreb to Belgrade and Budapest to Sarajevo. You might find yourself changing buses or trains here, as there are good onward connections to Osijek and Vukovar, but despite a clutch of eye-catching nineteenth-century buildings in the town centre, there's nothing that merits a specific visit. **Bus** and **train stations** stand next to each other 1km north of the town centre, where there's a serviceable modern **hotel**, the *Slavonija* (☎032/342-555, ☯www.son-ugo-cor.com; ❸).

Vukovar

Regular buses from Vinkovci and Osijek run through the wheat- and cornfields to **VUKOVAR**, 35km to the southeast, a once beautiful town hugging the west bank of the Danube, across which lies the Serbian province of Vojvodina. Until 1991 Vukovar was one of Yugoslavia's more prosperous towns, with a quaint Baroque centre, a successful manufacturing industry based around tyre-producing giant Borovo, and an urban culture that was lively, open and tolerant. However, proximity to the Serbian border and an ethnically mixed population (of whom 44 percent were Croat and 37 percent Serb) conspired to place Vukovar at the sharp end of the Croat–Serb conflict. The resulting **siege** and capture of Vukovar by the Yugoslav People's Army and Serbian irregulars left the centre of town in ruins, and did untold emotional damage to those lucky enough to escape. In January 1998 the town was returned to Croatia as part of the Erdut Accord, though Croats driven from Vukovar seven years before have been slow to return, either because their homes are still in ruins or because the local economy isn't yet strong enough to provide sufficient jobs. There are currently about 12,000 Serbs and 4000 Croats – about one-third of the original population – living in the shell of a town.

The siege of Vukovar

Inter-ethnic tension flared in Vukovar in April 1991, when barricades went up between the Croatian-controlled town centre and the Serb-dominated suburbs. The firing of a rocket at the Serb district of **Borovo Selo** by Croat extremists (an action in which the future Croatian defence minister Gojko Šušak was implicated) was a calculated attempt to raise the stakes. Croatian policemen patrolling Borovo Selo were shot at by Serbian snipers on May 1, and when a bus-load of their colleagues entered the suburb the following day, they were met by an ambush in which twelve of them lost their lives. The JNA (Yugoslav People's Army) moved in, ostensibly to keep the two sides apart, digging into positions that were to serve them well with the breakout of all-out war in the autumn.

On September 14, 1991, the Croatian National Guard surrounded the JNA barracks in town. Serb irregulars in the outlying areas, supported by the JNA, responded by launching an attack. Croatian refugees fled the suburbs, crowding into the centre. Aided by the fact that many of the outlying villages were ethnically Serb, the JNA swiftly encircled the town, making it all but impossible to leave (the only route out was through sniper-prone cornfields), and subjecting the population to increasingly heavy shelling. By the beginning of October the people of Vukovar were living in bomb shelters and subsisting on meagre rations of food and water, their plight worsened by the seeming inactivity of the government in Zagreb. The commander of the town's defence, Mile Dedaković Jastreb, accused President Tuđman of sacrificing Vukovar in order to win international sympathy for the Croatian cause. Vukovar finally fell on November 18, with most of the inhabitants fleeing back to the town hospital or making a run for it across the fields to the west. Of those who fell into Yugoslav hands, the women and children were usually separated from the men – many of the latter simply disappeared.

The worst atrocities took place after Yugoslav forces reached the **hospital**, which they proceeded to evacuate before the agreed arrival of Red Cross supervisors. Those captured here were bundled into trucks and driven away to be murdered, finishing up in a mass grave near the village of Ovčara, 7km southeast. About two thousand Croatian soldiers and civilians died in the defence of Vukovar, and a further two thousand are still missing, although the recovery of bodies from mass graves is going on all the time.

Despite a modest amount of renovation and rebuilding, Vukovar's siege-scarred buildings can still come as a profound shock to first-time visitors who are only used to seeing this kind of thing on TV. If you are interested in coming here, then bear in mind that it's not exactly a tourist mecca, and is probably best treated as a half-day trip from Osijek rather than a stopover destination in its own right.

The Town

Vukovar's bus station lies on the fringes of the twentieth-century town, opposite the main market. Walk through the market and turn left onto the town's main street, Strossmayerova, to reach the **Eltz Palace** (Dvorac Eltz), an imposing aristocratic seat built for a local landowning family in the early 1700s. Badly damaged but still standing, the palace is home to the **Town Museum** (Gradski muzej; Mon–Sat 7am–3pm; 10Kn), whose collections were expropriated by the Serbs in 1991. An agreement to return them was signed in 2001, and they've begun to trickle back, although it remains to be seen what will go on permanent dislay in the palace's surviving barrel-vaulted rooms.

Strossmayerova leads in the opposite direction towards the old town proper, crossing the River Vuka (which flows into the Danube a couple of hundred metres downstream) on the way. The first of the once-impressive civic buildings you come across on the opposite bank is the bombed-out shell of the **Radnički Dom** ("House of the Workers"), where the Yugoslav Socialist Party met to transform itself into the Yugoslav Communist Party in June 1920, only to be banned by the government five months later. Beyond lies the town's main street, lined with late Baroque buildings with arcaded lower storeys – some of which have already been tastefully restored. On high ground to the southeast stands the eighteenth-century **Franciscan monastery** (Franjevački samostan), faithfully reconstructed after almost total destruction. Beyond the monastery, the ice-cream cone shape of Vukovar's **water tower** thrusts skywards, preserved in its present shell-damaged form to serve as a symbol of the town.

Practicalities
The **tourist office** is on the way to the Eltz Palace at Strossmayerova 15 (Mon–Fri 7am–3pm; ℗032/442-889). Located near the heart of old Vukovar at the confluence of the Danube and the Vuka, the modern *Dunav* **hotel** (℗032/441-285 or 441-768, ℗441-762; ❸) has neat, functional en-suite rooms, many with views towards the rivers. There are few **eating** and **drinking** opportunities aside from the hotel's own café and restaurant, and a few more basic places offering grills and pizzas around the market.

Vukovar to Ilok
The main road east out of Vukovar runs parallel to the Danube, ploughing between vineyards and sunflower fields until, after about 25km, the western spur of the **Fruška Gora** hills emerges to break the monotony of the Slavonian plain. Squeezed between the hills and the riverbank, **Šarengrad** is a former fishing village full of little old houses – most of them war-damaged. Six kilometres inland from Šarengrad at the end of a minor road (Vukovar–Ilok buses sometimes make the detour here), **Bapska** is another photogenic little place full of indigenous architecture, although heavily scarred by artillery damage

---

Crossing into Serbia

Crossing from eastern Croatia **into Serbia** shouldn't present too many problems providing you check current visa regulations before setting out. A pilot scheme was introduced in 2002 allowing citizens from North America, Australasia and EU countries to enter Serbia without a visa – instead they were required to purchase a **tourist pass** (valid for 30 days) for about $5 at the border. If the scheme is not renewed, then all visitors to Serbia will need a **tourist visa** (also valid for 30 days), which will cost around $45 and is best obtained from the Serbian embassy in your home country (as it may not be available at border posts once you arrive).

The main road crossing points are at **Lipovac** on the Županija–Sremska Mitrovica stretch of the Autocesta, **Tovarnik** on the Vinkovci–Šid road, **Ilok** on the Vukovar–Novi Sad road, **Erdut** on the Osijek–Novi Sad road, and **Batina** on the Beli Manastir–Sombor road. Although there's not a great deal of traffic on any of these roads, crossing the border can still be a slow process.

Public transport between the two countries is returning to something approaching normality. There are a couple of daily **trains** from Zagreb to Belgrade, passing through Slavonski Brod and Vinkovci on the way. In addition, there's at least one daily Zagreb–Belgrade **bus**. If you're heading for Novi Sad, capital of the Serbian Vojvodina, then make your way to Vukovar and catch one of the four daily buses from there.

---

and subsequent pillaging. Thirty-five kilometres out of Vukovar, **Ilok** is the last town on the Croatian stretch of the Danube, a grey, half-forgotten place built around an old Turkish fortress which stands on a bluff overlooking the river. Thanks to the vineyards carpeting the slopes of the nearby Fruška Gora, Ilok is famous for the production of Graševina, an excellent dry white **wine** which has proved a big hit in Croatian supermarkets since harvests resumed in autumn 1999.

Samobor

Nestling beneath the eastern spur of the wooded Samobor hills around 25km west of Zagreb, **SAMOBOR** is every Croat's idea of what a provincial inland town should look like, a tidy, prosperous agglomeration of pastel-coloured houses, largely unsullied by industry and modern architecture, and with an abundance of hilly woodland on the doorstep. Samobor rivalled the capital as a trade and craft centre in the Middle Ages, though it's nowadays very much a dormitory suburb of its big neighbour, attracting a smattering of day-trippers keen to explore the woods above the town or sample the local delicacy, the *samoborska kremšnita* – a wobbly mass of vanilla custard squeezed between layers of flaky pastry.

The best time to be in Samobor is immediately preceding Lent, during the **Samobor carnival** (Samoborski fašnik; ⓦ www.fasnik.com), one of Croatia's best-known and most authentic festivals. On the weekend before Shrove Tuesday there are parades with floats, while hedonistic locals run around town in masks creating an impromptu party atmosphere, followed by a firework display on Shrove Tuesday itself.

The Town

The town centre revolves around the long, extended triangle of **Trg Kralja Tomislava**, beside which flows the Gradna – a minor tributary of the Sava, and here more of an swollen brook than a river – spanned by a succession of slender bridges. Lined by sober, beige town houses and overlooked by a canary-yellow parish church, the square has a character that's overwhelmingly Baroque, which renders the Art Nouveau pharmacy at no. 11 all the more striking – note the haughty, starch-winged angels high up on the facade. At the square's western end is the **Town Museum** (Gradski muzej; Tues–Fri 9am–3pm, Sat & Sun 9am–1pm; 8Kn), housed in Livadićev dvor, the nineteenth-century home of composer Ferdinand Weisner (1799–1879), whose enthusiasm for the liberation of the Slavs from the Habsburg yoke led him to change his name to the more Croatian-sounding Ferdo Livadić. An important meeting place for the leaders of the Illyrian movement in the 1820s and 1830s, his home now contains a modest collection of furniture, ceramics, and fusty portraits of local burghers. More interesting is the ethnographical section in an adjacent outbuilding, where a smattering of English-language texts help to tease meaning out of the rough wooden agricultural implements on display.

Leaving Trg Kralja Tomislava from the southern end, Langova curls its way up to a **Franciscan Monastery** with adjoining eighteenth-century church. Unassuming exterior notwithstanding, the church contains some worthwhile Baroque art by two of the most prolific local painters of the period: a monumental Dormition of the Virgin by France Jelovšek, and altar paintings by Valentin Metzinger.

Hiking in the Samobor hills

Samobor is a convenient staging post en route to the **Samoborsko gorje**, a ravine-scarred upland region which rises suddenly to the east of town, and backs directly onto the hills of the Žumberak (see p.140). Both ranges fall within the boundaries of the **Žumberak-Samobor Nature Park** (Park prirode Žumberak-Samoborsko gorje; ⓦwww.pp-zumberak-samoborsko-gorje.hr), which begins 5km west of Samobor and stretches 30km further west towards Ozalj (p.140). An area of deep forest interspersed with sub-alpine meadows, the eastern end of the Park is perfect for gentle uphill hikes, and is correspondingly busy with local families on summer weekends.

The best base for walks is **Šoićeva kuća**, a timbered cottage serving refreshments at the western end of the village of **Veliki Lipovec**, which is 9km west of Samobor along the road passing the (signposted) *Samoborski slapovi* hotel and restaurant. There's no public transport here. The most popular walk from Šoićeva kuća is the ascent of wooded **Japetić**, the Samoborsko gorje's highest point (1hr 30min–2hr). Two hundred metres southwest of Šoićeva kuća a road ascends steeply to the right, leading past cottages until asphalt gives way first to gravel track, then to footpath. After a steady climb through the woods you reach a plateau, where fairly obvious signs direct you either to Japetić's 879-metre summit, or to the Japetić mountain hut (weekends only) just to the south, which serves excellent *grah* and has good views of the Kupa valley to the southwest, with the forest-enclosed lakes of Črna Mlaka over to the left.

An alternative hike from Šoićeva kuća leads to the 752-metre peak of **Oštrc**, ninety minutes' walk to the south. Directly opposite Šoićeva kuća a marked path heads uphill into the woods, passing through the ruins of medieval Lipovec castle, continuing along a steep up-and-down path through the woods before eventually emerging onto the Preseka ridge, which runs above lush pastures. At the northeastern edge of the ridge lies Oštrc mountain hut (weekends only), serving good *grah* and simple cuts of meat. From here it takes only twenty minutes to reach the summit of Oštrc itself, where there are more fine views. From Oštrc you can either return to Šoićeva kuća the way you came, or follow a marked path to Japetić via a wooded saddle known as Velika vrata (the Oštrc–Japetić leg takes 1hr 30min), although the ascent of Japetić from Velika vrata is much steeper than the direct route from Šoićeva kuća.

An alternative access point to the Hills is **Slani Dol**, 10km west of Samobor, reached by leaving town along the Veliki Lipovec road but forking right after about 3km instead of carrying on to Šoićeva kuća. Here you'll find an **Ecology Centre** (Eko centar) maintained by the Žumberak-Samobor Nature Park, with displays of local flora and fauna. This is also the start of a long-distance hiking trail known as **Queen Beech Way** (Put kraljice bukve), a two- to three-day trek that leads from here to Sošice (see p.141) in the heart of the Žumberak. Recreational ramblers with limited time to spare can attempt the first leg, which ascends from Slani Dol through meadows and beech forest to the Sveti Bernard hut (2hr), where there's a good view and the chance of refreshments at weekends.

From the southern side of the square, Svete Ane climbs up past the parish church and town graveyard towards **Anindol**, a wooded hillside crisscrossed by paths. After about ten minutes, tracks lead off to the right towards the forest-bound chapel of St Anne (Crkvica svete Ana), from where you can choose between a steep route uphill to the chapel of St George (Crkvica sveti Jure) or a lateral path to Samobor's medieval **castle**. Both chapels are closed except for special masses, and the castle is no more than an overgrown ruin, but the tranquillity of the surrounding woods makes a walk here worthwhile. It was on Anindol that Josip Broz Tito (see p.104) organized the founding congress of the Croatian Communist Party on August 1, 1937, in an attempt to persuade the Croats that Yugoslav communists shared their nationalist aspirations. An annual hiking festival was used as a cover: with the whole area filling up with weekend visitors, party activists could infiltrate without arousing suspicion. Only sixteen communist agents actually made it to the "congress", and Tito was reduced to scratching the resolutions of the meeting on the back of a calendar with a penknife – or so the story goes.

Practicalities

Samobor's **bus station**, five minutes' walk north of the main square, is served by buses, run by Samoborček (every 20–30min; hourly on Sun), from both Zagreb's main bus station and the Černomerec tram terminal (at the end of tram lines #2, #6 and #11). The **tourist office**, Trg kralja Tomislava 5 (Mon–Fri 8am–3.30pm & 4.30–7.30pm, Sat & Sun 9am–noon & 4.30–7.30pm; ℡01/336-0044, ⓦwww.samobor.hr), hands out basic brochures and sells a town map. There are a couple of **pension**-type places in town: the *Golubić*, just behind the main square at Obrtnička 12 (℡01/33-60-937, Ⓕ33-60-030; ❸), offers unfussily decorated en-suite rooms with TV in a family house; while *Garni Hotel Samobor*, Josipa Jelačića 30 (℡01/33-66-970; ❸), delivers simple doubles in a suburban house in the leafy outskirts of town, about 800m northeast of the square. Moving up in the quality stakes, the *Livadić* **hotel**, Trg kralja Tomislava 1 (℡01/338-4062, ⓦwww.hotel-livadic.hr; ❺), is a friendly, family-run and rather plush affair, with spacious rooms furnished in nineteenth-century style offering all creature comforts. Three kilometres out of town to the northwest on the Lipovec road, *Samoborski slapovi*, Hamor 16 (℡01/33-84-059 or 33-84-061, Ⓕ33-84-062; ❹), has small, neat en-suite rooms with TV, but the real attraction is the location in a narrow wooded valley.

For **food and drink**, *Samoborska Pivnica*, in a barrel-vaulted chamber just off the main square at Šmidhenova 3, serves up cheap staples like *štrukli*, tasty local sausages and a full range of meat dishes. Slightly more upmarket, *Pri Staroj Vuri*, in a suburban street five minutes' walk above the square at Giznik 2 (go up Langova behind the parish church and bear right), specializes in traditional north Croatian cuts of meat, and is one of the best places in the region to tuck in to *lungić* (lean pork fillet) or *koljena* (knuckle of veal). The restaurant of the *Samoborski slapovi* has excellent trout and other freshwater fish (from their own pond). The best cafés in which to linger over coffee and cake are those on the main square (*U Prolazu* is said to offer the best *samoborske kremšnite*), while the narrow streets leading east from the square are well supplied with bars overlooking the River Gradna.

Zagreb to Karlovac

Croatia's busiest motorway zooms southwest from Zagreb towards the port city of Rijeka, gateway to the northern Adriatic coast. Thirty kilometres southwest of Zagreb the road brushes the northern fringes of the **Crna Mlaka** ("Black Marsh"), an area of forested wetland rich in birdlife, notably the blue-grey heron and the elusive black stork – which, unlike the more common white variety, is extremely sensitive to human disruption and only nests in the security of isolated forests. Visitors hoping to see these creatures usually head for the vast **fish farm** in the centre of the Mlaka, a series of ponds built at the end of the nineteenth century by Austro-Hungarian developers, who also constructed a (now sadly disused) narrow-gauge railway and a (now derelict) country house known as Ribograd, or "Fishville". Unfortunately, there are few clear walking itineraries; it's best to follow the gravelly tracks which lead round the fishponds to enjoy a taste of this calm, reed-shrouded environment. There's a plainly decorated but excellent **restaurant** inside the fish farm, the *Konoba Črna Mlaka*, which serves local carp, catfish and chewy, deep-fried frogs' legs (*žablji kraci*) at very reasonable prices.

To get to Crna Mlaka from the Zagreb–Karlovac motorway, turn off at the Jastrebarsko exit and follow the road, which heads left about 100m beyond the toll booths. This soon degenerates into gravel track; turn left at the sign for "IHOR Crna Mlaka". The only **accommodation** in the area is 6km east of Crna Mlaka in **DONJA ZDENČINA**, a village popular with nesting white storks, where *Seljački Turizam Šimanović*, Karla Vodopića 7 (☎01/62-88-102 or 62-89-096; ❷; full board available by prior arrangement), offers bed-and-breakfast accommodation in a modern house with simple but comfortable rooms, some decorated with embroidered textiles made on the family loom – the owner will provide a quick weaving display if you're interested. Donja Zdenčina is easily reached using the Zagreb–Karlovac commuter trains, although drivers will find it less straightforward: despite being close to the motorway, it's not served by an exit, so you'll have to stick to the old Zagreb–Jastrebarsko–Karlovac road (stara Karlovačka cesta) as far as Klinča Sela and take the southbound turning to Pisarovina, hitting Donja Zdenčina after 6km. The only drawback is that you can't actually drive from Donja Zdenčina to Crna Mlaka without taking a long roundabout route via **Jastrebarsko**, although you can walk there directly along forest tracks.

Donja Kupčina

The villages around Crna Mlaka still preserve a smattering of tumbledown wooden farmhouses, although the best examples are preserved at the village of **DONJA KUPČINA**, 15km southwest of Donja Zdenčina (head south to Jamnica, then west to Karlovac; there's no public transport to the village), in a small open-air **Folk Museum** (Zavičajni muzej; daily 9am–4pm; if the curator isn't around, ask in the nearby café or call ☎01/62-92-111). The museum has a lovely, unsanitized feel, featuring an ensemble of nineteenth-century oak farm buildings clustered around two houses in an overgrown glade. One of the houses contains implements once used in linen manufacture, a labour-intensive process in which the locally harvested flax was laboriously soaked, beaten and combed in order to produce fibres fine enough for weaving. Upstairs is a display of the garments produced, including the extravagantly embroidered dresses worn at wedding feasts – of which there were always two, one for each side of the family: the guests of bride and groom never mixed. A hundred years ago it wasn't unusual for girls in this part of Croatia to marry at the age of 12, although they slept in their mother-in-law's bed for the first few years of matrimony. The strangest exhibit in the museum is the system of winches used to raise village houses above the ground so that they could be moved on rollers to a new site, at times reaching speeds of 1km per day.

Karlovac

Less than an hour from Zagreb, **KARLOVAC** hides its provincial charms behind a screen of high-rise suburbs and light industry. The centre, however, is a minor delight: a compact grid of crumbling old houses which still preserves the street plan bequeathed to it by Habsburg planners. Initially a purely military settlement, Karlovac was built from scratch in 1579 in order to strengthen Austria's southern defences against Ottoman encroachment. It was deliberately sited between two rivers (the Kupa and the Korana) which had slightly different water levels, therefore providing a constant flow of water for the town's moat. Initially commanded by Archduke Karl of Styria and named Karlstadt in his honour, Karlovac gradually lost its strategic importance as Habsburg forces drove the Ottomans southwards in the late 1600s, and life within the fortress walls began to develop a civilian character. The town walls were demolished in the nineteenth century, but their shape – that of a six-pointed star – is still discernible in the earthworks and moats (now drained and transformed into parks) which surround the centre.

Karlovac is an easy day-trip from Zagreb, and onward connections to Rijeka, Zadar and Split are plentiful – which is a good job seeing as there's currently no reliable source of accommodation in town. A good time to be in Karlovac is for the **St John's Day Bonfire** (Ivanjski krijes) on June 23, when the inhabitants of two riverside suburbs, Gaza and Banija, stage competing bonfire-and-firework displays on either side of the Kupa.

The Town

A good way to start exploring the town is simply to follow the course of the old fortifications, nowadays marked by an almost unbroken circuit of tree-lined promenades surrounding the centre. Within lies a fine ensemble of eighteenth- and nineteenth-century town houses, although damage sustained in 1991 (when the front line was only about 5km away) is still painfully visible. The main square, Trg bana Jelačića, looks particularly shell-scarred and empty; that said, it's worth calling in at the **Holy Trinity Church** (Crkva presvetog Trojstva) on the corner, which has an unusually low barrel-vaulted ceiling decked out with bright Baroque frescoes. A block north of here on Strossmayerov trg, a small **Town Museum** (Gradski muzej; Tues–Fri 8am–3pm, Sat & Sun 10am–noon), set in the Baroque-style Frankopan winter palace, features scale models of old Karlovac and traditional costumes from the surrounding area. Local patriots will steer you towards the room devoted to the Karlovac-born nineteenth-century artist Vjekoslav Karas, who studied in Rome, joined the Nazarenes (a German movement roughly analogous to the British Pre-Raphaelites) and returned home to paint portraits of local worthies. Karas is as well known for his suicidal melancholy as for his paintings: he ended up drowning himself on account of an unrequited passion for local woman Irena Türk.

The main out-of-town attraction is the medieval stronghold of **Dubovac**, reached by following the banks of the Kupa to the north from central Karlovac before heading uphill to the left – a walk of about thirty minutes. Once held by the Frankopans, feudal lords of the island of Krk who extended their power to the Croatian mainland, it's a compact but well-preserved structure (now occupied by the *Stari Grad* restaurant) surrounding a triangular courtyard overlooked by three tiers of galleries. The grassy terrace outside affords an excellent view of Karlovac stretched out on the plain below.

Practicalities

Karlovac's **bus station** is about 500m southwest of the centre on Prilaz Vece Holjevca, the main north–south route through the town; the **train station** is about 1500m north of the centre along the same road. Tomislavova, next to the bus station, presents the most direct route into town, crossing the line of the former moat before arriving at the central square. There's a left-luggage office (daily 6am–8pm) in the bus station if you're just passing through, and a help-ful, if erratically open, **tourist office** just east of the centre at Petra Zrinskog 3 (usually Mon–Fri 8am–3pm; ☏047/615-115, ✉karlovac-touristinfo@ ka.hinet.hr). The only **hotel** in town is the *Carlstadt*, Vraniczanyeva 2 (☏047/611-111, ⓦwww.carlstadt.hr; ❹), providing plain but comfortable rooms with TV and private bathroom, and a reasonable buffet breakfast. There's an attractive **campsite**, the *Slapić*, 12km southwest of town in the village of **Belavići** (beyond Duga Resa on the road to Josipdol; ☏047/854-700), reached via an old wooden bridge beside a converted mill. You can swim in the Mrežnica river, and Belavići train station (served by Zagreb–Karlovac–Rijeka trains) is 300m away.

Back in town, snack **food** is plentiful around the bus station, and there's a rea-sonable pizzeria, the *Mona Lisa*, occupying a covered courtyard just west of the central square on Stjepana Radića. For a serious sit-down meal, try the *Kerempuh* restaurant a little way east of the bus station at Vladimira Nazora 4, where you can tuck into substantial veal, pork and turkey dishes in brick-lined rooms. There's a generous sprinkling of cafés just west of the centre around Petra Zrinskog: *Drmeš*, up a side street at Šebetićeva 3, is a brash, raucous place extravagantly decked out in pub bric-a-brac.

The Žumberak

North of Karlovac, the **Žumberak** is an area of steep, vineyard-clad hills and wooded vales punctuated by small plots of pasture and corn. The region's main appeal lies in its scenery – rather like a wilder version of the Zagorje, with denser forests, faster-flowing rivers and a higher degree of rural depopulation. Primarily given over to ageing smallholders and weekending city folk, the area's scattered **villages** – some of them so isolated that they're only connected to the outside world by gravel track – boast a high proportion of rickety half-timbered houses and open-sided wooden barns full of drying hay. Much of the local population is made up of so-called **Greek Catholics** (Grkokatolici), Orthodox Slavs who migrated to the area in the sixteenth and seventeenth centuries in the wake of Ottoman advances and were offered lands and security by the Habsburg court in return for accepting the primacy of the pope.

The main **road** into the Žumberak from Karlovac passes through the villages of **Ozalj** and **Krašić**, before working its way round the massif, close to the Slovenian border, and joining up with the other principal road into the region at Bregana, just north of Samobor. There's little **public transport** into the Žumberak proper, although Ozalj and Krašić are reachable from Karlovac by train and bus respectively. Beyond here you really need a car, and it's a delightful and rewarding region to drive through if you have a decent road map and a rea-sonable dose of patience – the Žumberak's minor roads provide excellent oppor-tunities for getting lost. **Accommodation** is thin on the ground, although well worth seeking out if you're looking for a rural break: *Seoski turizam Medven* (opposite) and *Eko-selo Žumberak* (p.142) are the only current possibilities.

Ozalj

Straddling the River Kupa some 16km north of Karlovac, **OZALJ** is a small rural spot located at the point where the green limbs of the Žumberak descend to meet the plain below. Just west of the village centre, **Ozalj Castle** is a Colditz-like lump of crumbling grey stone featuring temporary history exhi-bitions in its **museum** (Mon–Sat 7am–3pm; 10Kn). Returning to the centre of Ozalj, the main road to Krašić heads east over the Kupa, providing a fine view of the weirside **Munjara** (the "lightning factory"), a hydro-electric power station built in 1908; it's a charming Gothic-romantic folly whose crenellated turrets seem to echo the architecture of the castle above. Ten minutes' walk out of town to the east along the road to the village of Trg, the **Ozalj Ethno-Village** (Etno selo) comprises a couple of thatched farmsteads. You can wander freely around the small complex, although the simple peasant interiors are open only sporadically – ask at the museum in the castle.

Krašić

Ten kilometres northeast of Ozalj, the equally rustic village of **KRAŠIĆ** is fast emerging as one of Croatia's most important pilgrimage centres thanks to its status as the birthplace of **Alojzije Stepinac**, archbishop of Zagreb during World War II. After being imprisoned by the communists on trumped-up charges of collaboration, Stepinac lived out the last years of his life under house arrest in Krašić, where he was cared for by a pair of nuns and accompanied by a pet sheep – given to him by a kindly local and obviously intended as food, though Stepinac couldn't bear to have it slaughtered. Stepinac's two-room apartment, located in the parish priest's home just behind the village church, is now preserved as a **Memorial Museum** (Spomen-muzej; open Mon–Sat whenever the priest is around; donation requested), although the ascetic archbishop was not a great hoarder of personal effects – bedstead, writing table and church vestments are about all he left behind. The squat ochre **church** in which the ailing priest said mass was largely rebuilt in neo-Gothic style in 1913 by an architect who obviously had Jugendstil tastes – note the caryatids which peer down from the exterior walls. There's not much to see inside save for a side chapel which preserves some original chunks of medieval masonry.

There are a couple of **cafés** on the main square in front of the church, where you'll also find a small **tourist office** (Wed, Sat & Sun 9am–4pm; ☎01/62-70-910 & 48-46-690, ⓔtickrasic@hotmail.com), which has information on the Žumberak region and sells Stepinac-related souvenirs.

North into the Žumberak

Beyond Krašić, the road heads through a series of villages sunk deep in wooded valleys. First up is **PRIBIĆ**, an important centre of Greek Catholic culture where the splendid neo-Byzantine **Church of the Annunciation** (Crkva svetog Blagovijesta) rises up from a reedy islet at the entrance to the village. The interior is half derelict and rarely accessible, but the exterior presents a fine blend of Orthodox church architecture and Jugendstil, with fanciful eagles and gargoyles emerging from its domes.

Smothered in forest 5km northwest of Pribić, just beyond the hamlet of Medvenova Draga, the village of **ČUNKOVA DRAGA** is the site of the only reliable **accommodation** in this part of the Žumberak, *Seoski turizam Medven* (☎01/62-70-665; ❸). This comprises two self-catering apartments in a converted farmhouse, idyllically situated beside an old watermill.

Ten kilometres further on, a left turn after the village of **Kostanjevac** leads past wooden barns and ancient, tumbledown houses to the village of **SOŠICE**, grouped around two churches standing side by side, one Catholic and one Greek Catholic – the latter is the one with the taller, rocket-like belfry. Just downhill from the churches is a small **Ethnographic Museum** (Etnografski muzej; Mon–Sat 9am–5pm; donation requested) run by local Greek-Catholic nuns, who preside over a smartly arranged collection of farm implements, antiquated looms and traditional costumes. Of the female attire on display, the rich red-and-blue-striped aprons of the local Greek Catholics contrast sharply with the simpler whites of their Catholic neighbours, demonstrating how the two communities preserved separate traditions despite centuries of coexistence.

Back on the main northbound route, the road forges an ever more lonely path through thickening forest, wheeling eastwards towards **Bregana** along the Croatian–Slovene frontier. Twelve kilometres before Bregana a right turn – which rapidly deteriorates into a gravel track – leads deep up a narrowing side valley, arriving after 8km at the region's most popular weekend destination, **Eko-selo Žumberak** (Žumberak Eco-Village), a bizarre cross between a Wild West homestead and a nineteenth-century Croatian village complete with riding stables, a "cowboy saloon" and an excellent **restaurant**. The Eko-selo also offers **rooms** (⌖01/33-87-473; ❷), some in traditional wooden houses built from recycled timber taken from collapsing buildings throughout the region.

Returning to the Bregana route, you'll soon pass the popular recreation spot of *Divlje Vode*, a fish farm overlooked by a café-restaurant where you can eat local trout and frogs' legs (*žablji kraci*) on a shady terrace. From here it's a further 10km to Bregana and the main route southeast to Samobor (see p.135) and Zagreb.

West of Karlovac: the Gorski kotar

Road and rail routes from Karlovac to Rijeka follow a scenic route through the hills and mountains of the **Gorski kotar** (literally "wooded district") – a spectacular landscape of green river valleys and forested hillsides. It's a surprisingly untouristed area with a dearth of accommodation, although there's a nascent winter sports scene at the region's main holiday centre, **Bjelolasica**, and numerous summer hiking opportunities. The Karlovac–Rijeka road forges straight through the northern Gorski kotar, bypassing its main attractions, although the rail line initially breaks away southwards to pass through **Ogulin**, a gateway to the Bjelolasica region and a useful base from which to tackle one of the area's landmark peaks, **Klek**.

From mid-June to late September, a special **train**, the *Karlek*, runs from Zagreb to Ogulin on Saturday and Sunday mornings, returning the same evening. At Ogulin, connecting buses take *Karlek* passengers to Bjelolasica, Klek and other local beauty spots. It's possible to get to Ogulin using normal train services, but buses won't be laid on once you get there. From Ogulin there are three or four buses daily to the village of **Bijelsko** (see opposite), which is the most convenient jumping-off point for Klek.

Ogulin and around

Fifty-five kilometres southwest of Karlovac, **OGULIN** is an untidy small town built around a **castle** founded by the Frankopans in around 1500, and subsequently used as a prison. The structure still boasts an impressively turreted pair of towers, but the **museum** within (Mon–Fri 8am–2pm, Sat 9am–noon; 10Kn) is disappointing, with displays on the history of hiking in the region and a rather bare memorial cell where Josip Broz Tito was interned in 1932. Opposite the castle, a small viewing platform overlooks a canyon where the River Dobra flows into an underground passage, re-emerging several kilometres to the east before joining the River Kupa near Karlovac.

Ogulin's **train station** is ten minutes' walk from the centre (turn right outside the station and follow the main road). A new **bus station** is being built opposite the train station; in the meantime, buses stop outside the castle. The

tourist office on the main street at Bernardina Frankopana 2 (Mon–Fri 8am–3pm; ☎ & ℻047/532-278, ⓦwww.ogulin.hr) can help with local hiking information and may have maps for sale. There are a few **cafés** along the main street, but no decent places to eat unless you count the *Sabljaci* restaurant, on the eastern shores of Lake Sabljak, a five-kilometre drive south of town. The nearest accommodation is in Bjelolasica.

Klek

Seven kilometres due west of Ogulin, the 1184-metre **Klek** is not the highest of the Gorski kotar mountains, but is undoubtedly one of the most dramatic. Its summit – a tall rocky cylinder rising out of a forested ridge – dominates the local landscape for miles around and, somewhat appropriately, is said to be the place where local witches and demons meet on the eve of May 1. Klek has been one of inland Croatia's most important targets for hikers ever since 1838, when the future governor of Croatia, Josip Jelačić, scaled it in the company of King Friedrich August II of Saxony, adding a dash of aristocratic glamour to a pastime then in its infancy.

You can walk to Klek and back from Ogulin by following the Bjelolasica road west of town, although it's easier to drive as far as the village of **Bijelsko**, 8km west of Ogulin, thereby cutting a good ninety minutes off your journey. Arriving in the village from the direction of Ogulin, you'll see a house on your right with the legend "Klek: 1hr" helpfully painted on the wall. From here a well-marked trail ascends steadily through the woods, arriving at the Klek mountain hut (drinks and snacks available at weekends) after about 45 minutes. The path then coils its way round the stone barrel of Klek's upper reaches towards the summit, which should take you about another 25 minutes to negotiate, with a couple of steep, rope-assisted sections on the way up which may deter those who lack a good head for heights. The views from Klek's broad, flat top are magnificent, although take care – there are sheer drops on almost all sides.

Bjelolasica

Seventeen kilometres beyond Bijelsko, a right turn in the village of **Jasenjak** leads up a narrow wooded valley to the **Bjelolasica Olympic Centre** (Olimpijski centar Bjelolasica; ☎01/61-77-707, ℻6177-708; ❸) some 5km beyond. Laid out on meadows below steep, pine-covered slopes, this is a year-round tourist resort made up of several chalet-style accommodation blocks set beside a central administration and café-restaurant pavilion. As the name suggests, it's also a training camp for serious sportspeople, with numerous professional teams making use of its athletics track and indoor sports halls. Bjelolasica is Croatia's only real skiing resort, although the season is unpredictable and short (Dec–Feb, snowfalls allowing), so most winter sports fans tend to arrange ad hoc weekend breaks here rather than book skiing holidays in advance. Chairlifts run up the flanks of **Mount Bjelolasica**, immediately west of the resort, where there are slopes for beginners and intermediates, plus a single, five-hundred-metre run for advanced skiers; ski rental can be arranged. In spring and summer Bjelolasica is a good base for medium-to-strenuous hiking, with the primary targets being the 1531-metre peak of Bjelolasica itself (3–4hr each way), or the 1335-metre **Bijele stijene**, which crowns the next ridge to the west (3–4hr each way). Basic hiking maps can be picked up at the centre.

Delnice and Risnjak National Park

Twenty kilometres northwest of Ogulin the rail line rejoins the main Karlovac–Rijeka road route near the village of Vrbovsko, after which both continue to wind their way westward through craggy, densely forested hills. Most Rijeka-bound buses and trains stop at **DELNICE**, a rather featureless town about 60km past Karlovac, from where a minor road (served by two daily buses) runs 10km northwest to the village of **CRNI LUG**, the starting point for explorations of the **Risnjak National Park** (Narodni park Risnjak), which covers a mountain group centred on the 1528-metre Veliki Risnjak.

Food and **accommodation** are available in Crni Lug's *Nacionalni park Risnjak* **motel** (☏051/836-133; ❸), where you can pick up hiking maps and advice before setting out for the **park entrance** 1km west of the village. There's a range of walking possibilities; allow about three hours each way for an assault on Veliki Risnjak itself. West of Delnice, it's not long before the green, wooded scenery changes, and you're descending through an increasingly barren karst landscape to Rijeka and the coast.

South of Karlovac: the Plitvice Lakes

Beyond Karlovac, the main road to Dalmatia forges due south across the upland pastures of the **Kordun** and **Lika** regions, passing through a series of villages which are slowly returning to normality after wartime occupation by the Serbs. It's a busy route, choked with crawling coast-bound cars on summer weekends, and you'll come across innumerable roadside restaurants serving up spit-roast lamb or suckling pig to hungry travellers. Owing to the large volume of tourist traffic, an increasing number of local villagers are advertising private rooms for rent – hence the slightly surreal spectacle of newly renovated houses with cheery signs offering "zimmer" or "sobe" standing right next door to bombed-out homes whose owners have yet to return.

Perched on a hilltop 50km south of Karlovac, the small town of **SLUNJ** is unremarkable save for the confluence of the Korana and Slunjčica rivers just below, with the rushing waters of the latter dropping into the Korana gorge through a series of small waterfalls and burbling rapids. In times past this natural power source led to the development of a riverside watermilling settlement known as **Rastoke**. Several traditional millers' buildings still survive, solid structures with stone lower floors and timber upper storeys. It's a delightful area for a stroll, with excellent views of the gorge from the path above the north bank of the Korana, and everything is relatively easy to find: you'll glimpse Rastoke down to the right when entering the town by road from the north (buses stop 800m further uphill on Slunj's main square).

There's no other reason to hang around in Slunj, but the helpful **tourist office** just down from the square at Zagrebačka 12 (unpredictable hours, but usually Mon–Fri 8am–3pm; ☏47/777-630, ☼www.slunj.hr) can point you in the direction of private **rooms** (❶) in Slunj and outlying villages.

The Plitvice Lakes National Park

Forty kilometres south of Slunj, the **PLITVICE LAKES NATIONAL PARK** (Nacionalni park plitvička jezera; ☼www.np-plitvicka-jezera.hr) is the country's biggest single tourist attraction, and with some justification. The eight-kilometre string of sixteen lakes, hemmed in by densely forested hills, presents some of the most eye-catching scenery in mainland Croatia, with water rushing down from the upper lakes via a sequence of waterfalls and cataracts. This unique landscape came into being as a result of the action of travertine, calcium-rich material picked up by the river and then deposited downstream – a process which, when repeated over the course of several millennia, produced a terraced sequence of barriers behind which lakes formed. Nowadays these lakes – a bewitching turquoise when seen from a distance – teem with fish and watersnakes, while herons frequent the shores of the quieter, northern part of the system. Deer, bears, wolves and wild boar throng the wooded heights above.

Despite being occupied by Serb forces from 1991 to 1995, the national park is remarkably well organized: paths are easy to follow, regular shuttle buses and boats ferry visitors to major trailheads, and English-speaking staff are on hand with advice at the park's two major entry points. All this ensures that you can see a great deal in a short space of time, although keen walkers could easily spend a day or two exploring the whole area.

Practicalities

The park (daily: summer 8am–7pm; winter dawn–dusk; May, June, Sept & Oct 70Kn; July & Aug 90Kn; rest of year 45Kn) can be entered from two points on the main Zagreb–Split road: **Entrance 1** (Ulaz jedan) is at the northern (lower) end of the lake system, while **Entrance 2** (Ulaz dva) is 2.5km further south. Both serve as convenient gateways to a range of walks, but be aware that Entrance 2 may well be closed from October through to March, when it makes sense to head directly for Entrance 1. **Getting to Plitvice** is straightforward: most buses from Zagreb to Split or Zadar pass along the main road which fringes the park to the east, dropping passengers off at both entrances. **Moving on** can be a tricky business on summer weekends: there's no bus station at Plitvice where you can buy tickets, meaning that you have to wait at the roadside bus stop for one of the Split–Zagreb or Zadar–Zagreb inter-city services – as these are often full, you may have a long wait on your hands.

There are small **information offices** at both Entrance 1 (April–June & Sept 9am–5pm; July & Aug 8am–8pm; Oct–March 9am–4pm) and Entrance 2 (April–June & Sept 9am–5pm; July & Aug 8am–7pm), offering a wealth of advice but short on printed info and maps of the park.

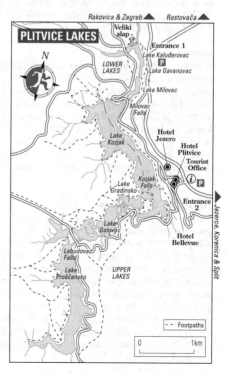

Accommodation

There's a cluster of **hotels** near Entrance 2, all of which are run by the park authorities: the *Bellevue* (☎053/751-015, ℗751-013, ℮np-plitvice@np -plitvice.tel.hr; ➍), which offers standard en-suite rooms; the *Plitvice* (same numbers; ➎), which has slightly plusher rooms with TV and minibar, and and the *Jezero* (same numbers; ❻), which offers the same comforts as the *Plitvice* but with slightly more modern furnishings and fittings.

The closest **campsite** is the *Korana*, on the main road about 7km north of Entrance 1, a large and well-organized place with bungalows (❶), restaurant and supermarket. Three kilometres further on, the *Autokamp Turist* in **Grabovac** is a smaller place with more trees (℡047/784-077, ⓦwww.slunjcica.hr). The same village is home to the roadside **motel** *Grabovac* (❸), which offers sparsely-furnished but comfortable rooms, and a big self-service restaurant.

There are private **rooms** (❶–❷) in the nearby villages of **Rastovača** (close to Entrance 1) and **Jezerce** (just south of Entrance 2). Vacancies at these are handled by the kiosks run by the National Park authorities at both entrances, but they only operate in July & August – at other times of the year the two park information offices can give you addresses of rooms, but won't make bookings for you. Additionally, the string of villages along the main road north of the park have an increasing number of private rooms, especially **Korana** (7km distant), **Grabovac** (9km), **Rakovica** (12km) and **Oštarski Stanovi** (18km). The majority of houses offering rooms are well signed from the main road – so if you're travelling through the area by car you shouldn't have too much difficulty tracking down vacancies. Inter-city buses pick up and drop off in these places too, but due to the paucity of on-the-spot timetable information, you can't rely on them to shuttle you in and out of the park once you've arrived. The **tourist office** in Rakovica, 12km north of the park, at no. 6 in the village's only street (℡047/784-450, ⓦwww.rakovica.hr), handles information and reservations for private rooms in Oštarski Stanovi, Rakovica and Grabovac, as does a kiosk by the roadside in Grabovac (June–Sept; ℡047/784-300), run by the AiS agency.

Eating

Entrance 2 has a **supermarket** opposite, and both entrances have **snack bars** offering a range of drinks and basic food. For more substantial fare, it's best to head for the *Lička kuća* **restaurant** opposite Entrance 1, a large, touristy place decked out with folksy wooden fittings and serving traditional Lika food such as spicy sausages, *đuveđ* (a paprika-flavoured ratatouille with rice) and roast lamb; the hotel restaurants at Entrance 2 are a bit bland. Look out for local women selling home-made cheese (the mild yellow *škripavac*) along the roadside. It's usually sold in large circular pieces weighing over a kilo, but you can ask for a half (*polovina*) or quarter (*četvrtina*) if you don't think you can manage a whole one.

Around the lakes

Entrance 1, situated at the point where the lake waters flow off into the Korana gorge, is ten minutes' walk away from **Veliki slap** (literally "the big waterfall"), a high wall of water that is the park's single most dramatic feature. Paths lead to the foot of the waterfall, passing alongside the top of the smaller **Sastavci** fall, which empties into the cliff-lined Korana gorge. From Veliki Slap you can proceed south on foot towards the lower group of cataracts, where wooden walkways traverse the foaming waters. Beyond lies **Kozjak**, the largest of Plitvice's lakes. By sticking to the western side of Kozjak you'll eventually emerge at the northern terminus of the **shuttle ferry** service (included in entrance ticket), which will take you south towards Entrance 2. Otherwise you can walk to Entrance 2 along the eastern bank of Kozjak, or take the bus from the road just above.

Entrance 2 is the best jumping-off point for the biggest group of cataracts, where waters from the highest of the Plitvice lakes, **Prošćansko**, tumble down into a succession of smaller pools and tarns before reaching Kozjak lower down. Exploring this part of the system can easily absorb at least half a day; to save time, you can take the **shuttle bus** (cost included in entrance ticket) to the southern-most stop (Labudovac) and take a stroll around the upper cataracts from there.

Travel details

Trains

Karlovac to: Ogulin (6 daily; 1hr); Ozalj (6 daily; 20min); Rijeka (6 daily; 3hr 20min); Split (2 daily; 7hr); Zagreb (hourly; 40min).
Savski Marof to: Kumrovec (6 daily; 55min).
Slavonski Brod to: Zagreb (8 daily; 2–3hr).
Zabok to: Gornja Stubica (8 daily; 30min); Krapina (9 daily; 25min); Stubičke Toplice (8 daily; 20min); Zagreb (14 daily; 40min–1hr); Zlatar Bistrica (14 daily; 20min).
Zagreb to: Čakovec (6 daily; 2hr 30min–3hr); Karlovac (hourly; 40min); Koprivnica (8 daily; 1hr 30min); Ogulin (6 daily; 1hr 40min); Osijek (4 daily; 5hr); Savski Marof (20 daily; 35min); Sisak (hourly; 1hr); Slavonski Brod (8 daily; 2–3hr); Varaždin (12 daily; 2hr–2hr 30min); Zabok (14 daily; 40min–1hr); Zlatar Bistrica (14 daily; 1hr–1hr 20min).

Buses

Đakovo to: Osijek (12 daily; 45min); Slavonski Brod (12 daily; 1hr 15min); Vinkovci (5 daily; 45min).
Karlovac to: Krašić (Mon–Fri 4 daily, Sat 2 daily; 35min); Ozalj (Mon–Fri 4 daily; 25min); Plitvice (hourly; 1hr 40min); Rijeka (20 daily; 2–3hr); Split (4 daily; 8hr); Zadar (4 daily; 4hr); Zagreb (every 30min; 50min).
Koprivnica to: Hlebine (Mon–Fri 6 daily; 30min); Varaždin (12 daily; 45min).
Marija Bistrica to: Stubičke Toplice (Mon–Sat 10 daily, Sun 6 daily; 35min); Zagreb (Mon–Fri 15 daily, Sat 8 daily, Sun 6 daily; 1hr 15min).
Osijek to: Bilje (every 30min; 10min); Đakovo (12 daily; 45min); Ilok (8 daily; 1hr 45min); Požega (Mon–Fri 6 daily, Sat 3 daily, Sun 1 daily); Slavonski Brod (12 daily; 2hr); Vukovar (10 daily; 45min); Zagreb (6 daily; 5hr 30min).
Požega to: Našice (Mon–Fri 6 daily, Sat 3 daily, Sun 1 daily; 1hr); Osijek (Mon–Fri 6 daily, Sat 3 daily, Sun 1 daily; 2hr);Slavonski Brod (4 daily; 1hr); Velika (Mon–Fri 9 daily, Sat 5 daily, Sun 1 daily; 30min); Zagreb (5 daily; 2hr 45min).

Sisak to: Čigoć (4 daily; 45min); Lonja (2 daily; 1hr 15min); Zagreb (Mon–Sat 24 daily, Sun 18 daily; 1hr 10min).
Slavonski Brod to: Đakovo (12 daily; 1hr 15min); Osijek (12 daily; 2hr); Požega (5 daily; 1hr); Vukovar (3 daily; 2hr); Zagreb (12 daily; 3hr).
Varaždin to: Čakovec (every 30 min; 20min); Koprivnica (Mon–Fri 11 daily, Sat 8 daily, Sun 4 daily; 45min); Krapina (Mon–Sat 2 daily, Sun 1 daily; 1hr); Osijek (Mon–Fri 1 daily; 5hr); Split (2 daily; 9hr); Trakošćan (Mon–Fri 10 daily, Sat & Sun 6 daily; 50min); Vukovar (Mon–Fri 1 daily; 5hr 40min); Zagreb (every 30min; 1hr 40min–2hr).
Vinkovci to: Đakovo (5 daily; 45min); Ilok (5 daily; 1hr 50min); Vukovar (12 daily; 50min).
Vukovar to: Ilok (Mon–Fri 20 daily, Sat–Sun 8 daily; 45min); Osijek (10 daily; 45min); Slavonski Brod (3 daily; 2hr); Vinkovci (Mon–Sat 24 daily, Sun 8 daily; 50min).
Zagreb to: Čakovec (10 daily; 2hr 30min); Desinić (Mon–Fri 8 daily, Sat–Sun 5 daily; 2hr); Karlovac (every 30min; 50min); Krapina (Mon–Fri 8 daily, Sat–Sun 5 daily; 1hr 10min–1hr 30min); Krapinske Toplice (12 daily; 1hr 20min); Marija Bistrica (Mon–Fri 15 daily, Sat 8 daily, Sun 6 daily; 1hr 15min); Osijek (6 daily; 5hr 30min); Plitvice (hourly; 2hr 30min); Požega (5 daily; 2hr 45min); Samobor (Mon–Sat every 20–30min, Sun hourly; 40min); Sisak (Mon–Sat 24 daily, Sun 18 daily; 1hr 10min); Slavonski Brod (12 daily; 3hr); Varaždin (12 daily; 1hr 40min–2hr).

International trains

Čakovec to: Budapest Déli (1 daily; 5hr); Budapest Keleti (1 daily; 5hr).
Varaždin to: Budapest Déli (1 daily; 5hr 20min).

International buses

Osijek to: Mohács (1 daily; 2hr 30min); Pécs (3 daily; 3hr).
Slavonski Brod to: Tuzla (5 daily; 5hr).
Varaždin to: Maribor (1 daily; 1hr 50min).
Vukovar to: Novi Sad (4 daily; 2hr 30min).

Istria

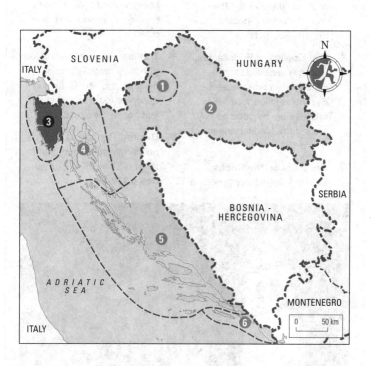

CHAPTER 3   # Highlights

✳ **The amphitheatre at Pula**
The Romans built things to
last, and this 2000-year-old
monument is still the dominating feature of Pula's landscape. See p.156

✳ **Rovinj** Italianate, chic, yet
relatively unspoiled – the
pick of the west-coast
resorts. See p.167

✳ **The basilica of Euphrasius,
Poreč** A venerable sixth-
century structure whose
Byzantine-influenced
mosaics are as good as any
around the Mediterranean.
See p.173

✳ **Our Lady on the Rocks,
Beram** Incandescent paint-

ings by medieval masters
light up this village chapel in
inland Istria's rustic heartlands. See p.178

✳ **Hill towns** Rich in historical
resonances, mellow towns
like Motovun and Oprtalj
seem a world away from the
heavily touristed coast. See
p.180

✳ **Truffles** The most celebrated
of Istria's gastronomic
delights, this smelly fungus
deserves to be tasted at
least once. See p.183

✳ **Dvigrad** This ruined city is a
hauntingly stark monument
to Istria's medieval glories.
See p.179

Istria

A large, triangular peninsula pointing down into the northern Adriatic, **Istria** (in Croatian, Istra) represents Croatian tourism at its most developed. In recent decades the region's proximity to Western Europe has ensured an annual influx of sun-seeking package tourists, with Italians, Germans, Austrians and what seems like the entire population of Slovenia flocking to the mega-hotel developments that dot the coast. Istrian beaches – often rocky areas that have been concreted over to provide sunbathers with a level surface on which to sprawl – do tend to lack the charm of the out-of-the-way coves that you'll find further south in Dalmatia or the Adriatic islands, yet the modern hotel complexes and sprawling campsites have done little to detract from the region's essential charm: development has left many of the Italianate coastal towns relatively unspoiled, while the interior, with its hilltop settlements pitched high in the mountains, is still amazingly unexplored.

Istria draws on a rich cultural legacy. A borderland where Italian, Slovene and Croatian cultures meet, Istria endured over four hundred years of Venetian rule before its incorporation into first the Austro-Hungarian Empire, then Fascist Italy, the Yugoslav Federation, and finally independent Croatia. Historically, an Italian-speaking population lived in the towns (most of which still bear Italian names – or at least Croatianized versions thereof), while Croatian-speakers occupied the rural areas. Despite post-World War II expulsions, there's still a fair-sized Italian community, Italian is very much the peninsula's second language, and the local dialect of Istria's Croats contains a liberal sprinkling of Italian words.

Nowhere is the region's complex identity better expressed than in its **cuisine**, where the seafood of the Adriatic meets the hearty meat-based fare of central Europe and the pasta dishes of Italy. *Fuži* (pasta twists) and *njoki* (gnocchi) are very much local staples; local delicacies include oysters (*oštrige*) from the Limski kanal, cured ham (*pršut*), wild asparagus (*šparoga*) and truffles (*tartufi*) from the hills inland. Istrian meats, such as *kobasice* (big, spicy sausages) and *ombolo* (lean pork loin chops), are often cooked on the *kamin* or open hearth, or braised slowly in a *padela* or *čripnja* – clay pots covered in embers. The latter method is the ideal way to prepare *janje* (lamb) or diced *jarić* (kid goat). Young donkey (*pulić*) was a local speciality until recently, when the beasts were made the subject of animal protection orders. One dish very much still on the menu is Istrian *supa*, red wine heated with sugar, olive oil and pepper then served in an earthenware jug (*bukaleta*), into which a slice of toasted bread is dipped.

With its amphitheatre and other Roman relics, the port of **Pula** at the southern tip of the peninsula is Istria's largest city and a rewarding place to spend a couple of days – rooms are relatively easy to come by and many of Istria's most interesting spots are only a short bus ride away. On the western side of the

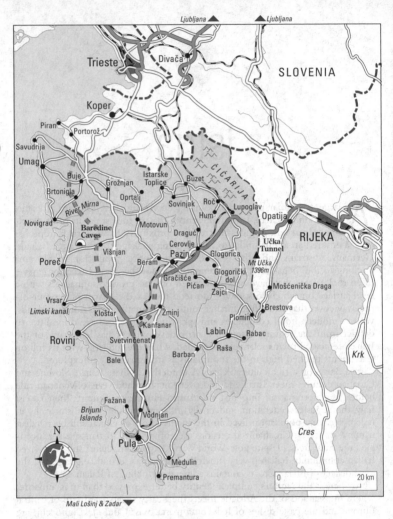

Istrian peninsula are pretty resort towns like **Rovinj** and **Novigrad**, with their cobbled piazzas, shuttered houses and back alleys laden with laundry. Poised midway between the two, the mammoth resort of **Poreč** has much less in the way of authentic Mediterranean charm, but offers everything in the way of tourist facilities. Inland Istria couldn't be more different – historic hilltop towns like **Motovun**, **Grožnjan**, **Roč** and **Hum** look like leftovers from another century, half-abandoned accretions of ancient stone poised high above rich green pastures and forests.

Regular **buses** connect Pula with Zagreb; otherwise, the city of Rijeka (see p.194) is the most convenient gateway to the region. There are also buses from Pula and Poreč to the Italian city of Trieste, and the Slovene resorts of Portorož and Piran on the north side of the peninsula. **Trains** from the Slovene capital Ljubljana to Pula (usually involving a change at Buzet) are another way of reaching the area, while **ferries** connect Pula with Lošinj and Zadar.

Some history

Istria gets its name from the **Histri**, an Illyrian tribe who ruled the region before succumbing to the **Romans** in the second century BC. The invaders left a profound mark on Istria, building farms and villas, turning Pula into a major urban centre and creating a Romanized population which would remain Latin-speaking even under subsequent rulers. Following the disintegration of the Western Roman Empire, Istria fell under the control first of Odoacer's Ostrogoth state in the fifth century, then of Justinian's Byzantine Empire in the sixth, a period which gave the region its greatest ecclesiastical monument, the Basilica of St Euphrasius in Poreč. **Slav tribes** began settling the peninsula from the seventh century onwards, driving the original Romanized inhabitants of the interior into the hills, where they preserved their Latin-derived dialects for generations before finally being Slavicized from the eighteenth century onwards.

Istria became a province of the Frankish Empire in 1040, but maritime and inland Istria began to follow divergent courses as the Middle Ages progressed. Most of the interior was presented as a feudal dependency to the Patriarchate of Aquileia – a virtually independent ecclesiastical city-state owing nominal fealty to Byzantium – in the twelfth century, while the coastal towns survived as independent communes until, one by one, they adopted **Venetian suzerainty** from the thirteenth century onwards. The lands of the Aquileian Patriarchs subsequently came under **Habsburg control**, ushering in centuries of intermittent warfare between Austrians and Venetians for control of the peninsula. The fall of Venice in 1797, followed by the collapse of Napoleon's short-lived Illyrian Provinces, left the Austrians in control of the whole of Istria. They confirmed Italian as the official language of the peninsula, even though Croats outnumbered Italians by more than two to one. Istria received a degree of autonomy in 1861, with Poreč becoming the seat of a regional diet, but only the property-owning classes were allowed to vote, thereby excluding many Croats and perpetuating the Italian-speaking community's domination of Istrian politics.

Austrian rule ended in 1918, when **Italy** – already promised Istria by Britain and France as an inducement to enter World War I – occupied the whole peninsula. When Mussolini's Fascist Party came to power in October 1922, prospects for the Croatian majority in Istria worsened still further: the Croatian language was banished from public life, while a law of 1927 decreed that Slav surnames were henceforth to be rendered in Italian. During World War II, however, opposition to Fascism united Italians and Croats alike, and Tito's Partisan movement in Istria was a genuinely multinational affair, although this didn't prevent outbreaks of inter-ethnic violence and tit-for-tat killings. The atrocities committed against Croats during the Fascist period were avenged indiscriminately by the Partisans, and the *foibe* of Istria – limestone pits into which bodies were thrown – still evoke painful memories for Italians to this day.

After 1945, the right of **Yugoslavia** to occupy the centre of the peninsula was more or less unquestioned by the victorious Allies, but both northern Istria and the port of Pula became the subject of bitter postwar wrangles between Yugoslavia and Italy. The Allies occupied Pula, and divided the north into two zones: Zone A, controlled by Anglo-American forces, included Trieste and its hinterland; while Zone B, controlled by the Partisans, comprised Koper, Piran, Umag and Novigrad. Pula was handed to the Yugoslavs in 1947, and in 1954 a compromise designed to appease both parties in northern Istria saw Zone A given to the Italians, while Zone B became part of Yugoslavia.

Despite promising all national minorities full rights after 1945, the Yugoslav authorities actively pressured Istria's Italians into leaving, and the region suffered serious **depopulation** as thousands fled – especially after the award of Zone B to Yugoslavia in 1954. In response, the Yugoslav government encouraged emigration to Istria from the rest of the country, and today there are a fair number of Serbs, Macedonians, Albanians and Bosnians in Istria, many of whom were attracted to the coast by the **tourist industry**, which took off in the 1960s and, despite a few lean years during the war-ridden 1990s, has never looked back.

Geographically distant from the main flashpoints of the Serb–Croat conflict, Istria entered the twenty-first century more cosmopolitan, more prosperous and more self-confident than any other region of the country. This state of affairs was not without problems, however, with local Istrian politicians tending to regard Zagreb as the centre of a tax-hungry state which took money out of Istria without putting anything back in. Growing regionalist sentiment in the early 1990s led to the rise of the **Istrian Democratic Party** (Istarska demokratska stranka, or IDS), a moderate, centrist party which has remained the peninsula's most influential political force ever since. One consequence of Istria's new-found sense of identity has been a reassessment of its often traumatic relationship with Italy, and a positive new attitude towards its cultural and linguistic ties with that country. Bilingual road signs and public notices are going up all over the place, and the region's Italian-language schools – increasingly popular with cosmopolitan Croatian parents – are enjoying a new lease of life.

Pula

Once the Austro-Hungarian Empire's chief naval base, **PULA** (in Italian, Pola) is an engaging combination of working port and brash Riviera town. The Romans put the city firmly on the map when they arrived in 177 BC, bequeathing it an impressive amphitheatre whose well-preserved remains are the city's single greatest attraction. Pula is also Istria's commercial heart and transport hub, possessing its sole airport, so you're unlikely to visit the region without passing through at least once. There's also an easily visited cluster of Classical and medieval sights in the city centre, while the rough-and-ready atmosphere of the crane-ringed harbour makes a refreshing contrast to the seaside towns and tourist complexes further along the coast. Central Pula can't boast much of a seafront, but there's a lengthy stretch of rocky beach about 3km south of the city centre, leading to the hotel complex on the Verudela peninsula, built in the 1980s to accommodate package-holidaying Brits.

Arrival, transport and information

Pula's **airport** is 6km northeast of the centre just off the main Rijeka road, but there's no bus link; a taxi into town will set you back 150–200Kn. The **train station** is a ten-minute walk north of the town centre at the far end of Kolodvorska. The main **bus station** is along Istarska, just south of the amphitheatre, although some intercity services also pick up and drop off at a terminal northeast of the amphitheatre at Trg 1. Istarske brigade, which is the main departure point for **local buses** to Fažana, Medulin and Puntižela. **City buses** also use the terminal on Trg 1. Istarske brigade, although most of them run through the central street, Giardini. Tickets for city buses cost 9Kn for two journeys if bought in advance from newspaper kiosks, 14Kn if bought from the driver.

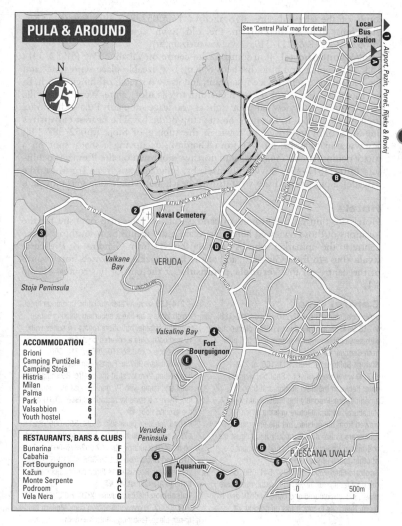

PULA & AROUND

See 'Central Pula' map for detail

Local Bus Station

Airport, Pazin, Poreč, Rijeka & Rovinj

N

Naval Cemetery

Valkane Bay

VERUDA

Stoja Peninsula

Valsaline Bay

Fort Bourguignon

Verudela Peninsula

Aquarium

PJEŠČANA UVALA

CESTA PREKOMORSKIH BRIGADA

0   500m

ACCOMMODATION

Brioni	5
Camping Puntižela	1
Camping Stoja	3
Histria	9
Milan	2
Palma	7
Park	8
Valsabbion	6
Youth hostel	4

RESTAURANTS, BARS & CLUBS

Bunarina	F
Cabahia	D
Fort Bourguignon	E
Kažun	B
Monte Serpente	A
Podroom	C
Vela Nera	G

The **tourist office**, Forum 3 (summer daily 9am–10pm; winter Mon–Fri 9am–7pm; ☎052/219-197, ⓦwww.pulainfo.hr), not only occupies the swankiest premises of any tourist association in Croatia but also offers most in terms of practical advice and free maps and brochures.

Accommodation

There's a stock of private **rooms** (❶) in the centre, as well as holiday **apartments** (❷–❸) in the beachside suburbs of **Stoja** and **Verudela**. The most conveniently located room **agencies** are Arenatours/Europa Istra, between the train station and the centre at Splitska 1a (in the ground floor of the *Riviera* hotel; daily 7am–9pm; ☎052/529-400, ⓦwww.arenaturist.hr); Atlas, just north of the amphitheatre at Starih Statuta 1 (☎052/214-172); Activa Travel, just south of the amphitheatre at Scalierova 1 (℡052/215-497, ⓦwww.activa-istra.com); and A-Turizam, in the old town centre at Kandlerova 24 (℡052/212-212 & 211-319, ⓦwww.a-turizam.hr).

Pula's **youth hostel**, 4km south of the centre on Valsaline Bay (℡052/391-133, ⓔhfhs-pula@pu.hinet.hr; beds 85Kn), is a sizeable place with four- and six-bed rooms, a self-service restaurant, and its own stretch of shingle beach. To get there, take bus #2 or #7 from Giardini to Vila Idola, a pre-World War I villa which comes into view on your right as you leave suburban Pula – the hostel itself is across fields to the right on the cusp of the bay. The nearest **campsites** are *Stoja*, 3km southwest of town in the suburb of Stoja (℡052/387-144, ⓦwww.arenaturist.hr; bus #1 from Giardini), occupying a shady spot on a rocky peninsula; and *Puntižela*, 8km northwest of town on the Puntižela penin-sula (℡052/517-490, ⓦwww.puntizela.hr; Puntižela bus from Trg 1. Istarske brigade), a big wooded site with its own beach, but which soon gets crowded.

Hotels

Hotels are thin on the ground in central Pula (see the map opposite for the locations of those reviewed here). There are more rooms 5km southeast of the centre in the upmarket suburbs of **Stoja** (bus #1 from Giardini) or **Pješčana uvala** (bus #6 from Giardini), and at the large package-oriented hotels south of the centre on the **Verudela peninsula** (at the end of bus routes #1 and #1A).

Central Pula

Omir Dobricheva 6 ℡052/210-614 or 218-186, ⓕ213-944. Small, friendly but rather plain hotel with serviceable en-suite rooms, slightly uphill from Giardini. ❹

Riviera Splitska 1 ℡052/211-166, ⓕ219-117, ⓦwww.arenaturist.hr. Shabbily genteel hotel between the train station and the amphitheatre. Probably the finest example of Habsburg-era architecture in Istria when viewed from the outside, but the en-suite rooms are rather dowdy. In July and August it's overpriced for what it is, but quite reasonable at other times of year. ❻

Scaletta Flavijevska 26 ℡052/541-599. One of the best family-run hotels in Croatia; rooms are plush, pastel-coloured and come with TV and bathroom. Needless to say, it fills up quickly. ❺

Out from the centre

Histria Verudela peninsula ℡052/590-000,

ⓕ214-175, ⓦwww.arenaturist.hr. Upmarket hotel which looks a bit like a suburban housing estate from the outside, but offers roomy en suites with TV and bath, plus a covered pool. ❼

Milan Stoja 4 ℡052/210-200, ⓕ210-500, ⓦwww.milan1967.hr. Family-run hotel in a suburban setting 2km west of the centre. Rooms are en suite and come with TV, minibar and air conditioning. There's a swanky restaurant (see p.161) on the ground floor. ❼

Palma Verudela peninsula ℡052/590-000, ⓕ214-175. Large, comfortable but bland package-oriented hotel. The nearby *Park* (℡052/375-001, ⓕ375-018) and *Brioni* (℡052/215-585, ⓕ213-671) are very similar. Rooms in all three can be booked through Arenaturist. All ❻

Valsabbion Pješčana uvala IX/26 ℡052/213-033, ⓕ208-033, ⓦwww.valsabbion.com. Modern family-run place, featuring attractive rooms, a fitness studio with small swimming pool, and a superb restaurant. ❻

The Town

According to legend, Pula was founded by the Colchians, who pursued the Argonauts here after the latter had stolen the Golden Fleece. The prosaic truth is that Pula began life as a minor Illyrian settlement, and there's not much evidence of a significant town here until the arrival of the Romans, who transformed Pula into an important commercial centre endowed with all the imperial trimmings – temples, theatres and triumphal arches – appropriate to its status. The chief reminder of Roman times is the immense **amphitheatre** (*amfiteatar* or *arena*; daily: summer 8am–8pm, 30Kn; winter 9am–5pm, 15Kn), just north of the centre, a huge grey skein of connecting arches whose silhouette dominates the city skyline. Built towards the end of the first century BC, it's the sixth largest amphitheatre in the world, with space for 22,000 spectators, although why such a capacious theatre was built in a small Roman town of only 5000 inhabitants has never been properly explained.

The outer shell is remarkably complete, although only a small part of the seating remains anything like intact, and the interior tiers and galleries were long ago quarried by locals, who used the soft limestone to build their own houses. It's lucky, in fact, that the amphitheatre survives here at all. Overcome by enthusiasm for Classical antiquities, the sixteenth-century Venetian authorities planned

► Local bus station (50ml & Poreč

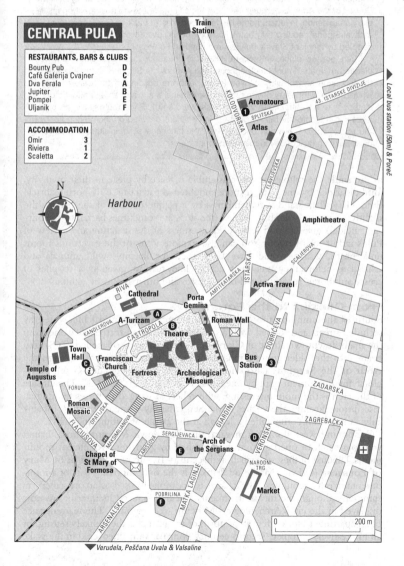

CENTRAL PULA

RESTAURANTS, BARS & CLUBS
Bounty Pub	D
Café Galerija Cvajner	C
Dva Ferala	A
Jupiter	B
Pompei	E
Uljanik	F

ACCOMMODATION
Omir	3
Riviera	1
Scaletta	2

Train Station

KOLODVORSKA

43 ISTARSKE DIVIZIJE

Arenatours ❶
SPLITSKA

Atlas
❷

FLAVIJEVSKA

N

Harbour

Amphitheatre

SCALIEROVA

ISTARSKA

AMFITEATARSKA

Activa Travel

RIVA
Cathedral
Porta Gemina
Roman Wall

KANDLEROVA

A-Turizam ⒶCASTROPOLA
Ⓑ Theatre

DORIĆEVA

Town Hall
Franciscan Church
Ⓒ
Fortress
Archeological Museum
Bus Station ❸

ZADARSKA

Temple of Augustus

FORUM

Roman Mosaic
OPATIJSKA

FLACIUSOVA

MAKSIMILANOVA

GIARDINI

ZAGREBAČKA

VERONSKA

SERGIJEVACA
CLABICSOVA
Arch of the Sergians
Ⓔ
Ⓓ

Chapel of St Mary of Formosa

NARODNI TRG

POBRILINA
MATKA LAGINJE
Market

Ⓕ

ARSENALSKA

| 0 | 200 m |

▼ Verudela, Peščana Uvala & Valsaline

James Joyce in Pula

In October 1904 the 22-year-old James Joyce eloped to mainland Europe with his girlfriend (and future wife) Nora Barnacle. He sought work with the Berlitz English language schools in Zürich and Trieste, but the organization found him a post in Pula instead, where he was paid £2 for a sixteen-hour week teaching Austro-Hungarian naval officers (one of whom was Miklos Horthy, ruler of Hungary between the wars). Despite their straitened circumstances, the couple enjoyed this first taste of domestic life, although Joyce viewed Pula as a provincial backwater and, eager to get away at the first opportunity, accepted a job in Trieste six months later.

Joyce had a productive time in Pula, writing much of what subsequently became *Portrait of the Artist as a Young Man*, but the city made next to no impact on his literary imagination. In letters home he described it as "a back-of-God-speed place – a naval Siberia", adding that "Istria is a long boring place wedged into the Adriatic, peopled by ignorant Slavs who wear red caps and colossal breeches".

There are few places in modern Pula which boast Joycean associations: a wall plaque on an apartment block opposite the Arch of the Sergians marks the site of the language school where Joyce taught, and the building of the *Café Miramar*, where Joyce went every day to read the newspapers, survives as a furniture store – it's opposite the entrance to the Uljanik shipyard on the Riva. You can always enjoy a drink in the café-bar *Uliks* ("Ulysses" in Croatian), situated on the ground floor of the apartment block which once housed the language school, although there's a disappointing lack of Joyce memorabilia inside.

to dismantle the whole lot and reassemble it piece by piece in their own city, until dissuaded by one of their more enlightened patricians, Pula-born Gabriele Emo. His gallant stand is remembered by a plaque on one of the towers, the slightly hair-raising climb up which (the steps are sometimes barred to discourage suicides) gives a good sense of the vastness of the structure and a view of Pula's industrious harbour. You can also explore some of the cavernous rooms underneath, which would have been used for keeping wild animals and Christians before they met their deaths. They're now given over to piles of crusty amphorae, reconstructed olive presses and other lacklustre exhibits.

From Giardini to the Forum

South of the amphitheatre, central Pula encircles a pyramidal hill, scaled by secluded streets and topped with a star-shaped Venetian fortress. Starting from the main downtown street of **Giardini**, **Sergijevaca** (also labelled Via Sergia) heads into the older, more atmospheric parts of town, running through the **Arch of the Sergians** (also known as Zlatna vrata, or Golden Gate), a self-glorifying monument built by one Salvia Postuma Sergia in 30 BC. The far side of the arch is the more interesting, with reliefs of winged victories framing an inscription extolling the virtues of the Sergia family – one of whom (probably Salvia's husband) commanded a legion at the Battle of Actium in 31 BC.

Continuing west along Sergijevaca, then left down Maksimilianova, brings you to a patch of open ground distinguished by a further two ancient monuments. The first of these, the small sixth-century Byzantine **Chapel of St Mary of Formosa** (Crkvica Marije od Trstika), is the only surviving part of a monumental basilica complex. The chapel is occasionally used as an art gallery in summer, although the mosaic fragments that once graced its interior are now displayed in the city's Archeological Museum (see opposite). The rear entrance of an apartment block a few steps north of the chapel is the unlikely setting for an impressively complete second-century floor **mosaic**, uncovered in the wake of Allied bombing raids in World War II. Now restored and on display behind a metal grille, it's largely made up of non-figurative designs – geometric flower-patterns and meanders – surrounding a central panel illustrating the legend of Dirce and the bull. From here it's worth making a brief detour southwards to the main **post office** on Danteov trg, an ambitious modern structure designed in 1933 by Angiolo Mazzoni – whose Futurist leanings are evinced by the stair-case spiralling awesomely upwards from the dark red vestibule.

At the western end of Sergijevaca, stepped streets lead uphill onto the city's central mound, one of them – Balde Lupetine – passing the severe, unadorned form of the thirteenth-century **Franciscan Church** (Crkva svetog Franja) on the way. There's a disorganized museum in the adjoining cloister (mid-June to mid-Sept: daily 9am–noon & 4–7pm; 10Kn), in which you'll find all kinds of stonework from Roman to late medieval times, and a display of mosaic frag-ments in a couple of side rooms.

Sergijevaca finishes up at the ancient Roman **Forum**, nowadays the old quarter's main square. On the far side is the **Temple of Augustus**, built between 2 BC and 14 AD to celebrate the cult of the emperor and one of the finest Roman temples outside Italy, with an imposing facade of high Corinthian columns. Inside there's a permanent exhibition (mid-June to mid-Sept: daily 9am–6pm; 10Kn) of the best of Pula's Roman finds, including the sculpted torso of a Roman centurion found in the amphitheatre, and a figure of a slave kneeling at the sandalled feet (more or less all that's left) of his mas-ter. The building next door began life as a Temple of Diana before being mod-ified and rebuilt as the **Town Hall** (Gradska vijećnica) in the thirteenth cen-tury – a Renaissance arcade was added later. Diagonally opposite the town hall, the **Cvajner Café and Art Gallery** occupies a medieval civic building which preserves a sixteenth-century wooden ceiling and some substantial late Gothic fresco fragments – swirling floral motifs in rich red and yellow hues.

The cathedral, fortress and Archeological Museum

Heading northeast from the Forum along Kandlerova brings you to Pula's sim-ple and spacious **Cathedral of St Mary** (Katedrala svete Marije; daily 7am–noon & 4–6pm), a compendium of styles with a dignified Renaissance facade concealing a Romanesque modification of a sixth-century basilica, itself built on the foundations of a Roman temple. Inside, the high altar consists of a third-century marble Roman sarcophagus that's said to have once contained the remains of the eleventh-century Hungarian King Solomon, though there's little else of interest.

From almost anywhere along Kandlerova you can follow streets up to the top of the hill, the site of the original Roman Capitol and now the home of a mossy seventeenth-century **fortress** (*kaštel*), built by the Venetians in the form of a four-pointed star. It now houses the sparse and uninformative **Historical Museum of Istra** (Povijesni muzej Istre; summer daily 8am–7pm; winter Mon–Fri 9am–5pm; 12Kn), with scale models of vessels built in local shipyards and a cabinet of Habsburg-era souvenir mugs decorated with the whiskery visage of Emperor Franz Josef and his World War I ally Kaiser Wilhelm II of Germany. However, the museum's real highlight is the chance to ramble around the fortress's ramparts, providing commanding views of Pula and its environs – with the cranes of the Uljanik shipyard clustered over to the west, and the spire of Vodnjan church (see p.165) a distant but discernible presence 12km away to the north.

A path leads round the south side of the fortress towards the other side of the town centre, passing the remains of a second-century **Roman Theatre** en route to the **Archeological Museum** (Arheološki muzej; May–Sept

Mon–Sat 9am–8pm, Sun 10am–3pm; Oct–April Mon–Fri 9am–2pm; 20Kn). The greater part of Pula's movable Roman relics have finished up in this rather old-fashioned museum, with room upon room of unimaginatively displayed ceramics, brooches and oil lamps. Excellent English-language labelling helps to ease your progress from one display case to the next. Highlights include the Roman gravestones arranged in the hallways and stairwells, many of which feature sensitive portraits of the deceased; and the pre-Roman artefacts from the Illyrian settlement of Nesactium – especially the enigmatic, squiggle-embellished tombstones, one of which takes the form of a man riding a horse, upon whose flanks an image of a fertility goddess has been carved. Just by the museum is the second-century AD **Porta Gemina**, smaller and plainer than the Arch of the Sergians, whose two arches give it its name: the Twin Gate.

South of the centre

Immediately south of Pula the city's dusty high-rise suburbs suddenly give way to a series of rocky promontories and forest-fringed inlets, culminating in the Verudela peninsula, 6km distant from the centre, where the city's package hotels are located. You can get to Verudela directly by taking bus #1 or #1A from Giardini, although a more leisurely approach will take you past several interesting sights on the way.

Taking bus #3 (destination Stoja), or walking southwest of the centre along Arsenalska (subsequently Bečka and then Katalinića Jeretova), brings you to Pula's finest graveyard, the Habsburg-era **Naval Cemetery** (Mornaričko groblje), 3km out of the centre at the western end of Katalinića Jeretova. Planted with dark cypresses and incongruously jaunty palms, this is a wonderfully strollable park as much as anything else, although there's a good deal of funerary sculpture to enjoy, too, with some imposing nineteenth-century memorials recalling Austrian sailors, and a civilian section where many of the Italian-speaking inhabitants of inter-war Pola were buried. From here ulica Stoja descends to concrete bathing platforms of **Valkane** bay, the nearest beach to the centre and a stylish seaside rendezvous in the inter-war years. It nowadays has a grubby, unkempt look about it, and it's far better to head left along the **Lungomare**, the road running southeast along the coast towards **Valsaline** bay, passing a succession of broad rock slabs which provide perfect spots for bathing. Heading uphill near the *Hotel Splendid*, just beyond Valsaline, brings you to a gravel track which leads to **Fort Bourguignon** (daily 11am–3pm; 20Kn), an enormous doughnut-shaped lump of stone built in 1861–66 and named after an Austrian Admiral. Inside, you can wander the galleries (used for rave parties on summer weekends, see p.162) and peruse a display documenting the eleven other forts built around the city by the Habsburgs, turning Pula into an impregnable fortress in the process.

Further south is the wooded **Verudela peninsula**, bordered to the east by the lovely Verudski kanal inlet, site of Pula's marina. The southern extremity of the peninsula, **Punta Verudela**, is home to a couple of good shingle beaches, of which the Havajka, on the west side of the peninsula behind the *Park* hotel, and the Ambrela, northwest of the *Brioni* hotel, are the most popular. The beaches are deluged with vacationing city folk during the summer, and remain a popular strolling area throughout the year. Another Habsburg fortress on high ground near the tip of the peninsula now houses an **aquarium** (daily 9am–7pm; 12Kn; ⊛www.aquariumpula-istra.hr), with an assortment of water-bound creatures gazing out of their tanks, and displays devoted to local marine ecology issues.

Eating and drinking

There's a healthy supply of serviceable **restaurants** in the centre of Pula, although – as so often in Croatia – the really outstanding eating places are in the suburbs. For snacks and supplies, the covered **market** and the surrounding cafés on Narodni trg, about 100m east of the Arch of the Sergians, are the best place for buying provisions or picking up sandwiches and pastries. Just north of the Forum, the Pekarna Jozef at Kandlerova 17 is a good place to stock up on bread and cakes.

Although the alfresco cafés and ice-cream parlours around the Forum provide plenty of opportunities for daytime **drinking**, central Pula doesn't really lend itself to a night-time bar-crawl. Most of the characterful hostelries popular with Puležani are spread throughout the city rather than concentrated in one central promenading area, and you'll have to be prepared to venture beyond the tourist-trodden areas in order to enjoy the city at its best.

Restaurants

Bunarina Verudela. Rough-and-ready but eternally popular grill, down by the marina where most Puležani keep their small boats. Good *ćevapi* (mincemeat rissoles) and *lignje* (squid).

Dva Ferala Kandlerova. Workaday bar and restaurant with wooden benches inside and out, handily situated on the main tourist trail. Good for grilled meats and cheaper fish dishes.

Jupiter Castropola 38. Traditionally regarded as being the best of the city's pizzerias, north of the fortress.

Kažun Vrtlarska 1. Traditional food in a suburban house ten minutes' walk east of the centre and well away from the main tourist trail. Friendly service and excellent Istrian fare such as *kobasice* (sausages) and *ombolo* (pork chops).

Milan Stoja 4 ☎052/210-200. Family-run restaurant in a modern suburban pavilion just opposite the Naval Cemetery, offering supreme seafood (especially the shellfish) and high-class service. Known also for its cakes, and an extensive international wine list.

Pompei Clearissova 1. Serviceable pizzas, excellent pasta dishes and generous salads, on a city-centre side street perfectly placed for a mid-sightseeing break.

Scaletta Flavijevska 26, A swish, intimate place attatched to the hotel of the same name, with top-quality seafood and meat dishes – try the *istarski odrezak* (veal stuffed with *pršut* and figs).

Valsabbion Pješčana uvala ☎052/222-991.

Upmarket place with a nationwide reputation for its fresh seafood and extravagant sweets, and a nouvelle-cuisine approach to presentation.

Vela Nera Pješčana uvala ☎052/219-209. Chic place on a terrace overlooking the marina, with the usual range of fish and shellfish, plus Istrian specialities like *rezanci sa tartufima* (noodles with truffles), or a very rich stewed *kunić* (rabbit).

Cafés and bars

Bounty Pub Veronska 8. An animated place with plenty of outdoor seating two blocks east of the Arch of the Sergians. Popular with the daytime coffee crowd as well as night-time revellers.

Cabahia Širolina. Cult drinking den on a side street 3km southwest of the centre, with a cosily eccentric interior, and an outdoor terrace with the feel of a bamboo hut. Mildly bohemian.

Café Galerija Cvajner Forum 2. The prime people-watching venue on the main square, next to the tourist office. Comfy sofas and contemporary art exhibits inside.

Monte Serpente Braće čeh 14. Stylish, roomy bar which turns into a club on weekend evenings, when it's a popular gathering point for beautiful young things. One drawback: it's 4km from the centre in the northeastern suburb of Monte Serpo.

Podroom Corner of Tomasinijeva and Budicinova. Lounge around on designer banquettes in Pula's funkiest interior, or mingle with a fun-seeking crowd on the standing-room-only outdoor terrace. Handily situated round the corner from Cabahia.

Entertainment and festivals

The **amphitheatre** hosts large-scale opera and pop performances in the summer, often featuring major international stars – the tourist office has details. The only reliable central **club** is *Uljanik*, Dobrilina 2, a counter-cultural club of many years' standing that holds DJ nights (anything from commercial techno to alternative rock) throughout the year, as well as live gigs on a big open-air terrace in summer – posters in town will provide an idea of what's on. Fort Bourguignon (@www.fortbourguignon.com) has been used as a venue for rave-style events in recent summers, but check the latest information before heading out there specially. Pula's main **cinema** is the Zagreb, bang in the centre at Giardini 12.

Ever since 1953 the Amphitheatre has hosted the Pula **Film Festival** (early Aug), which traditionally premieres the year's crop of domestic feature films. Back in the days when the Yugoslav film industry produced several big-budget features a year, the Pula Film Festival was a major international glam-fest which attracted big name stars – and guest-of-honour President Tito revelled in the opportunity of being photographed next to actresses like Gina Lollabrigida, Elizabeth Taylor and Sofia Loren. Now that the Croatia only produces a handful of (largely low-budget) films a year, the festival has rather lost its way – but attempts have been made to breathe new life into the event by including more international films. Contact the tourist office for further details. Other annual events of significance include **Valkana Beach** (@www.mtvvalkanabeach.com), an outdoor rave DJ event usually held in the town of **Medulin**, 12km southeast, in early August; and **IstriaEthnoJazz** (also Aug; @www.istraetnojazz.com), exploring the boundaries between traditional music and more contemporary styles, with concerts in Pula, Svetvinčenat and Pazin.

Listings

Airlines Croatia Airlines, Corrarina 8 (Mon–Fri 8am–4pm, Sat 9am–noon; ☎052/23-322).
Airport enquiries ☎052/530-511.
Bank Zagrebačka banka, M. Laginje 1 (Mon–Fri 7.30am–7pm, Sat 7.30am–noon). There's an ATM outside.
Car rental Avis, Dobricheva 1 ☎052/223-739; Budget, Carrarina 7 ☎052/218-252; Herz, Hotel Histria ☎052/210-868.
Ferry tickets Jadroagent, Riva 14 (Mon–Sat 8am–3.30pm, Sun 12.30–15.30pm; ☎052/210-431, @jadroagent@pu.tel.hr).
Hospital Gradska Bolnica, Zagrebačka 30 (☎052/214-433).
Internet access Cyber Caffe, Flanatička 14; Enigma, Kandlerova 19; Multimedialni centar Luka, Istarska 30.

Left luggage At the bus station on Istarska (daily 7am–9pm) and at the bus station on Trg 1. Istarske brigade (Mon–Fri 5–9am, 9.30am–4.30pm & 5–8pm, Sat 5–9am & 9.30am–1pm).
Mail and telephones The main post office is at Danteov Trg 4 (daily 8am–9pm), and there's a smaller branch just south of the amphitheatre at Istarska 7 (Mon–Sat 8am–3pm).
Pharmacy Ljekarna centar, Giardini 15 (24hr).
Police Trg republike 2 ☎052/532-111.
Taxis Try the rank on Giardini or call ☎052/223-228.
Travel agents Arenatours, Splitska 1, offers local excursions and accommodation reservations; GeneralTurist, Carrarina 4, sells international airline tickets.

The west coast

Istria's **west coast** represents the peninsula at its most developed. In itself it's attractive enough, with fields of rich red soil and pine woods sloping gently down to the sea, but a succession of purpose-built resorts has all but swallowed up the shoreline. Inland, the coastal strip fades imperceptibly into conifer-studded heathland and fields bounded by dry-stone walls and dotted with *kažuni*, the characteristic stone huts with conical roofs, traditionally used by Istrian shepherds for shelter when overnighting with their flocks. North of Pula, **Rovinj** is Istria's best-preserved old Venetian port, while the crumbling towns of **Vodnjan** and **Bale**, slightly inland, are also worth a look. Further north, the large resort of **Poreč** is package-holiday-land writ large, although it does boast the peninsula's finest ecclesiastical attraction in the shape of the mosaic-filled Basilica of St Euphrasius. The mega-hotels nearby offer undoubted comforts, but also a lot of concrete on the side.

The Brijuni Islands

North of Pula lie the **Brijuni** (Italian, Brioni), a small archipelago of fourteen islands that became famous as the private retreat of Tito, before being accorded national-park status and opened to visitors in 1983. Visitors are still only allowed on two of the islands, **Veli Brijun** and **Mali Brijun**, and travel here is strictly controlled due to the islands' status as a nature conservation area. You can visit the Brijuni on an organized day-trip – in which case you'll probably be whisked around Veli Brijun by tourist train – or book into one of the two upmarket hotels on Veli Brijun, in which case you'll have freedom to stroll around the island unsupervised.

The presidential playground

Although the islands were a popular rural retreat among wealthy Romans, the Brijuni's history as an offshore paradise really began in 1893, when they were bought by Austrian industrialist **Paul Kupelweiser**, owner of a steel mill in the Czech town of Vitkovice. Kupelweiser's aim was to turn the islands into a luxury resort patronized by the cream of Europe's aristocracy, and he brought in Nobel Prize-winning bacteriologist Robert Koch, who rid the islands of malaria by pouring petroleum on the swamps. Smart hotels and villas were built on Veli Brijun, and the Mediterranean scrub was cleared to make way for landscaped parks and a golf course. Brijuni's heyday was in the period immediately before World War I: Archduke Franz Ferdinand, Kaiser Wilhelm II and Thomas Mann all stayed on the islands, and struggling English-language teacher James Joyce came here to celebrate his 23rd birthday on February 2, 1905.

Following World War I, however, the islands lost their high-society allure, and Paul Kupelweiser's son and heir, Karl, committed suicide here in 1930 after being bankrupted by the cost of their upkeep. After World War II, **Tito** decided to make Veli Brijun one of his official bases, planting much of the island's subtropical vegetation and commissioning a residence – the White Villa (Bijela Vila) – in which he was able to entertain visiting heads of state in the style to which they were accustomed. It was here that Tito, Nehru and Nasser signed the Brioni Declaration in 1956, which paved the way for the creation of the **Non-Aligned Movement**. Far away from prying eyes, Brijuni was the perfect place from which to conduct secret diplomacy – Yugoslav-sponsored terrorist Abu Nidal was a house guest in 1978. Tito himself contrived to spend as much time on the Brijuni as possible, conducting government business from here when not busy hunting in his private game reserve or pottering about in his gardens and orchards, tangerines from which were traditionally sent to children's homes throughout Yugoslavia as a new year's gift. International stars attending the Pula Film Festival (see opposite) stayed on Brijuni as Tito's personal guests, bestowing his regime with a veneer of showbiz glamour.

After Tito's death in 1980 the islands were retained as an official residence, becoming the favoured summer destination of President Tuđman after 1990. Tuđman's rank ineptitude as a world statesman ensured that no foreign leader ever came to visit him here, however, and with Tuđman's successor Stipe Mesić declining to make use of the islands, the Brijuni look like losing their mythical status in Croatian politics.

The obvious gateway to the islands is the small fishing village of **FAŽANA**, 8km northwest of Pula (reachable from the city on bus #6). The national-park office on Fažana's harbourfront square (Mon–Sat 8am–8pm, Sun 8am–5pm; ☎052/525-888, ⊛www.np-brijuni.hr) sells tickets for day-trips to the biggest island and main tourist draw, Veli Brijun, as well as arranging transport to the hotels. There are about five such excursions daily from Fažana in summer, one daily in winter; each lasts roughly four hours and costs 170Kn in June, July and August, 130Kn in April, May, September and October, and 80Kn in other months. If you're staying in a package hotel in Istria you'll probably be paying around 250Kn for a Brijuni excursion, with transport to Fažana – and possibly lunch – thrown in. Trips to Brijuni are also offered by boats in Pula harbour (from around 160Kn per person), although these tend not to stop at Veli Brijun, heading instead for a bay on Mali Brijun for swimming and a fish picnic.

If you want to stay on the islands, be warned that the **hotels**, next door to each other on Veli Brijun's main bay, are deliberately overpriced in order to cultivate an aura of exclusivity: the *Neptun-Istra* (☎052/525-100; ⑨) is a standard three-star whose rooms come with TV, minibar and bath; while the *Karmen* (☎052/525-400; ❽) offers pretty much the same. Back in Fažana, the **tourist office**, right on the waterfront at Riva 2 (daily 8am–8pm; ☎052/383-727, ⊜tz-fazana@pu.hinet.hr), provides local information, and Stefani trade, Župni trg 2, doles out **private rooms** on the mainland (❶–❷).

Veli Brijun

After a fifteen-minute crossing of the Brijuni Channel, excursion craft from Fažana arrive at Kupelwiser's hotel complex on **Veli Brijun**'s eastern shore. From here a miniature train with English-speaking guide heads north through parklands to a **safari park** at the northern tip of the island. This was originally stocked with beasts given to Tito as presents by visiting dignitaries – the two elephants presented by Indira Gandhi are still here, alongside zebras, antelopes and camels. The train continues along the western side of the island to the **White Villa** and other official residences, including the Villa Jadran, where guests have included Queen Elizabeth II and Gina Lollobrigida, all watched over discreetly by liveried guards (Tito's personal quarters – together with his famous tangerine groves – were on the island of Krasnica, a few hundred metres off Veli Brijun's west coast). The train stops to allow exploration of a ruined **Byzantine fortress** at the southwestern corner of the island, its stark grey fortifications in bleak contrast to the green paradise it was built to defend.

The train then returns to the hotel complex via the scant remains of a first-century BC Roman villa at Veriga Bay. Beside the hotel complex an exhibition entitled **Tito on Brijuni** (Tito na Brijunima; daily summer 8am–7pm; winter 8am–2pm; free with excursion ticket) starts, on the ground floor, with a display of the animals given to Tito as presents and stuffed after their death, including four seven-week-old giraffes which contracted a virus soon after their arrival from Africa. Upstairs is a fascinating exhibition of photos documenting Tito's various personae: one moment a man of the people talking to Fažana fisherfolk, the next, sharing jokes with jet-setting house guests such as Sophia Loren, Elizabeth Taylor and Richard Burton, who played the part of Tito in the epic war film *Sutjeska* in 1970. Look out too for a photograph of Tito taking Ho Chi Minh for a spin in a motorboat, with both men sporting raffish panama hats – an experience which the Vietnamese leader appears to be enjoying somewhat less than the Marshal.

Vodnjan and Bale

Heading up the west coast from Pula, the main road runs inland through the historic town of **VODNJAN** (Dignano), 11km north of Pula, with its warren of weatherbeaten alleys gathered tightly around a time-worn main square. Vodnjan is famous for two things: the enduring presence of a large Italian-speaking community, and the well-preserved **Vodnjan mummies** – the desiccated bodies of various saints stored in the local **St Blaise's Church** (Crkva svetog Blaža; summer Mon–Sat 9am–7pm; winter, open when the priest is around), an eighteenth-century structure, built in imitation of Palladio's San Pietro in Castello, Venice, whose soaring campanile is the highest in Istria. Inside, the "mummies" are kept behind a burgundy-coloured curtain to the rear of the main altar. Originally stored in the church of San Lorenzo in Venice, they were brought to Vodnjan in 1818 for safekeeping after the monastic order that originally looked after them had been dissolved. Three complete and well-preserved bodies are laid out in glass cases, above which are stacked a range of smaller relics in a series of containers – one of which holds a twisted brown form reputed to be the torso and arm of St Sebastian. The most revered of the bodies is that of Leon Bembo the Blessed, a twelfth-century Venetian cleric and diplomat who gave up worldly pleasures for the monastic life, developing a reputation as a faith healer and sage. Beside him lie St Nikoloza of Koper (with a still-fresh-looking garland of flowers round her head) and St Ivan Olini of Venice, both renowned medieval healers – popular belief maintains that there's a link between the saints' healing powers and the subsequent failure of their bodies to decompose.

The **Collection of Sacral Art** (Zbirka sakralne umjetnosti; same times as the church; 10Kn) in the sacristy has innumerable smaller relics, including one glass jar which, it's claimed, contains the lower jaw and tongue of St Mary of Egypt, a sixth-century Alexandrian courtesan who converted to Christianity and thereafter opted for a life of asceticism in the desert. The star exhibit, however, is Paolo Veneziano's early fourteenth-century polyptych of St Bembo the Blessed, a wooden board which originally served as the lid of Bembo's coffin. A series of scenes show Bembo exercising his healing powers; mighty bishops and nobles visiting Bembo's deathbed; and pilgrims paying homage to Bembo's miraculously preserved body.

Buses from Pula to Pazin, Rovinj and Poreč all pick up and drop off on the western edge of town, a short walk from the main square, where you'll find Vodnjan's **tourist office** at Narodni trg 3 (June–Sept Mon–Fri 8am–3pm, Sat & Sun 9am–noon; Oct–May Mon–Fri 8am–3pm; ☎052/511-672, ⓦ www.vodnjan.hr). The cosiest place **to stay** in town is the *Pansion San Rocco*, Sveti Roko 41 (☎052/511-611; ❸), which has small, crisply furnished rooms with TV; the Wart agency on the opposite side of the road (Mon–Sat 9am– 4pm, Sun 9am–1pm; same phone number) has **rooms** (❷). For those with their own transport, *Stancija Negričani*, 8km north of Vodnjan and well signed from the northern end of town (☎052/391-084, ⓦ www.stancijane-gricani .com; ❸–❻ depending on room size), is one of the best rural hotels in the whole of Croatia. Set in a large stone farmhouse surrounded by forest, the en-suite rooms are all decorated in nineteenth-century style, with old

△ Window arches, Poreč

wooden bedsteads and rustic furniture – but pristine modern bathrooms and TV.

The *Stancija Negričani*'s **restaurant** is open to non-residents, though advanced reservations are required. Back in town, you can tuck into hearty Croatian food at *Pansion San Rocco*, or at the superior *Vodnjanka*, on the main Pula–Pazin road at Istarska bb (☎052/511-435). The latter, whose interior is like a cross between a nineteenth-century barn and a kooky art gallery, serves up the best in local cuisine, including some filling *fuži*- and *njoki*-based staples, and spicy Istrian sausages.

Bale

Ten kilometres beyond Vodnjan, **BALE** (Valle) occupies a hilltop site typical of the peninsula, with houses built in a defensive circle. Smaller and more deserted than Vodnjan, it's a good example of a town abandoned by its Italian population after 1945 and never properly lived in since. The most arresting edifice here is the **Soardo–Bembo Palace**, a fifteenth-century Venetian Gothic building with an elegant balcony built into its towered facade. It's currently being restored and will probably house a local history museum in future. Beside the palace, an arch topped by a clumsily rendered Venetian lion leads through into the core of the old town, which really amounts to a circular alleyway spanned by little arches, with rough stone buildings on either side. Follow this round in either direction to reach **St Elizabeth's Church** (Crkva svete Elizabete) in the central square, a largely nineteenth-century neo-Baroque building, although it preserves a Romanesque campanile and fragments from earlier sixth- and eighth-century churches in the crypt. Just outside the old town beside the road to Rovinj, the smaller, simpler, fifteenth-century **Church of the Holy Spirit** (Crkva svetog Duha) contains late Gothic frescoes and is sporadically open as a gallery in the summer months.

Pula–Rovinj buses stop on the main road just below the entrance to the old town, Trg palih boraca, where there's a small seasonal **tourist office** (summer daily 8am–8pm; ☎052/824-270). *Kamene Priče*, just above the Soardo-Bembo palace at Kaštel 57 (☎052/524-231, ℱ824-235; ❸), offers **bed and breakfast** in an atmospheric old stone house, although there are only three rooms, so ring well in advance. About a kilometre northwest of town, just off the Rovinj road and worth a stop, the *Sweet Bar* **café** is renowned for its excellent home-made cakes and biscuits.

Rovinj

There are few more pleasant towns in Istria than **ROVINJ** (Rovigno). Delicately poised between medieval port and modern tourist resort, it has managed better than anywhere else along the peninsula's west coast to preserve its character by keeping major development well away from its historic centre: its harbour is a likeable mix of fishing boats and swanky yachts, while its quaysides are a blend of sunshaded café tables and fishermen's nets. Spacious Venetian-style houses and elegant piazzas lend an overridingly Italian air to the town, and the festive mood the tourists bring only adds to the atmosphere. Rovinj is also the most Italian town on this coast: there's an Italian high school, the language is widely spoken, and street signs are bilingual.

Rovinj's urban core is situated on what was formerly an island. The strait separating it from the coast was filled in during the mid-eighteenth century, after which the town expanded onto the mainland, until then the site of a quite separate settlement of Croat farmers. Initially, the urban Italian culture of Rovigno assimilated that of the mainland Slavs, until industrial develop-

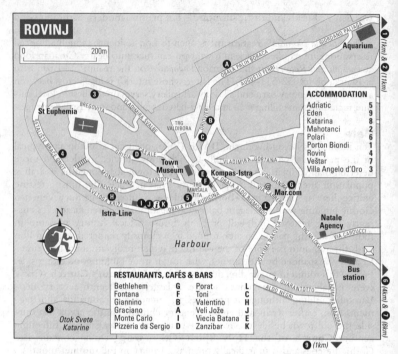

ROVINJ

| 0 | 200m |

Aquarium

① (1km) & **②** (11km)

St Euphemia

TRG VALDIBORA

BREGOVITA

VLADIMIRA SVALBE

OBALA PALIH BORACA

AUGUSTO FERRI

OBROVAC

Town Museum

Kompas-Istra

VLADIMIRA GORTANA

DRIOVIER

CASALE

GRISIA

MONTALBANO

GARZOTTA

SVETOGA KRIZA

TREVISOL

Istra-Line

OBALA PINA BUDICINA

TRG MARSALA TITA

Mar.com

VOD NJANSKA

VIA CARRERA

OBALA ALDO BISMONDO

Harbour

Natale Agency

VIA CARDUCCI

JOAKIMA RAKOVCA

N. QUARANTOTTO

ALDO NEGRI

TRG NA LOKVI

VLADIMIRA NAZORA

Bus station

ACCOMMODATION

Adriatic	5
Eden	9
Katarina	8
Mahotanci	2
Polari	6
Porton Biondi	4
Rovinj	1
Veštar	7
Villa Angelo d'Oro	3

③

Otok Svete Katarine

⑧

RESTAURANTS, CAFÉS & BARS

Bethlehem	G	Porat	L
Fontana	F	Toni	C
Giannino	B	Valentino	H
Graciano	A	Veli Jože	J
Monte Carlo	I	Viecia Batana	E
Pizzeria da Sergio	D	Zanzibar	K

⑥ (4km) & **⑦** (6km)

⑨ (1km)

ment in the late nineteenth century encouraged a wave of economic migrants, tipping the demographic scales in the Croats' favour. Playing a leading role in this was the Rovinj tobacco factory, founded in 1872, which still produces the bulk of Croatia's cigarettes. Rovinj's other claim to fame is as the "Montmartre of Istria" – a tag which stems from the painters and other artists who have gravitated here since the 1950s, whose studios fill the streets of the old town. For one day in August (usually the second Saturday), the main street, Grisia, is taken over by an open-air display of works in which anyone can take part, providing they register their works at the town museum on the morning of the show. The other annual event to look out for is St Euphemia's Day (Blagdan svete Eufemije) on September 16 – Euphemia being the town's patron saint – which provides the excuse for a week of cultural events and concerts.

Arrival, information and accommodation

It's five minutes' walk from Rovinj's **bus station** along the pedestrianized Via Carrera to the main Trg maršala Tita, which marks the junction of the old island and the mainland. The **tourist office**, just off the square at Obala P. Budičin 12 (mid-June to mid-Sept daily 8am–9pm; mid-Sept to mid-June Mon–Sat 8am–3pm; ☎052/811-566, ⓦwww.tzgrovinj.hr), should be able to provide a free map and English-language information booklet. **Bikes** can be rented from Bike Planet, Trg Na lokvi 3; **Internet access** is available at @Mar-com, Via Carrera 26.

There's a smattering of private **rooms** (**①**–**②**) and **apartments** (**③**) in the old town, although most are in the more modern areas. They can be booked through numerous agencies around town (usually open daily 8am–10pm in summer); try Natale, opposite the bus station at Carducci 4 (☏052/813-365, ✉natale@pu.tel.hr); Kompas-Istra, Trg maršala Tita 5 (☏052/813-211, ℗813-187); Generalturist, Trg maršala Tita 2 (☏052/811-402, ✉generalturist@generalturist.com); or Istra-line, near the tourist office at Vrata na obali 1 (☏052/811-209, ℗811-585).

The nearest **campsite** is the *Porton Biondi* (☏052/813-557, ⓦwww.cel.hr /porton-biondi), which occupies a roomy, pine-shaded site right by the sea 1km north of town. An alternative if you have your own transport is *Veštar* (☏052/811-431, ⓦwww.istra.com/jadranturist), on its own secluded bay 6km to the south. *Polari*, occupying a rocky cove 4km south of town, is a naturist camp (☏052/813-441).

Hotels

With so many well-appointed private rooms and apartments, Rovinj's mainstream package **hotels** are not worth the price unless you go slightly upmarket – luckily, a number of characterful places rise above the crowd. With your own transport, you could also try the *Matohanci*, Matohanci 16 (☏052/848-394, ⓦwww.agroistra.com/matohanci; ❸), a family-run bed and breakfast in a rustic spot 11km east of town; take the main road to Poreč and Pazin, and turn off into the village of **Brajkovići**. It offers cosy en-suite rooms with wooden floors and ceilings, as well as traditional home cooking in the ground-floor restaurant – half board arrangements are worth considering.

Note that many hotels are block-booked by package companies in July and August, when independent travellers will have to ring well in advance to secure a room.

Adriatic Corner of Trg maršala Tita and P. Budičin ☏052/815-088, ℗813-573, ⓦwww.istra.com/jadranturist. Venerable establishment right on the harbour, offering comfortable en-suite rooms with phone and TV. With only 27 rooms it has an intimate, almost genteel feel – so book very, very early. ❻
Eden L. Adamovića 66 ☏052/800-400, ℗811-349, ⓦwww.istra.com/jadranturist. One kilometre south of town, this is a vast modern complex backed by forest, with an outdoor pool and generous buffet breakfast. Closed Nov–March. ❾
Katarina Just offshore on the island of Sveta Katarina ☏052/804-100, ⓦwww.hotelinsel-katarina.com. Basically an early-twentieth-century villa-hotel (built by a certain Count von Korwin-

Milewski), with modern annexes either side. The recently modernized rooms have TV, a/c and their own bathroom, and there's an outdoor pool and plenty of wooded parkland out the back. Linked to town by half-hourly taxi-boat. Closed Nov–March. ❼
Rovinj svetog Križa 59 ☏052/840-757, ⓦwww.ipc.hr/hotel-rovinj. Unspectacular hotel offering functional rooms with attached bathroom, but worth considering because of the location – in the old town immediately beneath St Euphemia's church. ❻
Villa Angelo d'Oro Via Svalba 38–42 ☏052/840-502, ⓦwww.rovinj.at. Superbly restored town house on the north side of the peninsula, with luxurious rooms decorated with antique furnishings. Closed Jan & Feb. ❾

The Town

Northwest of the main square, **Trg maršala Tita**, the narrow pedestrianized alleyway of **Grisia** passes through a cute – if relatively unspectacular – Baroque archway before climbing steeply through the heart of the old town to **St Euphemia's Church** (Crkva svete Eufemije; daily 10am–noon & 4–7pm), which dominates Rovinj from the top of its stumpy peninsula. This eighteenth-century Baroque church is home to the sixth-century sarcophagus of St Euphemia, a Christian from Chalcedon in Asia Minor who was martyred during the reign of Diocletian – she was supposedly thrown to the lions in the Constantinople hippodrome after having survived various tortures, symbolized by the wheel which leans against her flanks. The church itself is a roomy three-aisled basilica with a Baroque altarpiece at the end of each. The altar of St

Euphemia is the one furthest to the right, behind which is a small sanctuary containing Euphemia's sarcophagus. A bare stone box, it was brought to Rovinj in 800 AD to keep it safe from the Iconoclasts, who were in the process of smashing up all the relics they could find in Constantinople. A seventeenth-century statue of the saint tops the church's 58-metre-high tower, said to be modelled on that of St Mark's in Venice.

It's below the church, and on either side of Grisia, that Rovinj's most atmospheric streets are to be found – narrow, cobbled alleyways packed with tiny craft shops, overlooked by high shuttered windows, spindly TV aerials and the thin, thrusting chimneys that have become something of a Rovinj trademark. Pressure on housing, so it's said, forced married sons to set up home in a spare room of their parents' house – before long every house in town accommodated several families, each with its own hearth and chimney.

Back on Trg maršala Tita, the **Town Museum** at no. 11 (Zavičajni muzej Rovinj; summer Mon–Sat 9am–12.30pm & 6–9pm; winter Tues–Sat 10.30am–1.30pm; 10Kn) has various archeological oddments, antique furniture and fine art. Among the numerous Madonna and Childs are several imposing Baroque works by anonymous Venetian artists, including a dignified *Deposition of St Sebastian*, and some older, Byzantine-influenced works, including the colourful pageantry of Bonifazio de Pirati's *Adoration of the Magi* (1430) and Pietro Mera's more subdued *Christ Crowned with Thorns* (early sixteenth century).

At its northern end, Trg maršala Tita opens out onto **Trg Valdibora**, site of a small fruit-and-vegetable market. A road leads east from here along the waterfront to the Marine Biological Institute at Obala Giordano Paliaga 5, home to an **aquarium** (Easter–Oct daily 9am–8pm; 10Kn) featuring tanks of Adriatic marine life and flora. Finally, just opposite the bus station, stands the often overlooked twelfth-century octagonal baptistry of the **Holy Trinity Church** (Crkva svetog Trojstva), a simple, functional structure that is rarely open.

Beaches and islands around Rovinj

Paths on the south side of Rovinj's busy harbour lead beyond the *Hotel Park* towards **Zlatni rt**, a densely forested cape crisscrossed by numerous paths and fringed by rocky **beaches**. Other spots for bathing can be found on the two islands just offshore from Rovinj – **Sveta Katarina**, the nearer of the two, and **Crveni otok** (Red Island), just outside Rovinj's bay, both of which can be reached on half-hourly ferries from the harbour. Neither is exactly deserted (there's a hotel on both), but the combination of pine-shaded shores and ultra-clean waters beats anything else the coast around Rovinj has to offer.

Eating

There are more seafood **restaurants** in Rovinj than you can shake a stick at, some of which have an Istria-wide reputation for good food. Many of the harbourfront establishments are bland, overtouristed and worth avoiding, although one or two of them have inexpensive fish specials chalked up on boards outside, and you can munch your way through serviceable pizzas almost everywhere.

Picnic ingredients can be had at the **supermarket** (Mon–Sat 7am–8pm, Sun 7am–11pm) on Trg maršala Tita or in the open-air **market** immediately to the north on Trg Valdibora. The *Martin* bakery on Trg maršala Tita, or the *Brionka* opposite the bus station at Carducci 6, are the best places to pick up bread and cakes.

Restaurants

Giannino A. Ferri 38 ☎052/813-402. The best place in town for grilled shellfish and fish, although moderately priced *njoki* and *fuži* dishes are available too. The cosy interior is filled with paintings and ceramics, while outdoors there are tables scattered across a cobbled street.

Graciano Obala palih boraca bb ☎052/811-515. Roomy portside pavilion with a menu covering all the fish and meat dishes you would expect, plus a few moderately priced risottos and pasta-and-seafood choices. The seafood platter (*riblja plata*) for two is worth trying.

Pizzeria da Sergio Grisia bb. On the old town's main artery, this is the best place for pizza; fills up quickly.

Porat Obala Aldo Rismondo. Unspectacular but cheap harbourfront restaurant serving up the simpler fish dishes, such as fried fillets of mackerel or hake.

Toni Driovier 3. Cosy mid-price joint down a narrow side street, tables crammed into a homely dining room. Good for fish and pasta.

Veli Jože svetog Križa 1. The over-designed interior looks like a nautical junk shop, but the food is first class, with excellent (expensive) seafood, as well as (cheaper) Istrian standbys such as *kobasice*, *teleća koljenica* (calf knuckles) and *fuži sa gulašom* (pasta with goulash).

Drinking

For daytime drinking, the harbour area is full of places where you can sit outside and enjoy coffee, ice cream and cakes, although the two cafés patronized by locals on the main square – *Fontana* and *Viecia Batana* – are both cheaper and more atmospheric. In the evening, head for the knot of convivial **bars** on and around Joakima Rakovca, just behind the seafront, where stools and tables are stuffed into narrow pedestrian alleyways: rather than aiming for a specific destination here, it's really a question of seeing who's hanging out where and what kind of music is playing. There's a trio of trendy establishments on the south side of the old-town peninsula: *Zanzibar*, on svetog Križa, serves up expensive cocktails in a loggia filled with comfy chairs; further along, *Monte Carlo* has outdoor seating perched right above the shore; and *Valentino*, further still, is a rather pretentious wine and cocktail place which nevertheless benefits from its unique position right on the rocks. For indoor drinking, *Bethlehem* on Vodnjanska is a convivial place crammed full of domestic and folksy trinkets – including a Christmas crib.

The Limski kanal and Vrsar

North of Rovinj, the main route detours inland around the **Limski kanal**, a turquoise fjord lined with thick woods rising sheer on either side, which cuts a deep green wedge into the Istrian mainland. In Roman times this marked the boundary between the Poreč and Pula regions – Lim is derived from *limes*, a Latin word meaning "border" or "limit"; later it became a favourite shelter of pirates, who used it as a base from which to attack the Venetians. An appealing local legend associates the *kanal* with pirate and adventurer **Captain Morgan**, who liked it so much he decided to settle down here with his crew, founding the village of **Mrgani** (which still exists 5km inland from the *kanal*) in the process.

Mussels and oysters are cultivated here – you can sample them, along with other fresh fish, in the *Viking* and *Fjord* restaurants, both expensive but highly rated by locals. If you've a car, you can get down to the northern side of the water (and the two restaurants) via the side-road which leaves the Rovinj–Poreč route near the village of **Kloštar**. The best way to see the inlet, however, is by boat. Numerous excursions, often including a fish picnic or a lunch stop en route, are advertised on the quaysides of Rovinj, Vrsar and Poreč; expect to pay around 150–180Kn for the trip.

Occupying high ground near the mouth of the Limski kanal is **VRSAR**, a hilltop village curled tightly around a campanile-topped summit. It's quieter than Rovinj and Poreč, although there's a marina and hotel on the shoreline below. A kilometre south of town on the coast is one of the world's largest nudist colonies, **Koversada**. Established in 1960, this was the first of the Adriatic's naturist communities, and is nowadays a self-contained mini-city where up to 15,000 residents can dress as nature intended on a 24-hour basis.

Stretching north of Vrsar there's a string of **campsites** on the coastal side of the main road to Poreč, beginning with *Autocamp Turist*, swiftly followed by the *Valkanela*, then *Camping Puntica*, which has a small bay to itself. Another couple of kilometres and you're in Plava Laguna, the first of Poreč's big package-hotel suburbs.

Poreč and around

The largest resort in Istria – and, indeed, in Croatia – **POREČ** (Parenzo) is one of those places that have been irredeemably spoiled by mass tourism but remain impossible to avoid. There's a huge influx of tourists here every summer, occupying a total, it's claimed, of 35,000 beds in the town and around – a staggering figure when you consider that Poreč's true population is just 3000. Happily, the hotels are mainly concentrated outside the town, in vast tourist settlements like Plava Laguna and Zelena Laguna to the south, and Pical to the north, but the town's central core of stone houses and mazey side streets – now overrun with ice-cream parlours and tacky souvenir shops – doesn't offer much respite from the hordes. If Poreč is no longer the characterful Mediterranean town you were expecting, however, it still has a couple of points in its favour: the romanesque **Basilica of Euphrasius** provides the town with at least one must-see attraction, and its tourist facilities and transport links make it a convenient base from which to visit the rest of the Istrian peninsula.

Arrival, information and accommodation

Poreč's **bus station** is just north of the town centre, behind the marina. From here, it's a five-minute walk to the **tourist office** at Zagrebačka 9 (daily 8am–10pm; ☎052/451-293, ⓦwww.istra.com/porec), where you'll probably receive a free map. You can surf the net at Cyberm@c, M. Grahalića 1 (daily 9am–midnight; 25Kn per half-hour). **Bikes** can be rented from any number of outlets along the seafront in Plava and Zelena Laguna.

For **hotels**, try the friendly and central *Poreč*, just south of the bus station at Rade Končara 1 (☎052/451-811, ⓦwww.hotelporec.com; ❺), which has poky but neat en-suite doubles and a more generous breakfast buffet than the slightly more comfortable and equally convenient *Neptun*, Obala maršala Tita (☎052/400-800, ⓕ431-351, ⓦwww.riviera.hr; ❻). The remainder of Poreč's hotels are in the big complexes north and south of town, and are virtually indistinguishable from one other apart from the two four-star places: the *Parentium* in Zelena Laguna, 5km south of town (☎411-500, ⓕ451-536, ⓦwww.plavalaguna.hr; ❻), and the *Pical* 3km to the north (☎052/407-000, ⓕ451-242, ⓦwww.riviera.hr; ❼). The hourly Plava Laguna bus from the bus station runs through Zelena Laguna en route. The closest **campsites** are *Zelena Laguna* at Zelena Laguna (☎052/410-541, ⓕ410-601) and, further south, *Bijela Uvala* (☎052/410-551, ⓕ410-600), also reachable by the Plava Laguna bus. The diving school at Plava Laguna (ⓦwww.plava-laguna-diving.hr) can sort out everything from beginners' courses (2050Kn for three days) to underwater expeditions to local caves and wrecks.

There are several agencies in the streets just north of the tourist office offering **rooms** (❷) and **apartments** (❷), most of which are in the modern

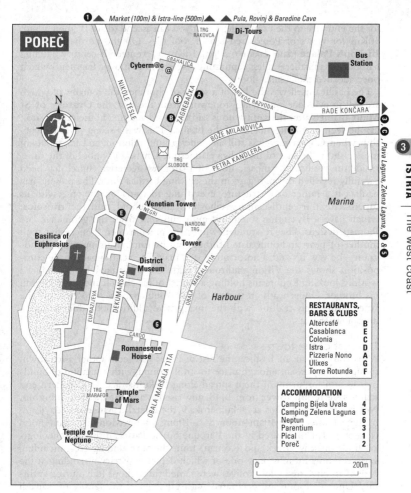

suburbs which fringe the old town; two of the best firms are DI-tours,
Prvomajska 2 (☎052/432-100, ⓦwww.di-tours.hr); and Istra-line, Partizanska
4 (☎052/451-067, ⓦwww.isra.com/istraline). Beware that stays of less than
four nights are subject to a thirty percent surcharge.

The Town and around

Poreč's star turn is the **Basilica of Euphrasius** (Eufrazijeva basilika; daily
7am–8pm; free), situated in the centre of the town just off Ljubljanska. This
sixth-century Byzantine basilica has incandescent mosaics that are comparable
with the celebrated examples at Ravenna, and is actually the centre of a religious complex, originally created by Bishop Euphrasius between 535 and 550,
which includes a bishop's palace, atrium, baptistry and campanile. Entry is
through the **Atrium**, an arcaded courtyard whose walls incorporate ancient
bits of masonry, although it was heavily restored in the last century. On the west
side of the atrium is the octagonal **Baptistry** (Baptisterijum), bare inside save

for the entrance to the campanile, which you can ascend (daily 10am–6.30pm; 10Kn) for views of Poreč's red-brown roof tiles. On the north side is the **Bishop's Palace** (daily 10am–6.30pm; 10Kn), a seventeenth-century building harbouring a further – if less captivating – selection of mosaic fragments which once adorned the basilica floor.

The basilica itself was the last of a series of churches, the remains of which are still in evidence. Surviving stonework from the first, the **Oratory of St Maur** (named after the saint who is said to have lived in a house on the site), can be seen on the north side of the basilica. This was a secret place of worship when Christianity was still an underground religion, and fragments of mosaic show the sign of the fish, a clandestine Christian symbol of the time. Inside the basilica, the mosaic floor of a later, less secretive church has been carefully revealed through gaps in the existing basilica floor. The present-day basilica is a rather bare structure, everything focusing on the apse with its superb late thirteenth-century ciborium and, behind this, the **mosaics**, which have a Byzantine solemnity quite different from the geometric late Roman designs. They're studded with semi-precious gems, encrusted with mother-of-pearl and punctuated throughout by Euphrasius' personal monogram – he was, it's said, a notoriously vain man. The central part of the composition shows the Virgin enthroned with Child, flanked by St Maur, a worldly-looking Euphrasius holding a model of his church and, next to him, his brother. Underneath are scenes of the Annunciation and Visitation, the latter surprisingly realistic, with the imaginative addition of a doltish, eavesdropping servant.

The rest of the town

After you've seen the basilica, the rest of Poreč can seem rather a let down, though it's a pleasant enough place to stroll around, with a handful of buildings to aim for, many of them spread along Dekumanska. At its eastern end stands a **Venetian tower** from 1448, now used as a venue for art exhibitions. Not far from the basilica at Dekumanska 9, the **District Museum** (Zavičajni muzej; summer daily 10am–noon & 6–10pm; winter Mon–Fri 10am–noon & 4–6pm; 10Kn), housed in the Baroque Sinčić Palace, displays archeological finds (mainly Greek and Roman) from the surrounding area, including various Roman tombstones, one of which depicts a patrician standing at the base of an olive tree – local olives were famed throughout Italy during antiquity. Upstairs, rooms are decorated with portraits of the family of Rinaldi Carli – Venetian ambassador to Constantinople in the late 1600s – dressed in Ottoman garb. Walk south towards the end of the peninsula and you'll find the distinctive thirteenth-century building with an unusual projecting wooden balcony known as the **Romanesque House** (Romanička kuća) – it's now another venue for art shows (mid–June to mid–Sept: daily 10am–noon & 6–10pm; free). Just beyond here, **Trg Marafor** occupies the site of the Roman forum and still preserves remains of temples to Mars and Neptune. Little is known about these, and they're now not much more than heaps of rubble.

The **beaches** around the old town, such as they are, are generally crowded and unpleasant, and it's better to take a boat from the harbour (daily 7am–11pm; every 30min; 12Kn) to the island of **Sveti Nikola**, though this too gets busy with sunbathers from its pricey hotel. Alternatively, staying on the mainland, walk south beyond the marina, where pathways head along a rocky coastline shaded by gnarled pines to reach several rocky coves; you'll eventually end up at Zelena Laguna, where there are concreted bathing areas.

The Baredine Cave

One of the most popular excursions from Poreč is to the **Baredine Cave** (Jama Baredine; daily: Jul–Aug 9.30am–7pm; May, June & Sept 10am–5pm; April & Oct 10am–4pm; 40Kn; ⊛www.istra.com/baredine), a series of limestone caverns 7km northeast of town just off the road to **Višnjan** – it's well signed if you're driving. During a 45-minute tour, guides will lead you through five exquisite chambers of dangling stalagtites and limestone curtains, and will also delight in telling you the legend of thirteenth-century lovers Gabriel and Milka, who got lost down here and died looking for each other. You'll probably also get to see a couple of captive specimens of the *Proteus anguineus*, a kind of salamander which is indigenous to the karst caves of Croatia and Slovenia, and looks like a pale-bodied worm with legs.

Eating and drinking

There's a decent sprinkling of places to **eat** in the old town. *Altercafé*, Zagrebačka, has reasonable croissants, sandwiches, pastries and pizza slices, while *Pizzeria Nono*, further up the same street at Zagrebačka 4, has cheap, good-quality pizza, salads and pasta dishes. The best place for traditional Istrian fare is the ever-popular *Istra*, on the corner of Obala maršala Tita and Bože Milanovića (reservations a good idea on summer weekends; ☎052/434-636), which offers top-of-the-range seafood including the local speciality *jastog sa rezancima* (lobster with pasta noodles), meaty alternatives such as *svinjski but* (roast pork in a rich sauce) as well as cheaper lunchtime favourites like *fuži* and *maneštra* (Istrian bean soup). *Ulixes*, Decumanus 2 (☎052/451-132), is another place which serves up top-quality seafood, either in a stone-clad interior stacked with rustic implements, or on an outdoor terrace in a walled garden. For picnic ingredients or self-catering supplies, head for the **market** just off Trg J. Rakovca.

Despite Poreč's status as a package paradise, the **drinking** scene remains remarkably old-fashioned, with a visit to one of the innumerable *slastičarnice* for ice cream and coffee providing the main source of after-dinner entertainment for many. There's less in the way of characterful cafés and bars, and the town can appear disastrously dead by the end of August, when the high-spending peak-season crowd is replaced by visitors of more modest means. The café-bars on Trg Mirafor are currently the fashionable places to hang out if the weather's good; otherwise, try the Bogey-memorabilia-fixated *Casablanca*, on Eufrazijeva, which crowds a healthy mixture of tourists and locals into its tiny bar area; or *Torre Rotunda*, housed in a medieval tower on the Riva, an atmospheric place with snug seating inside the tower wall, and a panoramic terrace on top. The best place to drink late, dance, and catch occasional live bands is *Colonia*, an open-air disco-bar set among pine trees, 1km east of the centre on the path to Plava Laguna.

Novigrad, Umag and Savudrija

Eighteen kilometres north of Poreč, and reached by regular bus, **NOVIGRAD** (Cittanova) is another pleasant peninsula-bound place with a Venetian-style campanile spearing skywards from its town centre, although it's lost most of its old buildings apart from a few toothy sections of town wall. There are a couple of privately run hotels that have more character than the accommodation in Poreč, and the atmosphere is more laid back all-round – this is one place on the west coast where you can safely wander the streets without being trampled to death by hordes of ice-cream-wielding promenaders. At the tip of the peninsula, the parish **Church of St Pelagius** (Crkva svetog Pelagija) was the seat of a bishop until the mid-nineteenth century, and still boasts a few luxuriant Baroque furnishings – notably the balustraded altar supporting a parade of porky cherubs. The crypt in which the bones of St Pelagius are kept is usually locked, but a grilled window provides glimpses of a vaulted eleventh-century ceiling supported by a cluster of stout columns. For **bathing**, the stretch of rock-and-concrete beach on the south side of town is outshone by the wonderful stretch of coastline to the north, where rocky reefs backed by woods are more attractive and less crowded.

Practicalities

Novigrad's **bus station** is 500m short of the town centre, where you'll find a helpful **tourist office** on the north side of the peninsula at Porporella 1 (daily 8am–8pm; ☏052/757-075, ⊛www.istra.com/novigrad). There are plentiful **private rooms** (❶–❷) in and around the centre: two accommodation agencies worth trying are Montak, in the bus station building at Murvi bb (☏052/757-603, ⊛www.montakso.hr), and Rakamtrade, midway between the bus station and the centre at ul. Mlinska 45 (☏052/757-047, ⊛www.rakam-trade.hr). *Torci 18*, Torci 43 (☏052/757-799, ⊛www.nautico.hr; ❹), is a family-run **pension** situated at the end of the peninsula behind the sea wall, offering prim en-suite rooms with TV grouped around a central restaurant-filled courtyard. *Cittar*, beside the entrance to the old town at Venecijanski prolaz bb (☏052/757-737, ⊛www.cittar.hr; ❻), was one of the first privately owned **hotels** established in Croatia and it shows: the rooms come with tasteful decor and wooden floors, TV, minibar, air conditioning and en-suite bath. There's a big area of packagey hotels just southeast of town alongside a big woodland **campsite** full of squirrels, the *Sirena* (☏052/757-159, ✉camping@laguna-novigrad.hr).

   Eating in Novigrad is generally first-rate, but comes at a price. The restaurant of the *Torci 18* does a decent range of meat and fish dishes, although *Mandrač*, on the harbour, is better, with quality seafood including grilled scallops (*jakopove kapice*) and dishes with lobster (*jastog*). Hidden away in the backstreets at Zidine 5, *Damir i Ornela* is something of a cult place to eat hereabouts, serving up simple but excellently prepared fish dishes, including some Japanese-influenced raw-fish recipes.

Umag and Savudrija

North of Novigrad, one road darts inland towards the hill town of **Buje** (see p.182), while the main coastal route forges across low hills crisscrossed with vineyards, passing the enormous **campsite** of *Ladin Gaj*, sprawled resplendently round its own stretch of coast some 7km north of town. Eight kilometres further on, **UMAG** (Umago) is typical of the settlements of Istria's west coast: a once attractive town, set on a tiny peninsula, now almost completely given over to the holiday business with its merciless profusion of concrete lidos, holiday chalets and autocamps. Most of the development is to the north of town, a long string of hotels and tourist settlements connected to Umag's centre by a regular miniature train. It's a better idea to go straight on to **SAVUDRIJA** (Punta di Salvore), a small fishing village about 5km away on the very northwestern tip of the Istrian peninsula. **Rooms** (❶) can be had through Istratours in the centre of the village, and there's a large **campsite** shaded by pines and with some fair stretches of beach.

Inland Istria

You don't need to travel away from the sea for long before the hotels and flash apartments give way to rustic villages of heavy grey-brown stone, many of them perched high on hillsides, a legacy of the times when a settlement's defensive position was more important than its access to cultivable land. The landscape is varied, with fields and vineyards squeezed between pine forests and orchards of oranges and olives. It's especially attractive in autumn, when the hillsides turn a dappled green and auburn, and the hill villages appear to hover eerily above the early morning mists.

Istria's hilltop settlements owe their appearance to the region's borderland status. Occupied since Neolithic times, they were fortified and refortified by successive generations, serving as strongholds on the shifting frontier between Venice and Hungary, or Christendom and the Ottoman Turks. They suffered serious depopulation in the last century, first as local Italians emigrated in the 1940s and 1950s, then as the rush for jobs on the coast began in the 1960s. Empty houses in these half-abandoned towns have been offered to painters, sculptors and musicians in an attempt to keep life going on the hilltops and stimulate tourism at the same time – hence the reinvention of Motovun and Grožnjan in particular as cultural centres.

Istria's administrative capital, **Pazin**, is the hub of the bus network and, although it's the least attractive of the inland towns, it's the nearest base for visiting the fifteenth-century frescoes in the nearby village of **Beram**. Of the hill settlements, **Motovun** and **Buzet** are accessible by bus from Pazin or Pula, but you'll need your own transport to make side-trips to the likes of **Grožnjan**, **Oprtalj** and **Hum**. The train line from Pula to Divača in Slovenia (where you change for Ljubljana or Zagreb) can be useful, visiting Pazin before passing close to Hum, Roč and Buzet, although a certain amount of walking is required to get to the last three.

The mass-tourist industry is much less evident here than on the coast: there are hotels in Motovun, Istarske Toplice and Buzet, and an increasing amount of the cosy farmhouse accommodation that the area seems to be made for. However, the relatively unspoiled nature of inland Istria has made it a magnet for aspirant second-home owners – cries of "Istria: the new Tuscany" are beginning to reverberate around central Europe, and real-estate prices are going through the roof as a result.

Pazin and Beram

Lying in a fertile bowl bang in the middle of the Istrian peninsula, unassuming **PAZIN** is an unlikely regional capital. A relatively unindustrialized provincial town, it was chosen following World War II by Yugoslavia's new rulers, who were eager to establish an Istrian administration far away from the Italianate coastal towns – the choice of Pazin was a deliberate slap in the face for cosmopolitan Pula. Although fairly bland compared to Istria's other inland towns, Pazin does boast a couple of attractions, most notably its medieval castle and the limestone gorge below, and it's also a useful base from which to visit the renowned frescoes in the nearby church at Beram.

Arriving at Pazin's **train** and **bus** stations, it's a straightforward downhill walk along the tree-lined Šetalište Pazinske Gimnazije towards the inoffensive, largely low-rise centre, beyond which rises the **castle**, a stern ninth-century structure, remodelled many times since, and one of the main reasons why Pazin never fell to the Venetians. Inside there's the **Istrian Ethnographic Museum** (Etnografski muzej Istre; summer Mon–Sat 10am–6pm, Sun 10am–3pm; winter Mon–Sat 10am–3pm; 12Kn; ⓦ www.emi.hr) with a fine collection of traditional Istrian costumes housed in atmospheric medieval galleries, along with a wide-ranging display of rural handicrafts and a mock-up of a kitchen featuring the traditional Istrian *kamin* (hearth), a fire laid on an open brick platform around which the cooking pots were arranged.

The castle overhangs the gorge of the River Fojba below, where a huge abyss sucks water into an underground waterway which resurfaces towards the coast. This chasm was supposed to have prompted Dante's description of the gateway to Hell in his *Inferno*, and inspired Jules Verne to propel one of his characters – Matthias Sandorf from the eponymous book, published in 1885 – over the side of the castle and into the pit. In the book, Sandorf manages to swim along the subterranean river until he reaches the coast – a feat probably destined to remain forever in the realms of fiction. Verne himself never came to Pazin, contenting himself with the pictures of the castle posted to him by the mayor. Back in the town centre, the plain exterior of **St Nicholas's Church** (Crkva svetog Nikole) conceals a thirteenth-century core; the sanctuary vaulting is filled with late fifteenth-century frescoes, mostly showing Old Testament scenes, although there's a fine depiction of a sword-wielding St Michael in the central panel.

Pazin's **tourist office**, just short of the castle at Franine i Jurine 14 (summer daily 8am–6pm; winter Mon–Fri 8am–3pm; ⓣ & ⓕ052/622-460, ⓦ www.tzpazin.hr), can help with town plans, information on central Istria, and accommodation in private **rooms** (❶) in Pazin and around. Otherwise **accommodation** in Pazin is limited to the *Motel Lovac*, Šime Kurelića 4 (ⓣ052/624-324, ⓕ624-219; ❸), just off the main road to Poreč at the western end of town, but within easy walking distance of the centre. For **food**, the *Fontana*, a few doors up from the tourist office at Franine i Jurine 6, is an unspectacular but cheap source of pizzas, sandwiches and other snacks; while the *Pod Lipom*, Trg Pod Lipom 2 (5min east of St Nicholas's church, along Muntriljska and behind the town bowling court), is a traditional restaurant popular with the locals, with cheap lunch dishes like *maneštra* and *fuži* chalked up on a board, and a regular menu of more substantial meaty fare.

Pazin's tourist office acts as the nerve centre of the town's **Jules Verne Club**, which publishes a newsletter and organizes various events, including a Jules Verne Day in Pazin on June 25. You can become a member by "donating a book or some other material connected to Jules Verne for the club collection" (information from the tourist office or ⓦ www.ice.hr/davors/jvclub.htm).

Beram

Six kilometres west of Pazin, just off the road to Poreč and Motovun, **BERAM** is an unspoilt hilltop village with moss-covered stone walls and some of the finest sacred art in the region. One kilometre northeast of the village is the **Chapel of Our Lady of the Rocks** (Crkvica svete Marije na škriljinah), a diminutive Gothic church with a set of frescoes dating from 1475, signed by local artist Vincent of Kastav. The key (*ključ*) to the chapel is kept by a villager, usually at house no. 22 or no. 33 in the centre (there are no street names). If you ask in Pazin, the tourist office may ring ahead to ensure that there's someone waiting in Beram for you. It's polite to give a small sum of money to the keyholder in lieu of an entrance fee.

Of the many well-executed New Testament scenes which cover the chapel interior, two large frescoes stand out. The marvellous, eight-metre-long equestrian pageant of the Adoration of the Kings reveals a wealth of fine detail – distant ships, mountains, churches and wildlife – strongly reminiscent of early Flemish painting, while on the west wall a Dance of Death is illustrated with macabre clarity against a blood-red background: skeletons clasp scythes and blow trumpets, weaving in and out of a Chaucerian procession of citizens led by the pope. A rich merchant brings up the rear, greedily clinging to his possessions while indicating the money with which he hopes to buy his freedom.

Dvigrad and Svetvinčenat

Southwest of Pazin, the main road and rail routes to Pula forge across a mixed landscape of woodland, cornfields and Mediterranean scrub. While you're unlikely to want to spend the night in any of the places along the way, a couple of them merit a stop-off.

Twenty kilometres out of Pazin, the frumpy town of **KANFANAR** was founded in the mid-seventeenth century by refugees from nearby **DVIGRAD**, a walled city suddenly abandoned by citizens demoralized by an outbreak of plague and raids by Uskok pirates. A cluster of moody grey ruins surrounded by farmland and forest, Dvigrad is nowadays a hugely evocative site, and well worth embarking on a half-day trip to see. It's reasonably easy to get to, with Pula–Pazin trains, as well as buses from Rovinj to Žminjg and Pazin, all stopping off in Kanfanar. Head west out of town along the Rovinj road, and turn right onto a well-signed minor road which leads downhill to the ruins (a three-kilometre walk in total). Despite its ruined state Dvigrad is immediately impressive, a huge crown of jagged grey battlements guarded by two massive towers. A path curls round one side of the battlements, passes through a ruined gate and leads into the city, its rough paving stones now overgrown with weeds. At its northern end looms the shell of the **Church of St Sofia** (Crkva svete Sofije), a twelfth-century basilica. The road on the western side of the fortress zigzags up the hillside, affording impressive views back towards the grizzled ruins.

Five kilometres southeast of Kanfanar, the tiny town of **SVETVINČENAT** (known in local dialect as "Savičenta") lies just off the main Pula-bound road and rail routes, but is well worth a detour if you're a fan of well-proportioned Mediterranean town squares. Svetvinčenat's is certainly among the most attractive in Istria, watched over by the trefoil facade of the **Church of the Assumption** (Crkva uznesenja), which harbours several mannerist altar paintings by sixteenth-century Venetians. Off to the left, the **castle** of the Grimani family sports a pair of grizzled-looking towers; unfortunately it can't be visited unless you attend one of the summer concerts held in its spacious courtyard. A fifteenth-century town hall and loggia complete the ensemble.

Gračišće and around

A much quieter road heads southeast from Pazin towards **Labin** (see p.187), passing through rolling, vineyard-covered hills and a succession of quiet hill villages. The fortified settlement of **GRAČIŠĆE**, 6km out of town, is perhaps the most interesting of these, its main gate leading through to a knot of gravelly streets and grey houses. Just inside the gate is the porticoed **Church of St Mary-on-the-Square** (Crkva svete Marije na Placu), whose fifteenth-century frescoes are usually visible through grilled windows even when the door is locked. The centrepiece is a stunning Adoration, in which mounted figures in medieval garb are greeted by a radiant Madonna and Child. A building behind the church sports a trio of Gothic windows, all that's left of the **summer palace of the bishops** of **Pićan**, a now-insignificant village 3km down the road, which was an important ecclesiastical centre in the Middle Ages (quite why its bishops chose to spend their summer holidays here must remain a mystery). A few steps beyond, the terrace behind the parish church provides terrific views of the surrounding countryside, with the western flanks of Mount Učka presiding over a landscape of sandy hills and mixed evergreen and deciduous forest.

There's nowhere to stay in Gračišće itself, but a couple of excellent farmhouse **B&Bs** lie in the vicinity. Head towards Pazin and turn left into the village of **Gržići** to find *Stari Kostanj*, Gržići 34 (☎052/687-037, ⊛www.agroistra .com/stari-kostanj), which has a rambling three- or four-person apartment in a stone barn set in meadows (420Kn per night). Slightly further afield, *Dol*, 5km east of Gračišće at Glogorički Dol 6 (☎052/684-625; ❷), offers a series of cosy en-suite rooms, each with wooden floors and ceiling beams, and a balcony overlooking the farmyard. There's a restaurant serving up Istrian staples – most of what you eat here will come from the owner's farm – and a mini-waterfall in the grounds, and the surrounding area is great for walks. Getting to **Glogorički Dol** can be a tricky business, however: either head southeast from Gračišće, turn left at **Zajci**, and head north for 5km; or double back to Pazin, make for Cerovlje, and head east through Glogorica.

Motovun and Oprtalj

Fifteen kilometres northwest of Pazin is perhaps the most famous of the Istrian hill towns, **MOTOVUN** (Montona), an unwieldy clump of houses straddling a green wooded hill, high above a patchwork of wheatfields and vineyards. The place has a genuine medieval charm, exuding a tranquil nobility unequalled in Istria. Like so many towns in Istria, Motovun was predominantly Italian-speaking until the 1940s (when racing driver Mario Andretti was born here), after which most of the inhabitants left for Italy. The problem of depopulation was partly solved by turning Motovun into an artists' colony – the godfather of Croatian naive art, Krsto Hegedušić (see p.115), was one of the first painters to move here in the 1960s – and several studios and craft shops open their doors to tourists over the summer.

A winding road zigzags its way up from the valley floor, eventually passing through two gates which breach the stout ramparts surrounding the old town. The first of the gates has a display of stone reliefs of Venetian lions inside the arch, while the second, 100m beyond, leads directly out onto a main square fronted by the Renaissance **St Stephen's Church** (Crkva svetog Stjepana), topped by a campanile whose crenellated top looks like a row of jagged teeth. The town's water supply used to be kept in a vast tank beneath the square, hence the medieval well in front of the church bearing a relief of Motovun's skyline with its five towers. At the far end of the square, a path leads to a promenade around the town battlements made up of two concentric walls with a tiny moat (nowadays dry) in between. From here there are fantastic views over the Mirna Valley and surrounding countryside, which produces some of the finest Istrian wines – Teran and Malvasija are among the better known.

There are five **buses** daily to Motovun from Pazin in July and August, although this dwindles to one a day out of season. The twice daily Pula–Buzet bus picks up and drops off at the bottom of Motovun's hill. Up on the main square, the *Kaštel* **hotel** (☎052/681-735 & 681-607, ⊛www.hotel-kastel -motovun.hr; ❸) offers simple en-suite rooms in a building of medieval origins, and also harbours a café and restaurant. All accommodation in the entire region is likely to be booked solid during the **Motovun Film Festival**

(@www.motovunfilmfestival.com), which usually straddles a long weekend at the end of July or beginning of August. Since its inception in 1999 the festival has established itself as Croatia's premier cinematic event, with feature films (European art-house movies for the most part) premiered on an open-air screen in the main town square. Featuring a minimum of segregation between stars and public, the festival is also one of the key social events of the summer, with thousands of celebrants ascending Motovun's hill – although most are here to enjoy the 24-hour party atmosphere rather than the films.

Oprtalj

Immediately north of Motovun the road reaches the Mirna Valley and a major crossroads: the right fork heads east towards Buzet; the left fork makes for Buje and the coast. Straight on, a minor road runs through the village of **Livade** before winding steeply and tortuously through thick forest to **OPRTALJ** (Portole), which straddles a grassy ridge high above the plain. The village is similar to Motovun but altogether more deserted: half its houses are in ruins, and tufts of grass grow from the walls of the rest. Both the fifteenth-century **St Mary's Church** (Crkva svete Marije) in the village centre, and the sixteenth-century **Chapel of St Rock** (Crkvica svetog Roka) at the entrance to town have some interesting fresco fragments if you can gain access (ask for the keys in the village); otherwise it's a good place for a peaceful wander and a quiet drink in the *Café Volta* near the town gate – which also has a couple of **rooms** (@052/644-216, @klaudio.ipsa@pu.hinet.hr; @).

Grožnjan

Eight kilometres west of the Mirna Valley crossroads, a side-road darts up towards **GROŽNJAN** (Grisignana), another hill village which was given a new lease of life when many of its abandoned properties were offered to artists and musicians as studios. There's also a summer school for young musicians, the Jeunesses Musicales Croatia (Hrvatska glazbena mladež), many of whom take part in outdoor concerts organized as part of the **Grožnjan Musical Summer** (Grožnjansko glazbeno ljeto; @www.hgm.hr), which takes place every August. Indeed high summer is the best time to come, when most of the artists are actually in residence and a smattering of galleries and gift shops open their doors. Outside this time, Grožnjan can be exceedingly quiet, but it's an undeniably attractive spot, with its jumble of shuttered houses made from rough-hewn, honey-brown stone, covered in creeping plants. Standing at the centre of the town is the **Church of St Vitus and St Modestus** (Crkva svetog Vida i Modesta), a largely unadorned eighteenth-century affair which harbours a much older pair of choir stalls, each carved with exuberant floral squiggles, and a lively modern altar painting of martyrs Vitus and Modestus being thrown to a collection of snarling felines. Slightly downhill from here, the graceful arches of a Renaissance **loggia** form one side of a tiny, gently sloping square, which looks out on what used to be the main town gate. Nearby battlements command superb views of the surrounding countryside, with Motovun perched on its hilltop to the southeast, and the ridge of Mount Učka dominating the horizon beyond it.

Unless you have your own transport, Grožnjan is difficult to get to: catching a Buzet–Buje bus as far as the hamlet of Bijele Zemlje, then walking uphill to Grožnjan via a signed minor road (3km), seems to be your best bet. Should you wish to **stay**, the *Černac* family, right in the centre at V. Gortan 5 (@052/776-122; @), offers a clutch of rustically decorated rooms and apartments, and also sells home-made olive oil, wine and *rakija*; while the Jeunesses Musicales Croatia sometimes has rooms available in July and August (☎052/776-106; ❶). *Art Café*, just east of the church, is a chic place to eat and drink, its terrace offering expansive views down the valley.

Buje

Proceeding northwest from Grožnjan towards the Slovene border, you'll pass through the much larger town of **BUJE** (Buie), its old quarter piled up on a hill with patches of newer development below. Buje was known as the "spy of Istria" for its hilltop site, and still commands an invigorating panorama, the cobbled streets looking out over fertile fields to the distant sea. The town ramparts, dating from the fifteenth to the seventeenth centuries, enclose a warren-like medieval centre which spreads uphill from the main road. Just down from the old town gate, the **Ethnographic Museum** (Etnografska zbirka; summer Mon–Sat 9am–noon & 5–8pm; 5Kn), displays a musty collection of kitchen utensils, wine presses and hand-operated looms. Roughly opposite, the **Church of the Madonna of Mercy** (Crkva majke milosrđa) contains a fine collection of Baroque paintings, including a series of eight bible scenes by eighteenth-century Venetian painter Gasparo della Vecchia. From here, alleyways wind uphill to the parish **Church of St Servolo** (Crkva svetog Cervula), built in the sixteenth century on the site of a Roman temple – bits of salvaged Roman masonry can still be seen poking out of the church's unfinished facade.

Buses pick up and drop off at the main crossroads through town, a few steps away from the **tourist office** at Istarska 2 (mid-June to mid-Sept Mon–Fri 8am–6pm, Sat 8am–2pm; ☎052/772-122, ✆www.tzg-buje.hr). There's no **accommodation** in Buje itself, although *Volpia*, 3km northwest of town just off the road to Portorož (follow signs to Slovenia and take the turn-off for the village of Volpija; ☎052/777-425, ✆777-424, ✆www.agroturizam-volpia.com; ❸), is one of the best rural hotels in the region. In a newly renovated stone house, it offers a supremely restful ambience with rooms decorated in contemporary rustic style: spanking new wooden floors, chunky wardrobes, and spacious bathrooms.

For **eating**, *Konoba Oliva*, just off Buje's main street on Via Giussepe Verdi 9, is a good place to sample local pasta dishes and fresh seafood on a shaded terrace. Otherwise the best options are out of town: the restaurant of the Volpia prides itself on traditional meat and fish recipes; while the *Konoba Astarea*, in the village of Brtonigla 5km southwest of Buje (it's right by the main road to Novigrad; ☎052/774-384) serves up some of the tastiest food in Istria, with meats prepared under a *peka* – a metal lid covered with embers. Buje stands at the centre of an important vine-growing area, the harvest of which is celebrated during the **Grape Festival** (Praznik grožđa), when parades, open-air concerts and wine-guzzling span a long weekend in mid-September.

Buzet, Roč, Hum and around

East of Motovun, the road to Buzet follows the course of the Mirna Valley as it gradually narrows, running between wooded crags. Roughly midway between Motovun and Buzet, the small settlement of **ISTARSKE TOPLICE** is inland Istria's most popular health resort, its sulphurous waters famous for alleviating back problems, rheumatism and skin complaints. The local **hotel**, the *Mirna* (☎052/664-300, ✆664-310; ❸), has smallish rooms with bath and TV and is a good base from which to visit the nearby hill towns, although most guests are here for the indoor swimming pool, fed by spring water which emerges ready warmed from the nearby cliffs at a temperature of 35°C.

Truffles: Istria's gold

The woods around Motovun and Buzet are one of Europe's prime hunting grounds for the **truffle** (*tartuf*), a subterranean fungus whose delicate taste – part nutty, part mushroomy, part sweaty sock – have made it a highly prized delicacy among the foodie fraternity. Truffles (which look like small tubers) tend to overpower whatever other ingredients they're mixed with, and so are used very sparingly in cooking – either grated over a freshly cooked dish, or used to give a defining flavour to a sauce.

The truffle-hunting season begins in late September and carries on through the autumn, with locals and their specially trained dogs heading off into the Istrian fog to sniff out the fungus. During this period most of the region's **restaurants** will have at least one truffle-based recipe on the menu, even if only a simple truffle-and-pasta dish or a truffle *fritaja* (omelette). Truffle dishes offered outside this period will most probably use preserved (rather than fresh) truffles – definitely worth trying, but not quite as mouthwatering as the just-unearthed variety.

To mark the start of the season, **Truffle Days** (Dani Tartufa) are organized in various places in the Motovun/Buzet region throughout September; these might involve truffle-tasting events, live music, or just lots of good-natured drinking. Best known of these fungus-fixated fiestas is the **Buzetska Subotina** ("Buzet Saturday"), when an enormous truffle omelette is fried up on the main square and then scoffed by an army of hungry celebrants (see below). You can buy truffles and truffle-based products throughout the year in the specialist shops run by Zigante (⊛ www.zigantetartufi .com) – they have outlets at J.B. Tita 12, Buje; Trg Fontana, Buzet; Livade 7, Livade; and Smareglina 7, Pula.

Buzet

From Istarske Toplice it's only 10km northeast to **BUZET**, the second largest town in the Istrian interior, whose original old hilltop settlement quietly decays on the heights above the River Mirna, while the bulk of the population lives in the new town below. Though it's not as pretty as Motovun or Grožnjan, Buzet has more accommodation and is a good base from which to explore the region. The town's importance as a truffle-hunting centre is celebrated by the **Buzetska Subotina** festival ("Buzet Saturday"; usually the first weekend of Sept), when an enormous truffle omelette is cooked and shared out, and local pop-rock bands play on a pair of outdoor stages – the tourist office has details. Another local speciality is *biska*, a mistletoe-flavoured brandy available in local hostelries; it can also be bought direct, along with other herbal firewaters, from Eliksir (Mon–Sat 11am–2pm & 5–10pm, Sun 11am–1pm), Vidaci 25, 3km out of town on the road to Cerovlje.

Old Buzet's cobbled streets and ruined buildings seem a world away from the new quarter down on the valley floor. A **plaque** affixed to a house on one of its tiny squares commemorates Stipan Konzul Istranin, a sixteenth-century Croatian writer active in the Reformation in Germany, and the first person to translate the New Testament into Croatian. The **Town Museum** nearby (Gradski muzej; Mon–Fri 12.30–3.30pm; 5Kn) has a small collection of Roman gravestones and a display of folk costumes, particularly strong on the functional wool and hemp garments worn by the hardy villagers of the **Ćićarija**, the ridge to the east which separates Istria from Slovenia. There's an expansive view from what remains of Buzet's ramparts of the Mirna Valley below, and east over lush green hills to the imposing grey ridge of the Ćićarija.

Buses arrive on Trg fontana, a small square in the new town. About 200m east of here, the **tourist office**, on the second floor of the town hall at II Istarske brigade 2 (Mon–Fri 8am–3pm; ☎ & ⓕ052/662-343), has information on private rooms (❷), most of which are in out-of-town farmhouses. The *Fontana* **hotel**, Trg fontana 1 (☎052/662-466, ⓕ662-306; ❷), is a plain but tolerable three-storey place; while the smaller *Sun Sport Motel* (☎052/663-140; ❸), on the corner of Sportska and Riječka just northeast of the tourist office, offers cosier, brighter, more modern en-suite rooms, although the ground-floor café can be noisy at weekends.

For **eating**, most local foodies head up to the *Toklarija* 5km south of town in **Sovinjsko polje** (see p.186). In town, you're limited to the *Bistro Panorama*, just off the old town's main square, which serves up grills and *fuži-* and *njoki*-based standards in a dining room with great views of the new town below. The bar at the Sun Sport motel is the liveliest place in town for a **drink**.

Roč

About 10km east of Buzet, framed against the backdrop of the limestone wall of the Ćićarija, the dainty village of **ROČ** sits snugly behind sixteenth-century walls so low that the place looks more like a child's sandcastle than an erstwhile medieval strongpoint. Roč has a strong **folk music** tradition, with performing skills passed down from one generation to the next, and almost the entire population is involved in some capacity or other with the local folk music society, Istarski željezničar ("Istrian railwayman"), which has a brass section, male and female choirs and an accordion band. Most members of the latter are devoted exponents of the Trieština, an archaic form of accordion which features push-buttons instead of a keyboard, and is rarely found outside Istria and northeastern Italy. The best time to catch them is during the international accordion festival (Z armoniku v Roč), which takes place on the second weekend in May: the tourist office in Buzet will have details.

With their neat rows of sturdy stone farmhouses, the narrow lanes of Roč provide a wonderful environment in which to savour the rustic atmosphere of eastern Istria. There's a small display of **Roman tombstones** inside the arch of the main gate into town, and the Romanesque **St Anthony's Church** (Crkva svetog Antuna) in the centre, an ancient, barn-like structure lurking behind an enormous chestnut tree and sporting an unusually asymmetrical bell tower.

Buzet–Rijeka **buses** will drop you off at the Roč turn-off 500m from the village, while the **train** station (on the Pula–Buzet line) is about 1500m east of the village. If you fancy staying in a local household, Marina Paladin, Roč 30 (☎052/666-716; ❷), and Drago Cerovac, Roč 58 (☎052/666-481; ❷), both rent out **rooms** – the latter is also the only reliable place in the Buzet region from which to rent out bikes (100Kn per day). For **food**, *Ročka konoba* in the centre of the village is a good place for asparagus and truffles in season, as well as the regular repertoire of *ombolo*, *kobasice* and *fuži*.

If you've got your own transport, you can follow the road leading northwest out of Roč to get up onto the summit of the Ćićarija ridge (follow signs to the village of Nugla, pass through it, and keep going for about 3km). Crossing heathland covered in conifers and sub-alpine meadows, the road ends up at **Raspadalica**, a local beauty spot which serves as an ideal launch-pad for local hang-gliding enthusiasts, and offers fine views to everyone else. There's a superb panorama of the Mirna valley, with Buzet down below and the hill town of Motovun in the distance.

Hum

Just 6km east of Roč, a minor road leads south through rolling pastures towards the minuscule settlement of Hum. The road itself is known as the **Glagolitic**

Alley (Aleja glagoljaša) after its series of open-air concrete sculptures by Želimir Janeš illustrating themes connected with Glagolitic (see box on p.222), an archaic form of Slavonic writing which was kept alive by priests in both Istria and the islands of the Kvarner Gulf before finally succumbing to Latin script in the nineteenth century. Positioned by the roadside every kilometre or so, the sculptures mostly take the form of Glagolitic characters – seductively decorative forms that look like a cross between Cyrillic and Klingon.

Heaped up on a hill surrounded by grasslands and broken up by deciduous forest, **HUM** is the self-proclaimed "smallest town in the world", since it's preserved all the attributes – walls, gate, church, campanile – that a town is supposed to possess, despite its population having dwindled to a current total of just seventeen. Originally fortified by the Franks in the eleventh century, Hum was a relatively prosperous place under the Aquileian Patriarchs and the Venetians, and it still looks quite an imposing place as you pass through a town gate topped by monumental, castellated bell tower. Beyond, the oversized, neo-Baroque **Church of the Blessed Virgin Mary** (Crkva blažene djevice Marije), built in 1802 as the last gasp of urban development in a shrinking town, lords it over a settlement which now amounts to two one-metre-wide streets paved with irregular, grassed-over cobbles, and lined by chunky grey-brown farmhouses. One of the latter holds a small **museum** (daily 11am–7pm; free), which displays essays and poems written in Glagolitic by local kids and sells souvenirs – including locally made honey, wine and *biska* brandy. Just outside the town walls, the Romanesque cemetery **Chapel of St Hieronymous** (Crkvica svetog Jeronima; get the key from *Konoba Hum*, see below) has a number of frescoes dating back to the late twelfth century, which display a melding of Romanesque and Byzantine styles typical of the northern Adriatic in the Middle Ages. As usual, the life of Jesus provides the subject matter: there's a fine Annunciation spanning the arch above the altar, together with a Crucifixion, Pietà and Deposition – the latter bordered by unusual rosettes and floral squiggles – on the walls. Most have been damaged by ancient, Glagolitic graffiti.

It's a bit awkward to reach Hum without your own transport. No buses venture this far, and Hum **train station** is a minor halt 5km downhill just beyond the village of **Erkovčići**. The only **rooms** in Hum are those provided by the Grabar family (℡052/660-004; ❶) – the tourist office in Buzet (see p.183) will act as an intermediary if you can't get through to an English speaker. With your own transport, you might consider staying at *Agroturizam Poljanice* (℡ & ℻052/684-150 & 684-367; ❷), 4km south at the end of a gravel track signed off the minor road to **Borut**. Housed in a farmhouse situated on high ground looking towards Mount Učka, it offers simple rooms with thick stone walls and timber floors, and a full range of local **food**. In Hum, the small but charming *Konoba Hum* serves good Istrian specialities and is very popular in summer.

Kotli

The half-abandoned hamlet of **KOTLI**, 2km northwest of Hum, has become something of a cult destination among summer bathers. It's here that the young River Mirna tumbles through a series of small depressions carved out of the smooth local limestone, creating a sequence of shallow, gurgling pools that some have compared to an open-air jacuzzi – although low water levels often leave visitors wondering what all the fuss is about. Whether you're in swimming mood or not, it's a fine spot for a riverside ramble. On the far side of the river, Kotli itself is a moody clump of farmhouses and barns, half-hidden by runaway vegetation. One of the buildings has been refurbished and turned into a café-restaurant, *Kotlić*, which serves up excellent *maneštra* and other local staples on a shady terrace.

Reached by a minor road that leaves the Glagolitic Alley midway between Roč and Hum, Kotli can also be reached on foot from Buzet (2hr), via a footpath that starts on the south side of town, on the far side of the bridge over the river Mirna – the Buzet tourist office might give you a rough-and-ready hiking map for free.

Sovinjak and Draguć

One of the most scenic routes heading out of Buzet is the one that climbs southwards to the hamlet of Svi Sveti (actually more of a road junction than a place), then follows a mountain ridge towards Cerovlje on the Pazin–Rijeka road. With the Mirna valley to the east and the Butoniga basin way down to the west, the ridge offers some of the best views of inland Istria's lumpish landscape, with pudding-basin hills rising up above a patchwork of forests, vineyards, pumpkin patches and cornfields. To see this landscape at its best, consider a brief detour to the hilltop village of **SOVINJAK**, 6km west of Svi Sveti on a side road that loops back towards Istarske Toplice. There's not much there apart from a corral of ochre and brown houses drawn tightly around a dumpy-looking church, but it's an undeniably beautiful spot, its grassy ramparts looking out over the bottle-green woodland of the Buzet region, busy with truffle-hunters and their dogs during the autumn. Two kilometres east of Sovinjak, the hamlet of Sovinjsko Polje is home to the *Toklarija* (reservations compulsory; ☎052/663-031), one of the nicest restaurants in Istria, if not the whole country. An atmospheric, intimate place housed in a venerable stone building with an oil press in the front room, it's famous for home-made pasta and seasonal local products – asparagus in spring, mushrooms and truffles in autumn – none of which comes cheap. If you can't get a table at *Toklarija*, then try *Konoba Volte*, by the roadside another 2km east in **Kozari**, which has tasty Istrian staples like *fritaja* (omelette with various fillings) and *njoki*, as well as truffle dishes in season.

Returning to Svi Sveti and rejoining the southbound route to Cerovlje brings you after 10km to **DRAGUĆ**, a tiny village stranded among haystacks and cornfields on a thin finger of highland pointing west towards the lowlands of the Mirna basin. At the end of the finger, the fourteenth-century **Chapel of St Rock** (Crkvica svetog Roka) contains frescoes similar to those in Beram, although slightly less well preserved – to get in, ask for the key (*ključ*) in the village square. There's a large Journey of the Magi on left as you enter, with an Annunciation above it, and a Martyrdom of St Sebastian and Flight into Egypt on the right, all rendered in vivid greens and ruddy browns redolent of the surrounding countryside.

The east coast

Compared with the tourist complexes of the west, Istria's east coast is a quiet and undeveloped area with few obvious attractions. East of Pula, the main road to Rijeka heads inland, remaining at a discreet distance from the shoreline for the next 50km. Half an hour out of Pula the road passes through **BARBAN**, a grey, largely forgotten village overlooking Krapan Bay. Barban's only claim to fame is as the home of the annual **Tilting at the Ring** festival (Trka na prstenac; mid-Aug), which involves locals on horseback attempting to spear a ring on the end of a lance; a sporting contest which was widespread through-

out the Mediterranean in the Middle Ages, it only survives in a few places –
notably the Dalmatian town of Sinj (see p.314).

From Barban, the road descends to cross the valley of Raška Draga before
entering the village of **RAŠA**, formerly the southernmost outpost of the Labin
coalfields before they were finally closed in 1999. Built by the Italians in 1937,
Raša still has the feel of a model industrial settlement, with its rows of identical barrack-like houses softened by trailing vines. It also boasts a fine example
of Mussolini-era architecture in **St Barbara's Church** (Crkva svete Barbare –
Barbara being the patron saint of miners), an austere but graceful structure featuring a campanile in the shape of a pithead, and a curving facade representing an upturned coal barrow.

Labin and around

Five kilometres beyond Raša, **LABIN** is divided into two parts, with the original medieval town crowning the hill above, and a twentieth-century suburb,
Podlabin, sprawling across the plain below. Labin was for many years Croatia's
coal-mining capital, and earned itself a place in working-class history in 1921,
when striking miners declared the "Labin Republic" before being pacified by
the Italian authorities. There's precious little sign of mining heritage nowadays
apart from the town museum and the one remaining pithead in Podlabin, the
top of which still bears the word "Tito" proudly spelt out in wrought-iron letters. Subsidence caused by mining led to Labin's old town being partially abandoned in the 1970s and 1980s, although the subsequent decline of the coal
industry, coupled with a thoroughgoing restoration programme, encouraged
people to return. The offer of cheap studio space also encouraged artists to move
to old Labin, and several ateliers and craft shops open their doors in summer. It's
consequently one of the more attractive of Istria's hill towns – all the more so
for its proximity to the beach at Rabac, only forty minutes' walk downhill.

The Town

Pula–Rijeka buses stop at the main bus station in Podlabin, from where it's a
twenty-minute walk up to the main square of the old town, **Titov trg**. From
here, a rough cobbled path leads through the city gate into the heart of the old
town, where steep alleys thread their way among a motley collection of town
houses attractively decked out in ochres, oranges and pinks. Head up the old
town's main street to find the **Church of the Birth of the Blessed Virgin
Mary** (Crkva rođenja blažene djevice Marije), on whose facade a fourteenth-century rose window is upstaged by a seventeenth-century Venetian lion, and by a
bust of patrician Antonio Bollari, who defended the town against Uskok pirates.
The burgundy Batiala-Lazarini Palace next door now holds the **Town Museum**
(Gradski muzej; June–Sept Mon–Fri 10am–1pm & 4–6pm, Sat 10am–1pm;
Oct–May Mon–Fri 10am–1pm; 12Kn), with a small collection of Roman tombstones and a display of local costumes, including examples of the enormous
woollen scarves which local women used to drape over their shoulders to cush-
ion the load when carrying water or other heavy burdens. There's also a small but
atmospheric re-creation of life inside a coal mine, which involves donning a
(totally unnecessary) hard hat and embarking on a stooping walk between pit
props. Directly opposite the museum, the **Municipal Art Gallery** (Gradska
galerija; June–Sept Mon–Fri 10am–1pm & 5–7pm, Sat & Sun 10am–1pm; free)
is the venue for interesting themed exhibitions during the summer.

From the gallery, continue up 1 Maja to reach the highest point of the hill,
marking the western boundary of the old town. There's a viewing terrace here

on the site of the (long demolished) medieval fortress, or **Fortica**, looking down towards Rabac on the coast, with the mountainous shape of Cres beyond. From here, you can descend the western flank of the old town's hill by walking down Guiseppine Martinuzzi, passing on the way the **Chapel of Our Lady of Carmel** (Crkvica Gospe od Karmene), nowadays pressed into service as an art gallery hosting high-profile contemporary displays in the summer season. At the bottom of the street stands the eighteenth-century Franković Palace, which now holds the **Memorial Collection of Matthias Flacius Illyricus** (Spomen-zbirka M.F. Ilirika; same times as the Town Museum, but ask there first to check there will be someone in attendance; 10Kn), with books and manuscripts published by Matija Vlačić (1520–75), local Protestant and right-hand man to Martin Luther. One typical engraving of the time depicts the Pope with the head of an ass, the torso of a woman and the legs of a dragon – the kind of image that would have pleased Vlačić's uncle and fellow reformist Baldo Lupetina, whose refusal to renounce his beliefs resulted in him being tied in a weighted sack and thrown into the Venetian lagoon.

Practicalities

Labin's **tourist office** (mid-June to mid-Sept Mon–Sat 8am–9pm, Sun 10am–1pm & 6–9pm; mid-Sept to mid-June Mon–Fri 8am–3pm; ☏052/855-560), on the corner of Titov trg and Boža Štemberge, can provide sundry brochures covering Labin and Rabac. Veritas, down some steps from here at svete Katarine 8 (☏052/885-007, ℮veritas@pu.hinet.hr), has **rooms** (❶) in and around the old town.

Of Labin's places to **eat**, *Kvarner*, just off Titov trg below the town gate, has a tourist-oriented menu of grilled fish in July and August, and offers cheap lunches and dinners at other times of year, with daily specials often chalked up on a board outside. The more expensive *Due Fratelli*, about 2km out of town on the road to Rabac at Montozi 6, offers top-notch seafood and grilled meats. For **drinking and nightlife**, there's a sprinkling of café-bars either on or just off Titov trg. Down in Podlabin, the buildings around the pithead have been transformed into a cultural centre, the Kulturni centar Lamparna, which organizes gigs, raves, theatre and art exhibitions and has a bar and Internet café.

Rabac

Buses run every two hours or so (starting at the main bus station in Podlabin before passing through Titov trg in Labin) to the resort village of **RABAC**, squeezed into a narrow bay on the coast; alternatively, you can walk there in about forty minutes by heading along the Rabac road then taking the path which leads right into the woods just behind the Portatours tourist agency on the edge of Labin. Initially developed by the Italians in the interwar years as a workers' holiday settlement, it nowadays has an almost totally modern appearance, its hillsides covered in apartment blocks and fringed by a line of hotels all run by the same company, Rabac Hotels (☏052/862-000, ⊛www.rabac-hotels.com). There's a reasonable shingle beach on the northern side of the bay, and the usual string of so-so bars and restaurants along the harbour. All in all it's a bit too sanitized to compete with the west-coast resorts, although the *Lanterna* hotel (☏052/862-220, ℻862-230; ❻) is one of the best on this part of the coast, and **rooms** (❷) are available from Veritas back in Labin (see above), or Kompas (June–Sept daily 8am–8pm; ☏052/856-599, ℮compas-rabac-labin@pu.tel.hr) on the southern side of the harbour. There's also the Oliva **campsite** (☏052/872-258), right on the beach and backed by attractive woodland.

Northeast of Labin

Northeast of Labin, the green edges of Istria drop steep and sheer into the sea, offering few viable places to build. Twelve kilometres out of Labin, the ancient and windswept hilltop settlement of **PLOMIN** is typical of the local villages – most of its inhabitants left for Italy in 1945, leaving the fishing port below to silt up; many of its old stone houses are now boarded up. Most Pula–Rijeka buses stop for a breather at the *Vidikovac* café 4km further on, a popular viewpoint high above the rocky shore, with the grey outline of the island of **Cres** (see p.208) rising to the east. Cres is reachable by regular car ferry from the tiny port of **Brestova**, to which a side-road descends a couple of kilometres further on. Beyond Brestova, the road continues to twist and turn above the shore before descending towards Mošćenička Draga, first in a string of resorts that make up the **Opatija Riviera** (see p.202).

Travel details

Trains

Pazin to: Buzet (4 daily; 50min); Hum (4 daily; 20min); Pula (6 daily; 1hr 10min); Roč (4 daily; 35min).
Pula to: Buzet (4 daily; 2hr); Hum (4 daily; 1hr 30min); Pazin (6 daily; 1hr 10min); Roč (4 daily; 1hr 45min).

Buses

Buje to: Buzet (4 daily; 1hr 30min); Novigrad (4 daily; 45min); Poreč (Mon–Sat 6 daily, Sun 2 daily; 1hr 30min); Pula (4 daily; 3hr); Rijeka (4 daily; 2hr 30min).
Buzet to: Buje (4 daily; 1hr 30min); Pazin (Mon–Fri 2 daily; 1hr 10min); Poreč (2 daily; 2hr 15min); Pula (Mon–Fri 2 daily; 2hr 30min); Rijeka (4 daily; 1hr 10min).
Novigrad to: Buje (4 daily; 45min); Buzet (2 daily; 2hr 15min); Poreč (7 daily; 30min); Pula (4 daily; 2hr 15min); Rijeka (4 daily; 4hr 30min); Umag (7 daily; 30min).
Pazin to: Buzet (Mon–Fri 2 daily; 1hr 10min); Labin (2 daily; 1hr 10min); Motovun (Jul & Aug: 5 daily, Sept–June: 2 daily; 45min); Poreč (9 daily; 1hr 15min); Pula (Mon–Sat 8 daily, Sun 4 daily; 1hr); Rijeka (6 daily; 1hr); Rovinj (Mon–Fri 6 daily, Sat 4 daily, Sun 2 daily; 1hr 10min); Zagreb (6 daily; 5hr 15min).
Poreč to: Buje (Mon–Sat 6 daily, Sun 2 daily; 1hr 30min); Buzet (2 daily; 2hr 15min); Lanterna (summer only; 5 daily; 30min); Novigrad (5 daily; 30min); Opatija (4 daily; 3hr 30min); Pazin (9 daily; 1hr 15min); Pula (12 daily; 1hr 30min); Rijeka (6 daily; 4hr); Rovinj (7 daily; 45min); Umag (6 daily; 45min); Višnjan (6 daily; 20min); Vižinada (8 daily; 30min); Vrsar (12 daily; 20min); Zagreb (6

daily; 6hr 30min); Zelena Laguna (9 daily; 25min).
Pula to: Bale (hourly; 45min); Buje (5 daily; 2hr 40min); Buzet (Mon–Fri 2 daily; 2hr 30min); Dubrovnik (1 daily; 16hr); Fažana (every 30min; 30min); Istarske Toplice (2 daily; 2hr 15min); Karlovac (10 daily; 5hr). Labin (15 daily; 1hr); Novigrad (3 daily; 2hr 10min); Opatija (hourly; 2hr); Pazin (Mon–Sat 8 daily, Sun 4 daily; 1hr); Poreč (12 daily; 1hr 30min); Rijeka (hourly; 2hr 30min); Rovinj (hourly; 1hr 15min); Šibenik (4 daily; 10hr); Split (4 daily; 12hr); Svetvinčenat (5 daily; 45min); Umag (4 daily; 2hr 25min); Varaždin (1 daily; 9hr); Vodnjan (hourly; 20min); Vrsar (4 daily; 1hr 30min); Zadar (4 daily; 6hr 30min); Zagreb (10 daily; 6hr 30min); Žminj (6 daily; 50min).
Rovinj to: Bale (Mon–Sat 18 daily, Sun 9 daily; 30min); Buje (3 daily; 1hr 20min); Buzet (1 daily; 3hr); Dubrovnik (1 daily; 17hr 30min); Kanfanar (Mon–Sat 8 daily, Sun 4 daily; 45min); Labin (5 daily; 2hr 25min); Novigrad (2 daily; 1hr 30min); Pazin (Mon–Sat 4 daily; 1hr 10min); Poreč (6 daily; 1hr); Pula (hourly; 1hr 15min); Rijeka (5 daily; 4hr); Split (2 daily; 13hr 30min); Varaždin (1 daily; 10hr 30min); Vrsar (4 daily; 25min); Zagreb (6 daily; 5hr 40min).

Ferries

Brestova to: Porozina, Cres; (hourly; 30min).
Pula to: Mali Lošinj (June–Sept 6 weekly, Oct–May 1 weekly; 2hr 25min); Silba (June–Sept 6 weekly, Oct–May 1 weekly; 5hr 20min); Zadar (June–Sept 6 weekly, Oct–May 1 weekly; 7hr 45min).

International trains

Pula to: Ljubljana (1 daily; 4hr 30min; change at Buzet).

International buses

Buzet to: Koper (1 daily; 1hr 30min).
Novigrad to: Koper (3 daily; 2hr); Trieste (1 daily; 3hr).
Pazin to: Trieste (Mon–Sat 1 daily; 2hr 30min).
Poreč to: Koper (2 daily; 2hr 30min); Ljubljana (1 daily; 4hr 30min); Piran (2 daily; 2hr); Portorož (2 daily; 1hr 50min); Trieste (Mon–Fri 3 daily; 2hr 50min).
Pula to: Koper (2 daily; 3hr 30min); Piran (1 daily; 3hr 30min); Portorož (1 daily; 3hr 20min); Trieste (1 daily; 4hr 30min).
Rovinj to: Koper (2 daily; 2hr 40min); Trieste (1 daily; 3hr 30min).

The Kvarner Gulf

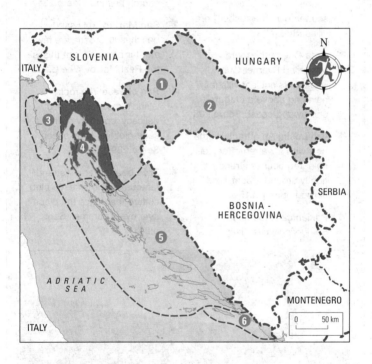

CHAPTER 4

Highlights

✳ **Eating in Opatija** This genteel watering hole boasts one of the finest collections of top-class seafood restaurants in the country. **See p.204**

✳ **Lovran** An Italianate, green-shuttered coastal town scattered with Habsburg-era villas. **See p.205**

✳ **Cres** One of the more unspoiled Kvarner Gulf islands, its ancient villages hovering above a craggy, uncrowded coast. **See p.208**

✳ **Veli Lošinj** An attractive little port with a warren of pastel-coloured houses strung tightly around a boat-filled harbour. **See p.215**

✳ **Paklenica National Park** Staggeringly beautiful mountain landscape offering an enticing mixture of karst wilderness, deciduous forests and fir-clad slopes. **See p.229**

✳ **Rab Town** Peninsula-hugging medieval town famous for its skyscraping church belfries. **See p.231**

✳ **San Marino** Truly sandy beaches in Croatia are few and far between, but this is the Real McCoy. **See p.238**

✳ **Pag cheese** The rocky island's most celebrated delicacy, courtesy of the sage-nibbling local sheep. **See p.239**

✳ **Zrće beach** Pebbly strand famous for the alfresco club culture that takes the place over every summer. **See p.241**

4

The Kvarner Gulf

The **Kvarner Gulf** – the large, deep bay which separates the Istrian peninsula to the north from Dalmatia to the south – is the first view of the coast for many visitors, as the main road from Zagreb sweeps down to the Adriatic at Rijeka. It's a region which brings together many of the features which make the coast so enticing: grizzled coastal hills and mountains, an archipelago of ochre-grey islands, and fishing villages with narrow alleys and gardens groaning under the weight of subtropical plants.

Croatia's largest port and the area's economic and political centre, **Rijeka** is more of a transit point than a destination in itself, and most people push straight on to the islands that crowd the gulf to the south. **Krk** is the most accessible of these, connected to the mainland by a road bridge just half an hour's drive from Rijeka, though the islands further out – **Lošinj**, **Rab** and most of all **Cres** – feel more removed from the urban bustle. Each has its fair share of historic towns, whose shuttered, Italianate houses recall the long centuries of Venetian rule, along with some gorgeous coves and beaches – especially the sandy ones at Baška on Krk and Lopar on Rab. Although lush and green on their western flanks, the islands are hauntingly bare when seen from the mainland, the result of deforestation during the Venetian period, when local timber was used to feed the shipyards of Venice; the fierce northeasterly wind known as the **Bura** (see box on p.225) has prevented anything from growing there again. This denuded landscape is particularly evident on the most southerly of the Kvarner islands, **Pag**, with its bare, stony hills.

The coast of the mainland which flanks the gulf was traditionally known as the **Hrvatsko primorje** (literally, "Croatian littoral") to distinguish it from the Adriatic islands and Dalmatia – largely because it never fell under Venetian control. Because of its proximity to Habsburg central Europe this stretch of the Adriatic shoreline was the first to develop as a tourist destination, with **Opatija**, **Crikvenica** and **Novi Vinodolski** emerging in the late nineteenth century as swish winter health resorts patronized by the Viennese upper crust. They're fairly bland tourist centres nowadays, although Opatija and neighbouring **Lovran** preserve something of the spirit of the *belle époque*. The southern part of the Kvarner coastline is dominated by the stark and majestic **Velebit** mountains, which can be seen at their best in the **Paklenica National Park** at the southern end of the range.

Getting around the region is straightforward, with buses zooming up and down the **Magistrala**, the main coastal road, at regular intervals. Rijeka, very much the hub of the transport system, is the main departure point for buses to the islands.

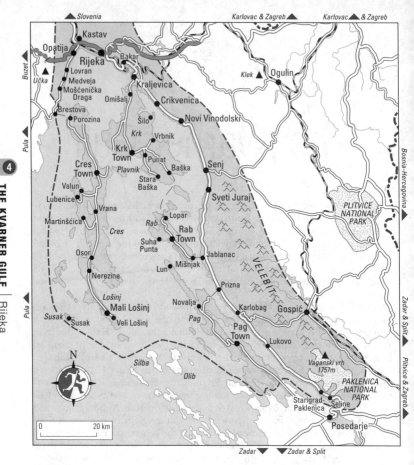

Rijeka

Rows of cumbrous cranes and rusty, sea-stained tankers front the soaring apartment blocks of Croatia's largest port, **RIJEKA** (pronounced "Ree-acre"), a down-to-earth industrial city which is the major ferry terminal along the Adriatic coast and an unavoidable transit point if you're travelling through the region by bus. Rijeka is far from beautiful, but it is the northern Adriatic's only true metropolis, mustering a reasonable number of attractions and an appealing urban buzz, while the hilltop suburb of **Trsat**, home to a famous pilgrimage church, is particularly attractive. Accommodation in town is limited to a few (mostly run-down) hotels, and if you want to stay in the area it may be better to aim for the Opatija Riviera to the west (see p.202), an area amply served by Rijeka's municipal bus network.

Some history

Although Trsat is built on an ancient hilltop site which was occupied by both Illyrians and Romans, the port below didn't really begin to develop until the thirteenth century, when it was known – in the language of whichever power controlled it – as St Vitus-on-the-River, a name subsequently shortened to the rather blunt "River" – which is what **Rijeka** (and its Italian version, Fiume) actually means. From 1466 the city was an Austrian possession, a prosperous port which remained under the direct control of Vienna until 1848, when Ban Jelačić (see p.410) brought it under Croatian administration. Rijeka became a bone of contention between Croatia and Hungary in the latter half of the nineteenth century, after the city was claimed by Budapest on the grounds that

Gabriele d'Annunzio in Rijeka

Following World War I, Italy's failure to win Rijeka by diplomatic means was seen by many right-wing Italians as proof of the essential weakness of Italian democracy, provoking calls for an overthrow of parliamentary government in favour of some form of dictatorship. Disgruntled army officers calculated that an attack on Rijeka would be enormously popular with the Italian public, thereby preparing the ground for a coup within Italy itself. To lead the attack they chose the flamboyant poet, novelist and pilot **Gabriele d'Annunzio** (1863–1938). D'Annunzio was a compelling figure: a decadent aesthete who reinvented himself as a war hero, he volunteered for the Italian cavalry in 1915 and went on to serve with distinction in both the navy and air force, becoming a bombastic nationalist ideologue in the process.

D'Annunzio marched into Rijeka on September 12, 1919, at the head of 297 volunteers – whose numbers were soon swelled by regular soldiers tacitly lent to the enterprise by their commanding officers. He immediately declared Italy's annexation of Rijeka, a deed that the Italian government in Rome, suspicious of the radical d'Annunzio, disowned. By September 1920, d'Annunzio – who now styled himself "Il Commandante" – had established Rijeka as an independent state entitled the **Reggenza del Carnaro**, or "Regency of the Kvarner", which he hoped to use as a base from which to topple the Italian government and establish a dictatorship.

Under d'Annunzio, political life in Rijeka became an experiment in totalitarian theory from which fellow Italian nationalist Benito Mussolini was to borrow freely. D'Annunzio's main innovation was the establishment of a **corporate state**, ostensibly based on the Italian medieval guild system, in which electoral democracy was suspended and replaced by nine "corporations" – each corresponding to a different group of professions – by which the populace could be organized and controlled. The Regency was also a proving ground for fascism's love of spectacle, with d'Annunzio mounting bombastic parades of extravagantly uniformed followers and mass meetings (often staged to make it appear as if the public had gathered spontaneously) featuring a call-and-response style of oratory which involved carefully scripted audience participation.

Successive Italian governments failed to take action against d'Annunzio, seeing him as a wild card with which to frighten the Allied powers still assembled at the Paris Peace Conference. Once Italian negotiators at the Conference had received what they thought was a reasonable chunk of Adriatic territory – Istria, Zadar and a couple of islands – they felt honour-bound to restore order to Rijeka, and Italian forces began a **bombardment of the city** on Christmas Eve 1920. D'Annunzio surrendered four days later, finally leaving town on January 18, thereby ending one of twentieth-century history's more bizarre episodes.

D'Annunzio's occupation of Rijeka had demonstrated to Mussolini how easy it was to mount a show of force against disorganized political opponents, providing him with the blueprint for his own successful coup, the **March on Rome** of October 1922. Once ensconced in power, Mussolini rewarded d'Annunzio for his Rijeka escapade with a seat in the Italian senate. Despite their political similarities, however, Mussolini and d'Annunzio never really got on: both were very much theatrical personalities, and each was afraid of having his thunder stolen by the other.

the Hungarian half of the Austro-Hungarian Empire should possess at least one outlet to the Adriatic. In 1868, an agreement between Croatia and Hungary – which was to have left the fate of Rijeka open to arbitration – was due to be signed by the Habsburg Emperor Franz Josef but, in a notorious piece of trickery, an additional clause presenting the port to Hungary was literally pasted in at the last moment without the Croats' knowledge.

Rijeka under Hungarian rule was a booming industrial port with a multinational population – the centre was predominantly Italian-speaking, while the suburbs were increasingly Croat – and both Italians and Croatians laid claim to the city when it once again came up for grabs at the end of World War I. The 1915 **Treaty of London** had promised Dalmatia – but not Rijeka – to the Italians as a reward for joining the war on the Allied side, a promise that Britain and France were unwilling to keep come 1918. The Italians demanded Rijeka as the price for giving up their claim to territories further south. In a plebiscite of October 1918, the city's inhabitants voted to join Italy (most of Rijeka's Croatian population actually lived outside the municipal boundary in the suburb of Sušak, and so were not represented), but the Allies remained firm, garrisoning the port with an Anglo-American and French force as a prelude to handing it over to the infant state of Yugoslavia. In September 1919, however, the Italian soldier-poet **Gabriele d'Annunzio** (see box on p.195) marched into Rijeka unopposed and occupied the city, establishing a proto-fascist regime which endured until January 1921. He was eventually forced to leave by an embarrassed Italian government, and February 1921's **Treaty of Rapallo** declared Rijeka a free city. Despite this, Rijeka was once again taken over by Italy following Mussolini's accession to power in 1922, an act which the Yugoslav government grudgingly accepted in the hope that it would deflect Italian territorial ambitions from the rest of the Adriatic.

Rijeka was returned to Yugoslavia after World War II, when most of the Italian population was induced to leave. In the years that followed, Rijeka's traditionally strong shipbuilding industry flourished anew, and the city acquired its high-rise suburbs. Rijeka's status as an economic powerhouse took a tumble in the immediate **post-independence** years, when the shipbuilding industry collapsed and the city's once-strong merchant fleet was sold off vessel by vessel. With traditional sources of employment drying up and a new postcommunist business culture emerging to fill the gap, it's a surprise to discover that Rijeka is still a town with solid socialist leanings. In contrast to Adriatic cities like Zadar, Split and Dubrovnik, most of the streets still carry their pre-1991 names: as well as squares and boulevards dedicated to Žrtava fašizma ("Victims of Facism") and President Tito, there's even a Šetalište XIII divizije or "Promenade of the Thirteenth Partisan Division" – the idea of battle-hardened guerillas strolling along its dull grey length is delightfuly absurd.

Arrival, information and transport

Rijeka's **train station** lies a few hundred metres west of the city centre on Krešimirova; **ferries** dock by the Riva, just south of the centre. The main **bus station**, handling all inter-city buses, is on the western fringe of the city centre at Trg Žabica. In addition, there are two smaller bus stations handling local services: buses to northern destinations (including Kastav, Opatija and Lovran) leave from Jelačićev trg on the east side of the city centre, while those heading south (to Bakar and Kraljevica) use a terminal a little way further east on the Delta. Rijeka's **airport** is 25km south of town on the island of Krk, and with only three flights a week from Zagreb, there's no public transport into town; a taxi will set you back 250–300Kn.

The **tourist office**, Korzo 33 (July & Aug Mon–Sat 8am–8pm, Sun 8am–2pm; Sept–June Mon–Fri 8am–8pm, Sat 8am–2pm; ☎051/335-882, ℱ214-706, ⓦwww.tz-rijeka.hr), has town plans and a wealth of information on the Kvarner region, including the English-language *Kvarner Info*, with listings of cultural events. Municipal **bus tickets** can be bought from newspaper kiosks (valid for two journeys) or from the driver (valid for one). **Fares** are calculated according to a zonal system: most city destinations, including Sušak and Trsat, fall within zone 1 (9Kn from the driver; 10Kn from a kiosk); Opatija is in zone 3 (12Kn; 17Kn); Lovran in zone 4 (14Kn; 20Kn).

Accommodation

There are no private rooms in the town itself, although there are plenty a short bus ride away along the Opatija Riviera (see p.202). Cheapest of the city's **hotels** is the *Neboder*, Strossmayerova 1 (☎051/373-538, ℱ373-551; ❸), an unkempt high-rise on the western fringes of the centre, some of whose decidedly tatty rooms come with en-suite facilities. You'll be more comfortable in the *Jadran*, 2km further east at Šetalište XIII divizije 46 (☎051/216-230, ℱ436-203; ⓦwww.jadran-hoteli.hr; ❸; bus #2 from the train station or from the Riva), a plain seafront block offering unexciting en-suite rooms, but with marvellous views across the water to the island of Cres. Back in the centre, the

Kontinental, Šetalište Andrije Kačića Miošića 1 (℡051/372-009, ℻372-009, ⓌＷww.jadran-hoteli.hr; ❹), is an old-fashioned, gloomy place offering passable rooms with attached bathroom and tired-looking brown furnishings. The businessman-friendly *Bonavia*, Dolac 4 (℡051/357-100, ℻355-969, Ⓦwww.bonavia.hr; ❽), is a fully renovated four-star affair, its rooms equipped with thick carpets, TV, minibar and air-con.

The nearest **campsite** is *Preluk* (℡051/622-249, ℻621-913), 8km north along the road to Opatija, on the cusp of the bay as the road wheels south towards Vološko; bus #32 (from Jelačićev trg or from opposite the train station) passes the entrance, but halts only on request – so remember to press the red button when you see the site approaching.

The City

Much of Rijeka was rebuilt after World War II, though a fair number of nineteenth-century buildings remain, many of them in solid ranks along the **Riva**, a neglected part of town which, the odd café excepted, lacks the vibrancy of other city waterfronts along the Adriatic. Just inland on Jadranski trg is one surviving symbol of inter-war Italian architecture, the russet-coloured **Veliki neboder** (literally "big skyscraper"), a boldly functional office block whose grid-like facade looks like a monumental CD rack – and has unsurprisingly earned the building the nickname of *ormar-ladičnjak* or "chest of drawers".

Running east from Jadranski trg, the pedestrianized **Korzo** is Rijeka's main shopping area and the focus of most of its streetlife. The one real landmark here is the **City Tower** (Gradski toranj), a medieval gateway topped by a later Baroque structure; its position marks the old seafront before the city was extended by landfills in the eighteenth and nineteenth centuries. Known locally as "Pod uriloj" (after the Italian word for clock, *orologio*), it has a relief on its street-facing side bearing the Habsburg double-headed eagle surmounted by busts of Austrian emperors Leopold I (on the left) and Charles VI (on the right). It was the latter's decision to declare Rijeka a free port in 1717 that kickstarted the city's economic growth.

The gate beneath the City Tower gives access to the **Old Town** (Stari grad), a rather hopeful description for an area of scruffy squares, peeling plaster and shiny, black glass-fronted department stores. Heading straight on uphill brings you out onto the sloping Trg Grivica, at the top of which stands **St Vitus' Church** (Crkva svetog Vida), surmounted by a rotunda built in 1638 in imitation of Santa Maria della Salute in Venice. Look out for the Gothic **crucifix** above the high altar: in 1296, the story goes, a gambler was losing at cards outside the church and ran inside in a rage, flinging stones at this crucifix, which began to bleed. In response to this blasphemy, the ground beneath the man's feet is said to have promptly opened up and swallowed him completely, except for one hand. The faithful claim that one of the stones he threw is still embedded in the side of the wooden Christ.

Not far from St Vitus' – make a left turn along Žrtava fašizma – rises the late nineteenth-century Gubernatorial Palace (Guvernerova palača), whose marvellously over-the-top state rooms now provide a sumptuous setting for the **History and Maritime Museum** (Pomorski i povijesni muzej hrvatskog primorja; Tues–Sat 9am–1pm; 10Kn). It was here that d'Annunzio installed himself for his short period of power, until shelling by the Italian battleship *Andrea Doria* on Boxing Day 1920 persuaded him to leave. Its huge echoing rooms hold costumes, period portraits, weaponry and a lot of colour-coordinated drapes and furniture, while the model ships on the second floor include replicas of the huge tankers formerly made by the local 3 Maj shipyard, whose gates you'll pass if entering the town from the northwest. In the palace grounds there's a modern pavilion holding the **City Museum** (Muzej grada Rijeke; Mon–Fri 10am–1pm, 5–8pm, Sat 10am–1pm; 10Kn), which hosts changing exhibitions relating to local history. Behind the Gubernatorial Palace to the northeast, the **Natural History Museum** (Prirodoslovni muzej; Mon–Fri 9am–7pm, Sat 9am–2pm; 10Kn) at Lorenzov prolaz 1 has displays on geology and marine life, including some ferocious-looking stuffed sharks.

Frana Supila, Dolac and the Capuchin Church

Returning downhill towards the Korzo along Frana Supila, you'll pass the **University Library** (Sveučilišna knjižnica; entrance round the corner on Dolac), which is home to two exhibition spaces: the **Modern Art Gallery** (Moderna galerija; Tues–Sun 10am–1pm & 6–9pm; 10Kn), which stages occasional temporary shows, and the **Glagolitic Exhibition** (Izložba glagoljice; in theory Mon–Fri 8am–3pm; in practice only open if you call in advance on ☎051/336-129; 10Kn), a worthy but less than riveting display of manuscripts written in the ecclesiastical script which was common to the Kvarner region in the Middle Ages (see box on p.222). Marking the western end of Dolac at no. 13 is the **Teatro Fenice** cinema, built in 1913 in Futurist style but nowadays looking somewhat uncared for – appropriately enough, this was where Futurist ideologue F. T. Marinetti addressed meetings in support of d'Annunzio in 1919.

Finally, opposite the bus station on Trg Žabica rises the huge, striped neo-Gothic bulk of the **Capuchin Church** (Kapucinska crkva), completed in 1908 and fronted by a large double stairway. It's said that the Capuchins – in particular a certain self-styled "Saint" Jochanza – collected money for the church with public shows of blood-sweating, making the site a minor place of pilgrimage until Jochanza was accused of charlatanry and arrested in 1913.

Sušak and Trsat

East of the old centre, the thick, pea-soup-coloured River Rječina marks the edge of central Rijeka, beyond which lies the suburb of Sušak; between 1924 and 1941, walking between the city centre and here meant crossing from Italy into the Kingdom of Yugoslavia. On the north side of Titov trg, a Baroque gateway marks the start of the **Trsatske Stube**, a stairway of 538 steps, built in 1531 at the bidding of Uskok commander Petar Kružić. This leads up to the pilgrimage centre of **Trsat** (also reachable on bus #1 or #1a from Fiumara or the Riva), nowadays a suburb of Rijeka, occupying a bluff high above the modern centre. According to legend, Trsat is where the House of the Virgin Mary and Joseph rested for three years during its miraculous flight from the infidel in Nazareth to Loreto in Italy, where it was set down in December 1294. At the top, the **Church of St Mary of Loreto** (Crkva svete Marije Lauretanske) supposedly marks the spot where the house rested. The church originally dates from the fifteenth century, but was almost completely rebuilt in 1824; it's now a place of almost exclusively female pilgrimage and worship – the more devout pilgrims sometimes scale Kružić's steps on their knees. The sanctuary features an altar with an icon of the Virgin, sent here by Pope Urban V in 1367, surrounded by necklaces and other trinkets hung there by grateful pilgrims, who are required to walk round the altar three times. At the side of the church is a **Franciscan monastery** whose chapel of votive gifts (*kapela zavjetnih darova*) is plastered with pictures and tapestries left by those whose prayers have been answered; the numerous enthusiastic paintings depicting events such as shipwrecks and car crashes in which the Virgin is supposed to have intervened are particularly striking.

Trsat Castle (Trsatska gradina; Feb, March, Nov & Dec daily 9am–3pm; April–Oct daily 9am–11pm), across the road from the church, is an ivy-clad hotchpotch of turrets and towers, walkways and parapets that give views backwards up a great grey tear in the mountains and forwards to Rijeka, under its dim yellowish haze of industrial smog. Beyond Rijeka is the island of Cres and, to the right, on the northwestern side of the Kvarner Gulf, the sheer mountain wall of Mount Učka. Parts of the castle date back to Roman times, when it was an important way-station on the trade routes linking the northern Adriatic with the Pannonian plain, but the fortress assumed its current shape mainly in the thirteenth century, when it became a stronghold of the Frankopans of Krk (see box on p.218). In 1826, an Austrian general of Irish descent, one Vice-marshal Laval Nugent, took the place over and restored it in Classical style, constructing the Doric temple in the middle which serves as his family's mausoleum; the castle is also used as a open-air theatre and houses a seasonal café.

Eating

Rijeka has less in the way of **restaurants** than a city of its size deserves, and most locals head for nearby Opatija if they want a slap-up meal. However, there's a handful of characterful eating places awaiting discovery by those prepared to venture beyond the main thoroughfares. There are plenty of snack and sandwich joints along the Korzo, and a bustling fruit and veg **market** just beyond the eastern end of the Riva.

Restaurants

Feral Matije Gupca 5b ☎051/212-274. Semi-formal seafood restaurant with high standards and higher-than-average prices – it's one of the best places in the region to eat *jakopske kapice* (scallops) and other shellfish. The brick-lined rooms have the feel of a cosy cellar. Closed Sun.

Moko Riva 14. Bright and breezy spaghetteria just round the corner from the bus station, offering inexpensive, satisfying pasta dishes in seemingly endless permutations of sauces.

Municipium Trg Riječke rezolucije 5. Smart city-centre establishment popular with a business crowd, and handy for downtown sightseeing. Standard Croatian repertoire of fish and meat dishes includes an excellent *pašticada* (spicy braised beef) alongside some slightly more pricey steaks. Closed Sun.

Na kantunu Demetrova 2. In a workaday grid of streets behind the market, this is a popular buffet serving up solid, satisfying and cheap seafood to an appreciative crowd of local port and office workers. Expect mackerel, sardines and other forms of *plava riba* (oily fish), as well as *oslić* (hake) and seafood and risottos. Closed Sun.

Trsatika Šetalište Joakima Rakovca 33. Right opposite Trsat's pilgrimage church, and with a spacious outdoor terrace that offers some excellent maritime vistas. The menu covers just about everything from inexpensive pizzas to lavish steaks and grilled fish, with some moderately priced pasta dishes (including *šurlice* from Krk; see p.217) in the middle.

Zlatna školjka Kružna 12a ☎051/213-782. Charming little seafood restaurant just off the Korzo, with an interior stuffed with nautical bric-a-brac. Plenty of shrimp and squid dishes (including an excellent and not too expensive *crni rižot*), as well as the full range of fish.

Drinking and entertainment

There's a range of lively **drinking** venues to choose from at night: take the steps leading uphill from the Korzo towards the Gubernatorial Palace to find the *River Pub*, Frana Supila 12 (enter from the alley round the back), a welcoming, wood-panelled place with Irish ales on tap. *Celtic Café Bard* also has Irish beers, though in a more intimate café-bar environment; it's opposite St Vitus' Church at Trg Grivica 68. *Svid Rock Café*, Riva 12–14, is an enormous, brash place decorated with pop bric-a-brac and hosting frequent live music.

The Rijeka carnival

On the last Sunday before Shrove Tuesday, Rijeka plays host to the biggest carnival celebrations in Croatia, culminating in a spectacular parade. Much of the parade centres on carnival floats and fancy-dress costumes, although there is one authentic older element in the shape of the **zvončari**, young men clad in animal skins who ring enormous cow bells to drive away evil spirits. Many of the villages in the hills north of Rijeka have their own groups of *zvončari*, a tradition which has survived since pre-Christian times. The Rijeka parade, which normally culminates with a large party of *zvončari* strutting their stuff, usually kicks off at around 1pm and takes around five hours to complete. Aftewards, participants and spectators alike troop off to the Delta (the estuary of the River Rječina), where there's a fairground and an enormous marquee, in which drinking and dancing continue into the early hours.

Palach, hidden away on Kružna, an alleyway which dives behind the Korzo just to the rear of the Riječka banka, has been the nerve centre of Rijeka's alternative scene ever since the late 1960s (when it was named, rather provocatively for the times, after the Czech anti-communist martyr Jan Palach): it currently comprises an art gallery, a cool matt-black bar area, and a space for live gigs and club nights. For daytime drinking, the pavement **cafés** lining the Korzo or those girdling the church in Trsat are the places to hang out. *Filodrammatica*, Korzo 28, has been one of the main city-centre coffee-supping venues for over a century, and has a good selection of cakes and pastries to boot.

Large-scale rock and pop performances take place at the Dvorana Mladost in Trsat, a modern multipurpose auditorium located slightly uphill from the church. The Croatian National Theatre (Hrvatsko narodno kazalište; ☎051/211-268, ⓦwww.hnk-zajc.hr), on Ivana Zajca, is the place for opera, orchestral concerts and theatre. For children, Gradsko kazalište lutaka, B. Polića 6 (☎051/212-090, ⓦwww.gklri.tripod.com), is the leading puppet theatre in this part of Croatia. Rijeka's two main **cinemas** are the Croatia, near the bus station at Krešimirova 2 (☎051/335-219), and the Teatro Fenice, at Dolac 13 (☎051/335-225).

The only spectator sport of note is **football**, with local team NK Rijeka playing at the all-seater Kantrida stadium, 6km west of the centre (bus #32 to Lovran passes by). Situated right by the sea, and with the imposing form of Mt Učka away to the west, it's a stirring arena in which to catch a game.

Listings

Airlines Croatia Airlines, Jelačićev trg 8a ☎051/330-207.
Beaches There are no beaches in Rijeka itself; most of the locals head for the Opatija Riviera or the nearby islands, or catch a local bus to Kostrena, an affluent suburb 6km to the southeast, which offers relatively clean water and a recently tarted-up seafront promenade.
Bookshop Nova, Trpimirova 9, has a small range of English-language paperbacks.
Exchange Riječka banka is at Jadranski trg 3a, with ATMs outside.
Ferry tickets Jadrolinija, Riva 16 (Mon, Wed, Fri & Sun 7am–8pm, Tue, Thurs & Sat 7am–6pm; ☎051/211-444 or 666-100).
Hospital Krešimirova 42 (☎051/658-111), on the

north side of the road, just west of the train station.
Internet access Internet Club Cont, ground floor of the Hotel Kontinental (daily 7am–11pm).
Left luggage There's a *garderoba* at the bus station (5.30am–10.30pm).
Pharmacy At Jadranski trg 1 (24hr).
Post office The most central post office is halfway down the Korzo (Mon–Fri 7am–9pm, Sat 7am–2pm); there's a 24hr branch beyond the train station at Krešimirova 7.
Taxi Both the train and bus stations have ranks outside; alternatively call ☎051/335-138.
Travel agents Generalturist, Trg Republike Hrvatske 8a ☎051/212-900; Kvarner Express, Trpimirova 2 ☎051/213-808; Maremonti, Korzo 40 ☎051/212-911.

The Opatija Riviera

Just to the west of Rijeka, the **Opatija Riviera** (Opatijska rivijera) is a twenty-kilometre stretch of sedate seaside resorts which lines the western side of the Kvarner Gulf. Protected from strong winds by the ridge of **Mount Učka**, this stretch of coast became the favoured retreat of tubercular Viennese fleeing the icy winter temperatures of central Europe. At the centre of the Riviera is the town of **Opatija**, whose success as a tourist resort in the latter half of the nineteenth century made it the Austro-Hungarian Empire's answer to the Côte d'Azur. The Habsburg ambience survives in some attractive *fin-de-siècle* architecture, the best of which is in the dainty town of **Lovran**, just southwest of Opatija. Beaches here tend to be of the concrete variety, unless you head for **Medveja** just beyond Lovran, which has a much more enticing stretch of shingle. There's an abundance of good accommodation throughout the Riviera, although private rooms and pensions tend to be cheaper in Lovran than in Opatija.

The main Rijeka–Pula road cuts right through the riviera. From Rijeka, **bus #32** (daily 4.30am–10.30pm from Jelačićev trg; every 20–30min) travels via Opatija to terminate in either Lovran or **Mošćenička Draga**, the latter just south of Medveja. If you're approaching from Pula, any Rijeka-bound bus will drop you off along here.

Kastav

The best view of the Opatija Riviera is from the village of **KASTAV**, a worthwhile side-trip 10km northwest of Rijeka on the karst ridge which overlooks the gulf. A windswept knot of cobbled alleyways hemmed in by scraps of surviving fortification, Kastav is strong on atmosphere but short of real sights. Head first for **St Helena's Church** (Crkva svete Jelene), from whose terrace there's an expansive panorama of the waters below. On the other, landward side of the village is the **Crekvina**, the stark remains of an enormous church begun by the Jesuits but never finished. Given the village as a fief by the Habsburgs, the Jesuits proved unpopular masters, greedy for taxes. One of their civilian administrators, Frano Morelli, was drowned in a well on the main square in 1666 – a crime which was committed en masse by the villagers and therefore proved unpunishable.

Kastav is easily accessible from either Rijeka (bus #18) or Opatija (bus #33), but there may not be any timetable information on display when you get here, so check schedules before setting out if you can. There's a **tourist office** beside the old town gate at Kastav 47 (Mon–Fri 7–11am & 11.30am–3pm; ☎051/691-425, ✆tz-kastav@kvarner.net) and a couple of good places to *eat*. *Vidikovac*, on the sea-facing side of the village, has a large outdoor terrace and simple grilled meats; while the considerably more chic *Kukuriku*, below the tourist office at Kastav 120 (☎051/691-417; reservations a good idea at weekends), offers an upmarket take on Istrian-influenced cuisine, serving up standards like *njoki* (gnocchi) and *fuži* (pasta noodles) with a range of imaginative and unusual sauces, alongside more substantial chicken, veal, game and horsemeat dishes. Cultural events include the **Kastav Cultural Summer** (Kastafsko kulturno leto), a programme of open-air classical concerts and theatre in July and August; and the **White Sunday and Monday** (Bela nedeja i beli pundejak) on the first Sunday and Monday in October, when new wine is tasted and there's folk dancing in the square.

Opatija

Fifteen kilometres out of Rijeka on the main coastal road to Pula lies **OPATIJA**, the longest established of the gulf's resorts. It's a town in the best tradition of seaside magnificence, pretty in an overpowering Austro-Hungarian sort of way, a monument both to genteel early twentieth-century tourism and to its subsequent decline. Opatija continues to be patronized by central Europeans of a certain age, and even in the height of summer there are times when you can stroll the length of the seafront without bumping into anyone under 40. However, Opatija's proximity to Rijeka (and, by extension, Zagreb) ensures a regular weekend influx of urban hedonists of all ages, when the shoreline promenade becomes jammed with strollers. Thanks to the big-spending habits of middle class Croats, top-quality seafood restaurants have taken off in a big way in Opatija, turning the town into a major target of gastro-pilgrims.

Opatija was little more than a fishing village until the arrival in 1844 of Rijeka businessman **Iginio Scarpa**, who built the opulent Villa Angiolina as a holiday home for his family and aristocratic Habsburg friends, such as the Archduke Maximilian, future Emperor of Mexico, and Maria Anna, wife of Emperor Ferdinand I. In 1882 the villa was bought by **Friedrich Schüller**, head of Austria's Southern Railways who, having supervised the completion of the line from Ljubljana to Rijeka, decided to promote Opatija as a mass holiday destination; the town's first hotels – the *Kvarner*, *Krönprinzessin Stephanie* (today's *Imperial*) and *Palace-Bellevue* – soon followed. Owing to its mild climate, Opatija was originally a winter health-resort, with a season running from October to May. It soon developed a Europe-wide reputation: Franz Josef of Austria and Kaiser Wilhelm II of Germany held talks here in 1894, while playwright Anton Chekhov holidayed at the *Hotel Kvarner* in the same year. A decade later Isadora Duncan installed herself in a villa behind the *Krönprinzessin Stephanie* and was inspired by the palm tree outside her window to create one of her best-known dance movements – "that light fluttering of the arms, hands and fingers which has been so much abused by my imitators".

Arrival, information and accommodation

Trains on the Ljubljana–Rijeka line stop at Matulji, 4km uphill from Opatija (regular local buses run from here down into town), though it's more convenient to arrive by **bus**; all buses stop at a central terminal on a small square facing onto the waterfront. Turn left from here and walk for five minutes up the main street, Maršala Tita, to reach the **tourist office** at no. 101 (mid-June to mid-Sept Mon–Sat 8am–10pm, Sun 6–10pm; mid-Sept to mid-June Mon–Fri 8am–3pm, Sat 8am–2pm; ☎051/271-310, ⓦwww.opatija-tourism.hr), which is well stocked with town maps and brochures. You can surf the **Internet** at Prive, Maršala Tita 83 (daily 8am–2am; 20Kn/hr).

Accommodation

Accommodation in Opatija is expensive unless you opt for the private **rooms** (②) and **apartments** (②) offered by numerous local agencies. The most helpful of these are easy to find along the central strip: head south of the bus station for DaRiva, Maršala Tita 162 (☎051/272-990, ⓦwww.da-riva.hr); and north of the bus station for Katarina Line, Maršala Tita 75/1 (☎051/272-110, ⓦwww.katarina-line.hr); and GIT, Maršala Tita 65 (☎051/271-967, ©gi -trade@ri.tel.hr). The nearest **campsites** are *Preluk* (see p.198), 5km to the north, and *Autocamp Opatija*, 3km south at Ičići (☎051/704-387, ℗704-046); the latter is a pleasant, wooded site on a terraced hillside about five minutes' walk above the main coastal road.

As for **hotels**, it's probably best to avoid the bland communist-era establishments which stretch a kilometre or so southwest of the centre, and opt instead for places strong on either *belle-époque* atmosphere or twenty-first century comfort. Bear in mind that the peak-season rates (as expressed in the price codes in the reviews below) fall by as much as fifty percent between October and May.

Galeb Maršala Tita 160 ☎ 051/271-177, ⓦ www.hotel-galeb.hr. Tastefully renovated nineteenth-century building in the centre, offering small, modernized rooms, all with TV, minibar, air-con and spanking-new bathrooms. The more expensive rooms have sea views. ❻

Ika ☎ 051/291-777, ⓦ www.hotel-ika.hr. Medium-sized, family-run hotel in Ika, 3.5km south of Opatija on the road to Lovran (bus #32 passes right by). Rooms are plain but comfy, all with en-suite shower, TV and air-con, and right beside Ika's pebbly beach. Rooms on the landward side are cheaper. ❹

Kvarner Park 1 Maja 4 ☎ 051/271-233, ℱ 271-202, ⓦ www.liburnia.hr. Grandest of the pre-1914 hotels, with comfy rooms, old-world furnishings, and a superb position right on the waterfront – can't be beaten for atmosphere. ❼

Millennium Maršala Tita 109 ☎ 051/202-000, ⓦ www.ugohoteli.hr. Recently modernized and rather swanky hotel bang in the centre, offering high standards of comfort and service. Calls itself a five-star but probably deserves four (some rooms have showers instead of bathtubs). ❼

Palace-Bellevue Maršala Tita 200 ☎ 051/271-811, ℱ 271-964). Cheapest of the Habsburg-era places, whose lobby and bar areas still convey a whiff of *fin-de-siècle* opulence, although the spacious en-suite rooms boast marvellously uncoordinated 1970s colour schemes. ❺

Paris Vladimira Nazora bb ☎ 051/271-911, ⓦ www.liburnia.hr. Smallish en-suite rooms in an unremarkable building just off the main street. Worth mentioning because it's one of the few habitable cheapies. ❹

Villa Ariston Maršala Tita 179 ☎ 051/271-379, ⓦ www.villa-ariston.net. Small-scale hotel occupying an elegantly restored building designed by Viennese architect Karl Seidl in Opatija's pre-World War I heyday. Most doubles are in the attic and come with atmospheric sloping roofs, as well as attached baths. ❼

The Town

Modern Opatija is a long, straggling resort which has lost much of its original *fin-de-siècle* character. The town's main attraction is the **Šetalište Franza Josefa**, a splendid tree-shaded promenade which runs along the rocky seafront all the way to the old fishing village of Volosko (2km to the north) and the sedate resort of Lovran (6km to the south), and offering a far better way of exploring the town than the rather tatty and traffic-choked main street, Maršala Tita. Squeezed between the promenade and Maršala Tita, about 500m north-east of the bus station, lie the flowerbeds and lovingly clipped shrubs of the **Park Angiolina**, surrounding Scarpa's original Villa Angiolina and boasting rows of exotic palms. On the western edge of the park is the oldest and grand-est of Opatija's hotels, the *Kvarner*, whose facade, complete with trumpet-blowing cherubs and bare-chested Titans, looks more like a provincial opera house than a hotel. Opatija's **beach** – a cemented-over lido opposite the bus station – is the biggest let-down in the Adriatic; it's better to walk 3km south to the gravelly beach at Ičići, or catch a bus to **Medveja**, where there's a much bigger, shingly affair (see p.207).

Offering a complete contrast to Opatija are the steep, narrow alleyways and shuttered houses of **Volosko**, once a separate village but now swallowed up by Opatija's suburban sprawl, an easy twenty minutes' walk along the coastal promenade. Again, specific attractions are thin on the ground, but it's an atmos-pheric place for a short wander, with its whitewashed buildings arranged into a kasbah-like maze of streets, and a small fishing fleet in its tiny *mandrać* (inner port).

Eating and drinking

Providing you stay well away from the bland fare served up in hotel restaurants, Opatija is an excellent place in which to sample Adriatic seafood at its best – and some of the town's restaurants are truly outstanding. There's no shortage of snack bars along the main strip – *Pomodoro*, up an alleyway beside Maršala Tita 136, is the place to pick up pizza slices.

Most of the **cafés** along Maršala Tita have had all trace of the *belle époque* ripped out of them by insensitive renovators, although the one beneath the *Palace-Bellevue* hotel has a good selection of cakes and a spacious terrace on which to see and be seen. The harbour, 1km northeast of the bus station, is the prime evening **drinking** area, where a forest of chairs, tables and parasol stands spreads out from a cluster of flash cafés and cocktail bars. Back in the centre, *Hobbiton*, Maršala Tita 136, is a bunker-like watering hole with a wide range of mainstream and alternative music. In Volosko, the *Kon-Tiki* is a chic and relaxing café right by the mandrać; while *Vološćica*, on the waterfront a little further north, is a smaller, standing-room-only kind of place inside, although it too has an outdoor terrace. The best club on this stretch of coast is the *Colosseum*, right by Opatija's concrete lido.

Restaurants

Amfora Črnikovica 4, Volosko ☏ 051/701-222. Succulent fresh fish in a pricey restaurant at the northern end of Volosko, its dining room overlooking a rocky, wave-bashed cove. Try the fish platter (*riblji pladanj*), usually featuring the grilled catch of the day garnished by the odd squid and shrimp.

Bevanda Lido ☏ 051/712-769. Superior-quality seafood served up by attentive, liveried staff in a Neoclassical pavilion near Opatija's harbour. Good for fresh lobster, and there's an extensive list of Croatian wines, plus the biggest choice of desserts in town.

Commodore Liburnijska bb, Ičići. Semi-formal dining in a pavilion beside the marina, serving up a range of dishes to suit all pockets: inexpensive pizzas and pastas, mid-price local favourites like *šurlice* (pasta from Krk), and top-class seafood.

Kanet Nova cesta 80 ☏ 051/712-222. Cosy little pub-restaurant uphill from the centre, with very few tables and pictures of old Opatija on the wall. Good place for an inexpensive lunch of pasta or goulash, or a more substantial meaty meal – traditional dishes like *buncek* and *koljenica* a speciality.

Madonnina Pava Tomašića 3 (signposted just off Maršala Tita near the tourist office). Best place in town for a filling, cheap feed, serving up pizzas, pasta dishes and salads in a bustling, convivial interior– there's also an outdoor terrace facing the *Kvarner* hotel.

Mali Raj Maršala Tita 191. The name of the restaurant means "little heaven", which is not a bad description of this clifftop terrace on the promenade between Opatija and Ičići. Splash out on lobster, grilled fish and shellfish, or tuck into more moderately priced grilled meats.

Plavi Podrum Obala Frane Supila 4, Volosko ☏ 051/701-223. Smart establishment right on Volosko's harbour, renowned for its expertly prepared seafood. You can opt for simple but effective meals like *fritaja* (omelette) sprinkled with a range of seasonal goodies, or linger over more substantial fish and lobster dishes while splashing out on the extensive wine list. If you can't get a table here, then the slightly less formal *Bevandica* restaurant, two doors down, is a worthy substitute.

Villa Ariston Maršala Tita 179 (also entered from the seafront promenade; ☏ 051/271-379). Top-of-the-range seafood, richly sauced pork and chicken dishes, and a big wine list. You can sit in what looks like a Second Empire drawing room inside, or a palm-packed garden outside.

Lovran and around

It's an easy hour's walk south along the coastal Šetalište from Opatija to **LOVRAN**, following a rocky shore punctuated by two pebbly coves at Ičići and Ika. On arrival you'll find an Italianate, green-shuttered little town with a small harbour, fringed by palatial *belle époque* villas, decorated with curly balustrades covered in green espaliers. Behind the main street, Maršala Tita, a small old quarter climbs the hill, where vine-shaded cobbled alleys converge on the fourteenth-century **St George's Church** (Crkva svetog Jurja). Some frescoes dating from 1479, reminiscent in style of the wall paintings at Beram (see p.178) and other Istrian churches, can be found behind the main altar. Opposite the church, the **House of St George** bears an eighteenth-century relief, above the doorway, of the saint slaying a dragon, which has become something of a town trademark.

Dominating the skyline above Opatija and Lovran is the long, forest-covered ridge of the **Učka massif**, which divides the Kvarner region from central Istria. A tunnel under Učka's northern limbs provides a fast road link between Rijeka and the Istrian hinterland, but there's an older, more scenic route which climbs from Rijeka via the village of Veprinac over the northern shoulder of the mountain, passing a turn-off to the 1396-metre summit of **Vojak** before zigzagging down to join the newer main road on the other side. Rather than driving all the way to Vojak, however, the best way to enjoy Učka's wooded slopes is to walk. Paths are well marked, and the free *Učka* map, available from the Lovran tourist office, is an invaluable guide.

Lovran is the starting point for the most direct **hiking route** up the mountain – the ascent takes around three and a half hours. A flight of rough-hewn steps begins immediately behind Lovran's old centre, leading to the small Romanesque Chapel of St Rock on the edge of the village of **Liganj**. Join the road into Liganj for a couple of hundred metres before heading uphill to the right through the hamlets of **Dindići** and **Ivulići** – semi-abandoned clusters of farmhouses and moss-covered dry-stone walls. From Ivulići it's a steady two-hour ascent through oak and beech forest before you emerge onto a grassy saddle where an expansive panorama of inland Istria suddenly opens up, revealing the knobbly green and brown forms of the peninsula's central hills; the peak of Vojak is another twenty minutes' walk to the right. At the top, there's an observation tower, TV mast and splendid views of Rijeka and the spindly form of Cres beyond. There's an **alternative ascent**, taking about fifty minutes longer, which starts just behind the **Medveja campsite** and ascends to the village of **Lovranska Draga** before climbing steeply up a wooded ravine to join the main path from Lovran.

From Vojak, a path descends north to **Poklon** (1hr), where you meet up with the old Rijeka–Istria road. There's a terrace offering another view of the Kvarner Gulf here, and a mountain hut and restaurant, though they're only sporadically open. Follow the road 1km west from Poklon to reach the *Dopolavoro* **restaurant** (closed Mon), invariably packed out with day-tripping Rijeka folk at weekends (when you might have to reserve; ☎051/299-641) who come to sample its top-notch Istrian cuisine and game dishes such as pheasant and boar. On Saturdays and Sundays, **bus #34** from Opatija climbs as far as Poklon twice a day, making this a good starting point from which to tackle Vojak if time is short. From Poklon, you can work your way southeast back to Lovran (roughly a 2hr walk) by a downhill path which ultimately joins the main route you came up on.

Habsburg-era villas are scattered all over Lovran. Many were taken over by the state and turned into flats after World War II; sadly, none is open to the public. Some of the best are concentrated northeast of the centre along Maršala Tita, where you can hardly miss the Secessionist **Villa Gianna** at no. 23, a pink-mauve confection built in 1904 by local architect Attilio Maguolo. It's embellished with ornate Corinthian columns and winged dragons clutching shields inscribed with the initials IP, a reference to the original owner, Iginio Persich. Further on, beyond the *Excelsior* hotel, a further group of villas lurks in shady seaside gardens. The most famous of these is the **Villa Frappart** on Viktora Cara Emina, another Secession-inspired work built for Viennese lawyer Michel Ruault Frappart by Karl Seidl in 1890. An eclectic Byzantine–Gothic building, whose colonnaded entrance gives it palatial pretensions, it's now an elite music school.

Practicalities

Buses pick up and drop off on Lovran's main street, where most of what you need is located. There's a helpful **tourist office** (summer Mon–Sat 8am–8pm, Sun 8am–noon; winter Mon–Fri 9am–4pm; ☎051/291-740, ⊛www.tz-lovran.hr)

which dispenses free town plans and so forth just off Maršala Tita, down a side-alley behind the harbour.

Accommodation

Plentiful private **rooms** (❶) and **apartments** (❸) are available from three agencies (usually open daily 8am–8pm in summer, Mon–Fri 9am–3pm in winter) on the main strip: T.A. Lovran, Maršala Tita 68 (☎051/291-041, ✉lovran@globalnet.hr); Hill, Trg slobode 15 (☎051/293-700); and Kvarner Express, Maršala Tita 39 (☎051/291-119). Fully equipped apartments in some of Lovran's more expensively restored turn-of-the-century villas can be arranged through Lovranske Vile, Poljanska 27, Ičići (☎ & ☎051/704-276, ⓦwww.lovranske-vile.com), although they don't come cheap and there's a minimum two-night stay, which will cost about 3000Kn for a four-bed apartment.

Hotels and pensions

Bristol Maršala Tita 27 ☎051/291-022, ☎292-049, ✉lrh@lrh.tel.hr. Looking somewhat like a French Riviera hotel that's gone to seed, the *Bristol* offers a charming array of creaky-floored rooms with Second Empire-style furniture. Inland-facing rooms come with en-suite shower and TV, while the more expensive sea-facing rooms have baths and balconies. ❺

Excelsior Maršala Tita 15 ☎051/292-233, ☎291-989, ⓦwww.liburnia.hr. Concrete tourist palace built in the Seventies, offering spacious rooms with TV and dowdy brown colour schemes, and indoor and outdoor pools fed by seawater. ❼

Primorka Maršala Tita 89 ☎051/292-770, ☎293-432. Medium-size hotel in the handsome *fin-de-siècle* Villa Mihaela, handy for the centre and the seafront. The parquet-floored rooms are simply furnished, but are quite spacious and have attached bathrooms. ❹

Villa Liana Maršala Tita 85 ☎ & ☎051/712-742, ✉marea@ri.tel.hr. Small but characterful hotel 1km southwest of Lovran along the coast road, with large, old-fashioned en-suite rooms in a creaky old folly. Breakfast can be taken on a terrace overlooking the sea. ❹

Villa Stanger 26. Divizije 2 ☎051/291-403, ☎294-345, ✉dragan.stanger@hinet.hr. Cosy bed and breakfast in a modern, three-storey house a stone's throw from the centre. Rooms are en suite and have tiny balconies. The owners speak Italian and German. ❸

Eating

The cheapest place to eat is probably *Oaza*, on Maršala Tita 37, which has a range of pizza and pasta dishes. Superior fare is on offer at *Knezgrad*, Trg slobode 12, which serves up good quality meat and fish at a moderate price, and often has cheap lunchtime menus chalked up on a board outside, and the slightly pricier *Grill Kvarner*, overlooking the harbour at Maršala Tita 65, which has excellent fresh seafood. Best of all is *Najade*, Maršala Tita 69 (☎051/291-866), with a big outdoor terrace, attentive service and freshly caught fish – the *punjene lignje* (squid stuffed with *pršut* and cheese) are exceptional. There are plenty of places offering coffee and ice cream along the main street; best of the venues for night-time **drinking** is *Lovranski Pub*, Maršala Tita 41, a cosy subterranean hideaway with a secluded outdoor terrace.

The Lovran area is famous for its chestnut trees, which were originally imported from Japan in the seventeenth century. They are harvested in mid-autumn, an event celebrated by the **Marunada Chestnut Festival** (call the tourist office for details) which takes place over three weekends in October: the first two weekends see festivities in hill villages above town, while the final weekend takes place in Lovran itself. The festival is used as an excuse for making a wide variety of cakes flavoured with chestnut purée, which are sold in all the local cafés.

Medveja and Mošćenička Draga

Three kilometres beyond Lovran, the small village of **MEDVEJA** has the area's best **beach** – a long crescent of shingle which can get crowded on summer weekends. Immediately behind the beach there's a small **tourist office** (June–Sept irregular hours, usually 8am–5pm; ☎051/291-296, ✆tzm-medve-ja@ri.tel.hr) and the New Sound agency (☎ & ℻051/292-111, ✆new-sound@ri.tel.hr), which has a few local **rooms** (❶–❷). There's also a well-appointed and spacious **campsite** (☎051/291-191, ✆ac-medveja@liburnia.hr), attractively tucked into a steep-sided valley, with a supermarket and grill restaurant on site. Four kilometres further on lies **MOŠĆENIČKA DRAGA**, the Riviera's last settlement, unattractively squeezed around the monster-sized *Marina* hotel. Here there's another popular stretch of pebbly beach, a **tourist office** on Aleja Slatina (☎051/737-533) and **rooms** (❷) from the AnnaLinea agency, which has offices by the main road and near the beach (☎ & ℻051/737-400).

Cres and Lošinj

The westernmost of the Kvarner islands, **Cres** and **Lošinj** (really a single island divided by a narrow artificial channel), together make up a narrow sliver of land which begins just south of the Istrian coast and extends most of the way across the Kvarner Gulf. Allegedly the place where Jason and the Argonauts fled with the Golden Fleece, the islands were originally known as the "Absyrtides"; according to locals, Medea killed her brother Absyrtus here as he pursued her and threw his remains into the sea, where two of his limbs became Cres and Lošinj.

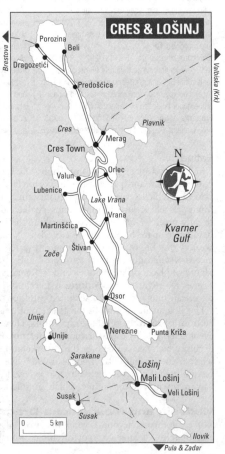

Cres (pronounced "tsress") is the second largest of the Adriatic islands, only beaten in size by neighbouring Krk. It marks the transition between the lush green vegetation of northern Croatia and the bare karst of the Adriatic, with the deciduous forest and overgrown hedgerows of northern Cres – the so-called **Tramuntana** – giving way to the increasingly barren sheep-pastures of the southern part of the island. Sheep apart, there's not much agriculture on the island, and the only other economic activities are fishing and tourism. Despite its proximity to the mainland, Cres is by far the wilder and most unspoiled of the two islands, boasting a couple of attractively weatherbeaten old settlements in **Osor** and **Cres Town**, as well as numerous villages and coves in which modern-day mass tourism has yet to make an impact.

Lošinj (pronounced "losheen") is smaller and more touristed than Cres, and has a thick woolly tree cover that comes as a relief after the obdurate grey-greenness of southern Cres. Long overshadowed by its neighbour, Lošinj developed a thriving maritime trade after the demise of the Venetian Republic, with a large fleet and several shipyards, and later emerged as a holiday destination – like Opatija on the mainland it started out in the late nineteenth century as a winter health-resort for sickly Viennese. Nowadays the island's main town, **Mali Lošinj**, is a magnet for package-holidaying Germans, Austrians, Italians and Croats, though even here you'll find a characterful old town and port relatively unsullied by concrete mega-developments. Its near-neighbour **Veli Lošinj**, which lies within walking distance, is smaller and offers more in terms of fishing-village charm – although it too can get crowded in August.

Access to the islands

Getting to the islands is relatively straightforward. **Ferries** run hourly from **Brestova** (see p.189), just south down the Istrian coast from Opatija, to Porozina in northern Cres, and from Valbiska on Krk to Merag on Cres. Most **buses** plying the Rijeka–Cres–Lošinj route use the Brestova ferry crossing, although at least one bus daily goes via Valbiska. If you're driving, bear in mind that both ferries attract lengthy queues on summer weekends – so it's best to arrive early or bring a good book. Heading to or from either Istria or Dalmatia, there are also six ferries weekly in each direction between Pula and Zadar, which call at Mali Lošinj on the way. Public transport runs up and down the main road along the island's hilly central spine, making travel between the main centres fairly easy, though to properly explore some of the smaller places on Cres – such as **Beli**, **Valun** and **Lubenice** – you'll need plenty of time and good walking shoes, or your own transport.

Cres Town

An oversized fishing village strung around a small harbour, **CRES TOWN** has the attractively crumpled look of so many of the towns on this coast: tiny alleys lead nowhere, minuscule courtyards shelter an abundance of greenery spilling over the rails of balconies, while mauve and pink flowers sprout from cracks in walls. **Trg F. Petrića**, which opens out onto the harbour, is the town centre, flanked by a small fifteenth-century loggia and a sixteenth-century clock tower. An archway leads through to the square known as **Pod urom** ("Beneath the clock"), where **St Mary's Church** (Crkva svete Marije) boasts a fifteenth-century Gothic–Renaissance portal featuring a fine relief of the Virgin and Child. Just south of here, set slightly back from the harbour, the Gothic Petris Palace holds a small **museum** which, once restored, will display piles of encrusted amphorae from the Roman trading post of Crepsa which once stood here, plus coins, manuscripts and sculpture from the town's days under Venetian and Austrian rule. From the northern end of the harbour, the main street, Creskog statuta, runs along the fringes of the town centre before finishing up at the **Porta Marcella**, a Renaissance gateway from 1595 that stands at one end of a stretch of old town wall dating from Venetian times. A couple of hundred metres south of here, past a peeling Partisan war memorial, another Renaissance gateway, the **Porta Bragadina**, leads back into the mazy centre of town via a collection of small piazzas.

Over on the southern side of town, just behind a rather ugly shipyard area, the **Franciscan monastery** (Franjevački samostan; Mon–Sat 10am–noon &

4–6.30pm; 5Kn) holds a shaded cloister and a small **museum**, in which flaky portraits of Franciscan theologians are outshone by Andrea de Murano's *Virgin and Child* of 1475, a warm depiction of a fat and mischievous Jesus with dove in hand. **Swimming** in Cres takes place along the concreted Lungomare promenade, which stretches west of town as far as the campsite some 1500m away; there's a naturist section on the far side.

Practicalities

Buses stop near the petrol station just off the harbour area, where a narrow alleyway leads to the **tourist office** at Cons 10 (June & Sept daily 7am–1pm & 2–9pm; July & Aug daily 8am–10pm; Oct–May Mon–Fri 8am–3pm; ☏051/571-535, ⓦwww.tz-cres.hr), which has a respectable stock of English-language brochures and can tell you just about everything you need to know about the island. Bikes (80Kn/day) and scooters (200Kn/day) can be rented from the Šumice kiosk in front of the *Hotel Kimen* (see below).

Rooms (❶) and apartments (❷) in the old town and in the suburb of **Melin**, 1km west, are available either from the Croatia travel agency (☏051/573-053, ⓦwww.cres-travel.com), next door to the tourist office, or the Cresanka Turist Biro round the corner on the harbour (daily 8am–8pm; ☏051/571-161, ⓦwww.cresanka.hr). Also in Melin is the *Kimen* **hotel**, set back from the Lungomare 1km from the town centre (☏051/571-322, ⓦwww.cresanka.hr; ❺), with box-like but acceptable en-suite rooms just above the Lungomare. Swisher en-suite rooms with modern furnishings, TV and air-con are available another 500m west along the Lungomare at the twelve-room *Kuća Kovačine* (☏051/571-423, ⓦwww.cresanka.hr; ❺), which lies inside the Kovačine **campsite** (☏051/571-423). The site itself occupies a terraced seaside area shaded by olives and other trees, is home to a popular diving school (crash courses start at 190Kn) and has a large naturist section on the far side.

There are plenty of **eating** opportunities around the harbour. Starting with snacks, *Slastičarnica Učka* does a reasonable *burek*, while the nearby *Pizzeria Palada* is probably the cheapest place to get a decent sit-down meal. *Konoba Bonaca*, Creskog statuta 13, is a homely tavern with wooden bench seating, and a range of budget fish dishes such as *srdele* (anchovies) and *skuša* (mackerel) as well as more expensive seafood. For classier fare, *Riva* has a prime waterside position and is the best place to try top-quality fish such as *orada* (gilthead) and *škrpina* (groper). Slightly further afield, *Gostionica Belona*, opposite the Partisan war memorial on Šetalište XX travnja, has a similar range of meat and seafood, and does a good *lignje na žaru* (grilled squid). There are plenty of **cafés** along the seafront although they can sometimes get a bit windy – in which case head for the more sheltered *Café Smack* beside the church on Pod urom.

Beli

North of Cres Town, the island narrows into a long, high ridge, descending steeply towards the sea on either side. The road dives from one side of the ridge to the other, swapping views of the Istrian peninsula to the west and the mainland from Rijeka to Velebit to the east. Thirteen kilometres north of Cres Town a minor road forks right off the main road, passing through half-deserted hamlets and oak and chestnut forests en route to the village of **BELI**. Huddled atop a knobbly hill high above the channel dividing Cres from Krk, Beli is an impressive agglomeration of ancient stone houses, many of them now left uninhabited as locals move away in search of work. It's gloriously rustic and peaceful, and there's a small shingle cove below the village at the end of a steep road.

The griffon vultures of Cres

The white-headed **griffon vulture** (*bijeloglavi sup*) formerly lived all over the Kvarner region, coexisting with a local sheep-farming economy that guaranteed the carrion-eating birds a constant supply of food. With the decline of sheep-rearing in the twentieth century, vulture numbers fell dramatically and communities of the birds are nowadays only found on the northeast coast of Cres and in a few isolated spots on Krk and the mainland. When conservationists first came to the area in the mid-1980s there were 24 pairs of vultures on the island; that number has now risen to about seventy, not least because locals have been educated to leave dead animals for the vultures to clear up rather than removing them from the fields themselves.

Fully grown griffon vultures have a wingspan of 2.5m, can weigh 8–10kg, live for up to 60 years, and can spot a sheep or donkey carcass from a distance of 6km. Their nesting area in the rocky cliffs on the eastern side of the island between Beli and Merag is now protected by law: it's forbidden to sail within 50m of the cliffs, as frightened young birds may fall out of their nests if disturbed. The vultures nest in December and produce one egg per pair, the young bird staying with its parents until August, when it begins a five-year roving period – which could take it to other vulture colonies in the Balkans or Near East – before returning to the island to breed. The main **threats** to the vultures are telephone wires, electricity power lines and contact with man-made poisons, such as the bait left out for vermin; the vulture population of Plavnik, an uninhabited island off the east coast of Cres, disappeared completely after the food chain had become contaminated in this way.

Beli is also home to the **Caput Insulae Ecology Centre** (Eko-centar Caput Insulae; daily 9–11am & 5–9pm; 10Kn; ⊛www.caput-insulae.com), established in the mid-1980s to monitor and protect the community of **griffon vultures** (see box above) indigenous to Cres. Located at the end of a stony road to the left as you enter the village, the centre has an exhibition on the vultures, with photographs and English-language text, and a small aviary in the back garden where sick vultures are often kept before being returned to the wild. They can also provide directions for the centre's **ecology path** (*eko-staza*), a hiking route which starts here and leads through the forest on a seven-kilometre circuit, passing through a mixed area of pasture, forest, abandoned villages and *gradine* (the small, walled-off areas of cultivable land typical to Croatia's limestone areas) on the way. The vultures themselves regularly scour the sparsely inhabited northern extremities of Cres in search of food – there's quite a good chance of spotting one, but don't count on it.

There are only two buses a week from Cres to Beli, and the much more regular Cres–Porozina–Rijeka buses only pass within 7km of the village. A **tourist information point** opens up in season (July & Aug daily 8am–7pm; ☎051/861-089) and allocates **rooms** (❶) – at other times enquire at the tourist office in Cres Town. There's a **campsite**, the *Brajdi* (☎ & ☎051/840-532), below the village near the beach, where there's also a small **grill-restaurant**. Back in the village, the *Gostionica Beli*, a cosy place decorated with agricultural implements, has a wider range of fish and meat dishes – including local roast lamb – and is also a good place for a drink.

Valun, Lubenice and Martinišćica

About eight buses a day leave Cres Town for Mali Lošinj (see p.213), a spectacular journey at times as the road hugs the island's central ridge before descending towards the sea at Osor. Eight kilometres south of Cres Town a minor road heads right towards the sparsely populated western side of the island. After 5km a side road descends to **VALUN**, a tiny fishing village with colourful houses crowding round its harbour, a quiet shingle beach and ultra-clear waters – it's very popular with weekending Italians, but remains more or less free from development. The **tourist office** just behind the harbour (June & Sept Mon–Sat 8.30am–2pm, Sun 8.30am–noon; July & Aug daily 8.30am–7pm; ☎051/525-084) has **rooms** (❶), and there's a very attractive small **campsite** 100m east of the harbour right on the beach (☎051/535-050, ℗535-085). For **eating**, *Konoba Toš Juna* has a terrace right on the harbourfront and is a good place to try the local *škampi* (shrimps) and *creška janjetina* (Cres lamb).

Roads lead southwest from Valun to **LUBENICE**, 5km away, a windswept village occupying a ridge high above the shore. Almost medieval in appearance, it's like a more extreme version of Beli – a depopulated cluster of half-ruined stone houses. The square at the entrance to the village, from which there's an invigorating view of the rugged western coast, hosts alfresco classical music concerts every Friday evening in July and August, and there's a pair of idyllic, secluded pebbly coves far below the village, though they're only accessible by boat or via a very steep and tiring path. There are only three Cres Town–Valun–Lubenice buses a week, so you'll need a car to explore thoroughly.

Back on the main road to Lošinj, you'll see **Lake Vrana** appear below and to the west, an emerald-green ellipse of fresh water that supplies both Cres and Lošinj – but for this lake, both islands would be utterly dry, and you can't swim here due to its importance as a source of drinking water. Shortly after you pass the lake, there's a turn-off to the right (west) running down to **MARTINIŠ-ĆICA**, a small village 9km off the main road with a long shingle beach. Modern and lacklustre in comparison to Valun or Lubenice, it nevertheless boasts a well-organized if over-large **campsite**, just west of the village on the Slatina peninsula (☎051/574-127, ℗574-167), with pitches set close to the shore between shrubs and pines.

Osor

Set beside the narrow strait which divides Cres from Lošinj, **OSOR** is an erstwhile cathedral town which has shrunk to the size of a hamlet. It's the oldest settlement on either island, a prosperous Roman city which some historians believe once had a population of fifteen thousand, although a couple of thousand seems more realistic. Osor's regional importance survived into the medieval era, thanks in part to the reputation of eleventh-century holy man (and later saint) Gaudentius, who established the now ruined monastery of St Peter here and turned Osor into a centre of Glagolitic manuscript production. Driven out by local nobles, Gaudentius died in exile in Rome – from where his remains miraculously returned to Osor in a sea-borne wooden chest. They're now kept on the high altar of Osor's cathedral. Under Venetian rule, Osor was a typical casualty of the decline in Mediterranean trade which followed the discovery of America and the opening up of the trans-Atlantic economy. Visiting in 1771, the Italian traveller Abbé Fortis described it as the "corpse of a town, in which there are more houses than inhabitants".

Osor nowadays is a small village with a permanent population of around seventy, its streets exuding a peace that, on a hot summer's day, it seems nothing will ever disturb. The cobbled kernel of the village stands just above the **Kavuada**, the narrow channel, just 11m wide, which divides Cres and Lošinj. Dug either by the Romans or their Illyrian predecessors, it's now spanned by a swing bridge which opens at 9am and 5pm every day to let boats through.

Presiding over a funnel-shaped main square is the **Church** (originally cathedral) **of the Assumption** (Crkva Uznesenja), completed in 1497 and boasting an elegant trefoil facade in smooth, pale stone. The small **Archeological Museum** (Arheološki muzej; summer daily 6–10pm; 10Kn) in the Venetian town hall opposite has Roman relics and a model of medieval Osor enclosed by extensive town walls, stretches of which survive in much reduced form.

On the other side of the square, a narrow street runs past the fifteenth-century **Bishop's Palace**, now a sporadically open lapidarium harbouring bits of masonry from Osor's many churches, several of which are covered with the *plutej*, a plait-like design characteristic of Croatian medieval art. The most imposing item on display is the **bishop's throne**, a composite work made from Romanesque stone fragments taken from the graveyard of St Mary's Church – the backrest is embellished with a fine carving of two birds hovering above a lion-like beast. Ten minutes north of the square, past the graveyard, lies Bijar Bay, where a small beach is overlooked by the ruins of the thirteenth-century **Franciscan monastery**, another important centre of Glagolitic culture in its day.

Rooms (❶) are available from Turist Biro on the main square (☎051/237-007), and there are two **campsites**: the beautifully situated *Bijar* (☎051/237-027), with a shady seafront position on the northern side of town, and *Preko Mosta* (☎051/237-350), just across the bridge on the Lošinj side. For **eating**, *Konoba Livio* serves up decent pizza in a pleasant courtyard, while *Konoba Bonifačić* has a wider range of local seafood, Cres specialities like *janjeći žgvacet* (lamb stew) and a lovely garden. The **Osor Evenings** (Osorske večeri) festival of chamber music stages performances in the Church of the Assumption from the second weekend of July to early August – the tourist office in Lošinj (see p.214) will have details.

Mali Lošinj

Straggling along either side of a deep sheltered bay, **MALI LOŠINJ** is a fast-growing resort whose outer layers of apartment and bungalow developments have failed to destroy the charm of its elegant core, where slender cypresses and spiky green palms poke up between tiers of peach and orange houses, covered in purple bougainvillea. Most of the hotels have been kept well out of the way on the Čikat peninsula just west of town, together with an enormous campsite and the island's most crowded beaches.

Most life in Mali Lošinj revolves around the quayside **Riva lošinjskih kapetana**, where rows of potted cacti and subtropical plants line a harbourfront overrun in summer with souvenir stalls and café tables. The Riva's southern end opens out into the triangular open space of Trg Republike Hrvatske, from where **Braće Vidulića**, the main street, runs inland through the oldest part of town. Once you've clambered around the stepped alleys and winding streets, there's not much to see save the **Art Collections** (Umjetničke zbirke; June–Sept daily 9–11am & 7–9pm; Oct–May Mon–Fri 10am–noon; 15Kn), displayed in the former House of Culture just behind the harbourfront at Vladimira Gortana 35. Inside lie the combined hoards of two private collectors, beginning with that of art critic Andro Vid Mihičić, which concentrates on Croatian twentieth-century works, notably the mottled cityscapes of Paris-trained Emanuel Vidović (1870–1953). The second collection, that of Giuseppe Piperata – a Lošinj doctor who emigrated to Italy in 1945 but was prevented from taking his most valuable paintings with him – inclines more towards the Baroque. Highlights include Francesco Solimena's busy and agitated *Meeting* *with Rebecca*, and Il Guercino's more contemplative *Allegorical Landscape with Female Figures*, a pastoral scene of washerwomen beside a duck-filled pond.

The best place to swim is around **Čikat Bay**, 3km west of town, where a coastal path runs past a succession of concreted bathing areas, rocky beaches and a couple of stretches of pebble. It's a laidback area, good for strolling whatever the season, with Habsburg holiday villas sheltering among wind-bent tamarisks and pines, and cafés and shacks renting out snorkelling gear and surfboards along the more popular stretches.

Practicalities

Ferries from Pula and Zadar and **buses** from Rijeka and Cres stop at the northern end of Mali Lošinj's harbour, near the **tourist office** at Riva lošinjskih kapetana 29 (mid-June to mid-Sept daily 8am–10pm; mid-Sept to mid-June Mon–Fri 8am–3pm; ⊤ & ⑤051/231-884, ⓦwww.tz-malilosinj.hr). Staff here have bundles of free brochures and sell local maps, including one of the town and another covering foot- and bike-paths all over the island.

Jadrolinija, Riva lošinjskih kapetana (⊤051/231-765), sells **ferry tickets** for the nearby islands of Susak, Ilovik and Unije; those for Pula and Zadar are handled by Lošinjska Plovidba, Riva lošinjskh kapetana 8 (⊤051/231-077, ⓦwww.losinjplov.hr). Mountain bikes and windsurf boards can be rented (both about 50Kn per hour) on the seafront promenade in Čikat, in front of the *Bellevue* hotel. The scuba-diving centre in front of the *Hotel Bellevue* on Čikat (⊤051/233-900, ⓦwww.diver.hr) rents out gear and organizes beginners' courses from 1800Kn. You can play computer games and surf the **Internet** at Klik, in an alleyway behind the fish market at Bočac 46 (Mon–Sat 10am–2pm & 7–11pm, Sun 7–11pm; 20Kn/hr).

Accommodation

There's a wealth of accommodation in town. Numerous agencies offer private **rooms** (❶–❷) and apartments (❷): easiest to find are Lošinjska Plovidba (see above) and Manora, on the opposite side of harbour at Priko 29 (⊤051/520-101, ⓦwww.manora-losinj.hr). Handily placed for those arriving by car is the Cappelli agency, on the main road at the northern entrance to town at Kadin bb (⊤051/231-582 or 231-178). At the northwestern end of Čikat, a thirty-minute walk from the town centre, the vast *Autocamp Čikat* **campsite** occupies a wooded site with good access to the beaches (⊤051/232-125, ⓦwww.camp-cikat.com.hr).

Most of the package **hotels** on the Čikat peninsula are run by Jadranka (central booking on ⊤051/661-101, ⓦwww.jadranka.com) and are all much of a muchness. Best is the *Bellevue* (⊤051/231-222, ⑤231-268; ❻), an enormous rectangle with an indoor pool, right on Čikat bay and within walking distance of the town centre. It's much better value than the twin concrete monster-hotels *Aurora* (⊤051/231-324, ⑤231-542; ❺) and *Vespera* (⊤051/231-304, ⑤231-402; ❺), which lie some way to the south. Also run by Jadranka, the *Villa Alhambra*, Čikat bb (⊤051/232-042; ❹), offers slightly dowdy rooms, but at least it occupies an attractive pastel-pink nineteenth-century villa surrounded by palms. Less packagey in style is *Villa Margarita*, Bočac 54 (⊤051/233-867, ⓦwww.vud.hr; ❻; Easter–Oct), in the winding alleyways above the harbour; it offers en-suite rooms with TV and air-con, as well as nifty apartments (1050Kn for four people). *Villa Anna*, Velopin 31 (⊤051/233-223, ⓦwww.vila-ana.hr; ❻), on the opposite side of from the bay to Lošinj's Riva, has smart rooms with modern furnishings, TV, attached bathroom and a small outdoor pool – although the recent addition of a ground-floor nightclub ensures that this is no longer the quiet hideaway it used to be.

Eating and drinking

The cheapest **restaurant** in town is the *Gostionica Miramare*, Vladimira Gortana 75, just behind the Riva, with a perfunctory but palatable range of fish and grilled meats. You'll get better quality at *Barracuda*, Priko 31, a friendly and popular place on the opposite side of the harbour to the Riva, with excellent seafood risottos and good fresh fish. *Konoba Corrado*, just off the eastern end of Braće Vidulića at Sv. Marija 1 (entrance round the corner on Sv. Martin) has a smallish menu of basic grilled meat and fish dishes, all excellently prepared, with seating in an intimate tree-shaded courtyard. Roast Cres lamb is a speciality here, but it has to be ordered 24 hours in advance. The best place for baked fish, as well as a reasonable repertoire of mainstream grills, is *Lanterna*, romantically situated on a small harbour in Sveti Martin bay, fifteen minutes' walk east of the town centre. *Ara*, right behind the harbour at Bočac bb, offers the tastiest in the pizza and pasta line.

For **snacks**, the Lo-Pek bakery, Priko 3, is a good source of bread, pastries and *burek*. There's a (not particularly cheap) fruit and veg **market** just uphill from the harbourfront on Braće Vidulića and a fresh-fish market (Mon–Sat am only) on Trg Republike Hrvatske. **Drinking** and nightlife are centred on the cafés along the Riva, a few bars on Braće Vidulića and tame euro-discos in the hotels.

Veli Lošinj

Despite the name (*veli* means "big", *mali* "little"), **VELI LOŠINJ** is actually a smaller, quieter version of Mali Lošinj, a warren of pastel-coloured houses strung tightly around a tiny natural harbour. It's a forty-minute walk from the centre of Mali Lošinj – follow Braće Vidulića uphill, head straight over the crossroads, and take the path downhill to the right to Baldarka Bay. From here you can pick up a wonderfully scenic shoreline path, which winds past a sequence of rocky bays before arriving at the Punta hotel, with Veli Lošinj's harbour just beyond.

Once you arrive, you can't miss the hangar-like Baroque **St Anthony's Church** (Crkva svetog Antuna), which contains a fine tempera-on-wood *Madonna with Saints* (above a side door on the left as you enter) painted by Bartolomeo Vivarini in 1475. Originally commissioned by the Venetian senate, the painting was paraded around Venice every year on the anniversary of the Battle of Lepanto to celebrate the famous naval victory over the Ottomans (October 7), until being bought by a Lošinj family shortly after the fall of the Venetian republic. Just behind the harbour, a crenellated **Venetian tower**, built in 1455 to discourage raids by the Uskoks, peers over the waterside houses. Restored in 2000, it now houses a small **museum** (daily: June & Sept 9am–6pm; July–Aug 9am–8pm; 10Kn) which tells the story of the island through an attractively displayed assemblage of nautical trinkets and paintings of old ships. The star exhibit is a replica of the Apoxymenos (which translates literally as the "man scraping himself off"), a Roman statue of a sporty youth conducting his ablutions with the aid of a dirt-removing body knife. The original, found off the coast of Lošinj in 1999, is currently being restored in Zagreb, and may well be displayed in Mali Lošinj in the near future. The best place to **swim** is at the rocks beside the path from Mali Lošinj, and there are a few concreted areas near the packagey *Punta* hotel on Veli Lošinj's northwestern fringes. In front of the hotel, the Mare2 scuba-diving base (☎051/662-044, ⓦ www.mare2.it) rents out gear and offers a two-day learn-to-dive programme for about 800Kn.

Rooms (❶) and **apartments** (❷) are available from Val, Obala Maršala Tita 34 (☎051/236-352, ⓦwww.losinj-val.com); or Palma, slightly inland from the port at Vladimira Nazora 22 (☎051/236-179, ⓦwww.losinj.com). The *Punta* **hotel**, Šestavina bb (☎051/662-000, ⓦwww.jadranka.hr; ❺), offers neat en-suite rooms but fills up quickly with package groups in summer. Cosier **pension**-style accommodation is available from the *Saturn*, which has neat, bright but cramped rooms right on the harbour (☎051/236-102; ❸); and the slightly roomier *Villa San*, just above the harbour at Garina bb (☎051/236-527, ⓔlaika@ri.hinet.hr; ❸). The *Villa San* has a good **restaurant**; otherwise head for the Rovenska harbour at the eastern end of town, where there's a trio of excellent grilled-fish restaurants by the waterside, best of which is the *Sirius*, Rovenska 4 (☎051/236-399).

Susak

About 9km west of Lošinj, **Susak** is one of the most interesting of the small-er Kvarner islands. Its clay and sand composition gives it an appearance quite different from the rocky terrain of the other Adriatic islands, while its isolation has produced a distinctive way of life: islanders still speak their own dialect and have retained many traditions and customs, including an unusual method of singing directly from the throat and a local costume which consists of gaudy green-and-yellow skirts worn with even brighter pink tights. Postcards and guidebooks would have you believe you'll see this all the time, though in fact most of the island's two hundred inhabitants are elderly and rarely dress up in their brightest garb, preferring a gentler version of the same costume in navy or black. The island's industry, fish-canning, has long since died out, and many islanders emigrated to the Americas in the early twentieth century (there's a sizeable Susak community in Hoboken, New Jersey). The remaining popula-tion relies on money sent back by relatives to supplement income from sales of, among other things, Susak's **wines** – the red *pleskunac*, and *trojišćina*, an intriguing, dry rosé. There's one village on the island but little of historical interest, though you might want to climb up to **St Nicholas's Church** (Crkva svetog Nikole), inside which there's a large wooden twelfth-century crucifix which the locals call *Veli Buoh* – the "Great God".

Susak gets its fair share of day-trippers; a Jadrolinija ferry does the rounds of the local islands daily in July and August (less often during the rest of the year), leaving Mali Lošinj early in the morning and returning in late afternoon. There are also excursions to Susak in smaller boats (from around 150Kn per person including lunch), leaving from Mali Lošinj's Riva. There's a limited number of private **rooms** (❶) on Susak but they're usually reserved months in advance – the tourist office in Mali Lošinj can give you a list of telephone numbers, but won't make bookings on your behalf. For snacks and drinks, there's a **café** in the village, also serving as the main local meeting place.

Krk

The largest of the Adriatic islands, **KRK** (pronounced "Kirk", with a strong-ly rolled *r*) is also one of its most developed, a result of its proximity to Rijeka, whose airport is situated on the island. Much of the north is industrial, and blighted by package-oriented mega-developments like those at **Omišalj** and **Malinska**; the south and east, by contrast, offer grey, furrowed mountain peaks, lustrous vineyards, olive plantations and sun-bleached villages. The main

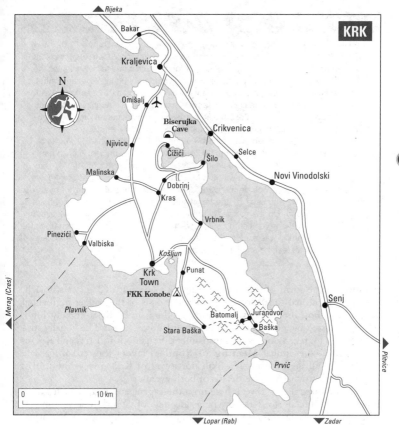

settlements are **Krk Town**, in the middle of the island, a historic little place with scraps of city wall surrounding a compact old centre, and **Baška** in the far south, a quirky fishing village with a spectacular sandy beach.

Krk was originally a Roman base called Curictum; Caesar is supposed to have had an encampment on the island, and was defeated by Pompey in a naval battle just offshore in 49 BC. Later, Krk fell under the sway of the Venetians, who in 1118 gave control of the island to the Dukes of Krk, subsequently known as the **Frankopans** (see box, p.218), one of the region's most powerful feudal families. Krk returned to the Venetian fold in 1480, after which it shared in the fortunes of the rest of the Adriatic: long, slow decline, followed by a sudden economic upsurge in the late twentieth century thanks to the tourist industry. In addition, the construction of the **bridge** linking Krk to the mainland enabled many locals to take jobs in Rijeka or elsewhere without having to move away from the island, thereby saving Krk from the rural depopulation which has afflicted other parts of the region.

Its proximity to the big city hasn't stopped Krk from preserving a few peculiarities of its own. Enduring **specialities** found nowhere else include *šurlice*, long, thin tubes of pasta dough, traditionally eaten *sa gulašom* (with goulash) or *sa žgvacetom* (lamb stew), and Vrbnička Žlahtina, the excellent white wine from Vrbnik on Krk's east coast. The island also preserves an archaic musical

The Frankopans

The story of the Frankopans on Krk begins with the shadowy **Dujmo I**, who was given control of the island by the Venetians in the twelfth century. His successors managed to turn the island into a hereditary fiefdom which came to be known as the *državina* ("statelet"), an autonomous territory only nominally under Venetian control. As the **Dukes of Krk**, Dujmo's descendants used the island as a base from which to extend their power to the mainland, grabbing a coastal strip stretching from Bakar to Novi Vinodolski in 1225 and expanding northeast into continental Croatia, establishing footholds in Ogulin and Ozalj to create an arc of family estates.

The name of **Frankopan** was officially adopted in 1430, when Duke Nikola received papal support for his claim to be descended from the ancient Roman patrician family of Frangepan – a move which, it was hoped, would accord the dynasty the prestige needed to compete with the other great houses of Europe. Frankopan power on Krk, however, was on the wane, and the defeat of **Duke Ivan VII** by the Hungarians in 1480 was used by the Venetians as an excuse to finally take back control of the island. On the mainland, branches of the Frankopan clan remained powerful well into the seventeenth century when, in 1671, **Fran Krsto Frankopan**, the head of the family, was executed alongside his brother-in-law Petar Zrinski (see box on p.113) after leading an anti-Habsburg rebellion.

tradition in the form of the *mijeh*, a bagpipe made out of a goat's stomach, whose shrill, atonal squalls of noise form the basis of the dances performed at the **Krk Folklore Festival** (Smotra folklora otoka Krka; usually July), which is hosted by a different town on the island each year. The equally strident *sopila* (a screechy oboe-type instrument indigenous to Istria and Krk) is celebrated at the annual **Meeting of Sopila Players** (Susret sopaca; late July) in the village of **Pinezići**, 8km northwest of Krk town – the tourist office in Krk town will have details of both events.

There are three flights a week here from the capital, and regular **buses** from Rijeka via Omišalj to Krk Town, a journey of about ninety minutes. Alternatively, passenger **ferries** run in summer from Crikvenica on the mainland to Šilo (though note that buses to the rest of the island from Šilo are infrequent), from Lopar on Rab to Baška (June–Sept only), and from Merag on Cres to Valbiska.

Krk Town

The island's main centre, and in the full throes of rapid expansion, modern **KRK TOWN** meanders over a series of hills in formless abandon, though at its heart there's still a small, partly walled city crisscrossed by narrow cobbled streets. The main fulcrum of the town is **Trg bana Jelačića**, a large open space just outside the town walls to the west, looking out onto a busy little harbour. Watching over the southeastern corner of the Trg is a hexagonal guard tower of thirteenth-century vintage although, like many of Krk's buildings, it makes much use of Roman-era masonry. A Roman gravestone is positioned halfway up one wall of the tower, portraits of the deceased peering down on passersby as if casually observing street life through an open window.

An opening on the western side of the square leads through to **Vela placa**, a smaller public space overlooked by another medieval guard tower, this time sporting a rare sixteenth-century 24-hour clock (noon is at the top, midnight at the bottom). Heading roughly east from here is the old town's main thoroughfare, J.J. Strossmayera, a two-metre-wide alleyway that becomes virtually impassable on summer nights, when the entire tourist population of the island seems to choose it as the venue for their evening corso. Even narrower alleys lead south from Strossmayera towards the town's Romanesque **Cathedral of the Assumption** (Katedrala Uznesenja; daily 9.30am–1pm), a three-aisled basilica built in 1188 on the site of a fifth-century church (and, before that, a Roman bath complex) incorporating pillars taken from a range of Roman buildings. There are two rows of ten columns fashioned in a variety of designs and materials – limestone, marble and red granite – with their capitals decorated with intricate floral patterns and scenes of birds eating fish. Among the altar paintings, look out for a sixteenth-century *Deposition* by Giovanni Antonio da Pordenone, and a largish *Battle of Lepanto* by A. Vicenti, showing the Madonna and Pope Pius V watching approvingly over victorious Venetian forces.

Built alongside the cathedral, from which it's separated by a narrow passageway, is another Romanesque structure, **St Quirinus' Church** (Crkva svetog Kvirina), whose campanile sports an onion dome topped by a trumpet-blowing angel. The campanile's lower storey is now a **Treasury** (Riznica; daily 9.30am–1pm; 10Kn) housing numerous artworks amassed by the bishops of Krk, most famously the *Madonna in Glory*, a silver-plated altarpiece made in 1477 by Venetian workshops for the last Duke of Krk, Ivan VII. It's a – literally – dazzling piece of craftsmanship, with central panels showing reliefs of the coronation of the Virgin and side panels depicting various saints. Behind the cathedral, a surviving stretch of wall incorporates the **Bishop's Palace** and an adjoining tower embellished with the Lion of St Mark – the symbol of Venetian sovereignty – although these sea-facing bastions were built in the fifteenth century under the Frankopans.

On the northern side of Strossmayera, steep cobbled streets seem to tunnel their way through a largely residential part of the old town which, largely devoid of cafés, shops and streetlighting, has the feel of a half-abandoned rural village. Standing at the northern apex of this maze, the **Church of Our Lady of Health** (Crkva majke božje od zdravlja) is worth a quick look if it's open – the nave is framed by two graceful lines of Romanesque arches, each held aloft by salvaged Roman columns. Diagonally opposite is the much larger church of the **Franciscan monastery** (Franjevački samostan), which rarely opens its doors outside mass times.

Krk's main **bathing** area lies to the east of town, where a sequence of small rocky coves provide a variety of atmospheric perches. There's a naturist beach about twenty minutes' walk east, by the *Politin* campsite.

Practicalities

Buses from Rijeka arrive at the **bus station** on the harbourfront, two minutes' walk west of Trg bana Jelačića. There's no public transport to and from Rijeka **airport**, 20km away at the northern end of Krk island; a taxi into Krk Town will cost 220–250Kn. The **tourist office**, up some steps in the northwest corner of Vela placa (Mon–Fri 8am–3pm, Sat & Sun 8am–1pm; ℡ & ℻ 051/221-414, ⓦ www.tz-krk.hr), has free town plans, a map of hiking paths on the Prniba peninsula just east of town, and information on cultural events. You can **surf the Web** at Multilink on Strossmayereva (daily 8am–noon & 7–11pm; 20Kn/hr).

Accommodation

Rooms (❶–❷) and two- and four-bed **apartments** (❷) are available from innumerable agencies around town, with only tiny variations in price from one to the next: most convenient are Autotrans in the bus station building (Mon–Sat

8am–9pm, Sun 8am–1pm & 6–9pm; ☎051/222-661, ✉krk@autotrans.hr), 500m west of Trg bana Jelačića on the other side of the harbour; and Aurea, at the northern entrance to town at Vršanska 26L (you'll see it on the right as you enter Krk from the Rijeka direction; May–Sept daily 8am–9pm; Oct–April Mon–Fri 8am–3pm, Sat 8am–1pm; ☎051/222-277, ⓦwww.aurea-krk.com).

The HI-affiliated **hostel** *Krk*, D.Vitezića 32 (☎051/220-212; 140Kn per person including breakfast, with a thirty-percent surcharge for stays of less than four days), is perfectly situated in a quiet corner of the old town, occupying the restored building of the island's first-ever hotel. Rooms (mostly quads and triples, although there are a few doubles available) are neat and tidy, and guests can use a washing machine. There's a large **campsite**, *Ježevac* (☎ & ⓕ051/221-081), ten minutes' walk southwest of town, and an exclusively naturist camp, *Politin* (☎051/221-351, ⓕ221-246), on the other side of town just beyond the *Koralj* hotel.

Krk's popularity with guests from northern Europe ensures that its **hotels** are overpriced for what they offer: the *Marina*, Obala hrvatske mornarice bb (☎051/221-128, ⓦwww.hotelikrk.com; ⑥), can't be beaten for convenience, offering acceptable if plain en-suite rooms slap-bang on the seafront. There's a line of package hotels hogging the water's edge to the east of town. The *Dražica*, Ružmarinska 6 (☎051/655-755, ⓦwww.hotelikrk.com; ⑦) offers eight storeys of prim en-suite rooms; nearby, *Tamaris*, Ružmarinska bb (same contact details; ⑥), is a more personable two-storey two-star offering neat rooms, with attached bathroom and most with TV as well, the bottom-storey ones opening straight out onto the seafront path. Best of the bunch is the three-star *Koralj*, Vlade Tomašića bb (☎051/221-044, ⓕ221-022, ✉zlatni-otok@ri.hinet.hr; ⑥), with bright, modern accommodation set among fragrant pine woods.

Eating, drinking and entertainment

There are plenty of **restaurants** offering fresh fish on the waterfront: *Corsaro*, Obala Hrvatske mornarice 1, is a good place for shellfish, squid risotto and seafood pasta, although there are other equally decent establishments on either side – all of which fill up fast on summer evenings. Just inland at Trg svetog Kvirina 1, *Frankopan* serves up similar fare in a slightly more formal atmosphere, with a restful terrace facing towards the cathedral. *Nono*, just east of the old town at Krčkih iseljenika 8, is the best place for authentic Krk recipes, augmenting the customary seafood fare with roast lamb, *šurlice* and other regional favourites – although the mock-rustic interior comes across as trashy rather than traditional. Picnic supplies can be picked up from the **supermarket** (Mon–Sat 7am–8pm, Sun 7am–1pm) opposite the bus station.

Slastičarnica Katarina, Matije Gupca 2, is the best place for **ice cream**, and there are a couple of busy **cafés** on the waterfront. Trendiest of the **bars** is *Jungle*, just up from Trg bana Jelačića on Stjepana Radića, which turns into a mainstream disco after 11pm.

There's a busy programme of cultural happenings in July and August, with folk, pop and classical **concerts** taking place in the Kaštel, or on Trg Kamplin just in front of it – the tourist office will provide a calendar of events. Two high-profile **festivals** attracting international performers are the Kamplin Jazz Festival (mid-Aug; ⓦwww.kamplinjazzfest.com) and the International Folk Festival (Međunarodna smotra folklora; late Aug). Depending on how many non-Croatian writers are invited, the Pontes Literature Festival (late Aug; ⓦwww.pontes.com) may feature prose readings and round-table discussions in English.

Punat to Baška

Four kilometres east of Krk Town, the village of **PUNAT** is set on the tranquil, enclosed bay of Puntarska draga. It's hardly the most evocative town on the island – a largely modern place made up of souvenir stalls, apartment blocks and a massive marina just to the north of town. However, there's a promising sequence of gravel beaches to the south, soon fading into quieter, rockier stretches of coast.

The main reason to come here is to take a taxi boat (boat owners tout for custom along the harbourfront; 20Kn return) across the bay to the islet of **Košljun**, about 1km offshore, where there is a **Franciscan monastery** (Franjevački samostan; Mon–Sat 9am–12.30pm & 3–6pm, Sun 10.30am–12.30pm; 10Kn) founded by monks settled here by the Frankopans in 1447. From Košljun's jetty, a path leads up to the monastery church, with a lofty, wooden-beamed interior. Look out for the 1532 polyptych by Girolamo da Santacroce on the high altar, showing scenes from the life of the Virgin. In one panel, a stocky and bearded St Quirinus holds a maquette of Krk Town, accompanied by St Catherine, whose right hand rests on the wheel on which she was tortured. Stretching across the arch above the altar is a large and dignified *Last Judgement*, executed in 1654 by E. Ughetto, whose swirling panoramas of heaven, hell and purgatory provide a contrast with the simpler but no less harrowing *Stations of the Cross* by the twentieth-century Expressionist Ivo Dulčić. A side gallery holds pen-and-ink drawings by the naive painter Ivan Lacković-Croata, and there are some rather more off-the-wall exhibits in the cloister outside, like a one-eyed sheep in a glass case and a two-headed lamb in a bottle. The adjoining **museum** has an interesting mishmash of stuff, including a selection of international banknotes and coins, some ancient typewriters and gramophones, and a display of local costumes. Outside, a confusing array of paths leads through the wilderness of the monastery gardens, although Košljun is so small that it's difficult to get really lost.

Practicalities

Krk–Baška **buses** pick up and drop off in a car park on the southeastern side of Punat. It's a short walk north along the seafront from here to the **tourist office**, housed in the same building as the post office (summer daily 7am–3pm; winter Mon–Fri 7am–3pm; ☎051/854-970, ⓦwww.punat.com), where you can collect a free town plan and the *Pastirske staze* map of local hiking routes in the green hills above town. Nearby, Marina Tours, on the seafront at Obala 81 (☎051/854-375, ⓕ854-340, ⓔmarina-punat@ri.tel.hr), is the place to enquire about **rooms** (❶). There's a simple **youth hostel**, *Ljetovalište OTC* (☎ & ⓕ854-037; 80Kn per person; May–Sept), in the centre, two blocks behind the market at Novi put 8, but in season it's invariably full of Croatian schoolkids. The spacious *Pila* **campsite** south of town has its own concrete beach (☎051/854-122, ⓕ854-101). Four kilometres south of town on the road to Stara Baška, a side-road descends to the *Konobe* naturist campsite (☎051/854-036, ⓕ854-101), a self-contained resort with its own restaurants and shops.

Stara Baška

A minor road heads south out of Punat towards **STARA BAŠKA**, 12km distant, a tiny place clinging to a narrow coastal strip at the base of the sage-covered slopes of the 482-metre Veli Hlam. This would be the most beautiful spot on the island if it wasn't for the unsightly holiday homes, and there are several small stretches of shingle beach – the best of which is in Oprna Bay 2km north of the village, visible from the road as you descend from the direction of Punat.

There aren't any buses to Stara Baška, so you'll need a car to get here – unless you want to walk here over the hills from Batomalj (see opposite), near Baška. The Zala agency in the centre of the village (☎ & ℱ051/844-605) has **rooms** (❶), and there's a **campsite**, the *Škrila*, on the shoreline at Stara Baška's northern end (☎051/844-678, ⊛www.skrila.hr). The *Nadia* **restaurant** is the best place to eat – fresh local fish like *škarpina* (groper) and *kovač* (John Dory) are pricey but worth it – and also has rooms (☎051/844-663, ℱ844-686; ❸).

Baška and around

Lying at the island's southern end, and connected by frequent bus to Krk Town, **BAŠKA** is set in a wide bay ringed by stark mountains. At the heart of a rapidly modernizing town lies the kind of fishing village that wouldn't look out of place in Brittany or Cornwall, a tangle of crooked alleyways and colourful

The Glagolitic script

The origins of Glagolitic go back to ninth-century monks **Cyril and Methodius**, chosen by the Byzantine emperor to convert the Slavs to Christianity. In order to translate the Gospels into the Slav tongue, Cyril and Methodius developed a new alphabet better suited to its sounds than either Latin or Greek. They began their missionary work with a trip to Moravia in 863, enjoying great success before the arrival of competing missions from Western Europe, and although their alphabet never caught on in Moravia, followers of Cyril and Methodius brought it to the Adriatic seaboard, where Croatian priests adopted it.

The script, which came to be known as **Glagolitic** (because so many manuscripts began with the words "*U ono vrijeme glagolja Isus*", "And then Jesus said"), is an extremely decorative 38-letter alphabet which borrowed some shapes from Greek, Armenian and Georgian, but which also contained much that was original. Other disciples of Cyril and Methodius made their way to Bulgaria, where they produced a modified version of the script, called **Cyrillic** in recognition of one of their mentors, versions of which are still used today in Russia, Ukraine, Bulgaria, Serbia and Macedonia.

Glagolitic took root in the areas of Croatia where Byzantine influence was at its strongest, and even with the growth of the power of the Roman Church, and Rome's use of Latin in church services, Croatian clerics stuck with the Glagolitic script and the Slav liturgy. The use of Glagolitic spread to the secular sphere too: the **Vinodol Codex** of 1288, drawn up by the Frankopans to delineate the rights and duties of their subjects around Novi Vinodolski, employed a flamboyant, cursive version of the script.

A succession of popes opted to tolerate Glagolitic rather than risk alienating the Adriatic clergy and driving them back into the embrace of Byzantium, and Glagolitic proved surprisingly enduring. Glagolitic prayer books were produced by clerics in Senj using the new printing technology from the 1490s onwards, and the script was still in use come the Reformation, when Croatian Protestants such as Stjepan Konzul Istranin from Buzet published Glagolitic books in Tübingen, prompting priests loyal to Rome to step up their own Glagolitic productions in response.

Ottoman advances finally brought an end to book production at Senj, and Adriatic Croatia's masters – whether Austrian or Venetian – increasingly regarded the use of Glagolitic as a sign of Slav resistance. Abbé Fortis, travelling round the Kvarner Gulf in the 1770s, noted that the Bishop of Rab was sending out Italian-speaking priests to counter the influence of local Glagolitic-using clergy. In inland Istria the script remained in use rather longer, but the Austrians prohibited its use in public documents in 1818, and the Glagolitic courses taught in Gorizia seminary were finally wound down in 1862. The growth of Croatian nationalism occasioned a Glagolitic revival in the late nineteenth century, but the universal dissemination of the Roman alphabet through secular education had by this stage condemned Glagolitic to obscurity.

houses perched on a steep slope facing the sea. Baška's star attraction, however, is its two-kilometre stretch of **beach**, a mixture of sand and fine shingle that from a distance looks like a long crescent of demerara sugar – not that you'll be able to appreciate this in July and August, however, when its entire surface is covered with parasols, beach towels, and pinky-hued north Europeans contentedly roasting themselves in the sun. Despite its popularity, it's undoubtedly one of the best beaches in the Adriatic, and the view from here – embracing the bare offshore island of Prvić and the Velebit mountains in the background – is dramatic whatever the time of year. In season, taxi boats shuttle bathers to and from the shingle coves of Prvić, or to the succession of bays east of Baška – of which long, shallow **Vela Luka** is the most alluring.

Twenty minutes' walk inland from Baška (back along the main road to Krk), **St Lucy's Church** (Crkva svete Lucije) in the village of **JURANDVOR** is the site of one of Croatian archeology's most important discoveries: the inscription known as the **Baška tablet** (Bašćanska ploča). Recording a gift to the church from the eleventh-century King Zvonimir, the tablet is the first mention of a Croatian king in the Croatian language and the oldest surviving text in the Glagolitic script (see box opposite). The original tablet is now in the Croatian Academy of Arts and Sciences in Zagreb, but there's a replica inside the church, and most places on the island seem to have sprouted copies.

Heading west from Jurandvor, a minor road leads to the hillside village of **BATOMALJ**, 1km away, the starting point for the path across the mountains to Stara Baška. The walk takes about three hours, rising steeply before skirting the 482-metre peak of Veli Hlam – it's well maintained and marked in either direction, although the going can be tough in wind or rain.

Practicalities

Buses terminate at a gravelly car park, from where it's a five-minute walk downhill to the town's main T-junction. Turn right here to find Baška's **tourist office** (July & Aug Mon–Sat 8am–9pm, Sun 8am–noon; Sept–June Mon–Fri 8am–3pm; ☎051/856-817, ℗856-544, ⓦwww.tz-baska.hr), which has a generous supply of brochures and town maps, and also provides an invaluable hiking map – drawn up by Czech tour guides who cleared and marked local goat-tracks to provide their own tourists with more in the way of outdoor activities. Private **rooms** (❶–❷) and **apartments** (❷) are available from agencies such as Primaturist, Kralja Zvonimira 98 (July & Aug daily 8am–10pm; ☎051/856-132, ℯprimaturist@ri.tel.hr) and Guliver next door (July & Aug daily 9am–10pm; ☎051/586-004, ℯpdm-guliver@ri.tel.hr), both of which are a few steps east of the main T-junction.

Baška's **hotel rooms** all fall under the aegis of the monstrous concrete *Corinthia* and its numerous annexes which stretch along the beach (☎051/656-111, ℗856-584, ⓦwww.hotelibaska.hr), offering accommodation ranging from sparsely furnished en-suite rooms (❹) to plush modern rooms with TV (❼) – the cheaper rooms will doubtless be booked solid by package tourists for the entire summer season. *Camping Zablaće* (☎051/856-909, ℗856-604) is an enormous, largely shadeless **campsite** which runs for about 1km along the southern end of the beach. At the eastern side of Baška, *Bunculuka* is a nudist site with its own stretch of beach in the next bay along (☎051/856-806, ℗856-595). Squatina Diving, at the far end of the beach at Zarok 88a (ⓦwww.squatinadiving.com), offers a one-day introductory course to scuba diving (475Kn) and plenty of other two- and four-day courses.

The best place **to eat** is *Cicibela*, on the seafront below the tourist office at Emila Geistlicha bb, offering excellently prepared seafood and a respectable range of steaks. *Konoba Kalypso*, Zvonimirova 51, is the poor man's alternative – a cosy harbourside bar which serves up plates of *srdele* (anchovies) and *girice* (whitebait), accompanied by good local wine.

Vrbnik, Dobrinj and around

There are no major resorts on the eastern side of Krk, but a succession of attractive small settlements provide reason enough to make a brief foray into the region. You'll need your own transport in order to explore the region in depth: towns in this part of the island are connected by infrequent bus to Krk Town, but not with each other, meaning that you can only visit one of them in the course of a day-trip.

East of Krk Town, a minor turning branches off the main road to Baška and climbs over a low ridge towards the fertile plain of the **Vrbničko polje**, where lush vineyards supply the wineries of **VRBNIK**, a small town perched on a fifty-metre-high sea cliff. The highly regarded local tipple, the dry white Vrbnička Žlahtina, is served in numerous local wine cellars, and the town itself – a network of narrow cobbled alleys which occasionally part to reveal views of Crikvenica and Novi Vinodolski across the water – is worth a quick amble.

There are two daily buses from Krk Town to Vrbnik – you'll have to catch the early morning service if you want to return the same day. The **tourist office** (☎051/857-479, ⓦwww.multilink.hr/vrbnik) on the main square has a list of private **rooms** (❶), and there's a newish, medium-sized **hotel**, the *Argentum*, in the eastern part of town at Supec 68 (☎051/857-370, ⓕ857-352, ⓔmesic.doo@hi.hinet.hr; ❹; May–Oct). *Nada*, at the sea-facing tip of the town at Glavača 22, has a good seafood **restaurant** upstairs and an evocatively fusty cellar hung with hams downstairs, where you can try the family's wine accompanied by local cheese and *pršut*. A couple of hundred metres east of the main square, *Gospoja*, Frankopanska 1, is a larger, more modern cellar with equally excellent wines and nibbles.

Šilo

Thirteen kilometres north of Vrbnik on the eastern side of Krk is the island's main harbour, **ŠILO**, a largely modern village with a couple of stretches of fine shingle beach. There's a ferry (foot passengers only) connecting Šilo with Crikvenica on the mainland, though if you're arriving on the island by this route, note that there are no direct buses to Krk Town. The **tourist office** on the seafront at Stara cesta bb (Mon–Fri 8am–3pm; ☎ & ⓕ051/852-107, ⓦwww.multilink.hr/dobrinj) handles **rooms** (❶) here and in Dobrinj, and there's a big beachside **campsite**, the *Tiha*, on the peninsula on the eastern side of the bay (☎051/852-170, ⓕ852-362).

Dobrinj and the Biserujka Cave

Five kilometres west from Šilo, **DOBRINJ** is an inland version of Vrbnik, a hilltop village from whose church there's an expansive view north towards the sprawl of Rijeka and Mount Učka, with the resorts of Lovran and Opatija lurking at its feet. Rather like the hill towns of nearby Istria, Dobrinj seems to be reinventing itself as a cultural centre, and there's plenty to see if you're here in summer, when everything's open. On the tiny main square, the former St Anthony's Church (Crkva svetog Antuna) now houses a **gallery** which hosts varied art shows in summer, while an impossible-to-miss creamy-pink town house round the corner hosts seasonal exhibitions of contemporary painting and sculpture. Between the two, a one-room **Religious**

Art Collection (Sakralna muzejska zbirka; summer daily 9am–noon & 6–9pm; 10Kn) boasts, among other trinkets, a fifteenth-century reliquary containing the head of St Ursula and a fourteenth-century altar cloth decorated with a Coronation of the Virgin sewn with gold thread. Just off the main square, the **Ethnological Collection** (Etnografska zbirka; summer daily 9am–noon & 6–9pm; 10Kn) contains three floors of agricultural tools, ceramics and costumes.

There's a single late-afternoon bus from Krk Town to Dobrinj on weekdays, but it doesn't return to town the same day. However it's just about feasible to treat Dobrinj as a day-trip from Krk Town by public transport, if you travel out via **Malinska** in the northwest – check times at the Autotrans desk at Krk Town's bus station before setting out. The homely *Zora* **restaurant** on Dobrinj's main square is one of the best places on the island to eat *šurlice*.

North of Dobrinj, it's 4km to the village of **Čižići** on the muddy Soline Bay, from where a well-signed road heads north to the **Biserujka Cave** (Špilja Biserujka; daily: March–June, Sept & Oct 10.15am–4.45pm; July & Aug 10am–7pm; 15Kn), a further 3km away on a coastal heath. The cavern is only about 150m long, but is well worth visiting – the stalagmite and stalactite formations are impressive, and you may also be lucky enough to catch sight of the cave's bat population.

Rijeka to Senj

Heading southeast, it's a while before you're finally free of Rijeka's industrial sprawl, which stretches way down the coast as far as the bridge to Krk. About 10km out of the city, nestling around the northern end of Bakar Bay, **Bakar** is a case in point, a once pretty place nowadays dominated by a vast oil refinery. It preserves its narrow streets, a derelict castle and a handful of crumbling town houses built by local mariners, but as a whole the place doesn't invite much more than a quick wander.

Ten kilometres further on, at the far end of Bakar Bay, **Kraljevica** is another example of an old coastal town almost entirely swallowed up by the industry of the Rijeka hinterland. It began life as the seventeenth-century strongpoint of Croatia's leading aristocratic families of the time, the Frankopans and the Zrinskis – the latter built two fortified palaces here, the Stari and Novi Grad, although they've since been much rebuilt and aren't open to the public.

The Bura

One of the Kvarner's most famous natural features is the **Bura**, a wind which is said "to be born in Senj, married in Rijeka, and die in Trieste". A cold, dry north-easterly, it blows across the central European plain and gets bottled up behind the Adriatic mountains, escaping through the passes at places like Senj, where it is claimed to be at its worst. It's said that you can tell the Bura is coming when a streak of white cloud forms atop the Velebit, the mountain ridge which stretches down the coast. At its strongest, it can overturn cars and capsize boats. When it's blowing, ferry crossings between the mainland and the islands are often suspended, and the road bridge to Krk will either be off limits to high-sided vehicles, or closed altogether.

Crikvenica and Novi Vinodolski

CRIKVENICA has been a tourist resort since the 1890s, when Archduke Josef, brother of Emperor Franz Josef, earmarked Crikvenica for development in a deliberate challenge to the pre-eminence of Opatija. He went so far as to name Crikvenica's first hotels – the *Erzherzog Josef* (now the *Therapia Palace*) and the *Erzherzogin Clothilde* – after himself and his wife. Following World War I, Crikvenica went on to prosper for a time as one of Yugoslavia's more modish playgrounds, though nowadays whatever charm it once possessed has been lost with the construction of the modern hotels and apartment blocks which straggle along its seafront. There really isn't anything to do but loll around on the succession of gravelly **beaches** which stretch northwest from the centre. Strossmayerovo Šetalište is the town's liveliest artery, leading along the waterfront from the main Trg Nikole Cara via a tangle of hotels, restaurants and tourist shops.

Crikvenica is easily reached by **bus** from Rijeka, while in July and August around ten **ferries** daily go to Šilo on Krk (see p.224). The **tourist office** is at Trg Stjepana Radića 1c (July & Aug daily 9am–7pm; Sept–June Mon–Fri 9am–3pm; ☎051/241-867, ⓦwww.crikvenica-tourist.com), a block north of the bus station; **rooms** (❶–❷) can be had from the Autotrans agency in the bus station, or from Kvarner Express just round the corner on Strossmayerovo Šetalište 3.

Nine kilometres south of Crikvenica, the resort town of **NOVI VINODOLSKI** ("Novi" for short) straggles along the main road for a couple of kilometres. It's actually of far greater historical significance than its rather suburban appearance might suggest, since it was here that the so-called **Vinodol Statute** (Vinodolski zakon), the oldest extant document in Croatian, was signed in 1288, recognizing the rule of the Frankopans over the surrounding district and the rights of the local citizens. Modern Novi is a dull sort of place, its waterfront lined with large hotels leading up to a scrappy harbour. Up above the main road there's a small old quarter, piled up on the hill, where you can view the austere sole remaining tower of the thirteenth-century Frankopan **castle** in a central square. Also on the square is a small **Town Museum** (Gradski muzej; Mon–Sat 9am–noon & 7–9pm, Sun 9am–noon; 10Kn) with a rather perfunctory display relating to the statute as well as folk costumes from the surrounding area. There's not much beach to speak of here, merely a string of concreted platforms near the hotels.

There's an enthusiastic **tourist office** on the main road, 200m south of the bus stop (daily 9am–10pm; ☎ & ℗051/244-306, ⓦwww.multilink.hr/novi -vinodolski); Adria Tourist, in the same building (☎051/244-307, ⓔinfo@hoteli-novi.hr), has **rooms** (❶–❷). Several shoreline **campsites** lie along the string of attractive bays south of Novi, all of them pleasant, isolated spots to stay, though you'll need your own transport. The first, *Povile* (☎051/793-083), is 3km south of Novi on the northern flanks of the Teplo inlet; 12km further on is *Sibinj* (☎051/796-905), followed after another 3km by *Bunica V* (☎053/616-718).

Senj

"May God preserve us from the hands of Senj." So ran a popular Venetian proverb, inspired by the warrior community known as the **Uskoks** (see box opposite), who in 1537 made **SENJ** their home and used it as a base from which to attack Adriatic shipping. Locals proudly claim the Uskoks as Croatian freedom fighters who helped slow the Ottoman advance, although their penchant for piracy earned the enmity of Venice and Dubrovnik, and contemporary historians tend to be more equivocal about the real nature of their activity.

The Uskoks

One result of the Ottoman Empire's steady advance into Bosnia and Croatia in the early sixteenth century was the creation of a mass of refugees who, forced from their lands in the Balkan interior, gravitated towards the Adriatic coast and began to organize themselves into military groups in order to repel further Ottoman encroachment. These anti-Turkish fighters were collectively known as **Uskoks**, although the name subsequently came to be applied to one particular group from Hercegovina, who took control of the fortress of Klis (see p.313) and defended it against Turkish forces until it finally fell in 1537.

The Uskoks subsequently withdrew to Senj, from where they mounted further resistance. Senj was under **Austrian rule** at the time, and the Uskoks were regarded as a useful component in the empire's defences. However, the Uskoks were consistently – perhaps deliberately – underpaid, forcing them to turn to piracy in order to survive. Harassing Adriatic shipping from their fifteen-metre-long rowing boats, they considered anything Turkish a legitimate target, which in practice meant attacking the (usually Venetian) ships on which Turkish goods were transported. The Austrians turned a blind eye, regarding Uskok piracy as a convenient way of challenging Venetian dominance of the Adriatic. The Uskoks also had few qualms about attacking Christian subjects of the Ottoman sultan, especially if they were Orthodox. The Rab-born churchman Markantun Dominis (see box on p.235), who briefly served as Bishop of Senj, even suggested that the Uskoks would abandon piracy if they were allowed to begin taking the Orthodox Serbs and Vlachs of the Turkish-controlled interior and sell them off as slaves.

Uskok commanders were often regarded as heroes fighting for the Catholic cause, but the lack of security for Adriatic shipping ultimately proved too much for the Venetians, who began a propaganda campaign accusing the Uskoks of eating the raw hearts of their enemies and dipping bread in their blood. In 1615 the Venetians provoked the so-called **Uskok War** with Austria in an attempt to bring an end to the problem. The Uskoks gave a good account of themselves until their Austrian protectors, eager for an accommodation with Venice, withdrew their support. According to the terms of the 1617 Treaty of Madrid, the Austrians agreed to destroy the Uskok fleet and resettle the Uskoks inland. Senj was occupied by the Austrian navy, and the Uskoks left for new homes in Otočac, just to the southeast, or in the Žumberak hills north of Karlovac.

Modern Senj is a quiet little town of mazy alleyways, worth a brief stop-off. It also stands at the beginning of the road which heads inland over the Vratnik pass towards the Plitvice lakes (see p.144) and Karlovac (p.138) – although there's little public transport on this route and it's much easier to reach the lakes from Split or Zadar. The only surviving reminder of the Uskoks in Senj nowadays is the **Nehaj Fortress** (daily: May, June, Sept & Oct 10am–6pm; July & Aug 10am–9pm; 12Kn) – the name means "fear not" or "heedless" – which looks over the town from a rubble-covered peak to the left of the harbour. It was constructed in 1558 under the auspices of Uskok commander Ivan Lenković, who obtained building materials by demolishing all the churches and monasteries which lay outside the town walls and so couldn't be defended against the Turks. Inside are three floors of exhibits illustrating the history of the Uskoks, featuring weaponry and costumes, with excellent English-language commentary. The view from the battlements justifies the climb, with the convoluted street plan of central Senj spread out immediately below, and the pale, parched flanks of Krk across the water.

The main focus of the town below is a scruffy harbourfront square, dotted with café tables, behind which lies a warren of alleyways and smaller piazzas. If you face inland and go left off the square, you'll come to the **Town Museum** (Gradski muzej; Mon–Fri 7am–3pm, Sat & Sun 10am–noon; 12Kn), housed in the fifteenth-century Vukasović mansion. It's a lacklustre display of archeological fragments and engravings illustrating the many literary figures to have come out of Senj over the centuries – foremost among them Pavao Ritter Vitezović (1652–1713), the poet and politician whose extravagantly titled *Kronika aliti spomen vsega i svieta vikov* ("Chronicle and Remembrance of Everything and the World from the Beginning") was one of the first history books to try to place the story of the Croats in a global framework. Just east of here, below a much-rebuilt cathedral of Romanesque origins, the rich **Religious Art Collection** (Sakralna baština; Mon–Sat mid-June to mid-Sept 9am–noon & 6–8pm; 12Kn) recalls the time when Senj was both the seat of a powerful bishopric and a major printing centre for Croatian-language religious texts. Among the Glagolitic missals, episcopal robes, paintings and silverware lie two exquisitely wrought fourteenth-century processional crosses, the biggest of which features a central relief of the Lamb of God surrounded by winged beasts symbolizing the evangelists – the lion for Mark, the bull for Luke, the eagle for John, and an angel for Matthew.

Practicalities

Buses plying the Rijeka–Zadar–Split coastal route pull up on the waterfront, close by the main square. The **tourist office**, about 400m north along the seafront at Stara cesta 2 (July & Aug daily 7am–9pm; rest of year Mon–Fri 9am–3pm; ☏053/881-068, ℻881-219, ⓔtz.senj@gs.hinet.hr), will help out with basic info and might even have a free town map.

Accommodation in Senj's numerous private **rooms** (❶) and **apartments** (❷) is organized by two agencies, Senia Tours (☏053/881-238, ⓔsenia-tours@ gs.hinet.hr) and Mokotours (☏053/881-769, ⓦwww.moko-tours.hr), operating out of roadside kiosks roughly opposite the tourist office. Of the town's brace of **hotels**, *Nehaj*, Obala kralja Zvonimira 8 (☏053/881-285, ℻882-636; ❷), offers simple unrenovated rooms with shared facilities right on the seafront; while *Art*, lurking behind a round harbourfront tower at Obala kralja Zvonimira 15 (☏053/884-377, ℻884-376; ❸), has spick-and-span en-suite rooms overlooking the water. The *Restaurant Martina*, beside the Magistrala (coastal highway) at the northern entrance to town (☏053/881-638; ❷), is a pension-style place offering small but homely rooms with their own bathroom. There are a couple of tiny **campsites**, Spasovac (☏053/882-941) and Ujča, squeezed into coves 3km and 4km south of town respectively: neither have much in the way of facilities, but both are superbly situated beside small pebble beaches.

The *Lavlji Dvor* **restaurant**, in the tangle of streets just east of the museums at Petra Preradovića 2, is a good place to enjoy seafood and grilled meats, although you"ll find better-quality fare at the *Martina*, offering a range of grilled meat, fish and shellfish on an outdoor terrace looking towards the sandy-coloured eastern shores of Krk. There are several pavement **cafés** on the main seafront square and numerous tiny **bars**, largely catering to the locals, in the narrow streets that wind away from here.

Senj to the Paklenica National Park

Continuing south from Senj, the Magistrala picks its way beneath the rocky slopes of the **Velebit**, the mountain chain which follows the coast for some 100km. It's initially a forbidding sight, a stark, grey, unbroken wall, although there are patches of green pasture and forest just below its string of summits. Some of the best views of the Velebit are to be had from the eastern coasts of Rab and Pag, from where it towers over the coast like the waves of a frozen sea. There are few coastal settlements of any size along this stretch of the Adriatic – understandably, given the steep and rocky terrain, which leaves precious little space for houses, agriculture or tourist resorts. It's also one of the trickiest stretches of the Magistrala to drive along, with the road twisting its way around a seemingly endless sequence of deeply indented bays and rocky spurs. The scenery, however, is magnificent, and there are some nice coves into which **campsites** have been attractively squeezed – *Rača* (☎053/885-250), on the southern side of Sveti Juraj, and *Žrnovica*, 5km further south, are two of the most pleasant.

About 20km south of Sveti Juraj a side-road descends to the port of **Jablanac**, from where regular ferries cross the narrow Velebit channel to Mišnjak on the island of Rab (see p.232). Most coastal buses don't make the detour to Jablanac, dropping off on the main highway 4km away instead, so if you're heading for Rab it's best to catch a direct Rijeka–Senj–Rab Town bus – Jablanac itself is small, unspectacular and not the kind of place you would want to get stuck in. Much the same could be said of **Prizna**, 13km south, another small harbour just off the Magistrala, from where hourly ferries leave for Žigljen on Pag (see p.240).

The larger but equally unrewarding town of **Karlobag**, another 13km south, is the starting point for a minor road which winds inland over the mountains, struggling up through the rugged terrain before arriving at **Gospić**, main town of the **Lika** region. This is another potential route up towards the Plitvice lakes (see p.144), although there's little to stop for en route other than the sheer barrenness of the landscape, which can be oddly riveting. Travelling through the area in the 1870s, the future archeologist Arthur Evans (then Balkan correspondent for the *Manchester Guardian*) described the area as the "Croatian Siberia" – "a strange, wild land . . . with its scattered oases of fertility, its chaotic rocks, underground rivers, and mysterious caverns; a country – as everywhere else in Illyria – presenting the most startling contrasts of nakedness and cultivation."

The Paklenica National Park

The coast south from Karlobag is similarly sparse on attractions until you reach the village of **STARIGRAD-PAKLENICA**. A straggling line of modern seaside houses and apartments, it constitutes the handiest base for the **PAKLENICA NATIONAL PARK**, the Velebit's last great flourish before the ridge trails inland to meet the Dinaric range on Croatia's border with Bosnia-Hercegovina. The park, designated in 1949, is the most accessible area for hiking in the Velebit and contains some of the country's finest karst landscapes, featuring gorges, grizzled mountains and caves. It also contains three quite different climate zones – coastal, continental and sub-alpine – which makes its weather unpredictable and, at times, extreme.

The park comprises two limestone gorges, Velika Paklenica and, 5km to the south, Mala Paklenica (literally, Big Paklenica and Small Paklenica), which run down towards the sea, towered over by 400-metre-high cliffs. **Mala Paklenica** has deliberately been left undeveloped in order to protect its status as a (relatively) untouched wilderness – paths are not maintained or marked with the same thoroughness as in Velika Paklenica, and you'll need good maps if you want to explore it.

Into the park

The entrance to the **Velika Paklenica** gorge is about 2km inland from Starigrad, reached by a road which heads east just south of the *Hotel Alan*; there's no public transport along this route. After you pass through the half-abandoned, stone village of Marasovići, there's a ticket booth where you pay an entrance fee (30Kn) and receive a basic free map, if you haven't already picked one up from the national park office (see below). A car park lies 2km further on inside the park, from where the gorge begins to narrow in earnest and everyone has to proceed on foot. The main path up the valley passes beneath towering cliffs and dramatic outcrops of rock, while a stream rushes down a boulder-strewn bed below.

After 45 minutes of moderate ascent, a well-signposted side-path heads right to **Anića kuk**, a craggy peak lying a steep climb to the south. Beyond here, the main path levels out for a while, passing through elm and beech forest – surprisingly lush after the arid Mediterranean scrub of the coast below. After another fifteen minutes, a second side-path ascends steeply to the left. A strenuous forty-minute walk up here will bring you to **Manita peć** (open three mornings a week in June and Sept; daily July & Aug; ask at the national park office in Starigrad or at the entrance gate to the park for details), a complex of stalactite-packed caverns about 500m long. From here you can either turn back the way you came, or head on for another hour and a half (the path leads from the left of the cave as you emerge), up some fairly steep and none too easy slopes to **Vidakov kuk**, an 800-metre-high peak that gives fine views over the coast and islands.

Back on the main path, it's about twenty minutes to the *Šumarska kuća* hut, where you can get food and drink on spring and summer weekends, and a further thirty minutes to the *Borisov Dom* mountain hut, the starting point for assaults on the major peaks above. The most prominent of these is **Vaganski vrh** which, at 1757m above sea level, is the southern Velebit's highest peak. The views from the top are spectacular, but you'll need to be reasonably fit, have a good map and make an early start if you're going to attempt the walk up.

A circular walk taking in the **Mala Paklenica** branches off the main trail some ten minutes after the turn-off for Anića kuk. Climbing steeply across the Jurasova glava ridge, this heads south to the neck of the Mala Paklenica gorge, which leads down towards **Seline** on the coast. The canyon is beautifully rugged, the trail not too difficult to follow, and there are some impressive rock formations en route. The whole hike takes about seven hours from entrance to exit, and you can do it in reverse from Seline if you prefer.

Finally, don't forget Paklenica's potential as a **beach** resort. The best spot for sunbathing is the shoreline stretching south of the *Hotel Alan*, where a narrow band of shingle backed by olive and fig trees culminates in a broad cape overlooked by a ruined medieval tower. The water is beautifully clear, there are good views of the tawny hills to the south and west, and even on August weekends it doesn't get too crowded.

Practicalities

All coastal buses plying the Rijeka–Zadar route run through Starigrad, stopping near the *Hotel Alan* (handiest for the national park) or at the northern end of the village, where there's a small harbour. The latter stop is convenient for the **tourist office**, on the landward side of the road at Trg Tome Marašovića 1 (July & Aug daily 8am–9.30pm; Sept–June Mon–Fri 8am–2pm, Sat 8am–noon; ☎023/369-245, ⑩www.rivijera-paklenica.hr), where you can pick up leaflets about the park and advice on what to see. The **national park office**, 500m south along the main highway (daily 8am–3pm; ☎023/369-202), is also useful if you're planning trips into the mountains – they sell detailed hiking maps, can advise on weather conditions and book rooms in Velika Paklenica's mountain hut, *Borisov Dom*. One popular local excursion is the boat trip up the **Zrmanja river** (see p.253). The tourist office and all the hotels will put you in touch with agencies organizing these – expect to pay around 250Kn per person including lunch.

For **eating**, all of the hotels listed below have good restaurants offering the usual repertoire of seafood risottos and fresh fish; in addition, there's a string of inexpensive grills along the main road through Starigrad, and stores in which to stock up on provisions.

Accommodation

The tourist office can fix you up with one of the plentiful private **rooms** (**①**) in Starigrad: otherwise look out for the *sobe* signs dangling outside most houses along the main highway. Camping isn't allowed in the park itself, but there's an abundance of **campsites** in Starigrad, including a large, well-tended site occupying a pleasantly shingly stretch of beach next to the national park office (☎023/369-202) and several smaller ones tucked neatly into private gardens on the access road to the entrance to Velika Paklenica.

Hotels

Alan Franje Tuđmana 14, Starigrad ☎023/369-236, ⓔalan@zadar.net. High-rise, 450-bed package hotel offering simple en-suite rooms – TVs might be installed soon and prices may rise accordingly. Convenient for the park entrance, a short walk from the best bits of beach, and also has a set of rather swanky tennis courts. May–Oct. **④**

Croatia put Jaza bb, Seline ☎023/369-190. Family-run small hotel at the northern end of Seline, on the shore, offering a couple of cosy en-suite doubles and several swanky two- or four-person apartments. **④**

Kiko Seline ☎023/369-784, ⓦwww.kikopansion -starigrad-seline.hr. Another small waterside hotel, offering with TV and attached bathroom, and some apartments. Staff are helpful and knowledgeable. **④**

Rajna Franje Tuđmana bb, Starigrad ☎023/369-130, ⓦwww.rajna-paklenica@inet.hr. Medium-sized place with standard en-suite rooms, on the main highway. The nearest hotel to the park entrance, it's popular with trekkers, and has an activity-sport shop on site. **③**

Vicko Jose Dokoze 20, Seline ☎023/369-304, ⓦwww.hotel-vicko-hr. Swanky but intimate family hotel on the main highway, just up from the tourist office, offering neat rooms with TV. About 1500m north of both the park access road and the best beaches. **⑤**

Rab

South of Krk and east of Cres, mainland-hugging **RAB** is the smallest but probably the most beautiful of the main Kvarner Gulf islands. Its eastern side is rocky and harsh, rising to a stony grey spine that supports little more than a few goats, but the western side is lush and green, with a sharply indented coast and some beautiful – if crowded – coves. Medieval **Rab Town** is the island's highlight, while the **Lopar peninsula** at the northern end of the island possesses some of the

231

sandiest beaches in the country. The place can get crowded, especially in July and August, but not disastrously so.

Rab's main link with the rest of Croatia is the **ferry** which connects Jablanac on the mainland with **Mišnjak** on the island's southern tip. The three daily Rijeka–Rab **buses** use this ferry, finishing up in Rab Town. If you miss the bus, you'll have to walk or hitch from the Magistrala (coastal highway) to Jablanac harbour (4km) and from Mišnjak to Rab Town (8km). You can also hop over to Rab by ferry from Baška on Krk to Lopar, though bear in mind that this leaves you a good 10km from Rab Town and buses don't always connect with the ferry arrivals, so you may have a wait on your hands.

Rab Town

Rab's main attraction is **RAB TOWN**, a perfectly preserved late-medieval Adriatic settlement squeezed onto a slender peninsula along which are dotted the city's trademark sequence of Romanesque campaniles. It's a genuinely lovely place: a tiny grey-and-ochre city, enlivened with splashes of green palm, huddles of leaning junipers and sprigs of olive-coloured cacti which push their way up between balconied palaces. The population today is only a third of what it was in Rab's fourteenth-century heyday, although it's swelled significantly by the influx of summer visitors, who create a lively holiday atmosphere without overly compromising the town's medieval character.

Starting out as a base for Roman and then Byzantine fleets, Rab Town (Arbe in Italian) grew into a prosperous, self-governing medieval commune until its incorporation into the Venetian state in 1409. Following this, the town's privileges were gradually eroded, trade was redirected towards the mother city and, after two outbreaks of plague in the mid-1400s, urban life went into a steep decline. Things did not improve until the late nineteenth century, when Rab began to benefit from central European society's growing interest in Adriatic rest cures. In 1889, Austrian professors Leopold Schrötter and Johann Frischauf launched a strategy to develop Rab as a tourist destination, and 1897 saw the formation of the Società d'abellimento di Veglia (Society for the Beautification of Rab), a kind of embryonic tourist board. Thanks to the efforts of Austrian and Italian naturists, Rab – or, more accurately, the Frkanj peninsula just west of town – was one of the first **nudist resorts** in Europe, a status popularized by the visit of English **King Edward VIII** (accompanied by future wife Wallis Simpson) in the summer of 1936. Whether Edward actually got his tackle out or not remains the subject of much conjecture, but his stay on Rab provided the inspiration for a recent Croatian musical, *Kralj je gol* (literally "The King is Naked", although in colloquial Croatian it means much the same thing as "The Emperor's New Clothes"). After visiting Rab, Edward and Wallis continued down the Adriatic aboard a luxury yacht packed with sundry toffs and royal hangers-on. Pursued by Europe's press, the trip turned into the celebrity media-fest of its day, with thousands of locals lining the streets to ogle the couple when they came ashore at Šibenik, Split and Dubrovnik. The only journalists who failed to follow the cruise were the British – the idea that their monarch was romancing an American divorcee was too mind-bogglingly scandalous to report.

Arrival, information and accommodation

Rab's **bus station** is in the shopping centre just northeast of the harbour, a five-minute walk from Trg svetog Kristofora. If you're **moving on** to Dalmatia from here by public transport, take a Rijeka or Zagreb bus as far as the Magistrala just above Jablanac, then wait by the roadside for a southbound bus.

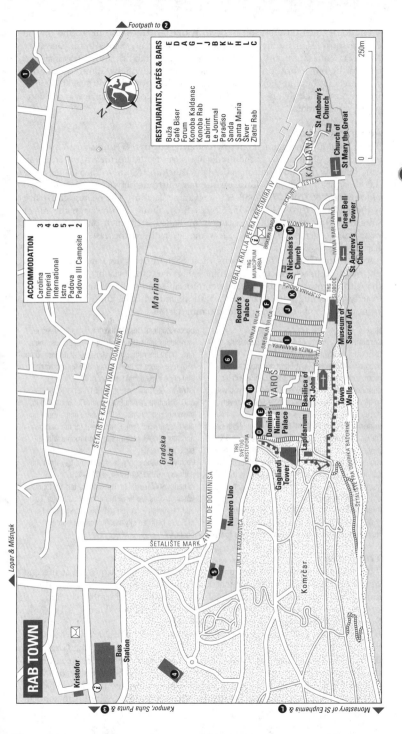

RAB TOWN

▲ *Footpath to* ❷

RESTAURANTS, CAFÉS & BARS

Buža	E
Café Biser	D
Forum	A
Konoba Kaldanac	G
Konoba Rab	J
Labirint	B
Le Journal	K
Paradiso	F
Sanda	H
Šanta Maria	L
Skver	C
Zlatni Rab	

ACCOMMODATION

Carolina	3
Imperial	4
International	6
Istra	5
Padova	1
Padova III Campsite	2

N

0   250m

❶

◄ *Lopar & Mišnjak*

ŠETALIŠTE KAPETANA IVANA DOMINISA

Marina

Gradska Luka

Kristofor

ⓘ

Bus Station

❹

ŠETALIŠTE MARK ANTUNA DE DOMINISA

JURJA BARAKOVIĆA

Numero Uno

❺

OBALA KRALJA PETRA KREŠIMIRA IV

TRG MUNICIPIUM ARBA

ⓘ

BISKUPA DRAGA

G

Rector's Palace

F

DONJA ULICA

SREDNJA ULICA

❻

TRG SVETOG KRISTOFORA

D

Dominis Nimira Palace

E

A   B

VAROŠ

C

Gagliardi Tower

Lapidarium

Basilica of St John

GORNJA ULICA

ULICA KNEZA BRANIMIRA

I

J

K

St Nicholas's Church

H

FLOJANOVA

STJEPANA RADIĆA

TRG SLOBODE

Museum of Sacred Art

IVANA RABLJANINA

St Andrew's Church

Great Bell Tower

Church of St Mary the Great

St Anthony's Church

KALDANAC

SVETNE A. TESTENA

Town Walls

ŠETALIŠTE FRA ODORIKA BADURINE

Komrčar

◄ *Kampor, Suha Punta & ❸*

◄ *Monastery of St Euphemia & ❶*

The local tourist association has two **tourist offices**, the main one on the central square, Trg municipium arbe (June–Sept daily 8am–10pm; Oct–May Mon–Fri 8am–3pm; ☎051/724-064, ⊚www.tzg-rab.hr), and a seasonal one behind the bus station on Mali Palit (June–Sept daily 8am–10pm). The shopping precinct behind the bus station serves as the town's main service centre, with a post office (Mon–Fri 7am–8pm, Sat 7am–2pm), pharmacy and a couple of supermarkets.

Accommodation

There are numerous agencies in town offering **rooms** (❶) and apartments (❷), either in the old town or in the modern suburbs to the northeast: try Kristofor, just behind the bus station at Mali Palit bb (☎051/725-543, ⊚www .kristofor.hr); or Numero Uno, on the harbourfront between bus station and old town (☎ & ☎051/724-688, ⊚www.dmmedia.com). The nearest **campsite** is the *Padova III* (☎051/724-355, ☎724-539), about 2km away in the resort suburb of **Banjol**, though it's a largely unshaded site which can get crowded in season; to get there, simply follow the sea path on the eastern side of the harbour.

As in many Croatian resort towns, most of the **hotels** here are run by a single mega-company (in this case Imperial; ⊚www.imperial.hr), which means that although they may be perfectly comfortable and well managed, they're not exactly brimming with character. Location, and whether the rooms have TV or not, seem to be the main differentiating factors.

Hotels

Carolina Suha Punta, on the Frkanj peninsula, 5km west of town ☎051/724-133, ⊚carolina@imperial.hr. A bit of a concrete mammoth, but the en-suite rooms are comfy and it's surrounded by pleasant woods. Perfect if you want to be near the coves of Frkanj. Served by seven buses a day from Rab bus station. ❻

Imperial Palit ☎051/724-522, ⊚imperial@impe-rial.hr. Sizeable three-star a short walk northwest of the old town, offering adequate if unexciting rooms, all with en-suite shower and TV. Its main advantage over the other hotels in town is that it's surrounded by the seductive subtropical lushness of Komrčar park. ❺

International Obala kralja Petra Krešimira IV ☎051/724-266, ⊚international@imperial.hr. Humdrum two-star which enjoys an enviable town-centre location. Despite the dowdy early Seventies furnishings the en-suite rooms are spacious, some have bathtubs rather than showers, and most come with nice views of the harbour. Due for renovation and price rises some time soon. ❹

Istra M. de Dominisa bb ☎051/724-134, ☎724-050, ⊚hotelistra@hotmail.com. The one hotel in town not run by Imperial, the *Istra* has a more intimate family-run feel. Convenient for the old town, and has simple, nicely renovated rooms with en-suite shower. ❺

Padova On the opposite side of the bay from the old town ☎051/724-444, ☎724-418, ⊚padova@imperial.hr. Recently tarted-up four-star whose rooms are largish and have bathtubs, TV and balconies – so you're likely to get a good view of Rab's belfryed skyline. Indoor and outdoor pools. ❻

The Town

The old town divides into two parts: **Kaldanac**, the oldest quarter, at the end of the peninsula, and **Varoš**, which dates from between the fifteenth and seventeenth centuries. Together they make up a compact and easily explored grid of alleyways traversed by three parallel thoroughfares: Donja ("Lower"), Srednja ("Middle") and Gornja ("Upper") ulica.

The old town is entered from **Trg svetog Kristofora** (St Christopher's Square), a broad open space overlooked by the jutting bastion of the **Gagliardi Tower** (Tvrđava Galijarda), built by the Venetians in the fifteenth century to defend the landward approaches to the town. From here, **Srednja** heads southeast, squeezing past rows of tightly packed three-storey town houses. The first of these is the Renaissance **Dominis-Nimira Palace**, where the scholar,

Rab's most famous son was **Markantun Dominis** (Mark Anthony de Dominis), a Jesuit-educated churchman whose anti-establishment rhetoric infuriated the Catholic hierarchy of the day. After studying philosophy at Padua, Dominis quickly gained a reputation in scientific circles for his work on optics and the influence of the moon on tides, while simultaneously rising speedily through church ranks, serving as bishop of Senj before being appointed archbishop of Split. However, Dominis's questioning of papal infallibility made him a target for the Inquisition, and after a brief sojourn in Venice he fled in 1614 to England and the Anglican Church, where he was feted as a prominent Catholic dissident and wrote his ten-volume *De Repubblica Ecclesiastica* – a vicious attack on the worldly nature of papal power.

Never wholly committed to Anglicanism, however (it's been suggested that he joined the Church of England because of the salary offered him by the English court), Dominis eventually decided to make his peace with Rome. He left England in 1622 and returned to Rome, where his hopes of fair treatment rested on his relative Pope Gregory XV. On Gregory's death in 1623, Dominis was accused of heresy and imprisoned, living out the rest of his days in a windowless cell in the Castel Sant'Angelo from where, he declared to visitors, "I can best contemplate the kingdom of heaven." Sympathy for Dominis was, nevertheless, at a low ebb. As Dr Fitzherbert, the Rector of the English College in Rome, told a visiting British aristocrat: "He was a malcontent knave when he fled from us, a railing knave while he lived with you, and a motley parti-coloured knave now he is come back." Dominis died before he could be brought to trial, and his body was burnt posthumously on Rome's Campo dei Fiori – an ignominious end for a man whose scientific and philosophical work was later to influence figures as diverse as Descartes and Newton.

priest and sometime archbishop of Split, Markantun Dominis (see box above), was born. The building is relatively plain save for some Gothic window frames, although a rather fine carving of the Nimira family crest, flanked by a small boy and rampant lion, adorns a doorway just down an alleyway to the left. After about five minutes' walk, Srednja opens out into a small piazza mostly taken up by a dinky Venetian loggia and, tucked away in the corner, the tiny Gothic **St Nicholas's Church** (Crkva svetog Nikole), which nowadays houses a sporadically open art gallery. Left from here lies Trg municipium Arbe, where the Venetian Gothic **Rector's Palace** (Knežev dvor) now houses the town council offices. The balcony facing the square is supported by three sculpted lions' heads sporting, from right to left, closed, half-open, and wide-open jaws – although they look more like overweight household pets than fearsome beasts of the savanna.

The Churches of St Mary and St Anthony

Southeast of Trg municipium Arbe lies the older part of town, **Kaldanac**, built on the site of the original Illyrian-Roman settlement of Arba. Kaldanac was largely abandoned after the plagues of the fifteenth century, and some of its older buildings still feature the bricked-up windows and doors which it was hoped would prevent the spread of disease. Occupying the highest part of Rab is the Romanesque **Church of St Mary the Great** (Crkva svete Marije Velike; still known locally as the Katedrala even though the bishopric was taken away from Rab in 1828). The west front is striped pale grey and pink, with a series of blind arches cut by a Renaissance doorway that supports a harrowing Pietà of 1414. Inside are crumbling, honey-grey walls with flecks of agate-coloured marble and a set of almost gaudily carved chestnut choirstalls, dominated by the main altar and its delicate ciborium of grey marble. A few steps away from the cathedral at the head of the peninsula, **St Anthony's Church** (Crkva svetog Antuna) preserves its original rib-vaulted apse and an imposing wooden sculpture of St Anthony (said to be twelfth century) flanked by fifteenth-century pictures of St Christopher and St Tudor – the latter clad in Roman armour.

The campaniles and more churches

Walk northwest along the ridge-top Ivana Rabljanina from the Church of St Mary and you pass the largest and most beautiful of Rab's campaniles, the perfectly symmetrical twelfth-century **Great Bell Tower** (Veli zvonik; daily 10am–1pm & 7.30–10pm; 5Kn). Topped by a balustraded pyramid, the 25-metre-high tower employs a simple architectural device: the windows on the lower storey have one arch, the windows on the second storey have two, those on the third have three, and so on. The tone of the tower's bell was mellowed – legend tells – by gold and silver dropped into the casting pot by Rab's wealthier citizens.

Rab's other three campaniles are spaced along Ivana Rabljanina and its continuation, **Gornja ulica**. The first, a smaller and more utilitarian piece of masonry from the late twelfth century, is attached to **St Andrew's Church** (Crkva svetog Andrije). The second – capped by a bulbous spire reminiscent of a bishop's mitre – is a seventeenth-century affair belonging to St Justine's Church (Crkva svete Justine), a small Renaissance structure that's now a **Museum of Sacred Art** (Muzej sakralne umjetnosti; June & Sept daily 7.30–9pm; July & Aug Mon–Sat 9am–12.30pm & 7.30–10pm, Sun 7.30–10pm; 5Kn). Inside there's an assortment of manuscripts, stonework and robes, and a mid-fourteenth-century polyptych by Paolo Veneziano showing a Crucifixion flanked by saints – St Christopher is on the right, standing beside St Thecla, shown wearing a glamorous green outfit despite the fact that she actually spent most of her life living in a cave. Pride of place goes to the reliquary holding the **skull of St Christopher**, a gold-plated casket made by a Zadar craftsman at the end of the twelfth century. Various scenes round the sides of the box depict the events surrounding the saint's martyrdom: he was beheaded by the Romans after an attempt to have him shot failed, the hand of God having turned the arrows back on his assailants. It's said that the head was brought to Rab by a local bishop in the eleventh century when the town was under attack from the Saracens – St Christopher kindly obliged, saving the town by hurling rocks back at the besiegers.

The final campanile, a simple thirteenth-century affair similar to the one belonging to St Andrew's, stands beside the ruined **Basilica of St John the Evangelist** (Bazilika svetog Ivana Evanđeliste), which probably dates from the sixth or seventh century. The church was abandoned in the 1830s and much of its masonry taken away to mend the town's other sacred buildings, although the graceful curve of its apse can still be seen. At the top end of Gornja ulica, steps lead up to St Christopher's Church on the right, which has a small **lapidarium** (July & Aug daily 9am–1pm & 6–10pm; ask at the tourist office at other times; 5Kn) containing tombstones and other masonry. From here, more steps scale a short fifty-metre stretch of Rab's medieval town **walls**, giving fine views back over the roofs and towers. A gate through the wall leads into the fragrant **Komrčar Park**, a shady place set on the ridge from where you can walk down to the concreted bathing spots on the west side of the peninsula.

The Monastery of St Euphemia

Thirty minutes' walk northwest of town along the seaside path is the Franciscan **Monastery of St Euphemia** (Samostan svete Fumije; June & Sept Mon–Sat 9am–noon & 3–5pm; July & Aug Mon–Sat 10am–noon & 4–6pm; 5Kn). Built in 1446, it has a delicate cloister and a museum in the library above, containing illuminated manuscripts, a headless Roman figure of Diana and a fifteenth-century wooden image of St Francis. The monastery has two churches: one dedicated to St Euphemia, and the larger church of St Bernardin, which has a gory late Gothic crucifix, a seventeenth-century wooden ceiling decorated with scenes from the life of St Francis, and a polyptych painted by the Vivarini brothers in 1458, showing a Madonna and Child flanked by two tiers of saints.

Beaches and coves

Šetalište Odorika Badurine, the waterside walkway on the west side of town (reached via steps down beside St Justine's Church, or from Komrčar Park), is actually one of the best urban beaches in Croatia – it doesn't amount to much save for a concrete stretch of strand, but the water is super-clear, and there's plenty of tree-shade if you're not in the mood to be grilled senseless. There are some attractive shingle beaches east of town beyond the *Padova* hotel, but far more popular is the **Frkanj peninsula**, 1km west of the town as the crow flies. The peninsula boasts numerous rocky coves backed by deep green forest, and there's a large naturist area on the far side. You can reach the peninsula from the harbour by taxi boat or by walking the 3km from **Suha Punta**, a tourist complex at its western end, comprising the *Eva* and *Carolina* hotels and accessible by a side-road which leaves the Rab–Kampor route just beyond the Monastery of St Euphemia. Beyond here lies a further sequence of bays and coves, slightly less busy than those of Frkanj and reachable by following tracks through the coastal forest.

Eating and drinking

There's a surfeit of good seafood **restaurants** in the old town, and although some are quite stylish they remain affordable – no one wants to price themselves out of a very competitive market. Of the **cafés**, *Zlatni Rab*, Jurja Barakovića 1, and *Café Biser*, on the corner of Trg svetog Kristofora and Srednja ulica, have the best cakes and sweets, while the latter is also an eternally popular daytime spot for coffee-sipping. The café-bars on Trg municipium Arba are classic spots for people-watching, although the nearby Donja ulica is the main venue for late-night supping; *Forum* and the *Le Journal* next door are lively, if not downright raucous, places to spend a summer weekend. Best of all is *Sanda* at the southeastern end of Donja ulica, which has tables and benches squeezed into the narrowest part of the street, and offers a decent list of cocktails.

Restaurants

Buža Ugalje bb. Sit-down snack bar in a narrow alley just off Trg svetog Kristofora, with a respectable range of sandwiches, as well as the more straightforward seafood dishes – grilled *lignje* and deep-fried *ribice* among them.

Konoba Kaldanac Biskupa Draga bb. Its wooden benches stuffed into a narrow alleyway just off the main square, this is a good place to try the cheaper fish dishes, and it also does simple risottos and seafood pasta. Fills up quickly.

Konoba Rab Kneza Branimira 3. Cosy split-level place with folksy touches – like dried herbs hanging from the thick stone walls – offering a good range of seafood and traditional meat dishes such as *teleća koljenica* (calf knuckle) and local speciality *janjetina pod peku* (pieces of lamb cooked in an ember-covered pot).

Labirint Srednja ulica 9. This place prides itself on having the longest fish menu in town – if it lives in the Adriatic, the chances are you can eat it here. A split-level collection of dining rooms, with good service and an extensive choice of Croatian wines.

Paradiso Stjepana Radića. Serves up reasonable pizza and pasta fare in a palm-shaded courtyard.

Santa Maria D. Dokule 6. Swish place in an atmospheric courtyard setting. Sumptuous range of seafood and a handsome selection of classic meat dishes (everything from wiener schnitzel to

fillet mignon), none of which will break the bank.

Škver Šetalište Odorika Badurine. On the seaside path on the west side of the peninsula, for much of the year this is an unpretentious place serving no-nonsense basics like *grah*, *lignje* and *ribice* to local fisherfolk. In July and August a tourist-oriented menu of grilled meats is introduced and the prices are tweaked upwards.

Kampor and the Lopar peninsula

Six kilometres northwest of Rab – and connected to it by seven buses daily – **KAMPOR** is a small, scattered village with a deep swath of shallow sandy beach. It doesn't get too crowded even in high season, and there are a couple of small **campsites** behind the beach, as well as private **rooms** (❶) available through agencies in Rab Town or by asking around. About 1km inland from Kampor, back along the road to Rab, lies the **Graveyard of the Victims of Fascism** (Groblje žrtava fašizma), a site commemorating the concentration camp established here by the Italian occupiers in 1942. It's referred to locally as the "Slovene Cemetery" owing to the large numbers of Slovenes who were imprisoned and died here, although it housed a wide range of Partisans, Jews and political undesirables, rounded up in the Italian-controlled portions of Slovenia and Croatia. Most of the internees were crowded together in flimsy tents – some five thousand died in the winter of 1942–43 alone, starved of food and drink by Italian officials. After the collapse of Italy in September 1943, most of the able-bodied survivors joined Tito's Partisans, who were briefly in control of the island before the arrival of a German garrison. The site is a dignified and restful place, with long lines of graves – one for every four people who died – surrounded by well-tended lawns, trees and shrubs.

The Lopar peninsula

Another road climbs out of Rab to the north, making its way down the island's broad central valley. After passing the sprawling settlement of Supetarska Draga, the main road reaches a T-junction at the neck of the Lopar peninsula. The left turn leads to the village of **LOPAR**, a handful of houses spread around a muddy bay from where the ferry leaves for Krk. The sandy beach here isn't particularly picturesque, but is usually empty. The right turn leads to **SAN MARINO**, 1km south, a largely modern village which nevertheless lays claim to being the birthplace of St Marin, a fourth-century stonemason who fled persecution by crossing the seas to Italy, founding the town that subsequently became the republic of San Marino. Today's settlement stretches around a vast expanse of sand known as **Veli mel** (*mel* being an archaic word for "beach", although it's also referred to hereabouts as Rajska plaža – "Paradise Beach" – or simply "Copacabana"), backed by cafés and restaurants and packed with families in July and August. The bay on which Veli mel is situated is unusually shallow, and you can paddle to an islet about 1km offshore. There's a sequence of smaller, progressively less crowded sandy beaches beyond the headlands to the north, beginning with Livačina Bay, followed by the predominantly naturist Kaštelina Bay slightly further up. Even more secluded sandy bays can be reached by heading northeast on foot from either Lopar or San Marino, where trails cross a sandy heath covered by prickly evergreens before dropping down into coves like Sahara and Stolac – the latter is reserved for naturists.

The Adriatic gulag: Grgur and Goli otok

While lounging around on the beaches of the Lopar peninsula you're sure to catch sight of the island of **Grgur**, little more than a kilometre offshore, site of a women's prison until the 1960s and once decorated with a giant "Tito" and *petokraka* (the five-pointed communist star), both carved painstakingly out of bare rock. Immediately to the southeast is the notorious **Goli otok** ("Bare Island"), an obstinate hummock of mottled rock that was used as an island jail for communists who remained loyal to the Soviet Union after Stalin's break with Tito in 1948. Over a period of five years in the late 1940s and early 1950s, a total of fifteen thousand *inform-burovci* (supporters of the Informburo, the Moscow-based organization which co-ordinated the work of communist parties worldwide) were "re-educated" on Goli otok through forced labour in the island's quarry. Few of the inmates were guilty of seriously plotting against the regime; the majority were minor figures who had simply spoken out against Tito in private and been betrayed by a colleague or friend. On arrival, prisoners were forced to pass through a chicken-run of lined-up guards bearing sticks, before submitting to a regime of beatings and torture; recalcitrant prisoners had their heads immersed in buckets of human excrement, while those who confessed their ideological errors were recruited to torture the others.

As ideological tensions lessened in the mid-1950s, Goli was used to incarcerate all manner of non-political prisoners, and the prison regime became more bearable. Sent here as an army deserter, Romany singing legend Šaban Bajramović (see p.434) played in goal for the prison football team and performed in the prison orchestra, going on to become a pan-Yugoslav musical superstar after his release. Despite being common knowledge, the existence of Goli otok was not officially admitted until the 1980s, by which time Tito – on whose personal initiative the camp had been established – was already dead.

There are seven **buses** daily from Rab to Lopar, and an equal number (summer only) to the beach at San Marino. All services pass by the **tourist office** (☎051/775-508, ⓦ www.lopar.com) at the T-junction between Lopar and San Marino, which shares premises with the Dedan tourist agency (☎051/775-105, ⓔ dedan-tours@ri.hinet.hr), offering private **rooms** (❶). The Numero Uno office at San Marino (☎051/775-073) also has rooms on offer. There's a large **campsite**, the *San Marino* (☎051/775-133, ⓕ775-290), just behind the Veli mel beach. The *Jadran* **pension**, right by the ferry dock in Lopar (☎051/775-153; ❺), has tasteful pine-floored rooms and a homely family-run feel.

Pag

Seen from the mainland, **PAG** is a stark and desolate pumice-stone of an island which looks as if it could barely support any form of life. Around eight thousand people live here, looking after three times as many sheep, who scour the stony slopes in search of the odd blade of grass. Hot afternoons always seem hotter here than anywhere else: nothing stirs, and, on the arid eastern side of the island, seemingly nothing grows except for a grey-green carpet of sage. The two main settlements are **Pag Town**, with its attractive historic centre, and **Novalja**, a bland modern settlement whose beach-based nightlife is fast earning it the title of the "Croatian Ibiza".

Pag's main claim to fame is its **cheese** (*paški sir*) – a hard, piquant sheep's cheese (with a taste somewhere between mature cheddar and parmesan) which you'll find in supermarkets all over the country. The distinctive taste is due to the method of preparation – the cheeses are rubbed with a mixture of olive oil and ash before being left to mature – and the diet of the sheep, which includes many wild herbs (notably the ubiquitous sage) flavoured by salt picked up from the sea by the wind and deposited on vegetation across the island. Indeed, Pag is a salty kind of place all round: the precious stuff is the island's main industry, with saltpans stretching out along the island's central valley, and even the tap water tastes slightly brackish. Pag's other traditional industry is **lace-making**, a craft that for the moment remains refreshingly uncommercialized. Small pieces are sold from doorways by the lacemakers themselves, often wearing the dark, full-skirted local costume which seems to have endured here more than anywhere else on the Adriatic.

Approaching Pag from the north, there's a **ferry** from Prizna, on the mainland 3km below the Magistrala, to **Žigljen**, 5km north of Novalja. The island's southern end is connected to the mainland via the **Pag Bridge** (Paški most), about 26km north of **Posedarje** on the Magistrala. The only public transport on the island is provided by daily Rijeka–Zadar **buses** (two daily in each direction) which pass through Novalja and Pag Town.

Pag Town

PAG TOWN originally lay about 3km south of its present site – the Pag salt industry was an attractive target for predatory neighbours and the inhabitants of Pag were able to play one aggressor off against another until the town was sacked by forces from Zadar in 1395 and many of its leading citizens killed. The Venetians, who had taken control of the area by the 1420s, hired the architect Juraj Dalmatinac (see p.278) to build a new island capital from scratch, creating the present town with its tight grid of narrow streets along one side of a deep bay. Abbé Fortis, visiting in the late eighteenth century, called it a dismal place, adding that "I found not a single man of good sense in all that town; everybody is interested in the salt pits, and whoever talks not of salt is not regarded."

Pag is the venue of two **carnivals**: the first an authentic local event immediately before Lent; the second, in late July or early August, a re-enactment of the first for the benefit of tourists. Both feature parades and a good deal of folk music and traditional dancing, and the pre-Lenten carnival culminates with the burning of the effigy known as Marko, whose ritual death is claimed to rid the community of all the bad things which have happened over the previous year. Both carnivals traditionally featured performances of *Paška robinja* ("*Slave Girl of Pag*"), a play of Renaissance origins concerning a captive of the Turks who is purchased and freed by a good Christian knight. Made up of rhyming couplets delivered in a monotone, it's nowadays considered too boring for the average audience, and is no longer performed every year.

The Town

Flanking the town's central square, Trg kralja Petra Krešimira IV, are two of Dalmatinac's original buildings: the **Rector's Palace** (Knežev dvor), now a café and supermarket, and the **Parish Church** (Župna crkva), on the other side of the square – the rose window on the church facade echoes the patterns found in Pag lace, while a relief above the main door shows the Virgin sheltering the townspeople (some wearing traditional Pag skirts) beneath her cloak. Inside, the columns sport capitals bearing a variety of carved beasts, including griffins, and dolphins drinking from cups.

A causeway-like strip of land connects central Pag with its suburbs on the western side of Pag bay, where you'll also find the town's main, pebble, beach. Behind it lies the Lokunjica, a muddy lagoon, and the saltpans, which stretch south for 6km. Walking along the west bank of the saltpans for 2.5km brings you to **Stari grad** (Old Town), the original town which was abandoned in the 1440s. There are a few ruined buildings here, including the cloister of a Franciscan monastery, and a church dating from 1392 with a fine Gothic relief of the Virgin above the portal – it served as the model for the relief adorning the parish church in the new town. A statue of the Virgin inside the old town church is taken in procession to the new parish church on August 15 (Assumption), where it's kept until September 8 (Birth of the Virgin).

Practicalities

Rijeka–Zadar buses stop at a car park on the northern edge of town, a short walk from the **tourist office** by the bridge across the Lokunjica (summer daily 8am–9pm; winter Mon–Fri 8am–3pm; ☎ & ☏023/611-286 & 611-301, ⓦwww.summernet.hr/pag). **Rooms** (❶) are available from Mediteran (☎023/611-238) or Suntourist (☎023/612-060) behind the bus stop, or from Meridian 15 (☎023/612-162, ⓔmeridijan-15@zd.tel.hr), on the other side of the car park next to the *Pagus* hotel. The *Pagus* itself, Ante Starčevića 1 (☎023/611-310, ☏611-101; ❹), is the least bland of the town's **hotels**, with spacious en-suite rooms and a small stretch of private beach. The *Biser*, on the opposite side of the bay at A.G. Matoša 8 (☎023/611-333, ☏612-224; ❹), is an adequate alternative. The nearest **campsite** is the *Šimuni* (☎023/697-440), occupying an attractive location on the island's western shore, 8km away on the road to Novalja; Pag–Novalja buses will drop you near the site's access road.

The best places for traditional **food** are *Konoba Bile*, up from the parish church on Jurja Dalmatinca, and *Konoba Bodulo*, just to the north on Vangradska. There are numerous **café-bars** on the main square and along the waterfront, and a **disco**, *Peti magazin*, in one of the old salt warehouses over the bridge from the tourist office.

Novalja and around

Twenty kilometres north of Pag Town, **NOVALJA** is the island's main resort, much more developed and crowded than Pag Town. Originally a Roman settlement dating from around the first century AD, it preserves a few ancient remains, including an underground **water conduit** (*vodovod*; summer daily 9am–7pm; 8Kn), known by the locals as the "Italian Hole", a stretch of which you can walk along – it's clearly signposted just north of the seafront. There's a curving gravel beach at the south side of town, from where a stony path leads south to the much larger, pebbly **Straško beach**. Two kilometres south of town on the road to Pag Town, a side-road descends to the east-facing **Zrće beach**, a vast, gravelly expanse with a view of the pale ochre hills of eastern Pag and the greenish Velebit mountains beyond. There's a sandier beach in the next bay to the north, about ten minutes' walk, although it's more exposed to the wind.

In recent years a string of alfresco DJ bars have set themselves up on Zrće beach in the summer, turning the area into a dance-till-dawn paradise for Croatian clubbers. Zagreb-based establishments like *Papaya* (see p.87) and *Aquarius* (p.88) decamp here for the holiday season, although it's local outfit *Calypso* that has been on the beach the longest – and has developed a cult following in the process. Food and drink is served round the clock, so you can just about spend 24 hours partying and chilling on the beach if you want to.

Buses stop on Novalja's seafront, from where it's a short walk uphill to the **tourist office** at Zvonimirova bb (summer daily 8am–7pm; winter Mon–Fri 8am–3pm; ☎ & ℗053/661-404, ⓦwww.novalja.hr). Sunturist, near the bus stop at Kranjćićeva bb (☎053/663-257, ⓦwww.sunturist.hr), can fix you up with **rooms** (❶) and **apartments** (❷). The **campsite** at Straško beach (☎053/661-226, ⓦwww.turistdd.hr) is like a small town in its own right, with shops, bars and spaces for four thousand campers – a third of which are reserved for nudists. There are plenty of places along Novalja's waterfront serving up inexpensive if undistinguished **food**. *Steffani*, in the town centre at Petra Krešimira IV 28, is definitely worth the extra expense, cooking up a superlative range of fish, shellfish, Pag lamb either stewed or roasted – and local snails.

Travel details

Trains

Rijeka to: Zagreb (5 daily; 4–5hr).

Buses

Cres Town to: Beli (2 weekly; 30min); Lubenice (3 weekly; 40min); Mali Lošinj (8 daily; 1hr); Rijeka (4 daily; 2hr 30min); Valun (3 weekly; 30min); Zagreb (2 daily; 6hr 30min).
Krk Town to: Baška (8 daily; 40min); Punat (10 daily; 10min); Rijeka (12 daily; 1hr 40min); Zagreb (2 daily; 5hr 30min).
Lovran to: Liganj (8 daily; 15min); Lovranska Draga (8 daily; 20min); Rijeka (every 30min; 45min).
Opatija to: Kastav (hourly; 20min); Lovran (every 30min; 15min); Rijeka (every 30min; 30min).
Pag Town to: Novalja (2 daily; 30min); Rijeka (2 daily; 3hr); Zadar (2 daily; 1hr); Zagreb (5 daily; 5hr).
Rab Town to: Kampor (Mon–Sat 7 daily, Sun 1 daily; 15min); Lopar (7 daily; 30min); Rijeka (3 daily; 3hr 30min); Senj (3 daily; 2hr); Zagreb (July & Aug 2 daily; 6hr).
Rijeka to: Buzet (4 daily; 2hr); Cres (4 daily; 2hr 30min); Crikvenica (hourly; 45min); Dubrovnik (2 daily; 13hr); Karlobag (12 daily; 2hr 45min); Kastav (every 30min; 25min); Krk Town (12 daily; 1hr 40min); Lovran (every 30min; 45min); Mali Lošinj (4 daily; 3hr 30min); Novi Vinodolski (hourly; 1hr); Opatija (every 30min; 30min); Pag (2 daily; 3hr); Pazin (4 daily; 1hr 10min); Poreč (6 daily; 4hr); Pula (hourly; 2hr 30min); Rab Town (3 daily; 3hr 30min); Rovinj (5 daily; 4hr); Senj (hourly; 1hr 20min); Šibenik (11 daily; 7hr); Split (11 daily; 8hr 30min); Starigrad-Paklenica (11 daily; 3hr 35min); Umag (3 daily; 4hr 25min); Zadar (11 daily; 4hr 30min); Zagreb (20 daily; 3–4hr).

Ferries

Baška to: Lopar (May, June & Sept 2 daily; July & Aug 5 daily; 50min).
Crikvenica to: Šilo (July & Aug 10 daily; 30min).
Jablanac to: Mišnjak (every 30min: summer 5am–10pm, winter 6am–7pm; 30min).
Mali Lošinj to: Pula (6 weekly; 2hr 35min); Zadar (6 weekly; 5hr 20min).
Porozina to: Brestova (hourly; 30min).
Prizna to: Žigljen (hourly; 20min).
Rijeka to: Dubrovnik (summer daily; winter 2 weekly; 22hr); Hvar (summer daily; winter 2 weekly; 12–14hr); Korčula (summer daily; winter 2 weekly; 18hr); Rab Town (summer 1 weekly; 3hr); Split (summer daily; winter 2 weekly; 10–12hr); Zadar (summer daily; winter 2 weekly; 6hr).
Valbiska to: Merag (hourly; 30min).

Domestic flights

Rijeka to: Zagreb (3 weekly; 35min).

International trains

Rijeka to: Ljubljana (2 daily; 2hr 30min).

International buses

Rijeka to: Ljubljana (2 daily; 2hr 30min); Medjugorje (1 daily; 14hr); Sarajevo (5 weekly; 16hr); Trieste (5 daily; 6hr 30min).

International ferries

Rijeka to: Bari (3 weekly in summer; 25hr); Igoumenitsa (1 weekly in summer; 38hr).

Dalmatia

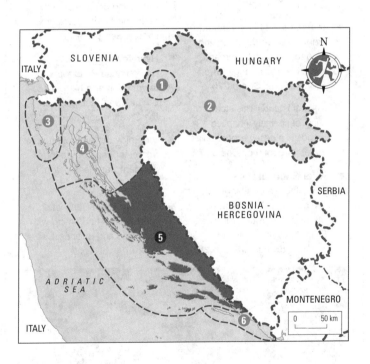

CHAPTER 5

Highlights

✳ **Nin** Composed of real sand and backed by duney heath, this is the best beach in Dalmatia by far. **See p.253**

✳ **Zadar** Bustling port city whose narrow pedestrianized alleys are bursting with café life. **See p.255**

✳ **Telašćica Bay** Compact natural wonderland comprising rugged coastline, dramatic sea cliffs and a tangle of offshore islands. **See p.270**

✳ **Kornati islands** This stark chain of sparsely inhabited islands is a deservedly popular target for boat trips. **See p.272**

✳ **Krka National Park** Tumbling waterfalls, gurgling rapids and a beach-party atmosphere at central Dalmatia's most-visited natural attraction. **See p.281**

✳ **Trogir** A warren of stone-paved streets presided over by a stunning Romanesque cathedral. **See p.285**

✳ **Split** With their unique tangle of Roman and medieval remains, the streets of the Dalmatian capital are a living textbook of Mediterranean history. **See p.292**

✳ **Hvar Town** Beautifully proportioned Renaissance town which also happens to be the swankiest resort on the Croatian coast. **See p.324**

✳ **Vis** Enjoy the unspoilt nature and clear seas of the independent traveller's favourite island. **See p.333**

✳ **Korčula Town** Captivating medieval port brimming with churches and palaces. **See p.340**

5

Dalmatia

tretching from Zadar in the north to the Bay of Kotor (now part of Montenegro) in the south, **Dalmatia** possesses one of Europe's most dramatic shorelines, as the stark, grey wall of the coastal mountains sweeps down towards a lush seaboard ribbon dotted with palm trees and olive plantations. Along the coast are beautifully preserved, Venetian-influenced medieval towns that wouldn't look out of place on the other side of the Adriatic, poised above some of the clearest waters in Europe, while further out are myriad islands adorned with ancient stone villages and enticing coves. The tourist industry mushroomed hugely in the 1970s and 1980s before collapsing during the 1991–95 war and, though visitor numbers have risen rapidly since the return of peace, the crowds are rarely difficult to avoid: the Adriatic islands can swallow up any number of sightseers, while tourist settlements on the mainland have been kept well away from the main towns.

The contrast between the arid maquis of Dalmatia's stony interior and the fertile seaboard is reflected in the region's dual personality: the towns on the coast and islands have long enjoyed a thriving Mediterranean civilization, while their unsettled hinterland has been much more prone to the political uncertainties and population movements of the Balkan interior. People on the coast have traditionally been able to make a living through fishing, olive-growing, wine-making or trade, whereas life in the interior – the more arid parts of which are often called *kamenjar* ("stone-field") in Croatian – has always been much harsher.

Dalmatia's long history of Roman, Venetian and Italian cultural penetration has left its mark on a region where children still call adult males *barba* ("beard" – Italian slang for "uncle") and respected gents go under the name of *šjor* (the local version of *signore*), but modern Dalmatia's identity is difficult to pin down. People from northern Croatia will tell you that life is lived at a much slower pace in Dalmatia, whose inhabitants are joshingly referred to as *tovari* ("donkeys") by their compatriots, though the briefest of visits to bustling regional centres like Zadar will be enough to persuade you that these clichés are somewhat wide of the mark. What is true is that Dalmatia is slightly poorer than the north: local industries took a battering in the war and recession of the 1990s, and tourism – the mainstay of the local economy – is yet to reattain its pre-1991 levels.

Although Dalmatia is culturally and historically a unified region, we've divided the following account into two halves, recognition in part of the regional roles played by the province's two great cities, **Zadar** and **Split**. Almost everything in **northern Dalmatia** revolves around Zadar, whose busy port sends ferries out to the myriad islands of the **Zadar Archipelago**, many of which

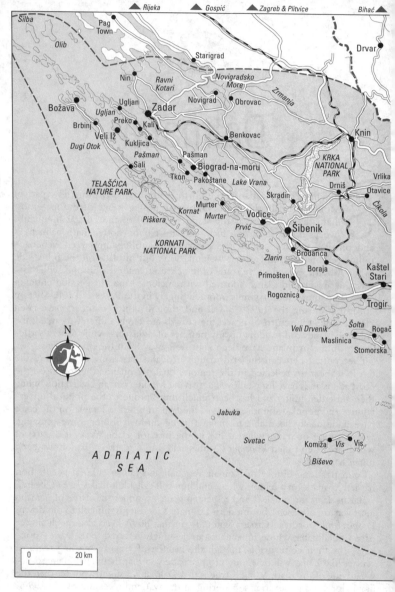

are blissfully unspoiled. Zadar's bus station funnels passengers south to the cathedral city of **Šibenik**, a useful gateway to the natural splendours of the **Kornati Islands** and **Krka National Park**. Life in **southern Dalmatia** is largely dominated by Split, a teeming, chaotic but ultimately addictive city which controls ferry access to the tourist-deluged islands of **Hvar**, **Brač** and **Korčula** – as well as relatively off-the-beaten-track places like **Vis** and **Lastovo**. Road traffic pours out of Split and onwards along the coast, passing

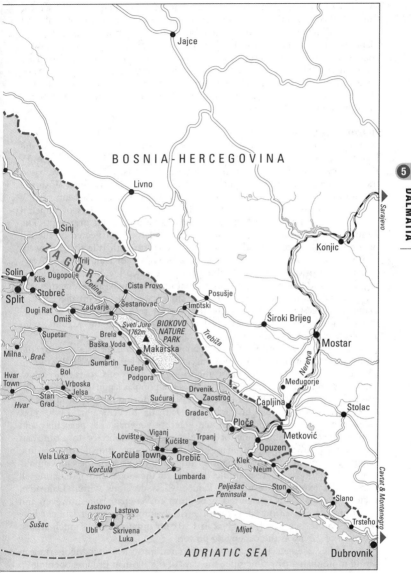

through the pebbly-beached resorts of the **Makarska Riviera** before arriving in Dubrovnik (which forms the subject of chapter 6).

Getting around Dalmatia is quite straightforward. There's one main road, the Jadranska **Magistrala**, or Adriatic Highway; frequent **buses** run up and down it every day of the week, connecting all the major centres – you can travel from Zadar to Dubrovnik in around seven hours – though be aware that picking up buses in smaller centres often involves waiting by the side of the

Magistrala until something turns up. There are also a number of **ferries**, most run by Jadrolinija, although an increasing number of seasonal hydrofoils and catamarans are being run by smaller operators. Just about every inhabited island is connected by some kind of regular local ferry, and there's also a coastal service which cruises up and down from Rijeka to Dubrovnik daily throughout the summer (twice a week in winter), calling at most of the major ports and islands en route and continuing to Bari in Italy and Igoumenitsa in Greece at least once a week in summer. Ferries also ply the Zadar–Ancona route in summer.

Some history

Although initially colonized by the **Greeks**, who established themselves on the islands of Vis (Greek Issa) and Hvar (Pharos) at the start of the fourth century BC, the area was first called Dalmatia by the **Romans**, who may have based the name on the Illyrian word *delmat*, meaning a proud, brave man. With the imposition of Roman rule over local Illyrian tribes in the first century BC, power drifted away from the old Greek towns to new centres of imperial power on the mainland like **Jadera** (Zadar) and **Salona** (Solin, near Split). The Latinate urban culture which grew up here was largely unaffected by the fall of the Roman Empire and the brief period of Ostrogoth rule that followed, and was soon reorganized into the Byzantine Theme of Dalmatia. The Avar-Slav invasion of 614 did considerable damage to town life, however, weakening Zadar and completely destroying Salona (although a new settlement founded by the fleeing Roman-Illyrian citizenry would eventually become Dalmatia's largest city, Split). The Byzantines soon re-established nominal control of the region, but increasingly left the hinterland to the **Croats**, who arrived here soon after the Avars.

By the eleventh century, the Croatian state – and later its successor, the Hungaro-Croatian kingdom – was successfully challenging both Byzantium and Venice for control of the coast. Increasing numbers of Croats moved into the towns, and Croatian entrenched itself as the popular language, even if Latin was still used in writing. When Ladislas of Naples, during his brief stint as King of Hungary-Croatia, sold his rights to Dalmatia to Venice in 1409, most Dalmatian towns were given a choice – accept Venetian rule peacefully and retain a degree of autonomy, or submit by force. Contrary to Dalmatian expectations, however, the Venetians kept the towns on a short leash, muzzling traditions of municipal government by imposing on each of the cities an all-powerful rector (*knez*) responsible directly to the doge, and redirecting all import and export trade through Venice. Class divisions within Dalmatian society prevented any concerted opposition to Venetian rule, however, and rebellions were few and far between – the commoners' revolt launched by **Matija Ivanić** (see p.324) on Hvar in 1510, for instance, was as much against the local oligarchy as the occupying power.

Under the Venetians, Dalmatia was integrated into the wider Mediterranean world more than at any time since the days of the Roman Empire, opening up its cities to Renaissance culture and Italianate architecture. But however many fine loggias and campaniles the Venetians built, it would be a mistake to think that the locals had turned into good Venetians – the urban elite of fifteenth-century Dalmatia clearly saw themselves as Croats, and were keen to develop the local language as a medium fit for their patriotic aspirations. Prime movers were **Marko Marulić** of Split, whose *Judita* (Judith) of 1521 was the first ever epic tale "composed in Croatian verse", as its own title page proclaimed; and **Petar Zoranić** of Zadar, whose novel *Planine* (Mountains) of 1569 contains a scene in which the nymph Hrvatica (literally "Croatian girl") bemoans the lack of Dalmatians who show pride in their own language.

Venetian political control went largely unchallenged, however, because of the growing threat of the **Ottoman Turks**. The Venetians did their best to live in peace with the Turks in order to ensure the smooth functioning of trade, although major conflicts – notably the **Cyprus War** (1570–71) and the **Candia War** (1645–69) – occasionally brought roving armies to the Dalmatian hinterland. The Ottoman **defeat** outside Vienna in 1683 finally provided Venice with the opportunity to push the Turks back into Bosnia, but by this stage decades of conflict had changed the make-up of the Dalmatian population, as Croats from the interior had fled to the coast. Much of the hinterland itself had been devastated and repopulated with migrants from the Balkan interior, most of whom were classified as **Vlachs** (*vlah* or *vlaj* in Croatian) – a name which was sometimes applied to the nomadic tribes descended from the original Roman-Illyrian population, at others to all migrant stockbreeders from the interior. More important than the niceties of ethnic distinction, however, was the fact that the majority of Vlachs belonged to the Orthodox faith and, largely because they came under the jurisdiction of the Serbian Orthodox Church, came increasingly to regard themselves as Serbs.

Questions of ethnic identity are further complicated by the fact that the Venetians referred to all inlanders, regardless of who they were, as **Morlachs** (*morlacchi*), a term thought to originate in the combination of the name Vlach with the Greek word *mavro*, meaning "black" or "dark". The Morlach label came to be applied to all the inhabitants of Dalmatia who lived outside the cultured world of the coastal towns and islands and, although the hard life of the Morlachs was romanticized by foreign travellers (see box on p.250), they were shunned by the urban population on the coast, who were rarely aware of their existence except at fairs and markets. Until the twentieth century even educated Croats knew little about the hinterlanders, referring to them all as *morlaci*, *zagorci* (highlanders) or *vlaji* (a term still used as a put-down in Split, where anyone who can't see the sea from their house is a *vlaj*; see box on p.293), regardless of where they came from or what religion – Catholic or Orthodox – they professed.

For over 350 years Venice gave the Dalmatian towns peace, security and – ultimately – economic and political stagnation. The fall of the Republic in 1797 was followed by a brief Austrian interregnum until, in 1808, **Napoleon** incorporated Dalmatia into his **Illyrian Provinces**, an artificial amalgam of Adriatic and west Slovene territories with its capital at Ljubljana. The reforming French played an important role in pulling Dalmatia out of its torpor, building roads, promoting trade and opening up the region to modern scientific and educational ideas. There's little evidence that the French were popular, however: their decision to close down the monasteries deeply offended local Catholic feeling, and they also dragged Dalmatia into wars with the Austrians and the British, who occupied Vis in 1811 and shelled Zadar in 1813.

Hopes that Dalmatia would be unified with the rest of the Croatian lands after its incorporation into **Austria** in 1815 were soon dashed. Instead, Dalmatia became a separate province of the Habsburg Empire, Italian was made the official language, and German- and Italian-speaking bureaucrats were brought in to run the administration. By mid-century Dalmatia had just over 400,000 inhabitants, of whom 340,000 were Slavs and only 16,000 were Italians, and yet the first Croatian language schools didn't open until the 1860s. Many Croats living in the coastal towns still saw fluency in Italian as a mark of social and cultural superiority, and felt that they had little in common with

Images of Dalmatia: Alberto Fortis and the Morlachs

Western images of Dalmatia owe much to the writings of the Italian **Alberto Fortis**, a lapsed priest, natural scientist and tireless traveller who contributed more to the outside world's knowledge of the eastern Adriatic than anyone before or since. Fortis was particularly taken by the **Morlachs** (see p.249), the inhabitants of inland Dalmatia who had never been assimilated into the coast's urban Mediterranean culture. Although the Morlachs were well known to the Venetian administrators who controlled the coast, Fortis was the first outsider to visit Morlach villages and write about them with any sympathy. He described the Morlachs' often abysmal living conditions, noting the tiny houses in which families slept alongside their cattle, adding that in households which actually possessed a bed, the husband slept on it while the wife was relegated to the floor. He admired their capacity for honesty, hospitality and lifelong friendship, as well as their code of honour – which allowed plenty of room for blood feuds and vengeance. He was particularly taken by the epic poems which Morlach bards recited to the accompaniment of the *gusla* (a hideously droning bowed instrument). For Fortis, the Morlachs weren't just living examples of the noble savages he had read about in Jean-Jacques Rousseau, they were the nearest thing that Europe still had to the heroic ideals of Homeric Greece.

Fortis was travelling at a time when **epic poems** were all the rage in Western Europe. His journeys were partly financed by Scottish laird, the Earl of Bute, whose interest in heroic folk tales had been fired after reading *Ossian*, an epic poem thought to be the work of third-century Celtic bards (although it was subsequently revealed to be a forgery). Both Bute and Fortis reckoned that the study of oral literature in inland Dalmatia would prove that all the valiant hero-nations of Europe had somehow been shaped by their epic poetry, and their enthusiasm soon caught on. Fortis's *Travels into Dalmatia* (1774) was an international sensation, provoking a craze for all things Morlach which lasted well into the next century. His translation of the epic poem *Hasanaginica* – a tale of conflict on the Croatian–Ottoman border – was rendered into German by Goethe, and into English by Sir Walter Scott. Romantic novelist Prosper Merimée included Hasanaginica – alongside numerous

those from inland. Things began to change in 1848, when the newly formed Croatian **Sabor** (Parliament) in Zagreb renewed calls for the reunification of Dalmatia with the rest of Croatia. The Viennese court quashed the idea, but could no longer prevent the growth of Croatian national consciousness in the Adriatic towns.

The creation of a Dalmatian Assembly in 1861 opened up a political arena which was dominated by the **Narodnjaci** (Nationalists), who wanted the reunion of Dalmatia with the historic heartlands of continental Croatia, and the **Autonomaši** (Autonomists), who regarded Dalmatia as a unique cultural entity populated by "Slavo-Dalmatians" rather than Croats. The Autonomaši tended to be supported by Italians or Italianized Croats who looked to Italy – which had emerged as a unified kingdom in 1861 – rather than Austria, although the Austrian defeat of an Italian navy off the island of Vis in 1866 put paid to any immediate likelihood that Dalmatia was about to be swallowed up by the new state across the Adriatic. The importance of the Battle of Vis was not lost on the local Croats, who began to celebrate its anniversary with much pomp in order to annoy their Italian neighbours. The Narodnjaci won control of the Dalmatian Assembly in 1870, and Croatian became the official language in the Assembly in 1883, though it wasn't introduced into the civil service or the law courts until 1912.

Despite Italian claims, the whole of Dalmatia except Zadar and Lastovo fell to the Kingdom of Serbs, Croats and Slovenes (subsequently Yugoslavia) in purportedly Morlach poems which he simply made up himself – in his collection *La guzla ou choix de poésies illyriques recueillies dans la Dalmatie, la Bosnie, la Croatia et l'Hercegovinie* (The Gusla, or a Selection of Illyrian Poetry from Dalmatia, Bosnia, Croatia and Hercegovina; 1827). As great a figure as Pushkin was taken in by Merimée's book, reprinting some of the Frenchman's fraudulent epics in his *Poems of the Western Slavs*.

Nineteenth-century travel writers tended to use Fortis's work as a guidebook, uncritically repeating his comments on the Morlachs. Even Balthasar Hacquet, whose *L'Illyrie et la Dalmatie* (Illyria and Dalmatia; 1815) was in many ways better informed than Fortis about the South Slavs, still managed to include a fair share of *Arabian Nights*-style nonsense about the Morlachs, such as the assertion that "When local gendarmes capture a *haiduk* [bandit], there is no need to tie them up: it suffices to cut the waist cord of his ample trousers, which fall around his ankles and prevent him from taking flight."

What none of these travellers got to grips with was the question of who the Morlachs actually were, though the term itself became increasingly redundant as the Morlachs began to identify themselves as Serbs and Croats rather than submitting to the labels applied to them by others. Dalmatia could still be a place of dramatic contrasts, however. The sight of men in embroidered jackets and with pistols stuck in their belts made a big impression on Maude Holbach, whose tellingly entitled *Dalmatia: the Land Where East meets West* (1908) gushingly informed readers that "the Dalmatians look more like stage brigands than peaceful subjects of the Austrian Empire". The Fortis effect probably reached its high-water mark, however, with *Black Lamb and Grey Falcon* (1937) by **Rebecca West**, whose prose was always more enthusiastic when she was writing about the macho types of the Balkan hinterland rather than the civilized urbanites of the Adriatic coast. This type of response to Dalmatia is less popular now than it was, not least because the events of 1991–95 suddenly made traditional Western views of southeastern Europe appear naive and over-romanticized.

1918. However, the threat of **Italian irredentism** remained strong, especially after Mussolini came to power in 1922. The Italian occupation of Dalmatia between 1941 and 1943 only served to worsen relations between the two communities, and at the war's end most remaining Italians fled.

The advent of socialism in 1945 failed to staunch major **emigration** to the New World and Australasia. After World War II, the traditional olive-growing and fishing economy of the Adriatic islands and villages was neglected in favour of heavy industry, producing a degree of rural depopulation which has only partly been ameliorated by the growth of tourism. The arrival of package tourists in the 1960s brought Dalmatia hitherto unimagined prosperity (although much of the money earned from tourism went to the big Yugoslav travel companies based in Belgrade), while urban-dwellers from inland cities like Zagreb and Belgrade increasingly aspired to **vikendice** ("weekend houses") on the coast, changing the profile of the village population and turning the Adriatic into a vast recreation area serving the whole of Yugoslavia.

Many of the holiday homes owned by Serbs ended up being abandoned, sold or blown up by right-wing thugs after the **collapse of Yugoslavia**, in which Dalmatia suffered as much as anywhere else in Croatia. After securing control of the hinterland areas around Knin and Benkovac, Serbian forces never quite reached the sea – despite attempts to subdue Zadar. Coastal hotels soon filled with refugees, however, and the tourist industry wound down owing to lack of custom. With the resumption of peace, Slovene, Italian and German tourists were quick to return to their former stomping grounds, and by the turn of the century they had been joined by Hungarians, Poles, Czechs and Brits – making Dalmatia one of the most cosmopolitan summer playgrounds in the whole of Europe.

Northern Dalmatia

The main urban centre of northern Dalmatia is **Zadar**, an animated jumble of Roman, Venetian and modern styles that presents as good an introduction as any to Dalmatia's mixed-up history. It's within day-trip distance of the medieval Croatian centre of **Nin**, and is also the main ferry port for the unassuming northern Dalmatian islands of **Silba**, **Ugljan**, **Pašman** and **Dugi otok**, where you'll find peaceful villages, laidback and fairly empty beaches, and relatively few package hotels.

The next major town south of Zadar is **Šibenik**, with a quiet old town and a spectacular fifteenth-century cathedral, and the most convenient base from which to visit the tumbling waterfalls of the **Krka National Park**. The main natural attraction in this part of Dalmatia is the **Kornati archipelago**, a collection of captivatingly bare and uninhabited islands accessed from the village of **Murter**. Further down the coast, ancient **Trogir** is one of the loveliest towns on the entire seaboard, an almost perfectly preserved example of a Veneto-Dalmatian town of the late Middle Ages.

Along the coast to Nin

Approaching from the north, your first sight of Dalmatia is the lofty concrete span of the **Maslenica Bridge** (Maslenički most) as it sweeps across the **Maslenica Gorge**. The original bridge was destroyed by Serb forces in autumn 1991 in an attempt to sever Dalmatia's communications with the rest of the country, and it wasn't until January 1993 that the Croatian army regained control of Maslenica (breaking a UN-brokered ceasefire in the process). The new Maslenica Bridge, opened in 1996, is notoriously susceptible to strong winds – if the Bura is blowing it's often closed to high-sided vehicles, bikes and trailers, and in bad storms it's shut altogether.

To the south of the Maslenica Bridge is the **Novigradsko more** ("Novigrad Sea"), a large, sheltered lagoon bordered by grey-brown hills. Just beyond the bridge, past the village of Posedarje, there's a southbound turning for the little town of **NOVIGRAD**, tucked away on the west side of the lagoon beneath a ruin-crowned hill. Novigrad has something of a history of being a front-line town: it was an important point in Venice's line of defences against the Turks, and held out successfully except for a short period in 1646–47, when Ibrahim Pasha seized the fortress. More recently it was occupied by the Serbs until won back in the Maslenica Bridge operation of 1993, although it remained so close to the front line that the locals couldn't return to their houses for another two years.

Nowadays Novigrad is a pleasant little place, with an S-bend of solid stone houses following a quay lined with small fishing craft, and narrow streets winding uphill. The otherwise unremarkable **parish church** (*župna crkva*) contains a Gothic statue of the Pietà which is paraded around town on the third Sunday of September. Above the church you can pick up paths to the hilltop **castle** (*fortica*), where Elizabeth Kotromanić, Queen of Hungary, was murdered in 1386. The castle is now in ruins, but the climb is worth it for the views north over the Novigradsko more to the ridge of the Velebit mountains.

The main coastal buses don't make the detour to Novigrad, so those dependent on public transport will have to make for Zadar (see p.255) first and pick up local services from there. These pull up on Novigrad's Riva, where the **tourist office** (Mon–Sat 8–11am & 6–9.30pm, Sun 8–11am; ☎023/375-051) has information on local **rooms** (❶). There's a nice **pension**, *Osam ferala*, on the right as you enter town (☎023/375-114 & 375-122; ❷); and a neat, Austrian-run **campsite**, the *Mulić* (☎023/375-111, ✉office@adriasol.com), on the eastern side of town, which sits on a pleasant stretch of pebbly **beach**.

On the eastern side of the Novigradsko more, huge rock portals announce the entrance to the narrow canyon of the **Zrmanja Gorge**, one of the most remarkable karst formations in the country, its sheer sides rising as high as 200m. The best way to see the gorge is by **boat**: departures are usually advertized on Novigrad's harbourfront; otherwise the tourist office will arrange for a local boatman to take you up the gorge if you give them 24 hours' notice. It's also possible to take a **raft trip** down the upper stretches of the Zrmanja, with excursions beginning at Kaštel Žegarski 25km upriver from Novigrad, and finishing at Muškovci a further 10km downstream. Details of these trips are advertized in the tourist office in Novigrad, or at hotel receptions in Starigrad-Paklenica (see p.229) or Zadar (p.256) – expect to pay 220–250Kn per person.

Nin

To the west of the Maslenica Bridge, the Magistrala forges across the **Ravni kotari** (literally "flat districts"), a fertile expanse of farmland and one of the few places in Dalmatia where you'll see cows, sheep and pumpkins alongside more commonplace Mediterranean features such as vineyards, olive groves and maquis. About 15km beyond Posedarje, another side-turning leads north to **NIN**, erstwhile ecclesiastical capital of Croatia and now a sleepy, beach-fringed town, set on a broad bay facing the southwestern extremities of the island of Pag. Initially settled by the Liburnians followed by the Romans, Nin later became a royal residence of the early Croatian kings and a major see of their bishops from 879. Like everywhere else along the coast it fell under Venetian rule in the fifteenth century, and was soon threatened by Ottoman advances, until in 1646 the Venetians evacuated the town and then shelled it from the sea, after which it slipped quietly into decay. By the time T.G. Jackson got here in 1887 Nin was no more than a large village whose inhabitants were so wan and unwholesome from malaria that his guides wouldn't let him stay there overnight.

The malaria has gone, but apart from that Nin can't have changed much since Jackson's visit, preserving a scattering of Roman ruins, crumbling walls and a clutch of quaint old churches which give evidence of Nin's former importance. Nin also boasts some decent **beaches**, with alluring sandy stretches north and east of town, and a more pebbly affair at the tourist settlement of Zaton to the west.

The Town

The town is built on a small island connected to the mainland by two bridges: Gornji most and Donji most ("upper bridge" and "lower bridge"). Donji most is your most likely starting point, across which lies the main street, which leads past the plain-looking **St Aselus's Church** (Crkva svetog Azela), an eighteenth-century structure built on the site of Nin's former cathedral and dedicated to a first-century martyr held by local tradition to be the town's first bishop. Inside, a small chapel to the right of the main altar holds a fifteenth-century statue of the Madonna of Zečevo, which commemorates an apparition of the Virgin on a nearby island. A copy of the statue (the original is too fragile) is borne in a procession of boats to Žečevo on May 5, the anniversary of the vision. Next door, the **treasury** (*riznica*; summer only; Mon–Sat 10am–noon & 5.30–9pm; 10Kn) houses an extraordinary collection of gold- and silver-plated reliquaries, beginning with a ninth-century chest of Carolingian origin containing the shoulder blade of St Aselus, and decorated with reliefs of SS Marcela, Ambrozius and (on the extreme left with hands raised) Aselus himself. Fourteenth-century Zadar goldsmiths produced the nearby reliquary for Aselus's arm, as well as skull reliquaries for Aselus and Marcela – their lids embossed with angels and griffins. The treasury's collection of St Aselus's body parts is rounded off by a dainty casket in the shape of a foot.

A little further up the main street and just off to the right, the small cruciform **Church of the Holy Cross** (Crkva svetog Križa) is the oldest church in the country, with an inscription on the lintel referring to Župan (Count) Godezav dated 800 AD. A simple whitewashed structure with high, Romanesque windows and a solid dome, it's sometimes open in summer, though it's bare inside apart from the simple stone slab which serves as an altar – ask at the tourist office or at the **Archeological Museum** at the top of the main street (Arheološki muzej; Mon–Sat: June–Aug 9am–noon & 6–10pm; Sept–May 8am–1pm; 10Kn). This small but excellently presented museum at the head of the main street kicks off with an ancient Liburnian *peka* (a cooking pot on top of which embers are piled) which looks identical to those still in use in Dalmatian kitchens today. The imported ceramics dredged up from Liburnian wrecks in Zaton harbour include a wealth of north Italian tableware and a dog-faced ornamental jug from Asia Minor. One room is devoted to two eleventh-century Croatian ships (one of which has been fully reconstructed) rescued by marine archeologists from shallow waters nearby. Possibly sunk in front of Nin port in order to prevent attack, these were easily manoeuvrable, eight-metre-long vessels which could be used either for fishing or fighting, and could easily be pulled up onto land or hidden in small bays. A collection of early medieval stonework culminates with a large stone font sporting a clumsily engraved inscription honouring Višeslav, one of the first Christian rulers of the embryonic Croatian state. There's also a model of the Roman **Temple of Diana**, whose scrappy remains lie round the corner from the museum. Beyond the temple ruins lie a surviving stretch of town wall and the Gornji most, over which the austere, barn-like thirteenth-century **St Ambrose's Church** (Crkva svetog Ambroza) stands silent guard.

Entering Nin on the main road from Zadar, you'll notice another tiny church, **St Nicholas's** (Crkva svetog Nikole), an eleventh-century structure. Surrounded by slender Scots pines, it was built on an ancient burial mound and later fortified by the Turks – the resulting crenellations give it the appearance of an oversized chesspiece. The interior is almost always locked, but it's an impressive site nevertheless, with a fine view over the blustery lowlands to the worn shape of Nin and the faint, silver-grey ridge of the Velebit mountains in the distance.

Nin's superb **beach** is an easy three-kilometre walk from town – head north from the landward side of Donji most, passing a small-boat harbour before ascending to meet a small crossroads, where you carry straight on. After a while you'll pass *Camping Ninska Laguna* (see below), then branch off on a path which leads through a purply-green, heather-like carpet of grasses and reeds before emerging onto a duney shore. The beach is genuinely sandy, and there's another fine view of the Velebit mountains across the water.

Practicalities

The only way to reach Nin by public transport is from Zadar, with local **buses** (approximately every 45min) dropping passengers at an unmarked road junction at the western, mainland side of town. There's unlikely to be any timetable information here, although the **tourist office** (summer Mon–Sat 8am–9pm, Sun 8am–noon; winter Mon–Fri 8am–3pm; ☎023/264-280 & 265-247, Ⓔtzg-nina@zd.tel.hr), just downhill from the bus stop, can advise on return services to Zadar, or book you into a private **room** (❶) or **apartment** (❷). *Perin Dvor* is a cosy **pension** on the old town's main street beside Donji most (☎023/264-307; ❸), offering simply-furnished rooms, some of which are en suite. *Camping Ninska Laguna*, on the way to the beach (☎023/264-265), is an orderly little place with a reasonable amount of shade, although it tends to get cramped in season. For **food**, there are a couple of places offering grills on the square in front of the Archeological Museum, and a wider range of meals at either *Gostionica Sokol* or the *Perin Dvor*, both beside the Donji most – where you'll also find a couple of cafés.

Zadar

The ancient capital of Dalmatia, **ZADAR** is a bustling town of around 100,000 people, but it preserves a relatively small-town feel, with a compact historic centre crowded onto a tapered thumb of land jutting northwest into the Adriatic. Pretty comprehensively destroyed in the last war by the Allies – it was bombed no fewer than 72 times – it lacks the perfectly preserved, museum-like quality of so many of the towns on this coast, displaying instead a pleasant muddle of architectural styles, where lone Corinthian columns stand alongside rectangular 1950s blocks, and Romanesque churches compete for space with glassy café-bars. Zadar is a major ferry port, so you'll pass through here if travelling on to the islands of the Zadar archipelago – Ugljan, Pašman, Dugi otok and a host of smaller islets. As the major urban centre between Rijeka and Split, Zadar can boast a university and a smattering of cultural distractions, and the presence of big hotels on the outskirts of town ensures that the central streets are swarming with life in July and August; outside that time, Zadar's relaxing café culture is left very much to the locals.

Long held by the Venetians (who called it Zara), Zadar was for centuries an **Italian-speaking** city, and you'll find the Latin influence still strong – Italian is widely understood, particularly by older people, and the place has much of the vibrancy of an Italian coastal town. It was ceded to Italy in 1921 under the terms of the Treaty of Rapallo, before becoming part of Tito's Yugoslavia in 1947, when many Italian families opted to leave.

Postwar reconstruction resulted in the current patchwork of old and new architectural styles, although further damage was meted out in 1991, when a combination of Serbian irregulars and JNA (Yugoslav People's Army) forces came dangerously close to capturing the city. As the country slid towards all-out war in early autumn 1991, JNA artillery units quickly took control of the low hills around Zemunik airport east of the city, leaving Zadar open to bombardment. JNA–Serb forces reached the high-rise suburbs but never pressed on towards the centre, possibly fearing the heavy losses that would be incurred in hand-to-hand street fighting. Despite the UN-sponsored ceasefires of 1992, Zadar remained exposed to Serbian artillery attack right up until 1995, when the Croatian Oluja offensive finally drove them back.

After some years spent in the economic doldrums, today's Zadar has a more dynamic feel than some of the other Dalmatian cities. Major money earners are the tuna-fishing fleet, with most of the catch exported directly to Japan, and the almost totally refurbished Borik hotel development – built in the 1980s, this was given a wide berth by tour operators throughout the 1990s, but looks like becoming a fashionable destination once again.

Arrival, information and accommodation

Arrivals at Zadar's **airport**, 10km southeast of town at Zemunik, are met by Croatian Airlines buses into town (25Kn). **Ferries** arrive at the quays lining Liburnska obala, from where the town centre is a five-minute walk uphill. Zadar's **train** and **bus stations** are about 1km east of the town centre, a fifteen-minute walk or a quick hop on municipal bus #5. For local bus rides, pay the driver (6Kn flat fare) or buy a ticket (8Kn) in advance, valid for two journeys, from newspaper and tobacco kiosks. The **tourist office** is in the southeast of the old town at Ilije Smiljanića 5 (summer daily 8am–10pm; winter Mon–Fri 8am–3pm; ☎023/212-412 & 212-222, ✉tz-zadar@zd.tel.hr).

Accommodation

There's a reasonable stock of private **rooms** (❶–❷) in the old town, and plenty of **apartments** (❸) in the coastal suburbs to the west, although they're speedily snapped up in summer. They can be booked through two agencies near the ferry quays: Aquarius, Nova Vrata bb (☎023/212-919 and 224-120, ⓦwww.jureskoaquarius.com) and Miatours, Vrata sv. Krševana (☎023/254-400 & 254-300, ⓦwww.miatours.hr).

The *Borik* **campsite**, next to the hotel complex of the same name 4km northwest of town (bus #5 from the train and bus stations; ☎023/332-074), is large, tidy and shaded by a variety of deciduous and coniferous trees. Croatia's biggest HI-affiliated **youth hostel** lies on the nearby waterfront at Obala kneza Trpimira 76 (bus #5; ☎023/331-145, Ⓕ331-190), with 280 places in everything from double rooms (❷) to six-bed dorms (95Kn per person, 110Kn with breakfast), a cheap alfresco café-restaurant and a relaxing, laid-back atmosphere.

Hotels

Hotels in central Zadar are in short supply, but there's plenty of choice in the seaside suburb of Puntamika.

Albin put Dikla 47 ☎023/331-137, Ⓕ332-172. Family-run hotel in a residential area 3km north of the centre, handy for the beach facilities at Borik. Rooms come with TV and a/c, and there's a dinky pool out the back, plus an excellent seafood restaurant on the ground floor. Bus #5 or #8 from the bus/train stations. ❹

Borik Puntamika, 4km northwest of the centre ☎023/206-637, ⓦwww.hoteliborik.hr. A seafront holiday complex with a clutch of bland concrete-box hotels. The *Adriana*, *Novi Park* and *Puntamika* have already been refurbished and awarded four-star ratings; the others are sure to follow. Save for the chic, stylish *Adriana*, the atmosphere inside the hotels is a bit antiseptic – but the complex is set in well-tended gardens and has a long pebble beach.

CENTRAL ZADAR

RESTAURANTS, CAFÉS & BARS

Atrij	C
Café Central	G
Danica	F
Donat	A
Dva Ribara	J
Foša	O
Fast Sandwich Bar	H
Forum	N
Galerija Dina	K
Konoba Martinac	B
Kult	M
Malo Misto	D
Marival	E
Stomorica	L
Toni	I

ACCOMMODATION

Kolovare	2
Verona	1

Train Station

Bus Station

▼ Borik

Hospital

Basketball Stadium

Vladimir Nazor Park

ZRINSKO-FRANKOPANSKA

ZAGREBAČKA

Jazine

Footbridge

Foša

St Simeon's Church

St Michael's Church

Land Gate

VAROŠ

Market

Aquarius

Guard House

Loggia

Port Gate
Miatours

Ferries to Ugljan

St Mary's Church

Archeological Museum

Jadrolinija Office

St Chrysogonus's Church

FORUM

St Donat's Church

Cathedral

St Elijah's Church

Franciscan Monastery

Jadrolinija Office

Ferries to Dugi Otok, Iž & Silba

Ferries to Italy, Rijeka & Dubrovnik

LIBURNSKA OBALA

ISTARSKA OBALA

OBALA KRALJA PETRA KREŠIMIRA IV

Zadar Channel

N

0   100m

5

DALMATIA | Zadar

▼ 2 (200m)

There's not much room for individual travellers in July and Aug, when Borik is block-booked by package companies. Bus #5 from the train and bus stations. March–Oct. *Barbara, Donat & Zadar* ❹, *Puntamika* ❺, *Adriana & Novi Park* ❻

Kolovare Bože Peričića 14 ☎023/203-200, ☏203-300, ✉hotel-kolovare-zadar@zd.tel.hr. Five minutes south of the bus and train stations, this is currently the only mid-range/business class hotel within convenient walking distance of the centre. Rooms are in different stages of renovation, but all have private bathroom and TV. ❻

Mediteran Matije Gupca 19 ☎023/337-500, ⓦwww.hotelmediteran-zd.hr. Small and rather swish private hotel north of the beach at Borik. All rooms come with balcony, en-suite shower and TV;

some of the more expensive ones have a/c and minibar. Bus #5 to *Camping Borik*, then a 5min walk uphill. ❹–❺

President Vladana Desnice 16 ☎023/333-696, ⓦwww.hotel-president.hr. Intimate-sized luxury hotel in the environs of Borik, featuring plush Second Empire furnishings and conscientious staff. Dine on caviar, snails and other choice delicacies in the on-site restaurant. Doubles from 1350Kn. ❾

Verona Šime Ljubića 4a ☎023/370-264. A pension-style place (really an accommodation agency with rooms above the office) situated in the heart of the Varoš, central Zadar's most atmospheric quarter. Rooms are rather minuscule but are neat and comfortable, and come with en-suite shower. ❸

The Town

Much of central Zadar remains a network of narrow medieval streets, barred to motor traffic. The two sides of the peninsula are quite different in feel: the **northern waterfront**, lined by a surviving section of city wall, is busy with the hustle of ferry traffic, while the **southern side**, along Obala kralja Petra Krešimira IV, seems somewhat neglected, despite its fine nineteenth-century buildings and views of offshore islands. On the eastern side of the peninsula lies the **Jazine**, the sheltered harbour beyond which lie the modern parts of town, uneventful save for a snazzy yacht club and a few marinas.

The Forum and cathedral

Zadar's main square, the **Forum**, is a messy expanse with a gravelly parking lot rubbing up against remnants of the original Roman forum, now reduced to a few hastily dumped sarcophagi and a single standing column – the only surviving pillar of a colonnade which was once the size of a football pitch. The Forum's southwestern side joins up with the seafront boulevard of Obala kralja Petra Krešimira IV, where there's a fine view across the water to the hilly island of Ugljan.

Much of the original stone from the Forum found its way into the adjacent ninth-century **St Donat's Church** (Crkva svetog Donata; summer only: daily 9am–10pm; 5Kn), a hulking cylinder of stone built – according to tradition – by St Donat himself, an Irishman who was bishop here for a time. It's an impressive example of Byzantine church architecture, resembling from the outside San Vitale in Ravenna and Charlemagne's Palatinate Chapel in Aachen. The cavernous, bare interior has a pleasing simplicity, a high-ceilinged circular space with a gallery held up by six chunky supports and two Corinthian columns. It stopped being a church in 1797, subsequently serving as a shop, military store and museum, but for the moment it lies empty, used only occasionally for summer concerts.

The modern, concrete **Archeological Museum** opposite (Arheološki muzej; Mon–Sat 9am–1pm; in summer also Mon–Sat 6–9.30pm, Sun 6–9.30pm; 10Kn) has a neatly displayed collection beginning with the Neolithic period on the top floor and moving on through Liburnian, Roman and medieval Croatian periods as you descend. There are several examples of the characteristic Liburnian gravestone or *cipus*, a tapering bollard-like affair crowned with carved leaf shapes, rather like a fat stalk of asparagus (there are a few more stacked up in the yard at the back). The medieval Croatian stonework also catches the eye, particularly the fancifully rendered griffins; these flank the depiction of Christ and his angels on the eleventh-century carved doorway which once adorned the portals of the (long since demolished) St Lawrence's Church.

St Mary's Church and the Church Art Exhibition

On the same side of the square as the museum, **St Mary's Church** (Crkva svete Marije) dates from 1066 and includes some salvaged Roman and medieval pillars in the nave, though its trefoil Renaissance frontage was added in the sixteenth century, and the interior was given a thorough refurbishment in the eighteenth, when the rippling stucco balconies of the gallery were added. The Romanesque bell tower next door is the oldest in Dalmatia, having been built in 1105.

The adjacent **convent** is of more interest, having recently been converted to house a **Permanent Exhibition of Church Art** (Stalna izložba crkvene umjetnosti; Mon–Sat 10am–1pm; in summer also Mon–Sat 6–8pm, Sun 10am–1pm; 20Kn), a storehouse of Zadar's finest church treasures and very much the pride of the city. The first floor has numerous reliquaries, including a richly ornamented twelfth-century casket containing the arm of St Isidore and a thirteenth-century reliquary for the shoulder blade of St Mark, which resembles a small grand piano mounted on three clawed legs. Some very diverse iconic representations of the Madonna and Child include a Paolo Veneziano work from the 1350s, in which the rigidity of sacred painting is

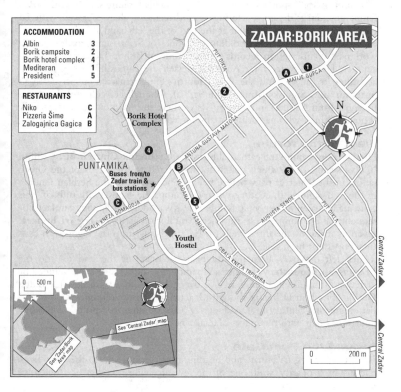

softened with a touch of naturalistic portraiture, with the eyes of the Virgin fixing the viewer. On the second floor there's a large fifteenth-century gang of apostles carved in wood by the Venetian Matej Moronzon in 1426, and an early six-part polyptych by Vittore Carpaccio, one panel of which features a much-reproduced picture of a youthful, tousle-haired St Martin of Tours lending his cloak to a beggar. Altogether, it's a fabulous museum, subtly arranged, beautifully lit and just small enough to be manageable in a single visit.

The cathedral

On the northwestern side of the Forum, the twelfth- and thirteenth-century **Cathedral of St Anastasia** (Katedrala svete Stošije) is a perfect example of the late Romanesque style, with an arcaded west front reminiscent of the churches of Pisa and Tuscany. Around the door frame stretches a frieze of twisting acanthus leaves, from which various beasts emerge – look for the rodent and bird fighting over a bunch of grapes – while to either side hang figures of four apostles, engagingly primitive pieces of stonework which were probably taken from the facade of an earlier church on this site. The cathedral's **campanile** was only finished in the 1890s by the English writer and architect T.G. Jackson; if you've been to Rab you may find it familiar – he modelled it on the cathedral bell tower there.

The **interior** is high and capacious, with the nave greedily out of proportion to the narrow aisles hidden away on each side. The lofty arcade is pretty enough, with pillars picked out in red marble, but it can't help but look a little lost in the broad expanses of flat, grey stone. At the eastern end, the Gothic ciborium of 1332 sports a series of deftly chiselled columns, each with a different geometric design, enclosing a ninth-century altar engraved with fat crosses and palms. The side altar at the end of the left-hand aisle is surmounted by a plain marble casket holding the bones of St Anastasia, made – as the workmanlike inscription records – in the time of Bishop Donat in the ninth century. Details concerning Anastasia herself are impossible to pin down: according to one legend she was a fourth-century martyr put to death in Sirmium (now Sremska Mitrovica in Serbia), although her cult probably came to Zadar from Aquileia in northern Italy, where she was honoured as a saintly Roman woman who performed many miracles.

West of the forum

Hidden away behind the cathedral lurks the **Orthodox Church of St Elijah** (Crkva svetog Ilije), which originally ministered to the needs of the Greek sailors in the Venetian navy before being handed over to the Serbian Church in the mid-eighteenth century, when the campanile – now with tufts of grass growing between its heavy blocks of stone – was added. Following Široka (subsequently J. Bjankinija) west from here, you'll soon arrive at **Trg tri bunara**, given its name by the three wells (*tri bunara*) dating from the eighteenth century on its northern side.

Turn left down A. Papavije and bear left again at the end to find the **Franciscan monastery** (Franjevački samostan), said to have been founded by St Francis himself when he visited Zadar in 1219, and purportedly the oldest Gothic church in Dalmatia, though it's actually a fairly dull renovation with a flat eighteenth-century roof. A doorway leads through to a plain but pleasing courtyard lined with the graves of Zadar nobles.

Around the Port Gate

Returning to Trg tri bunara and heading north brings you to the ferry dock and a length of **city wall**, one of the few surviving stretches of a defensive system completed in 1570, just in time to save Zadar from a two-year Turkish siege. You can follow these fragments of wall southeast towards the **Port Gate** (Lučka vrata), a Roman triumphal arch which was later topped with a relief of St Chrysogonus, the city's protector, on horseback.

Slightly uphill from the gate is **St Chrysogonus' Church** (Crkva svetog Krševana), a more impressive building outside than in, with a west front similar to the cathedral's and a superb colonnaded east end. To one side stands a squat, unfinished tower which never rose above the height of the church's facade, and an angular, musclebound modern statue of the Zadar-born writer **Petar Zoranić** (1508–c.1560), whose Arcadian romance *Planine* (Mountains) is often credited with being the first novel written in Croatian. On the other side of the street, the interior of the **Zagrebačka banka** incorporates elements of the medieval St Thomas's Church (Crkva svetog Tome), which once stood on this spot, with stubby remains of columns running along the floor and gravestones mounted on one of the walls.

Cut southeast along Krnarutića to reach the **market** (mornings only), which fills a small square hard up against the walls. Here you'll find all manner of fruit and vegetables brought in daily from the surrounding countryside, while traders in an adjacent hall sell freshly caught fish. It's a colourful scene, though no longer as exotic as it was when Maude Holbach travelled through Dalmatia in the early 1900s, remarking on the peasants who, "seated on the ground in the fashion of the East, offered their eggs and vegetables for sale in the strangest tongue that ever assailed my ears. At first glance they seemed to me more like North American Indians than any European race."

Narodni trg and St Simeon's Church

Just beyond the market, another gate leads through to the pedestrian bridge which leads across the Jazine into modern Zadar. In the other direction, Jurja Barakovića heads up to **Narodni trg**, which took over from the Forum as the main focus of civic activity in the Middle Ages. It's overlooked by the sixteenth-century **Guard House** (Gradska straža), a low, single-storey building with a soaring square clock tower, built in 1562. The niche to the left of the main entrance houses a fine bust of the Venetian governor G.G. Zane from 1608, sporting stylized furrowed brows and a veritable carpet of a beard. Immediately opposite, the **Town Loggia** (Loža; daily 9am–1pm & 5–7pm) has been enclosed in plate glass and transformed into an art gallery.

Southeast of Narodni trg, on Trg Petra Zoranića, the Baroque **St Simeon's Church** (Crkva svetog Šimuna) was rebuilt in the seventeenth century to act as a fitting shrine for the bones of St Simeon, a minor saint who is supposed to have held the Christ Child in the Temple. The body was originally stored in the Church of St Mary the Great until its demolition to make way for the city walls in 1570.

St Simeon's silver-gilt **reliquary** now forms the main feature of the high altar, where it's held aloft by two Baroque angels cast in bronze from captured Turkish cannons. An extravagant work of art, ordered by Queen Elizabeth of Hungary in 1377, the reliquary was fashioned from 250 kilos of silver by a team of local artisans working under the supervision of a Milanese silversmith. The story goes that Elizabeth so wanted a piece of the saint's body that she broke off a finger and hid it in her bosom, where it immediately began to decompose and fill with maggots – a process only reversed when she returned the finger to its rightful place. The creation of the reliquary was her way of atoning for the theft, though it also had a political dimension: her patronage of the cult of St Simeon increased the local popularity of her husband, King Louis of Anjou, then engaged in keeping Zadar free from the clutches of Venice. The lid of the reliquary shows the bearded saint in high relief; on the front, two panels dramatize the discovery of St Simeon's body in a monastery on the outskirts of Zadar and Louis of Anjou's triumphant entry into the city after relieving Zadar from an eighteen-month Venetian siege. The centre panel is a rough copy of Giotto's fresco of the Presentation in the Temple in Padua. The reliquary is opened every year on the feast of St Simeon (Oct 8).

Trg pet bunara and the Varoš quarter

Beyond St Simeon's Church a low flight of steps leads to the five wells that give **Trg pet bunara** its name and which were the city's main source of drinking water until the late nineteenth century. Completely repaved in 1998, the square still has an antiseptic aspect which seems out of keeping with the grizzled pentagonal **Captain's Tower** (Kapetanova kula) which overlooks it from the north. Immediately southeast of here lies the entrance to the city park, laid out on a jutting, arrow-shaped bastion which once formed the landward side of Zadar's defences.

Southwest from Trg pet bunara is the **Land Gate** (Kopnena vrata), a triumphal arch topped by a row of eight cattle skulls – thought to be a death symbol intended to ward off would-be invaders – and a monumental winged lion of St Mark; tellingly, this symbol of Venetian power dwarfs the civic emblem – another relief of St Chrysogonus on horseback – immediately below it. On the far side of the gate lies the **Foša**, a narrow channel which once fed Zadar's moat and is now a small harbour crowded with pleasure boats. Follow this around and you're back on Zadar's southern waterfront, Obala kralja Petra Krešimira IV.

Alternatively, heading northwest from the Land Gate along Špire Brušine (subsequently Plemića Borelli, then Madijevaca) leads you back into the city centre through the charming **Varoš quarter**, whose narrow alleys are packed with little boutiques and cafés. On the corner of Špire Brušine and M. Klaića, the main portal of **St Michael's Church** (Crkva svetog Mihovila) is topped by an animated fourteenth-century relief of St Michael spearing a demon, flanked by Zadar's ubiquitous patrons, Anastasia and Chrysogonus. Peering out from the facade higher up are three fish-eyed male heads, the remains of a crudely carved late Roman gravestone. Continuing along Borelli and Madijevaca, passing the yellow brick Austrian courthouse (Sudska palača), you'll eventually emerge beside St Mary's Church on the corner of the Forum.

Eating and drinking

While central Zadar would never feature in any gourmet's grand tour, there are plenty of unpretentious sit-down places serving up simple grills and fish dishes. The swankier seafood restaurants are all located in the city's northwestern suburbs. For **snacks** and **picnics**, the daily market just inside the old town walls off Jurja Barakovića is the place to get fruit, veg, local cheeses and home-cured hams. There's a **supermarket**, Zadranka (daily 6.30am–9pm), on the corner of Široka and Dalmatinskog sabora, and a larger branch just across the footbridge over the Jazine on Josipa Jurja Strossmayera. The *Fast Sandwich Bar*, M. Klaića, is the place to get a sandwich filled with local *pršut* or Slavonian *kulen* sausage.

For **drinking**, the central strip from Narodni trg to the Forum is well supplied with terrace cafés and ice-cream parlours. However, many of the more atmospheric café-bars are in the Varoš quarter: from Narodni trg, head down

Klaiča and its continuation, Varoška, before bearing right into Stomorica – en route you'll pass a string of tiny establishments with outdoor seating crammed into narrow alleys. On warm summer evenings most customers end up either perching precariously on benches or standing in the street.

Restaurants

Central Zadar

Dva Ribara Borelli 7. Conveniently placed city-centre place with a general meat and fish menu, but particularly known for its pizzas – which keep the locals coming in droves. The spacious terrace gets busy in summer.

Foša Kralja Dimitra Zvonimira 2. Dependable fish and seafood restaurant, with an outdoor terrace right on the small harbour outside the Land Gate.

Konoba Martinac A. Papavije 7. Cosy little place in the alleyway leading to the Franciscan monastery, offering fresh fish, excellent squid and scampi, and a small garden terrace.

Malo Misto Jurja Dalmatinca 3. Neighbourhood bar-restaurant which keeps the locals happy with inexpensive staples like *grah* and *girice* during the winter, and opens up a terrace serving moderately priced grilled meats in the summer.

Marival Don Ive Prodana 3. Another small, cramped restaurant serving up cheap, traditional lunches to the locals in winter, grilled fish and fries to the tourists come July and Aug. Informal, fun, but soon fills up.

Stomorica Stomorica 12. No-nonsense working men's tavern with a couple of benches out front, serving *girice* and other salty snacks, washed down with Dalmatian wines.

In and around Borik

Niko Obala Kneza Domagoja 9 ☎023/331-138. Upmarket seafood restaurant hidden away in an anonymous street just west of Borik, serving superbly prepared fish and shellfish – the kind of place where Zadar people go for a special meal.

Pizzeria Šime Matije Gupca 15. Monster-sized terrace restaurant uphill from Borik, known for its filling, inexpensive fare. Can get packed out in July and Aug.

Zalogajnica Gagica Antuna Gustava Matoša bb. Cult Zadar snack bar opposite the entrance to the Borik complex, doling out *burek* and cheap grills such as *ćevapi* and *pljeskasvice*. At night the terrace attracts a lively cross section of Zadar folk and is a good place for a drink.

Cafés and bars

Atrij Jurja Barakovića. on the way to the footbridge from the old town, featuring fine views, good coffee, French-style pastries, and piano-tinkling in the evening.

Café Central Široka bb. Zadar's principal café and meeting point ever since the 1890s, still attracting a broad cross section of Zadar's population during the daytime. At night it attracts a decidedly younger clientele with loudish music, moody lighting and a long list of cocktails.

Danica Široka bb. Café and cake shop next door to the *Central*, with the biggest range of sweets and pastries in the city.

Donat Trg sv Stošje. The best of Zadar's ice-cream parlours, with outdoor seating right by the cathedral and a full range of non-alcoholic drinks. Both *Donat* and the café next to it (*Lloyds*) are popular vantage points from which to observe the ebb and flow of the evening *korzo*.

Galerija Đina Varoška. Chic and comfy café in one of the tightest-packed alleyways of the Varoš quarter – where you can savour the unique Zadar experience of listening to music simultaneously pumped out by three or four cafés.

Kult Stomorica. Another popular Varoš hangout, this time with lots of outdoor seating in an attractively tatty residental courtyard.

Toni M. Klaića. Tiny but enduringly popular café-bar occupying a key junction on the route into the Varoš quarter, attracting a slightly older crowd than *Galerija Đina* or *Kult*.

Nightlife and entertainment

Popular **clubs** include *Forum*, a youth-oriented disco on three floors, right by the basketball stadium on Obala kralja Tomislava; and *Gotham*, 2km northeast of the old town at Marka Oreškovića 1a, which has themed DJ nights, and live gigs (anything from Croatian pop to jazz) on the terrace in summer. The Croatian Playhouse (Hrvatska kazališna kuća; ☎023/314-586), on the corner of Široka and Dalmatinskog sabora, is the main venue for serious **drama** and **classical music**; the churches of St Donat and St Chrysogonus are also used as chamber-music venues from early July to mid-August. Zadar's **Puppet**

Theatre (Kazalište lutaka), Sokolska 1 (☎023/212-754), is among the best in the country.

Most prestigious of the mainstream arts festivals is the **Zadar Theatrical Summer** (Zadarsko kazališno ljeto; mid-July to mid-Aug) featuring theatre groups from all over the country, and although most performances are in Croatian, imaginative use of the city's open spaces (venues include Trg pet bunara and various courtyards) makes for some striking visual entertainment. More accessible for non-Croatian audiences is **Zadar Dreams** (Zadar snova; July or Aug), a festival of alternative theatre, performance art and music held in old-town churches and squares.

Although Zadar has a first-division football team, most locals (like all good Dalmatians) support Hajduk Split in preference to their underachieving home-town side. However the local **basketball** team, Zadar, is one of the major forces in the Croatian game, and a source of fanatical local pride. Look out for posters advertising game, usually played on Saturdays from September to April at the Košarkaško igralište, on the eastern fringes of the old town just off Obala kralja Tomislava.

Listings

Airlines Croatia Airlines, Natka Nodila 7 ☎023/250-101.
Banks Dalmatinska banka, J. Bjankinija 2 (Mon–Fri 8am–7pm, Sat 8am–noon).
Ferry tickets Jadrolinija, Liburnska obala 7 (Mon–Fri 7.30am–7.30pm, Sat 7.30am–5pm, Sun 7am–noon & 4–8pm; additional late-night opening to coincide with the arrival and departure of the coastal ferry; ☎023/212-003, ☎311-151); Jadroagent, Natka Nodila bb (☎023/251-052, ✉jadroagent-zadar@zd.tel.hr).
Hospital Just east of the centre, opposite the *Kolovare* hotel, at Bože Peričića 5 ☎023/315-677.
Internet access Cybercafe Internet, Špire Brušine 8 (daily 7am–midnight).

Left luggage At the bus station (daily 6am–10pm).
Opticians Ghetaldus, just off the Forum at Knezova Šubića Bribirskih 9.
Pharmacy Donat, just off Široka at Braće Vranjana 14, has a counter open 24hr.
Post office/telephones Just off the Forum on Šimuna Kožičića Benje (Mon–Sat 7am–9pm).
Taxis Try the ranks on Liburnska obala or phone ☎023/251-400.
Travel agents Atlas, Obala kneza Branimira 12 (☎023/235-850); Croatia express, Široka bb (☎023/250-502); and Kompas, Široka bb (☎023/251-892), sell plane tickets and organize local excursions – including trips to the Kornati islands (see p.272).

The Zadar archipelago

The small, often bare islands of northern Dalmatia – sometimes called the **Zadar archipelago** – see much less in the way of mass tourism than those in the south, and their unspoiled, largely rural nature provides them with bags of off-the-beaten track allure. The northern end of the archipelago is full of semi-abandoned islands boasting beautiful bays and lush inland scenery, although few other than **Silba** posess significant tourist facilities. Unsurprisingly considering its proximity to Zadar, **Ugljan** is the most urbanized island of the group, although it's still a soothingly laid-back kind of place, as is its neighbour **Pašman**, to which it is connected by road bridge. Hidden away on the far side of Ugljan, little **Iž** provides the perfect venue for a bout of pure relaxation. Further out, the long and barren island of **Dugi otok** shelters the rest of the archipelago from the open sea, and offers most in the way of stunning scenery, including the beautiful **Telašćica Bay** – the archipelago's most celebrated natural beauty spot.

The northern archipelago: from Zadar to Silba

There are two main Jadrolinija-operated catamaran routes from Zadar into the northern islands of the archipelago. The first calls in at the barren islets of Rivanj, Sestrunj and Zverinac before arriving at the larger and slightly more touristed islands of Molat and Ist – the latter, with its main settlement squatting on a beautiful shallow bay, is particularly worthy of a day-trip, although at the time of writing this can only be done on Sundays. A second catamaran heads via **Olib** for the green island of Silba, which has a reasonable amount of private accommodation and is the one place in this part of the Adriatic you're likely to want to stay for a couple of days. You can also get to Silba via the Zadar–Mali Lošinj–Pula car ferry (4 weekly) run by Lošinjska plovidba.

Silba

Eight kilometres in length and only 1km wide at its narrowest point, **Silba** probably gets its name from the Latin word *silva* (wood) and is still covered with trees (notably *crnika* or Mediterranean black oak), giving it an atmosphere quite different from that of its largely scrub-covered neighbours. The island's one settlement, **SILBA TOWN**, has an air of relaxed luxury, its palm-shaded stone houses and their walled gardens serving as reminders of the island's erstwhile commercial wealth, when sailing ships from Silba dominated the carrying trade between Dalmatia and Venice – only to be put out of business by the steam-powered ships of the nineteenth century. Nowadays a permanent population of about 300 is swelled tenfold in summer, when weekenders from Zadar and independent travellers from all over Croatia come to enjoy the island's uniquely relaxing rural atmosphere.

Silba Town straddles the island's narrowest point, its narrow car-free streets sloping down towards two bays. The one on the western side of town contains the ferry dock and has some splendid sections of pebble beach – great places from which to observe the sun setting over the open sea. The bay to the east is home to a yachting marina and a broad, shallow beach with a luxuriantly sandy sea floor. Although there's no official nudist beach on the island, Uvala Mavrova, fifty minutes' walk south of the village, is the place to let it all hang out.

Silba's **tourist office** is currently in the village school a few steps north of the church, although it may soon move to a new location (July & Aug Mon–Sat 7am–noon, Sun 8–11pm; ☎023/370-010). Private **rooms** (❶) are available from the Silba agency (☎023/370-264), which doesn't currently have an office – ring them in advance and they'll make sure someone meets you at the ferry dock. For **eating**, *Jadran*, just uphill from the dock, succeeds in being all restaurants to all men, with cheap pizzas, moderate grills, and full-price fish of the day – specialities of the house are octopus or lamb baked *ispod peke*. *Konoba Mul*, by the marina, serves up succulent grilled fish on a terrace decorated with fishing nets and other maritime nick-nacks.

Ugljan and Pašman

Just 5km west of Zadar, long, thin **Ugljan** is the most densely populated of all the Adriatic islands, yet remains largely rural in feel. Despite the presence of small colonies of package tourists on the island, the bulk of the tourist industry here revolves around Croatian independent travellers, and there's plentiful private accommodation, offering ideal places to vegetate if you want to leaven the urban bustle of Zadar with a dollop of rustic peace. Beaches on both islands are modest – usually no more than concreted quays with short stretches of shingle – but they have one major advantage over those on the mainland: once you get in the water, the feel of the sea bed beneath your feet is distinctly sandy rather than rocky. Much of the island luxuriates under a green covering of olive plantations, which produce some of Croatia's best olive oil (the name Ugljan comes from the Croatian word for oil, *ulje*), although you're unlikely to find it on sale in the local shops – most of the island's farmers produce only a small surplus, and the whole business is surprisingly uncommercialized.

The fourteen daily **ferries** from Zadar to Ugljan drop you at the town of Preko, from where there are buses (usually coordinated to meet incoming ferries) running north to Ugljan village and Muline on the tip of Ugljan island, and south to the resort of Kukljica and to Pašman island.

Preko and Kali

Standing opposite Zadar, **PREKO** (literally "on the other side") is Ugljan's largest village, and feels very much like a dormitory suburb of Zadar – a quiet, unspectacular settlement, comprising a few residential streets and a small harbour. Locals swim from **Jaz**, a wide shallow bay 1km north of the harbour, or the rocky coast of **Galevac** (also known as Školjić, or "little island"; accessible by taxi boat in season from the quayside in Preko), an islet 80m from the shore, where there's also a Franciscan monastery set in its own park. It was once the site of a Croatian-language printing press, moved here from Zadar in 1925 to escape Italianization, but there's little to see here now, although an exhibition of monastic treasures is under construction. The pleasant surrounding subtropical vegetation is like a little piece of Eden gone to seed. Overlooking the town to the west (and looking deceptively close) is the **Fortress of St Michael** (Tvrđava svetog Mihovila), an hour or so's walk along the road that heads uphill from the main island road on the western fringes of Preko. The fortress, which dates from 1203, was already largely ruined by the time the JNA – fearing it might be used as an observation post – shelled it in 1991. The views east to Zadar and west to the long, rippling form of Dugi otok – and, on a clear day, Ancona and the Italian coast – are marvellous.

Heading south, Preko runs gently into **KALI**, spread around a small hillock a kilometre or two down the coast. More immediately picturesque than Preko, Kali is also firmly committed to the local fishing industry, with trawlers crammed into the two harbours which stand on either side of its peninsula. There's little to do beyond wandering the pinched, sloping streets, although the sight of Kali's fishing boats setting sail into the evening twilight is an evocative one – something that you won't see in the more touristy islands further south.

Practicalities

The Zadar **ferry** docks midway between Preko and Kali – turn left and walk along the seafront for ten minutes to get to Preko's main harbourside square. At the far end of the square, set back slightly from the waterfront, the **tourist office** (July & Aug daily 8am–9pm; Sept–June Mon–Fri 8am–2pm; ☎023/286-108, ℗286-383) is friendly and informative, but low on brochures and maps. **Rooms** (❶) and **apartments** (❸) in Ugljan are available from Turistička Agencija Rušev, right on the waterfront (June & Sept 8am–1pm & 5–7pm; July & Aug daily 8am–9pm; Oct–May irregular hours but probably open mornings; ☎ & ℗023/286-085, ⊛www.rusev.croadria.com), who also have their own **pension** (same telephone number; ❷), offering cosy rooms with attached bathroom and TV, five minutes' uphill from here. If you want a **hotel**, the *Preko*, up some steps from the harbour (☎023/286-041, ℮hotel-preko@zd.tel.hr; ❹), has simple, sparsely furnished en-suite rooms, some with good sea views. *Konoba Barbara*, which you'll pass when walking from the ferry dock to the village centre, is a good place to **eat** fish, and there are numerous harbourside **cafés** from which to admire the twinkling lights of Zadar across the water. **Bikes** and small **boats** can be rented from the Turistička Agencija Rušev or from other ad hoc operators on the harbourfront during the season.

Around Ugljan island

Ten kilometres north of Preko, and served by six daily buses from the ferry dock, **UGLJAN VILLAGE** is smaller and much more rustic, and its broad pebbly bay is an attractive spot for swimming. The *Ugljan* **hotel** (☎023/288-004, ⑩www.dalmacija3d.com; ❸) is a fairly standard concrete box, but has a lovely position on Ugljan's harbour, and offers basic but bright en-suite rooms, some with sea-facing balconies; you can rent bikes and boats here too. There are also – at the last count – about nine **campsites**, mostly small affairs hidden away in private gardens. Also accessible from Preko by bus, the village of **MULINE**, 4km beyond Ugljan at the northern tip of the island, has three more campsites about a kilometre's walk from the bus stop, set side by side amid picturesque woodland, together with an attractive bay with a quiet beach.

Five kilometres south of Preko on the road to Pašman lies **KUKLJICA**, a small fishing hamlet on a wide green bay. In season it's normally full of central European tourists, who block-book the bungalow complex on the pine-covered eastern side of the bay, but even so things rarely get too busy. A well-signed path leads from the southern end of Kukljica's harbour to **Sabušica Bay** on the western edge of the island, where there's a quieter, concreted bathing area with naturist sections on its fringes. The **tourist office** (daily 8am–3pm; ☎023/373-276, ⓔtz-kukljica@zd.hinet.hr), just behind the harbourside market, has a choice of **rooms** (❶) and **apartments** (❷). Most package tourists stay at the *Zelena Punta* complex (☎023/373-337, ⑤373-319, ⓔhut-kukljica@zd.tel.hr) on the eastern side of the bay, which has cubicle-like **bungalows** (❸) and swisher **apartments** (❺) sheltering under pines and surrounded by concrete and stone beach areas. **Eating** and **drinking** in Kukljica is limited to a couple of cafes and pizzerias on the harbour, or the restaurant at the *Zelena Punta*.

Kukljica is famous for the festivities marking **Our Lady of the Snows** (Gospa od sniga) on August 5, which celebrate a "miraculous" summer fall of snow here some four hundred years ago. Every year a statue of the Madonna is carried in a procession of small boats from Kukljica to a seaside chapel lurking behind the headland to the south – a regatta in which the entire village takes part. Quite why the August snowfall should have been adopted as a Catholic miracle is unclear, beside its usefulness in providing the excuse for another feast day dedicated to the Virgin.

Pašman

Immediately south of Ugljan, and linked to it by a road bridge, the island of **Pašman** is even sleepier than its neighbour, with local activity confined to a few low-key fishing villages strung out at the base of a green central ridge. About eight buses a day make the journey from Preko to **PAŠMAN VILLAGE**, 15km south of the Ždrelac strait, the first real settlement on the island. A faded little place, the village has a pleasant shallow bay, Lučina, on its northern side. The **tourist office**, on the dusty road that passes for a seafront (June & Sept 8am–noon; July & Aug 8am–8pm; ☎ & ⑤023/260-155) will direct you towards private **rooms** (❶), and there are two **campsites** on Lučina Bay, the *Lučina* and

Kod Jakova, and a **pension**, the *Ružmarin* (☎023/260-231 or 260-381; ❷), also on Lucina Bay, offering small en-suite rooms and breakfast. Just round the corner from the tourist office is the *Lanterna* **restaurant**, whose terrace is a bit too exposed to southerly winds, but it has a basement where food, including all the local fish specialities, is cooked over a stone hearth.

Just beyond the next hamlet, Ugrinći, a lane to the right winds up onto Ćokovac hill, site of the **Monastery of SS Cosmas and Damian** (Kuzma and Damjan; daily 4–6pm). Initially a twelfth-century Venetian fortress, it was taken over by Benedictines fleeing Biograd-na-moru in 1394, when that town was razed by the Venetians. An important centre of Glagolitic culture until it was closed down by the French in 1808, the monastery was reoccupied in the 1930s and is currently the only permanently occupied Benedictine establishment in Croatia (though Benedictine nunneries, for some reason, are more widespread). The main reasons to visit are the late-fourteenth-century crucifix above the altar, and the view of modern Biograd-na-moru on the mainland.

The bus terminates in **TKON**, the island's main centre, which is directly connected to Biograd-na-moru (see p.270) by ten ferries daily. Tkon is less developed than Biograd, and is a much better place to stay if you don't like package resorts: the **tourist office** on Tkon's main street (Mon–Sat 7am–9pm, Sun 7am–noon; ☎023/285-213, ✉tz-opcine-tkon@zd.hinet.hr) will help you find a **room** (❶). For a place **to swim**, follow the road south out of Tkon to find a string of sandy coves.

Iž

Engulfed by maquis and untended olive trees, the little island of **Iž** is ideal for connoisseurs of islands that not many other people get to. It's easily reached from Zadar, although the daily car ferry leaves you stranded at **Bršanj** (a bay rather than a village in its own right) at the south end of the island, and it's preferable to catch one of the two weekly ferries (currently Fri & Sun) to the settlement of **Veli Iž** 7km further north. Friday's ferry only gives you a couple of hours in Veli before heading back to Zadar, while the Sunday service allows you to spend the whole day there. It's a scenic sea voyage whenever you come, with the boat squeezing through the channel that divides Ugljan from Pašman before working its way round the sheer western side of Ugljan.

A delightfully uneventful agglomeration of ruddy-brown fishermen's houses strung around a deep bay, **VELI IŽ** itself sees a modicum of low-key tourism in July and August, falling back into a deep sleep the rest of the year. There's a small marina popular with the Italian yachting contingent at one end of the bay, and a couple of cafés and restaurants strung along the harbourfront. Private **rooms** (❶) can be booked at the **tourist office** in the Dom Kulture (House of Culture) on the harbour, although it's only sporadically open in July and August; simple en-suite rooms are available at the **Hotel Korinjak** (☎023/277-064, ✆277-248; ❹; May–Sept only), a standard four-storey concrete block on a small peninsula north of the ferry dock. Activities on Iž boil down to exploring the paths leading up onto the wooded hillsides behind the village, or indulging in a swim – you can splash around in the shallow water in front of the hotel, or walk north past the next bay to find a long stretch of rocks, where the coastline – and the people – get barer the further you go.

Dugi otok

Dugi otok ("Long Island") is the largest of the islands of the Zadar archipelago, 52km long, though nowhere more than 5km wide. Only 1500 people live here, and parts of the island are very remote – some settlements are accessible only by sea. It's a wilder and more dramatic landscape than either Ugljan or Pašman, with sheer cliffs on its western side and a rugged, indented coastline that is justifiably popular with the yachting fraternity. Dugi otok's main attraction is **Telašćica Bay**, which is best approached from the island's main settlement, **Sali,** although the quiet villages and headlands of the northern part of the island are also worth a visit. It's also a possible base from which to visit the Kornati archipelago (see p.272), with boat captains in Sali offering trips, although the archipelago is more usually approached from Murter (see p.271).

There are only a couple of **ferries** daily during summer, making it impossible to visit without staying overnight, while outside summer it's difficult to get to the island at all. Sali and **Brbinj** are the main entry points, but there are no buses linking one to the other, so you'll need a car if you want to explore the island's single north–south road, with its spectacular views of the rest of the Zadar archipelago to the east. In addition to the regular Zadar–Sali and Zadar–Brbinj services, there are weekly Ancona–Brbinj ferries in summer, plus weekly Rijeka–Brbinj and Ancona–Brbinj hydrofoils and a weekly Zadar–Božava–Ancona catamaran. There are no campsites on the island, but private **rooms** aplenty. If you're driving, note that the island's only petrol station is just north of Sali in Zaglav.

Northern Dugi otok

Despite **BRBINJ**'s importance as a ferry port there's nothing much here, and it's a good idea to catch one of the buses which head north to **BOŽAVA**, a small fishing village with an attractive harbour and a path leading round the headland to the east to a rocky coast overlooked by swooning trees. **Rooms** (❶) are available from the **tourist office** (☎023/377-607) at the northern end of the harbour, while the *Božava* **hotel** complex (☎023/377-684, ⓦwww.bozava.zadar.net; ❹), set among pines on the west side of the harbour, offers tastefully refurbished rooms with TV and en-suite facilities.

Driving northwest out of Božava on the road to the village of Soline, you get a good view of the north of the island as it finishes in a flourish of bays and peninsulas. Follow the road up the westernmost of these peninsulas, Veli rat, then take a left turn onto an unmarked gravel track about 3km out of Božava and proceed about 1km through fragrant forest (drivers will have to park about halfway down) until you reach one of the island's best beaches, **Sakarun**, a 500-metre-long bar of pebbles commanding a shallow bay. Carrying on up Veli rat, the road terminates beside a stumpy, ochre lighthouse, built by the Austrians and now a popular spot for bathing, with an attractively rocky coastline stretching away on both sides.

Southern Dugi otok

The island's largest village and the centre of a prosperous fishing industry, **SALI** is a quiet place, with nothing really to see or do, though the smattering of cafés round the harbour provide the requisite air of Mediterranean vivacity on warm summer nights. The **tourist office**, on the western side of the harbour (July & Aug daily 8am–8pm; Sept–May Mon–Fri 8am–3pm; ☎ & ⓕ023/377-094), has **rooms** (❶) and **apartments** (❷), and there's also a **hotel**, the *Sali* (☎023/377-049, ⓕ377-078; ❹), over the hill from the harbour in the next bay to the north, Sašćica. The best time to be in Sali is the first weekend in August, when the Saljske užance **festival** takes place, with outdoor concerts, drinking and feasting, and performances of *tovareća muzika* ("donkey music" – so called because it's a tuneless racket that sounds like braying), which features the locals raucously blowing horns.

It's about 3km from Sali to the northern edge of **Telašćica Bay**, a seven-kilometre channel overlooked by smooth hills interspersed with numerous smaller bays which run down to the tangle of islands at the northern end of the Kornati archipelago (see p.272). The flora along the shoreline marks the transition from the green vegetation of the Zadar archipelago to the bare wilderness of the Kornati – banks of deep forest slope down towards the western shore of the bay, where maquis-covered offshore islands rise like grey-brown cones from the water – and the whole place has been designated a **nature park**.

Telašćica can't quite compete with the Kornati in terms of stark beauty, but it's much more accessible. To get there, take the signposted minor road which heads west from the Sali–Božava route about 1500m out of town. The road terminates at one of Telašćica's numerous small bays, from where a path leads southwards to the appropriately named **Uvala mir** ("Bay of Peace") about 4km beyond and a short distance from the park's main attractions. There's a bar and restaurant here, and a path which leads, after five minutes' walk up a wooded hillside, to a stretch of ruddy clifftop looking out towards the open sea. Five minutes south of the restaurant lies **Jezero mir**, a saltwater lake cut off from the sea by a narrow barrier of rock at the lake's southernmost end. The rock is a favourite with naturists, while the lake itself is popular swimming territory, although it's full of shrimps which nibble your legs if you stand still long enough – not as unpleasant an experience as it sounds.

Zadar to Šibenik

About 20km southeast of Zadar, **BIOGRAD-NA-MORU** was one of the towns developed by Croatia's medieval kings to challenge the pre-eminence of Zadar and Split. Petar Krešimir IV moved the archiepiscopate of Split here in the mid-eleventh century, and it was in Biograd that the Hungarian kings were crowned monarchs of Croatia after 1102. Biograd's period of greatness came to an end on Good Friday 1126, when the Venetians razed the town to its foundations, a catastrophe from which it never really recovered. Modern Biograd is one of the major package resorts on this part of the coast, though there's little of an old town left, and the uninspiring beaches tend to get crowded in season. It's mainly of interest as a base for visiting Lake Vrana (see opposite) or the Kornati islands (p.272), and as the ferry port for Tkon on the island of Pašman (see p.268).

The **tourist office** is hidden in a courtyard just off Trg hrvatskih velikana (Mon–Fri 9am–5pm; ☎023/383-123), where buses arrive. From here it's a short walk to the seafront and the Ilirija agency (daily 8am–8pm; ☎023/383-120), which will fix you up with a **room** (❶) or an **apartment** (❸). The recently renovated *Bolero*, 1km out of town on Ivana Meštrovića 1 (☎023/386-888, ⓦwww.hotel-bolero.hr; ❹), is the best of the **hotels**. The *Aquarium* **restaurant** on the Riva is the best place for a slap-up seafood feast, although there are numerous cheaper grill houses and pizzerias in the streets behind it. *In Vino Veritas*, in an alleyway beside the parish church, is a wonderfully atmospheric place dishing out *pršut*, *srdele* and local wine to an appreciative cross section of tourists and locals.

Most of the travel agencies on Biograd's Riva offer **boat trips to the Kornati islands**, although it's worth noting that many of these "Kornati" trips actually aim for Telašćica Bay on Dugi otok (see p.268) – a beautiful and worthwhile destination in its own right, but not, strictly speaking, part of the

Kornati archipelago. Ask to be shown on a map precisely where the trip is going in order to avoid disappointment. The Šangulin agency on the Riva (℗023/383-738) runs daily trips to the (real) Kornati from 200Kn per person.

Pakoštane and Lake Vrana

Five kilometres south of Biograd and a short hop by local bus, **PAKOŠTANE** is an inoffensive little resort with a few stretches of pebbly beach next to its small harbour. There's a well-appointed *Club Mediterranée* resort on the northern outskirts, but little else to get excited about save for the presence of **Lake Vrana** (Vransko Jezero), the largest natural lake in Croatia, just 2km inland. This thirteen-kilometre-long, reed-shrouded stretch of water is especially popular with wading birds such as herons and ibises, alongside bullfinches, terns and (in winter) large numbers of ducks and coots. Now a nature reserve (Park prirode Vransko Jezero; ⓦwww.vransko-jezero.hr), the lake and its shores still support human activities such as farming, tourism and fishing, save for one area near the northwestern corner of the lake specifically designated as a strict ornithological reserve, due to the presence of a colony of purple herons.

The most accessible parts of the lake are on the northwestern shore, on either side of the strict reserve: here numerous farm tracks branch off the road from Pakoštane, passing through dense reed beds towards the shore. The village of **Vrana**, straggling along the northern shoulder of the lake about 5km out from Pakoštane, was occupied by the Serbs in 1991–95 and still presents a disconcerting picture of ruin and reconstruction. In the sixteenth century it was one of the westernmost outposts of Ottoman power in the Adriatic, evidence of which exists in the shape of a derelict **caravanseray**, built in 1644 by order of local-born Jusuf Mošković, and reputedly the largest in Europe at the time.

There are two daily **buses** (one on Sundays) from Biograd to the northwestern end of the lake and Vrana village, although you could just as easily hike there in forty-five minutes from Pakoštane, which is served by much more frequent buses from Biograd and Zadar. **Cycling** is also an option: a map of biking routes round the lake is available from the tourist office in Biograd, and bikes can be rented for about 80Kn per day from the Ilirija agency in Biograd (see opposite) or from Cat, next to the bus stop in Pakoštane (℗023/381-401, Ⓔcat-centar-adria-tours@zd.hinet.hr). Dalmaturist, on Trg Kraljice Jelene beside the church (℗023/381-990, Ⓕ381-991), can sort out **private rooms** (❶) in Pakoštane, and there's a **campsite**, the *Crkvine*, on the northern shore of Vrana Lake, complete with café-restaurant and a small stretch of beach.

Murter and the Kornati archipelago

Around 25km south of Biograd, a side-road heads west towards the small island of **Murter**, linked to the mainland by bridge. The main settlement, **MURTER TOWN**, at the northern end of the island, is a frumpy little place that soon gets choked by visitors and their cars in July and August – largely as a result of the town's status as the main gateway to the Kornati archipelago. Day-trips to the latter are organized by most of Murter's travel agencies, but once you've been on one of these there's little in town to justify a longer stay. Murter's waterfront is not exactly designed for leisurely strolling: most of it is just a grubby car park. There's a hideous concrete **beach** at the western end of town, and an infinitely more attractive pebble affair at **Slanica Bay** fifteen minutes' walk further west – there's rarely enough room to swing a bikini here on summer weekends, but it's an enchanting place from which to watch the sun set over the Kornati once the crowds have thinned.

There are eight **buses** a day from Šibenik to Murter, passing through **Vodice** (the place to change if you're approaching from the north) en route before pulling into Murter's main square, Trg Rudina. There's a small **tourist office** on the square (July & Aug daily 8am–10pm; Sept–June Mon–Fri 8am–noon; ☎022/434-995 & 434-950, @www.tzo-murter.hr), which doles out free town plans, sells a national-park-approved map of the Kornati, and advises on which agents are offering the best trips to the islands.

Rooms (❶) are available from the Coronata bureau on Trg Rudina (daily: June & Sept 8am–1pm & 5–8pm; July & Aug 8am–11pm; ☎022/435-089, @www.coronata.hr), Kornat Turist on the same square (☎022/435-855, @www.kornatturist.hr), or from Atlas, just inland from the square at Hrvatskih vladara 8 (☎022/434-999). The marina, ten minutes' walk to the east, has a small **hotel**, the *Hramina* (☎022/434-411, ☎435-242, @www.marina-hramina.hr; ❸), with simple, cosy, balconied en-suite rooms overlooking the yacht berths; alternatively, the four-storey, box-like *Colentium* offers comfortable, smart rooms overlooking the beach at Slanica (☎022/431-100, ☎435-255; ❼). There's a small **campsite** at Slanica, and a string of larger ones south of town: the *Plitka Vala* (3km away), *Kosirina* (4km away on a lovely rocky bay) and *Jezera* (5km away) – Šibenik–Murter buses pick up and drop off at each of them.

There are a couple of places **to eat** on the town's main westbound alleyway, Luke. The friendly and unpretentious *Konoba Ćo* offers fresh fish as well as cheap and hearty stews like *mućkalica* (paprika-flavoured braised beef), while *Barbara* a little further along concentrates on standard pizza and pasta fare – including several vegetarian options. *Mate*, on the corner of Luke and Kornatska, offers some excellent, moderately priced seafood pasta and risotto dishes, alongside expertly grilled (and more expensive) fresh white fish.

Slastičarna Zelena, Trg Rudina, is the place to pick up doughnuts and pastries at breakfast time, as well as cakes and ice cream throughout the day. Both Trg Rudina and ul. Matije Gupca, an alleyway immediately east of it, have their fair share of café-bars, although the best place for late-night **drinking** is *Lantarna*, a beach bar 4km southwest of town that has frequent gigs and DJ nights. Eseker, just east of Trg Rudina on the marina side of town (@www.esekertours .hr), is the place to rent small **boats** (from 240Kn/day), **scooters** (240Kn/day upwards) and **bikes** (70Kn/day).

The Kornati archipelago

Scattered like pebbles to the south of Dugi otok lie the ninety or so islands of the **Kornati archipelago**, grouped around the 35-kilometre-long island of Kornat. A national park since 1980, the Kornati archipelago comprises a distinctively harsh and bare environment, almost devoid of life. The islands range in colour from stony white to pale ochre or green, sometimes mottled with patches of low shrub and hardy sage. They were once covered in forest until it was burned down to make pasture for sheep, who proceeded to eat everything in sight. The dry-stone walls used to pen them in are still visible, although the sheep themselves – save for a few wild descendants – are no more.

The islands were originally owned by the nobles of Zadar, who allowed the peasants of Murter to raise flocks and grow olives on the islands in return for a share in the cheese and oil thus produced. When the Zadar nobility fell on hard times in the nineteenth century, the islands were sold to the Murterians – and their descendants (the Kurnatari) remain the owners of most of the land on the Kornati to this day. Despite the number of stone cottages scattered over the islands (**Vruje**, on Kornat, is the biggest single settlement with 50 houses), most Kurnatari actually live in Murter nowadays – returning to the islands for a few months in the summer, when they come to relax, fish, or take advantage of the growing opportunities offered by tourism. The popularity of the Kornati with the international yachting fraternity is having a profound impact on the archipelago's development, with shoreline restaurants serving up top-quality seafood springing up in every available cove. There's a fully equipped yachting marina on the island of Piškera, on the western side of the archipelago, and an even bigger one on the island of Žut, which lies just outside the park boundaries to the east.

Unless you have access to a boat, the easiest way of seeing the Kornati is to go on one of the **day-trips** arranged by one of the travel agents in Murter; Atlas, Coronata and Kornatturist are among the most reliable. Travel agencies in Biograd-na-moru (see p.270), Sali (p.269) and Zadar (p.264) also offer similar trips. Wherever you start, excursions are likely to set off at 8 or 9am and return around 5pm, weaving in and out of the islands on the western side of the archipelago, stopping a couple of times so that you can stretch your legs, swim and consume some of the local food and drink. Prices start at around 190Kn per person if you're travelling from Murter, 250Kn if you're approaching from Biograd, Sali or Zadar, and include the national park entrance fee, and probably lunch with wine too. If you're approaching the islands independently, look out for the rubber dinghies operated by national park wardens, which cruise the area selling entrance tickets (50Kn). If you need more information, the Kornati national park office is just off Murter's main square at Butina 2 (Mon–Fri 8am–3pm; ☎022/434-166, ⊛www.tel.hr/np-kornati).

Staying in one of the island's **stone cottages** is popular with visitors who want a period of complete peace and quiet, and it's marketed by local agencies under the name "Robinson turizam" in order to lend it the requisite desert-island-like appeal. You'll have to arrange accommodation through Coronata, Kornatturist or Atlas in Murter (see above) well in advance, however, and commit yourself to a reasonably lengthy stay because of the logistics involved (the arrangements offered by Atlas, for example, run from Saturday to Saturday, while Coronata and Kornatturist are more flexible). Prices work out at about 400–500Kn per day for a two-person apartment, 600–800Kn per day for a four-person apartment, plus 500–600Kn for boat transfer there and back. Once you're there provisions will be delivered to you by boat every two or three days – you'll be able to eat out if you've chosen one of the islands with a marina or restaurant; otherwise, you're on your own. Some of the growing number of UK-based travel agencies offering stays in Kornati cottages are listed on pp.12–13.

Vodice

The rapidly expanding town of **VODICE**, 9km south of the Murter turn-off, is, unaccountably, central Dalmatia's most successful package-holiday destination, but also one of its least atmospheric – there's not much of an old town and most of the beaches are concrete. It has good bus connections with Murter and a convenient ferry link with the alluring islands of Zlarin and Prvić (see p.280), but is otherwise an unwieldy behemoth of a resort which may not prove to be the characterful Dalmatian getaway you were looking for.

Most coastal buses call in at Vodice's **bus station**, at the eastern end of the waterfront; the **tourist office** is two minutes' walk to the west in the market area (May, June & Sept 8am–noon & 2–8pm; July & Aug daily 8am–9pm; Oct–April Mon–Fri 8am–3pm). Private **rooms** (❶) and **apartments** (❷) can be booked through the Turist Biro (☎022/443-110) in the same building as the bus station, or Nik, Ante Poljička 2 (☎022/200-550, ✉nik-ta@si.tel.hr). If you want **hotel** comforts and are prepared to pay for them, the high-rise, three-star *Punta* (☎022/451-451, ⊛www.vodicanka.com; ➐) is a good choice, offering smart en-suite rooms on a pine-covered peninsula. For **eating**, you'll find innumerable cafés and pizzerias along the harbour, together with several restaurants offering German-language menus and slightly higher than average prices. One of the more atmospheric places is *Santa Marija*, on the waterfront, serving up some of the best seafood in town in what looks like a disorderly nineteenth-century parlour.

Šibenik and around

ŠIBENIK is one of the few towns on the Adriatic not to have a Greco-Roman heritage. Originally founded around an eleventh-century Croat fortress, it fell firmly under the control of the Venetians in the fifteenth century, becoming an important strongpoint in their struggles against the Ottomans. As the main town of middle Dalmatia, Šibenik was a thriving industrial port until the 1990s, when war and recession conspired to close down the aluminium and chrome factories, and the city entered the new century as one of Dalmatia's most economically depressed areas. It's not a resort, and there's little point in stopping if you're looking for somewhere quiet with a beach, though the mazelike medieval centre is good for idle wandering and the cathedral is one of the finest architectural monuments on the coast. As a transport hub, Šibenik isn't as important as Zadar or Split, but there are ferries to a handful of offshore islands, and buses inland to the waterfalls of the **Krka National Park** and the medieval castle at **Knin**.

Arrival, information and transport

Šibenik's **bus station** is just southeast of the city centre on Obala Hrvatske mornarice, with a left luggage office in the ticket hall (daily 6am–10pm). The **train station**, for what it's worth (trains run from here only to the inland town of Knin, where there are infrequent connections to Split or Zagreb), is ten minutes' walk further south. The **tourist office**, perched above Trg palih šibenskih boraca at Fausta Vrančića 18 (July & Aug Mon–Sat 8am–10pm, Sun 8am–noon & 4–10pm; Sept & Oct Mon–Fri 8am–2pm; ☎022/212-075, ⨍219-073; ✉tzg-sibenika@si.tel.hr), is a helpful source of information on the whole Šibenik area, and has a free city map.

Travel agents offering **excursions** from Šibenik include Atlas, Trg Republike Hrvatske 2 (☎022/330-232, ✉atlas-sibenik@si.tel.hr), and Ivante, Obale Hrvatske Mornarice bb (on the sea-facing side of the bus station; ☎022/200-433, ⊛www.ivante.hr), which organize day-trips to the Kornati islands and the Krka National Park. Slaptours, opposite the train station at Fra Jerolima Milete 31a (☎022/310-593, ⊛www.slaptours.hr), specializes in rafting trips on the Zrmanja and Cetina rivers (see p.253 and 354 respectively).

Moving on from Šibenik is relatively straightforward: all coastal **buses** running between Zadar and Split (some carry on all the way to Dubrovnik) stop off here, and although the main coastal **ferry** doesn't call at Šibenik, there are four daily departures to Vodice calling at the minor islands of Zlarin and Prvić. Tickets can be bought from the Jadrolinija office on the waterfront at Obala Franje Tuđmana bb (Mon–Sat 4.45am–8.30pm, Sun 7am–noon & 5.30–8.45pm; ☎022/213-468).

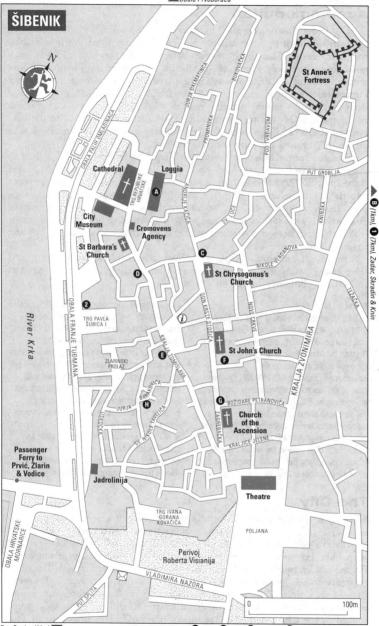

ŠIBENIK

St Anne's
Fortress

Cathedral   Loggia

City
Museum
         Cromovens
         Agency
St Barbara's
Church

St Chrysogonus's
Church

St John's
Church

Church
of the
Ascension

River Krka

Passenger
Ferry to
Prvić, Zlarin
& Vodice

Jadrolinija

Theatre

TRG IVANA
GORANA
KOVAČIĆA

POLJANA

Perivoj
Roberta Visianija

VLADIMIRA NAZORA

0   100m

Bus Station (50m) ▼   Train Station (500m), ❸ (6km), ❹ (7km), ❺ (7km), ▼❻ (9km), Brodarica & Split

ACCOMMODATION				RESTAURANTS, CAFÉS & BARS					
Jadran	2	Solaris Hotel Complex	4	Bobis	G	Kavana Medulić	E	Uzorita	B
Panorama	1	Solaris Lučica Campsite	5	Četvorka	F	Maestro	D	Vijećnica	A
Pension Petričević	3	Solaris Zablaće Campsite	6	Da Noi	H	Tinel	C		

Accommodation

With only one functioning hotel in the centre, and a handful in suburban areas, **accommodation** in Šibenik is pretty limited. Things aren't much helped by the *Solaris* **resort** 7km south of town, which is a bit too isolated for its own good (buses run only every 2hr to Šibenik bus station from here), and isn't within walking distance of anywhere particularly interesting. The nearest **campsites** are run by the resort: *Solaris-Lučica* is a mammoth-proportioned camp next to the resort's yachting marina; while *Solaris-Zablaće* is 2km north of the main *Solaris* complex, situated in a wooded peninsula next to the harbour of **Zablaće** village (Šibenik–Zablaće buses run every 1–2hr). Both sites are on the seashore, but have concrete beaches.

Either the tourist office or Cromovens, Trg Republike Hrvatske 4 (July & Aug Mon–Fri 9am–2pm & 5–8pm, Sat 9am–2pm; Sept–June Mon–Fri 9am–2pm; ☎022/212-515, ⓦwww.cromovens.hr) will sort out **private rooms** (❶) in the centre of Šibenik, although these too are in very short supply. There's a bigger stock of rooms in the scruffy seaside settlement of **Brodarica**, 7km south of town (see p.279) and linked to Šibenik by urban bus – if you arrive late on a summer weekend you might save time by heading straight there.

Otherwise, if you want to explore Šibenik and its surroundings in depth, consider basing yourself anywhere between Vodice (see p.273) and Primošten (p.284) and commuting in by bus.

Hotels

Jadran Obala Franje Tuđmana 52 ☎022/212-644, ⓕ212-480. Medium-sized place offering nondescript but perfectly comfy en-suite rooms with TV. Right on the Riva, a 5min walk away from everything you might want to see. ❺

Panorama na mostu ☎022/213-398. Functional cube of 1970s vintage, with simple no-nonsense en-suite rooms. Situated 7km north of town beside the main road bridge across the Krka estuary, a renowned local beauty spot offering truly magical views downstream towards Šibenik – a vista shared by at least some of the hotel's south-facing rooms. Buses plying the Šibenik–Vodice route stop off in the adjacent car park. ❹

Pension Petričević Podsolarsko 78 ☎022/350-494, ⓕ022/351-071. Small family-run bed and breakfast 6km south of town, with simply furnished rooms with private facilities, as well as a good ground-floor restaurant. It's just off the main road to Split, on the approach road to the *Solaris* resort, but you'll need a car as buses don't stop nearby. ❸

Solaris ☎022/361-007, ⓦwww.solaris.hr. Bland holiday development 7km south of the centre, boasting five three-star hotels (*Excelsior*, *Mirage*, *Meridien*, *Holiday Beach* and *Millennium Club*), all of which look and cost the same. It's girdled by undistinguished beaches consisting of either concrete or car-park-style gravel. Buses every 2hr to Šibenik represent the only form of escape. ❺

The City

Clinging to the side of a hill, Šibenik's ancient centre is a steep tangle of alleys, steps and arches bisected by two main arteries, **Zagrebačka** and **Kralja Tomislava** (the latter popularly known as Kalelarga), which run between Trg Republike Hrvatske, the core of the city, and the modern square known as Poljana (which until recently rejoiced in the name of Poljana maršala Tita, until reference to the former communist autocrat was quietly dropped). Entering the old town along Zagrebačka from Poljana, it's not long before you emerge into the first of Šibenik's tiny medieval squares, Božidara Petranovića, overlooked by the **Church of the Ascension** (Crkva Uspenja Bogomatere). The main feature of this Baroque building is the belfry built onto the facade, a curious but elegant structure which resembles a pair of bay windows. The church is now the seat of a Serbian Orthodox bishop, whose see extends inland to cover the traditionally Serb-inhabited area around Knin. A few steps further on lies **St John's Church** (Crkva svetog Ivana), with a balustraded outside stair-case said to be the work of sculptor Nikola Firentinac (who also worked on the cathedral) linking the ground floor to a gallery. The church's four-storey bell tower holds Šibenik's first mechanical clock, a contraption dating from 1648. Beyond here, Zagrebačka becomes Don Krste Stošića, a stepped street which leads up to the small, plain **St Chrysogonus' Church** (Crkva svetog Krševana), now home to seasonal art exhibitions.

Heading down one of the alleys leading off to the left brings you out onto Kralja Tomislava, where a sharp right delivers you to **St Barbara's Church** (Crkva svete Barbare), site of a modest **Collection of Church Art** (Zbirka crkvene umjetnosti; summer Mon–Fri 9am–noon & 6–8pm; 5Kn). Its star exhibit is a small fifteenth-century polyptych of the Madonna and Child flanked by saints, painted by Blaž Jurjev of Trogir, the leading Dalmatian artist of his day, who is credited with introducing Italian Renaissance styles to the eastern Adriatic. Down an alley beside the church, the fifteenth-century **Rector's Palace** (Kneževa palača) is nowadays home to the **City Museum** (Gradski muzej; Mon–Sat 10am–1pm & 8–10pm; 10Kn), which has an unspec-tacular display of local archeological finds from Neolithic to early medieval times, though little English information to help with interpretation.

The cathedral and around

Immediately to the north of the County Museum lies Trg Republike Hrvatske and the Gothic Renaissance **St James's Cathedral** (Katedrala svetog Jakova; daily 8.30am–7pm), the product of a long-running saga that stirred the imag-inations and emptied the pockets of the townspeople here during the fifteenth century. Plans for a new cathedral were originally drawn up in 1402, but war, lack of funds and disputes over the site delayed the start of work until 1431, when a group of Italian architects oversaw the erection of the Gothic lower storey of the present building. In 1441, dissatisfaction with the old-fashioned Gothic design led to the appointment of a new architect, **Juraj Dalmatinac** (see box p.278), who presided over three decades of intermittent progress, interrupted by perennial cash shortages, two plagues and one catastrophic fire. The cathedral was just below roof height when he died in 1473 and his Italian apprentice **Nikola Firentinac** ("Nicholas of Florence" – he is thought to have been a pupil of Donatello) took over, completing the roof and the octagonal cupola, although both may have been designed by Dalmatinac. The resulting edifice is an intriguing mixture, with Venetian Gothic portals and windows at ground level and a Florentine Renaissance dome at the top.

Entry to the cathedral is by the north door, framed by arches braided with the leaves, fruit and swirling arabesques which led to Dalmatinac's style being dubbed "floral Gothic". Two lions roar companionably at each other, support-ing remorseful and rather crudely carved figures of Adam and Eve. Inside, the church is a harmonious blend of Gothic and Renaissance forms; the sheer space and light of the east end draw the eye towards the soft grey Dalmatian stone of the raised sanctuary. Follow the stairs down from the southern apse to the **Baptistry**, Dalmatinac's masterpiece. It's an astonishing piece of work, a cubbyhole of Gothic carving, with four scallop-shell niches rising from each side to form a vaulted roof, beneath which cherubim scamper playfully.

Back outside the cathedral, around the exterior of the three apses, Dalmatinac carved a unique **frieze** of 71 stone heads, apparently portraits of those who refused to contribute to the cost of the cathedral and a vivid cross section of sixteenth-century society. On the north apse, beneath two angels with a scroll, he inscribed his claim to the work with the words *hoc opus cuvarum fecit magister*

Juraj Dalmatinac

Juraj Dalmatinac (George the Dalmatian; c.1400–73) was the most prolific stone-mason of the Dalmatian Renaissance, but little is known of the man save for the works he left behind. Born in Zadar some time around 1400, he learnt his trade in Venice, setting up a workshop there which made his reputation as a mason. The Šibenik town authorities engaged him to supervise completion of the cathedral in 1441, paying him 150 golden ducats a year as well as covering his family's moving expenses and providing free housing.

Work on the cathedral frequently stalled owing to lack of cash, and Dalmatinac filled in his time by working on commissions elsewhere, notably in Split, where he sculpted the **sarcophagus of St Anastasius** in the cathedral (see p.303), and at Ancona, where he completed the facade of the cathedral. In 1464 he replaced Michelozzo Michelozzi as the overseer of fortification work in Dubrovnik, where he finished the finest of the system's many bastions, the **Minčeta Fortress** (p.376). Following working visits to Urbino and possibly Siena, he returned to Šibenik, where he died in 1473, the cathedral still unfinished.

Dalmatinac's great skill was to blend the intricate stoneworking techniques of the Gothic period with the realism and humanism of Renaissance sculpture. His stylistic innovations were carried over to the next generation by his pupils **Andrija Aleši** and **Nikola Firentinac**, who were involved in the completion of Šibenik cathedral before going on to produce their own masterpieces in Trogir.

Georgius Mathei Dalmaticus – "these apses have been made by Juraj Dalmatinac, son of Mate." Given the narrowness of Šibenik's central streets, it's difficult to get a reasonable view of the cathedral's barrel roof, made from a line of enormous stone slabs and considered a marvel of construction at the time, though you should be able to catch sight of the statue high up on the southeast corner – a boyish, curly-haired Archangel Michael jauntily spearing a demon.

Trg Republike Hrvatske itself is lined with historic buildings including, directly opposite the cathedral, the town hall with its sixteenth-century **loggia**, much restored after World War II bombing, part of which now houses a café. Climb the alleyways leading up to the northeast, you'll eventually emerge at **St Anne's Fortress** (Tvrđava svete Ane), the nearest and most accessible of the system of fortifications constructed by the Venetians to keep Šibenik safe from the Turks. Built on the ruins of the earlier Croatian citadel, there's not much inside except for rubble, although the ramparts afford a panorama of the old town (including a clear view of the cathedral's roof), Šibenik bay beyond, and the endless green ripple of offshore islands in the background. From the fortress, what remains of Šibenik's **city walls** plunge downhill to meet the sea, forming the old town's northern boundary.

Eating and drinking

There's a growing number of reasonable **restaurants** in and around the tourist-trodden old town, although most local foodies head for out-of-town establishments such as *Zlatna Ribica* in Brodarica (see opposite). Plentiful pastries, cakes and ice cream can be picked up from *Bobis*, on the corner of Zagrebačka and Petranovićeva, or *Maestro* on Kralja Tomislava. If you want to buy fresh fruit and veg, there's a **market** just uphill from the bus station. For **drinking**, try the small knot of cafés on Obala oslobođenja, or the other, more youth-oriented stretch of café-bars just north of here, past the *Jadran* hotel, on Obala prvoboraca. *Da Noi*, slightly inland from Obala oslobođenja at Jurja

Barakovića 5, is one of the cosiest places in town for an intimate drink, and doubles as an Internet café.

Restaurants

Četvorka Trg Dinka Zavorovića 4. Chic little place with good steaks, and outdoor seating in a tiny Baroque square.

Kavana Medulić Trg palih šibenskih boraca. Pavement café convenient for old-town sightseeing, offering a range of snacks, pasta concoctions and more substantial meat and fish dishes.

Tinel Corner of Andrije Kačića and Nikole Vladanova. Occupying a dainty tree-shaded terrace opposite the Church of St Chrysogonus, this bar-restaurant serves up simple lunches like *fažol sa kobasicom* (beans with sausage), mid-price staples like *brodet* and *pašticada*, as well as more expensive steaks and fish.

Uzorita bana Jelačića 58. Characterful establishment featuring dining rooms hung with hams and cooking pots, specializing in seafood specialities such as baked octopus, and shellfish from the nearby Krka estuary. A little out of the way (it's 1km uphill from the centre near the NK Šibenik football ground) but well worth the trip.

Vijećnica Trg republike Hrvatske. Smart and stylish restaurant occupying the arcaded front of the former town hall, and with excellent views of the cathedral. Good pastas and salads, and lavish main courses utilizing the best of the local seafood.

Brodarica and Krapanj

South of Šibenik along the Magistrala, the first place you come to is **BRODARICA**, an undistinguished village which stretches along the road for some 3km. Unlike Šibenik, however, Brodarica can boast a huge stock of private accommodation – and with Šibenik–Brodarica buses shuttling back and forth every 30 minutes, and Šibenik–Split services trundling through roughly every hour, it makes a handy if rather functional base from which to tour the region.

The modest **tourist office** at the southern end of the village, beside the Magistrala at Krapinjskih Spužvara 1 (July & Aug 9am–9pm; ☎022/350-612, ⓦwww.tz-brodarica.hr), can provide bus times and details of the ferry to Krapanj (see below). A privately run Turist Biro situated in a roadside kiosk at the northern entrance to Brodarica (July & Aug daily 9am–8pm, at other times call to check; ☎022/350-300 & 351-160, ⓦwww.crotours.com/tudic) arranges **rooms** (❷) and **apartments** (❸); if coming from Šibenik, get off at the first bus stop in the village; coming from Split, get off at the third. The same firm runs the *Pansion Zlatna Ribica*, down beyond the tourist office at Krapanjskih Spužvara 46 (same telephone number; ❸), which offers cosy rooms with TV and a top-notch **restaurant** famous for its superbly grilled fish – it's probably the best (and most expensive) place to eat seafood in the whole Šibenik region.

Krapanj

Brodarica is largely populated by families from **Krapanj**, a few hundred metres across the water, which has the minor distinction of being the smallest inhabited island in the Adriatic. Boats cross from Brodarica hourly, arriving at a sleepy harbour backed by an enjoyable warren of grey-brown houses. The one bona-fide attraction is the fifteenth-century **Franciscan monastery** (Franjevački samostan) ten minutes' walk north of the harbour, where a **museum** (June–Sept Mon–Sat 9am–noon & 5–7pm; 10Kn) contains a couple of Renaissance paintings and a collection of sponges. Diving for sponges used to be the main occupation on Krapanj, although there's not much evidence of this now, save for a couple of shops on the harbour selling spongy souvenirs. Krapanj fills up with Croatian weekenders in July and August, when there's a fair number of sunbathers sprawled out on either side of the quay – the rest of the time women clad in traditional black widows' weeds outnumber other residents four to one.

Zlarin and Prvić

Neither Šibenik nor Brodarica offer much in the way of beaches, and unless you fancy squeezing onto the horrendously overcrowded strands at nearby Vodice (see p.273), your best bet is to head for the nearby islands of **Zlarin** and **Prvić**, where you stand a good chance of finding a secluded bit of rocky shoreline and crystal-clear water. There's no mass tourism on the islands, and precious few cars – merely a succession of orderly and neat little villages kept alive by a trickle of independent tourists and weekending Croatians. The islands are served by the four daily Šibenik–Vodice passenger ferries, which call in at Zlarin before proceeding to Prvić Luka on the southeastern side of Prvić, and Šepurine on the island's northwestern shore. From either Šibenik or Vodice, you could feasibly fit all three villages into a single day's sightseeing, although most visitors favour a more relaxing approach. If you're planning **to stay** on the islands, note that private rooms on Prvić can be booked in advance through the Turist Biro in Vodice (see p.273).

The ferry trip from Šibenik is a treat in itself, with the boat ploughing its way through **St Anthony's Channel** (Kanal svetog Ante), a narrow, cliff-lined waterway which leads from the bay of Šibenik out into the open sea. At the far end of the channel lies the sixteenth-century **St Nicholas's Fortress** (Tvrđava svetog Nikole), a monumental triangular gun battery placed here by Venetian engineers to keep enemy shipping away from Šibenik's port. Classical music is sometimes performed in summer, with concertgoers ferried to the venue by a flotilla of small boats.

The islands

Twenty-five minutes out from Šibenik, the boat docks at the village of **ZLARIN**, an attractive huddle of houses at the apex of a broad bay. There's a tourist office on the harbour (July & Aug daily 9am–1pm & 6.30–9pm; ☎022/553-557)

Faust Vrančić (1551–1617)

Renaissance Šibenik produced many learned minds, most famously **Faust Vrančić** (Faustus Verantius), the author of *Machinae novae* (1615) – a book of machines and contraptions whose inventiveness rivalled the mechanical fantasies of Leonardo da Vinci. The album of 49 copper engravings included pontoon bridges, suspension bridges, wind-powered flour mills with rotating roofs and, most famously, **Homo volans** – a picture of a man jumping from a tower with a primitive parachute. Equipped with a square of sail-canvas, Vrančić opined in the accompanying text, "a man can easily descend securely and without any kind of danger from a tower or any other high place". It is not known whether Vrančić ever tried this at home.

Machinae novae was written towards the end of a busy intellectual life. The young Faust studied in Bratislava and Padua before becoming administrator of the Hungarian city of Veszprém, and in 1581 was appointed secretary to the court of **Emperor Rudolf II** in Prague – a renowned meeting place for humanists from all over Europe. He subsequently retired to become a Pauline monk in Rome, where he probably became acquainted with Leonardo's drawings, and was moved to compile his *Machinae*. Vrančić's other major (and, in terms of Croatian culture, far greater) work was his *Dictionarium quinque nobilissimarum Europae linguarum* ("Dictionary of the five most noble languages of Europe", 1595), a lexicon including Latin, Greek, German, Hungarian and "Dalmatian" (Croatian). It was the first real Croatian dictionary, setting a standard which all future language reformers would be obliged to follow.

doling out private rooms (**①**), and a brace of shops selling souvenirs fashioned from coral, which existed in some abundance off the shores of Zlarin until being over-harvested in the early twentieth century. Paths on the western side of the bay will take you to an abundance of rocky bathing areas backed by pines. Zlarin's rarely open **parish church** is famous for housing the body of fourth-century Roman martyr St Fortunatus, a relic obtained for the island by a resourceful local priest in 1781. Every fifty years the remains are paraded through the village on April 23 – the next celebration is due in 2050, so there's no need to pack your bags just yet.

A fifteen-minute ferry journey away, the main settlement of Prvić, **PRVIĆ LUKA**, is another unassuming, bay-hugging village with a charmingly soporific atmosphere. The only sight of note is the **parish church** just up from the harbour, which boasts an extrovert collection of Baroque altarpieces as well as the tomb of Šibenik-born humanist and all-round brainbox Faust Vrančić (see box opposite). Private **rooms** (**①**) are available from the sporadically open **tourist office**, just beyond the church; and the nearby *Art Pension* (☎022/448-220; **②**) has a small stock of cosy en suites. You can **bathe** on the rocks on either side of the bay.

A single road leads northwest out of Prvić Luka, passing olive groves before arriving after fifteen minutes in **ŠEPURINE** (which is also the next stop for the Vodice-bound ferry), an attractive fishing village spread beneath a mushroom-topped church tower. Šepurine has the best **beach** in the area, a wonderful S-bend of shingle stretching away south of the ferry dock. The **tourist office** (Mon–Sat 9am–noon & 7–9pm; ☎022/448-103), 200m south of the landing stage and housed in the local primary school, will put you in touch with local landladies offering **rooms** (**①**). The nearby *Ribarski dvor* **restaurant** offers some of the best grilled fish and shellfish in the region, and has prices to match.

The Krka National Park

Šibenik stands at the mouth of the River Krka, which rises just outside Knin and flows through a sequence of gorges, lakes and rapids before meeting the sea. Although the whole stretch of the **Krka valley** between the towns of Knin and Skradin has national park status (Nacionalni park Krka; ⓦwww.npkrka.hr), it's the section of the park just east of Skradin, only 12km out from Šibenik, that most visitors gravitate towards. Here the river descends via a sequence of mini-waterfalls at Skradinski buk (Skradin Falls) before flowing through a small but picturesque canyon to the town of Skradin itself. The upper reaches of the river are much less swamped by crowds, although there's a good deal worth seeing here, including two historic monasteries and another stretch of falls – all of which are accessible by national-park-operated excursion boats.

Visiting the park

There are two main entrance points to the national park: the town of **Skradin** itself, 4km north of Skradinski buk, from where national park boats ferry visitors to the falls, and **Lozovac**, on the hill just above Skradinski buk, from where a bus shuttle shuttle service leads down to the river. There are five **buses** daily from Šibenik to Skradin, passing through Lozovac on the way, making it an easy day-trip from the city – although there's little information on return services once you arrive, so it's a good idea to check the relevant times at Šibenik bus station before setting out. An early start is advised if you want to explore more than just the area around Skradinski buk – boat timings mean that a full day is required if you want to venture into the upriver sections of the park. The **entrance fee** (April, May & Oct 40Kn; June–Sept 45Kn; Nov–March 20Kn), payable at pavilions sited on the main approaches to Skradinski buk, includes travel on the shuttle boats and buses, but lengthier boat excursions to the upper stretches of the river cost extra.

Skradin

The classic approach to the park is via **SKRADIN**, a pleasing, one-street town of stone houses with a marina squeezed into one of the river's small inlets. It's the only place with any **accommodation** in the environs of the park: the **tourist office**, on the waterfront at Obala bana Šubića 1 (July & Aug: daily 8am–8pm; Sept–June: Mon–Fri 9am–3pm; ☎022/771-306), has information on **private rooms** (❶), while the *Skradinski buk* **hotel**, bang in the centre of the village at Burinovac bb (☎022/771-771, ⓕ771-770; ❹), is much swankier than similarly priced places back in Šibenik, its small en-suite rooms coming with cool Scandinavian-style furnishings, TV and air conditioning. There's a string of **cafés** along the waterfront, and a superb seafood **restaurant** in the shape of the *Bonaca*, which serves up local fish and shellfish on an outdoor terrace slightly uphill from the marina.

Into the park

National park boats leave Skradin's harbourfront hourly for the trip up to **Skradinski buk**, a twenty-minute journey; should you miss the boats, you can walk by following the road from Skradin along the river's right bank, taking you between steep, scrub-covered hills (50min). Skradinski buk itself is a bit like a smaller Plitvice (see p.000) – a five-hundred-metre sequence of seventeen mini-cascades spilling over barriers of travertine (limestone sediment), behind which lie pools surrounded by reeds and semi-submerged forest. One of the more dramatic sequences is just up from the boat landing, with several tiers of waterfall tumbling into a broad, shallow pool – it's the only part of the park where swimming is permitted, and is correspondingly full of frolicking holiday-makers on warm summer days. From here the main path crosses over to the eastern side of Skradinski buk, climbing past a collection of poky stone watermills positioned directly above the rushing Krka. There's also a network of short wooden walkways which break off from the main path, leading you above the gurgling waters and through the thick riverine vegetation. It's a beautiful location, and you could spend an entire day here, lolling around on the rocks beside the tumbling water.

After climbing past the cataracts for 1km or so the path levels out, arriving at the bus stop used by the national park's shuttle services to Lozovac. A kiosk here handles information and tickets for the boat excursions to the northern stretches of the river (a fairly obvious path descends from the kiosk to the quay from which these boats depart). The most popular northbound trip (reckon on 2hr for the journey there and back) takes you to the islet of **Visovac** just upstream from Skradinski buk, where you can visit a Franciscan monastery nestling amongst a thick cluster of cypresses. The monastery has a small collection of seventeenth-century paintings and, in its valuable library, some incunabula and a beautifully illustrated fifteenth-century *Aesop's Fables*, one of only three such in the world. From here another boat continues 10km further upstream to **Roški Slapovi** (2hr return), a set of falls only slightly less dramatic than those at Skradinski buk. Finally, another boat takes you from Roški slapovi through a rugged canyon-scape to the ruins of **Nečven**, a fourteenth-century Croatian fortress just short of Knin (another 2hr return), pausing en route at **Krka monastery**, a Serbian Orthodox foundation nestling in a lovely rustic setting on the western bank of the river, the monastery church rich in incense and icons. If you want to fit the entire Skradinski buk–Visovac–Roški slapovi–Nečven itinerary into one day, you'll need to be at the Skradinski buk excursion-boat quay by about 10am.

Drniš and Knin

Thirty-four kilometres inland from Šibenik, the small market town of **DRNIŠ** has little to recommend it. It was occupied by Ottoman forces during the sixteenth century, when it was known as "little Sarajevo", though most of the relics of the Turkish period were obliterated when they were driven out, and the only surviving reminder is a sixteenth-century mosque, since incorporated into St John's Church (Crkva svetog Ivana). There's also a ruined tower picturesquely located above the River Čikola, and an irregularly open **Town Museum** (10Kn), which has a rather limited collection of works by local sculptor Ivan Meštrović (see box on p.308); some pieces disappeared during the Serbian occupation in 1991.

Meštrović hailed from the village of **OTAVICE**, 10km east, where he is buried in the hilltop **Meštrović Mausoleum**, a simple cube topped by a dome designed by Meštrović himself. He began the work in 1926, intending it as a family mausoleum, and was buried here after his death in the USA in 1962. Inside, an Art Nouveau-inspired sculpture of the Crucifixion is watched over by a pale, Buddha-like face, hinting at the religious syncretism towards which Meštrović leaned throughout his life. During the Serbian occupation, the bronze doors (bearing touching portraits of the Meštrović family) were stolen, reliefs were damaged, and the tombs desecrated; restoration is in progress.

Drniš is the centre of a large area devoted to the making of *pršut* (home-cured ham), and most local families keep a few pigs. Late November's *svinokolja* or **pig slaughter** is the key event of the local agricultural year, when up to ten thousand of the beasts meet their deaths.

Knin

Some 20km inland from Drniš is the rather plain town of **KNIN**, which became notorious as the epicentre of the Serbian rebellion of 1990–95, when it was the capital of the Serbian-controlled parts of Croatia, the so-called **Republic of the Serbian Krajina** (Republika srpske krajine, or RSK). Something like ninety percent of Knin's population was Serbian by the early 1990s, making it the obvious focus for Serbian discontent in the Dalmatian hinterlands. Control of Knin was always important to Serbian military planners: the town stands on the rail line between Zagreb and Split, and to remove the town from Zagreb's control – it was argued – would seriously weaken Croatia's bargaining power should Yugoslavia ever fall apart.

Many of the key players in the ensuing Serb-Croat conflict came from Knin: Jovan Rašković, founder of the Serbian Democratic Party; Milan Babić, the RSK's first leader; Milan Martić, the Knin police chief who built up the Krajina's first armed forces; and Colonel Ratko Mladić, commander of the Knin military garrison, who practised ethnic cleansing here, forcibly ejecting Croat families from nearby villages, before becoming head of the Bosnian Serb army in 1992. The Serbian irregulars based in Knin during 1991–95 – who called themselves the *knindža*, in imitation of ninja-style comic strip heroes – melted away when the Croatian army launched the Oluja ("Storm") offensive in August 1995, and Knin's recapture on the morning of August 5, 1995, brought the war in Croatia to a rapid conclusion: Serbian resistance elsewhere in the country collapsed within two days, and pictures of President Franjo Tuđman kissing an enormous Croatian tricolour flying from **Knin fortress** were seen on TV across the world. Most Serb civilians fled in the wake of their defeated army in August 1995 and, though many have returned, the present population is still only a fraction of what it was, the local economy is in recession, and an atmosphere of despondency prevails. The castle is worth visiting if you're passing through, but there's little else to keep you, and certainly no tourist facilities.

Knin's **train** and **bus stations** are next to one another on the main street, and it's easy to pick a route up to the fortress on the hill above. There's been a castle here since at least the tenth century, and it was the seat of the medieval Croatian state's last effective king, Zvonimir, towards the end of the eleventh century. The castle's fall to the Turks in 1522 hastened a change in the demographic profile of the area, with fleeing Catholics being replaced by a predominantly Orthodox population from the Balkan interior. The fortress has been impressively restored, with a central keep surrounded by concentric rings of walls, and outlying towers squatting on outcrops of rock. The battlements offer an extensive panorama of the surrounding countryside, with a view of Knin below in its bowl of brownish hills and the grey ridge of the Dinaric mountains to the northeast on the border with Bosnia-Hercegovina – the best place to enjoy it is from the terrace of the **café-restaurant** inside the fortress.

From Šibenik to Trogir

Heading south from Šibenik most traffic follows the coastal Magistrala, although there's an inland route which cuts through the arid mountains before rejoining the main road at Trogir. It's worth taking if you like spit-roast lamb – a couple of roadside restaurants in the village of **Boraja**, 15km outside Šibenik, are famous for it.

The small town of **PRIMOŠTEN**, 20km south of Šibenik, is the best place on this part of the coast to rest up and do nothing for a while. Heaped up on an island that's joined to the mainland by a short causeway, it's enchanting when seen from a distance, although on closer inspection most of the houses are twentieth century, and there's nothing of specific interest. There are extensive pebble and rock **beaches** lapped by ultra-clear water on the wooded promontory to the north of the town, where there are also a number of hotels.

Primošten's small **bus station** is uphill on the landward side of the causeway, a short walk from the **tourist office** in the small square that marks the entrance to the old town (June & Sept daily 8am–7pm; July & Aug daily 8am–10pm; Oct–May Mon–Fri 8am–3pm; ☎ & ⓕ 022/571-111, ⓦ www.summernet .ht/primosten). Private **rooms** (❶), available from Turist Biro at the bus station (daily 7am–9pm), are probably a better deal than the package-style *Zora* **hotel** (☎ 022/581-111, ⓕ 570-048; ❹), a typical 1960s seaside establishment with functional en-suite rooms located on the wooded promontory north of town. Providing a cosy small-hotel alternative is *Villa Koša*, right on the seashore just east of town at Bana Jelačića 4 (☎ 022/570-365, ⓦ www.villa-kosa.hinet.hr; ❹), offering bright modern rooms with pine flooring and private bathroom, as well as a handful of swanky apartments (❺). The *Adriatik* **campsite**, about 3km north of town on the Magistrala, has good tree cover and an attractive rocky beach.

For **food**, the *Buffet Aligator* in a nameless alley just uphill from the tourist office is good for cheap fried-squid snacks; the nearby *Gostiona Dalmacija* has a more extensive range of seafood risottos, grilled scampi and fish; and there are loads of café-pizzerias on the harbour. Wherever you eat, be sure to try the local Primošten wine, Babić – a smooth, dry red. *Aurora*, 2km from the town centre (follow the Magistrala in the Split direction and then head uphill), is one of the best **clubs** in central Dalmatia, with a string of European techno and house DJs guesting here over the summer – look out for posters in Primošten, Split and Šibenik.

Trogir and around

Thirty kilometres east of Primošten and about 20km west of Split, **TROGIR** is one of the most seductive towns on the Dalmatian coast, a compact brown-beige welter of palaces, jutting belfries and shambling streets fanning out from an antique central square. Founded by Greeks from Vis in the third century BC, Trogir can compare with any of the towns on the coast in terms of historic sights, and its **cathedral** is one of the finest in the Adriatic. It's also a good base for further exploration: the swarming city of Split is a short ride away on the #37 bus, and in between lies a string of attractively time-worn fishing villages known collectively as **Kaštela**, after the little "castles" built here by Trogir nobles to serve as country retreats.

Arrival, information and accommodation

Trogir's **old town** is built on an oval-shaped island squeezed between the mainland and the larger island of Čiovo, while modern Trogir has spread onto the mainland, stretching along the coast for several kilometres. Intercity **buses** pick up and drop off on the main street in the new town, just opposite the bridge

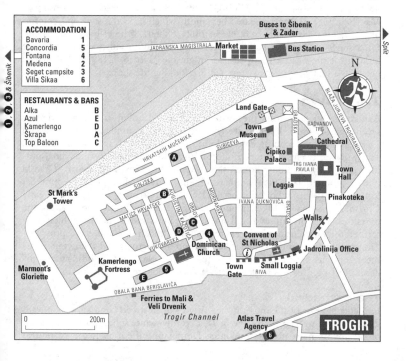

which leads over to the old town. Also on the mainland side of the bridge is a small bus station, where the #37 bus from Split terminates. Head over the bridge and straight through the town centre to find the **tourist office** at the southern end of Gradska, the main thoroughfare (summer daily 8am–2pm & 6–9.30pm; winter Mon–Fri 8am–3pm; ☎021/881-412 & 885-628, ⓔtzg -trogir@st.tel.hr), which has basic town maps. **Ferries** to the nearby islands of Mali and Veli Drvenik (see p.290) depart from the eastern end of Trogir's Riva (Obala bana Berislavića), although tickets must be bought from Jadrolinija at the western end, at Obala bana Berislaviča 4 (Mon–Fri 6.15am–1.45pm, Sat 6.30–9am, and daily 1hr before the departure of the boat).

Rooms (❶) and **apartments** (❷) are available from the Čipiko agency, in the Čipiko Palace opposite the cathedral at Gradska 41 (summer daily 8am–9pm; winter Mon–Fri 9am–1pm; ☎021/881-554), or from Atlas, a little way south of the old town in Čiovo at Obala kralja Zvonimira 10 (Mon–Sat 8am–9pm, Sun 8am–noon & 5–9pm; ☎021/884-279, ⓕ884-744, ⓔatlas .trogir@st.tel.hr). There are two good **hotels** in old town houses on the Riva, both with friendly staff and smart en-suite rooms with TV: the *Fontana*, Obrov 1 (☎021/885-744, ⓦwww.tel.hr/fontana-commerce; ❺); and slightly more cramped *Concordia*, Obala bana Berislavića 22 (☎021/885-400, ⓦwww.tel.hr/concordia-hotel; ❹). Across the water in Čiovo, the *Villa Sikaa* **pension**, above the Atlas office at Obala kralja Zvonimira 13 (☎021/881-223, ⓔstjepan.runtic@st.tel.hr; ❸), offers snug rooms with TV and bathroom, many with excellent views of the old town.

There's more accommodation 3km northwest of town in the seaside suburb of **Seget** – any buses operating the Šibenik–Split route will drop you off here; local Trogir buses to Najevi, Dogradi, Vinišće, Sevid and Vranjica also pass through. The *Medena* hotel, Seget donji bb (☎021/880-588, ⓦwww.hotelmedena.com; ❹; May–Sept) is a package-oriented behemoth which lacks the style and comfort of the *Bavaria*, Hrvatskih žrtava 133 (☎021/880601, ⓔhotel-bavaria@st.tel.hr; ❻), a show-off modern building with plush en-suite rooms. Seget is also the location of the nearest **campsite** to Trogir, the *Seget* (☎021/880-394), which occupies a sequence of grassy terraces overlooking the shore.

The Town

Across the bridge from the mainland, the old town is entered via the seventeenth-century **Land Gate** (Kopnena vrata), a simple arch topped with a statue of the town's protector, St John of Trogir (Sveti Ivan Trogirski), a miracle-working twelfth-century bishop. Straight ahead, the outwardly unassuming Garagnin palace now houses the disappointing **Town Museum** (Gradski muzej; summer daily 9am–noon & 6–9pm; winter Mon–Fri 7am–3pm, Sat 9am–noon; 10Kn), whose downstairs lapidarium boasts a few chunks of early Christian masonry and Renaissance family crests which once hung above the portals of patrician houses. You'll also see a giant wooden cockerel which once formed the figurehead of a sixteenth-century Turkish ship and was captured by Trogirans serving in the Venetian navy. Amid the pictures and yellowing documents upstairs are proclamations issued by the Napoleonic authorities, condemning Trogir leaders to death after a failed anti-French uprising in 1807.

The cathedral

Immediately east of the museum lies Trogir's main street, Gradska, which leads straight down to **Trg Ivana Pavla II**, a creamy-white square flanked by some of the town's most historic buildings. Dominating them all is the **cathedral**

(Mon–Sat 9am–noon & 3–7pm), a squat Romanesque structure begun in 1213 and only finished with the addition of a soaring Venetian Gothic campanile some three centuries later. A previous church on this site had been damaged by Saracen raiders in the twelfth century, but the town's control of lucrative trade routes with the Balkan interior helped pay for the construction of a new one.

The cathedral's most distinctive feature is its **west portal**, an astonishing piece of work carved in 1240 by the Slav master-mason **Radovan**. Radovan laid claim to his work in an immodest inscription above the door, calling himself "Most excellent in his art" – a justifiable claim given the doorway's intricate mix of orthodox iconography with scenes from ordinary life and legend, showing figures of apostles and saints, centaurs and sirens, woodcutters and leather-workers jostling for position in a chaos of twisting decoration. Roughly speaking, there is a gradual movement upwards from Old Testament figures at the bottom to New Testament scenes on the arches and lunette. Adam and Eve frame the door and stand with anxious modesty on a pair of lions. On either side, a series of receding pillars sit upon the bent backs of the undesirables of the time – Jews and Turks – while above is a weird menagerie of creatures in writhing, bucking confusion, laced together with tendrilled carvings symbolizing the months and seasons. The sequence begins with March (the year started with the Annunciation as far as the Church was concerned), symbolized by a man pruning vines, and a wild-haired youth blowing a horn (a reference to the March winds). Further on, a man killing a pig represents the autumn (pig-slaughtering and sausage-making still form an important part of the Croatian calendar), while another character in clogs cooks what look like sausages. The lunette above comprises two scenes fringed by curtains, in imitation of the two-level stages on which medieval miracle plays were often presented. The Nativity is portrayed on the upper level, and the Bathing of Christ below, with shepherds and magi crowding the wings. Above the lunette, the uppermost arch is decorated with scenes from the life of Christ.

Left of the portal, small circular windows are framed by a serpent tearing apart a half-naked libertine. Further over to the left lies the fifteenth-century **Baptistry**, a fine piece of Renaissance stonework executed by **Andrija Aleši** of Dürres, who is thought to have been an Albanian noble who fled the Turks and had to learn a trade in order to earn a living. He was apprenticed to Juraj Dalmatinac (see box on p.278) at Šibenik, and was in many ways his stylistic successor. The portal, topped by a relief of the Baptism of Christ, gives way to a coffer-ceilinged interior, where a frieze of cherubs carrying a garland leads round the walls, overlooked by a relief of St Hieronymous in the cave in smooth milky stone.

The **interior** of the cathedral is atmospherically gloomy, its pillars hung with paintings illustrating scenes from the life of St John of Trogir. At the head of the nave stand a Romanesque octagonal pulpit, its capitals decorated with griffins and writhing snakes, and a Baroque high altar canopied by an ornate thirteenth-century ciborium; the beautiful set of mid-fifteenth-century choirstalls were carved in Venetian Gothic style by local artist Ivan Budislavić. The north aisle of the cathedral opens up to reveal **St John of Trogir's Chapel** (Kapela svetog Ivana Trogirskog), another spectacular example of Renaissance work, mostly carried out by Juraj Dalmatinac's other pupil Nikola Firentinac, together with the Trogir sculptor Ivan Duknović. God the Creator is pictured at the centre of barrel-vaulted ceiling, from which a hundred angels gaze down. The space below is ringed by life-size statues of saints, each of which occupies a niche framed by cavorting cherubs. Firentinac's statues of St John of Trogir and St Paul, both portrayed as bearded sages pouring over their prayer books, are masterpieces of sensitive portraiture. Duknovic's equally impressive statue of St John the Evangelist, here depicted as a curly-haired clean-shaven youth, is thought to bear a deliberate resemblance to a favourite son of Trogir-based aristocrat Koriolan Čipiko, who may well have had a hand in commissioning the sculptures for the chapel. At floor level there are more cherubs, this time peeping cheekily from behind half-open doors – which here symbolize the passage from life to death.

Finally, further along the north aisle from St John's Chapel lies the sacristy, which houses the **treasury** (*riznica*; summer 9am–noon & 5–8pm; 10Kn), a mundane collection of ecclesiastical bric-a-brac. The best exhibits are the fine inlaid storage cabinets carved by Grgur Vidov in 1458, a fourteenth-century Gothic jug, scaled and moulded into snake-like form, and a silver-plated reliquary of St John of Trogir which is paraded round on his feast day.

The rest of the old town

Opposite the cathedral entrance is the **Čipiko Palace**, a well-worn fifteenth-century Venetian Gothic mansion whose balustraded triple window – with Venetian Gothic arches held aloft by florid corinthian capitals – is said to be the work of Andrija Aleši. There's nothing inside except the Čipiko tourist agency, though it's noteworthy for being the erstwhile home of the Čipikos, Renaissance Trogir's leading noble family. Their best-remembered representatives are the aforementioned Koriolan Čipiko (1425–93), Venetian admiral and author of *De bello asiatico*, an account of his wartime experiences with the fleet, and Alviz Čipiko, who commanded a galley from Trogir at the Battle of Lepanto in 1571. It was in the Čipiko family library that the first known manuscript of "Trimalchio's Feast", a hitherto undiscovered fragment of Petronius' *Satyricon*, was discovered in 1653, sending a frisson of excitement through literary circles all over Europe.

On the other side of the square, the **Town Loggia** (Gradska loža), with its handsome clock tower and classical columns, dates from the fifteenth century, though its pristine appearance is explained by a late nineteenth-century restoration. The large relief on the east wall of the loggia, showing Justice flanked by St John of Trogir and St Lawrence (the last holding the grill on which he was roasted alive), is another work by Firentinac, identifiable by the presence of his personal "signature", the flower-covered pillars on either side. The relief was damaged in 1932, when a Venetian lion occupying the (now blank) space beneath the figure of Justice was dynamited – an act carried out by locals keen to erase Italian symbols from a town which was still coveted by Italian nationalists. Mussolini, eager to resurrect territorial claims in Dalmatia, raged against "Yugoslav barbarism" and forced the Yugoslav government into a grovelling apology. The loggia's south wall has been disfigured by a surprisingly lifeless Meštrović relief of Petar Berislavić, sixteenth-century Bishop of Zagreb and Ban of Croatia, who fought a losing battle against the advance of Ottoman power.

Just off the square to the southeast is the Church of St John the Baptist (Crkva svetog Ivana Krstitelja), a bare thirteenth-century structure which now holds the **Pinakoteka** (July & Aug daily 8am–noon & 6–9pm; 10Kn), a display of sacred art from the best of Trogir's churches. Among a number of painted crucifixes and the like is Blaž Jurjev's polyptych showing a Madonna and Child flanked by six saints, in which the Virgin proffers an ivory breast to the infant. There are also canvases of John the Baptist and St Jerome, painted for the cathedral organ by Gentile Bellini in 1489.

South of Trg Ivana Pavla II, the ever-narrowing Gradska leads on to the **Convent of St Nicholas** (Samostan svetog Nikole; May–Sept 9am–noon & 3–7pm; Oct–April on request at the tourist office; 10Kn), whose treasury is famous for the outstanding third-century Greek relief of Kairos, discovered in

1928. Sculpted out of orange marble, it's a dynamic fragment representing the Greek god of opportunity – once past he's impossible to seize hold of, and the back of his head is shaved just to make it even more difficult. The rest of the collection focuses on Byzantine-influenced sacred paintings from the sixteenth century, and the painted chests in which girls new to the convent brought their "dowries" (gifts to the convent in the form of rich textiles and ornaments) in anticipation of their wedding to Christ.

Along the Riva

Gradska makes a sudden dog-leg to the right before emerging through the **Town Gate** (Gradska vrata) onto the Riva, a seafront promenade facing the island of Čiovo. Hard up against the gate stands the so-called **Small Loggia** (Mala loža), nowadays occupied by souvenir sellers. On either side of the gate are a few stretches of what remain of the medieval **town walls**, large chunks of which were demolished by the Napoleonic French, who hoped the fresh sea breezes would help blow away the town's endemic malaria. To the right, past a gaggle of cafés, is the campanile of the **Dominican Church** (Crkva svetog Dominika), a light, high building with a charming relief in the lunette above the main door; it shows a Madonna and Child flanked by Mary Magdalene, clad in nothing but her own tresses, and Augustin Kažotić (1260–1323), Bishop of Trogir and subsequently Zagreb. A small praying figure next to Kažotić represents his sister Bitkula, who commissioned the work. The main feature inside is the tomb of Šimun and Ivan Sobota, which bears a Firentinac relief of the Pietà surrounded by mourners. The coffin below is decorated with more of Firentinac's trademark flowery, pinapple-topped pillars.

Further along, the fifteenth-century **Kamerlengo Fortress** (summer daily 11am–1pm & 2–5pm; 10Kn) was named after the Venetian official – the *kamerling* – who ran the town's finances. An irregular quadrilateral dominated by a stout octagonal tower, it's a wonderfully atmospheric venue for a quick stroll on the battlements. Beyond lies the town's football pitch, on the opposite side of which looms the tapering cylinder of **St Mark's Tower** (Kula svetog Marka), a sandcastle-style bastion built at the same time as the Kamerlengo.

Finally, at the far end of the island is **Marmont's Gloriette**, a graffiti-covered, six-pillared gazebo which looks out onto Čiovo's rusting shipyard. It was built for Marshal Marmont, the French governor of Napoleon's Illyrian Provinces; just and progressive, Marmont was probably the best colonial ruler the city ever had, and the Gloriette serves as some sort of modest tribute.

Eating, drinking and entertainment

Eating out in Trogir is a joy, with dozens of restaurants tucked away in the courtyards of the centre. There's also a hugely enjoyable **market** opposite the bus station, where you'll find fruit, veg, cheeses, hams and home-made wines and spirits offered by local farmers, haphazardly bottled into all kinds of containers. As far as **drinking** is concerned, all the old town's squares are stuffed with café tables in summer, and it's really a question of picking a space that suits. In the evening, head for Radvanov trg behind the cathedral, which soon fills up with drinkers drawn by the trio of stylish café-bars around its edges. *Azul*, on the Riva beside the Kamerlengo fortress, is a cool place for cocktails.

The *Formula 1* **disco**, 4km east of town at the junction of the Magistrala and the Split airport road, organizes techno parties and performances by Croatian pop stars. The Trogir **Summer Festival** (early July to mid-Aug) features pop music and folklore events on various outdoor stages in the town centre.

Restaurants

Alka Augustina Kažotića 15. Don't be fooled by the touristy signs pointing the way, this is one of the longest-established and best seafood restaurants in Trogir, serving up suberb grilled fish and shellfish. Also does a mean *pašticada*.

Kamerlengo Vukovarska 2. Top-class fish and scampi cooked on an outdoor charcoal grill in an L-shaped courtyard.

Konoba Fontana Obrov 1. With an outdoor terrace right on the Riva, this is one of the classiest places in town, offering the widest range of meat and fish dishes, all excellently prepared and presented.

Škrapa Augustina Kazotića. Cheap and cheerful feeding station serving up seafood risottos, *lignje na žaru* (grilled squid) and other standards, with wooden bench seating on the street outside. Fills up early.

Top Baloon Obrov. Pizza joint in a pleasantly flower-decked courtyard up behind the *Fontana* hotel. Does decent pasta and lasagne dishes – as does the similar *Kristian* restaurant next door.

Mali Drvenik and Veli Drvenik

There's little in the way of decent beaches around Trogir, and it's well worth considering a ferry trip to **Mali Drvenik** or **Veli Drvenik** if a lazy day by the sea is what you're after. Lying some 12km west of town, these small, sparsely populated islands are increasingly popular with yachtspeople, but are little visited by other travellers, making them perfect for a quiet getaway. Passenger-only boats sail from Trogir twice a day on at least five days of the week (Mon–Thurs & Sat at the time of writing), ensuring that you can spend a day on one of the islands and be back in town by nightfall. There are precious few roads on the islands (wheelbarrows and mini-tractors provide the only forms of transport), but they're crisscrossed by farm tracks, making them perfect for relaxed rambling. You'll find accommodation, food and drink on Veli Drvenik should you wish **to stay**.

Although Mali Drvenik is slightly further away from Trogir than Veli Drvenik, it's Mali that the ferry visits first, calling in at the island's only real settlement, the aptly named **MALI DRVENIK**. A grubby little place with few amenities, this is no more than a staging post on the way to **Vela Rina**, a broad bay twenty-minute's walk away on the other side of the island. There's not much here apart from bare rocks and a view of the open sea, but it's an undeniably beautiful spot – you could easily while away several hours here if you come well prepared (there's precious little shade here and certainly no cafés).

Veli Drvenik

Twenty minutes' sailing time from Mali Drvenik, **VELI DRVENIK** is a much more lively island, with its eponymous main village sprawling attractively on either side of a deep bay. The village itself is popular with second-home owners from the mainland, while its harbour frequently fills with touring yachts – all of which helps to keep the village shop and a couple of cafés in business. The water in the bay is clean enough to swim in, and there are several attractive coves elsewhere on the island – **Krknjaši bay**, a forty-five-minute walk to the east, has a partly pebbly beach and views southeast towards the island of Šolta. The interior of the island, covered in prickly bushes, abandoned olive plantations and fig trees, is a great place for walks – there's little real tree cover, however, so bring a hat.

There's no tourist office on the island, but private **rooms** (❶) can be arranged in advance through the tourist office in Trogir. There's also an excellent family-run **pension** in the shape of *Mia*, overlooking the harbour at Bobovišće 5 (☎021/893-038, ⊛www.geocities.com/apartmanimia; contact the tourist office in Trogir if the owner's English isn't up to making a reservation; ❷–❹), which offers a range of cosy rooms and apartments, and scrumptious home cooking if you pay a few extra kuna for half board. The owner will drive you round the island on his tractor buggy for a small extra fee. There are a couple of harbourside **restaurants** serving up fresh fish, although they tend to only open up when yachts appear in the bay. The coolest place to hang out in the village is *Atelje* (evenings only), an art gallery just below the Mia pension run by a Finnish–Croatian couple, which also serves wine in the garden courtyard.

Kaštela

East of Trogir the coastline swings around towards Split in a wide, curving bay, sheltered from the open sea by the island of Čiovo and Split's jutting peninsula. During the fifteenth and sixteenth centuries, local nobles lined this fertile sweep of coast with country houses, fortified against pirate raids to give them the appearance of castles – the settlements which have grown up in their wake go under the collective name of **KAŠTELA**. The castles were built to protect the agricultural lands to which the nobles owed their wealth, but they were also rural retreats where their owners spent the summer months and received guests. Koriolan Čipiko was the first of the Trogir worthies to move out here, in 1481; his house subsequently earned the epithet Kaštel stari ("Old Castle") in order to differentiate it from those which followed, and seven summer houses survived to become the nuclei of the fishing villages that exist here now. Most of these castles were converted into flats years ago and can't be visited, but the villages look endearingly time-worn and have accessible places **to swim** if you're staying in Trogir. The villages are only separated from each other by a kilometre or two, and strolling from one to another makes for a wonderful seaside walk whatever the time of year. The #37 Trogir–Split bus links them all – the best thing to do is to hop off at, say, Kaštel Štafilić, head for the waterfront and proceed eastward along the coastal path; you can return to the main road to pick up a bus when you've had enough.

The road from Trogir passes Split airport before arriving at the first of the villages, **KAŠTEL ŠTAFILIĆ**. There's a pleasant shingle **beach** on Štafilić's western fringes, although the castle around which the village grew is now crumbling and derelict. **KAŠTEL NOVI**, immediately beyond, is perhaps most typical of the villages – an agreeable if unremarkable huddle of ancient houses with a simple, fortified tower at its centre, and not much else to speak of – save for the attractive octagonal tower of the church of St Rock (Crkva svetog Roka). **KAŠTEL STARI**, a short walk away, has a decent stretch of stony **beach**, and a reasonable two-star **hotel** in the shape of the *Palace*, Obala kralja Tomislava 82 (℡021/206-222; ❹), a venerable pre-World War I establishment with a modern accommodation block tacked on the side. **KAŠTEL LUKŠIĆ**, just beyond, is marginally livelier, with several cafés scattered along its seafront. The castle itself, a chunky brown cube right at the water's edge, has been tastefully restored, and now serves both as a seasonally open **art gallery** and home to the **tourist office** (June–Sept Mon–Fri 8am–6pm, Sat 9am–1pm; Oct–May Mon–Fri 8am–3pm; ℡021/227-933, ✉tzg -kastela@st.tel.hr), which has information on the whole Kaštela region. The Ostrog Tourist Agency (Mon–Fri 8am–noon & 5–8pm; ℡021/227-594), 100m further along the shore, can organize **rooms** (❶) in the village. Kaštel Lukšić runs imperceptibly into **KAŠTEL KAMBELOVAC**, where you'll find the *Baletna Škola* **restaurant** near the harbour; serving up cheap lunchtime soups and stews as well as the best fresh seafood, this has something to suit most tastes and pockets. A kilometre beyond, **KAŠTEL GOMILICA** is the most picturesque of the villages, its fortress squatting impressively on a small islet joined to the mainland by a bridge. It's probably not worth covering the remaining 3km to the last outpost of Kaštela, **KAŠTEL SUĆURAC**, which is just 10km short of Split and within alarming proximity of the city's industrial installations.

Southern Dalmatia

The hub around which everything in **Southern Dalmatia** revolves is **Split**, Croatia's second city and the most vibrant centre on the coast. It grew out of the Roman palace of Dalmatian-born Emperor Diocletian, and successive layers of ancient, medieval and modern architecture have given the centre a unique – albeit chaotic – urban character. Inland from the city, the ruins of the Roman city of **Salona**, and the medieval Croatian stronghold of **Klis**, are the main draws.

The coast south of Split is probably mainland Dalmatia's most enchanting stretch, with the mountains glowering over a string of long pebble beaches, although a sequence of modern tourist resorts is beginning to put the squeeze on the fishing villages. If you want to join the crowds, the resorts of the **Makarska Riviera** are justifiably popular family holiday centres, but it's the southern **islands** which are the real highlight of any trip to Dalmatia. Easiest to reach from Split is **Brač**, boasting some nice beaches at **Supetar** and a truly wonderful one at **Bol**, while lying off the southern coast of Brač is the long thin island of **Hvar**, whose capital, **Hvar Town**, rivals Dubrovnik and Trogir in the number of venerable stone buildings lining its ancient alleys. It's also a fashionable hangout for urbane Croats: chic bars rub shoulders with Gothic palaces and chapels, and water taxis convey bathers to idyllic offshore islets. Much the same can be said of the island of **Korčula**, south of Hvar, whose fascinating medieval capital, **Korčula Town**, offers a mixture of urban tourism and lazy beachcombing.

Further out, but still only a few hours by boat from Split, the islands of **Vis** and **Lastovo** were only opened up to foreign tourists in 1989, after previously serving as naval bases. Wilder and less visited, both are obligatory destinations for travellers who want a piece of the Adriatic to themselves. You can rejoin the mainland from Korčula by a short ferry-ride to the **Pelješac peninsula** – virtually an island itself – which is joined to the coast by a slim neck of land at **Ston**, whose magnificent town walls were built to defend the northernmost frontiers of the Dubrovnik Republic.

As in northern Dalmatia, most public transport in the region is provided by the frequent intercity **buses** which plough along the coastal highway, the Magistrala. In addition, Split has good bus links with all the large towns of inland Croatia, and is also the main **ferry** port for all the islands in this section. Hopping from one island to the next is feasible up to a point: Hvar is a good base for onward travel to Korčula and Lastovo; moving on from Brač and Vis usually involves heading back to Split first.

Split

SPLIT is one of the Adriatic's most vibrant cities: an exuberant and hectic place full of shouting stall-owners and travellers on the move. At the heart of the city, hemmed in by sprawling estates and a modern harbour, lies the crumbling old town, which grew out of the former **palace** of the Roman Emperor Diocletian. The palace remains the central ingredient in the city's urban fabric – lived in almost continuously since Roman times, it's gradually been transformed into a warren of houses, tenements, churches and chapels by the various peoples who came to live here after Diocletian's successors had departed.

Modern Split is a city of some 220,000 inhabitants, swollen by post-World War II economic migrants and post-1991 refugees – a chaotic sprawl of hastily planned suburbs, where factories and high-rise blocks jangle together out of an undergrowth of discarded building material. As Croatia's second city it's a hotbed of regional pride, and disparagement of Zagreb-dwellers is a frequent, if usually harmless, component of local banter. The city's two big industries – shipbuilding and tourism – suffered immeasurably as a result of war and the economic slump which followed the collapse of communism, and municipal belt-tightening has led to a decline in subsidies for the city's traditionally rich cultural scene. This is more than made up for by the vivacious outdoor life that takes over the streets in all but the coldest and wettest months: as long as the sun is shining, the swish cafés of the waterfront Riva are never short of custom.

Not surprisingly, Split is home to one of the more authentic **carnival seasons** in Croatia – a tradition which has only recently been revived – when masked revellers take over the streets and squares of the old town on the night of Shrove Tuesday and during the weekend before it. Split's other big day is May 7, when the **Feast of St Domnius** (Sveti Dujam or, more colloquially, Sveti Duje), the city's protector, is celebrated with processions, masses and general festivity. Domnius is also the patron saint of woodwork, and you'll see craftsmen selling chairs, tables, barrels and carvings in Split market on the days surrounding the feast.

Some history

According to conventional wisdom, Split didn't exist at all until the emperor Diocletian (see box on p.294) decided to build his retirement home here, although recent archeological finds suggest that a Roman settlement of sorts was founded here before Diocletian's builders arrived. **Diocletian's Palace** was begun in 295 AD and finished ten years later, when the emperor came

Diocletian (245–312)

Born the son of slaves, **Diocletian** was a native of Dalmatia – and possibly grew up in Salona, next door to Split. Despite his humble origins he proved himself quickly in the Roman military, becoming emperor in 284, at the age of 39. For 21 years he attempted to provide stability and direction to an empire under pressure – goals he achieved with some measure of success, even organizing the last triumph imperial Rome was ever to see. In the belief that the job of running the empire was too big for one man, Diocletian divided the role into four, the **Tetrarchy**, carefully parcelling out responsibility among his partners – a decision which some historians believe led directly to disintegration and civil war. Diocletian was also renowned for his persecution of Christians: those martyred during his reign included the patron saints of Split, Domnius and Anastasius, along with many other leading religious figures, Sebastian, George, Theodore and Vitus among them.

The motives for Diocletian's early **retirement** have been the subject of much speculation. It was obviously planned well in advance by a man who feared his health was no longer up to the rigours of government. As a highly innovative emperor, Diocletian obviously saw the very concept of retirement – a total novelty among Roman rulers – as a logical adjunct to his other reforms. However the power-sharing system he left behind soon disintegrated once he was no longer at the helm. The Tetrarchy had been welded together by inter-family marriage: after her father's retirement, Diocletian's own daughter, Valeria, stayed in Rome as the wife of Galerius, one of the Tetrarchs. On Galerius's death she received a proposal of marriage from his nephew Maximinus Daza, but was banished to Syria when she refused. When Diocletian tried to intercede on her behalf, he was cold-shouldered by his heirs – and the embittered ex-emperor appears to have poisoned himself in despair. Licinius, the new strongman in the eastern half of the Empire, arranged the murder of both Valeria and Diocletian's wife Priscia in 314.

back to his native Illyria to escape the cares of empire, cure his rheumatism and grow cabbages. But this was no simple retirement, and the palace no ordinary retirement home. Diocletian maintained an elaborate court here in a building that mixed luxurious palatial apartments with the infrastructure of a Roman garrison: the northern half of the palace was occupied by servants and the garrison; to the south lay the imperial suites and public buildings. The palace as a whole measured some 200m by 240m, with walls 2m thick and almost 25m high, while at each corner there was a fortified keep, and four towers along each of the land walls.

The palace was home to a succession of regional despots after Diocletian's death, although by the sixth century it had fallen into disuse. In 614, it was suddenly repopulated by refugees fleeing nearby Salona, which had just been sacked by the Avars and Slavs. The newcomers salvaged living quarters out of Diocletian's neglected buildings, improvising a home in what must have been one of the most grandiose squats of all time. They built fortifications, walled in arches, boarded up windows and repelled attacks from the mainland, accepting Byzantine sovereignty in return for being allowed to preserve a measure of autonomy. The resulting city developed cultural and trading links with the embryonic Croatian state inland, and was absorbed by the Hungaro-Croatian kingdom in the eleventh century.

By the fourteenth century, Split had grown beyond the confines of the palace, with today's Narodni trg becoming the new centre of a walled city that stretched as far west as the street now known as Marmontova. **Venetian rule**, established in 1420, occasioned an upsurge in the city's economic fortunes, as the city's port was developed as an entrepot for Ottoman goods. Turkish power was to be an ever-constant threat, however: Ottoman armies attacked Split on numerous occasions, coming nearest to capturing it in 1657, when they occupied Marjan hill before being driven off by reinforcements hastily shipped in from Venice, Trogir and Hvar.

During the nineteenth century, **Austrian rule** brought industrialization and a railway to the city. Austrian stimulation of Adriatic shipping also helped speed the development of Split's port facilities, while the Italian seizure of Rijeka in 1919 (see box on p.195) caused the Yugoslav government to deliberately develop Split as an alternative centre of maritime trade. Split's biggest period of growth occurred after World War II, when the development of heavy industry attracted growing numbers of economic migrants from all over the country. Many of these newcomers came from the Zagora, the rural uplands stretching from the central Dalmatian coast to the Hercegovinian border, and ended up working in the enormous shipyards – colloquially known as the "Škver" – on Split's northwestern edge, providing the city with a new working-class layer. It was always said that productivity at the Škver was directly related to the on-the-pitch fortunes of **Hajduk Split** (see box on p.306), the football team which more than anything else in Split served to bind traditional inhabitants of the city with recent arrivals. Beginning with the big televised music festivals of the 1960s, Split also became the nation's unofficial **pop music** capital, when it was promoted as a kind of Croatian San Remo, since when generations of balladeering medallion men have emerged from the city to regale the nation with their songs of mandolin-playing fishermen and dark-eyed girls in the moonlight.

The city was briefly **shelled** by the Yugoslav Navy in 1991 but was otherwise largely untouched by Serb–Croat hostilities, although refugees have added to the city's housing problems. None of this has damaged the spirit of the Splićani themselves, who remain famous for their self-deprecating humour, best exemplified by the writings of **Miljenko Smoje** (1923–95), a native of the inner-city district of Veli Varoš. Smoje's books, written in Dalmatian dialect, document the lives of an imaginary group of local archetypes and brought the wit of the Splićani to a nationwide audience. An adaptation of his works, *Naše malo misto* (Our Little Town), was the most popular comedy programme in Croatian – and probably Yugoslav – television history. The city's tradition of irreverence lives on in the weekly newspaper and national institution **Feral Tribune**, a mixture of investigative reporting and scathing political satire which has been a thorn in the side of successive recent administrations.

Arrival, information and city transport

Both the **train** and **intercity bus stations** are five minutes' walk southeast of the centre on the main harbourfront road, Obala kneza Domagoja, along which are ranged all the **ferry** and **hydrofoil** berths. Split's **airport** is around 20km northwest of town between Kaštela and Trogir. Croatia Airlines buses (25Kn) connect with scheduled flights, dropping passengers on the waterfront Riva, near the Croatia Airlines office; alternatively, the #37 Trogir–Split bus (13.50Kn) runs from in front of the airport to the suburban bus station on Domovinskog rata, twenty minutes' north of the centre. A taxi from the airport will cost 160–200Kn.

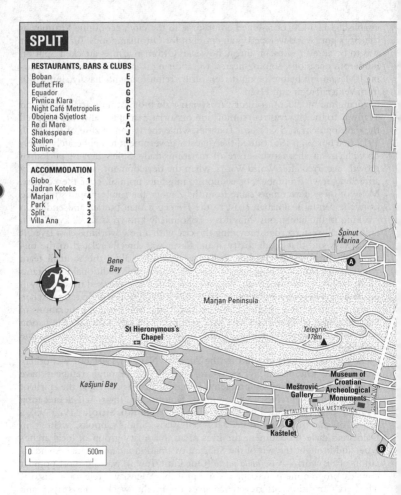

SPLIT

RESTAURANTS, BARS & CLUBS

Boban	E
Buffet Fife	D
Equador	G
Pivnica Klara	B
Night Café Metropolis	C
Obojena Svjetlost	F
Re di Mare	A
Shakespeare	J
Stellon	H
Šumica	I

ACCOMMODATION

Globo	1
Jadran Koteks	6
Marjan	4
Park	5
Split	3
Villa Ana	2

N

Špinut
Marina

Bene
Bay

Marjan Peninsula

St Hieronymous's
Chapel

Telegrin
178m

Kašjuni Bay

Meštrović
Gallery

Museum of
Croatian
Archeological
Monuments

ŠETALIŠTE IVANA MEŠTROVIĆA

Kaštelet

0   500m

The city's **tourist office** is located right in the heart of the old town, in the Chapel of St Rock on the Peristyle (June–Sept Mon–Sat 9am–8pm, Sun 9am–1pm; Oct–May Mon–Fri 9am–5pm; ☏021/342-606, ⓦwww.visitsplit.com). The staff can probably provide a free map and a list of museums and their opening times, as well as giving out general advice. However, the privately run **Turist Biro** on the Riva (see "Accommodation" below) is usually much better informed about accommodation options in the city.

As for **city transport**, it's generally easiest to walk, though for journeys out to the Marjan peninsula and some of Split's museums you may need to take one of the city's **buses**. These are frequent and operate between 5am and midnight; tickets can be bought from the driver or conductor (7Kn) or from newspaper and tobacco kiosks (7Kn, valid for two journeys) and should be punched when you board. Tickets for Kaštela and Trogir (see p.291 and p.285) are priced according to a zonal system – most of Kaštela is in zone 3 (13.50Kn one-way from the conductor or 20.50Kn return from a kiosk); Trogir is in zone 4 (16.50Kn one-way from the conductor or 27Kn return from a kiosk). The prin-

Map labels:

Poljud Stadium

Archeological Museum

HRVATSKE MORNARICE
TRG HRVATSKE BRATSKE ZAJEDNICE

Suburban Bus Station

HERCEGOVAČKA

DOMOVINSKOG RATA

ŠIBENSKA

VELEBITSKA

Stari plac **B**

M A N U Š

Tvrdava Gripe

Dom omladine **C**

VELI VAROŠ

Vrh Marjana ▲ 123m

St Nicholas's Chapel **D**

see Central Split map

Train Station

Bus Station

Ferry Terminal

KRALJA ZVONIMIRA

ACI Marina

5

G H

Hospital **+**

E

Bačvice Bay

I

Firule Bay

J Zenta Bay

Tennis Club

cipal nodal points for the municipal bus network are Trg republike, at the western end of the Riva (for the Marjan peninsula and Solin); Zagrebačka, opposite the market on the eastern side of the old town; and the suburban bus station on Domovinskog rata (for Kaštela and Trogir). There are **taxi** ranks outside the train and bus stations, and at both the eastern and western ends of the Riva.

Accommodation

There are plenty of private **rooms** (❶–❷) in Split, and it's easy to find one even in high season providing that you arrive early in the day – contact the Turist Biro on the waterfront at Riva 12 (Mon–Fri 7.30am–9pm, Sat 8am–8pm; ☎ & ℻021/342-544 & 342-142, ℮turist-biro-split@st.hinet.hr). There are very few rooms in the old town, though the nearby residential districts of Manuš and Veli Varoš can be equally atmospheric. Single travellers usually have to pay for a double room, or be prepared to team up with a stranger. The unregistered rooms offered by touts at the bus station may work out

Moving on from Split

Split is an excellent base for onward travel, with **buses** to every conceivable destination in Croatia, as well as daily services to Mostar and Sarajevo in Bosnia-Hercegovina. There are two daily **trains** to Zagreb, calling at Knin and Karlovac on the way.

Split is the Dalmatian coast's main Jadrolinija terminal, with regular **local ferries** to the islands of Brač, Vis, Lastovo, Hvar and Korčula; it's also a major stop on the summer **coastal ferry** service, which connects Split with Rijeka, Rab, Zadar and Dubrovnik. In summer, the coastal ferry carries on to Bari in Italy (1 or 2 weekly) and Igoumenitsa in Greece (1 weekly), while from June to September there are ferries roughly every day to Ancona in Italy. For the main coastal ferry, pre-booking is recommended. Tickets and reservations for all the above ferry services can be made through Jadrolinija, which runs a couple of ticket kiosks along Obala kneza Domagoja, and a larger sales counter in the main passenger terminal at the end of Obala kneza Domagoja (☏021/355-399, ℻362-050, ⊛www.jadrolinija.tel.hr). An alternative Ancona service is runs by Adriatica Navigazione: reservations are handled by Jadroagent (☏021/338-335, ⊛www.jadroagent.com) in the main passenger terminal.

In addition, SMC runs daily **hydrofoils** (slightly faster than regular ferries) to Brač, Hvar, Šolta and Vis (mid-May to mid-Sept), and the Italian port of Ancona (Jan to late Oct); there's an SMC ticket counter in the main ferry terminal (☏021/338-219, ℻338-267, ⊛www.sem.hr).

cheaper, but bear in mind that there's no quality control, and many are miles out of the centre.

There's not as great a choice of **hotels** as you'd expect in a city of this size, and you should book ahead in July and August. All the hotels listed below include breakfast in the room price; those in central Split are marked on the map opposite.

Hotels

Central Split

Adriana Obala Hrvatskog Narodnog Preporoda 8 ☏021/340-000. Superbly situated small hotel offering modern doubles and swanky apartments, located above the seafront café-pizzeria of the same name. Complete with deep carpets, minibars and air-con, the rooms are plush enough to satisfy both comfort-conscious tourists and business travellers – but demand is high, so book early. ⑥

Bellevue Bana Jelačića 2 ☏021/585-701, ℻362-383. A once elegant nineteenth-century pile superbly situated at the western end of the Riva, with some rooms overlooking the flagstoned expanse of Trg republike. Rooms are adequate but dowdy, and come with TV and attached bathroom. ⑤

Prenočište Slavija Buvinina 3 ☏021/347-053, ℻591-558. The only budget place in town, occupying a gloomy and characterless building, although it has a couple of saving graces, notably its proximity to the sights and its fourth-floor terrace, from where there's a good view out over Split's red-tiled skyline. It features plain, unadorned rooms (a mixture of singles, doubles and triples), some en suite. ②

Out from the centre

Globo Lovretska 18 ☏021/481-111, ⊛www.hotel.globo.com. New three-star place with smart, comfortable en-suite rooms. It's located in a characterless area of grey blocks north of the centre, a 10min walk from the old town. ⑥

Jadran Koteks Sustjepanski put 23 ☏021/398-622, ⊛www.dalmacija3d.com. Smallish hotel, a 15min walk southwest of the old town, with smart rooms, all with TV. ⑤

Marjan Obala kneza Branimira 8 ☏021/302-111, ⊛www.hotel-marjan.com. Dowdy 1960s high-rise which is much nicer inside than out. Functional but comfortable rooms with TV, bath and balcony, some with views back towards the old town (a 5–10min walk away). ⑥

Park Hatzeov perivoj 3 ☏021/406-400, ℻406-401. Recently renovated hotel 500m southeast of the centre, directly above Bačvice beach. Smart rooms and chic reception areas give the place a somewhat more exclusive air than the rest. Formerly known as the *Imperial*, it was Split's top hotel in the 1920s and 30s, and the place where Italian forces formally surrendered Split to the Partisans in 1943. ⑦

Split Put Trstenika 19 ☎ & ☏ 021/303-011, ⓦwww.hotelsplit.hr. Concrete, three-star 3km east of the centre, on a bluff overlooking the shore. Rooms come with TV, minibar, bath and disconcertingly bright blue-and-white 1980s decor. All have small balconies, some looking across the water to the island of Brač, and there's a small open-air pool. Bus #17, or a 30min walk along the coastal path. ❻

Villa Ana Vrh Lučac 16 ☏021/482-715. Refurbished stone house in the atmospheric Radunica district, just east of the old town and ideally situated for the port and stations. Rooms are bright, spacious, pine-floored affairs with en-suite shower, TV and minibar – but there are only eight of them, so ring in advance. ❺

The City

Split may be the largest town in Dalmatia, but nearly everything worth seeing is concentrated in the compact **old town** behind the waterfront Riva, made up in part of the various remains and conversions of Diocletian's Palace itself, and the medieval additions to the west of it. You can walk across this area in about ten minutes, although it would take a lifetime to explore all its nooks and crannies. On either side the old town fades into low-rise suburbs of utilitarian stone houses grouped tightly around narrow alleys – **Veli Varoš**, west of the old town, and **Manuš**, to the east, are the most unspoiled – and, although there are no specific sights, worth a brief wander. West of the city centre, the wooded **Marjan peninsula** commands fine views over the coast and islands

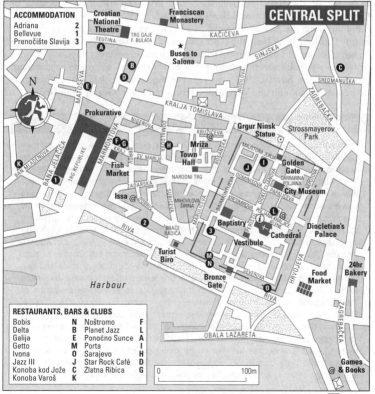

Bus Station, Train Station & Ferry Terminal (200m) ▼

from its heights. The best of the beaches are on the north side of Marjan, or east of the ferry dock at **Bačvice**.

The palace

Despite its importance, don't expect **Diocletian's Palace** to be an archeological "site": the shape and style of the palace have to be extrapolated from what remains, which itself is obscured by centuries of addition and alteration – the map opposite gives an idea of the palace's original ground plan, but doesn't show contemporary features. The palace occupies the eastern half of the old town, though apart from certain set-piece buildings – notably the cathedral (originally Diocletian's mausoleum) and the baptistry (once a temple) – it has been built upon so much by successive generations that it is no longer recognizable as an ancient Roman structure. Little remains of the imperial apartments, although the medieval tenements, shops and offices which have taken their place were built in large part using stones and columns salvaged from Diocletian's original buildings. Despite its architectural pedigree, the palace area hasn't always been the most desireable part of the city in which to live. During the inter-war period it was dubbed the *get* ("ghetto") and – abandoned to the urban poor, down-at-heel White Russian emigres and red-light bars – became synonymous with loose morals and shady dealings. Nowadays the palace area is once more the centre of urban life, hosting a daily melee of tourists and shoppers.

The best place to start exploring is on the seaward side, at Split's broad and lively waterfront, the **Riva** (officially the Obala hrvatskog naradnog preporoda, or Quay of the Croatian National Revival, although hardly anyone ever calls it that). Running along the palace's southern facade, into which shops, cafés and a warren of tiny flats have been built, the Riva is where a large part of the city's population congregates day and night to meet friends, catch up on gossip or idle away an hour or two in a café. It's also the obvious venue for mass gatherings and celebrations, most notably on July 10, 2001, when tens of thousands flocked here to welcome home native Splićanin and Wimbledon tennis champion **Goran Ivanišević**.

Robert Adam and Diocletian's Palace

The rediscovery of Diocletian's Palace owes much to the eighteenth-century Scottish architect **Robert Adam**, who believed that contemporary European builders had much to learn from their Roman forebears. Adam arrived in Split in 1757 with a team of draughtsmen, spending five weeks in the city despite the hostility of the Venetian governor, who almost had them arrested as spies. This didn't prevent Adam from enjoying the trip: "the people are vastly polite, everything vastly cheap; a most wholesome air and glorious situation" was how he summed the town up. The resulting book of engravings of the palace caused a sensation, offering inspiration to Neoclassical architects all over Britain and Europe. Mindful of Adam's success, Austrian Emperor Josef II commissioned Frenchman **L.F. Cassas** to supply a wider-ranging set of engravings of Dalmatia's ancient buildings, which was also published to great acclaim. A sign that attitudes towards Dalmatia were beginning to be coloured by imperial rivalries in the region came in the French edition of Cassas's book, the accompanying text accusing Adam of having travelled "like an Englishman, that is to say with that national egoism which counts England for everything and the rest of the world for nothing". "When the English travel", it went on, "the desire to appropriate precedes the desire to instruct." Whatever its original motive, Adam's work was seminal in the development of the Georgian style in England, and large chunks of London, Bath and Bristol may be claimed to owe something of their space, symmetry and grace to Diocletian's buildings in Split.

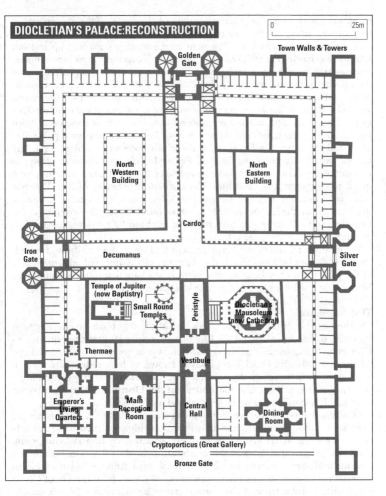

DIOCLETIAN'S PALACE:RECONSTRUCTION

0   25m

Town Walls & Towers

Golden Gate

North Western Building

North Eastern Building

Cardo

Iron Gate

Decumanus

Silver Gate

Temple of Jupiter (now Baptistry)

Small Round Temples

Peristyle

Diocletian's Mausoleum (now Cathedral)

Thermae

Vestibule

Emperor's Living Quarters

Main Reception Room

Central Hall

Dining Room

Cryptoporticus (Great Gallery)

Bronze Gate

The main approach to the palace from the Riva is through the **Bronze Gate** (Mjedena vrata), an anonymous and functional gateway that originally gave access to the sea, which once came right up to the palace. Inside is a vaulted space which once formed the basement of Diocletian's central hall, the middle part of his residential complex, now occupied by arts and crafts stalls. On either side of here stretch the **subterranean halls** (*podrum*; daily: summer 8am–8pm; winter 8am–noon & 4–7pm; 10Kn), built in Diocletian's time to support the apartments above – until 1956 they remained unexplored and full of centuries of debris. Parts have now been cleared out and opened to the public, and though there's nothing actually to see, they give an idea of what the palace must have once looked like, since their ground plan is an exact mirror of the imperial living quarters that formerly stood above. The long corridor which stretches east and west of the Bronze Gate corresponds to the **cryptoporticus**, or great gallery, along which the emperor would have promenaded. The large hall off the western end of the corridor stood beneath Diocletian's main reception room, while the cruciform group of chambers off the eastern end of the corridor stood beneath the triclinium, or dining room.

At the northern end of this basement area, imposing steps lead up and out into the **Peristyle** (Peristil), once the central courtyard of the palace complex, opening out from the point where the cardo and decumanus meet. These days it's a lively square and meeting point, crowded with café tables and surrounded by considerable remnants of the stately arches that once framed the courtyard. The Peristyle has been the site of two major cultural scandals in modern times, the first in 1968, when three students used the cover of darkness to paint the square's paving stones red – the colour of both revolutionary socialist idealism and the ossified political elites in socialist states such as Yugoslavia. The action, which became known as **Red Peristyle**, has gone down in history as one of the key events in Croatian conceptual art, although the authorities were quick to condemn it as vandalism. The thirtieth anniversary of Red Peristyle was marked on the night of January 10, 1998, when Igor Grubić painted a black circle in the centre of the Peristyle (black being the colour of the extreme right and, by implication, the Croatia of the 1990s) – a gesture which engendered much the same official response.

At the southern end of the Peristyle, steps lead up to the **vestibule**, a round, formerly domed building that is the only part of the imperial apartment area of the palace that's anything like complete. It was here that subjects would wait before being admitted to the presence of Diocletian himself.

The cathedral

On the east side of the Peristyle stands one of the two black granite Egyptian sphinxes, dating from around 15 BC, that originally flanked the entrance to Diocletian's mausoleum, an octagonal building surrounded by an arcade of Corinthian columns. Diocletian's body is known to have rested here for 170 years until it mysteriously disappeared – no one knows where. The building was later converted into the **Cathedral of St Domnius** (Katedrala svetog Dujma; Mon–Sat 7am–noon & 4–7pm) and a choir added.

The cathedral porch is entered through an arch guarded by two Romanesque lions with a motley collection of human figures riding on their backs, including Greek-born Maria Lascaris, wife of Hungarian King Bela IV, who briefly took refuge from the Tatars in the nearby stronghold of Klis. The walnut and oak main **doors** – carved in 1214 by local artist Andrija Buvina with an inspired comic-strip-style sequence showing 28 scenes from the life of Christ – are scuffed and scraped at the bottom, but in fine condition further up. On the right looms the six-storey **campanile** (same times as cathedral; 5Kn), begun in the thirteenth century but not finished until 1908 – the climb up is worth the effort for the panoramic view over the city and beyond.

Inside, the **dome** is ringed by two levels of Corinthian columns dating from the first century BC, while a frieze depicting racing chariots, hunting scenes and, in one corner, portraits of Diocletian and his wife Priscia, runs around the base. The rest of the constricted interior is stuffed with miscellaneous artworks. Immediately to the left of the entrance, the **pulpit** is a beautifully proportioned example of Romanesque art, sitting on capitals tangled with foliage, snakes and strange beasts. Moving clockwise round the church, the next feature is the **Altar of St Domnius**, honouring the first bishop of Salona's underground Christian community, who was beheaded in 304. Built by Giovanni Morlaiter in 1767, the altar features a pair of angels holding a reliquary on which a group of celestial cherubs cavort – a symbol of man's journey to the afterlife.

Further around lies the church's finest feature, the **Altar of St Anastasius** (Staš), which preserves the bones of a Christian contemporary of Domnius who, on Diocletian's orders, was thrown in a river with a stone tied to him. Sheltering under an extravagant canopy, the saint's sarcophagus bears Juraj Dalmatinac's cruelly realistic relief, the *Flagellation of Christ* of 1448, showing Jesus pawed and brutalized by some peculiarly oafish persecutors, while just above is a figure of St Anastasius with a millstone round his neck. The Baroque **high altar**, occupying the arch which leads through to the choir, features a pair of delicate, gilded angels supporting what looks like a cherub-encrusted carriage clock bearing paintings on each of its faces; an ornate coffered ceiling with ten paintings on Old Testament themes by Matej Ponzoni-Pončun fills the arch above. Further around is Bonino of Milan's fifteenth-century **Altar of St Domnius**, where the saint's bones were once kept. Sheltered beneath a flowery Gothic ciborium, this uses an ancient Roman sarcophagus bearing a relief of a man with hunting dogs as a base, on which rests a larger sarcophagus etched with a reclining figure of the bishop.

Behind the high altar, the **choir** was tacked onto the mausoleum in the seventeenth century, and still feels a very different part of the church. It's worth peering closely at the latticed choir stalls, which include some particularly delicate wood-carving – the oldest in Dalmatia, dated to about 1200. To the right, a flight of steps leads up to the **treasury** (*riznica*), sporting a melange of chalices, handwritten missals, thirteenth-century Madonnas and reliquary busts of the city's three great martyrs – Domnius, Anastasius and Arnerius (Arnir), a bishop of Split who was stoned to death in 1180.

Opposite the cathedral, a narrow alley runs from a gap in the arched arcade down to the attractive **baptistry** (opening times vary, check at the cathedral), a temple built in Diocletian's time and variously attributed to the cults of Janus or Jupiter, with an elaborate ceiling and well-preserved figures of Hercules and Apollo on the eastern portal. Later Christian additions include a skinny statue of John the Baptist by Meštrović (a late work of 1954) and, more famously, an eleventh-century baptismal font with a relief showing a Croatian king trampling on a figure thought to represent either a devil or a pagan foe. Above the two figures runs a swirling pleated pattern known as *plutej*, a design typical of the Croatian Romanesque which has subsequently been adopted as a national symbol – you'll also see it around the bands of policemen's caps.

At the southern end of the Peristyle, steps lead up to a cone-shaped, roofless chamber which once served as the palace **vestibule**, in which visitors would wait before being summoned into the presence of the ex-emperor. On the far side of the vestibule, the area once occupied by Diocletian's private apartments is nowadays one of the poorest parts of the city, where medieval tenement buildings brush up against the sea-facing walls of the palace. The sequence of interlocking small squares here have a desolate, half-forgotten air which seems miles away from the tourist-tramped areas nearby. The area used to be the favoured meeting-place of Split's prostitutes and drug addicts, and is still fondly referred to by locals as the *kenjara* ("shit-hole"). At the south end of this area, along Severova, windows in the palace wall provide an excellent vantage point from which to spy on goings-on down on the Riva while, to the west, Alješijeva threads its way through one of the most abandoned and mysterious parts of the palace, eventually bringing you out at Mihovilova širina (see below).

The rest of the palace
North of the Peristyle, Dioklecijanova follows the line of the former cardo past rows of tottering medieval houses. A right turn down Papalićeva leads to the

Juraj Dalmatinac-designed **Papalić Palace**, a typical example of the sturdy Gothic town houses built by Split's fifteenth-century aristocracy. An unobtrusive gateway leads through to a secluded, ivy-covered courtyard centred on a well adorned with the star and feathers symbol of the Papalić family, with a delicate loggia at ground level and an outdoor stone stairway leading to the first-floor apartments. It now houses the **City Museum** (Gradski muzej; Tues–Fri 9am–noon & 5–8pm, Sat & Sun 10am–noon; 10Kn), with well-laid-out displays of medieval weaponry, figureheads from eighteenth-century galleys and sculptural fragments – including a serene Pietà by Nikola Fiorentinac. The reconstructed Papalić dining room on the first floor contains pictures and manuscripts relating to Marko Marulić (1450–1524), author of the biblically inspired epic *Judita* and the first Dalmatian poet to abandon Latin in favour of Croatian.

Continuing north along Dioklecijanova soon brings you to the grandest and best preserved of the palace gates, the **Golden Gate** (Zlatna vrata). This was the landward – and therefore most important – entrance to the palace, and the beginning of the main road to Salona. The arched niches (now empty) originally contained statues, and the four plinths on top of the gate once supported likenesses of Diocletian and the three other tetrarchs.

Just outside the gate there's another Meštrović work, the gigantic statue of the tenth-century Bishop **Grgur Ninski**. It was completed in 1929 to mark the 1000th anniversary of the Synod of Split, at which Grgur, Bishop of Nin, fought for the right of his people to use their own language in the liturgy instead of Latin. Catching the bishop in stiff mid-gesture, it's more successful as a patriotic statement than as a piece of sculpture. This mammoth used to stand in the Peristyle before it was moved during World War II, when the Italian occupiers attempted to cleanse the town centre of anything resembling a Croatian national symbol.

Narodni trg to Marmontova

Returning to the Peristyle and heading west along the ancient decumanus, now Krešimirova – a shop-lined alley which, despite its narrowness, is the old town's main thoroughfare – takes you out through the Iron Gate (Željezna vrata) into **Narodni trg** ("People's Square", usually known as "Pjaca", the local version of the Italian word *piazza*). This replaced the Peristyle as the city's main square in the fourteenth century, and is overlooked to the east by a Romanesque clock tower with the remains of a medieval sundial, behind which looms a taller, older belfry. The north side of the square is dominated by the fifteenth-century **Town Hall** (Gradska vijećnica), with a ground-floor loggia of three large pointed arches supported by stumpy pillars – it's now home to an ethnographic museum, currently closed for refurbishment.

West of the square lie the bustling narrow streets and passages of the medieval town. To the south, Marulićeva leads down towards **Mihovilova širina**, a small square whose café-bars get packed on warm summer evenings, and the adjoining Trg braće Radića, more popularly known as **Voćni trg** (Fruit Square) because of the market that used to be held here. There's a large statue of Marko Marulić, supplied by the industrious Meštrović, in the middle, and an octagonal tower that once formed part of the fifteenth-century Venetian castle, or *kaštel* – most of which has now either disappeared or been incorporated into residential buildings. A passageway to the left of the tower brings you back out onto the Riva.

Amble west along the Riva to reach the foot of **Marmontova** – the pedestrianized thoroughfare which marks the western boundary of the medieval town. Near the southern end of Marmontova is **Trg republike**, an elongated square set back from the water and surrounded on three sides by the grandiose neo-Renaissance city council buildings known as the **Prokurative** – it's put to good use as a venue for outdoor concerts in summer. From here, Marmontova heads north, passing the animated **fish market** on Kraj svete Marije – the scene of shopping frenzy most mornings, especially Fridays – and a few remaining bastions of the star-shaped seventeenth-century fortifications which once surrounded the town, before arriving at Trg Gaje Bulata. This broad open space is overlooked by the **Croatian National Theatre** (Hrvatsko narodno kazalište, or HNK), a plain brown construction much rebuilt after a fire in 1971 and unadorned save for a group of statues on the third floor representing the arts.

On the northern side of the square, the church of the **Franciscan monastery** (Franjevački samostan) is worth a peek for the large fresco behind the high altar, a flamboyantly expressionistic work by contemporary religious artist Ivan Dulčić. A central figure of Jesus hovers above the Adriatic coastline, offering salvation to the matchstick forms below, most of which are dressed in colourful Dalmatian costumes. On his left are Cyril and Methodius, inventors of Glagolitic, the script used by the medieval Croatian church, while floating in the sky are a bull, lion and eagle – symbolizing SS Luke, Mark and John the Evangelist respectively.

North of the old town

Immediately to the west of the theatre is another modern square, Ujevićeva poljana, from which Zrinsko-Frankopanska spears north towards the city's modern residential districts. Appearing almost immediately on your left is the **Stari plac**, a scruffy sports ground that was home to football team Hajduk Split until 1979, when they moved to a brand new stadium up the road (see below). Despite its nondescript appearance, the Stari plac has an almost religious significance to the locals, and many of the cafés around the ground retain a strong sporting theme, their walls covered with Hajduk memorabilia and TVs permanently tuned to sporting channels. The Stari plac now serves as the ground of Split rugby club – it's only in Split and nearby Makarska (see p.357) that the sport seems to be played with any seriousness in Croatia.

Continue up Frankopanska for ten minutes to reach the **Archeological Museum** at no. 25 (Arheološki muzej; Tues–Sat 9am–1pm & 5–8pm, Sun 10am–noon; 20Kn), with its comprehensive displays of Illyrian, Greek, medieval and – particularly – Roman artefacts, mostly plucked from the rich excavation sites at nearby Salona. Exhibits include delicate votive figurines, amulets and jewellery embellished with tiny peep-shows of lewd love-making. Outside, the arcaded courtyard is crammed with a wonderful array of Greek, Roman and early Christian stelae, sarcophagi and decorative sculpture. There are three key exhibits. Two of these, to the left of the entrance, are Salonan sarcophagi from the third century AD: one depicts the Hippolytus and Phaedra legend and is in superb condition – the marble still glistens – while the other is of a Calydonian boar hunt, which in Robert Adam's pictures stood outside Split's baptistry. The third, another sarcophagus, is much later, dating from the fourth century. Known as the "Good Shepherd", it has been the subject of much speculation on account of its mixing up of the Christian motif of the shepherd with pagan symbols of Eros and Hades on its end panels.

Carry on up the road for another five minutes and you'll catch sight of the **Poljud Stadium** over the brow of the hill. Built for the 1979 Mediterranean Games and now home to Hajduk Split football team (see box, p.306), it's a strikingly organic structure, the curving roofs of its stands suggesting the sides of a fishing boat's hull or a gargantuan seashell.

Hajduk Split

Few football teams are as closely associated with their home city as **Hajduk Split**. Formed in February 1911 by Croatian students returning from Prague – who had witnessed the fervour created by Czech teams Sparta and Slavia – the club is named after the Robin Hood-like brigands who opposed both Ottoman and Venetian authority from the Middle Ages onwards. Hajduk was an explicitly Croatian team at a time when Split was still part of the Austro-Hungarian Empire and, later, in World War II, the team reflected the popular mood of resistance by joining the Partisans en masse. They were also the first team in Yugoslavia to play with a *petokraka* (Communist five-pointed star) on their jerseys, and the first team to remove it when it became clear that Yugoslavia's days were numbered.

A large part of the Hajduk mystique comes from their success on the pitch: they were Yugoslav champions twice in the 1920s, three times in the 1950s, four times in the 1970s, and went on to become champions of Croatia in 1992, 1994 and 1995. They're also famous for their loyal fans, known as the **torcida** (after the Brazilian fans that Hajduk supporters had seen footage of during the 1950 World Cup). Split's version of the *torcida* launched itself in October 1950, providing the team with maximum, Rio-style support for the title-decider against Red Star Belgrade – the first time that torches, banners and massed chanting had been seen on the terraces of mainland Europe. Hajduk won the match, but football purists were shocked by the levels of popular frenzy displayed. The Yugoslav regime, which had since 1945 condescendingly regarded Hajduk as "their" club, was horrified by the idea that football supporters could organize themselves without the leadership of the Party. *Torcida* founder Vjenceslav Žuvela was given a three-year prison sentence and the captain of the team was expelled from the Communist Party. Today, Hajduk and the *torcida* remain an unavoidable part of the urban landscape, and victories over traditional enemies like Dinamo Zagreb are still celebrated with city-wide rejoicing. Some would argue that the team has become all-important to the local population as other symbols of Dalmatian identity are gradually eroded and the act of supporting Hajduk becomes one of the few communal experiences left.

Tickets for matches (20–50Kn) are sold from kiosks at the southern end of the ground. Most of the *torcida* congregate in the northern stand (*tribina sjever*), while the poshest seats are in the west stand (*tribina zapad*). Beer and popcorn are available inside, and there are numerous snack bars offering drinks and grills immediately outside. Remember to bring a sheet of newspaper to sit on: the seats are filthy. The official club website (❀www.hajduk.com) is Croatian-language only, but the *torcida* site (❀www.torcida.org) has some information in English.

The Marjan peninsula

Crisscrossed by footpaths and minor roads, the wooded heights of the **Marjan peninsula** offer the easiest escape from the bustle of central Split. From the old town it's an easy ten-minute walk up Senjska, which ascends westwards through the district of Veli Varoš, arriving after about ten minutes at the *Vidilica* **café** on Marjan's eastern shoulder. There's a small Jewish graveyard round the back of the café, and a terrace out front offering good views of Veli Varoš immediately below and the old town beyond. To the right of the café a stepped path climbs towards **Vrh Marjana**, where there's a wider view of the coast and islands, although there's an even better panorama from the peninsula's highest point, 175-metre-high **Telegrin**, about 1km further west.

Keeping to the left of the *Vidilica* brings you to a path which heads round the south side of the hill, arriving after about five minutes at the thirteenth-century **St Nicholas's Chapel** (Sveti Nikola), a simple structure with a sloping belfry tacked on to one side like a buttress. From here, the path continues for 2km, with wooded hillside to the right and the seaside sub-urbs of Marjan's south coast on the left, before arriving at **St Hieronymous's Chapel** (Sveti Jere), a simple shed-like structure pressed hard against a cliff – medieval hermits used to live in the caves which are still visible in the rock above. From here you can descend towards the road which leads round the base of the peninsula, or cross its rocky spine to reach Marjan's fragrant, pine-covered northern side. Paths emerge at sea level near **Bene** bay, where you'll find a combination of rocky and concreted bathing areas and a couple of cafés. You can also get to Bene by taking bus #12 from Trg republike (every 30min).

The Museum of Croatian Archeological Monuments

Marjan's main cultural attractions are on its southern side, in the suburbs of Zvončac and Meje, about twenty minutes' walk from the centre or a short ride on bus #12 from Trg republike. Heading west along Šetalište Ivana Meštrovića brings you first to the **Museum of Croatian Archeological Monuments** (Muzej hrvatskih arheoloških spomenika; Tues–Sat 9am–4pm, Sun 9am–noon; 20Kn), housed in an oversized concrete edifice with huge open-plan halls and piped-in organ muzak. The museum makes a concerted attempt to remind people of Split's medieval Croatian heritage, a phase of local history that's often forgotten in the enthusiasm for all things connected with Diocletian. Displays include a motley collection of jewellery, weapons and fragmentary reconstruc-tions of chancel screens and ciboria (the canopies built over a church's main altar) from ninth- and tenth-century Croatian churches.

The Meštrović Gallery and the Kaštelet

A couple of minutes further along Šetalište Ivana Meštrovića at no. 39, the **Ivan Meštrović Gallery** (Galerija Ivana Meštrovića; Tues–Sun 11am–6pm; 20Kn) is housed in the ostentatious Neoclassical building that the country's most famous modern sculptor (see box, p.308) planned as his home and studio. Fronted by a portentous veranda supported by Ionic columns, the house was completed in 1939 – Meštrović lived in it for just two years before fleeing to Zagreb to escape the Italian occupation in 1941.

Even if you're not mad about Meštrović, this is still an impressive collection, although the emphasis is on smooth female nudes and tender Madonnas rather than the ideological and historical subjects with which he made his reputation. Some of the religious pieces (look out for a particularly tortured *Job* from 1946) have considerable emotional depth, although his other work can some-times appear facile – such as the slightly daft *Joyful Youth* or the giant and ungainly *Adam and Eve*. Portraits of members of his immediate family in the ground-floor drawing room are refreshingly direct, especially the honest and sensitive *My Mother* from 1909.

Meštrović's best work can be seen in the so-called **Kaštelet** ("little castle"; in theory Tues–Sun 10am–5pm, but check at the Meštrović Gallery first; admis-sion with gallery ticket) about 200m further up the road. Built in the sixteenth century as the fortified residence of the Capogrosso family, but long used for other purposes (it was at various times a tannery and a hospital), the Kaštelet was virtually a ruin when Meštrović bought it in 1939 to house his **Life of Christ** cycle, a series of reliefs in wood that he'd been working on since 1916. Presided over by a mannered but moving *Crucifixion*, the cycle spreads like a frieze across all four walls of the church, borrowing stylistically from Assyrian bas-reliefs, Egyptian tomb paintings and Archaic Greek art. The result is an immensely powerful piece of religious sculpture, with rows of rigidly posed, hypnotically stylized figures in which the sum of Meštrović's eclecticism is for once greater than its parts. It's said that Meštrović began the cycle in response to the horrors of World War I, which may go some way to explaining its spiritual punch.

Ivan Meštrovic (1883–1962)

Ivan Meštrović was born in Slavonia to a family of itinerant agricultural labourers, but his parents soon moved back to their native Dalmatia, settling in Otavice near Drniš. Meštrović was too busy tending sheep on Mount Svilaja to attend school, and had to teach himself to read and write. At the age of 16 he displayed some drawings in a local inn, prompting locals – including the mayor of Drniš – to apply to art schools on his behalf. He was turned down, but managed to land a job with a Split stone-mason, thus beginning his training as a sculptor.

Awarded a place at the **Viennese Acadamy** in 1901 (quite a feat considering his background), he was soon exhibiting with the Art Nouveau-influenced Secession group. At the age of 22, Meštrović was already receiving big public commissions – like the Secession-influenced *Well of Life* (1905) which still stands outside the Croatian National Theatre in Zagreb. By the time he moved to Paris in 1907 a distinctive Meštrović style was beginning to emerge, blending the earthy Romanticism of Rodin with the grace of Classical sculpture and the folk motifs of southeastern Europe. This **eclecticism** may help explain why Meštrović – considered too daring by traditionalists but not daring enough by the moderns – never enjoyed the reputation abroad which he did at home.

Like many men of his generation, Meštrović was convinced that the Austro-Hungarian state could not survive, and that the expanding Kingdom of Serbia would provide the basis of a future Yugoslav state in which all South Slavs could live as equals – he had grown up in an area of mixed Serb–Croat settlement and was familiar with the folk culture of both communities. When the Austrian government invited Meštrović to represent them at the Rome International Exhibition of 1911, he chose to exhibit in the Serbian pavilion instead (of the 23 artists in the Serbian pavilion, incidentally, 14 were Croat).

On the outbreak of World War I Meštrović moved to Italy, until Italian designs on Dalmatia led to him moving to London, where his involvement with the Yugoslavist cause helped land him a one-man show at the Victoria and Albert Museum in 1915. The exhibition was an enormous success – Britain and Serbia were allies at the time, and attendance at the show was seen as a sign of support for the war effort. In 1918 Meštrović hailed the creation of Yugoslavia as the "greatest accomplishment that our people have hitherto performed", although his enthusiasm would subsequently wane. He was made Rector of the Academy of Fine Arts in Zagreb in 1923, and was in constant demand as an artist over the next two decades, working on monumental public projects such as the *Grgur Ninski* sculpture in Split (1928) and two vast, muscular Indians on horseback for Grant Park in Chicago (1928). His **architectural work** was in many ways more innovative than his sculptural, developing a cool, sepulchral style which found expression in the Račić mausoleum in Cavtat (1923), the Meštrović family mausoleum in Otavice (1927–31) and the Art Pavilion in Zagreb (1939).

In 1941, Meštrović was **imprisoned** by the Ustaše because of to his history of pro-Yugoslav activity, but after four months Ante Pavelić summoned the sculptor to his office, apologized and told him he was free to emigrate. Meštrović eventually made his way to America, where he became Professor of Sculpture at the University of Notre Dame, Indiana. Much of his **later work** was religious, although he'd been tackling sacred subjects on and off ever since 1916, when the cycle of reliefs displayed in Split's Kaštelet was begun.

East of the centre

There's not much of interest east of the old town save for the main city beach of **Bačvice**, a few minutes' walk south past the railway station. This simple crescent of shingle can't compare with the beaches further south, but it remains a popular – and crowded – destination for Splićani of all ages. Bačvice is also the home of *picigin*, a game (only played in and around Split) rather like a netless version of volleyball played in the sea, involving a lot of acrobatic leaping around as players try to prevent a small ball from hitting the water. The front has recently been given a facelift thanks to the chic modern three-tier pavilion that curves gracefully round the beach, like a cross between an Art Deco seaside building and a hi-tech metal tent. There are several cafés and a couple of swanky eating places inside (see opposite).

A coastal path leads east from Bačvice past a couple of smaller bays, passing the tennis club where Goran Ivanišević honed his skills. Beyond the Firule yachting marina the path culminates at **Žnjan**, a large waterside expanse which was levelled so that the pope could hold a vast outdoor mass here in 1998. There are several more cafés along the way, and the whole stretch is a popular strolling area all year round.

Eating

Surprisingly, good sit-down **restaurants** are in short supply along the well-worn tourist trail of the old town, although there are several good places a short walk away. Restaurants tend to stay open until 11pm or midnight unless stated otherwise; some have a separate menu of *marende* (cheap brunches), which is often chalked up on a board outside. For self-catering and snacks, the daily **market** at the eastern edge of the old town is an excellent place to shop for fruit, veg and local hams and cheeses, while there's a handily placed Gavrilović **supermarket** (daily 7am–11pm) at the ferry terminal on Obala kneza Domagoja. The 24-hour Prerada **bakery** directly opposite the market on Zagrebačka offers a dizzying array of fresh buns, cakes and strudels. *Delta*, next to a certain American hamburger joint at Marmontova 7, is a good place to pick up takeaway pizza slices and pastries. The best **cakes** and sweets are from *Bobis*, which has a large café on the Riva and a smaller outlet on Marmontova. Decent ice cream is available almost everywhere; *Ivona*, Riva 25, serves up some of the best.

Restaurants

Central Split

Galija Kamila Tončića 12, on the corner with Matošića. The best of the city's pizzerias – a small, unpretentious and cheap place with breezy service and wooden-bench seating on the western fringes of the old town.

Konoba kod Jože Sredmanuška 4. A 10min walk northeast of the old town in a back alley (head north along Zagrebačka and turn right into Sredmanuška after you've passed Strossmayerov park), this is one of Split's best seafood restaurants – with a homely, intimate atmosphere and fishing nets hung from the walls – and not too expensive. Choose between quick and cheap meals like *crni rižot* (squid risotto) or opt for the best fresh fish and lobster.

Konoba Varoš Ban Mladenova 7 ☎021/396-138.

Handily situated just west of Trg republike – it's up an alley behind the *Hotel Bellevue* – this is a good place for reasonably priced *marende* as well as expensive slap-up evening meals – featuring the best fresh fish. Much patronized by locals and soon fills up.

Noštromo Kraj svete Marije 8. Upper-crust seafood restaurant right on the edge of the old town, with a swish designer interior and attentive service. Good for lobster, but you can't go wrong whatever you order here.

Ponoćno Sunce Teutina 15. Minimally decorated but rather cosy, this is a good source of moderately priced meat and fish dishes, with the welcome addition of some filling pasta dishes, and a usually excellent salad bar. Popular with both performers and punters at the nearby Croatian National Theatre.

Sarajevo Domaldova 6. In the heart of the old

town, this elegant place is one of Split's few old-fashioned downtown restaurants. Tuck into a full range of moderately expensive Dalmatian fish and meat dishes, including an excellent *pašticada*.

Zlatna Ribica Kraj svete Marije 12. No-nonsense stand-up buffet by the fish market on Marmontova offering cheap seafood snacks. Mon–Fri till 9pm, Sat & Sun till 2pm.

Out from the centre

Boban Hektorovićeva 49 ☎021/543-300. Smart and rather formal restaurant with a long tradition of serving top-notch seafood, in residential streets some 2km east of the old town. Superb fish dishes, elegantly presented, and an extensive wine list.

Buffet Fife Trumbićeva obala 11. Unpretentious but characterful feeding station just west of the old town, with a tightly packed wooden-benched interior and a glass-enclosed porch. It's renowned among the Split cognoscenti for its inexpensive home cooking – usually served up in enormous portions – with cheap standards such as *ribice* (small fish, deep-fried) and *fažol*, augmented by daily seafood specials.

Re di Mare Špinut. In the marina on the north side of the Marjan peninsula, and handy if you're on the way back from Bene beach. It does upmarket grills and a good range of reasonable pizzas, and there are views of Mount Kozjak on other side of the bay.

Stellon Bačvice. Chic but not overpriced pizza and pasta restaurant in the pavilion above Bačvice beach. A safe bet for vegetarians, with some satisfying main courses (try the penne with broccoli) and good salads.

Šumica Put Firula 6 (☎021/389-897). Long-established rendezvous for the smart set just east of Bačvice beach, with a big outdoor terrace and a formal, starched-napkin interior. They serve excellent seafood and a full range of shellfish, as well as succulent schnitzel-style meals typical of inland Croatia. Higher-than-average prices, but deservedly so.

Drinking

There are plenty of **pavement cafés** along the waterfront and around the Peristyle for daytime and evening drinking. The Riva is the classic venue for hanging out and people-watching; there's not much to choose between the numerous cafés along it, although those at its western end are slightly more posey and expensive than those to the east. From the Riva, evening crowds flow into the old town, where crumbling palaces and squares provide the perfect ambience for late-night supping. More café-bars can be found in the pavilion at Bačvice beach, and in the next two bays along the coastal path to the east.

Cafés and bars

Equador Bačvice. Snazzy latin-themed bar in the pavilion above Bačvice beach, with deep, comfy chairs and a range of cocktails, nibbles and salads.

Getto Dosud 10. Arty bar occupying a quiet courtyard in the palace area.

Jazz III Vuškovićeva. Dimly lit, relaxing drinking haunt in the northwest quarter of the palace, attracting a predominantly laid-back arty crowd. Admire the medieval brickwork in the cosy inner sanctum, or choose a table in the glass-enclosed front yard. Might close for a month or two during summer.

Pivnica Klara Kavanjinova 5. A pub-like pair of rooms which can get packed and raucous on Fridays and Saturdays, although you can always cool off in the beer garden-style courtyard. It's a little way north of the old town: head up Zrinsko-Frankopanska and look out for Kavanjinova on the right.

Planet Jazz Grgura Ninskog. Tightly-packed L-shaped bar with outdoor seating in a time-weathered courtyard, immediately northeast of the Peristyle, attracting a young-ish cross section of Split society.

Porta Majstora Jurja. Cosy café-bar with jazzy music, decent cocktails, and outdoor seating crammed into an atmospheric old-town alleyway.

Puls, Puls 2 & Song Mihovilova Širina. This small square just behind the Riva is crowded with the tables of these three popular and vibrant café-bars – the place to be on warm summer weekends, if you can find a space.

Star Rock Café Marmontova. Brash, roomy bar decked out in rock memorabilia in *Hard Rock Café* style. A magnet for young wannabes.

Nightlife and entertainment

There are several **discos** offering a diet of commercial techno: *Night Café Metropolis*, in the Koteks shopping centre east of the centre on Osječka, and

Shakespeare, just east of Bačvice beach at Uvala Zente 3, being the best – beware that they may close for long periods during July and August, when most local clubbers leave town for the islands. *Obojena Svjetlost*, on the beach beneath the Meštrović gallery, is an animated open-air disco-bar that stays open until the early hours in summer and often stages live Croatian rock-pop.

Top-class **drama**, **classical music** and **opera** is staged at the prestigious Croatian National Theatre (Hrvatsko narodno kazalište, or HNK), Trg Gaje Bulata 1 (☏021/585-999, ⓦwww.hnk-split.hr). The **Split Summer Festival** (Splitsko ljeto; mid-July to mid-Aug; details and tickets from the HNK) hosts a spate of cultural events – including top-quality theatre, a lot of classical music and at least one opera – many of which take place on outdoor stages in the Peristyle and other old-town squares. Slightly more subcultural tastes are catered for during the **Festival of Creative Disorder** (Festival kreativnog nereda; mid-Aug), which brings together various counter-cultural events and happenings. One longer-established alternative event is the **Festival of New Film and Video** (Festival novog filma i videa; late Sept to early Oct), featuring independent short films from Croatia and full-length foreign releases. The prime venue for this is Kinoteka Zlatna Vrata **cinema**, Dioklecijanova 7 (☏021/361-255), which also has a regular programme of art-house and cult films. Mainstream movies are shown at the Marjan cinema on Trg republike (☏021/347-838).

There are numerous open-air pop concerts in summer, when both the Prokurative and the inner courtyard of **Tvrđava Gripe** (an old Venetian fortification 1km east of the centre) are pressed into service as venues. Also look out for occasional gigs, events and exhibitions at the monstrous concrete **Youth Centre** (Dom omladine) on Savska, just northeast of Tvrđava Gripe.

The best way to find out **what's on** is to keep an eye out for posters or consult the back pages of local newspaper *Slobodna Dalmacija* – good for serious culture and cinema listings, though not so well informed about pop or alternative happenings.

Listings

Airlines Adria, Obala kneza Domagoja bb ☏021/338-445; Croatia Airlines, Riva 9 ☏021/362-997.
Airport enquiries ☏021/203-506.
Banks Hypo Banka, Peristil (Mon–Fri 8am–8pm, Sat 8am–noon); Splitska banka, Sinjska 2 (Mon–Fri 7.30am–8.30pm, Sat 8am–noon); Zagrebačka Banka, Riva 10 (Mon–Fri 7.30am–7pm, Sat 8am–noon). All the above have ATMs outside.
Bookshops A small selection of English-language paperbacks can be found at Algoritam, Bajamontijeva, or at Morpurgo, Narodni trg.
Car rental Avis, airport ☏021/895-320, ⓦwww.avis.hr; Budget, Obala kneza Branimira 8 ☏021/399-214; Hertz, Tomića stine 9 ☏021/360-455.
Consulates Italy, Riva 10, 2nd floor ☏021/348-155; UK, Riva 10, 3rd floor ☏021/341-464.
Hospital Spinčićeva 1 (☏021/556-111).
Internet access Games and Books, Obala kneza Domagoja 1; Internet Caffe, Grgura Ninskog 9 (Mon–Sat 10am–10pm); Issa, Dobrić 12; Mriža,

Kružićeva 3 (Mon–Sat 9am–9pm, Sun 9am–2pm).
Left luggage At the bus station (daily 6am–10pm) and the train station (daily 6–10.30am, 11am–5pm, 5.30–10pm).
Pharmacy Dobri, Gundulićeva 52, just south of the suburban bus station, is open 24hr.
Police Trg hrvatske bratske zajednice 9 (☏021/307-022), west of the suburban bus station.
Post office Northwest of Diocletian's Palace at Kralja Tomislava 7 (Mon–Sat 7am–9pm) and southeast of the palace at Obala kneza Domagoja 3 (daily 7am–9pm).
Taxis There are taxi ranks at the eastern and western ends of the Riva, or ring ☏970.
Travel agencies Atlas, Nepotova 4 (☏021/355-833, ⓦwww.atlas.hr), east of the Golden Gate, organizes yacht charter, rafting on the River Cetina, and trips to Međugorje, as well as handling international airline tickets. Split Tours, Obala Lazareta 3 (☏021/885-856), at the eastern end of the Riva, offers canyoning trips on the Cetina alongside other local excursions.
Telephones At the post office.

Inland from Split

The most direct route between mid-Dalmatia, the Plitvice lakes and Zagreb heads inland from Split towards the **Zagora**, a highland area which stretches from the mountain ridge just behind the coast to the Hercegovinian border further east. A rocky, scrub-covered plateau, scattered with villages eking a living from thin and unproductive soil, the Zagora is economically poorer than the coastal strip, and many of its inhabitants (the "Vlaji" of Split lore – see box on p.293) have decamped to seek work in the big city nearby.

Most people breeze through the area en route for northern Croatia, although there's a smattering of worthwhile sights. The Roman city of **Salona** and the medieval fortress of **Klis** are only a few kilometres outside Split, and easily reached on local buses while, slightly further afield, the Marian pilgrimage centre of **Sinj** can also be visited on hourly buses from the city.

Salona

Five kilometres inland from Split, at the foot of the mountains which divide the coastal plain from the Zagora, is the sprawling dormitory suburb of Solin, a characterless modern town which has grown up beside the ruins of **SALONA**, erstwhile capital of Roman Dalmatia and probable birthplace of Diocletian. The town once boasted a population of around 60,000 and was an important centre of Christianity long before Constantine legalized the religion throughout the empire – prominent leaders of the faith (future saints Domnius and Anastasius among them) were famously put to death here by Diocletian in 304. It was later the seat of a powerful Byzantine bishopric until 614, when the town was comprehensively sacked by a combined force of Slavs and Avars, and the local population moved off to settle in what would subsequently become Split.

Located on the northwestern fringe of Solin, the **ruins of Salona** (June–Sept Mon–Fri 7am–7pm, Sat 10am–7pm, Sun 4–7pm; Oct–May Mon–Fri 8am–3pm; 10Kn) stretch across a hillside just above the main road to Kaštela and Trogir. Bus #1 (Mon–Fri every 20–30min, Sun every hr) from Trg Gaje Bulata in central Split passes the main entrance to the ruins. En route you'll see stretches of the **aqueduct** built by Diocletian to bring fresh water to his palace from the hills to the north – numerous refurbishments later, it's still very much in use. Salona itself was extensively excavated at the end of the nineteenth century, and although most movable remains were packed off to museums years ago there's still a great deal to see. Pretty much an overgrown meadow scattered with weathered stones, the location is a peaceful and evocative one, giving views to the hazy industrial suburbs across the bay.

The part of the site closest to the entrance is **Manastirine**, an early necropolis for Christian martyrs piled high with sarcophagi around the impressive ruins of a fifth-century basilica. Within its walls are the graves of Domnius and his nephew Primus, Salona's first bishop. Nearby, the former summer villa of Don Frane Bulić (the doyen of Croatian archeology, who spent the first half of the twentieth century digging here) incorporates various Roman fragments, including gravestones, in its walls. Below Manastirine, the path leads along a stretch of old city wall as it zigzags across scrubby fields through a confusion of necropoli and ruined basilicas – most complete of which is Salona's fifth-century **cathedral**. Downhill to the south, the arched form of the first-century **Porta Caesarea** is easily identified, marking the boundary between the oldest quarters of Salona (to the west) and the so-called Urbs Nova ("New Town") to the east. What was once Salona's main east–west street heads through the gate, disappearing into modern vineyards and olive groves. Sticking to the wall-top path instead takes you westwards, past another early Christian basilica before arriving at the second-century **amphitheatre**. A reasonably well-preserved structure, it originally seated around 18,000 spectators and is probably the most extensive relic on the site – the grassy central space is now used to graze goats. From here you can descend to the busy Split–Zadar highway and catch a bus back to town (there's a stop served by the #37 Split–Trogir service 100m to the right), or return the way you came.

Klis

The town of **KLIS** grew up around a strategic mountain pass on the trade routes linking the coast with the hinterland of the Zagora. The steep rock pinnacle around which the modern town huddles was first fortified by the Romans before being taken over by the expanding medieval kingdom of the Croats; kings Mislav (835–45) and Trpimir (845–64) both based their courts here. Klis remained in Hungaro-Croatian hands until the sixteenth century, when the Turks, already in command of Bosnia, began pushing towards the coast. Commanded by Captain **Petar Kružić**, who paid for the Trsat staircase in Rijeka (see p.199), Klis withstood sieges in 1526 and 1536, but finally succumbed to Ottoman attack in 1537, when attempts to relieve the citadel ended in farce. Badly drilled reinforcements sent by the Habsburgs fled in fear from the Turks, and their attempts to re-board their boats in Solin bay caused many vessels to sink. Kružić himself – who had left the fortress to make contact with the hapless reinforcements – was captured and executed: the sight of his head on a stick was too much for Klis's remaining defenders, who gave up the fortress in return for safe passage north, where they resumed the struggle from the security of Senj (see box on p.227).

The present-day town straggles up the hillside beneath the fortress and is divided into three parts: **Klis-Varoš**, on the main road below the fortress; **Klis-Grlo**, at the top of the hill where the Drniš and Sinj roads part company; and **Klis-Megdan**, off to one side, where you'll find the main gate to the site (June–Sept daily 9am–7pm; Oct–May Sat–Sun 9am–5pm; 10Kn). The **fortress** (*tvrđava*) is a remarkably complete structure, with three long, rectangular defensive lines surrounding a central strongpoint, the Položaj maggiore ("Grand Position", a mixed Croatian–Italian term dating from the time when Leonardo Foscolo captured the fortress for the Venetians in 1648), at its eastern, highest end. You can't see inside many of the buildings apart for one dusty old stone chapel, but there are lots of grassy bastions to scramble around on and impressive views of the coast, with the marching tower blocks and busy arterial roads of suburban Split sprawling across the plain below, and the islands of Šolta and Brač in the distance.

Driving to Klis, take the old road which heads inland from Solin (rather than the new dual carriageway which skirts Klis to the east), go through the tunnel that separates Klis-Varoš from Klis-Grlo, and turn left when you see the sign for the *tvrđava*. **Buses** #34 and #36 go from Split to Klis-Megdan, but they're relatively infrequent, so it may be better to catch any Sinj bus, get off opposite the *Castel* café in Klis-Varoš, and walk up the hill via a network of steep zigzagging alleyways (15min). There's an enthusiastic **tourist office** (⊕021/240-578) behind the *Belfast* **café**, on the square just below the fortress entrance, but staff shortages ensure that it's only sporadically open in summer. Klis is famous for the three **restaurants** by the road junction in Klis-Grlo selling spit-roast lamb (*janjetina na ražnju*), each of which advertises its wares by having a carcass or two slowly revolving over open fires by the roadside. Portions are priced by the kilogram and are invariably served with spring onion (*kapulica*).

North to Sinj

From Klis, the road forges across the stony uplands of the Dalmatinska Zagora towards Sinj, 20km further on. It's a route traversed by frequent buses from Split, although you'll need your own transport to make the worthwhile side-trip to the **Vranjača Cave** (Špilja Vranjača; Easter–Oct daily 9am–5pm; ask at the nearby post office if there's no caretaker at the entrance; 15Kn), along a side-road to the east. To get there turn right about 3km beyond Klis and head through the village of **Dugopolje** ("Long Field", so named because it's in a typical *polje*, or fertile depression, common to karstic areas) towards a group of hamlets known collectively as Kotlenice. In the first of these, **VLADOVIĆI**, there's a small car park from which a gravel track leads to the cave. Discovered by the grandfather of the cave's current caretaker and guide, the cave is explored via a steep stairway which descends some 100m down into a chamber about 150m long, filled with honey-brown stalactites and stalagmites. The 65-million-year-old formations grow at a rate of 1mm every thirty-five years and include fluted limestone curtains and forms resembling the bunched heads of cauliflowers.

Sinj and beyond

Back on the Split–Sinj route, the road crosses infertile heath before descending into **SINJ**, a provincial market centre laid out in a bowl between the hills. It's famous locally for the **Sinjska gospa** (Our Lady of Sinj), a supposedly miraculous image of the Virgin dating from around 1500 which hangs in the local parish church (on the last altar on the left-hand side as you enter). It's claimed that prayers to the Sinjska gospa saved the town on Ascension Day 1715, when the locals drove away a superior force of Ottoman Turks – it still draws pilgrims from all over Dalmatia, and is paraded through the town every year on August 15.

Victory over the Turks is also celebrated annually by the **Sinjska alka** (usually the first weekend of August) – a sort of medieval joust in which contestants, clad in eighteenth-century cavalry costume, gallop down a steeply sloping street at the southern end of town, and attempt to thread their lances through a ring dangled from a rope. First recorded in 1715, the Alka is one of the few remaining examples of the equine contests which once took place in all the Adriatic towns and cities, and its survival in Sinj is seen as a powerful symbol of regional identity by the locals. Membership of the Alkarsko Društvo, the association of riders allowed to take part in the Alka, is still seen as a badge of knightly prowess in a part of the country where traditional patriarchal values still rule. Indeed the Alka has in recent years become a focus for nationalist groups disillusioned with a Croatia run by centre-left parties. In 2001 the event was taken over by right-wing supporters of alleged Croatian war criminal Mirko Norac (who himself hails from the local village of Otok), prompting President Mešić to withdraw state support for the Alka in 2002. Politics apart, however, it remains an authentic expression of living folklore, a riotous, boozy business involving all the surrounding villages and taking up the whole day in a blaze of colour, costume and procession. Tickets for the main spectator stand are hard to get hold of (costing from 70Kn to 150Kn, they usually go on sale in travel agents in Split and Makarska a few weeks before the contest), but the atmosphere is worth savouring whether you get a grandstand view or not. More details can be had from the small **tourist office** (Mon–Fri 9am–3pm; ☏021/826-352) next to the modern and central *Alkar*

△ Šibenik cathedral

hotel (☎021/824-474 or 824-488, ☏824-505; ❸), which has neat, recently refurbished en-suite rooms.

Beyond Sinj, the main road heads northwest towards Knin (see p.283), while an alternative route heads southeast towards the small town of Trilj (see p.355), a useful base for exploring the landscapes around the River Cetina (p.354).

Šolta

Though one of the closest islands to Split, **ŠOLTA** can't compare with neighbours Brač and Hvar in terms of attractions or holiday facilities. Indeed it's the lack of any meaningful mass tourist industry that gives the place its charm. The island was used by the Romans to dispose of political exiles, and later by the Christian church to banish heretics, and on the face of it seems to have changed very little since either era. A fertile island of red soil, with several compact, hive-like villages and an agricultural economy that's somewhat gone to seed, it's more a place for quiet escape than high-level tourism.

About five ferries and two catamarans arrive daily from Split at **ROGAČ**, which is little more than a dock and a bar, although there's a small **tourist office** (July & Aug Mon–Sat 8–10am & 3–5pm, Sun 8–10pm & 6–8pm) by the quayside which can fix up rooms (❶). Ferries are met by two buses, one heading east towards Maslinica, the other west to Stomorska. Both go through **Grohote**, perched on a hill overlooking the harbour and the largest settlement on Šolta – a pleasant, peaceful village whose half-ruined houses are a monument to rural depopulation.

Seven kilometres to the west, **MASLINICA** is the perfect antidote to the more commercialized places up and down the coast, an attractively becalmed fishing village of green-shuttered stone houses sporting colourful wallflowers and windowboxes – all squeezed into a narrow bay. There are a few concrete bathing areas, private **rooms** (❶) from the **tourist office** on the front (mid- to end June & early to mid-Sept daily 8–10am & 7–8pm; July & Aug daily 8am–8pm), and a **restaurant**, the *Avlija*, housed in a fortified eighteenth-century villa which once functioned as a hotel.

East of Rogač, the bus passes through the small tourist complex of **NEČUJAM**, a pine-shaded **bungalow settlement** (☎021/650-149, ⓦwww.soltaht.hr; ❸) which stretches away from a crescent-shaped shingle beach. Hard by the bus stop, there's a **tourist office** (July & Aug daily 8–11.30am) housed in a rickety stone house where Renaissance man of letters **Marko Marulić** stayed as a guest while penning his magnum opus *Judita*,

Five kilometres further east lies the village of **Stomorska**, a slightly less cosy version of Maslinica; another narrow harbour with a **tourist office** (July & Aug 8am–noon & 5–7pm) doling out **rooms** (❶); a **campsite** squeezed into a private garden near the village entrance; and a couple of pizzerias.

Brač

The third largest of Croatia's Adriatic islands, **BRAČ** is the nearest of the major islands to Split, and is correspondingly busy in season. The south coast fishing village of **Bol**, with its spectacular beach, is the main attraction, although the beaches at **Supetar** (where ferries from Split arrive) on the north coast are no mean substitute. Away from the coast, the island's starkly beautiful interior has undoubted allure, its scrub-covered karst uplands dotted with fertile depressions containing vines, olives and orange trees, or by the great man-made piles of limestone that characterize the Dalmatian islands, built up over centuries by smallholders clearing a place in which to grow crops.

Brač is famous for its stone, and was until the development of the tourist trade dependent on the export of its milk-white **marble**, which was used in Berlin's Reichstag, the high altar of Liverpool's Catholic cathedral, the White House in Washington and, of course, Diocletian's Palace in Split. The island's other major source of wealth was the grape harvest, though the *phylloxera* (vine lice) epidemics of the late nineteenth and early twentieth centuries forced many winemakers to emigrate. Even today, the signs of this depopulation are all around in the tumbledown houses and overgrown fields of the interior.

Bol is served by **flights** from Zagreb between April and September inclusive. There are several **ferries** a day from Split to Supetar, plus **catamarans** from Split to Bol and to Milna, on the western side of the island, daily between mid-June and mid-September; there's also a ferry from Makarska on the mainland to Sumartin on the eastern tip of the Brač, although there are only two or three connecting buses from here to Supetar daily. Supetar is the main hub of the island **bus** network, with frequent departures southwest to Milna, east to Pučišća, and south to Bol. If you're travelling on **to Hvar**, note that some excursion operators in Bol offer trips there (they'll be chalked up on signboards in the harbour), which may be more convenient than going all the way back to Split to pick up a regular ferry.

Supetar

Despite being the largest town on the island, **SUPETAR** is a sleepy place onto which package tourism has been painlessly grafted. Something of an old town survives, its mottled, rust-brown stone houses grouped around a horseshoe-shaped harbour, from where a line of modern hotels leads west along a shallow, pebble-fringed bay. The small **town museum** (Gradski muzej; daily 10am–noon & 7–11pm; 10Kn), next to the Baroque parish church, is a mundane affair, and you'd do best to head out to the **beaches** west of town, long stretches of pebble around a very shallow bay.

Standing on a peninsula screened by dark cypresses just beyond the beaches, the **town cemetery** is as much a sculpture park as a burial site, thanks in large part to **Ivan Rendić** (1849–1932), whose eclectic amalgam of Egyptian, Classical and Byzantine styles can be seen on many of the family tombs here.

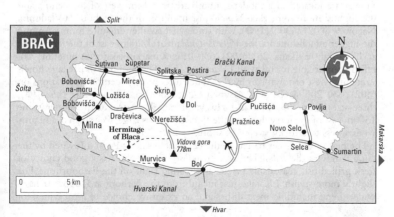

Rendić was one of the leading Croatian sculptors at the turn of the twentieth century and, as a native of Supetar, was repeatedly commissioned by wealthy families to design funerary monuments here, giving the cemetery a uniquely unified sculptural style. The first tomb, belonging to the Čulić family, is immediately inside the gate – a dome supported by four squat pillars and bursting with eccentric knobbly accretions which seems almost Aztec in inspiration. More tombs lie east of here in the lower part of the cemetery, where the cupola-crowned Rendić family mausoleum raises a sarcophagus to the skies on solid pillars in a manner reminiscent of Lycian tombs in southern Turkey.

Ironically, Rendić was passed over when the cemetery's grandest sepulchural monument, the **Petrinović Mausoleum**, was commissioned. Ivan Meštrović turned down the job in protest at the way in which Rendić had been snubbed, and the task eventually fell to Meštrović's contemporary **Toma Rosandić**. The resulting structure is a beautiful piece of sepulchral art: a neo-Byzantine dome pokes above the trees, topped by a kneeling angel, his long wings spearing skywards. The four external pillars carry reliefs of mourners, some playing musical instruments, others bearing flowers. Behind the mausoleum is a well-head, also by Rosandić, bearing a relief of bare-backed strongmen gripping rams by their horns.

The clear waters around Supetar are perfect for **diving**. The Dive Center Kaktus (T & F 021/630-421) in the *Kaktus Hotel* complex – one of the packagey places west of town – rents out gear and arranges crash courses from around 220Kn.

Practicalities

Ferries from Split arrive at the modern quay just off Supetar's old harbour, roughly opposite the **bus station**. In between lies the **tourist office** at Porat 1 (June & Sept daily 9am–4pm; July & Aug daily 8am–10pm; Oct–May Mon–Fri 9am–1pm; T & F 021/630-551, W www.supetar.hr), which is well supplied with tourist bumph. There are several places renting out **bikes**, including M&B just outside the bus station.

The best places to try for private **rooms** (❶) and **apartments** (❷) are Atlas (Mon–Sat 8am–2pm & 3–10pm, Sun 8am–noon & 6–9pm; T 021/631-105, F 631-088) and Brač Tours, Kala bb (Mon–Sat 9am–9pm, Sun 9am–noon & 6–9pm; T 021/757-316 or 757-317, E bractours@hi.hinet.hr), both on the harbourfront. Best of the small family-run **hotels** are the *Palute*, at Put pašika 16 (T 021/631-541; ❸), a friendly bed and breakfast whose simple rooms with shower are located in a modern suburban street 1km west of the centre, and the slightly more upmarket *Mandić*, just uphill from the harbour at Vladimira Nazora 9 (T 021/630 911; ❹), with somewhat swisher en-suite rooms. Among the bigger establishments, the *Villa Britanida* **hotel**, 200m east of the ferry dock at Hrvatskih velikana 26 (T 021/630-017, E markitojaksic@st.hinet.hr; ❹), offers comfortable rooms with TV and air-con. There's a line of package hotels stretching west of town run by the Supetrus company (central reservations on T 021/630 200, F 631 344, E svpetrvs@st.hinet.hr): the two-star *Palma* (❹), three-star *Kaktus* (❺), and all-inclusive *Adria* (❼). **Autocamp** *Supetar*, some 1500m east of the ferry dock on the Pučišća road, is large, well shaded, and provides access to a rocky stretch of shore.

The best of the places **to eat** in the centre is *Palute*, at Porat 4 (owned by the same family as the *Palute* bed and breakfast), which also has a good choice of fresh grilled fish, reasonable prices, and seating right on the harbourfront. The slightly more stylish *Vinotoka*, just inland from the harbour at Dobova 6, has a wider menu including meat dishes and an extensive choice of local wines; for steaks and schnitzel, the restaurant of the *Villa Britanida* is the best place to go. Most expensive is the *Jastog*, in the residential streets west of town at Josipa Jelačića 9, which excels in the preparation of lobster and shellfish.

As far as **drinking** is concerned, *Barbara*, on the eastern side of the harbour near the tourist office, is the coffee-supping venue of choice for locals and visitors alike, while *Ben Quick*, west of the harbour on Put Vele Luke, attracts a wide range of night-time tipplers with its relaxing outdoor terrace and list of cocktails. Follow Put Vele Luke further uphill to find a brace of bars belting out loud music to a youngish crowd.

West from Supetar

Fifteen minutes west of Supetar, the village of **SUTIVAN** straggles along the shore behind its rocky beach. Almost all the buildings here are made out of the local marble and, although there are no specific features of interest, it's a pretty enough little settlement of narrow alleys and ancient houses. The **tourist office** (July–Sept 7am–10pm; ☎021/638-357), near the bus stop, can arrange accommodation in private rooms (❶).

The road to the southwest of Sutivan heads inland through **Ložišća**, a picturesque settlement spread across a steep ravine, with narrow, cobbled alleys hugging the hillside. Thrusting up from the valley floor is a parish church belltower, built in 1920 and sporting a fanciful, onion-domed belfry by Rendić. Beyond here the road crosses the island's empty uplands before twisting down to the sea at **MILNA**. The capital of a short-lived Russian protectorate over Brač during the Napoleonic wars, Milna is a tiny, neat and unremarkable port that curves round one of the island's many deep bays. The old village climbs uphill from the shore, a pleasant enough ensemble of narrow lanes and stone houses on either side of an eighteenth-century parish church and an adjacent nineteenth-century loggia. Behind the loggia looms an ancient crumbling house that's curiously known as *Anglešćina* after a local myth connecting its construction with an English crusader. All in all it's a relaxing little place, and the **tourist office** (June & Sept Mon–Sat 8am–1pm & 3–8pm, Sun 8am–noon & 4–8pm; July & Aug daily 8am–10pm; ☎021/636-233, @tzo -milna@st.tel.hr) in the main square has plenty of **rooms** (❶) and **apartments** (❷) if you want to stay. The Riva has a sprinkling of **cafés**, and you can **eat** local specialities such as roast lamb and baked octopus at *Konoba Dupini*, hidden away in a narrow street just behind the harbour.

East from Supetar

Three buses daily make the short detour inland from Supetar to the village of **ŠKRIP**, the oldest continually inhabited settlement on Brač. Founded by the Illyrians, it's now a sleepy nest of stone houses with heavy stone roof tiles that seem in permanent danger of slipping off, while its hilltop position affords views towards the terraced ridges of the Mosor massif on the mainland. The eastern end of the village is the oldest bit, with a ruined sixteenth-century castle overlooking a smaller fortified stone residence which now serves as the **Museum of Brač** (Brački muzej; daily 10am–6pm in theory, if not always in practice; 10Kn), displaying a well-preserved Roman relief of Hercules discovered locally, and sundry nineteenth-century agricultural tools. Outside the museum lie the remains of Iron Age walls and a Roman mausoleum, which local legend says contains a wife or daughter of Diocletian.

Škrip is a restful, rustic place **to stay**: the *Konoba Herkules* hotel (☎ & ☎021/350-098; ❷) offers simple but bright rooms in a modern three-storey house built in traditional Brač marble, and also has a **café–restaurant** with cypress-shaded terrace and a delicious menu of fresh seafood and Brač lamb. The sea is a thirty-minute downhill walk from here – either by road to Splitska or by track to Postira, both of which have a few stretches of rocky strand. A better place to swim if you have your own transport is **Lovrečina Bay**, some 7km east of the Škrip turn-off (it's 4km beyond the next settlement along the coast, Postira), where there's a fine shingle beach overlooked by the remains of an early Christian basilica.

Bol and around

Brač's second town, **BOL** has long been the only significant settlement on the island's southern side – an isolated community stranded on the far side of the Vidova gora, the mountain ridge which overlooks this stretch of coast. In the seventh century, its isolation attracted Romans fleeing the Croat invasion, but over the following centuries Bol was attacked repeatedly by pirates, Saracens, Turks and just about anybody else who happened to be passing. Nowadays there's no denying the beauty of Bol's setting, or the charm of its old stone houses. The problem is that it's very small, and is easily swamped by the influx of tourists that grows yearly. But if you can go out of season, or are immune to crowds, it's well worth the trip.

Bol's main attraction is its beach, **Zlatni rat** (Golden Cape), which lies to the west of the centre along the wooded shoreline. Composed of fine shingle and backed by pines, the cape juts out into the sea like an extended finger, changing shape slightly from one year to the next according to the action of seasonal winds. It lies a little over 2km west of the harbour, although the walk there – along a tree-lined promenade – is part of the attraction. With a series of large hotels positioned behind the promenade, the cape can get crowded during summer, but the presence of extra beach space on the approach to the cape, and rockier coves beyond it, ensures that there's enough room for everyone. Naturism is tolerated on the far side of the cape, and in the coves beyond.

Bol itself isn't much more than a seafront backed by a couple of rows of old houses, although newer apartment blocks are continually sprouting up on the hillside behind. The main attraction along the seafront is the **Branislav Dešković Gallery**, housed in a former Renaissance town house, which contains a good selection of twentieth-century Croatian art. Most big names get a look in – sculptor Ivan Meštrović, the religiously inspired expressionist Ivan Dulčić and contemporary painter Edo Murtić among them. Further east lies the late fifteenth-century **Dominican monastery** (Dominikanski samostan; daily 10am–noon & 5–9pm; 10Kn), dramatically located high on the promontory just beyond Bol's centre. Its **museum** holds crumbling amphorae, ancient Greek coins from Hvar and Vis, Cretan icons and an imposing Tintoretto *Madonna with Child* from 1563 among its small collection. An archway leads through the accommodation block to the superbly maintained monastery gardens overlooking the sea.

Practicalities

Most flights into Brač **airport**, 15km northeast of Bol, are met by a minibus into town; otherwise a taxi will set you back 150–200Kn. Buses from Supetar stop just west of Bol's harbour, at the far end of which stands the **tourist office** (June–Aug daily 8.30am–10pm; Sept–May Mon–Fri 8.30am–3pm; ☎021/635-638, ☏635-972, ⓦwww.bol.hr), which has free leaflets, maps of the island (useful if you're walking to Blaca; see p.322), and also doubles as an Internet café.

There are a couple of **windsurfing** centres on the shore west of town, on the way to Zlatni rat, offering board rental (about 250Kn per day) and a range of courses (about 600Kn for eight hours). Reputable outfits include Big Blue, in front of the *Hotel Borak* (Ⓦwww.big-blue-sport.hr), and Orca, a little further west on the way to Zlatni rat (Ⓣ021/635-650, Ⓦwww.orca-sport.com). Next to Orca, Diving Centre Bol (Ⓣ021/635-367, Ⓦwww.nautic -center.bol.com) organizes **scuba-diving** courses from around 2000Kn, and rents out gear. Boltours (see below) and Big Blue also rent out **mountain bikes** (from 70Kn/day) and there are plenty of smaller outfits on the path to Zlatni rat renting out cheaper bicycles (from 60Kn/day) and scooters (260/360Kn a day).

Accommodation
The best of the **hotels** is the *Kaštil*, housed in a historic building right on the waterfront at Frane Radića 1 (Ⓣ021/635-995, Ⓦwww.kastil.hr; ❻), and featuring tastefully modernized en-suite rooms with TV and air-con – all rooms come with a sea view. The *Villa Giardino*, just uphill from the centre at Novi Put 2 (Ⓣ021/635-286; ❺), is a cosy place with, as the name suggests, a soothing garden out the back, but it's booked up well in advance during July and August. There's a trio of three-star package hotels nestling among the pines on the way to Zlatni rat, all run by the Zlatni Rat company (Ⓣ021/635-288, Ⓦwww.zlatni-rat.hr); from east to west, these are the *Borak* (❼), *Elaphusa* (❻) and *Bonaca* (❼), all recently refurbished and offering good access to the beach. There are several **campsites** in the new part of town uphill from the centre: both *Ranč* (Ⓣ021/635-635) and the adjacent *Meteor* (Ⓣ021/635-630) are pleasantly situated in olive groves on Hrvatskih domobrana, well signed from the main road into town.

Private **rooms** (❷) and **apartments** (❸) can be obtained from Boltours, 100m west of the bus stop at Vladimira Nazora 18 (mid-April to mid-Oct daily 8.30am–9pm with possible afternoon break; Ⓣ021/635-693 or 635-694, Ⓕ635-695, Ⓦwww.boltours.com), or from Adria, 100m further west at Vladimira Nazora 28 (daily 8am–9pm; Ⓣ021/635-966, Ⓕ635-977, Ⓔadria -tours-bol@st.tel.hr).

Eating, drinking and nightlife
Given that so many guests have half-board arrangements in their hotels, it's not surprising that central Bol has a relatively meagre roster of places **to eat**. *Konoba Gušt*, above the square at Frane Radića 14, has a wide range of fresh fish, traditional Dalmatian dishes (such as a reasonable *pašticada*), and a cosy interior with agricultural implements and old photographs hanging from the wall. *Mlin*, midway between the harbour and the Dominican monastery on A. Rabadana, is another rustically decorated place, but this time with a big olive-shaded terrace overlooking the sea – tasty eats include *brodet* (spicy fish soup), seafood risottos and all manner of grilled mussels. *Mali Raj*, set in a garden just beyond Zlatni rat, is the place to go for grilled meats.

For **drinking**, there are several cafés and ice-cream parlours along the front: *Café Loža*, at the eastern end near the tourist office, is the perfect place to observe goings-on in the port, with seating built into the curving harbour wall. In the evenings you can lounge around in wicker sofas sipping drinks at *Varadero* at the western end of the harbour, or peruse the impressive list of cocktails at *Papaya*, just uphill on Frane Radića.

If you don't fancy the easy-listening crooners who seem to be on permanent duty in Bol's hotels, the best **nightlife** on offer is at *Pivnica Moby Dick*, a late-opening bar just above the tourist office, featuring DJ-driven sounds and frequent rock-pop performances, or at *Faces* **disco**, a circular concrete structure at the northern entrance to the town owned by footballer Igor Štimac – Croatian pop stars perform here over the summer.

Around Bol

Looming over Zlatni rat to the north is the 778-metre peak of **Vidova gora**, the highest point on any Adriatic island. It's accessible via an asphalt road which leaves the Supetar–Bol road just south of the village of Nerežišća, and there's also a marked walking trail (2hr each way) from the centre of Bol, which heads uphill about 100m beyond the *Faces* discotheque. There's a small tavern at the summit which sometimes serves roast lamb during summer, but most people come simply to savour the view, encompassing Zlatni rat and Bol down to the left, with the islands of Vis and Hvar visible further out.

Tucked away at the head of a valley on the western flanks of the Vidova gora is the **Hermitage of Blaca** (Pustinja Blaca; Tues–Sun 8am–5pm, though check in the tourist office at Bol or Supetar as times can vary; 20Kn), about 12km out of Bol. You can walk there by following the road (which later degenerates into a track) west from Bol, passing the village of Murvica before heading inland at Blaca bay. The route is easy to follow and takes about three hours each way – a worthwhile but unshaded walk along a rugged hillside with the sea far below. You can cut out some of the effort by taking a boat trip (advertised in Bol harbour in high season) to Blaca bay and continuing from there. If you're driving, take the turn-off for Vidova gora midway between Supetar and Bol, then turn right after about 2km onto the signed gravel track for Blaca (just about passable for cars, but rough on the suspension). From the end of the track, walk along the path which heads downhill past deserted hamlets before arriving at the monastery after about forty minutes.

The hermitage was founded in 1588 by monks fleeing the Turks; the last resident – Niko Miličević, an enthusiastic astronomer who left all sorts of bits and bobs, including an assortment of old clocks and a stock of lithographs by Poussin – occupied the hermitage in the 1930s. You can also look around the ascetic living quarters and the kitchen, with its forest of blackened iron utensils surrounding an open hearth. But the principal attraction is the setting, with the simple buildings hugging the sides of a narrow, scrub-covered ravine. Islanders from all over Brač attend the **pilgrimage** to Blaca on the first weekend after Assumption (Aug 15).

Hvar

HVAR is one of the most hyped of all the Croatian islands. People talk of its verdant colour, fragrant air and mild climate, and at one time local hoteliers even had enough faith in the weather to offer a money-back guarantee if the temperature ever dropped below zero. And Hvar is undeniably beautiful – a slim, green slice of land punctured by jagged inlets and a steep central ridge streaked with the long grey lines of limestone spoil heaps built up over the centuries by farmers attempting to carve out patches of cultivable land. The island's main crop is lavender, which was introduced in the 1930s and covers the island in a spongy grey-blue cloak every spring, before finding its way onto souvenir stalls across the island.

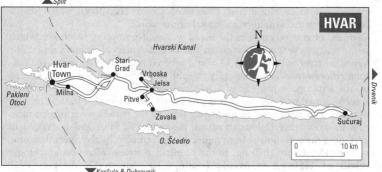

Intensively but tastefully developed as a tourist resort, the island's capital, **Hvar Town**, is one of the Adriatic's most bewitching – and best preserved – historic towns, and is a good base from which to explore the rest of the island, which is fairly low-key in comparison. Buses out of Hvar Town either take the old road across the central ridge, or speed through the recently built tunnel to reach the northern side of the island, where **Stari Grad** and **Vrboska** boast some good beaches, old stone houses and an unhurried, village feel. **Jelsa**, further east, can't quite compete with its two neighbours in terms of rustic charm, but has more accommodation than Vrboska, which is only a forty-minute walk away. East of Jelsa, the island narrows to a long, thin mountainous strip of land that extends all the way to isolated **Sućuraj**, which is linked to the mainland by regular ferries, although there's virtually no public transport between here and the rest of the island.

The daily Split–Vela Luka–Lastovo **ferry** stops at Hvar Town six days a week; on the remaining day (currently Tues), the Split–Vis ferry calls in instead (but note that only foot passengers can get off in Hvar Town). There are also daily **catamarans** to Hvar Town from Split between mid-May and mid-September. The regular Split–Stari Grad ferry is the easiest way of getting a car on and off the island – foot passengers using this service can catch local buses from the quay to the centre of Stari Grad, Hvar Town or Jelsa. The main **coastal ferry** (daily in summer) also stops at Stari Grad, connecting the island with Split and points to Rijeka in the north, Korčula and Dubrovnik to the south. During summer there are also ferries from **Ancona** in Italy to Stari Grad. You can also reach the island on one of several daily ferries from Drvenik (see p.360) on the mainland to Sućuraj – though the poor bus connections mean that this approach is only really of use if you're travelling by car. Lastly, throughout the season there's a daily **catamaran** service from Jelsa to Split via Bol on Brač.

Travelling on from the island, you'll find that queues for car ferries build up fast in summer, so arrive early. Advance reservations can be made at the Jadrolinija office on the quayside in Hvar Town.

Some history

Around 385 BC, the Greeks of Paros in Asia Minor established a colony on Hvar, naming it **Pharos** (present day Stari Grad). After a period of Roman then Byzantine control, the island was thoroughly Slavicized in the eighth century, when it was overrun by the **Narentani**, a Croatian tribe from the Neretva delta. The new arrivals couldn't pronounce the name Pharos, so the place became **Hvar** instead. The settlement nowadays known as Hvar Town began life as a haven for medieval pirates. The Venetians drove them out in 1240, and encouraged the citizens of Stari Grad to relocate to Hvar Town, which hence-forth became the administative capital of the island.

For the next two centuries the island was a self-governing commune which swore fealty to Venetian, Hungarian and Bosnian rulers at different times. The Venetians returned to stay in 1420 and ushered in a period of urban and cultural efflorescence. The aristocracy's wealth still came from the estates located on the fertile plain just east of Stari Grad, but the ascendancy of Hvar Town was confirmed by a rule stipulating that nobles had to spend at least six months of the year there in order to qualify for seats on the island's governing council.

As in most other Dalmatian towns, the nobles of Hvar had succeeded in excluding the commoners from municipal government by the fifteenth century. The most serious challenge to this oligarchical state of affairs came with the **revolt of 1510** led by **Matija Ivanić**, a representative of the non-noble shipowners and merchants who felt that real wealth and power had been denied to them. The revolt got off to a bad start when a priest in Hvar Town claimed that the crucifix on which the plotters had sworn an oath had begun to sweat blood in a divine warning of the violence to come. The townsfolk lost their enthusiasm for the revolt but it took off elsewhere on the island, especially around Vrbanj, Vrboska and Jelsa. Ivanić himself led a raid on Hvar Town, sacking the houses of the nobles and killing many of the occupants, and Hvar's surviving aristocrats fled to the mainland and awaited Venetian intervention.

Venetian emissary Sebastiano Giustignan initially failed to quell the rising. His troops (mostly Croats from the mainland) were an unruly lot, and looted Vrboska before being driven out of the town in August 1512. In control of the bulk of the island for two years, Ivanić led another attack on Hvar Town in August 1514, massacring those noble families who had returned. Fearful that the revolt might spread to other Dalmatian cities, the Venetians this time reacted with swift effectiveness, defeating the rebels and hanging their leaders from the masts of their galleys. Ivanić himself escaped, dying in exile in Rome.

Despite all this, sixteenth-century Hvar went on to become one of the key centres of the Croatian Renaissance, with poets like **Hanibal Lucić** and **Petar Hektorović** (see box on p.331) cultivating intellectual links with Dubrovnik and penning works which were to have a profound influence on future generations. This golden age was interrupted in 1571, when the notorious corsair **Uluz Ali** (see box on p.327) sacked Hvar Town on behalf of the Turks and reduced it to smouldering rubble. Rebuilt from scratch, the town soon reassumed its importance as an entrepot on the east–west trade routes. Later, the movement of trade to the west and the arrival of steamships becalmed Hvar Town, which drifted into quiet obscurity until the tourists arrived in the late nineteenth century – largely due to the efforts of the Hvar Hygienic Society, founded in 1868 by locals eager to promote the island as a health retreat. The first ever guide book to the town, published in Vienna in 1903, promoted it as "Austria's Madeira", and it has been one of Dalmatia's most stylish resorts ever since.

Hvar Town

The best view of **HVAR TOWN** is from the sea, with its grainy-white and brown scatter of buildings following the contours of the bay, and the green splashes of palms and pines pushing into every crack and cranny. The harbour is alive with a constant hum of activity, whether it be the Rijeka ferry lumbering into port, catamarans buzzing insect-like around the bay, or tiny water taxis ferrying people to bathe on the nearby Pakleni islands. Once you're on terra firma, central Hvar reveals itself as a medieval town full of pedestrianized alleys overlooked by ancient stone houses, providing an elegant backdrop to the main leisure activity: lounging around in cafés and watching the crowds as they shuffle round the harbour. After Dubrovnik, Hvar is probably the most fashionable of the Adriatic resorts among the Croats themselves, and there's something of southern France in the chic *korzo* that engulfs the town at dusk.

Arrival and information

Ferries dock on the eastern side of Hvar Town's bay on Obala oslobođenja. From here, it's a couple of hundred metres to the **tourist office** (June & Sept Mon–Sat 8am–1pm & 4–9pm, Sun 10am–noon & 6–8pm; July & Aug daily 8am–2pm & 3–10pm; Oct–May Mon–Sat 8am–1pm; ℡ & 📠021/741-059, 🕸www.hvar.hr), on the corner of the main square, Trg svetog Stjepana. The **bus station** is a few steps east of the main square on Trg M. Miličića, and the **Jadrolinija** office (daily 7am–1pm & 2–9pm) is on the ferry dock, with an ATM just outside. You can surf the Net at Internet Access (daily 9am–midnight) on Ivana Vucetića, one of the narrow stepped streets leading uphill from Obala Oslobođenja. Luka Rent, Dolac (℡021/742-946, 🕸www.lukarent.com) rents out bikes (70Kn/day), boats (300Kn/day) and scooters (300Kn/day). The Jurgovan Diving Centre in front of the *Hotel Delfin* rents out gear, organizes courses for beginners, and also rents out boats and bikes (℡021/742-490, 🕸www.jurgovan.com).

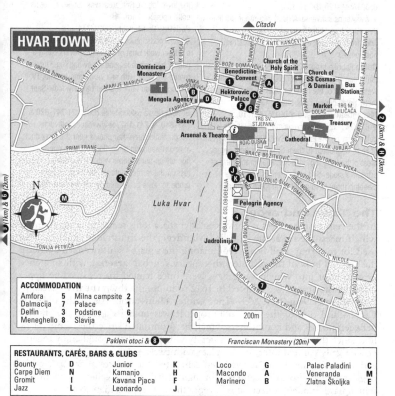

ACCOMMODATION

Amfora	5	Milna campsite	2
Dalmacija	7	Palace	1
Delfin	3	Podstine	6
Meneghello	8	Slavija	4

RESTAURANTS, CAFÉS, BARS & CLUBS

Bounty	D	Junior	K	Loco	G	Palac Paladini	C
Carpe Diem	N	Kamanjo	H	Macondo	A	Veneranda	M
Gromit	I	Kavana Pjaca	F	Marinero	B	Zlatna Školjka	E
Jazz	L	Leonardo	J				

Accommodation

Private **rooms** (**①**) and **apartments** (**③**) are available from the Mengola agency on the waterfront, diagonally opposite the tourist office (Mon–Sat 8.30am–12.30pm & 4.30–10pm, Sun 10am–noon & 6–9pm; ☎021/742-099, ⓦwww.mengola.hr), or from Pelegrin Tours, near the ferry dock on Obala oslobođenja (Mon–Sat 8am–10pm, Sun 6–8pm; ☎ & ⓕ021/742-743, ⓔpelegrini@inet.hr). The nearest **campsite** is in the quiet cove of Milna, 3km east of Hvar Town. Most (but not all) Hvar Town–Stari Grad buses pass along the main road just uphill from the site – ask the driver to set you down.

Hvar Town is oversupplied with characterless package **hotels**, most of which belong to the Sunčani Hvar conglomerate – although there are a couple of characterful, independently run choices outside the centre or on nearby islets. None is particularly cheap unless you travel out of season, and they all fill up quickly in July and August – when you might be forced to consider staying in Stari Grad or Jelsa instead. The hotels listed below are open all year round unless stated otherwise.

Amfora Tonija Petrića bb ☎021/741-202, ⓕ741-711, ⓦwww.suncanihvar.hr. Monstrously proportioned, seven-hundred-bed lump of concrete, west of town on the Veneranda headland. Rooms are swish and comfortable, however, and there's an indoor pool, gym and casino. **⑦**

Dalmacija Obala Ivana Lučića-Lavčevića bb ☎021/741-120, ⓕ741-160, ⓦwww.suncanihvar.hr. A good mid-range choice, this attractive whitewashed building is a 5min walk from the centre and has a good seafront position. **⑤**

Delfin Fabrika bb ☎021/741-168, ⓦwww.suncanihvar.hr. Simple concrete box over on the western side of the harbour, offering plain but perfectly habitable en-suite rooms. **⑤**

Meneghello Palmižana ☎091/478-3110, ⓕ021/741-427, ⓦwww.palmizana.hr. Luxury villa settlement on the island of Sveti Kliment 5km west of Hvar, connected to town by regular boat shuttle. Most of the accommodation comes in the form of attractive stone-clad self-catering bungalows sleeping three or four, although there are also some two-person apartments, all surrounded by lush Mediterranean vegetation. In high season only seven-day bookings (from Sat to Sat) are accepted. **⑤**

Palace Trg svetog Stjepana bb ☎021/741-966, ⓕ742-420, ⓦwww.suncanihvar.hr. Habsburg-era hotel on the harbourfront, part of which occupies the town loggia. Still preserves something of its belle-époque charm. **⑦**

Podstine Podstine bb ☎021/741-118, ⓦwww.podstine.com. Mellow, medium-sized hotel a 20min walk west of the centre, overlooking a pebbly bay which is good for swimming. The rooms are cosy, with sea views and satellite TV, and some also have a small balcony. May–Sept. **⑥**

Slavija Obala oslobođenja bb ☎021/741-820 & 741-840, ⓕ741-147, ⓦwww.suncanihvar.hr. Respectable three-star choice near the ferry dock, in an unassuming three-floor building offering homely en-suite rooms with TV. You can eat breakfast on the terrace right by the harbour. Sometimes prone to noise generated by nearby bars. **⑤**

The Town and around

At the centre of the town is Trg svetog Stjepana, a long, rectangular main square which meets the sea at the so-called **Mandrač**, the balustraded inner harbour used for mooring small boats. Dominating the square's southwestern corner is the arcaded bulk of the seventeenth-century Venetian **arsenal**, with an arched ground floor into which war galleys were once hauled for repairs. The upper storey of the arsenal was adapted in 1612 to house the town **theatre** (*kazalište*; daily: summer 9am–1pm & 5–11pm; winter 11am–noon; 10Kn), the oldest in Croatia and one of the first in Europe. It was built to assuage the distrust between nobles and commoners which had continued since the Ivanić rebellion, since the theatre was a civic amenity which all classes could enjoy together. The gaily painted interior, complete with two tiers of boxes, dates from the early 1800s, when locals revived and renovated the theatre after a period of neglect. The auditorium is entered through a small picture gallery (same times), which has a modest collection of twentieth-century Croatian work.

Uluz Ali and the raid on Hvar

As one of the archetypal bad guys of Dalmatian history, the corsair **Uluz Ali** gets a passing mention in most of the local museums – and yet few make an effort to explain who he actually was. Born Luca Galeni in Calabria in 1508, he was captured by the Ottoman Turks off Naples and became a galley slave, until conversion to Islam won him his freedom. He made his name as a corsair, raiding Mediterranean shipping from the safety of Ottoman-controlled North Africa, was appointed *bey* (viceroy) of Algiers in 1568 and captured the city of Tunis from the Spanish the following year. In 1571, with the maritime forces of the **Holy League** (Austria, Venice and Spain) massing to take on the Ottoman navy in the eastern Mediterranean, Uluz Ali assembled a fleet of eighty ships to mount a diversionary attack on Venetian possessions in the Adriatic. After an unsuccessful raid on Korčula he arrived off Hvar Town on August 17. The population fled to the safety of their hilltop citadel and could only watch helplessly as Ali's men torched their dwellings below. The raiders meted out similar punishment to Stari Grad, Jelsa and Vrboska before withdrawing to rejoin the rest of the Ottoman fleet.

In an important postscript to the raid, the ships of the Holy League eventually caught up with the Ottomans at **Lepanto**, near Corfu, on October 7. The Turkish fleet was scattered, but it was something of a Pyrrhic victory for the Western powers. The Holy League began to fragment and the Venetians, weakened by their losses, had to give up Cyprus to the Turks in order to secure peace.

The Cathedral and treasury

Towering over the eastern end of the square is the trefoil facade of **St Stephen's Cathedral** (Katedrala sveti Stjepan; no fixed opening hours – try mornings), a sixteenth-century construction whose spindly four-storey campanile employs the typical Venetian device of having one window on the first floor, two windows on the second, and so on up to the top. The interior is fairly unremarkable save for two notable artworks: a Venetian *Madonna and Child* (on the fourth altar on the right), a Byzantine-influenced, icon-like image painted in around 1220, which exudes a spiritual calm quite different from the tortured Baroque altarpieces nearby; and a touching fifteenth-century Pietà by Spanish artist Juan Boschetus (in the opposite – south – aisle), although its power is somewhat lessened by being framed within a larger and later work.

Immediately next door to the cathedral, the **Bishop's Treasury** (*riznica*; summer daily 9am–noon & 5–7pm; winter 10am–noon; 10Kn) houses a small but fine selection of chalices, reliquaries and embroidery. Look out for a nicely worked sixteenth-century bishop's crozier, carved into the shape of a serpent encrusted with saints and embossed with a figure of the Virgin, attended by Moses and an archangel.

North to the citadel

The rest of the old town backs away north from the square in an elegant confusion of twisting lanes and alleys hiding a series of understated architectural gems. Just uphill from the cathedral, the diminutive **Church of the Holy Spirit** (Crkva svetog Duha) has a small but striking Romanesque relief of God the Creator above the portal, while just down the steps from here the **Church of SS Cosmas and Damian** (Crkva svetog Kozme i Damjana) sports a fine barrel-vaulted roof. West of here lies the main "street" in this quarter of town – actually more a flight of steps – the steep Matije Ivanića. The striking roofless **palace** at its southern end – a grey shell punctuated by delicately carved Gothic windows – is popularly ascribed to the Hektorović family, but was more likely commissioned by another noble family, the Užičić, in 1463, and never finished. Behind it, the **Leporini Palace** is identifiable by a carving of a rabbit – the family emblem – halfway up the wall. Further up Ivanića lies the **Benedictine convent** (Benediktinski samostan; Mon–Sat 10am–noon & 5–7pm; 10Kn), founded by the daughter-in-law of the sixteenth-century Hvar poet Hanibal Lucić, which occupies the poet's former town house. Inside there's a small display of devotional paintings, and lace made by the nuns.

Head to the top of Ivanića to find the path which zigzags its way up an agave-covered hillside to the **Citadel** (Kaštil; June–Sept 8am–midnight; 10Kn), built by the Venetians in the 1550s and strengthened by the Austrians three centuries later. There's a marine archeology collection in one of the halls, with an attractively presented display of amphorae and other sediment-encrusted Greco-Roman drinking vessels, although the real attraction is the view from the citadel's ramparts. Largely intact stretches of defensive wall plunge down the hillside towards the terracotta roofs of Hvar Town below, while beyond stretch the deep green humps of the Pakleni islands just offshore and the bulky grey form of Vis further out to the southwest.

The Dominican monastery

A couple of hundred metres west of Trg svetog Stjepana, slightly set back from the shoreline, are the remains of a **Dominican monastery** (you can see its surviving bell tower from the citadel), an important centre of religious and political life until it was expropriated by French administrators in 1811 and allowed to fall into ruin. It was here in 1525 that Friar **Vinko Pribojević** famously addressed the Hvar nobility with his paper *De origine successibisque slavorum* (Of the Origin and History of the Slavs), a landmark text in the development of Croatian national self-consciousness. Pribojević floated the not unreasonable idea that all Slavs were ethnically related, but added the improbable hypothesis that they had their origins in Dalmatia, from where the Croatian brothers Čeh, Leh and Rus set out to found the Czech, Polish and Russian nations respectively. The tale of the three brothers is a common theme in Slavic folklore: it crops up in Poland and Russia as well as in the Croatian Zagorje town of Krapina.

The surviving apse of the monastery church now holds a small **archeology collection** (*arheološka zbirka*; daily 10am–noon & 8.30–10.30pm; 10Kn), with exhibits from prehistoric through to Roman times. Besides flint arrows and axe-heads from two of the island's caves – the Grapčeva and Markova – where the island's first Neolithic inhabitants holed up, there are ceramics from the late Neolithic Hvar Culture, including an anthropomorphic four-legged brazier, the most arresting item in an unassuming collection.

The Franciscan monastery

Occupying a headland just southeast of Hvar Town's ferry dock is the **Franciscan monastery** (Franjevački samostan; Mon–Fri 10am–noon & 5–7pm; 10Kn), founded in 1461 by a Venetian sea captain in thanks for deliverance from shipwreck. There's a small collection of paintings in the former refectory, including a melodramatic, near life-size seventeenth-century *Last Supper* by Matteo Ingoli of Ravenna, which covers almost the entire back wall, though in terms of expressive power it's outdone by the smaller and more tranquil *Mystical Wedding of St Catherine* painted in around 1430 by a follower of Blaž Jurjev of Trogir.

Next door is the pleasingly simple monastic **church**, with beautifully carved choir stalls and a fanciful partition of 1583. Built to separate the commoners from the nobility, the latter is decorated with six animated scenes of the Passion by Martin Benetović, a local seventeenth-century painter, and a brace of less expressive polyptychs by Francesco da Santacroce. Look out for the extravagant dragon candle-holders that push out above the panel detail below. The floor is paved with gravestones, including that of poet and playwright Hanibal Lucić by the altar, identifiable by the fleur-de-lys and dove's wing of the family crest. In the small side chapel, there's a moving *Christ on the Cross* by Leandro Bassano.

The Pakleni otoci

There are 3km of rock and concrete **beaches** east of Hvar Town in front of the big hotels, although if you want to swim it's better to head for the **Pakleni otoci** ("Islands of Hell"), a chain of eleven wooded islands just to the west of town, easily reached by water taxi from the harbour (10–20Kn each way). Only three of the islands have any facilities, and even then only a few simple bars and restaurants: **Jerolim**, a naturist island, is the nearest; the others are **Marinkovac** (with two popular beaches, Ždrilca on the northern side and U Stipanska on the south) and **Sveti Klement**, the largest of the Pakleni, with a sandy beach at Palmižana. A smaller number of water taxis serve the other islands, but your need to take your own food and drink.

Eating, drinking and nightlife

There are dozens of places to eat in Hvar Town, none of them too expensive. For a daytime **snack**, the **bakery** on the harbour, near the Mengola travel agency, is the best places for *burek*, pizza slices and pastries. Among the **restaurants**, expect to see plenty of seafood pasta, seafood risotto, and expertly grilled fish – you can make a good meal out of one of the first two even if your budget doesn't stretch to the latter.

For **drinking**, the cafés and bars around the main square and along the harbour are packed from mid-morning onwards. Trade thins out for a few hours during the hottest part of the day, until the crowds return for the evening *korzo*. Those who aren't interested in imbibing – or who simply can't afford the local café prices – sit on the walls of the Mandrać, observing the ebb and flow of well-dressed promenaders. Some bars stay open until 1–2am in July and August – but all close up much earlier outside this period.

Restaurants

Bounty Fabrika bb. Heavily touristed but reasonably priced place serving up simple grilled fish, grilled meat and seafood risottos. The main attraction is the location, with outdoor tables arranged right on the inner harbour.

Junior Pučkog ustanka 4. Informal, easy-going place offering the usual seafood dishes, none of which are too expensive, with tables scattered across a narrow medieval street.

Kamanjo Milna. Located in the centre of the bay-hugging hamlet 3km east of Hvar, this cosy restaurant cooks up suberb seafood, accompanied by locally grown vegetables and herbs.

Leonardo Obala oslobođenja. One of the more consistent of the innumerable pizzerias in Hvar. Nice position on the harbourfront, too.

Macondo Avelinija. This place has got style and quality, yet remains informal, and for a slap-up

seafood feast there are few better places: their *škampi buzara* (unpeeled prawns in wine sauce) is excellent. It's tucked away in a backstreet uphill from the main square (head up Matije Ivanića and take the second right).

Marinero Vinka Pribojevića. A reliable and popular source of mid-price dishes such as seafood spaghettis and fried squid, as well as weightier fish items. Up a side alley behind the Mengola travel agency, with tables ranged across a relatively quiet courtyard.

Palac Paladini Matije Ivanića. Serves a good range of medium-expensive seafood and other Croatian standards, with outdoor seating in a garden courtyard shaded by orange trees.

Zlatna Školjka Hektorovića. Top-notch restaurant which augments its regular seafood menu with other specialities, such as lamb stewed in a variety of different ways. On the expensive side, unless you stick to gnocchi and pasta.

Cafés, bars and clubs

Carpe Diem Obala oslobodenja. Prime meeting place for Hvar's beautiful people, with relaxing wicker chairs and cushions outside, brash and often crowded bar inside. Has a long list of (expensive) cocktails, and late opening hours.

Gromit Obala oslobodenja. Day- and night-time café-bar on the Riva, and a popular vantage point from which to admire the expensive yachts moored in the harbour. A decent choice of pastries and cakes makes this the ideal stop-off either for breakfast or afternoon snacking.

Jazz Pučkog ustanka. Laid-back, intimate bar in the tangle of streets leading south of the main square. Dark decor, and more than just top-forty sounds on the playlist.

Kavana Pjaca Trg svetog Stjepana. Classic people-watching café on the main square, which has so far resisted any temptation to transform itself into a garish tourist trap. Decent coffee, ice cream and cakes as well as the full range of alcoholic drinks.

Loco Trg svetog Stjepana. Relaxing, quirky and chic. Best of a long line of stylish youth-oriented bars, running from the main square in the east to the *Hotel Delfin* in the west.

Veneranda Hillside behind the *Hotel Delfin*. Occupying the surviving fortifications of a Venetian fortress, this outdoor club comes into its own at the weekends, when international DJs are shipped in to entertain the crowds until dawn. Different styles of music on different nights – so look out for posters.

Stari Grad

Twenty kilometres east across the mountains, **STARI GRAD** is a popular and busy resort, though more laidback than Hvar Town, straggling along the side of a deep bay. The old part of Stari Grad has been pleasantly renovated, and backs onto the main street as it wings its way along the waterside. Just back from the water is Stari Grad's most famous sight, the **Tvrdalj** (June & Sept daily 10am–1pm; July & Aug daily 10am–1pm & 5–8pm; 10Kn), the summer house and walled garden of the sixteenth-century poet and aristocrat Petar Hektorović (see box opposite). Those expecting a stately home will be disappointed: the original crenellated structure disappeared behind the present plain facade in the nineteenth century, and Hektorović's extensive gardens – which once featured clipped rows of box and medicinal herbs, as well as cypresses and oleanders sent by fellow poet Mavro Vetranović of Dubrovnik – have now been largely divided up into allotments, although a portion has been tidied up and returned to its former glories. It's still a remarkably restful location, however, built around a central cloister with a turquoise pond fed with sea water and packed with mullet. Hektorović littered the place with inscriptions (carved round the pond and on the walls of the house in Latin, Italian and Croatian) to encourage contemplation: "Neither riches nor fame, beauty nor age can save you from Death" is one characteristically cheerful effusion.

The narrow streets behind the Tvrdalj are as atmospheric as anywhere in the Adriatic: a warren of low stone houses decked in windowboxes, with alleyways suddenly opening out onto small squares. The lane to the right of the Tvrdalj as you face it leads up to the **Bianchini Palace** (Palača Biankini; June–Sept daily 10am–noon & 7–9pm; 10Kn), where there's a display of finds from ancient Pharos, including pottery fragments, and a *louterion* – a stone basin used for washing before a ceremony or sacrifice. To the left of the Tvrdalj a lane leads up to the **Dominican monastery**, a fifteenth-century foundation half-heartedly fortified with the addition of a single sturdy turret after Uluz Ali's attack of 1571. Rooms off the cloister house a **museum** (Mon–Fri 10am–noon & 6–8pm; 10Kn), which contains an absorbing collection of Greek gravestones from Pharos, Creto–Venetian icons and a *Deposition* by Tintoretto. According to local tradition, the figures of Joseph of Arimathea, Mary Magdalene and the young man leaning over Christ's body in the picture are portraits of Hektorović, his granddaughter Julija, and her husband Antun Lucić – although more sober analysts have pointed out that many of the stock figures in the

Petar Hektorović and the Tvrdalj

Renaissance poet and Hvar noble **Petar Hektorović** (1487–1572) is primarily remembered for his *Ribanje i ribarsko prigovaranje* ("Fishing and Fishermen's Conversations"), the first work of autobiographical realism in Croatian literature. Written in 1556, when he was already an old man, the 1680-line poem was inspired by a three-day boat trip to Brač and Šolta in the company of two local fishermen, Paskoje and Nikola, who despite being commoners are accorded a dignity which was rare for the literature of the period. Hektorović had lived through the Ivanić rebellion of the early sixteenth century, and perhaps intended *Ribanje* as a message to his fellow aristocrats – treat the lower orders with a bit of humanity, and the bonds of society will hold.

This sense of *noblesse oblige* also underpinned Hektorović's plans for the **Tvrdalj**, which he began in 1514 and carried on building for the rest of his life. As well as a place of repose for himself, it was intended to be a fortified refuge for the locals in time of attack – a self-sufficient ark which would provide food from its garden and fresh fish from the mullet pond. Hektorović's typically Renaissance fondness for order and balance was reflected in the symbolic inclusion of a pigeon loft in the main tower, to emphasize the point that the Tvrdalj was a refuge for creatures of the sky as well as the sea and earth. The house was built in simple unadorned style, both because Hektorović had a taste for rusticity and because he didn't want to provoke the locals with a display of lordly luxury. Local Venetian commanders actually sanctioned the diversion of manpower resources from Hvar Town to assist Hektorović in its construction, since it freed them from the responsibility of defending the people of Stari Grad from pirates.

The Tvrdalj never fulfilled its intended purpose: it was damaged during Uluz Ali's raid of 1571, and Hektorović died the following year before finishing the thing off, though it was renovated and preserved by his descendants until the nineteenth century, when new owners arrived and its shape was radically changed. Ironically, the one thing which most people find so memorable about the Tvrdalj – the restful arched cloister surrounding the fishpond – wasn't part of Hektorović's original plan, added instead by the Niseteo family in 1834.

---

artist's paintings possess similar faces. There's also a small display of Hektorović's effects, including a 1532 edition of Petrarch's *Sonnets* and a copy of Polybius's *Histories*.

In the fields immediately south of the monastery, the Chapel of St Nicholas (Crkvica sveti Nikole) was the scene of an extraordinary demonstration of religiosity in 1554, when the hermit **Lukrecija of Brač** chose to be walled into a small side-room, where she lived on bread and water until her death 35 years later. Heading east from the monastery and then turning left back towards the town centre brings you past **St John's Church** (Crkva svetog Ivana), a twelfth-century Romanesque church with some sixth-century mosaics inside, and **St Stephen's Church** (Crkva svetog Stjepana), a plain, weatherbeaten example of Dalmatian Baroque with a fine Venetian campanile. Embedded in a wall opposite the church is a Roman-era gravestone relief of Winged Eros leaning nonchalantly on an upside-down torch – a classic symbol of death.

There are rock and concrete **beaches** on the northern side of the bay in front of the hotels, from where a path carries on beyond the *Arkada* mega-hotel to a much less sanitized area of rocks backed by pines. Much better is the bay favoured by locals on the other (southern) side of the bay – simply walk along the Riva to the end of town and you'll find a shallow rocky bay perfect for snorkelling.

Practicalities

Buses from the ferry terminal (3km west of town) and from Hvar Town drop you on the edge of the centre, a short walk from the Riva. You'll find the **tourist office** in the harbourside market at Nova Riva 2 (July & Aug daily 8am–2pm & 5–9pm; Sept–June Mon–Fri 8am–2pm, Sat 10am–noon; ☏ & ℻021/765-763, ✆tzg-stari-grad@st.tel.hr). The Mistral agency (Mon–Sat 9am–12.30pm & 6.30–8.30pm, Sun 7–9pm; ☏021/765-281), and Hvar-Touristik (daily 9am–1pm & 6–8pm; ☏021/717-580, ✆antun.balic@st.hinet .hr), both on the Riva, can arrange accommodation in private **rooms** (❶) and **apartments** (❷). Stari Grad's concrete **hotels**, grouped around the north side of the bay, are a pretty characterless bunch all round: the two-star *Helios* (☏021/765-555, ⓦhoteli-helios@st.tel.hr; ❸) is plain but adequate, while the three-star *Arkada* (same numbers as the Helios; ❹) and *Adriatic* (same numbers as the Helios; ❹) are slightly plusher. On the south side of town, *Autocamp Jurjevac* occupies a partly shaded site in what used to be the town park, and rents out en-suite four-person **bungalows** for 390Kn.

The handiest of the town's **restaurants** are the *Pizzeria San Marino* next to the Tvrdalj, and the *Konoba Herakleia* on Vagonj, which has the customary range of Dalmatian seafood dishes. Slightly better is *Ermitaž* on the north side of the harbour on the way to the package hotels, serving up excellent grilled fish in an ancient building with a shaded terrace out front. The *Sunčani Hvar* **bakery** on the Riva (daily 7am–10pm) has anything you might need for breakfast.

Jelsa and Vrboska

The tiny port and fishing village of **JELSA** sits prettily by a wooded bay 10km east of Stari Grad. Tucked away behind a nineteenth-century waterfront, the old quarter climbs up the hill, a maze of ancient alleys and lanes; the two big hotels on either side of the bay, fronted by concrete bathing platforms, seem oddly out of place. Just off the quayside is the charming octagonal sixteenth-century **Chapel of St John** (Crkva svetog Ivana), squeezed into one of the old squares and overhung by the balconies of the surrounding Renaissance buildings. Up from here is the town's fortified **parish church**, which managed to resist Uluz Ali's attack of 1571, though it's hard to make out the original design as the facade and bell tower were added in the nineteenth century. Opening times are unpredictable – if you do manage to get in, look out for the wooden Gothic statue of the Madonna (brought here from the mainland in 1539 to keep it safe from the Ottomans) on the high altar. You can avoid the crowded **beaches** by taking a taxi boat to the Glavica peninsula near Vrboska (see opposite).

Buses stop about 300m inland from the harbour, where you'll find a **tourist office** on the western side (June & Sept Mon–Sat 8.30am–12.30pm & 6.30–8.30pm, Sun 9am–noon; July & Aug Mon–Sat 7am–10pm, Sun 9.30am–12.30pm & 6.30–9.30pm; Oct–May Mon–Fri 9am–noon; ☏021/761-017). Private **rooms** (❶) and **apartments** (❷) are available from Odisej, in the bus station (daily 8am–10pm; ☏021/761-888, ⓦwww.odisej -travel.com), and Globus, in between the bus station and the harbour (daily 8am–noon & 4–11pm, ☏021/774-151). Among the most characterful places to stay is the family-run *Pansion Murvica* (☏021/761-405, ✆pansion-murvica@ st.hinet.hr; ❸), located in a residential street behind the bus station, and offering nifty studio apartments with TV and kitchenette. Also worthwhile is the *Hotel L'Accento*, Slatina 1 (☏021/761-236, ⓦwww.free-st.hinet.hr/laccento; ❹), a medium-sized place with modest, comfortable en-suite rooms. Best of the packagey hotels is the *Mina* on the south side of the bay (☏021/761-122,

ⓦwww.hoteli-jelsa.hr; ❺), a concrete eyesore of 1980s vintage which just about deserves two-and-a-half stars – but not the three advertised. There's a **campsite**, the *Mina* (ⓣ021/761-210, ⓕ761-227), on a pine-shaded promontory overlooking the sea at the eastern end of town – beyond which lies a pebbly beach.

The *Pansion Murvica* serves up decent **food**; otherwise the best of the restaurants is the friendly, family-run *Konoba Pelago*, near the Chapel of St John at Trg Ivana bb, a reliable source of good quality seafood. *Dgigibaoo*, a little further east on the way to the Mina hotel and campsite, is a lively café with a respectable line in pizzas and cakes.

Vrboska

The sleepy little village of **VRBOSKA** strings along the side of another of the island's deep bays, about 4km from Jelsa and easily reached by bus or water taxi, or by following the coastal path. The bus stop is on the edge of the old village, five minutes' walk along the quayside from the **tourist office** (Mon–Sat 8am–noon & 6–9pm, Sun 10.30am–noon & 6.30–8pm; ⓣ021/744-137), which has a small cache of **rooms** (❶).

The two sides of Vrboska, on either side of the inlet, are joined by three small and picturesque bridges. Perched above the quayside is the unusual, fortified **St Mary's Church** (Crkva svete Marije; Mon–Sat 10am–noon & 6–7pm), dating from 1580, which was extensively fortified to resist attacks from pirates and the Turks. The result is a high, unadorned structure with a crenellated tower on the southeast corner, and a hefty bastion on the northwest – a protruding, angular structure that looks like the prow of a beached dreadnought. The interior is partly paved with grave slabs and from the sacristy you can get onto the roof for a view of the town below. A couple of minutes away, the Baroque **St Lawrence's Church** (Crkva svetog Lovre; Mon–Sat 10am–noon & 6–7pm) has a small art collection, including a stagy-looking polyptych depicting St Lawrence flanked by John the Baptist and St Nicholas on the high altar, nowadays attributed to Paolo Veronese, although local tradition ascribes it to Titian. To the right, there's a *Madonna of the Rosary* by Leandro Bassano.

There's a series of **beaches**, including a couple of naturist ones, on the Glavica peninsula 2km northeast of town. You can find quieter spots by walking north from Vrboska, straight over Kaštilac hill (where there's a ruined tower), to the isolated bays of Hvar's north coast. From here there's a great view of the southern flanks of Brač and, away in the distance, the stark ridge of Mount Biokovo on the mainland.

Vis

A compact hump rearing dramatically out of the sea, **VIS** is situated further offshore than any of Croatia's other inhabited Adriatic islands. Closed to foreigners for military reasons until 1989, the island has never been overrun by tourists, and with only two or three package-oriented hotels on the whole island, this is definitely one place in Croatia where the independent traveller rules the roost. Croatian holiday-makers have fallen in love with the place over the last decade, drawn by its wild mountainous scenery, some interesting historical relics and two good-looking small towns – **Vis Town** and **Komiža**. The latter is the obvious base for trips to the islet of **Biševo**, site of one of Croatia's most famous natural wonders, the **Blue Cave**. The island is also famous for a brace of fine local

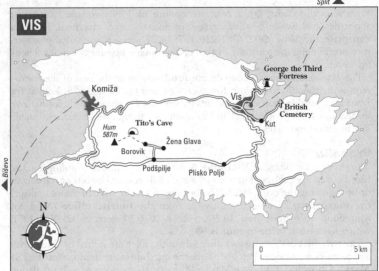

wines – the white Vugava and the red Viški plavac – and the *pogača od srdele* (anchovy pasty, also called *viška pogača* or *komiška pogača* depending on which town you're staying in), which is sold by local bakeries and cafés.

Vis's history has been shaped by its strategic position on the sea approaches to central Dalmatia. The **Greeks** settled here in the fourth century BC, choosing the island as a base because of its convenience as a stepping-stone between the eastern and western shores of the Adriatic, and founding **Issa** on the site of present-day Vis Town. When the fall of Venice in 1797 opened up the Adriatic to the competing navies of France, Britain, Russia and Austria, Vis was again much fought over, eventually falling under the control of the **British**, who fortified the harbour and founded the Vis Cricket Club. The British defeated Napoleon's navy off Vis in 1811, and the **Austrians** – who inherited the island from the British in 1815 – brushed aside Italian maritime ambitions in another big sea battle here in 1866. Vis's position was once more exploited during World War II (see box on p.338), when Josip Broz **Tito**'s Partisan movement was briefly based here. After the war, the island was heavily garrisoned and used for military training, a situation which, along with the decline of traditional industries like fishing and fish canning, encouraged successive waves of **emigration**. The island had 10,000 inhabitants before World War II; it now has fewer than 3000. According to local estimates, there are ten times more Komiža families living in San Pedro, California, than in the town itself.

Ferries run year round between Split and Vis Town (1 or 2 daily; 2hr 30min; once a week these call in at Hvar on the way) though in winter the trip can get mighty rough. From mid-July to late August there are also two weekly ferries from Ancona in Italy.

Vis Town

VIS TOWN's sedate arc of grey-brown houses stretches around a deeply indented bay, above which looms a steep escarpment covered with the remains of abandoned agricultural terraces. There's not much of ancient Issa to be seen apart from a few chunks of unadorned masonry – most of which have been absorbed into the dry-stone walls of local gardeners – on the hills above town.

The most attractive parts of town are east of the ferry landing (to the right as you get off the boat). A five-minute walk along the front brings you to the venerable **Church of Our Lady** (Gospa od Spilica), a squat sixteenth-century structure harbouring a *Madonna and Saints* by Girolamo da Santacroce, just beyond which is the Austrian defensive bastion known as Gospina baterija (Our Lady's Battery). A barrack block at the rear of the bastion has been transformed into the **Town Museum** (Gradski muzej; Tues–Sun 9am–1pm & 5–7pm; 10Kn), a small but well-organized collection mixing Greco-Roman finds with nineteenth-century wine presses and domestic furniture. The star exhibit is the bronze head of a Greek goddess, possibly Aphrodite, from the fourth century BC, which is claimed to be by a student of Praxiteles, although only a replica is on display – the original is locked up in the town vaults.

Another 500m east along the seafront lies the suburb of **Kut** (literally "quiet corner" or "hideaway"), a largely sixteenth-century tangle of narrow cobbled streets overlooked by the summer houses built by the nobility of Hvar – the stone balconies and staircases give the place an undeniably aristocratic air. Kut's **St Cyprian's Church** (Crkva svetog Ciprijana) squats beneath a campanile adorned with unusual sun and rose motifs. There's a fine wooden ceiling inside, although it's difficult to gain access outside mass times.

Continuing round the bay from Kut for another fifteen minutes brings you to a small wooded peninsula, and a tiny walled garden containing a **British Cemetery** – inside lie a couple of unobtrusive monuments honouring the war dead of both 1811–15 and 1943–44. The marvellous pebble **beach** on the far side of the cemetery is one of the best on the island.

Heading west around the bay from the ferry landing takes you past an equally diverse collection of monuments, beginning after some 200m with an **Ancient Greek Cemetery** (daily 5–9pm) behind the municipal tennis courts. There's only a handful of tombstones bearing faded inscriptions, but it's an evocative place, heavy with the scent of wild fennel. Another 200m further on lie the rubbly remains of the **Roman Baths** (you're free to wander round if the gate is open), a smallish second-century complex centred on some exquisite abstract floor mosaics in what was the main hall. Beyond here it's impossible to miss the campanile of the **Franciscan monastery** (Franjevački samostan), rising gracefully from a small kidney-shaped peninsula. Flanked by a huddle of cypresses, this sixteenth-century foundation was built on the remains of a Roman theatre, and some of its interior walls follow the curving lines of the original spectator stands, although you can't get inside to have a look. The adjacent **municipal graveyard** is similar to the one in Supetar (see p.317) in featuring some elegant nineteenth-century funerary sculpture, including a particularly fine statue of a maiden stooping over a cross, dating from 1899, by Supetar sculptor Ivan Rendić, which can be seen adorning the grave of a certain Toma Bradanović.

Beyond the monastery, the road continues along the shoreline past the *Hotel Issa*. After twenty minutes, a track breaks off to the left and heads uphill to **Fort Wellington**, a ruined white tower constructed by the British after 1811, which crowns a blustery ridge providing fine views back towards Vis Town to the south, or out towards the island of Hvar over to the northwest. A ten-minute walk east from Fort Wellington brings you to the **George the Third** fortress, built in 1813 to guard the entrance to Vis harbour. At the time of writing visitors can wander at will through this remarkably well-preserved complex (although access may become more difficult once the authorities decide what to do with it), entering the main courtyard through a doorway topped by a crude carving of the Union Jack. A passage leads through the sturdily built barrack blocks, emerging onto a sea-facing gun terrace shaded by palms and agaves.

Practicalities

Just to the right of the ferry dock as you step off the boat, Vis's **tourist office** (summer Mon–Sat 9am–1pm & 6–9pm; winter Mon–Fri 9am–1pm; ☎ & ⓕ021/711-144, ⓦwww.tz-vis.hr) is a mine of local information and can help with directions to out-of-town beaches, which might be quieter than the ones here or in Komiža. The most reliable source of **rooms** (❶) and **apartments** (❷) is the Ionios agency, on the Riva 200m left of the ferry dock (daily 8am–10pm; ☎021/711-531, ⓔionios@st.hinet.hr). You can **rent bikes** (30Kn/day) and scooters (60Kn/day) from Ionios, or from the nearby Dodoro agency at Riva 24a.

The best of the town's **hotels** is the stately, Habsburg-era *Tamaris*, on the waterfront at Obala sv. Jurja, east of the ferry dock (☎021/711-350, ⓕ711-349; ❸), which has cosy en-suite rooms with TV, air con and squeaky parquet floors, as well as a handful of self-catering attic apartments for 700Kn for two or three people. The smaller, pension-like *Paula*, Petra Hektorovića 2 (☎021/711-362, ⓔpaula_hotel@st.tel.hr; ❸), offers smart modern rooms with TV amid the picturesque alleyways of Kut. *Pansion As*, Korzo 16 (☎021/711-474; ❸), has slightly plainer en-suite rooms but enjoys an excellent position near the ferry dock – it soon fills up, however. About 800m west of the ferry dock at Apolonija Zanelle 5, the modern *Issa* (☎ & ⓕ021/711-450; ❸) is owned by the same firm as the *Tamaris* and costs the same, but hasn't received the same amount of investment: the en-suite rooms are adequate but slightly tatty and lack TV.

Vis's harbour is a popular overnight stop-off for yachtspeople, which helps to explain why the standard of **restaurants** in town is so high. *Pojoda*, in Kut at Don C. Marasovića 8, is one of the best places in southern Dalmatia for traditional fish recipes (zestfully flavoured with caper or wine sauces rather than simply grilled), all served up in a garden shaded by mandarin-orange and lemon trees. The nearby *Vatrica*, sheltering under a vine-shaded terrace at Obala kralja Krešimira IV 13, does a memorable baked octopus) as well as the usual seafood risottos, fish and shellfish. If a unique ambience is what you're after, consider *Kaliopa*, Vladimira Nazora 32, with tables buried amid the palms and shrubs of a walled garden – the seafood here is as excellent as you would expect, but be prepared to splash out. For a quick, uncomplicated feed, your best bet is *Buffet-Pizzeria Katarina*, right opposite the ferry dock, with workmanlike pizzas, cheap *ćevapi* and other grilled-meat standards. Next door, *Bejbi* ("baby" to you and me) is the most laid-back **drinking** hangout in town, with a funkily decorated café indoors, and bamboo-shaded bar in the yard. For **snacks**, *Pekarna Kolđeraj*, Trg Klapavica, offers all you need in the fresh bread-and-pastry line, and is the place to seek out Vis's famous *pogača od srdele* – although they don't bake them every day.

Komiža and around

Buses leave Vis harbour five times daily for the 25-minute trip to the pleasant town of **KOMIŽA**, the island's main fishing port. Compact and intimate, Komiža's curved harbourfront is lined with palm trees and fringed by sixteenth- and seventeenth-century Venetian-style houses with intricate wrought-iron balconies. Dominating the southern end of the harbour is the **Kaštel**, a stubby sixteenth-century fortress whose appearance is slightly unbalanced by the slender clock tower which was built onto one of its corners at the end of the nineteenth century. It now holds a **Fishing Museum** (Ribarski muzej; June–Sept Mon–Sat 10am–noon & 7–10pm, Sun 7–10pm; 10Kn), whose worthy displays of nets and knots are enlivened by the presence of a reconstructed *falkuša*, one of the traditional fishing boats with triangular sails which were common hereabouts until the early twentieth century. At the other end of the harbour, on a tiny square known as the **Škor** (local dialect for *škver*, the part of the harbourfront onto which fishing boats were pulled up for repairs), the mid-sixteenth-century **Palača Zanetova** is a stately but dilapidated building which was once a ducal mansion – look out for the carved Virgin and Child high up on the front wall.

Among the town's churches, the most notable is the sixteenth-century **Gospa Gusarica**, whose name loosely translates as "Our Lady of the Pirates" – it's said that a painting of the Virgin was stolen from the church by pirates, but floated back into port when they were shipwrecked. The church is set amid trees on a little beach at the northern end of town near the *Biševo* hotel, and has an eight-sided well adorned with reliefs of St Nicholas, protector of fishermen and patron of Komiža.

About a kilometre southeast of the town on a vineyard-cloaked hillock is the seventeenth-century **Benedictine monastery** (known as *mušter*, the local dialect word for monastery), fortified in the 1760s to provide the townsfolk with a refuge in case of attack by pirates. Surrounded by defensive bastions, it's a good vantage point from which to survey the bay of Komiža below. Most of the island's population congregate beneath the monastery every year on St Nicholas's Day (Sveti Nikola; Dec 6), when an old fishing boat is hauled here by hand and then set alight – the idea of sacrificing a boat to the patron saint of seafarers reveals just how much pre-Christian practice is preserved in Mediterranean Catholicism.

The best of the **beaches** are south of town: head past the Kaštel, follow the road round for ten minutes, head round the back of the fish canning factory, and you'll find yourself on a coastal path that leads past a sequence of attractive coves.

Practicalities

Buses from Vis Town terminate about 100m behind the harbour, from where it's a short walk south to the **tourist office** (summer Mon–Sat 8am–noon & 6–10pm; winter Mon–Fri 8am–1pm; ☎021/713-455), on the Riva just beyond the Kaštel. Staff here can point you in the direction of agencies offering excursions to the Blue Cave on Biševo (see p.339). Adventure specialists Alternatura, Jončićeva 3 (☎021/717-239, ⊛www.alternatura.hr), are the people to ask about scuba diving, pony trekking, and hang-gliding from nearby Mt Hum.

The town's only **hotel** is the *Biševo* (☎021/713-095, ℱ713-098; ❹), a comfortable package-tour-oriented place about five minutes' walk from the centre at the northern end of the bay. **Rooms** (❶) and **apartments** (❷) are available from a number of agencies in the centre, most reliably Darlić & Darlić, on the harbourfront (daily 10am–noon & 5–7pm; ☎021/717-205, ⊛www.darlic -travel.hr), and Srebrna, a little way back from the harbour on Ribarska (daily 8am–noon & 4–9pm; ☎021/713-668). There are a couple of pizzerias on the harbourfront, and one very good seafood **restaurant** just off Ribarska, *Bako*, which has a vine-shaded terrace right on the beach. *Jastožara*, Gundulićeva 6, is the place to go for lobster, prepared in any number of ways – although they do the usual grilled fish dishes too. For **drinkers**, the day begins and ends on the central Škor, which is ringed by lively and friendly café-bars.

Mount Hum and the south coast

Rearing up above Komiža to the southeast is **Mount Hum**, at 587m Vis's highest point. You can scramble up to the top by following the tracks from behind the Benedictine monastery, although there's also a road of sorts, accessed by following the old Komiža–Vis Town route (not the new one traversed by buses), which works its way round the southern side of the island. About 6km out of Komiža, take a left to the hamlet of Žena Glava followed by a second left to Borovik, from where a deteriorating asphalt road heads uphill to the summit. There's a small chapel at the top, and a panorama of the

Vis in World War II

The collapse of Italy in the autumn of 1943 led to a power vacuum in the Adriatic, with both the Germans and Tito's Partisans racing each other to take control of the region's major ports and islands. Eager to support the Partisan effort, the British occupied Vis in early 1944, and in June of that year Vis was chosen as the temporary headquarters of the Partisan high command, headed by Tito himself. Having narrowly escaped a German attack on his previous stronghold, Drvar in western Bosnia, Tito was evacuated to Italy by the Allies at the end of May. He sailed for Vis on board the HMS *Blackmore* on June 7, entertaining the officers' mess, it is said, with a near-perfect rendition of "The Owl and the Pussycat".

Tito immediately took up residence in a cave on the southern flanks of Mount Hum, while his staff meetings took place in another cave next door. British officers who had never met Tito before entertained all kinds of wild ideas about who this shadowy guerilla leader really was. Novelist **Evelyn Waugh** (then a British liaison officer) was obsessed with the idea that Tito was a lesbian in disguise, and continued to spread this rumour for reasons of personal amusement even after meeting the partisan supremo in person – it's said that Tito upbraided Waugh about this during a trip to the beach, the Marshal's skimpy trunks leaving no room for further doubt about his gender.

Vis soon became a vast **armed camp**, hosting 10,000 Partisans and 700 British and American commandos. The island was an excellent base from which to harry German positions on nearby islands, although commando raids on rugged Brač (where the Scottish Highlanders indulged in a *Guns of Navarone*-style attempt to capture Vidova Gora) were extremely costly in terms of Allied lives. Despite the need for constant vigilance against German attacks, the daily existence of those stationed on Vis was made more than bearable by the the endless opportunities for swimming, sunbathing and drinking the local wine. For the local population, things were not quite so jolly: all men between the ages of 15 and 50 were called up by the Partisans, while women, children and the elderly were evacuated to a tent-camp in British-controlled Egypt, where many died in the stifling heat.

Vis was the site of the first meeting between Tito and the head of the royalist Yugoslav government in exile, Ivan Šubašić, who arrived there on June 16. After concluding the Tito–Šubašić Agreement, which provided de-facto recognition of Tito's primacy in Yugoslavia, the signatories went on a motor-boat excursion to the Blue Cave on Biševo, where they indulged in skinny dipping, followed by a lunch of lobster and wine. Fitzroy Maclean, Winston Churchill's personal envoy at Partisan HQ, noted that the sea was choppy on the way back and that "several of the party were sick".

Ultimately Tito feared that he would lose his political independence if he accepted British protection on Vis for too much longer, and chose to reassert himself with a show of disobedience. On September 18 he abandoned Vis in the dead of night, flying to join the Soviet Red Army in Romania in a Russian plane. Vis's brief period in the political limelight was over.

Adriatic that reveals just why Vis was so strategically important: you can pick out the pale grey stripe of the Italian coastline far away to the west, and the mountains of the Croatian mainland to the east. Also visible are many of the uninhabited islands of the mid-Adriatic: the hump of Svetac immediately to the west, the unearthly volcanic pyramid of Jabuka beyond it and, to the south-east, Croatia's farthest-flung Adriatic possession, **Palagruža** – according to legend, the last resting place of Diomedes, King of Argos and leading participant in the siege of Troy.

Nearing Hum's summit by road, you'll pass an overgrown concrete stairway leading to **Tito's Cave** (Titova špilja), a group of caverns from which the Marshal directed the war effort during 1944. Once a popular attraction, the caves fell into disuse after 1991, although local enthusiasts occasionally open them up for visitors in July and August – the tourist offices in Komiža and Vis Town will have up-to-date information.

Returning to the road along the south of the island, another 5km from the Žena Glava turn-off is the village of **PLISKO POLJE**, where the British constructed a speedily improvised airstrip in 1944 by linking together innumerable metal plates. It was long ago pulled up and replaced by vineyards, the fruits of which can be sampled at *Konoba Roki* in the village – a great place to sit in a shady courtyard trying out the local *rakija* (flavoured with *rogač*, carob) and red and white wines, accompanied by *pršut*, home-made cheese, and fishy main courses baked *ispod peke*.

Biševo and the Blue Cave

Each morning small boats leave Komiža harbour for the short crossing to **Biševo**, a tiny islet just to the southwest of Vis. There's a seasonally inhabited hamlet just up from Biševo's small harbour, and a couple of attractive coves, but the main attraction here is the **Blue Cave** (Modra špilja; 25Kn) on the island's east coast, a modestly sized but entrancing grotto which can only be reached by sea. It's been a tourist attraction since the 1880s, when a minor Viennese painter Eugen von Ransonnet-Villet dynamited the entrance to the cave to widen it for boat access, and the Lloyd steamer company began advertising it as the "Austrian Capri". It probably deserves the hype: when the sun is at its height, water-filtered light shines in through a submerged side entrance to the cave to bathe everything in the cavern in an eerie shimmering blueness. Due to the narrowness of the entrance, the cave can't be entered when the sea is choppy, which can happen on all but the calmest of summer days; ask the tourist office in either Komiža or Vis Town about conditions.

There are two ways to visit the cave; the easiest is to take an excursion from either Komiža or Vis Town (all the private room agencies offer tours, costing 80–100Kn including the cave entrance fee), although it's also possible to take a taxi boat from Komiža harbour to the island, from where you can walk to a spot near the cave entrance. Either way, you'll be transferred to a small boat and ferried into the cave. You can take a dip in the cave if you want – although be warned that the volume of tourist traffic often means that you won't be able to spend as long there as you might wish.

Korčula

Like so many islands along the coast, **KORČULA** was first settled by the Greeks, who gave it the name Korkyra Melaina, or Black Corfu, for its dark

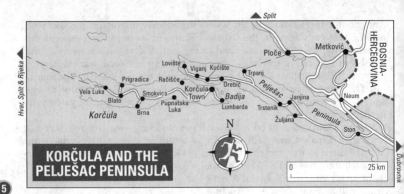

and densely wooded appearance. Even now it's one of the greenest of the Adriatic islands, and one of the most popular, thanks almost entirely to the charms of its main settlement, **Korčula Town**, whose surviving fortifications jut decorously out to sea like the bastions of an overgrown sandcastle. There are good beaches at the village of **Lumbarda** 7km away, but the rest of the island lacks any obvious highlights.

The main Rijeka–Dubrovnik **ferry** drops you right at the harbour at Korčula Town. In addition, local ferries travel daily between Split and Vela Luka at the western end of Korčula island, from where there's a connecting bus service to Korčula Town. There's also a daily **bus** service from Dubrovnik, which crosses the narrow stretch of water dividing the island from the mainland via car ferry from Orebić (see p.349), just opposite Korčula Town on the **Pelješac peninsula**. Orebić is the obvious gateway to Korčula if you're approaching from the south: there are several daily ferry sailings from there to Dominće, 3km south of Korčula Town, and a regular passenger-only **boat service** in summer (daily 6am–8pm) that brings you to the centre of town. If you arrive at Dominće on one of the ferries from Orebić, you can avoid the thirty-minute walk into town by waiting for one of the Lumbarda–Korčula buses, which call in at the Inkobrod shipyard just uphill from the harbour.

Korčula Town

KORČULA TOWN sits on an oval hump of land, a medieval walled city ribbed with a series of narrow streets that branch off the main thoroughfare like the veins of a leaf – a plan designed to reduce the effects of wind and sun. Controlling access to the two-kilometre-wide channel which divides the island from the Pelješac peninsula, the town was one of the first Adriatic strongpoints to fall to the Venetians – who arrived here in the tenth century and stayed, on and off, for over eight centuries, leaving their distinctive mark on the culture and architecture of the town. Korčula's golden age lasted from the thirteenth to the fifteenth centuries, when the town acquired its present form and most of its main buildings were constructed, but a catastrophic outbreak of plague in 1529 brought an end to Korčula's expansion. Further disaster was narrowly averted in 1571 when, in the run-up to the Battle of Lepanto, Uluz Ali (see box on p.327) turned up outside the town. The Venetian garrison withdrew without a fight, leaving the locals to defend themselves under the command of local priest Antun Rožanović – they managed to repulse Ali, who went off to destroy Hvar Town instead.

With the decline of Mediterranean trade that followed the discovery of America, Korčula slipped into obscurity. The twentieth century saw the development of shipyards east of town, and the emergence of tourism. The first guests arrived in the 1920s, although it wasn't until the 1970s that mass tourism changed the face of the town, bequeathing it new hotels, cafés and a yachting marina.

Korčula's most famous event is the performance of the **Moreška** sword dance (see box on p.343), which traditionally falls on St Theodore's Day (July 29) – although these days it's re-enacted weekly throughout the summer for the benefit of visitors. Another good time to be in town is **Easter Week**, when the religious brotherhoods (charitable associations formed in medieval times) parade through the town with their banners – individually on the days preceding Good Friday, then all together on Good Friday itself. A comparatively recent event – but planned to become an annual feature if funds permit – is the seaborne re-enactment of the 1298 **Battle of Korčula** (Sept 7 or

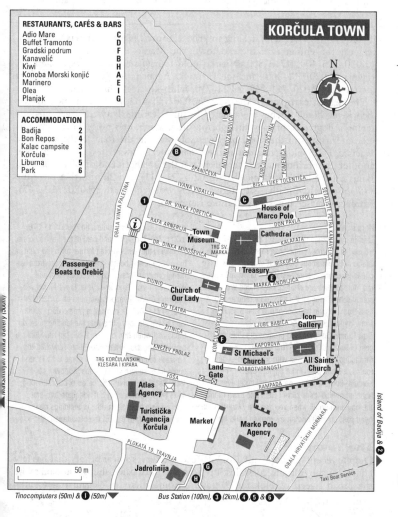

RESTAURANTS, CAFÉS & BARS

Adio Mare	C
Buffet Tramonto	D
Gradski podrum	F
Kanavelić	B
Kiwi	H
Konoba Morski konjić	A
Marinero	E
Olea	I
Planjak	G

ACCOMMODATION

Badija	2
Bon Repos	4
Kalac campsite	3
Korčula	1
Liburna	5
Park	6

KORČULA TOWN

Tinocomputers (50m) & ❶ (50m) ▼   Bus Station (100m), ❸ (2km), ❹,❺ & ❻ ▼

nearest convenient date), when the Genoese under Admiral Lamba Doria defeated a numerically superior Venetian fleet, capturing Marco Polo in the process.

Arrival, information and accommodation

Korčula's **bus station** is 400m southeast of the old town. The **tourist office** (June–Sept Mon–Sat 8am–8pm, Sun 8am–3pm; Oct–May Mon–Sat 8am–noon & 5–8pm, Sun 8am–noon; ☎020/715-701, ℱ715-866, ℯtzg-korcule@du.tel.hr), over on the western side of the peninsula, can tell you almost everything that there is to know about the island.

Bikes can be rented from outside the *Park* hotel (15Kn per hour, 75Kn per day). If you're moving on from Korčula by boat, you can book **ferry tickets** through the Jadrolinija office on Plokata 19. travnja (Mon–Fri 7.30am–8pm, Sat 7.30am–2pm, Sun 8am–1pm). You can check your emails at Tinocomputers, midway between the old town and the bus station on Prolaz tri sulara.

Accommodation

There are three agencies dealing in private **rooms** (❷) and **apartments** (❸), all near the entrance to the old town: the Marko Polo agency at Biline 5 (☎020/715-400, ℱ715-800, ℯmarko-polo-tours@du.tel.hr); Atlas, Plokata 19. travnja (☎020/711-060); and the Turistička Agencija Korčula, just off Plokata 19. travnja (☎020/711-067, ℱ711-710, ℯhtp-korcula@du.tel.hr).

The nearest **campsite** is the *Kalac* (☎020/711-182, ℱ711-746), next to the *Bon Repos* hotel. Pitches are situated in tiny clearings between trees, guaranteeing a degree of privacy, though the site is sometimes noisy. There are quieter alternatives in the small bays west of town on the road to the village of Račišće. Four kilometres out is the *Palma*, tucked away in a private garden; another 2km brings you to the *Vrbovica*, at the northern end of village of Luka Banja on the lovely Vrbovica bay (☎020/721-311); and 2km further on is the *Oskorušica*, idyllically situated among olive trees (☎020/710-747). Korčula–Račišće buses pass all three campsites.

Hotels

Badija otok Badija ☎020/711-115, ℱ711-746. Housed in a former Franciscan monastery on the island of Badija about 2km east of town, this is the cheapest option around – but the rooms are spartan and facilities are shared. Often filled with sporty school groups. It's served by regular taxi boat from Korčula harbour and is well placed for some rocky beaches. ❷

Bon Repos On a wooded promontory 2km southeast of town ☎020/711-102, ℱ711-122. Straggling hotel complex with simple en-suite rooms, a small pool and a shingle beach. The Korčula–Lumbarda bus passes the hotel every hour, otherwise it's a 25min walk into town round the bay: turn uphill when you see the *Liburna*, then head past an inlet and an overgrown park. ❺

Korčula Obala Vinka Paletina bb ☎020/711-078, ℱ711-746. The oldest and best of the town's hotels, occupying the Austrian-built former town hall right in the old town, and boasting an elegant waterfront terrace. Former guests include Rebecca West and World War I stormtrooper-novelist Ernst Jünger. ❻

Liburna Obala Hrvatskih Mornara bb ☎020/726-006, ℱ711-746. Occupying a promontory 1500m east of the old town, this was the leading hotel on the island when first built in 1985, but now looks a bit like a socialist-era period piece. However, the en-suite rooms are comfy and come with TV, and some have superb views of the old town. ❻

Park Šetalište Frana Kršinića bb ☎020/726-004, ℱ711-746. Uninspiring but adequate two-star occupying a box-like huddle of buildings on the coastal path 1km east of the bus station. ❺

The Town

Despite recent development, Korčula Town preserves a neat beauty that has few equals on the Adriatic coast. Just up from the quay, cafés, shops and banks line the broad sweep of Plokata 19. travnja, from where an elegant nineteenth-

Korčula Town is famous for its **Moreška**, a traditional sword dance and drama that was once common throughout the Mediterranean. Judging by the name, the dance probably originated in Spain and related to the conflict between the Moors and the Christians, although in Dalmatia its rise was probably connected with the struggles against the Ottoman Turks, in particular the victory over them at the Battle of Lepanto. Whatever its origins, the Moreška has become a major tourist attraction, and its annual performance on St Theodore's Day (July 29) has been transformed into a weekly summer event, held every Thursday evening between May and September at a pitch just outside the Land Gate or – if the weather is bad – in the local cinema near the bus station. Tickets (50Kn) are available from Marko Polo Tours.

Basically the dance tells the story of a conflict between the White King and his followers (actually dressed in red) and the Black King. The heroine, Bula (literally "veiled woman"), is kidnapped by the Black King and his army, and her betrothed tries to win her back in a ritualized sword fight that takes place within a shifting circle of dancers. The adversaries circle each other and clash weapons several times before the evil king is forced to surrender, and Bula is unchained. The strangest thing about the dance is the seemingly incongruous brass band music that invariably accompanies it – a sign that the present-day Moreška falls somewhere between medieval rite and nineteenth-century reinvention.

Similar sword dances are still performed throughout the island, although once outside Korčula Town you're more likely to find them accompanied by traditional instruments such as the *mijeh* (bagpipe). The most important of these are the **Moštra**, performed in Postrana on St Rock's Day (Aug 16), and the **Kumpanjija**, staged in several places at different times of year: Blato on St Vincent's Day (April 28), Čara on St James's Day (July 25), Smokvica on Candlemas (Feb 2) and Pupnat on Our Lady of the Snows (Aug 6). Many of these dances are performed in Korčula Town over the summer under the banner of the **Festival of Sword Dances** (Festival viteških igara), with performances running throughout July and August; the tourist office will have details.

In the past many of these dances would have been followed by the beheading of an ox, which was then roasted and divided among the participants. The practice was banned during the communist period, and its revival in Pupnat in 1999 was followed by lurid – and largely negative – reporting in the Croatian press. It's unlikely that ritual slaughter will ever form part of the dances again.

century flight of steps sweeps up to the **Land Gate** (Kopnena vrata), the main entrance to the tiny old town. Begun in 1391, the gate was completed a century later with the addition of the **Revelin**, the hulking defensive tower that looms above it. The northern side of the gate takes the form of a triumphal arch built in 1650 to honour the military governor of Dalmatia, Leonardo Foscolo, who led Venetian forces against the Turks during the Candia War – a struggle for the control of Crete – of 1645–69.

Inside the gate lies a well-ordered grid of pale-grey stone houses, most dating from before 1800. On the far side of the gate lies Trg braće Radića, a small square bordered on one side by an elegant loggia belonging to the sixteenth-century town hall and, on the other, **St Michael's Church** (Crkva svetog Mihovila). This is connected to a neighbouring building by a small bridge which was used as a private entrance to the church by members of the medieval Brotherhood of St Michael – one of many such charitable brotherhoods formed during the Middle Ages throughout the Adriatic. From here, Korčulanskog statuta 1214 leads on into the town centre, passing the **Church of Our Lady** (Crkva Gospojina; summer daily 9.30am–12.30pm & 7–11pm) on the left, a simple structure whose floor is paved with the tombstones of Korčulan nobles – it's used as a picture gallery selling works by local artists in summer. Above the high altar is a mosaic of the Virgin and Child, a dazzling confection of yellows, blues and pinks completed by Dutchman Louis Schrikkel in 1967.

The cathedral and treasury

Immediately beyond the church lies **St Mark's Cathedral** (Katedrala svetog Marka), squeezed into a diminutive space that passes for a main town square. The cathedral's facade is decorated with a gorgeous fluted rose window and a bizarre cornice frilled with strange beasts. In the centre, a matronly lady looks down with half-closed eyes; no one knows for sure who she is – suggestions have ranged from the emperor Diocletian's wife to one of a number of Hungarian queens who helped finance the church. The main figure directly above the porch is St Mark, flanked by lions pawing smaller, more subservient animals, while the door is framed by statues of Adam and Eve.

The cathedral's **interior** is one of the loveliest on the coast, in a curious mixture of styles developed over three hundred years, from the Gothic nave to the Renaissance north aisle. Local stonemason Marko Andrijić completed the elegant ciborium some time in the 1490s, topping its Corinthian columns with statuettes of Archangel Michael and the Virgin, and adding a pagoda-like roof. Beneath its canopy you can just about make out an early Tintoretto altarpiece, depicting St Mark flanked by SS Hieronymus and Bartholomew. There's a wealth of interesting clutter in the south aisle, including some of the pikes used against Uluz Ali, another Tintoretto (an *Annunciation*, with the Archangel appearing to the Virgin in a shower of sparks), and a thirteenth-century icon of the Virgin. This was once kept on nearby Badija island and is credited with offering miraculous assistance to the Venetian fleet at the Battle of Lepanto in 1571; accompanied by a flotilla of small boats, the icon is taken back to Badija every year on August 2 to preside over a special thanksgiving mass. At the end of the south aisle lie the fine Renaissance tomb of Bishop Malumbra and an altar featuring a murky, time-darkened allegory of the Holy Trinity by Venetian painter Leandro Bassano.

Many of the church's treasures have been removed to the **Bishop's Treasury** (*riznica*; July & Aug: daily 10am–noon & 5–7pm; rest of year apply at the tourist office; 10Kn), next door. This is one of the best small art collections in the country, with an exquisite set of paintings which takes in a striking *Portrait of a Man* by Carpaccio, a perceptive *Virgin and Child* by Bassano, a tiny *Madonna* by Dalmatian Renaissance artist Blaž Jurjev of Trogir, plus some Tiepolo studies of hands, and drawings by Raphael. Oddities include an ivory statuette of Mary Queen of Scots, whose skirts open to reveal kneeling figures in doublet and hose – what it's doing in Korčula remains a mystery. A modest annexe to the treasury, entered just round the corner on Marka Andrijića (same times; 5Kn), displays Roman and Byzantine pottery retrieved from offshore wrecks.

The rest of the town

Opposite the cathedral, a Venetian palace houses the **Town Museum** (Gradski muzej; July & Aug: daily 9am–1pm & 5–7pm; rest of year Mon–Sat 9am–1pm; 10Kn), whose modest display includes a copy of a fourth-century BC Greek tablet from Lumbarda – the earliest evidence of civilization on Korčula – and, upstairs, a re-creation of a typical Korčula peasant kitchen, with an open hearth surrounded by cooking pots and bed warmers.

Close by the main square, down a turning to the right, is another remnant from Venetian times, the so-called **House of Marco Polo** (Kuća Marka Pola;

daily 10am–1pm & 5–7pm; 10Kn). Korčula claims to be the birthplace of Marco Polo – not as extravagant a claim as it might seem, since the Venetians recruited many sea captains from their colonies, and Marco Polo was indeed captured by the Genoese in a sea battle off the island in 1298. Whatever the truth of the matter, it seems unlikely that he had any connection with this seventeenth-century house, which is little more than an empty shell with some terrible twentieth-century prints on the walls; it's worth visiting only for the outstanding view from the tower over Korčula's terracotta-coloured rooftops.

From here you can descend towards Šetalište Petra Kanavelića, the seafront walkway which leads round the outside of the peninsula. Walk south to the junction with Kaporova to find the **Icon Gallery** (Galerija ikona; July & Aug daily 10am–noon & 5–7pm, rest of year apply at the tourist office), where there's a permanent display of icons in the rooms of the All Saints' Brotherhood. Most of the exhibits were looted from Cretan churches at the end of the Candia War (on the pretence of saving them from falling into infidel hands), when Venice had to hand over the Mediterranean island to the Ottoman Turks. Among the Pantokrators and Virgins emblazoned in gold leaf is a haunting fifteenth-century triptych of the Passion.

From here, a covered bridge similar to the one outside St Michael's Church takes you into **All Saints' Church** (Crkva svih svetih), with its brooding Renaissance interior and one of the most impressive Baroque altarpieces in Dalmatia – an eighteenth-century Pietà carved from walnut wood by Austrian master George Raphael Donner, enclosed by a fifteenth-century ciborium in imitation of the one in the cathedral. On the far side of the altar is another of Blaž Jurjev's fifteenth-century masterpieces, a polyptych centred on a chilling *Deposition*, below which the tiny figures of the All Saints' Brotherhood – identifiable from their trademark white robes – kneel in prayer.

If you're in the mood for more paintings, head west from the old town along Put sv. Nikole to the **Maksimilijan Vanka Gallery** (Galerija Maksimilijana Vanke; July & Aug daily 6–9pm; 5Kn), some five minutes' distant, which hosts summer exhibitions by prominent Croatian artists.

Beaches and islands

The nearest **beaches** to the old town are on the headland around the *Hotel Marko Polo*, though they're crowded, rocky and uncomfortable. The shingle beach in front of the *Bon Repos* hotel and *Kalac* campsite is much nicer, and there's a sandy beach a short bus ride away in Lumbarda (see opposite). Alternatively, take a water taxi (15Kn) from the harbour on the eastern side of town on the way to the bus station to one of the **Skoji islands** just offshore. The largest and nearest is **Badija**, where you can either disembark at the *Hotel Badija* – from which tracks lead to secluded beaches and a couple of elementary snack bars – or continue onwards to the naturist part of the island round the corner. The long shingle beaches of Orebić (see p.349) are also only a fifteen-minute ferry ride away; boats run roughly hourly from the pier opposite the *Hotel Korčula* throughout the day.

Eating and drinking

There are more pizzerias than you can shake a stick at in the old town, and a number of decent **restaurants** too; wherever you eat, try some of the excellent local white **wines**: Grk from Lumbarda, and Pošip and Rukatac, both from the area around the villages of Čara and Smokvica, are the best. For picnics, there's a fruit and vegetable **market** just below the Land Gate, where you'll also find the Mediator supermarket.

Drinking in Korčula is quite animated during the day. The cafés on Plokata 19. travnja are busy with locals and tourists alike; while *Kiwi*, just off Plokata, is good for ice cream. At night, however, Korčula becomes Snorečula – there's an almost total lack of decent bars in the Old Town, and the string of flashy places just behind the bus station on Šetalište Frana Kršinića are a curiously joyless bunch. The only place which regularly gets packed out is *Olea*, between the Old Town and bus station at Prolaz tri sulara, a friendly if at times chaotic bar which attracts most local and visiting youth on summer evenings. A nightlife of sorts – tame discos or warbling crooners for the most part – can be found in the hotels.

Restaurants

Adio Mare Svetog Roka. Located just by the alleyway leading down to Marco Polo's House, this is a tourist favourite of long standing, offering top-quality fare in an atmospheric, high-ceilinged room of medieval vintage. As well as the obvious seafood, look out for Korčulanska *pašticada*. Arrive early to make sure of a table – the queue of would-be diners makes the street outside virtually impassable.

Buffet Tramonto Top of the stairway beside the tourist office. A good choice of pizza and pasta, including a couple of vegetarian options.

Gradski podrum Trg Antuna i Stjepana Radića. Superbly situated, with tables strewn across one of the old town's most atmospheric open spaces, and a very wide menu, featuring local fish as well as continental-Croatian meat dishes.

Kanavelić Šetalište Petra Kanavelića. Formal dining in a highly regarded restaurant; the fresh fish and grilled scampi are quite delicious, but a shade more expensive than elsewhere in town.

Konoba Morski konjić Šetalište Petra Kanavelića. Situated right on the northern tip of the peninsula (and not to be confused with the flashier *Morski konjić* restaurant on the eastern side), this is a small and intimate place with good fresh fish, although the benches outside are a bit exposed to sea breezes.

Marinero ul. Marka Andrijića. Exemplary seafood dishes including delicious grilled fish, served up in cosy rooms with bits of maritime junk hanging from the ceiling – or at outdoor tables crammed into a narrow stepped street.

Planjak Plokata 19. travnja. Moderately priced, unpretentious place offering the full range of local grill fare and plenty of outdoor seating.

Around the island

The beauty of Korčula Town only serves to emphasize just how short on appeal the rest of the island is. The only other major attraction are the beaches just beyond **LUMBARDA**, 8km south of Korčula Town and accessible by regular buses (Mon–Sat hourly; 5 daily on Sun). It takes about twenty minutes to walk to the beaches from Lumbarda. First, continue along the main road south until you reach a small chapel. From here, the track on the right leads to **Prižna bay**, a glorious two-hundred-metre stretch of sand backed by a couple of cafés, while the track on the left goes to **Bilin Žal**, a far rockier strand with brief sandy stretches and dramatic views of the coastal mountains.

The **tourist office**, in the centre near the bus stop (July & Aug Mon–Sat 8am–10pm, Sun 10am–10pm; ☎020/712-005, ✉tz-lumbarda@du.hinet.hr), will help locate private **rooms** (❶) and point you in the direction of the growing number of family-run **pensions** in the suburban villa zone on the north side of town. Of these, *Pansion Lovrić*, Lumbarda bb (☎020/712-052; ❷), offers comfortable en-suite rooms and an excellent restaurant. There's also the *Vela Postrana* **campsite** between the centre and the beaches, although it's in an open field with not much shade.

Heading in the other direction out of Korčula Town, a single road (served by six buses daily) runs the length of the island west to Vela Luka, passing most of the island's major settlements en route. These are a series of largely bland villages, often connected by rough road to the nearest strip of coast, where there are usually a few holiday villas, some sort of rocky beach, a store and – sometimes – private rooms, though they're almost impossible to reach without your own transport.

Forty kilometres west of Korčula Town, **BLATO** is something of an antidote to all this, an old-fashioned country town that's easily the most agreeable of Korčula's inland settlements. First colonized by the Greeks, Blato (literally "mud" or "swamp") is at the centre of a wine-growing district and is attractively bisected by a magnificent avenue of lime trees. At the western end of the island, **VELA LUKA** may be your first view of Korčula if you're arriving by ferry, but it's not really of any interest apart from a string of vivacious seafront cafés which sadly fail to overcome the town's all-round charm deficit. There's a **tourist office** (Mon–Sat 8am–8pm, Sun 8am–noon; ☎020/813-619, ✉tzo-vela-luka@du.tel .hr) at the rear of the triangular waterfront square which has **rooms** (❶).

Lastovo

Directly south of Korčula, tiny **LASTOVO** lies at the centre of an archipelago of 45 uninhabited islets some five and a half hours from Split. Remote and virtually self-sufficient in food, Lastovo feels much more isolated that any of the other Adriatic islands, and there's a sense of pride and independence here, most obviously expressed in the annual **Poklad** festival (see box on p.348) at the beginning of Lent. Like Vis, Lastovo was closed to foreigners from 1976 until 1989 owing to its importance as a military outpost, and organized tourism has never caught on, but what it lacks in hotels and amenities it more than makes up for in its extraordinary sense of isolation and in its natural, wooded beauty. The island has only one major settlement, **Lastovo Town**, where most of the remaining 1500 islanders live.

Vukodlaci and other vampiric houseguests

Express an interest in **vampires** in today's Dalmatia and you'll probably be told that you've come to the wrong country – and yet belief in the supernatural creatures was widespread hereabouts until a couple of centuries ago. One of the last recorded outbreaks of vampire mania in Croatia took place on Lastovo in 1737, when officials from Dubrovnik had to dissuade the local populace from carrying out mass exhumations of those suspected of walking with the undead.

According to Croatian folk belief, the most common form of vampire was a **vukodlak** (often translated as "werewolf", although it clearly means something quite different), which basically consisted of the skin of a human corpse puffed up with the breath of the devil and further bloated with the blood of its victims. The *vukodlak* was an all-purpose bogeyman whose existence could explain away all manner of crises and conflicts: anything from listlessness among the local livestock to marital problems were blamed on the bloodsuckers (it was said that *vukodlaci* visited the beds of bored wives and pleasured them in the night). A **mora** was a female equivalent of a *vukodlak*, nightly sapping the strength of the menfolk; while **macići** were mischievous young *vukodlaci* who created envy and discord by bringing good luck to some villagers, misfortune to others – if a farmer got rich, neighbours would say that he had a *macić* in the house.

People were said to turn into *vukodlaci* after their death if a dog, cat or mouse passed under their coffin while it was being borne to the grave. The only cure was to dig up the body and cut its hamstrings to prevent it from wandering about at night. Visiting the Dalmatian hinterland in the 1770s, the intrepid Venetian traveller Alberto Fortis discovered that some of the locals asked their families to carry out this operation as soon as they died, just to be on the safe side.

Ferries leave Split for the island's port at **Ubli** once or twice daily all year, calling at Hvar Town and Vela Luka on Korčula en route. There's a petrol station and a couple of shops opposite the ferry dock, while the incongruously chic *Lounge Lizard* **café** on the harbour rents out mountain bikes, but not much else. You're better off making your way directly to Lastovo Town – all ferries are met by a connecting bus – or to the hamlet of **PASADUR** 3km north of Ubli, where the island's only hotel, the *Solitudo* (℡020/805-014; ❹), offers simple en-suite rooms, a restaurant and a late-night bar.

Lastovo Town and around

Unusually for the capital of a Croatian island, **LASTOVO TOWN** faces away from the sea, spreading itself over the steep banks of a natural amphitheatre with a fertile agricultural plain below. There's a road at the top, a road at the bottom, and a maze of narrow alleys and stone stairways between. The town's buildings date mainly from the fifteenth and sixteenth centuries – although depopulation has left many empty and dilapidated – and are notable for their curious chimneys shaped like miniature minarets, although there's no record of Arab or Turkish raiders ever making it this far.

The fifteenth-century parish **Church of SS Cosmas and Damian** (Crkva svetog Kuzme i Damjana) in the centre of town is worth a look for its interior, richly adorned with sixteenth- and seventeenth-century paintings and icons, with a dainty fifteenth-century loggia opposite the entrance. Above the town lie the remains of the old French **fort**, built in 1810 above some much older fortifications and now used as a weather station – it's a stiff walk up, but worth it for the views from the top, with Lastovo on one side and the sea on the other. Heading downhill from the main square a road hairpins its way to two tiny harbours: **Lučica**, a tiny hamlet with a mix of derelict houses and renovated holiday homes, and, a little further on, the quieter **Sveti Mihovil**.

The Poklad

Lastovo's carnival is one of the strangest in Croatia, featuring the ritual humiliation and murder of a straw puppet, the **Poklad**. After a long weekend of preparation things come to a head on Shrove Tuesday, when the Poklad is led through town on a donkey by the men of Lastovo, who dress for the occasion in a uniform of red shirts, black waistcoats and bowler hats. Following this, the Poklad is attached to a long rope and hoisted from one end of town to the other three times while fireworks are let off beneath it. Each transit is met by chanting and the drawing of swords. Finally, the Poklad is put back on the donkey and taken to the square in front of the parish church, to the accompaniment of music and dancing. At the end of the evening, the villagers dance the **Lastovsko kolo**, a sword dance similar to the Moreška in Korčula (see box on p.343), and the Poklad is impaled on a long stake and burnt. Drinking and dancing continues in the village hall until dawn.

Local tradition has it that the Poklad symbolizes a young messenger who was sent by Catalan pirates to demand the town's surrender, although it's more likely that the ritual actually derives from ancient fertility rites. Whatever its roots, the islanders take the occasion very seriously, and it's certainly not enacted for the benefit of outsiders. Lastovčani from all over the world return to their home village to attend the Poklad, when accommodation is at a premium. If you do want to attend, contact the tourist office well in advance.

Ask at Lastovo's tourist office whether any local boatmen are offering excursions to **Šaplun**, an uninhabited islet to the south which has a lovely fine shingle beach. Otherwise, you can walk to **Zaklopatica**, a hamlet 3km away on the northern coast of the island with a yachting harbour and a couple of *konobe*, or to **Skrivena Luka** 5km south, a deep bay backed by sandy hills and cleared of vegetation by forest fires, where there are several rocky places to swim.

Practicalities

The bus from the ferry dock at Ubli stops on the main square right outside the **tourist office** (variable opening times, but always open when the bus from the boat arrives; ☎ & ℗020/801-018), where you can pick up a basic map and book **rooms** (❶). You'll probably be asked whether you want full board; consider this carefully, since there are precious few eating places on the island and the home cooking you'll be offered is usually exceptionally good, and served in enormous portions. Needless to say, fish features heavily, along with an array of the island's vegetables and wild mushrooms, washed down with local wine.

There are a couple of bars, a bank and a grocery store on the square. Hiding in the back alleys at the bottom end of the village is the town's one **restaurant**, the *Konoba Bačvara*, serving up freshly caught seafood in a snug indoor room or on a terrace hung with fishing nets. For those prepared to wander further afield, the *Triton* in Zaklopatica is another great place for grilled fish. Back in Lastovo Town, there's a **café-bar** down in Sveti Mihovil bay which often stays open until the last customer staggers home.

The Pelješac peninsula

Just across the Pelješac channel (Pelješki kanal) from Korčula is the **PELJEŠAC PENINSULA**, a slim, mountainous finger of land which stretches for some 90km from Lovište in the west to the mainland in the east. Parts of the peninsula are exceptionally beautiful, with tiny villages and sheltered coves rimmed by beaches, but although it's a reasonably popular holiday area development remains low-key. The downside is that public transport is meagre except along the main Korčula–Orebić–Ston–Dubrovnik route, and most of the smaller places are impossible to get to without a car.

Orebić

A short ferry-hop from Korčula, the small town of **OREBIĆ** was a subsidiary trading outlet of the Dubrovnik Republic for almost five hundred years, and later enjoyed a brief period of extraordinary prosperity during the nineteenth-century revival of Adriatic trade, during which the town's merchants set up a maritime society, built a huge church and constructed their own shipyards to supply an independent merchant fleet. The bubble soon burst, however, and the society and yards were wound up in 1887, after which the town slipped back into obscurity until the emergence of mass tourism. Orebić has featured in the package brochures ever since, largely on account of its long shingle **beaches**.

Today, Orebić straggles along the seashore on either side of its jetties, an aimless but attractive mixture of the old and new. The best part of town is along Obala Pomoraca, just east of the quays, where generations of sea captains built a series of comfortable country villas, set behind a luscious subtropical screen of palms and cacti. The **Maritime Museum** (Pomorski muzej; Mon–Fri 9am–noon & 6–8pm; 5Kn) at Trg Mimbeli 12 sports a few crusty amphorae and a dull collection of naval memorabilia relating to the Orebić fleet. Far better to head up to the **Franciscan monastery** (Franjevački samostan; Mon–Sat 9am–noon & 4–6pm, Sun 4–6pm; 10Kn) on a rocky spur twenty minutes' walk out of town – to get there, head west from the ferry quay as far as the *Bellevue* hotel, then bear right onto the road which snakes up the hillside. The monastery was built in the 1480s to house a miraculous icon known as Our Lady of the Angels, brought here by Franciscans from the Bay of Kotor, just south of Dubrovnik. The icon was thought to protect mariners from shipwreck – Orebić ship captains would sound their sirens on passing the monastery on their way into port. The picture still occupies pride of place in the church: a stylized, Byzantine-influenced Madonna and Child surrounded by an oversized frame in which gilded angels cavort in a sky full of bluish cotton-wool clouds. The monastery **museum** displays votive paintings commissioned by crews who were saved from pirates or storms after offering prayers to the Virgin, and models of ships once owned by Orebić magnates such as the Mimbeli brothers, whose onion-domed mausoleum can be seen in the graveyard outside. There's also a wonderful view of the Pelješac channel from the monastery's terrace.

There are even better views from the 961-metre summit of **Sveti Ilija**, the bare mountain which looms over Orebić to the northwest. A marked path to the summit (4hr walk each way) strikes uphill just before you get to the monastery (look out for the red-and-white paint marks on the rocks), although it's largely unshaded. There are some lovely pebble **beaches** stretching west from the ferry terminals in front of the hotels, although the best of Orebić's beaches is twenty minutes' walk east from the ferry terminal at Trstenica, where you'll find a crescent of shingle just about fine enough to make sandcastles out of, and views of the distant island of Mljet's ragged coast.

Practicalities

Buses pull up beside the **ferry quay**, from where the **tourist office** is five minutes' walk east on Trg Mimbeli (July & Aug daily 8am–9pm, Sept–June Mon–Fri 9am–1pm; ☎020/713-718); an additional information kiosk right by the quay may be open in summer. The main office deals in **rooms** (❶), both in Orebić and in the nearby villages of Kučište and Viganj (see below). Alternatively, there's a string of medium-rise concrete **hotels** spreading out west of the landing stage, looking onto a long stretch of pebble beach. Best of the bunch is the all-inclusive *Orsan* (☎020/713-026; ❼), with cramped but comfy rooms with TV and balcony, and a dinky outdoor pool. Simpler, but still serviceable, are the nearby *Bellevue* (☎020/713-148; ❹) and *Rathaneum* (☎020/713-022; ❹). There are two **campsites** behind Trstenica beach and several more in private suburban gardens further east. For **food**, the *Bistro Jadran*, on Obala pomoraca just beyond the tourist office, does a decent range of pizzas and inexpensive grill food; *Taverna Mlinica*, midway between the tourist office and Trstenica beach, serves up traditional dishes baked *ispod saća* (under an ember-covered lid) amid rustic furnishings – expect pay 150Kn for a slap-up meal.

Kučište and Viganj

West of Orebić, the road follows the coast past the relatively unspoiled villages of Kučište and Viganj, both of which have shingle beaches, a string of shore-side campsites, and – in the case of Viganj at least – a burgeoning windsurfing scene. There's little in the way of package holiday development along this stretch of coast but plenty of private rooms (which can be booked through the tourist office in Orebić, see above), making it a laid-back, low-key alternative to the bustle of Orebić and Korčula. There are only three buses a day from Orebić (one on Sundays), but the presence of a privately operated boat service from Kučište and Viganj to Korčula Town ensures that you can still get round and see the sights.

Five kilometres out of Orebić, sleepy **KUĆIŠTE** presents a wiggly line of rust-coloured stone houses facing the water. The tourist office midway through the village (July & Aug daily 9am–noon & 5–8pm) provides information on boat departures to Korčula and doles out local rooms (❶). There's a soothing lack of things to do in Kučište, save for sunbathe on the small-boat jetties strung out along the shoreline, stroll in the scrub-covered foothills of Mount Sveti Ilija above the village, or admire the view of Korčula's woolly tree cover from a brace of waterfront cafés.

It's only a fifteen-minute walk from Kučište to the next village along, **VIGANJ**, which lies on the far side of a pebbly spur of beach from which windsurfers launch themselves into the Pelješac channel. Most of the surfers stay at one of the three campsites immediately behind the beach: the straggling and largely unshaded *Ponta*, the large, well-organized *Liberan*, or the orchard-like *Anthony Boy*. *Camping Liberan* boasts a windsurfing school (☎020/719-330) where it's possible to rent boards (60Kn/hour or 250Kn/day) or sign up for courses (four-day beginners' courses start at 970Kn). A little further on in the village itself, the tourist office (July & Aug daily 8am–noon & 5–8pm) will sort you out with a room (❶). There's a cheap restaurant serving pizzas and grills in front of the *Ponta* campsite; while the plant-filled veranda of *Bistro Karmela*, next to the tourist office, is the perfect place to relax over a drink.

East to Ston

East of Orebić, the main road twists up into the mountains before reaching, after 15km, the turning to the lazy port of **TRPANJ** (served by 4 buses daily from Orebić), which lies at the end of a ravine on Pelješac's northern coast. It's not a bad place in which to get stuck, with a couple of cafés on the Riva, a tree-shaded pebble beach at the end of the harbour and views of the Makarska Riviera's dramatic mountain backdrop on the other side of the water. The **tourist office** (Mon–Sat 8am–2pm & 4–8pm, Sun 8am–2pm; ☎020/743-433) on the front has plenty of **rooms** (❶), and there are **ferries** to **Ploče** on the mainland proper, where you can pick up buses north to Split or south to Dubrovnik.

Back on the main road, it's another 18km to the turn-off for **TRSTENIK**, on the peninsula's southern side, another pleasant destination set tight against the hills behind a couple of tiny beaches. A further 14km along the main road at Dubrava there's a minor road (not served by bus) down to one of the best beaches on the coast at **Žuljana**, 6km away – a tiny resort built round a sheltered bay at the foot of a steep rocky gorge. There's a **tourist office** (☎020/756-227) with unreliable opening times right on the beach, plenty of private **rooms** (❶) and a reasonable **campsite**, the *Brijezi*. For **food**, there are a couple of unpretentious bar-restaurants on the harbourfront, where you'll also see signs advertising boat trips to even more remote beaches.

Ston and Mali Ston

About 20km beyond Dubrava, the twin settlements of Ston and Mali Ston straddle the neck of land which joins Pelješac to the mainland. **STON** (sometimes called Veliki – or "Great" – Ston to differentiate it from Mali Ston), an important salt-producing town, was swallowed up by Dubrovnik in 1333, becoming the most important fortress along the republic's northern frontier. Piled up above the saltpans of its long sea inlet, the town is framed by its dramatic and unusually shaped fourteenth-century walls, whose V-shaped apex is on the hillside high above the town's narrow streets. You can walk along the stretch of walls immediately above the town, and potter around the alleyways below, among a mix of Renaissance- and Gothic-style houses laid out on a gridiron plan. If central Ston looks a bit ramshackle it's probably the result of the 1996 earthquake, when almost all of the town's buildings suffered structural damage – many remain uninhabited to this day. Just west of Ston, the pre-Romanesque **St Michael's Church** (Crkva svetog Mihovila) squats atop a conical hill overlooking the saltpans and has twelfth-century frescoes inside; however, it's only infrequently open, so ask at the tourist office before making your way up.

Fifteen minutes' walk northeast of Ston, **MALI STON** began life as the outermost bastion of Ston's defensive system, and the line of fortifications linking Ston with Mali Ston can still be seen trailing majestically across the adjacent hillsides. It's now a sleepy little village of old stone houses pressed within its walls, looking out onto Mali Ston bay, where the village's **oyster beds** are marked out by wooden poles, hung with ropes on which the oysters are encouraged to grow prior to harvesting in May and June. The village's traditional popularity as a seafood centre has been augmented by its growing reputation as a venue for romantic weekend breaks – perhaps something to do with the oysters' aphrodisiac effect. Following the narrow lanes up from the harbour, you'll soon reach a crescent-shaped fortress which marked the north-easternmost extent of Ston's sophisticated network of defences. Nowadays it's an uninhabited shell, though steps lead up to a parapet from where there are good views.

There's no **beach** in Mali Ston, but the jetties and rocks around the harbour are pleasant places to sunbathe and the water is clean enough to swim in. Otherwise the nearest pebble beach is by the *Prapratno* campsite (see below) to the southwest.

Practicalities

Buses pull up on Ston's main street, where there's a **tourist office** (Mon–Fri 7am–1pm & 5–7pm, Sat 7am–1pm; T & F 020/754-452) which can fix up local **rooms** (❶). There are a couple of lovely family-run **hotels** on Mali Ston's harbour: the *Villa Koruna* (T 020/754-359, F 754-642; ❹) is a six-room pension whose small but stylish rooms boast air conditioning and TV, while the slightly grander *Ostrea* (T 020/754-555, F 754-575, E ostrea.info@ostrea.hr; ❺) offers posher rooms with a slap-up evening meal included in the price. The nearest **campsite** is the *Prapratno* (T 020/754-000), about 4km southwest of town, down a steep side-road just off the main route to Orebić. It has its own beach, a couple of grill-restaurants and impressive views of the mountains of Mljet across the water.

Mali Ston also has several upmarket **restaurants** offering top-quality fish and shellfish; in terms of quality and service there's little to choose between the *Koruna*, the *Ostrea* (both in the hotels of the same name) or the *Kapetanova Kuća* which, as the oldest of the three, boasts a loyal clientele of local big-spenders – all are close to each other on the waterfront. Cheaper fare is available in Ston, where *Konoba kod Bače* on the main street has a range of inexpensive *marende* (brunches), as well as meaty grills.

The Southern Dalmatian coast

The coast south of Split is perhaps the most dramatic in the country, with some of the Adriatic's best beaches sheltering beneath the papier-mâché heights of the karst mountains, all easily accessible on the frequent coastal bus service. Most of the beaches are pebble or shingle, and all are served by at least one campsite and (usually) a stock of private rooms.

The coastline immediately south of Split is uninspiring, a twenty-kilometre stretch of modern apartments and weekend houses culminating in one of south Dalmatia's most prominent industrial white elephants, the ferro-chrome plant at **Dugi rat**. Once beyond here things improve markedly, with the historical town of **Omiš** marking the entrance to the rugged **Cetina gorge**, and a useful base from which to visit the strange and wonderful lakes at **Imotski** inland. South of Omiš stretch the celebrated beaches of the **Makarska Riviera** – which runs from Brela to Gradac – dramatically perched at the base of the **Biokovo mountains**. **Ploče**, the one other big town between Makarska and Dubrovnik, is an industrial port rather than a resort, and the rest of southern Dalmatia is a relatively low on attractions until you get to Dubrovnik itself, covered in chapter 6.

Plentiful **buses** zoom up and down the Magistrala between Dubrovnik and Split, though Makarska and Ploče are the only places along this stretch of coast which have proper bus stations with timetable information; elsewhere, you'll just have to wait by the roadside until something turns up (during the day, it's unlikely you'll have to wait more than an hour). Makarska and Ploče are also useful **ferry** hubs: the former has links with Sumartin on Brač, the latter has regular services to Trpanj on the Pelješac peninsula. Note that travelling between Makarska and Dubrovnik entails passing through a small chunk of **Bosnia-Hercegovina** – visas aren't required for this, but be prepared for passport checks.

Omiš and around

The first town of any size south of Split is **OMIŠ**, at the end of the Cetina Gorge, a defile furrowed out of the bone-grey karst by the River Cetina. For centuries, Omiš was an impregnable pirate stronghold – repeated efforts to winkle them out, including one expedition in 1221 led by the pope himself, all failed. These days the town is rather dominated by the Magistrala, which passes just south of the old quarter, a huddle of cramped alleys spread out along a pleasant central street, Knezova Kačića. Remnants of the old city walls survive, and two semi-ruined Venetian fortresses cling to the bare rocks above. The lowest of these is the **Mirabela**, reached by a zigzagging path that begins behind Omiš parish church. A steep scramble up staircases affords access to the roof of its tower (June–Sept daily 8am–noon & 4.30–8.30pm; 10Kn), which offers a good view of the offshore island of Brač. Perched more precariously on a pinnacle of rock higher up is a slightly more ruined stronghold, the **Fortica**. It can be reached from the town centre via a steeply ascending road, then goat track, in about 45 minutes – you'll be rewarded with a stunning panorama of the offshore islands. The new town lies to the south, a featureless stretch of post-World War II buildings behind the main town **beach**, composed of hard and uninviting sand – you're better off heading for the long shingle beaches of **Duće**, about 2km back along the Magistrala, or for the nice shingle beach at the village of **Nemira**, 3km southeast.

Omiš is famous for its festival of local **klape** – the traditional male-voice choirs of Dalmatia – which takes place on weekends throughout July, usually culminating on the last weekend of the month with open-air performances in the old town. *Klape* are an important feature of Dalmatian life, and almost every town or village has at least one of them. Songs deal with typical Dalmatian pre-occupations like love, the sea and fishing, and are usually sung in local dialect. It's well worth a trip from Split; the Omiš tourist office will have details.

As well as the intercity buses plying the Magistrala, Omiš is also served by local bus from Split (#60, caught from the Lazareti bus stop at the eastern end of the Riva). The **tourist office**, just off the Magistrala on Trg kneza Miroslava (mid-June to mid-Sept Mon–Fri 8am–8pm, Sat 8am–noon; mid-Sept to mid-June Mon–Fri 8am–3pm; ☎ & ℱ 021/861-350, ✉ tz-omis@st.tel.hr), has details of local excursions up the Cetina Gorge (see below). Omiš is a popular place in July and August, when **rooms** (❶) can be hard to find unless you arrive early in the day or reserve in advance – Active Holidays, Knezova Kačića bb (☎ 021/861-829, ⓦ www.activeholidays-croatia.com), and Slap, Trg Poljički bb (☎ 021/871-108 & 757-336, ✉ slap@st.hinet.hr), are the places to make enquiries. The nearest **campsite** is the *Galeb* (☎ 021/862-130), just north of town and handy for the beaches of Duće. There are plenty of places **to eat** on Knezova Kačića; the atmospheric *Konoba u našeg Marina* serves up simple snacks like *pršut* and local cheese, while the nearby *Milo* has a wider range of meaty grills and seafood. The **cafés** of Trg Stjepana Radića, at the eastern end of Knezova Kačića, are lovely places to sit outside in the summer.

Inland from Omiš: the Cetina Gorge and Imotski

The River Cetina rises just east of Knin (see p.283) and flows down to meet the sea at Omiš, carving its way through the karst of the Zagora to produce some spectacular rock formations on the way. The most eye-catching portions are those just outside Omiš, and 23km upstream near Zadvarje, although there's no public transport along the valley so you'll need a car to see all the interesting bits. Over the summer, boat trips are advertised on Omiš's quayside (20Kn per person; they depart when full), but they only go about 5km upstream before stopping at one of the riverbank restaurants. You can also **raft** down the upper stretches of the gorge (see "Rafting down the River Cetina", below).

Out of Omiš, the first few kilometres of the Cetina gorge are truly dramatic, with the mountains pressing in on a narrow winding valley. Further up, the valley floor widens, making room for some swampy stretches of half-sunken deciduous forest. There's a string of good waterside **restaurants** along this part of the gorge: *Kaštil Slanica*, 4km out of Omiš, specializes in freshwater fish as well as *žablji kraci* (frogs' legs) and the tasty *brudet od jegulje* (spicy eel soup), while the larger *Radmanove Mlinice* (boat trips from Omiš often end up here), about 1500m further on, is known for its trout, as well as lamb baked *ispod peke*.

Rafting down the Cetina

Rafting down the River Cetina is fast becoming the premier activity-holiday attraction in southern Dalmatia, with a growing number of local travel agents offering the trip. Excursions usually start at Penšići, 16km upstream from Omiš, and end up at Radmanove Mlinice 10km further down. The river only gets wild after strong rains, so most trips involve a gentle descent rather than a white-knuckle, whitewater ride – giving you plenty of time to admire the dense riverine vegetation and rugged cliffs on either side. Rafting excursions can be arranged in Omiš through Active Holidays or Slap (see above), or Adria Tourist, Trg kralja Tomislava 4 (ⓦ www.rafting-pinta.com). If you're based in Split, Trogir or Makarska, local branches of Atlas will organize the trip. Expect to pay 200–250Kn per person.

Soon after the *Radmanove Mlinice* the road turns inland, twisting its way up onto a plateau surrounded by dry hills streaked with scrub. The village of **ZADVAR-JE**, at the top of a steep sequence of hairpins, offers views of the most impressive stretch of the gorge. Follow a sign marked *Vodopad* (Waterfall) in the centre of the village to a scruffy car park on the edge of a cliff, from where there's a view north-east towards a canyon suspended halfway up a rock face, with the river plunging down via two waterfalls to a gorge deep below. The cliffs lining the canyon sprout several more minor waterfalls whenever the local hills fill up with rain.

From Zadvarje, you can either head south to rejoin the Magistrala, or carry on northwards through **Šestanovac** to a major T-junction 7km beyond at **Cista Provo**, where you're faced with a choice of routes – eastward to the lakes of Imotski (see below), or westward to **TRILJ**. This otherwise unassuming rural town offers some of the best accommodation in the area in the shape of the *Sveti Mihovil* **hotel**, Bana Jelačića 8 (℡021/831-790, ⓦwww.avanturist -club.com; ❹), which offers smart rooms with private bathroom and TV, and excellent dining in the attached *Čaporice* **restaurant**, with Zagora specialities such as *arambašići* (stuffed cabbage leaves) and the ubiquitous *žablji kraci*. The hotel is an excellent base for adventure tourism, arranging rafting and kayak-ing on the Cetina, horse-riding in the hills, and mountain bike rental (100Kn/day). Beyond Trilj you can continue northwest towards Senj (see p.226), or head east along the road to Livno in Bosnia-Hercegovina.

Imotski

Many of the buses that pass through Omiš from Split are bound for **IMOTS-KI**, a provincial town set amid stony hills hard up against the Hercegovinian border. Unfortunately these buses don't follow the Cetina gorge route, but it's a highly scenic ride nevertheless, climbing over scrub-covered mountains south of Omiš before ploughing through fertile valleys thick with vineyards. Buses drop you at the eastern end of town, from where it's a short walk downhill to a main square hemmed in by green-shuttered stone houses. However most vis-itors come to Imotski to gawp at the two lakes on the outskirts of town, reached by following Ante Starčevića westward from the square. A ten-minute walk brings you to the first of these, the so-called **Modro Jezero** or Blue Lake, which occupies a monstrous hole in the karst formed by the collapse of under-ground caverns. The depression is 290m deep, and fissures near the bottom keep the lake fed with water whenever the local rock is saturated with rainfall. In dry summer weather the water level drops dramatically, revealing a deep basin with sheer cliffs on one side and steep scree-covered slopes on most oth-ers. A path switchbacks its way down into this veritable moon-crater of a place, offering several vantage points en route before arriving at the water's edge. The going is rough and gravelly, so don sensible footwear (and try and ignore the locals nonchalantly traipsing down in their flip-flops). Fifteen minutes' walk further west from the Modro Jezero, the **Crveno Jezero** ("Red Lake") is if anything an even more gob-smacking sight, owing its name to the fact that it gets less sunlight than the Blue Lake, and reflects only the sombre russet and grey hues of the surrounding cliffs. The lake stands at the bottom of a pit some 300m wide and 500m deep – water usually fills the lower 250–300m. You can't get down to the water's edge, but you get a marvellous view of this awesome hole in the ground from the rim of the depression.

There are plenty of **cafés** on Imotski's main square and along Šetalište Stjepana Radića, the street that leads off it. The *Imota* **hotel**, Stjepana Radića 15 (℡021/841-402; ❸), has been subjected to long periods of closure due to own-ership disputes, so ring in advance before setting your heart on staying there.

The Makarska Riviera

South of Omiš the road twists round the headlands of the Biokovo mountains into the section of coast known as the **MAKARSKA RIVIERA**, a string of resorts boasting long pebble beaches ranging from the over-exploited to the relatively unknown. Most of the villages here were originally based a kilometre or two inland until the growth of tourism, when families abandoned their old homes and built new houses down on the coast. With a few exceptions, therefore, the shoreline resorts are predominantly modern and charmless, but if all you want is a beach and cheap beer and pizza, then the Makarska Riviera is a decent place to get them.

The town of **Makarska**, roughly in the middle of the region, has the best nightlife and is a good base from which to tackle the ascent of the **Biokovo range**, while **Brela**, just to the north, has managed to preserve something of its chic, coastal-village-made-good atmosphere. The south of the Riviera is quite bland in comparison, attracting tourists mainly from the former Eastern Europe and working out slightly cheaper than the north.

Brela

Surrounded by aromatic pine groves, the northernmost settlement of the Makarska Riviera, **BRELA**, sports a fine strand of beach next to a steep warren of alleyways, where a mixture of old stone houses and modern holiday homes pokes out from a blanket of subtropical vegetation. The beach, backed by a clutch of hotels, stretches for a couple of kilometres to the north of the town centre before being broken up by little rocky headlands.

The **tourist office** lies just behind a parade of shops midway along the seafront (irregular opening times; ☎ & ℻021/618-337, ✉tz-brela@st.tel.hr, ⓦwww.brela.hr) and has **rooms** (❷), as do the Adria-service (☎021/618-393) and Bonavia (☎021/619-019) tourist agencies nearby. The best of Brela's **hotels** are the *Maestral* (☎021/603-671, ℻603-688; ❻) and the ziggurat-like *Soline* (☎021/603-207, ℻603-208; ❻), both large and comfortable package-oriented complexes 500m north of the centre along the coastal path, with good beach access.

Two **restaurants** worth eating at for their locations are the *Punta Rata*, about ten minutes' walk north of the centre along the beach, and the restaurant of the *Hotel Berulia*, which has a beautiful elevated position on the beach between Brela and Baška Voda – both have a decent range of fresh and reasonably priced seafood.

Baška Voda

BAŠKA VODA, 3km southeast along the Magistrala (though you can just as easily walk along the coastal path), is less charming and more commercialized than Brela. The town is modern and unexciting, although the **Archeological Collection** (Arheološka zbirka; Mon–Sat 6–9pm; 5Kn) just off the Riva has a small but imaginatively presented selection of finds from Gradina, the hillock immediately west of the centre, which was the site of a settlement from the Bronze Age to late Roman times. There's a re-creation of a late Roman hearth, and some simply decorated storage vessels and glassware.

Some Split–Makarska buses pass right along Baška Voda's waterfront, although most coastal services pick up and drop off high above the centre on the Magistrala, from where it's a fifteen-minute walk down Put kapelice to the seafront. Here you'll find a helpful **tourist office** at Obala svetog Nikole 31 (daily 8am–9pm; ☎ & ⓕ021/620-713, ⓦwww.baskavoda.hr) and a string of agencies – Duga, Obala svetog Nikole 9 (☎021/620-207, ⓔduga-bv@st.tel .hr); Bonavia, Obala svetog Nikole 83 (☎021/620-400, ⓔbonavia@st.hinet .hr); and Mariva, Obaa svetog Nikole 29 (☎021/620-463, ⓔmarivaturist@ podgora.net) to name but three – offering **rooms** (❷) and apartments (❸). Of the **hotels**, the *Slavija* (☎021/620-003, ⓔhotels-baskavoda@st.tel.hr; ❻) is a central beachfront establishment of 1930s vintage with TV in all the rooms, while the more modern *Horizont* (☎021/604-555, ⓔhotels-baskavoda@st .tel.hr; ❼), a few steps south, is one of the best hotels on the Dalmatian coast and earns its four-star rating, with spongy carpets, gleaming bathrooms and air conditioning. There's a **campsite**, the *Baško Polje* (☎021/612-329), at the south end of town near the exit off the Magistrala – if approaching by bus, get off at the Baško Polje stop (rather than the central Baška Voda one) and walk downhill.

For some of the best **food** in the area, catch a taxi to *Konoba Biston*, 5km uphill from Baška Voda in the hillside village of **Bast**, where you can dine on succulent *pršut*, tasty home-made bread, and an excellent *pašticada*.

Makarska

MAKARSKA, 10km south of Baška Voda, is a lively seaside town ranged round a broad bay, framed by the Biokovo massif behind and two stumpy pine-covered peninsulas on either side. A leading package holiday centre since the Sixties, Makarska offers some of the liveliest nightlife on the coast, and is exceedingly popular with the youth of Croatia and Bosnia-Hercegovina as a result. Makarska's seafront can be frenetic with activity in July and August, but the place can be soothingly quiet in May, June and September, when it makes the perfect base for exploring the arid, rocky landscapes of Mount Biokovo (see box, p.359).

Despite being the home town of Hajduk, Lazio and Middlesbrough foot-baller Alen Bokšić, Makarska is more famous for its **rugby** than its soccer. The popularity of the oval ball here is largely due to the efforts of New Zealanders and Australians of Croatian stock, who came home in search of their roots and decided to form a team. Makarska consistently finish the season as Croatian rugby champions – although, to be honest, they've only got about six other teams in the country to play against.

Arrival, information and accommodation

The town **bus station** is on the Magistrala, a five-minute walk from the seafront, where you'll find the **tourist office** at Obala kralja Tomislava bb (June–Sept daily 7am–9pm; Oct–May Mon–Fri 9am–3pm; ☎ & ⓕ021/612-002, ⓦwww.makarska.com). It's a well-organized outfit whose output includes a free town map, advice on hiking on Biokovo mountain, and a leaflet detailing local mountain bike trails.

Innumerable central agencies offer **rooms** (❷) and **apartments** (❸). Grouped on or near the seafront are Atlas, Kačićev Trg 9 (Mon–Sat 8am–1pm & 5–9pm, Sun 8am–noon & 6–9pm; ☎021/617-038, ⓔatl.makarska@atlas.hr); SB tours, Obala kralja Tomislava 11 (daily 8am–10pm; ☎021/611-005, ⓕ611-955); and Turist Biro, Obala kralja Tomislava 2 (daily 8.15am–9pm; ☎021/611-688, ⓔturist_biro@hotmail.com); while Eurotours is 100m west of bus station at Ante Starčevićeva 48 (daily 8am–8pm; ☎021/611-062, ⓔeurotours-makarska@ st.hinet.hr). The nearest **campsite** is the *Baško Polje* on the southeastern out-skirts of Baška Voda (see above).

The town's **hotels** are mostly package-oriented establishments dating from the Seventies and Eighties, which have undergone various levels of refurbishment in recent years. In many cases the process of renovation is ongoing, so expect star ratings (and prices) to rise as time goes on. All of the hotels listed below can be full to the rafters in July and August, so don't bank on getting a room if you're just turning up on spec. They're open all year unless otherwise stated.

Hotels

Biokovka Put Cvitačke 9 ☎021/602-200, ⓔbiokovka@st.tel.hr. Sizeable two-star 2km west of the centre, offering plain en-suite rooms, an indoor pool, and a health-spa treatment centre. ❹

Biokovo Obala kralja Tomislava ☎021/615-244, ⓕ615-081, ⓔhotel-biokovo@st.tel.hr. Hogging a waterside position right on the Riva, this is the handiest hotel for the town centre, although its popularity with tour groups ensures that it fills up fast. The rooms are tastefully decorated and en suite, with shower. ❻

Dalmacija ☎615-777, ⓕ612-211, ⓦwww.hoteli-makarska.hr. Plain high-rise 1km west of the cen-

tre, much improved inside after recent renovations, offering neat rooms with attached bathroom (most with shower). April–Oct. ❺

Makarska Potok 17 ☎021/616-622, ⓦwww.makarska-hotel.com. Medium-sized, well-looked-after place about 5min uphill from the Riva, with simple en-suite rooms, some of which are rather frumpily furnished. May–Oct. ❸

Meteor ☎021/615-344, ⓕ611-419, ⓦwww.hoteli-makarska.hr. Pale concrete ziggurat 1km west of the centre, offering modernized rooms with en-suite bathtubs, minibar and a/c. There's also an outdoor pool and a sauna on site. Prices vary according to room position and size of balcony. ❺

The Town and the beaches

Despite two hundred years of Turkish occupation, little of Ottoman vintage survives, and the Venetian and Habsburg-era buildings on the seafront Riva coexist with modern apartment blocks thrown up after the tourism boom. All that survives of the old town is one central square, **Kačićev trg**, which slants up just behind the waterfront to the Baroque St Mark's Church (Crkva sveti Marko). Outside is Ivan Rendić's statue of **Andrija Kačić–Miošić** (1704–60), the Franciscan friar whose *Razgovor ugodni naroda slovinskoga* ("A Pleasant Conversation of the Slav People") was the most widely read book in the Croatian language until the twentieth century, after which its archaic style fell out of fashion. Kačić's work, a history of the Croats written in verse, and containing material taken from folk poems recounting Slav heroism in the face of the Ottoman Turks, was a landmark in the creation of a modern Croatian consciousness.

There's a rather pedestrian **Town Museum** (Gradski muzej; Mon–Fri 9am–noon & 8–10pm, Sat 9am–noon; 10Kn) on the Riva, featuring old nautical relics and photographs. The **Franciscan monastery** (Franjevački samostan), just east of the centre, is worth visiting for the enormous contemporary mosaic in the apse of its church. Completed by Josip Biffel in 1999, it's rich in greens and turquoises, with Christ the Pantokrator presiding over an array of colourful sea-creatures. The **Seashell Museum** (Malakološki muzej; Mon–Sat 10am–noon & 5–7pm, Sun 10am–noon; 10Kn) in the monastery courtyard is more engrossing than you might expect, its colourful exhibits shown to maximum advantage in a stylish and well-planned display.

The main **beach** is west of town, where a seafront path backed by the main package hotels stretches for some 2km. Far more attractive is **Nugal**, an enticing stretch of pebble squeezed between red-streaked cliffs 3km southeast of town – to get there, head to the eastern end of Makarska's Riva and pick up the marked trails leading up into the woods.

Mount Biokovo

The long grey streak of the **Biokovo** ridge hovers over the Makarska Riviera for some 50km, and its highest point – 1762m **Sveti Jure** just above Makarska – is the highest point in Croatia. Much of it falls within the boundaries of the **Biokovo nature park** (Park prirode Biokovo; ⊛www.biokovo.com), formed in order to preserve the area's unique combination of lush pine forests, Mediterranean scrub and arid, almost desert-like fields of stone. It takes about about four hours to climb Sveti Jure from Makarska: head uphill from St Mark's Church, cross the Magistrala and continue to the village of Makar, from where a marked path leads to the 1422-metre-high subsidiary peak of **Vošac** (3hr). It's a steep climb, but there's a stunning panorama of Makarska and its beaches at the top. Unless you fancy breaking your journey at the Vošac mountain hut (weekends only; ☎021/615-422), it's another two hours' hike to Sveti Jure itself, where you'll be rewarded with a beautiful view of the Dalmatian islands.

Be warned, however, that Biokovo is not suitable for occasional hikers, and ill-prepared tourists are more likely to come to grief on its slopes than anywhere else in Croatia. The ascent is strenuous, slippery and prone to swift weather changes, so you'll need proper footwear, waterproofs, plenty to drink and an accurate weather forecast from the tourist office in Makarska. Another essential item of equipment is the 1:25000 map of Biokovo published by SMAND and available from Makarska tourist office free of charge (some kiosks and travel agents in town sell it).

You can **drive** to the top in summer by taking the road to Vrgorac and Mostar just south of Makarska, then turning left after 7km up a steeply ascending track which works its way up to the summit from the southeast – although you'll require nerves of steel to negotiate the hairpins. Biokovo Active Holidays, Obala kralja Tomislava 2, Makarska (☎021/615-352 & 611-688, ⓔbiokovo-ah@st.tel.hr), organizes guided walks up Sveti Jure and early morning jeep trips to watch the sunrise.

Eating and drinking

The town centre has scores of **restaurants** along the Riva, although in many of these establishments price and quality tend to vary from one season to the next. Decima, just behind the Riva on Trg Tina Ujevića, seems to keep both tourists and locals satisfied with a filling and not-too-pricey range of Croatian standards such as *grah*, *girice* and grilled fish. Moving up in price and quality, *Peškera*, at Šetalište Donja luka bb, on the way to the package hotels and beach, is unrivalled for the choice and quality of its seafood. The *Susvid*, Kačićev trg, is owned by the same company and has much the same menu. Supremely good fish and shellfish in a formal ambience are offered by *Jež*, tucked away behind the *Dalmacija* and *Meteor* hotels at Kralja Petra Krešimira IV 90 – a seafood starter here will set you back as a main course elsewhere, but will probably justify the price tag. *Tempet*, midway along the Riva at Obala kralja Tomislava 11, and *Ivma*, at the eastern end of the Riva at Marineta 3, are the best places for **ice cream**.

Simply cruise the Riva to find a place to **drink**. The terrace of the *Biokovo* hotel is as good a place as any to start, with good coffee and a respectable selection of cakes. East of here, a nightly *korzo* flows past the string of lively café-bars crowded into the Lištun, the narrow pedestrian street which connects Kačićev trg with the far end of the Riva. Most of the bars are indistinguishable from each other save for the music they're blaring out – and it can get so crowded here at weekends that the main priority is simply to grab a table wherever you can. For a change of style try *Art Café*, just above Kačićev trg at Don M. Pavlinovića 1, which offers more soothing sounds in a tranquil garden, and occasional live music or DJ nights in a club-like space inside.

Opera, just beyond the Riva's eastern end at Šetalište fra Jure Radića bb, is currently the most stylish of the **clubs**, though *Grota* enjoys a more exotic location, occupying a sea cave just west of the Riva at Šetalište svetog Petra bb. Running throughout July and August, the **Makarska Cultural Summer** (Makarsko kulturno ljeto) features concerts and theatre performances in town squares, chamber music in the town church, and carnival-style events on the Riva – pick up a schedule from the tourist office.

The southern Makarska Riviera

The strip of coast immediately south of Makarska is one of the most inten-sively developed in Croatia, reminiscent of the Spanish *costas* in the number of hotels and apartment blocks that straggle along the coast. **Tučepi** and **Podgora**, a few kilometres south of Makarska, are fairly typical, with nice beaches backed by a soulless straggle of holiday homes and hotels. Podgora is the more characterful of the two, if only because it retains a still-functioning fleet of trawlers (fishing on an industrial scale has disappeared almost every-where else in southern Dalmatia), many of which turn themselves into tourist excursion boats in summer.

The next cluster of resorts begins with the small, unremarkable port of **Drvenik**, 15km past Drasniče. It's really two settlements separated by a small headland – Donja Vala to the north, and Gornja Vala to the south – each of which has a pebble beach. There's a **tourist office** in Donja Vala (Mon–Sat 8am–noon & 5–7pm, Sun 8am–noon) with **rooms** (❶). Four kilometres fur-ther on is the quiet and charming village of **ZAOSTROG**, built around a sixteenth-century **Franciscan monastery** (Franjevački samostan), with a simple, plant-filled cloister and a small **museum** (daily 4.30–7.30pm; 10Kn) displaying church silver and traditional agricultural implements. There's a long **beach** in front of the monastery, and the path leading north out of Zaostrog back towards Drvenik leads past some attractive rocky coves. Zaostrog has two **campsites**, the slightly scruffy *Viter* at the centre of the village, and the more attractive *Uvala Borova* site occupying pine-shaded terraces about 1500m to the south. The Makarska Riviera peters out at **Gradac**, 8km beyond Zaostrog, a frumpy but inoffensive little town with a shingle beach on each side of the central church-topped peninsula.

Ploče to Dubrovnik

Eleven kilometres further south of Gradac the industrial port of **PLOČE** (which, for a brief period in the 1980s, was named Kardeljevo in honour of the bespectacled Slovene ideologist and Tito sidekick Edvard Kardelj) is one of the few genuine eyesores on the Adriatic coast. Developed to provide the cities of the Balkan interior with an outlet to the sea, Ploče lost its raison d'être with the break-up of Yugoslavia, and the town's ill-planned ensemble of tower blocks and dockside cranes slid into stagnation. It's still of marginal importance as a transport hub, however: **rail** services to the Bosnian capital Sarajevo have recently been re-established (currently summer only, but check for the latest information locally), and there are also a few daily **ferries** to Trpanj on the Pelješac peninsula, where you can pick up buses to Orebić (see p.349). Ploče's **bus** and **train stations** are next to each other just off the seafront, about two minutes' walk from the **ferry dock**.

Bosnia-Hercegovina, or **BiH** (pronounced "bey-ha"), as it is colloquially known, is in theory a unified state comprising two "entities" – the so-called **Serbian Republic** (Republika srpska; RS), which roughly covers the east and northwest of BiH, and the **Muslim-Croat Federation**, which covers the rest. Within the Muslim–Croat entity, Croatian-dominated Hercegovina is virtually a state within a state, paying little heed to the government in Sarajevo. Travel between the entities is officially unrestricted, although it would still be unwise for the driver of, say, a Croatian-registered car to stray too far into Serbian areas. Most of what you are likely to want to see – dramatic, still-beautiful Sarajevo, Ottoman-influenced Mostar, and the Catholic pilgrimage centre of Međugorje – are all in the Muslim-Croat Federation.

EU, US and Canadian citizens do not need a **visa** to enter Bosnia-Hercegovina; Australians and New Zealanders need a tourist visa – you'll need to apply at the Bosnian embassy in Canberra (☎02/6232 4646, ⑩www.bosnia.webone.com.au). The visa requirement is waived if you're just travelling through the **Neum corridor**, the nine-kilometre stretch of Adriatic coast which falls within Bosnia-Hercegovina's borders.

Public transport from Croatia to the Muslim-Croat Federation is relatively straightforward. The Ploče–Mostar–Sarajevo **rail** line was reopened in 1999 to bring Bosnian holiday-makers to the Adriatic coast, but may remain a summer-only line for the time being. There are, however, numerous **buses**, with at least one departure a day from Zagreb, Split and Dubrovnik to destinations like Sarajevo, Mostar and Međugorje. The official **currency** of Bosnia-Hercegovina is the convertible mark (konvertabilna marka; KM), although you'll find that in Croatian-dominated Hercegovina, euros and Croatian kuna are the only currencies accepted.

Bosnia-Hercegovina is still heavily **mined**. Stick to roads and pavements, and never go wandering off across waste ground or into the countryside.

From Ploče, the Magistrala cuts inland to Opužen, where the main road to Mostar and Sarajevo in Bosnia-Hercegovina (see box above) breaks off to the east, passing through the small town of Metković before arriving at the border. Meanwhile, the Magistrala ploughs on across the broad, green delta of the **Neretva River**, once an expanse of marsh and malarial swamp but now – after reclamation – some of the most fertile land in the country. Despite intensive cultivation, significant patches of reedy wetland still survive, providing the perfect habitat for nesting marsh harriers, crakes and bitterns. The area is crisscrossed by streams and irrigation channels, and it's possible to take a **boat trip** through the waterways, although these have to be booked in advance through one of the travel agencies on the coast (notably Atlas, who have offices in Makarska, see p.357, and Dubrovnik, "Listings", p.391) – a day-long trip including lunch will set you back upwards of 330Kn.

South of the delta the Magistrala rejoins the coastline at **Klek**, a delightful village squatting beside a wonderful crescent of shingle beach. If you fancy a quick swim before resuming your journey southwards, this is the place to take it. Immediately beyond Klek, the road enters the nine-kilometre stretch of coast which is actually part of **Bosnia-Hercegovina** (keep passports handy). This corridor was awarded to the Republic after 1945 in order to give it access to the sea, although it has no strategic or economic value at present – Bosnia-Hercegovina's trade, such as it is, still goes through Ploče. The corridor's only real settlement is the ghastly holiday village of **Neum**. Food and cigarettes here are slightly cheaper than on the Croatian side of the border, and most Croatian intercity buses make a pit-stop here so that passengers can do a spot of shopping. Continuing south, the lumpy mountains of the Pelješac peninsula close in against the coast until the turn-off for Ston (see p.351), where the mountains join the mainland and the dividing strip of water peters out in a chain of aquamarine salt flats.

Travel details

Trains

Split to: Zagreb (July & Aug 2 daily; Sept–June 1 daily; 8hr).
Zadar to: Knin (5 daily; 2hr 30min).

Buses

Bol to: Supetar (Mon–Sat 7 daily, Sun 5 daily; 1hr).
Brbinj to: Božava (1–2 daily; 25min).
Hvar Town to: Jelsa (Mon–Sat 5 daily, Sun 2 daily; 55min); Stari Grad (Mon–Sat 8 daily, Sun 4 daily; 35min); Sućuraj (Mon & Fri 1 daily; 1hr 10min); Vrboska (Mon–Sat 5 daily, Sun 2 daily; 45min).
Imotski to: Dubrovnik (1 daily; 4hr); Split (12 daily; 2hr 15min); Zagreb (3 daily; 8hr).
Korčula Town to: Dubrovnik (1 daily; 3hr 30min); Lumbarda (Mon–Sat hourly, Sun 5 daily; 20min); Pupnat (Mon–Sat 7 daily, Sun 4 daily; 20min); Račišće (Mon–Sat 6 daily; 20min); Ston (1 daily; 2hr); Vela Luka (at least 4 daily; 1hr 20min); Zagreb (1 daily; 13hr).
Orebić to: Dubrovnik (2 daily; 2hr 40min); Kućiše (Mon–Sat 3 daily, Sun 1 daily; 10min); Lovište (Mon–Sat 3 daily, Sun 1 daily; 35min); Ston (3 daily; 1hr 10min); Trpanj (Mon–Sat 4 daily, Sun 2 daily; 45min); Viganj (Mon–Sat 3 daily, Sun 1 daily, 15min); Zagreb (1 daily; 12hr).
Ploče to: Dubrovnik (hourly; 2hr 15min); Split (hourly; 2hr 30min).
Preko to: Kukljica (10 daily; 10min); Muline (6 daily; 25min); Pašman (8 daily; 20min); Tkon (8 daily; 30min); Ugljan (6 daily; 15min).
Makarska to: Baška Voda (8 daily; 20min); Brela (8 daily; 30min); Gradac (hourly; 50min); Split (hourly; 1hr 10min); Zaostrog (hourly; 40min).
Šibenik to: Drniš (10 daily; 40min); Knin (8 daily; 1hr 20min); Murter (7 daily; 1hr); Pula (4 daily; 10hr); Skradin (6 daily; 45min); Split (hourly; 2hr); Trogir (hourly; 1hr 30min); Vodice (20 daily; 25min); Zadar (hourly; 1hr 30min).
Split to: Dubrovnik (hourly; 4hr 40min); Gradac (hourly; 2hr); Imotski (12 daily; 2hr 15min); Klis (every 30min; 35min); Makarska (hourly; 1hr 10min); Omiš (every 30min; 40min); Plitvice (8 daily; 6hr 30min); Ploče (hourly; 2hr 30min); Rijeka

(hourly; 8hr); Šibenik (hourly; 2hr); Sinj (hourly; 1hr); Trsteno (hourly; 4hr); Zadar (hourly; 4hr); Zagreb (8 daily; 9hr); Zaostrog (hourly; 1hr 50min).
Stari Grad to: Hvar Town (Mon–Sat 4 daily, Sun 2; 35min); Jelsa (Mon–Sat 10 daily, Sun 4; 20min); Sućuraj (Mon–Sat 2 daily, Sun 1; 35min); Vrboska (Mon–Sat 10 daily, Sun 4; 10min).
Ston to: Dubrovnik (3 daily; 1hr 30min); Korčula Town (1 daily; 2hr); Orebić (3 daily; 1hr 10min).
Supetar to: Bol (Mon–Sat 7 daily, Sun 5; 1hr); Milna (Mon–Sat 5 daily, Sun 4; 35min); Postira (Mon–Sat 5 daily, Sun 3; 1hr 15min); Povlja (Mon–Sat 3 daily, Sun 2; 1hr 10min); Pučišća (Mon–Sat 5 daily, Sun 3; 45min); Škrip (Mon–Sat 2 daily; Sun 1; 25min); Sumartin (Mon–Sat 3 daily, Sun 2; 1hr 20min).
Trogir to: Šibenik (hourly; 1hr 30min); Split (every 20min; 30–50min); Zadar (hourly; 3hr).
Vodice to Murter (9 daily; 35min); Šibenik (20 daily; 25min).
Trsteno to: Dubrovnik (hourly; 40min).
Vela Luka to: Korčula Town (at least 4 daily; 1hr 20min).
Vis Town to: Komiža (5 daily; 25min).
Zadar to: Biograd-na-moru (Mon–Fri 17 daily, Sat–Sun 9 daily; 1hr); Dubrovnik (9 daily; 8hr 30min); Murter (2 daily; 2hr); Nin (Mon–Fri 15 daily, Sat–Sun 10 daily; 45min); Novalja (2 daily;); Novigrad (Mon–Fri 5 daily, Sat–Sun 1 daily; 30min); Pag (2 daily; 1hr); Plitvice (hourly; 3hr); Pula (4 daily; 6hr); Rijeka (13 daily; 4hr 30min); Šibenik (hourly; 1hr 30min); Split (hourly; 3hr 30min); Trogir (hourly; 3hr); Zagreb (hourly; 5hr).

Ferries

Biograd-na-moru to: Tkon (10 daily; 15min).
Drvenik to: Sućuraj (summer 9 daily, winter 4 daily; 20min).
Hvar Town to: Lastovo (6 weekly; 3hr); Split (1–2 daily; 1hr 50min); Vela Luka (6 weekly; 1hr 15min); Vis (weekly; 1hr 15min).
Makarska to: Sumartin (summer 5 daily, winter 3 daily; 30min).
Orebić to: Dominče (summer 14 daily, winter 7 daily; 15min); Korčula Town (foot passengers only;

summer 8 daily; 15min).

Ploče to: Trpanj (summer 7 daily, winter 3 daily; 1hr).

Šibenik to: Prvić Luka (Mon–Sat 4 daily, Sun 2 daily; 45min); Šepurine (Mon–Sat 4 daily, Sun 2 daily; 1hr); Vodice (Mon–Sat 4 daily, Sun 2 daily; 1hr 20min); Zlarin (Mon–Sat 4 daily, Sun 2 daily; 30min).

Trogir to: Mali Drvenik (2 daily; 50min); Veli Drvenik (2 daily; 1hr 10min).

Split to: Dubrovnik (summer 1 daily, winter 2 weekly; 9hr); Hvar Town (1–2 daily; 1hr 50min); Lastovo (1 daily; 5hr); Rijeka (summer 1 daily, winter 2 weekly; 11hr); Stari Grad (3–5 daily; 2hr); Supetar (summer 13 daily, winter 7 daily; 1hr); Vela Luka (2 daily; 3hr 45min); Vis (1–2 daily; 2hr 30min); Zadar (summer 4 weekly, winter 2 weekly; 5hr 15min).

Stari Grad to: Dubrovnik (July to mid-Sept 1 daily; 7hr); Korčula Town (July to mid-Sept 1 daily; 3hr 30min); Rijeka (July to mid-Sept 1 daily; 11hr 30min); Split (summer 5 daily, winter 3 daily; 2hr); Zadar (July to mid-Sept 4 weekly; 6hr 45min).

Vela Luka to: Hvar Town (6 weekly; 1hr 15min); Split (2 daily; 2hr 40min–3hr 45min).

Zadar to: Brbinj (2 daily; 1hr 30min); Ist (2 weekly; 3hr 15min); Iž (Bršanj; 1 daily; 1hr 20min); Iž (Veli Iž; 2 weekly; 1hr 30min); Molat (6 weekly; 2hr 55min); Preko (hourly; 30min); Sali (2 daily; 1hr 30min); Zaglav (2 daily; 1hr 45min).

Catamarans

Split to: Bol (June–Sept 1 daily; 45min); Jelsa (June–Sept 1 daily; 1hr); Korčula Town (July & Aug 3 weekly; 2hr 15min); Lastovo (July & Aug 1 weekly; 2hr 45min); Vela Luka (July & Aug 1 weekly; 2hr).

Zadar to: Božava (mid-June to mid-Sept 1 weekly; 40min); Ist (1 daily; 2hr 30min); Molat (1 daily; 1hr 30min); Silba (daily; 1hr 40min).

Hydrofoils

Hvar Town to: Split (mid-May to mid-Sept 2 daily; 1–2hr).

Split to: Hvar Town (mid-May to mid-Sept 2 daily; 1–2hr); Vis (mid-May to mid-Sept 2 daily; 1hr 40min).

Vis to: Split (mid-May to mid-Sept 2 daily; 1hr 40min).

Domestic flights

Bol to: Zagreb (April–Sept 1 or 2 weekly; 50min).

Split to: Zagreb (April–Sept 4 daily, Oct–March 3 daily; 45min).

Zadar to: Zagreb (April–Sept 2 daily, Oct–March 1 daily; 30min).

International buses

Split to: Mostar (10 daily); Sarajevo (5 daily; 7hr).

Zadar to: Ljubljana (1 daily; 8hr); Sarajevo (1 daily; 10hr).

International trains

Split to: Ljubljana (July & Aug 1 daily; 10hr 30min).

International ferries

Brbinj to: Ancona (mid-June to mid-Sept 1–2 weekly; 5hr).

Korčula Town to: Bari (mid-June to Sept 1–2 weekly; 11hr); Igoumenitsa (mid-June to Sept 1 weekly; 24hr).

Šibenik to: Ancona (July & Aug 3 weekly, June & Sept 2 weekly; 9hr).

Split to: Ancona (1 daily; 10hr); Bari (mid-June to late Sept 1–2 weekly; 15hr); Igoumenitsa (mid-June to late Sept 1 weekly; 28hr).

Stari Grad to: Ancona (July & Aug 6 weekly, June & Sept 1 weekly; 9hr); Bari (Aug 1–2 weekly; 12hr).

Vis to: Ancona (mid-July to Oct 3 weekly; 9hr).

Zadar to: Ancona (June & Sept 3 weekly, July & Aug 5 weekly; 7hr).

International catamarans

Božava to: Ancona (mid-June to mid-Sept 1 weekly; 1hr 40min).

Zadar to: Ancona (mid-June to mid-Sept 1 weekly; 2hr 30min).

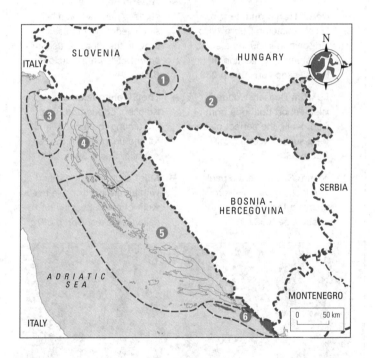

6

Dubrovnik and around

CHAPTER 6

Highlights

✳ **Dubrovnik's city walls**
A well-trodden walkway leads the full circuit of the battlements, providing the ideal vantage point from which to enjoy the city's medieval and baroque splendours. **See p.376**

✳ **Dominican monastery**
Quiet cloister in Dubrovnik's old town, harbouring a small but stunning collection of Renaissance art. **See p.383**

✳ **Lokrum** Densely wooded islet a short boat ride from Dubrovnik, the perfect place for a sunbathe or a stroll. **See p.386**

✳ **Mount Srđ** Scale the peak overlooking Dubrovnik to enjoy fantastic views of the coast. **See p.387**

✳ **Dubrovnik's Summer Festival** The annual cultural shinding brings top-class drama and music to the old-town courtyards, and adds a dash of glamour to the streets. **See p.390**

✳ **Trsteno** Renaissance gardens perched on a hill-side overlooking the sea provide the ideal excuse for an out-of-town excursion. **See p.392**

✳ **The Elaphite Islands** Koločep, Lopud and Šipan are among the most beautiful and unspoiled in the Adriatic. **See p.394**

✳ **Mljet** Lush, forested island with an easily strollable network of paths beside its two saltwater lakes. **See p.397**

Dubrovnik and around

D
UBROVNIK's motto, *Libertas* ("liberty"), which is plastered across the sides of buses and the city's tourist literature, speaks volumes about the city's self-image and the idealized way in which it is perceived by others. For several centuries the city-state of Dubrovnik – or **Ragusa** as it was then known – managed to hang on to a modicum of independence while the rest of this coast fell under the sway of foreign powers. The Venetian Lion of St Mark is conspicuously absent, while statues of **St Blaise** (Sveti Vlaho), the symbol of Dubrovnik's independence, fill every conceivable crack and niche in the city. At its sixteenth-century height, the Ragusan Republic had the third largest merchant fleet in the world, and its galleons gave us the word "argosy", a corrupted form of the city's name.

An essentially medieval city reshaped by Baroque town planners after a disastrous earthquake of 1667, Dubrovnik's **historic core** seems to have been suspended in time ever since. Set-piece churches and public buildings blend seamlessly with the green-shuttered stone houses to form a perfect ensemble untouched by the twenty-first century – even modern shop signs are so strictly regulated in the old town as to be almost invisible. Outside the city walls, modern Dubrovnik is comparatively bereft of sights but exudes a Mediterranean elegance: gardens are an explosion of colourful bougainvillea and oleanders, with trees weighted down with figs, lemons, oranges and peaches.

Few visitors will notice any remaining signs of the 1991–92 **Siege of Dubrovnik**, during which over two thousand enemy shells fell on the old city. Reconstruction has been undertaken with astonishing speed, and the old town is pretty much back to its normal self. The fact that conflict took place here at all only reveals itself through subtle details: the vivacious orange-red hues of brand-new roof tiles, or the contrasting shades of grey where damaged facades have been patched up with freshly quarried stone.

Dubrovnik is worth a visit at any time of year, although late spring and summer – when life spills out onto the streets and café tables remain packed well into the night – bring out the best in the city. Croatia's cultural luminaries visit the town during the **Dubrovnik Summer Festival** in July and August, bringing an added dash of glamour to the streets, while the main event in winter is the **Feast of St Blaise** on February 3, when the patron of the city is honoured by a parade and special Mass, followed by much drinking and eating.

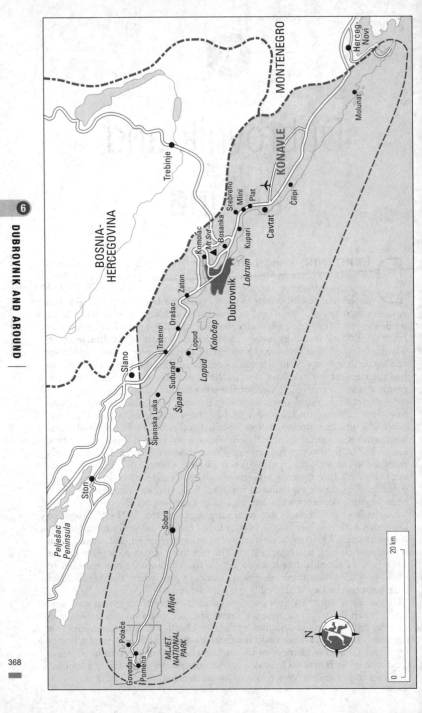

The main tourist resorts south of Dubrovnik, **Mlini** and **Cavtat**, are within easy reach of the city by public transport. In addition, Dubrovnik's port is the natural gateway to the southernmost **islands** of the Croatian Adriatic, with the sparsely populated, semi-wild islands of **Koločep**, **Lopud** and **Šipan** providing beach-hoppers with a wealth of out-of-town bathing opportunities. Slightly further out to sea, the green island of **Mljet** is one of the most beautiful on the entire coast – you'll need a day or two to do it justice.

Some history

Dubrovnik was first settled in the early seventh century by Greco-Roman refugees from the nearby city of Epidaurum (now Cavtat) after it was sacked by the Slavs. The refugees took up residence in the southern part of what is now the old town, then an island known as **Laus** – a name which later metamorphosed into **Ragusa**. The Slavs, meanwhile, settled on the wooded mainland opposite, from which the name **Dubrovnik** (from *dubrava*, meaning "glade") comes. Before long the slim channel between the two was filled in and the two sides merged, producing a symbiosis of Latin and Slav cultures unique in the Mediterranean. Ethnically, the city was almost wholly Slav by the fifteenth century, although leading families consistently claimed Roman lineage, and the nobility actively preserved the use of both Latin and Italian in official circles, if not always in everyday speech. They also held on to the name Ragusa, which remained in use until the early twentieth century.

Initially the city owed allegiance to **Byzantium**, but came increasingly under the influence of the **Venetians**, who gained control of the city in 1204. Protected by Venice from the expansionist Slav states of the Balkan hinterland, the city developed trade links with its inland neighbours, such as the fourteenth-century Serbian empire of Tsar Dušan. The Venetians stayed until 1358, when they were squeezed out of the southern Adriatic by Louis of Hungary. Officially, Dubrovnik became a vassal of the Hungaro-Croatian kingdom, paying an annual tribute, although it effectively became an independent city-state.

The emergent **Ragusan Republic** was run by an elected senate – fear of dictatorship meant that the nominal head of state, the Rector (*knez*), was virtually a figurehead. However, the republic was by no means a democracy: the city's nobility was the only section of society allowed to vote. Civic peace was ensured by allowing the rest of the citizenry full economic freedom and the chance to grow rich through commerce. Dubrovnik's network of maritime contacts made it one of the major players in Mediterranean trade, but the key to the city's wealth was its unrivalled access to the markets of the Balkan hinterland. The Ottoman Empire, having absorbed the kingdoms of both Serbia and Bosnia, granted Dubrovnik this privileged trading position in return for an annual payment of 1000 ducats, an arrangement that remained essentially unchanged until the Ragusan Republic's fall. Dubrovnik established a network of trading colonies stretching from the Adriatic to the Black Sea, from where wheat, wool, animal hides – and, for a time, slaves – could be shipped back to the mother republic before being re-exported to the West at a fat profit. As commerce grew, so did the need to protect it, and the republic extended its borders to include the whole of the coast from Konavle in the south to Pelješac in the north, as well as the islands of Mljet and, to its west, Lastovo.

Mercantile wealth underpinned an upsurge in culture, producing a fifteenth- and sixteenth-century **golden age** when the best artists and architects in the Adriatic were drawn to the city. It was during this period that many of the urban landmarks of present-day Dubrovnik were completed: Juraj Dalmatinac and Michelozzo Michelozzi worked on the town **walls**, Paskoje Miličević drew up plans for the **Sponza Palace**, and Onofrio della Cava designed the **Rector's Palace**, as well as the two **fountains** that still bear his name. Florentine styles influenced the work of painters such as Nikola Božidarević, and successive generations of writers – playwright Marin Držić and poet Ivan Gundulić among them – abandoned Latin in favour of their native tongue, breathing life into the Croatian literary Renaissance in the process.

Suzerainty over Dubrovnik had passed from the Hungaro-Croatian kingdom to the Ottoman Empire by the early sixteenth century, but shrewd diplomacy and the regular payment of tributes ensured that the city-state retained its virtual independence. Every year two envoys would visit Istanbul, hand over the agreed cash and stay for a year in fawning acquiescence until someone arrived to relieve them. In the sixteenth and seventeenth centuries Dubrovnik enjoyed the protection of both Spain (Dubrovnik ships sailed with the Armada in 1588) and the papacy, but usually avoided being dragged into explicitly anti-Turkish alliances. In fact, wars between the Ottomans and the West usually led to increased revenues for Dubrovnik, which played on its role as the only neutral port in the Adriatic.

Decline set in with the **earthquake of 1667**, which killed around five thousand people and destroyed many of the city's buildings. Bandits from the interior looted the ruins, and Kara Mustafa, Pasha of Bosnia, demanded huge tributes in return for keeping the robber bands under control. Kara Mustafa's death during the Siege of Vienna in 1683 allowed the city the chance to rebuild, producing the elegantly planned rows of Baroque town houses which characterize the centre of the city to this day. However, the Austro–Turkish conflict of 1683–1718 seriously affected Dubrovnik's inland trade, a blow from which it never really recovered. By the eighteenth century Dubrovnik's nobility was dying out, and commoners were increasingly elevated to noble rank to make up the numbers; anachronistic **feuds** between the Sorbonnesi (old patricians) and Salamanchesi (newly elevated patricians) – named, for some unknown reason, after the universities of Sorbonne and Salamanca – weakened the traditional social fabric still further.

The city-state was formally **dissolved by Napoleon** in 1808. The French occupation of the city provoked a British naval bombardment, while Russian and Montenegrin forces laid waste to surrounding territories, destroying much of suburban Dubrovnik in the process. In 1815 the **Congress of Vienna** awarded Dubrovnik to the Austrians, who incorporated the city into the newly formed province of Dalmatia. Political and economic activity was henceforth concentrated in towns such as Zadar and Split, leaving Dubrovnik on the fringes of Adriatic society.

The symbolic importance of Dubrovnik long outlived the republic itself. For nineteenth-century Croats the city was a Croatian Athens, a shining example of what could be achieved – both politically and culturally – by the Slav peoples. It was also increasingly a magnet for foreign travellers, who wrote about the city in glowing terms, save for Rebecca West, for whom it was too perfect and self-satisfied: "I do not like it," she famously wrote. "It reminds me of the worst of England."

Already a society resort in West's time, Dubrovnik enhanced its reputation for cultural chic with the inception of the **Dubrovnik Festival**, one of Europe's most prestigious, in 1949, while the construction of big hotel complexes in Lapad and Bubin Kuk to the north, and Mlini to the south, helped make Dubrovnik one of the most popular tourist destinations in Yugoslavia in the 1970s and 1980s. Much of the damage done during the **1991–92 siege** was repaired with remarkable speed, and Dubrovnik is once again fully prepared to welcome the vacationing hordes.

Few thought that Dubrovnik would be directly affected by the **break-up of Yugoslavia**: no significant Serbian minority lived in the city, and its strategic importance was questionable. However, in October 1991 units of the JNA (Yugoslav People's Army), supported by volunteers from Montenegro and Serb-dominated eastern Hercegovina, quickly overran the tourist resorts south of Dubrovnik and occupied the high ground commanding approaches to the city. The **bombardment of Dubrovnik** began in early November and lasted until May 1992. Despite considerable damage to the town's historic core, Dubrovnik's medieval fortifications proved remarkably sturdy, with the fortresses of Revelin and St John (more familiar to tourists as the site of the aquarium) pressed into service as shelters for the civilian population.

The logic behind the attack on Dubrovnik was confused. Belgrade strategists unwisely considered it an easy conquest, the fall of which would damage Croatian morale and break the back of Croatian resistance elsewhere on the Adriatic. The attack on Dubrovnik also presented an effective way of dragging both the Montenegrins and the Serbs of eastern Hercegovina into the conflict, not least because it seemed to promise them ample opportunities for pillage.

Attacking forces employed a mixture of bad history and dubious folklore to justify their actions. Dubrovnik's links with medieval Serbia, and the fact that so many leading Ragusan families had originally come from the Balkan interior, were unconvincingly offered up as evidence that the early republic had been part of the Serbian cultural orbit. Far from treating present-day Dubrovnik as a symbol of Mediterranean civilization, opportunist Serbians painted the city as a cesspit of urban corruption that stood in decadent opposition to the pure, martial values of the Balkan male. In a bizarre sideshow to the siege, Serbian forces in occupied Cavtat attempted to establish a quisling regime that would run the city once they captured it, declaring a new Dubrovnik Republic headed by Aleksandar Aco Apolonijo, former chief of the Dubrovnik tourist association.

Contrary to Serbian expectations, Dubrovnik's hastily arranged defences held out. In the end, the siege was broken in July 1992 by a Croatian offensive from the north – one of the first big morale-boosting victories of the war. Once Dubrovnik's land links with the rest of Croatia had been re-established, Croatian forces continued their push southwards, liberating Cavtat and Čilipi.

Direct reminders of the siege are few and far between in Dubrovnik today, but the price of reconstruction has left the city shouldering a considerable burden of debt. Almost every hotel in Dubrovnik suffered some kind of damage, whether owing to enemy shelling or to the more long-term wear-and-tear involved in hosting large numbers of refugees, and the loans incurred in putting all this right will take years to pay off.

Arrival, information and accommodation

Dubrovnik's **airport** is situated some 22km east of the city, close to the village of Čilipi (see p.391). Croatia Airlines buses meet all arrivals (even the late night ones), dropping off at the main western entrance to the old town, **Pile** (pronounced *pee-lay*) **Gate**, before terminating at the bus station (25min; 25Kn each way). A taxi into town all the way from the airport will cost about 200Kn. Buses back to the airport leave the bus station ninety minutes before each flight departure. The **ferry** and **bus terminals** are located about 500m apart in the port suburb of Gruž, 3km west of the old town. Pile Gate is a forty-minute

slog along Ante Starčevića from Gruž, and you'd be better off catching a bus – #1a and #3 from the ferry terminal, #1a, #3 or #6 from behind the bus station. Flat-fare **tickets** for local buses can be bought either from the driver (10Kn; exact change only) or from newspaper kiosks (7Kn).

Dubrovnik's tourist association (ⓦ www.tzdubrovnik.hr) operates **information points** at Miha Pracata bb in the old town (summer daily 8am–8pm; winter daily 9am–4pm; ☎020/323-587); Ante Starčevićeva 7, near the Pile gate (daily 8am–8pm; ☎020/427-591); and at Gruška obala bb, opposite the ferry dock (☎020/417-983). They're a good source of advice on local attractions and public transport details, and give away copies of the *Dubrovnik Guide* (also available from most hotels), a monthly listings booklet which contains museum opening times, details of cultural events, ferry timetables, and Yellow Pages-style information on local services.

Accommodation

Hotel accommodation in Dubrovnik is generally more expensive than elsewhere in Croatia, leaving budget travellers with little option but to settle for private rooms. Demand for all beds is high in July and August, so you should be prepared to arrive early in the day or reserve in advance.

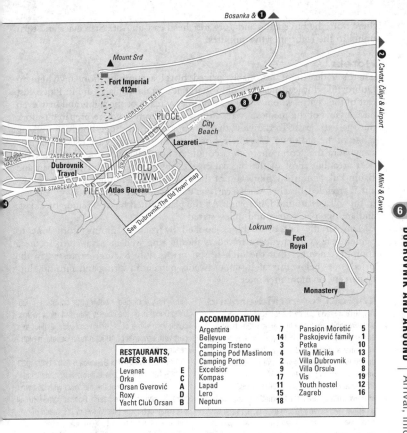

Bosanka & ❶ ▲

❷ Cavtat, Ćilipi & Airport

Mount Srd ▲

Fort Imperial
412m

JADRANSKA CESTA

FRANA SUPILA

❾ ❽ ❼   ❻

PLOČE

City
Beach

GORNJI KONO

ZAGREBAČKA

Lazareti

ADMIRA
HAZORA

Dubrovnik
Travel

OLD
TOWN

ANTE STARČEVIĆA

PILE   Atlas Bureau

See 'Dubrovnik–The Old Town' map

Milini & Cavat

Lokrum

Fort
Royal

Monastery

**RESTAURANTS,
CAFÉS & BARS**

Levanat	E
Orka	C
Orsan Gverović	A
Roxy	D
Yacht Club Orsan	B

ACCOMMODATION

Argentina	7	Pansion Moretić	5
Bellevue	14	Paskojević family	1
Camping Trsteno	3	Petka	10
Camping Pod Maslinom	4	Vila Micika	13
Camping Porto	2	Villa Dubrovnik	6
Excelsior	9	Villa Orsula	8
Kompas	17	Vis	19
Lapad	11	Youth hostel	12
Lero	15	Zagreb	16
Neptun	18		

There are numerous accommodation agencies handling private **rooms** (❷) and **apartments** (❸), many of which accept reservations by email. The most conveniently located ones are Gulliver, just opposite the ferry terminal at Obala Stjepana Radića 31 (summer Mon–Sat 8am–8pm, Sun 8am–noon; winter Mon–Sat 7am–7pm; ☎020/313-300, ⓦwww.gulliver.hr); Dubrovnikturist, 100m east of the bus station at put Republike 7 (☎020/356-959, ⓦwww.dubrovnikturist.hr); Dubrovnik Travel, a short but steep walk uphill from Pile gate at Zagrebačka 13 (☎020/311-733, ⓦwww .dubrovniktravel.com); and Perla Adriatica, right by Ploče gate at Frana Supila 2 (May–Oct only; ☎020/422-766, ⓔperla-adriatica@du.hinet.hr). Travellers arriving at the bus station may well be besieged by aggressive landladies offering unlicensed rooms, but these are often a long way from the centre, and various "extra costs" may be subsequently added to any price you think you've agreed.

Dubrovnik's friendly all-year **youth hostel**, just off bana Jelačića at V. Sagrestana 3 (☎020/423-241, ⓕ412-592, ⓔdubrovnik@hfhs.hr; 90Kn per person), is perfectly poised between Gruž and the old town. Providing bunk-bed accommodation in neat four- or six-person dorms, it fills up fast in summer, so arrive early or ring in advance. Breakfast and other meals, available for an additional charge, are served up on an attractive outdoor terrace. To get there from the bus station and port area, head east up Ante Starčevića and turn uphill to the right after five minutes.

Hotels

There's a dearth of reasonably priced **hotel** accommodation anywhere in Dubrovnik, not least near the old town. The swankiest places are in Ploče, just east of the centre, where you'll be within easy reach of the sights and may even have a view of the medieval walls from your balcony if you're prepared to fork out the extra cash. To the west, there's a brace of mid-range hotels in walking range of the old town. Elsewhere, however, you'll probably be a short bus ride away from the action: there are a couple of hotels handily placed in the Gruž port area, but most of the big package establishments are on the Lapad and Babin kuk peninsulas, 5km west of the Pile Gate, where there are some pleasant, if crowded, beaches. With a car, you could consider the pension–style places in the villages around Dubrovnik. All the places listed below include breakfast, and are open all year round unless stated.

Many of the hotels are block–booked by package groups from June to September, so independent travellers should ring well in advance to secure a room. Remember that the high-season prices (July & Aug) expressed in the price codes below can fall by about twenty percent in spring and autumn, thirty percent or more in winter.

The old town and around

Argentina Frana Supila 14 ☏ 020/440-555, ⊛ www.hoteli-argentina.hr. Large 1920s hotel a 10min walk east of the old town, recently renovated to five-star standard. It has all the creature comforts, including its own concrete beach and a small swimming pool. **❾**

Bellevue Pera Čingrije 7 ☏ 020/413-095, ⊛ www.wrensgroup.com. Dramatically situated on a clifftop overlooking Miramare Bay, a 15min walk from Pile Gate, and with a wonderful shingle beach immediately below. Completely renovated in 2002 to provide neat en-suite rooms with TV and a/c. April–Oct. **❼**

Excelsior Frana Supila 12 ☏ 020/353-353, ⊛ www.hotel-excelsior.hr. Just east of the old town, and recently modernized, this five-star place offers plush en-suite rooms, indoor pool and fitness centre. The terraces of the hotel's bar and restaurants have excellent views back towards the town, as do some of the room balconies. Doubles start at about 1300Kn, rising to 2150Kn with sea view. **❾**

Lero Ive Vojnovića 14 ☏ 020/332-022, ⊛ www.hotel-lero.hr. Recently renovated hotel a 20min walk (or a short ride on bus #4) from Pile Gate. Rooms are neat and modern with en-suite shower and TV. **❻**

Pucić Palace od Puča 1 ☏ 020/324-111, ⊛ www.thepucicpalace.com. Currently the only hotel within the old town walls (it's marked on the map on p.377), this is a five-star place in a recently renovated eighteenth-century palace, offering plush, fully equipped – but slightly cramped – doubles. Decor is on the chintzy side, but most rooms come with views of old-town streetlife. Expect to part with upwards of 4000Kn for a double in high season. **❾**

Villa Dubrovnik Vlaha Bukovca 6 ☏ 020/422-933, ℻ 423-465, ⊛ www.villa-dubrovnik.hr. Small, intimate hotel 1km east of the old town with its own gardens and concrete beach. Rooms come with all the usual comforts, plus views of the island of Lokrum. Doubles from 1500Kn. **❾**

Villa Orsula Frana Supila 14 ☏ 020/440-555, ⊛ www.hoteli-argentina.hr. Compact, plushly furnished rooms in a 1930s villa sandwiched between the *Argentina* and *Excelsior* hotels. Great views of the old town, a lovely terraced garden and a small concrete beach. Doubles start at around 2600Kn. **❾**

Gruž, Lapad and Babin kuk

Kompas Šetalište kralja Zvonimira 56, Lapad ☏ 020/435-777, ⊛ www.hotel-kompas.hr. One of the better package-oriented hotels on the Lapad peninsula, this is a well-run place used by German and British tour groups. All rooms are en suite and have cable TV; many also have views of Lapad Bay. Take bus #6 (destination Dubrava) from either Pile or opposite the bus station to Lapad post office, then walk downhill along Šetalište kralja Zvonimira. **❻**

Lapad Lapadska obala 37 ☏ 020/432-922 or 413-576, ⊛ www.hotel-lapad.hr. Large early twentieth-century hotel overlooking Gruž harbour and nicely restored, with modern annexes tacked on. Most of the two hundred en-suite rooms come with a/c and TV – it may be worth asking when making a reservation. There's a small swimming pool in the courtyard, and Lapad beach is a 15min walk away. Within walking distance of both the bus station and the port, and on the #6 Pile–Dubrava bus route. ⑥

Neptun Kardinala Stepinca 31 ☎020/440-100, ⓔhotel-neptun@du.tel.hr. Handiest of the Babin kuk hotels, this is a modern concrete structure offering functional rooms with TV and attached bathroom. The semi-wild vegetation of the Babin kuk peninsula is perfect for walks, and the hotel is right beside the waterfront path to Lapad beach. Sea-facing rooms have wonderful views of craggy offshore outcrops. Take bus #5 (destination Neptun) from Pile, or bus #6 (destination Dubrava) from Pile or the bus station, and alight at the end of the line. April–Oct. ⑥

Petka Obala Stjepana Radića 38, Gruž ☎020/418-008, ⓔhotel-petka@du.hinet.hr. Medium-rise concrete affair opposite the ferry landing. The rooms are plain and feature furniture that has been around a bit, but they're spick and span, with shower, TV and phone; front-facing rooms have marvellous views of the port. A walkable 500m northwest of the bus station; otherwise catch bus #1a from Pile. ④

Vila Micika Mata Vodopica 10, Lapad ☎020/437-332, ⓔbooking-vila-micika@email.hinet.hr. Family-run villa with garden, a short walk uphill from Lapad Bay, offering hostel-style arrangements (a bed in a clean and comfortable two- or three-person room) as well as bright en-suite doubles. No breakfast, but you do have access to a fridge. Bus #6 to Lapad post office. ①–②

Vis Masarykov put 4, Lapad ☎020/437-303,

ⓦwww.hotelimaestral.com. On the eastern side of Lapad Bay, this modern hotel has simple en-suite rooms as well as pleasant restaurant and café terraces overlooking a generous stretch of private beach. Take bus #4 (destination Hotel Palace) from opposite the bus station. May–Sept. ⑥

Zagreb Šetalište kralja Zvonimira 31, Lapad ☎020/431-011, ⓔhot-sumratin@du.hinet.hr. Plain en-suite rooms in a pleasant, early twentieth-century building surrounded by stately palms, a 5min walk from Lapad beach. Directions as for Hotel Kompas. May–Sept. ⑥

Outside the city

Pansion Moretić na Pržini 10, Orašac ☎020/891-507, ⓦwww.i-reception.net/moretic. This bed and breakfast in a rustic village 12km west of town, just off the main road to Split, has simple en-suite doubles, some with balconies looking out upon vineyards, olive trees and orange groves. It's a 15min walk from the sea, and handily placed for the botanical gardens at Trsteno (see p.392). The owner speaks German and Italian. The pension is well signed from the main road, and there's a bus stop (most intercity buses will pick up and drop off here) nearby. ③

Paskojević family Bosanka bb ☎020/411-245. In a village set on a scrub-covered, goat-grazed plateau, high above the city on the shoulder of Mount Srđ. Rooms are bright, comfortable and come with TV, attached bathroom and pine floors; the use of a kitchen is included. You'll need a car to get here: head out of town on the Cavtat road and then take the battered side-road that leads to Mount Srđ. Once you get settled in, you can walk down to Dubrovnik in under an hour, though getting back up again can be rather more time-consuming. ②

Campsites

There are no **campsites** in Dubrovnik itself, but several lie within a short bus ride of the city.

Camping Trsteno In the hillside-hugging village of Trsteno, 15km northwest of Dubrovnik ☎020/751-060. An idyllic tree-shaded site next door to the famous botanical gardens (see p.392), and a short walk from a rocky stretch of beach. Intercity buses plying the Dubrovnik–Split route pass through Trsteno every hour or so.

Pod Maslinom Orašac. In a terraced olive grove 12km northwest of Dubrovnik, 50m from the Magistrala, and at the top of a steep path down to

the seashore. There's a bus stop right outside served by Split–Dubrovnik services.

Porto Srebreno, 8km southeast of town, right by the main road for Cavtat ☎020/487-078. With Dubrovnik–Cavtat buses trundling past at roughly hourly intervals until around midnight, this is the most convenient site for those dependent on public transport, though it's in an uninspiring area of mass-tourism development. If it's full, try the Matkovica campsite virtually next door.

The City

With a population of a little over 30,000, Dubrovnik isn't as large a city as you might think, and although it sprawls along the coast for several kilometres, its real heart is the walled and surprisingly compact **old town**. Doing the circuit of the city walls is the one Dubrovnik attraction you really can't miss out, and it's worth doing this early on in order to get the feel of the place. The rest of the old town can easily be covered in a day and a half – although once you begin to soak up the atmosphere of the place you'll find it difficult to pull yourself away. Running above the town to the east is the bare ridge of **Mount Srđ**, the summit of which provides expansive views of the town and the coast. The best place for swimming and sunbathing is the islet of **Lokrum**, a short taxi-boat ride from the old town.

The city walls

The **Pile Gate**, where city buses from the ferry and bus terminals arrive, is the logical place to start exploring the old town. The northernmost of the two main entrances to the medieval city, the gate – a simple archway reached through a plain, pillbox-like bastion – is accessible by a stone bridge dating from 1471 which crosses the former moat, now a park full of fruit trees. From here, the best way to get your bearings is by making a tour of the still largely intact **city walls** (Gradske zidine; daily: summer 9am–7.30pm; winter 10am–3pm; 15Kn), 25m high and stretching for some 2km, completely surrounding the old town. They are encrusted with towers and bastions, and it's impossible not to be struck by their remarkable size and state of preservation. Some parts date back to the tenth century, but most of the original construction was undertaken in the twelfth and thirteenth centuries, with subsequent rebuildings and reinforcements carried out in the mid-fifteenth century when fear of Ottoman expansion was at its height. Once you're on top, the views over the town are of a patchwork sea of terracotta tiles, punctuated by sculpted domes and towers and laid out in an almost uniform grid plan – the Ragusan authorities introduced strict planning regulations to take account of the city's growth as early as the 1270s, and the rebuilding programme which followed the earthquake of 1667 rationalized things still further.

Clockwise around the walls from the Pile Gate, it's a gentle two-hundred-metre climb towards the fat, concentric turrets of the **Minčeta Fortress**, which guards the old town's northern corner. It was begun in 1455 by the Florentine architect Michelozzo Michelozzi and was replaced by Juraj Dalmatinac (see box on p.278), who designed the eye-catching crown of battlements that has made Minčeta such a landmark. From Minčeta it's a further 500m around the walls to the **Ploče Gate**, where you have an excellent view of the old port area, and another 200m to **St John's Fortress**, a W-shaped curve of thick stone facing out to sea. It's probably as you return towards Pile Gate along the southern, sea-facing walls that you get the best views of old Dubrovnik's tiled roofs and narrow, tunnel-like streets. At the western corner of the old town you'll pass the **Bokar Fortress**, also by Michelozzi and Dalmatinac, a jutting bastion which once guarded sea-borne access to the moat.

Along Stradun

Inside the Pile Gate, **Stradun** (also known as Placa), the city's main street, runs straight across the old town, following the line of the channel that originally separated the island of Ragusa from the mainland. A constant surge of tourists

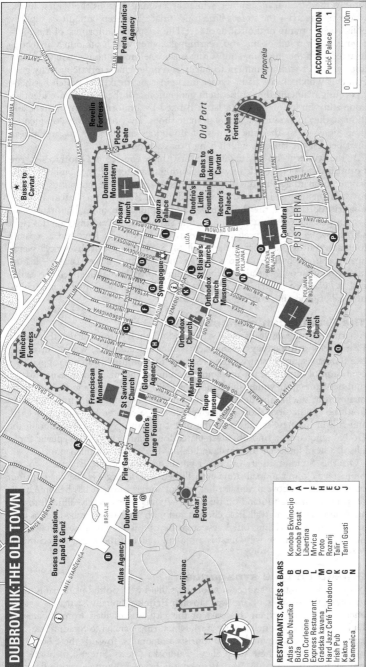

DUBROVNIK: THE OLD TOWN

Lazareti & Museum of Modern Art

ACCOMMODATION
Pucić Palace **1**

Perla Adriatica Agency

Revelin Fortress

Ploče Gate

Dominican Monastery

Rosary Church

Sponza Palace

Onofrio's Little Fountain

Rector's Palace

St John's Fortress

Old Port

Boats to Lokrum & Cavat

Synagogue

St Blaise's Church

Orthodox Church Museum

Cathedral

Jesuit Church

Orthodox Church

Marin Držić House

Rupe Museum

Minčeta Fortress

Franciscan Monastery

St Saviour's Church

Globetour Agency

Onofrio's Large Fountain

Pile Gate

Dubrovnik Internet

Bokar Fortress

Buses to bus station, Lapad & Gruž

Atlas Agency

Lovrijenac

Buses to Cavtat

Porporela

N

0   100m

RESTAURANTS, CAFÉS & BARS

Atlas Club Nautika	B
Buža	Q
Don Corleone	D
Express Restaurant	L
Gradska kavana	M
Hard Jazz Café Trubadour	O
Irish Pub	K
Kaktus	G
Kamenica	N
Konoba Ekvinocijo	P
Konoba Posat	A
Libertina	I
Mrvica	F
Proto	H
Rozarij	E
Talir	C
Tanti Gusti	J

throngs the Stradun in summer, while the evening *korzo* is the busiest in the whole of Croatia – the street's limestone surface has been buffed to a slippery polish by the tramp of thousands of feet. The set-piece uniformity of this thoroughfare is a result of the 1667 earthquake, after which Stradun was reconstructed with the imposing, outwardly unadorned town houses you see today, displaying a civic commitment to purity and order characteristic of a city government which always had a rather disciplinarian streak, and which has been rigorously maintained by subsequent generations. All the houses have identical door and window frames, the latter flanked by uniform green shutters, and though they're nowadays full of tourist shops, laws forbidding conspicuous shop signs mean that the names of boutiques and restaurants are instead inscribed on the lanterns which hang over each doorway.

At the western end of Stradun, the first thing you see is **Onofrio's Large Fountain** of 1444, a circle of water-spouting heads topped by a bulbous dome where, to guard against the plague, visitors to this hygiene-conscious city had to wash themselves before they were admitted. Built by the Italian architect Onofrio de la Cava, the fountain was the culmination of an elaborate water system that delivered water from Mount Srđ to public washing facilities right across town – though even in this relatively liberal city Jews had a separate fountain. Across the street is the small **St Saviour's Church** (Crkva svetog Spasa), a simple but harmonious Renaissance structure whose facade – featuring a rose window beneath a trefoil roof line – may have influenced the cathedral at Hvar (see p.327). The church's bare interior is now used as an exhibition gallery showing contemporary work.

The Franciscan monastery

A narrow passageway leads from St Saviour's Church to the fourteenth-century **Franciscan monastery** (Franjevački samostan) complex, whose intriguing late Romanesque cloister is decorated with rows of double arches topped by a confusion of human heads and fantastic animals. The attached **treasury** (daily: summer 9am–4pm; winter unpredictable; 5Kn) is also worth a look, with some manuscripts tracing the development of musical notation, together with relics from the apothecary's shop at the entrance to the cloister. Established in 1317, and still in business, it calls itself the oldest pharmacy in Europe. Among the Gothic reliquaries, a smooth, silver-plated fourteenth-century receptacle for St Ursula's head looks far too small and dainty to contain a human skull.

On the Stradun itself, on the right-hand side of the entrance to the monastery cloister, a small stone embellished with a gargoyle-like face juts out of the wall just above pavement height. For some reason, it has become a test of male endurance to stand on this stone – which is extremely difficult to balance on – facing the wall, bare chested and with arms outstretched, for as long as possible before falling off. A few steps beyond is the entrance portal to the monastery church, above which is a moving relief of the Pietà, carved by the Petrović brothers in 1499.

Prijeko and the synagogue

North of the Stradun a succession of alleys filled with potted plants runs uphill towards the city walls, on the way crossing **Prijeko** (literally "across" – a reference to the time when this part of the city was divided from the rest of Dubrovnik by a channel of sea water), which runs parallel to Stradun and contains many of Dubrovnik's more touristy restaurants. Towards the eastern end of Stradun, one of these steep alleys, Žudioska ("Jews' Street"), is home to a tiny **synagogue** (Mon & Wed 10am–noon, Fri 5–7.30pm) – dating from the fifteenth century and said to be the second oldest in the Balkans. The present-day interior dates from the nineteenth century, its heavy brass lamps and candelabras hanging from a bright blue ceiling dotted with star of David motifs. Unlike other Christian powers, Dubrovnik welcomed many of the Jews expelled from Spain in 1492, although anti-Semitism was not unknown. Even before their arrival in the city, scapegoating of Jews formed part of Dubrovnik's medieval carnival, most notably in the practice known as the *džudijata*, in which an unfortunate lunatic or criminal was dressed as a Jew before being hauled through the streets in an ox cart and either ritually killed or made to act out a make-believe death – historians are divided on how far things actually went.

Luža Square

The Stradun's far end broadens into the pigeon-choked **Luža Square**, the centre of the medieval town and even today a hub of activity, with its pavement cafés and milling tourists. Overlooking it is the fifteenth-century municipal **bell tower** (*gradski zvonik*), a smooth pillar of pale stone topped by an unassuming pimple-like cupola. On the left, the **Sponza Palace** (usually open mornings and evenings if there's an exhibition on), once the city's custom house and mint, grew in storeys as Dubrovnik grew in wealth, with a facade that features broad Renaissance arches on the ground floor and florid Venetian Gothic windows on the first floor. It was designed by Paskoje Miličević in 1522, although much of the stone-carving was done by Josip Andrijić, who also worked on Korčula's cathedral (see p.344) as well as Dubrovnik's St Saviour's Church.

Inside, the majestic courtyard is given over to art exhibitions and occasional concerts in summer. A Latin inscription on the far wall refers to the public scales that once stood here, and puts God firmly on the side of trading standards: "Cheating and tampering with the weights is forbidden, and when I weigh goods God weighs me." The splay-legged, spear-wielding figures underneath (known as the *zelenci*, or "greenies", because of to their weather-beaten-bronze appearance) were cast in 1578 and used to strike the bell on the near-by clock tower.

St Blaise's Church and Orlando's Column

Across the square, the Baroque **St Blaise's Church** (Crkva svetog Vlaha), completed in 1714, is in graceful counterpoint to the palace, boasting a fine facade topped by saintly statuettes which seem poised to topple down onto the square below. Twentieth-century stained glass bathes the interior with dappled light, although it's hard to make out the statuette of St Blaise on the high altar, surrounded by a supporting cast of swooning Baroque statuary. Originally an Armenian martyr, Blaise is said to have appeared in a vision to a local priest to warn of impending Venetian attack in 791. Although the whole story is a piece of anti-Venetian propaganda cooked up in around 1000 AD, it was enough to ensure the Saint's adoption as patron of the city.

Outside the church, plumb in the middle of the square, stands the carved figure of an armoured knight on top of a small column, usually referred to as **Orlando's Column**. Surprisingly for such an insignificant-looking object, erected in 1418 as a morale-boosting monument to freedom, this was the focal point of the city-state: it was here that government ordinances were promulgated and punishments carried out. Nowadays, a flag bearing the *libertas* motto flies from atop the column, and the start of the Dubrovnik Summer Festival is formally proclaimed here every July. Orlando's right arm was also the Republic's standard measurement of length (the Ragusan cubit or Dubrovački lakat, equivalent to 51.2cm); at the base of the column you can still see a line of the same length cut in the stone. The medieval cult of Orlando (or Roland) was born in the twelfth century thanks to the popularity of the epic poem, the *Song of Roland*, which told of the knight's heroic defence of a Pyrenean pass during the Arab invasion of Europe in the eighth century. The cult was a predominantly north European affair, brought to Dubrovnik at the time the city was under the protection of the Hungarian king, Sigismund of Luxemburg, who passed through the city after his defeat by the Turks at Nicopolis in 1396. The legend of Orlando was subsequently adapted to Ragusan requirements by making him the saviour of Dubrovnik in battles against the Saracens, during which he fought a duel with a pirate called Spuzente ("Smelly breath") – nobody seemed to mind that the real Saracen siege of Dubrovnik took place almost a century after Orlando's time.

The eastern side of Luža is flanked by a loggia, to the right of which is **Onofrio's Little Fountain**, an altogether more dainty affair than the same sculptor's fountain at the other end of Stradun, decorated with frivolous cherub reliefs courtesy of Onofrio's contemporary, Pietro di Martina of Milan. Along from the fountain, facing the bare southern flank of St Blaise's church, the terrace of the **Gradska kavana** (literally "town café") is where Dubrovnik's more stolid burghers traditionally sit to exchange gossip and observe the ebb and flow of tourists below. The rear of the café, where another terrace looks out onto the small port on the other side of the walls, was once the city **arsenal**, into which galleys were hauled for repairs.

The Rector's Palace

From Luža you can head either northeast via the Dominican monastery and Ploče Gate to the Revelin Fortress (see p.386), or south to the **Rector's Palace** (Knežev dvor), the seat of the Ragusan government. The building was effectively a prison: the rector, elected for just one month, had no real power and could only leave on state occasions with the say-so of the nobles who elected him; after the end of his period of duty, he was ineligible for re-election for the next two years. The palace housed all the major offices of state, plus a dungeon and a powder store (which caused the palace to blow up twice in the fifteenth century). Begun in the 1460s after the second of the powder explosions, the current palace, put together by a loose partnership of architects (including Dalmatinac and Michelozzi), is a masterpiece of serene proportion, fringed by an ornate arcaded loggia held up by columns with delicately carved capitals. Furthest to the right as you face them is the so-called **Asclepius Column**, bearing a relief of a bearded figure – presumably the Greco–Roman god of medicine, Asclepius – sitting in a pharmacist's laboratory. Asclepius was thought to be the patron of the ancient city of Epidauros (modern-day Cavtat, 20km south of Dubrovnik), from which the original population of Dubrovnik came, making him something of a distant guardian of the Ragusan state.

The palace's Renaissance atrium is a popular venue for summer recitals. At its centre is a bust of **Miho Pracat** (1522–1607), a rich shipowner and merchant from the island of Lopud who left most of his wealth to the city-state on his death – and was consequently the only citizen the republic ever honoured with a statue. An imposing staircase leads from the atrium to the balcony and, off here, the former state rooms, including the rooms of the city council, the Rector's study and the quarters of the palace guard. Today these are given over to the **City Museum** (Gradski muzej; June–Sept daily 9am–7pm; Oct–May

Mon–Sat 9am–1pm; 15Kn), a badly labelled three-floor collection of furniture and paintings which manifestly fails to tell the story of the republic in any meaningful or accessible way. It works quite well as a picture gallery though, with a respectable hoard of (mostly anonymous) Baroque works amassed by the city's aristocracy, and several imposing portraits of eminent Ragusans to whom moderately interesting stories are attatched. On the ground floor, look out for pictures of Nikola Bunić (1635–78), the statesman who died as a hostage in Silistra jail while trying to renegotiate the tribute paid by Dubrovnik to the Turks. Also here is an image of a kaftan-clad Marojica Kaboga (1630–92), who murdered his father-in-law in front of the Rector's Palace but escaped from prison in the chaos following the 1667 earthquake and, finding that there were few other capable nobles left, took charge of the defence and reconstruction of the city. Hidden away on the middle floor is an idealized picture of Cvijeta Zuzorić (1552–1648), a poetess and legendary beauty who held contemporary men of letters in thrall – notably philosopher Nikola Gucetić, who immortalized Zuzorić in his *Dialogues*.

The cathedral and St John's Fortress

Across the square from the palace is Dubrovnik's **Cathedral** (Katedrala), a plain but stately Baroque structure designed by Andrea Bufalini of Urbino in 1672, and built under the supervision of a succession of architects imported from Italy (the first three of whom gave up due either to illness or non-payment) before it was finally completed by local Ilija Kalčić in 1731. According to legend, the original church – destroyed in the 1667 earthquake – was funded by a votive gift from Richard the Lionheart, who may well have been ship-wrecked (and saved) off Ragusa on his way back from the Third Crusade, though traces of the original church's foundations have revealed that it actually predated Richard's visit by a couple of decades. Inside the cathedral are a couple of Italian paintings, including Titian's polyptych *The Assumption* behind the main altar, a work originally purchased by the Brotherhood of the Lazarini – a sign of how rich some of Dubrovnik's commoners' associations really were. The west side of the nave holds the icon of Our Lady of the Port, a Veneto-Byzantine Madonna once carried through the streets in time of drought on account of its rain-making powers.

To the left of the altar, the **treasury** (*riznica*; Mon–Sat 8am–5pm, Sun 11am–5pm; 5Kn) occupies a specially built room hidden behind heavy wooden doors with three locks – the three keys were held separately by the rector, the bishop and a nobleman. Now packed with gilded shelves and small paintings, the treasury originally grew from two collections, one of which was attached to the now destroyed St Stephen's Church, while the other belonged to the old pre-earthquake cathedral. Stored in the Revelin Fortress after the earthquake, both were brought to their current home in a grandiose procession in 1721. One of the prime exhibits is a twelfth-century skull reliquary of St Blaise, fashioned in the shape of a Byzantine crown, studded with portraits of saints and frosted with delicate gold and enamel filigree work. Nearby are both hands and one of the legs of the same saint, the left hand having been brought here from Constantinople by merchant Tomo Vicijan. Even more eyecatching is a bizarre fifteenth-century *Allegory of the Flora and Fauna of Dubrovnik*, a jug and basin festooned with snakes, fish and lizards clambering over thick clumps of seaweed.

From the cathedral, it's a short walk east along Kneza Damjana Jude towards the monolithic hulk of **St John's Fortress**, now refurbished to house a gloomy **aquarium** (*akvarium*; summer daily 10am–8pm; winter Mon–Sat

10am–1pm; 15Kn) full of Mediterranean marine life, including a pair of sad-looking sea turtles occupying pools into which visitors throw coins for good luck. Upstairs, the **Maritime Museum** (Pomorski muzej; summer daily 9am–7pm; winter Tues–Sun 9am–1pm; 15Kn) traces the history of Ragusan sea power through a display of marine artefacts, ranging from the well-stocked medicine chests of nineteenth-century ships' doctors to an excellent collection of models of Dubrovnik boats throughout the ages.

Pustijerna and Gundulićeva poljana

Walking back from St John's Fortress along Pustijerne, you'll find yourself round the back of the cathedral, south of which stretches one of the city's oldest quarters, **Pustijerna**; much of this predates the seventeenth-century earthquake and preserves a medieval feel, with crumbling, ancient houses crowding in on narrow lanes spanned here and there by arches. Dominating the western side of Pustijerna, the **Jesuit Church** (Isusovačka crkva), Dubrovnik's largest, is modelled, like most Jesuit places of worship, on the enormous church of the Gesù in Rome. It certainly boasts Dubrovnik's most frivolous ecclesiastical interior, with pinks and blues swirling across the ceiling, and a bombastic main altar with scenes from the life of St Ignatius, founder of the Jesuit order – the central panel shows the man renouncing all worldly things (here symbolized by a bevy of comely Baroque ladies).

The steps that lead down from here also had a Roman model – the Spanish Steps – and sweep down to **Gundulićeva poljana**, the square behind the cathedral which is the site of the city's morning fruit and vegetable market. In the middle stands Ivan Rendić's **statue of Ivan Gundulić** (1589–1638), the poet whose curly locks adorn one side of the 50Kn banknote. Gundulić's epic poem *Osman*, celebrating the victories of the Poles over the Turks, revealed a typical Ragusan paradox: despite growing rich through trade with the Ottoman state, the locals always sympathized with the empire's enemies, especially if they were Slavs. Gundulić's poetry found a nationwide audience in the nineteenth century, when a burgeoning sense of cultural patriotism generated new pride in the literary traditions of the past. The unveiling of the statue in 1893 occasioned one of the biggest demonstrations of solidarity the nation had ever seen, with the cream of Croatian society converging on the city to indulge in what amounted to a week-long street party.

Along Od Puča

Running parallel to Stradun, **Od Puča** leads west from Gundulićeva poljana, with stepped alleys branching off to meet the sea-walls. At no. 8 there's an **Orthodox Church Museum** (Muzej pravoslavne crkve; Mon–Sat 9am–1pm; 10Kn) containing a display of icons packed with Virgins, Christ Pantokrators and St Georges, mostly anonymous works hailing from Crete, Greece and the Bay of Kotor in Montenegro. A couple of paces beyond is the **Orthodox Church** itself, whose simple icon screen and functional interior are not of great artistic merit, but nevertheless exude an air of peaceful harmony.

A northward turn off Puča brings you to the **House of Marin Držić** at Široka 7 (Dom Marina Držića; Mon–Fri 9am–1pm, Sat 10am–noon; 10Kn), where Croatia's greatest sixteenth-century playwright (see box opposite) is commemorated in an imaginative audiovisual display (with English commentary). This makes a brave, if not entirely successful, stab at evoking Renaissance Dubrovnik, somewhat hampered by a lack of genuine exhibits – there's not much to actually see apart from a few facsimile manuscripts.

In many ways Marin Držić is to Croatia what William Shakespeare is to the English-speaking world: a seminal figure who transformed the knockabout theatrical entertainments of the day into something approaching modern drama, employing an unprecedented richness of vocabulary and metaphor that helped turn the dialect of sixteenth-century Dubrovnik into a literary medium equal to the other tongues of Renaissance Europe. Držić is an important symbol of Dubrovnik's contribution to Croatian – and European – culture, and his works almost always enjoy a central role in the annual Summer Festival.

Born into a family of merchants, Držić was never a member of the aristocratic elite that ran the republic, though the city did award him a scholarship to study at the University of Siena, where his involvement with the theatre began – he was thrown out in 1542 after taking part in a banned theatrical performance. Držić returned to Dubrovnik, and in 1545 entered the service of Graf Rogendorf, an Austrian then working as a diplomat for the Ottoman Empire.

It's not known precisely how and when Držić got involved with the drama troupes active in Dubrovnik. As in other Renaissance cities, satirical, farcical and moralizing performances were put on to entertain the populace at carnival time, or were given at the private parties and wedding feasts of the wealthy. It was in this environment that Držić's bawdy, but subtly plotted, comedies appeared. His first play, the now-lost *Pomet*, was performed in Dubrovnik in 1548. *Dundo Maroje* (1551), a ribald farce set among the expatriate Dubrovnik community in Rome, is the most frequently performed work today. His only tragedy, a reworking of Euripides' *Hecuba*, was interpreted as an anti-aristocratic allegory by the city authorities.

Držić left Dubrovnik for Venice in 1562, where he became an outspoken critic of the Ragusan Republic – his final literary oeuvre took the form of five letters to Cosimo de Medici asking for Florentine help in overthrowing the Dubrovnik aristocracy. The letters went unanswered, and Držić died an embittered and lonely figure. Ragusan men of letters who had rubbished Držić's reputation while he was alive wrote glowing obituaries after his death, and his work was swiftly enshrined as the literary standard against whom other Croatian writers were all measured.

Go a little way south from here up Domina to reach the **Rupe Ethnographic Museum** (Etnografski muzej Rupe; Sun–Fri 9am–1pm; 5Kn), whose dull display of regional crafts isn't half as interesting as the building itself, a former municipal grain store built in 1548 and featuring fifteen huge storage pits – the *rupe* or "holes" after which the building is named – carved out of bare rock. The Dubrovnik Republic was almost wholly reliant on imported grain, and the city imposed food-carrying responsibilities on shipowners as much as twelve months in advance. On arrival, wheat was dried in the upper storeys of the building before being sent down chutes into the storage pits below.

The Dominican monastery and museum

Back on Luža, a Gothic arch leads off the northeastern corner of the square to the twisting lane which first passes the entrance to the **Old Port** (Stara luka) – nowadays given over to pleasure boats, and the ferries which run across to the island of Lokrum, just offshore (see p.386) – before reaching the **Dominican monastery**. Begun in 1301, the construction of the monastery was very much a communal endeavour: due to its position hard up against the fortifications, the city authorities provided the Dominicans with extra funds, and ordered the citizenry to contribute labour. The monastery is approached by a grand stairway with a stone balustrade whose columns have been partly mortared in, an ugly modification carried out by the monks themselves in response to the loafers who stood at the bottom of the staircase to ogle the bare ankles of women on their way to church. At the top of the steps a doorway leads through to a fifteenth-century Gothic Renaissance cloister, filled with palms and orange trees.

The attached **museum** (daily: summer 9am–6pm; winter 9am–5pm; 10Kn) has some outstanding examples of sixteenth-century religious art from Dubrovnik, including three canvases by **Nikola Božidarević**, the leading figure of the period, who managed to combine Byzantine solemnity with the humanism of the Italian Renaissance. Immediately on the right as you enter, Božidarević's triptych with its central Madonna and Child is famous for its depiction of Dubrovnik prior to the earthquake of 1667, when both Franciscan and Dominican monasteries sported soaring Gothic spires. On the panel to the left, St Blaise holds a model of the city, while, on the right, St Dominic (accompanied by St Augustine) brandishes a model of the medieval cathedral. Nearby, Božidarević's *Annunciation* of 1513, commissioned by shipowner Marko Kolendić, contains more local detail in one of its lower panels, showing one of the donor's argosies lying off the port of Lopud. The most Italianate of Božidarević's works is the *Virgin and Child* altarpiece, also of 1513, ordered by the Đorđić family (the bearded donor kneels at the feet of St Martin in the lower right-hand corner) – note the concerted attempt at some serious landscape painting in the background.

Much more statically Byzantine in style is the largest work on display, a polyptych of 1448 in dazzling gold-leaf by Lovro Dobričević Marinov, the most illustrious of Božidarević's predecessors. It shows Christ's Baptism in the River Jordan, flanked from left to right by SS Michael, Nicholas, Blaise and Stephen – the last was put to death by stoning, hence the stylized rock shapes which the artist has rather awkwardly placed on his head and shoulders. Alongside a fine but rather statuesque *St Nicholas* (1512) by Mihajlo Hamzić, there's a smaller, much simpler, but rather more gripping *Martyrdom of St Vincent* by Frano Matkov, in which the saint is roasted on a bed of hot coals. Cabinets full of precious silver follow, including the cross of the Serbian king, Stefan Uroš II Milutin (1282–1321), inscribed with archaic Cyrillic lettering, and a reliquary which claims to contain the skull of King Stephen I of Hungary (975–1038). The Baroque paintings in the next-door room are all fairly second-rate, save for Titian's *St Blaise and St Mary Magdalene* – Blaise holds the inevitable model of Dubrovnik while sinister storm clouds gather in the background. The youth holding a fish on the right of the canvas is St Tobias, here accompanied by the donor, Ragusan noble Damjan Pucić, kneeling in prayer.

After all this fine art, the adjoining monastery **church** is a bit of a disappointment. The best artworks are a fine pastel *St Dominic*, by the nineteenth-century Cavtat artist Vlaho Bukovac, and a dramatic Veneto-Byzantine crucifix, attributed to the fourteenth-century Paolo Veneziano, which hangs over the main altar.

Right beside the main monastery entrance, an unassuming doorway leads to the **Rosary Church** (Rozarijo), formerly belonging to the Dominicans and nowadays sporadically used as an art gallery. The intimate Renaissance interior, divided by arcades topped by angels' heads, is definitely worth a peek.

The Revelin Fortress to the Museum of Modern Art

Beyond the monastery, the lane emerges at the **Ploče Gate**, the main eastern entrance to the old town. It's larger than the Pile Gate, with another statue of

△ Franciscan monastery, Dubrovnik

St Blaise in the niche above (the oldest in the city) and a bridge across the moat dating from 1449. The **Revelin Fortress**, just beyond, was begun around the same time, but not finished until 1539, when fears of a coming war between the Turks and the Western powers impelled the Ragusans to hastily strengthen their defences. All other building work in the city was cancelled for four months, leaving the city's builders free to concentrate on the fortress, and leading families had to send their servants to work as labourers, or pay a fine.

Beyond Revelin is the modern suburb of **Ploče**, until the beginning of the twentieth century the scene of a large market where cattle and other goods arrived by caravan from the Balkan interior. Fear that such caravans brought disease prompted the construction in 1590 of a series of quarantine houses, or **Lazareti**, a row of brick-built accommodation blocks and courtyards which can still be seen on the right-hand side of the road. During times of pestilence, visitors entering the Dubrovnik Republic from the Ottoman Empire were obliged to stay here for forty days before proceeding any further. Ottoman traveller Evliya Çelebi, quarantined here in 1664, likened it to a comfortable and homely inn, although he regretted not being allowed out to enjoy Dubrovnik's nightlife. Sanitary concerns were still uppermost in Ragusan minds in the mid-nineteenth century, when British traveller A.A. Paton reported with satisfaction that the market here was penned in by a chest-high stone partition in order to "permit commerce and conversation without contact".

Beyond the Lazareti, Frana Supila leads gently uphill to the **Museum of Modern Art** (Umjetnička galerija; Mon–Sat 10am–1pm & 5–8pm; 10Kn) at no. 23, which hosts high-profile exhibitions on the ground floor, and showcases local painters upstairs. Of the latter, the most important is considered to be the Cavtat-born, Paris-trained Vlaho Bukovac (1855–1922), a stiff Victorian realist whose portraits of late nineteenth-century worthies are considerably less colourful than near-contemporary Marko Rešica's Post-Impressionist Adriatic landscapes, featuring wind-teased cypresses and tamarisks. A couple of post-World War II names are worth picking out: Ivo Dulčić (1916–75), whose blood-red landscape, *Crveni otok* ("Red Island"), verges on the abstract, and Antun Masle (1919–67), painter of the dreamy, Chagall-esque *Lapad*, which is one of the smallest – but best known – pieces in the entire collection.

Lokrum

Facing the suburb of Ploce is the wooded island of **LOKRUM**, 1km to the southeast. Reputedly the island where Richard the Lionheart was shipwrecked, it was bought in 1859 by Maximilian von Habsburg, Archduke of Austria (and subsequently Emperor of Mexico). He transformed a former Benedictine monastery here into his summer palace, created a botanical garden which he stocked with exotic plants and cacti, and wrote bad verse about the island's beauty. After Maximilian's death in 1867, the Habsburgs sold the island to a local businessman eager to turn it into a health resort, only to buy it back on behalf of Emperor Franz-Josef's son Rudolf, who wintered here to soothe his bronchial chest.

Boats leave for Lokran from the old town's port every half-hour, and take ten minutes (May–Oct 9am–6pm; 12Kn). Unfortunately you can't visit the monastery – just up from the island's jetty – although you can look around the cloister (now home to a restaurant) and wander around Maximilian's **Botanical Garden** next door, where odd varieties of giant triffid-like cactus look as if they could swallow you whole. The best of the (largely rocky) **beaches** are beyond the monastery on the island's southwest side, where you'll find a small salt lake just inland, and a naturist beach at the island's southern tip.

Shady paths overhung by pines run round the northern part of the island, with tracks leading uphill towards **Fort Royal**, a gun position left by the Napoleonic French whose grey, menacing ramparts rise rather suddenly from the jungle-like greenery covering the island's central ridge.

North and west of the old town

West of the old town, just outside Pile Gate, steps descend towards a small harbour overlooked by the Bokar Fortress on one side and by the monumental, wedge-shaped fortress of **Lovrijenac** on the other (daily 9am–2pm; 10Kn). Originally built in 1050, but assuming its current shape in the sixteenth century, it was the most important component of the city's south- and west-facing defences, commanding both land and sea approaches from atop a craggy cliff. In recent times Lovrijenac has become famous as the venue for performances of Shakespeare's *Hamlet* during the Dubrovnik Summer Festival, when it becomes the perfect double for Elsinore castle.

A statue of St Lawrence brandishing a model of the fort watches over the fortress entrance, above which there's a typically proud Ragusan inscription: *Non bene pro toto libertas venditur auro* ("All the gold in the world cannot buy freedom"). There's not much to see inside the fortress, though the triangular courtyard framed by chunky arcades is impressive enough on its own, while the upper level gives a fine view of the city and its walls.

Gruž and the Rijeka Dubrovačka

Spearing westwards from the Pile Gate, Ante Starčevića heads towards the suburb of **Gruž** and Dubrovnik's main port, tucked between the mainland on the eastern side and the Lapad peninsula to the northwest. Dominating the western end of Gruž is the **Franjo Tuđman Bridge** (Most Franja Tuđmana), a breathtakingly elegant suspension bridge spanning the mouth of a four-kilometre inlet known as the **Rijeka Dubrovačka**. Opened in 2002, the bridge is the first thing that travellers see when approaching the city from the west: as such, it's a marvellously futuristic counterpoint to the historic old town beyond. The Rijeka Dubrovačka itself was once one of the Ragusan Republic's favourite pleasure resorts. Noble families built summer villas here, a number of which still stand – though these days the look of the place has been largely spoiled by the modern city's industrial and residential sprawl. It's not an area you're likely to make a special trip to see (buses #1A and #1B run here from Pile Gate), unless you're heading for the large yachting marina near the suburb of **Komolac** at the end of the inlet, where the slightly unkempt gardens and fishponds of the **Sorkočević Palace** (the interior can't be visited) offer a distant echo of the horticultural splendours of the Ragusan Renaissance.

One kilometre beyond Komolac, on the right-hand side of the road, the inlet itself emerges dramatically from a limestone cliff at **MLINI**, the next settlement along, a slightly scruffy area that seems to have missed out on development as a beauty spot.

Mount Srđ

Towering above the town to the north, **Mount Srđ** was a much-visited attraction until 1991, when Yugoslav forces destroyed the cable car that used to deliver tourists to its 412-metre-high summit. A handful of people still make the trip, either by the winding footpath (the aptly named *serpentina*) which heads up to the top from Jadranska cesta, or via the badly surfaced road which leaves the Cavtat-bound highway 1km southeast of Dubrovnik, clambering its way to the village of Bosanka and thence on to the shoulder of the mountain. If you're walking, bear in mind that the *serpentina* is unshaded, and the ascent can be a hellish experience in hot weather.

Whichever way you get there, you'll be rewarded with a stunning view of the walled town below, with a panorama of the whole coast stretching as far as the Pelješac peninsula to the northwest. The summit-crowning **Fort Imperial** was built by Napoleon's occupying army in 1808 and served as a disco in the 1980s before reverting to its original military purpose in 1991, when it was successfully held by Dubrovnik's defenders. Seriously smashed up by Serbian artillery, however, it's now derelict and can't be visited. The mountain seems a world away from the lush subtropical world of the coastal strip; nothing much grows here apart from sage, which is hungrily devoured by the sheep sent here to graze by the farmers of Bosanka.

Eating, drinking and nightlife

There's no shortage of **restaurants** in Dubrovnik, and culinary standards are reasonably high. The choice of food doesn't significantly differ from what's on offer in the rest of maritime Croatia, with grilled fish, squid and shellfish forming the backbone of local culinary culture. However certain places have become tourist traps and are worth avoiding: Prijeko, the street running parallel to Stradun to the north, is lined with establishments offering identical menus at identical prices, aggressively selling their indifferent fare by sending staff out onto the streets to ambush hungry tourists with dubious offers of free house wine or family discounts. Luckily, there are plenty of other places in the tourist-trodden old town that base their reputation on good cooking rather than the hard sell.

Most restaurants are open until 11pm unless otherwise stated, although many extend their hours until midnight in season. We've included the telephone numbers of those restaurants where it might be a good idea to reserve in advance. Restaurants in Dubrovnik often charge a cover of 5–10Kn, although you don't always get much in return for this except a few indifferent hunks of bread.

For **snacks**, try the sandwich bars lining the alleys running uphill from Stradun, notably *Kaktus* on Vetranovićeva, and *Mrvica* on Kuničeva, both of which are a good place for a *pršut* sandwich. *Don Corleone*, Boškovićeva 4, serves up the best pizza slices, as well as filling portions of lasagne in its backroom restaurant. *Tanti Gusti*, Između polače, a 24-hour bakery just off the Stradun, always has fresh bread and tasty pastries. There are fruit and vegetable **markets** (Mon–Sat mornings) on Gundulićeva poljana and on the waterfront in Gruž, and there are a pair of **supermarkets** on Gundulićeva poljana.

Restaurants

The old town and around

Atlas Club Nautika Brsalje 3 ☎020/442-526. Long considered the best place in town for quality seafood, this is an upmarket environment with two floors of formal dining rooms, each with a small outdoor terrace. Liveried waiters, napkins folded with origami-like precision, and a large list of top international wines complete the picture. Expect to pay around 200–300Kn a head for full meal.

Express Restaurant M. Kaboge 1. Self-service canteen food in antiseptic surroundings just off the Stradun, including vegetarian options, filling stews, and a salad bar. Tasty fare at rock-bottom prices. Closes 10pm.

Kamenica Gundulićeva poljana 8. Unpretentious and cheap seafood restaurant popular with locals and tourists alike, with a cramped, functional interior, and outdoor seating on one of the old town's finest squares. Favourites include *girice* (tiny fish deep fried and eaten whole), *kamenice* (oysters) and *mušule* (mussels).

Konoba Ekvinocijo Ilije Sarake 10. Family-run restaurant in the warren of streets south of the cathedral, offering the usual fish and meat dishes, but with a bit more friendliness and style than the tourist-trap places on Prijeko. The squid stuffed with ham and cheese rarely fails to disappoint. There are two levels of outdoor seating, but no indoor dining room, so this is really a warm-evenings-only affair.

Konoba Posat uz Posat 1. Restaurant with a large and pleasant garden terrace just outside the city walls, slightly uphill from the Pile Gate, offering views towards Minčeta Fortress. Good for grilled meats, and not too expensive.

Proto Široka 1 ☎020/323-234. Top-notch establishment bang in the heart of old Dubrovnik, with a formal indoor dining room, a rather more relaxed outdoor terrace upstairs, and attention-to-detail service. As usual fish is the main attraction, although this is one place in Dubrovnik where the meat dishes are prepared to the same level of excellence as the seafood – you can't really go wrong here whatever you order. The site has been occupied by a fish restaurant ever since 1886, and it's claimed that Edward VIII and Wallis Simpson (see p.232) ate here during one of their visits to Dubrovnik in the 1930s. Expect to exceed the 200Kn mark for main course, sweet and drinks.

Rozarij Corner of Prijeko and Zlatarska. Cosy and intimate restaurant, with outdoor tables crammed into a quaint corner just uphill from Luža. Good for fish and seafood, and also has a small selection of schnitzel-type meat dishes. If you have to eat on Prijeko, this is the place to do it.

Lapad, Babin kuk and outside the city

Levanat Nika i Meda Pucića 15 ☎020/435-352. Family-run restaurant on the coastal path between Lapad and Babin kuk, with chic interior and an outdoor terrace with a marvellous view of jagged offshore outcrops. The imaginative seafood menu features a lot of boiled and baked fish recipes, often with unusual sauces, as well as the plain grilled variety. A café as well as a restaurant, Levanat is one of the most relaxing places in this part of Dubrovnik to stop off for a drink. A full meal will set you back 200–250Kn with drinks.

Orsan Gverović Zaton Mali bb ☎020/891-267. Cult seafood restaurant 5km northwest of town, right beside the coastal Magistrala at the entrance to the village of Zaton. The owner adopts a no-nonsense approach: there's little on the menu save for expertly grilled fresh fish and shellfish – all served up on a terrace within bone-spitting distance of the sea. Popular with the arty set drawn to Dubrovnik by the summer festival, but less expensive than the top-of-the-range seafood places back in town.

Yacht Club Orsan Ivana Zajca 2. Situated on the northern side of the Lapad peninsula, right on the marina where Dubrovnik folk are wont to tether their boats, this is as pleasantly peaceful a spot as you will find in this part of town. The menu concentrates on the tried and tested meat and fish favourites, but standards are high and prices a good ten percent lower than in the old town.

Drinking

Drinking in Dubrovnik, is for much of the year, a question of finding an outside table from which to see and be seen. The pavement cafés of Stradun are the best places for daytime and early evening imbibing, providing the classic people-watching and postcard-writing venues. Nearby Bunićeva poljana, just behind the cathedral, becomes one vast outdoor bar on summer nights, with rows of tables spread out between the *Jazz Café Trubadour* on one side and *Café Mirage* on the other. You could also try the streets leading uphill from Stradun, notably Zamanjina, Kunićeva and Antuninska, where you'll find locals sitting on the steps outside tiny bars with blaring music.

The other main area for drinking is northwest of the centre, between the old town and Gruž, where a strip of flashy bars lining bana Jelačića has been dubbed "Bourbon Street" by the locals – for whom it remains the venue of choice for Saturday-night drinking and flirting.

Bars and cafés

Buža iza Mira. One of the most atmospheric places to drink in Dubrovnik, this is an unpretentious outdoor bar perched on the rocks just outside the old town's sea-facing walls. It's approached through a hole in the wall – advertised by a sign which simply reads "cold drinks". Doesn't bother opening if the weather is cold or windy.

Gradska kavana prid Dvorom. Cavernous but characterful café with dowdy decor and a loyal clientele of older generation, coffee-supping locals. Good for cakes and ice cream. Live demonstrations of piano-tinkling skills are a frequent occurrence in summer.

Hard Jazz Café Trubadour Bunićeva poljana. Small and intimate pub-like space which explodes out onto the surrounding square as soon as the weather's warm enough for outdoor drinking. If you're a well-known face in Croatia, you have to be seen drinking here at least once in the summer. Owned by a former member of the Dubrovački Trubaduri (a big-time Sixties beat group that had the dubious honour of representing Yugoslavia in the Eurovision Song Contest), it hosts impromptu live jazz music most nights in summer – when drink prices rise according to the status of the performers.

Irish Pub Između polača 5. There's nothing particularly Irish about this place apart from the ales, but the laid-back atmosphere and reasonable beer prices ensure a healthy influx of tourists and local students. Quite a crush on summer weekends, and the most likely place to show midweek football on TV.

Libertina Zlatarska. Tiny watering hole in a side-street next to the Sponza Palace which, despite being located in Dubrovnik's tourist-tramped centre, still has the feel of a neighbourhood bar. A cosy place, stuffed with domestic nick-nacks and garrulous local drinkers.

Orka Lapadska obala 9. Cosy café-bar in the Lapad/Gruž area, with a lively, late-opening upstairs terrace (reached via a separate entrance two doors down). Often packed with students from Dubrovnik University's nearby Faculty of Tourism. Not worth a special trip, but a welcoming bolt hole if you're staying in this part of town.

Roxy bana Jelačića. Most characterful of the bars on "Bourbon Street", good for either a quick coffee break or a lengthy drinking session. It was once an important music venue, but gigs are few and far between nowadays – although the Croatian rock memorabilia crowding the interior makes this an enduring shrine to the local music scene. There are plenty of other bars within crawling distance: the next-door *Planet Sport* harbours a fascinating gallery of sport-related photographs.

Talir Antuninska. Legendary post-performance hangout for actors and musicians during the summer festival – the walls are plastered with photographs of Croatian celebrities past and present. It's a small place, in a side-street midway down Stradun, and most people end up sitting on the steps outside.

Nightlife and entertainment

During the summer, the rich cultural diet provided by the **Summer Festival** (see below) is augmented by informal open-air pop and jazz concerts in the old town. Outside summer, look out for regular performances mounted by the town's two main cultural institutions: the **Marin Držić Theatre** (℡020/426-437), Pred Dvorom 3, which specializes in serious drama in the Croatian language; and the **Dubrovnik Symphony Orchestra**, whose concert hall is at Ante Starčevića 29 (℡020/417-101). Local folk ensemble Linđo perform in the Lazareti (see p.386) at least twice a week in summer – tourist offices and hotels will have details. The most central **cinema** is Kino Sloboda on Luža.

Most of the **clubbing** venues lack either a regular clientele or a strong identity. *Esperanza*, near the bus station at Put Republike 30, is a popular venue for Croatian pop concerts; *Exodus*, near the *Argosy* and *Tirena* hotels on the Babin kuk peninsula, has more in the way of cutting-edge house and techno. Club nights and **live gigs** (rock, ethno and jazz) are occasionally organized at the Lazareti. Listings information in the local press is inadequate, so you'll have to look for posters to get an idea of what's on.

Festivals

The **Dubrovnik Summer Festival** (Dubrovačke ljetne igre; July & Aug; ⓦwww.dubrovnik-festival.hr) stages classical concerts and theatre performances in Dubrovnik's courtyards, squares and bastions in the old town – sometimes offering the only chance to see inside them. The emphasis is very much on high culture: the festival usually includes plays by Shakespeare and Marin Držić (see box on p.383), a major opera, symphonic concerts and a host of smaller chamber-music events. Seats for some of the more prestigious events often sell out well in advance, but it should be possible to pick up tickets for many performances at fairly short notice. The full programme is usually published in April: for further details and advance tickets contact Dubrovačke ljetne igre,

Poljana Paska Miličevića 1, 20000 Dubrovnik (☎020/412-288 or 426-351, ℱ427-944, ✉program@dubrovnik-festival.hr). Once the festival starts, tickets (30–200Kn) can be bought from festival information points at the Pile Gate and on Stradun.

As a kind of riposte to the festival, the Otok Cultural Centre organizes the **Karantena Festival** of alternative theatre, performance art and happenings in August, with performances taking place in the Lazareti. Advance information from Otok, Pobijana 8, 20000 Dubrovnik (☎ & ℱ020/423-497).

Listings

Airlines Croatia Airlines, Brsalje 9 (Mon–Fri 8am–4pm, Sat 9am–noon; ☎020/413-777).

Airport ☎020/773-377.

Banks and exchange Dubrovačka banka, Stradun (Mon–Fri 7.30am–1pm & 2–7pm, Sat 7.30am–1pm); Gospodarsko-Kreditna banka, Pile Gate (daily 8am–8pm); Zagrebačka banka, Gundulićeva poljana (Mon–Fri 8.30am–noon & 6–8pm, Sat 8.30am–noon).

Bookshop English-language paperbacks are available from Algoritam, Stradun 8.

Bus station ☎020/23-088.

Car rental Budget, Obala S. Radića 20, Gruž ☎020/411-649; Gulliver, Obala S. Radića 31, Gruž ☎020/411-088.

Ferries Tickets from Jadrolinija, opposite the ferry terminal, at Obala S. Radića 40, Gruž (Mon–Thurs & Sat 8am–2pm, 3–4.15pm & 7–8pm; Fri 8am–2pm, 3–4.15pm & 7–11pm, Sun 7–10am &

7–8.30pm; ☎020/418-000), and Globetour, Stradun (☎020/428-992).

Hospital At Roka Mišetića, Lapad, 4km west of the old town ☎020/431-777.

Internet access Dubrovnik Internet Centar, round the back of the *Dubravka* café, Pile; and Internet, Prijeko 15, close to the *Don Corleone* pizza place.

Left luggage At the bus station (daily 4.50am–9.30pm).

Pharmacy Kod Zvonika, Stradun, is open 24hr.

Post office and telephones Ante Starčevića 2 (Mon–Fri 7am–8pm, Sat 7am–7pm, Sun 8am–2pm).

Taxis There are ranks outside the bus and ferry terminals and at Pile Gate, or call ☎020/24-343.

Travel agents The Atlas offices at Lučarica 1 or Svetog Đurđa 1 (near the Pile Gate) handle air tickets and excursions (Mon–Sat 8am–9pm, Sun 9am–1pm; ☎020/442-222, ⊛www.atlas-croatia.com).

The coast around Dubrovnik

Standing on the coastal highway 13km northwest of Dubrovnik, the straggling village of **Trsteno** is an essential day-trip destination if you're at all interested in things horticultural, as it's the site of an arboretum stocked with hundreds of varieties of trees. Heading south instead from Dubrovnik, you immediately run into what was once one of the most heavily developed parts of the coast, with a string of purpose-built resorts edging the road and obscuring all sight of the sea. The area was occupied by Serb and Montenegrin troops in the winter of 1991–92 and most of the hotels looted, although all but a small proportion have now been spruced up and put back in service. Starting with Kupari, and followed swiftly by Srebreno, Mlini, Soline and Plat, the resorts merge to form a six-kilometre line of apartment blocks, weekend villas, angular hotels and waterside cafés. The beaches here are not worth making a special visit for, and it's best to press on to **Cavtat**, 3km beyond Plat, which preserves a modicum of traditional architecture fringed by lush Mediterranean vegetation, or the village of **Čilipi**, where you can hear folk music on summer Sundays. Thirty-five kilometres south of Dubrovnik the road arrives at the border with **Montenegro** (Crna Gora in Croatian and Serbian), although you should check visa requirements before attempting to cross it.

Trsteno

It was in **TRSTENO** in 1502 that Dubrovnik noble Ivan Gučetić built his summer villa, surrounded by decorous gardens which spread along a terrace overlooking the sea. Such gardens were considered de rigeur by the aristocracy of sixteenth-century Dubrovnik – sadly, those of Trsteno are the only ones which can still be enjoyed in something approaching their original form. Maintained by successive generations of the Gučetić family, the villa and its gardens were confiscated in 1948 by a communist regime eager to destroy any latent prestige still enjoyed by the Dubrovnik nobility. The Yugoslav (now Croatian) Academy of Sciences took the place over and expanded it, turning it into an arboretum.

Trsteno is relatively easy to get to, with Dubrovnik–Split **buses** dropping off and picking up in the centre of the village. Standing by the roadside just next to the bus stop is a majestic pair of 400-year-old plane trees, some 50m high and 15m in circumference. From here a path drops you down to the main entrance to the **arboretum** (daily: summer 8am–9pm; winter 8am–3pm; 12Kn), where Gucetić's former villa overlooks the oldest part of the estate, a typical Renaissance garden in which patches of lavender, rosemary, oleander, bougainvillea, myrtle and cyclamen are divided up by lines of box hedge to form a complex geometrical design. A nearby orchard sports bushy grapefruit and mandarin trees, but beyond here the garden has a wonderfully lush, uncontrolled feel, as pathways begin to lose themselves in a dense woodland environment comprising trees from around the world. Amidst it all, a trident-wielding statue of Neptune overlooks a pond packed with goldfish. Running northwest from the villa, an avenue of palm trees leads to yet more semi-wilderness areas, thick with cypresses and pines. The effects of two recent fires (the first resulting from Yugoslav artillery in 1991, the second starting accidentally in summer 2000), can be seen in the shape of blackened tree trunks and waste ground, dotted here and there with areas of new planting. Once you've seen the gardens, however, there's not much to keep you here, save for the little **café** attached to the campsite just uphill from the garden entrance.

Cavtat

Twenty kilometres south of Dubrovnik, and 3km off the main coastal highway, **CAVTAT** is a dainty coastal town and package resort which began life in the third century BC as Epidaurum, a colony founded by Greeks from the island of Vis. There's nothing left to see of the antique town: Epidaurum was evacuated in favour of Dubrovnik after a thorough ransacking by the Slavs in the seventh century, and the pretty fishing village of Cavtat subsequently grew up in its place. Discovered by Austro-Hungarian holiday-makers at the beginning of the twentieth century, Cavtat was a favourite haunt of the wealthy until a rash of high-rise hotel building in the 1980s changed the place's profile. Happily, the hotels are set apart from the palm-dotted seafront of the original village, ranged across the neck of a sweet-smelling wooded peninsula.

Much of Cavtat's former charm survives in the old part of town, which straddles the ridge behind the waterfront. The showpiece here is the **Račić Mausoleum** (Mon–Sat 10am–noon & 5–7pm, Sun 10am–noon; 4Kn), built on a prime spot high above the town in 1921 by Ivan Meštrović for a local shipowning family. It's one of Meštrović's more successful stabs at architectural eclecticism: a simple, Byzantine-inspired, domed structure guarded by stern, archaic Greek angels and decorated with dog-faced gargoyles, Teutonic-looking eagles and what look like neo-Assyrian winged lambs just below the cupola.

Downhill from here on the waterfront's northern end, the rather plain-looking **Monastery of Our Lady of the Snow** (Samostan snježne Gospe) contains a couple of early Renaissance gems in its small church: the first, Vičko Lovrin's triptych of 1509 at the back of the church, shows a gold-clad Archangel Michael slaying a demon while John the Baptist and St Nicholas look on from the wings; the second, Božidar Vlatković's *Madonna and Child* (1494) on the main altar, is a small piece somewhat overpowered by its fussy Baroque frame. Walking south along the Riva and heading up Bukovčeva (a narrow, stepped alleyway rather than a street) brings you to the **Vlaho Bukovac gallery** at no. 5, honouring the Cavtat-born painter (1855–1922) with a selection of his stolid portraits of self-confident, early twentieth-century middle-class types. More of his paintings can be seen in the **Baltazar Bogišić Collection** (Zbirka Baltazara Bogišića; Mon–Sat 9.30am–1pm; 10Kn), which occupies the former Rector's Palace at the southern end of the Riva. Lawyer and cultural activist Bogišić (1834–1908) spent a lifetime promoting Croatian literature and learning, at a time when Italian was still considered the language of civilized discourse along the coast. Books from Bogišić's collection crowd the display cabinets, although the stand-out exhibit is Bukovac's immense canvas of local carnival celebrations in 1901 – with the cream of Cavtat society gamely got up in fancy dress for the occasion. If you're in the mood for more Bukovac, head just uphill to **St Nicholas's Church** (Crkva svetog Nikole), where his paintings of the Four Evangelists look down on the main altar.

A brace of fine shingle **beaches** lies about 1km east of the town centre in an area known as **žal** (literally, "beach"), although the proximity of the package hotels ensures that they're usually crowded. Quieter spots, if you don't mind perching on rocks, can be found at the far end of the peninsula, ten minutes' walk north from town, or on the Sustjepan peninsula immediately to the west. The latter has a naturist section, just on the other side of the *Croatia Hotel*.

Practicalities

Bus #10 runs here roughly every hour from Dubrovnik. Privately operated **boats** from Dubrovnik's Old Port (see p.387) do the same trip for about 20Kn. Cavtat's **tourist office**, a short walk east of the **bus station** at Tiha 3 (summer daily 8am–7pm; winter Mon–Fri 8am–3pm; ☏020/479-025, ⓦwww.tzcavtat-konavle.hr) offers an ocean of town maps and brochures in every conceivable language. Ample private **rooms** (❶) and **apartments** (❷) are available from the Adriatica agency (Mon–Sat 8am–8pm, Sun 9am–noon; ☏020/478-713, Ⓔadriatica@du.hinet.hr), just by the bus station. There's an old harbourfront **hotel** in the centre, the slightly dowdy *Supetar* (☏020/475-555, Ⓕ478-213; ❸), and a string of three more modern package-oriented hotels in the *žal* area: the *Cavtat* (☏020/478-246; ❻), the *Albatross* (☏020/471-333; ❼) and the *Epidaurus* (☏020/471-444; ❻), all owned by the same company (ⓦwww.hotelicavtat.hr) and offering similar standards of beachfront comfort, although the *Albatross* has a large private swimming pool and plusher, air-conditioned rooms. On the other side of town, the five-star *Croatia* (☏020/475-555, ⓦwww.hoteli-croatia.hr; ❽) is a vast multi-tiered concrete affair hogging the ridge of the Sustjepan peninsula. It's easy to get lost in its seemingly endless corridors, but it has modern air-conditioned rooms with TV, a swimming pool and a private beach facing the Cavtat waterfront.

There are numerous **restaurants** on or near the waterfront, offering everything from cheap pizza to more expensive local specialities; best of the lot is *Galija*, tucked in an alleyway behind the monastery, offering succulent seafood starters and fishy main courses (often baked or boiled rather than grilled) in a cosy semi-rustic interior or a shaded upstairs terrace. Slightly inland, the *Konoba Kolona* offers cheap and tasty eats on a small but shady garden terrace just by the bus stop.

Čilipi

Six kilometres south of Cavtat, just beyond Dubrovnik's airport, **ČILIPI** is the main village of the **Konavle** region, a small area known for the colourful costumes of its inhabitants, characterized by the small pillbox hats donned by unmarried girls and the enormous white scarves worn by married women. The latter are still very much in use (for the benefit of tourists as much as anything), and Čilipi has become something of an excursion spot for tour operators from Dubrovnik because of the **folklore shows** which take place on the village's flagstoned central square every summer Sunday. Organized by the local folklore society, performances are held in the late morning immediately after mass, when locals and tourists alike perch on the church steps to observe a forty-minute medley of local songs and dances. Foremost among the latter is the *linđo*, which employs rigid, stylized gestures to mimic the rites of courtship, and is accompanied by the *lirica*, an archaic, droning fiddle.

Trips to Čilipi from Dubrovnik are run by the ubiquitous Atlas agency (see "Listings", p.391), although you can get here independently using the three daily buses which run from Dubrovnik via Čilipi to Gruda or Molunat. There are a couple of cafés just off the main square, and a largely tourist-oriented Sunday **market** selling folksy embroidery and textiles.

The Elaphite Islands

The string of islands that crowd the sea between Dubrovnik and the Pelješac peninsula to the north are known as the **Elaphites** ("deer islands"), a name apparently first coined by Pliny the Elder in his 37-volume *Historia Naturalis*. The Elaphites became part of the Dubrovnik Republic from the fourteenth century, sharing in its prosperity and then its decline – by the middle of the eighteenth century many island villages lay abandoned and depopulation had become a major problem. Today, only three of the islands are inhabited – **Koločep**, **Lopud** and **Šipan** – each of which supports a modest tourist industry. Of the three, Lopud is perhaps the most developed, although tourism everywhere is fairly low key, the almost total absence of cars contributing to the mellow feel (private vehicles are not allowed on any of the islands except Šipan, but almost all the ferries that go there are passenger-only).

All three islands are linked to Dubrovnik by a **ferry** which runs up to Šipan and back again (up to 4 daily in summer; 1 daily in winter), and are great places for getting away from it all – whether for a day-trip or an extended stay. As you leave Gruž harbour you'll pass the first of the Elaphiti, tiny uninhabited **Daksa** – just off Babin Kuk, it's notorious as the site of a 1945 massacre when over two hundred political opponents of the new communist regime were liquidated.

Koločep

Just half an hour from Dubrovnik by ferry, the islet of **Koločep** is a little over 2.6 square kilometres in area, and has a population of under 150 concentrated in two main hamlets: **Donje Čelo**, on the north side of the island where the ferry docks, and **Gornje Čelo** to the southeast. There are no special sights, but Donje Čelo is a pleasant cluster of stone houses which boasts an excellent curving sandy beach. Just uphill from the waterfront, a concreted path strikes inland towards Gornje Čelo, a huddle of vegetation-choked houses overlooking two small bays. From here you can follow innumerable paths into the dense, fragrant pine and deciduous forest that covers the southern part of the island.

Accommodation is limited to the *Hotel Koločep* (☎020/757-025, ℱ757-027; ❺; May–Oct), an ensemble of eight modern blocks ranged across a hillside just above Donje Čelo's beach. There's also a waterfront **café–restaurant** in Donje Čelo offering simple grills and seafood.

Lopud

In Dubrovnik's heyday, **Lopud** was the seat of one of the republic's vice-rectors and, with a population of some 4000 (today it's 400), was a favoured watering hole of the city's nobles. A large part of Dubrovnik's merchant fleet was based here, and the ruined palaces of shipowners still occupy crumbling corners of the island's only village. Tourism here dates back to the 1920s, and the island's hotels were used by the Italians to intern Jews from Dubrovnik and Bosnia in 1942. They were shipped off to the notorious concentration camp on Rab (see p.238) the following year, though many managed to escape to join the Partisans after the collapse of Italy in 1943.

Located on the northern side of the island, the village of **LOPUD** is strung around a wide, curving bay which boasts a long, crowded and reasonably sandy **beach**. Its most prominent monument is the fortified **monastery** which overlooks the village from a promontory just east of the quay where ferries dock. Built by the Franciscans (and funded by Lopud merchants) in 1483, it's now mostly derelict, although there's long been talk of inviting a foreign investor to take the place over and put it to some use. For the time being all that can be visited is the erstwhile monastery (and now parish) **Church of Our Lady of the Cave** (Crkva Gospe od Špilice), which boasts a rich collection of altar paintings. Among these is a triptych (to the right as you face the main altar) by Nikola Božidarević or his workshop, depicting the Virgin and Child accompanied by a bevy of saints, the ubiquitous St Blaise among them. The main altar is separated from the main body of the church by a delicately carved stone screen, on which small mammals munch away happily on berries, and are in turn menaced by snarling dragons.

West along the seafront from the quay, steps lead up to the **Đorđić-Mayner Park** (Perivoj Đorđić-Mayner), grouped around enormous pines, with the inevitable range of palms basking beneath. A few steps beyond lies the ruined palace of **Miho Pracat**, the sixteenth-century merchant and shipowner whose bust stands in the Rector's Palace in Dubrovnik (see p.380). Lopud folk tales sought to explain how Pracat came by his fabulous wealth. Somewhat improbably, he is said to have robbed Dubrovnik cathedral's treasury to pay for his business ventures, one of which involved exporting the city's cats to North Africa, where he had chanced upon a plague of rodents. Paths at the back of the village lead up onto the high ground at the centre of the island, one of which (look for signs reading "Kaštio" or "Tvrđava") climbs towards the Ragusan **fortress**, a forty-minute walk away, which looms above Lopud village to the southeast. It's a complete ruin nowadays, but the view from its crumbling ramparts is magnificent, with stark grey coastal mountains to the east, and the green, cone-shaped hills of Šipan and Pelješac to the north. The best of Lopud's beaches is **Šunj Bay** (Uvala Šunj), a lovely shallow cove backed by a grove of pines; it's 2km south of Lopud village and easily reached via an asphalt path.

Rooms (❶) are available from the **tourist office** on the seafront (June–Sept daily 8am–1pm & 6–9pm; ☎020/759-086). A few hundred metres west of the jetty is the *Lafodia* **hotel** (☎020/759-022, ⓕ759-026; ❺; June–Sept), a modern affair whose en-suite rooms have small balconies, many with excellent views towards the harbour. An altogether more intimate place is the *Villa Vilina* (☎020/759-333, ⓔvilla-vilina@inet.hr; ❽; April–Oct), situated in an old stone house up by the Franciscan monastery, offering a handful of tastefully furnished, plush-carpeted rooms with TV.

Šipan

The largest and least developed of the populated Elaphites, the island of **Šipan** is a delightful combination of craggy hills strung out around a long, fertile plain thick with olive trees and vines and dotted with the occasional hamlet. There are no special sights and there's certainly no nightlife, but if you're after some peace and quiet and gentle hikes, this is one of the best places to be on the coast.

Ferries terminate at the island's main settlement, **ŠIPANSKA LUKA**, a pretty little place buried at the end of a deep inlet at the island's northern end. The settlement contains the odd relic of former glories: best are the remains of the Magistrate's Palace, ten minutes along the road to Suđurađ, and the neglected villa on the harbourfront, which boasts a balcony supported by carved lions, and seems to be crying out for restoration. Šipanska Luka's main **beach** is about 500m away from the harbourfront, a tiny strip of sand pressed against a thread of rock that separates the western side of the bay from the sea. More isolated spots for bathing can be found by following the path which extends beyond the ferry jetty on the opposite side of the bay, threading its way between rocky shoreline and shady olive groves before petering out in dense undergrowth after a couple of kilometres.

Incoming ferries are often met by locals offering private **rooms** (❶) – if not, just ask around. Otherwise, the harbourfront **hotel**, the *Šipan* (☎020/758-000, ⓕ758-004, ⓔhotel-sipan@mail.inet.hr; ❹; May to mid-Oct), offers standard en-suite rooms – the attic rooms on the top floor are the cosiest – and also rents out **bikes**. **Eating** and **drinking** possibilities are limited to the hotel restaurant and the couple of bars nearby.

Heading south out of Šipanska Luka, the seven-kilometre walk to **SUĐU-RAĐ** (also traversed by occasional minibus) takes you past some lovely inland scenery. Suđurađ itself – little more than a clump of houses grouped around a bay – is overlooked by an imposing pair of stone **towers**, all that's left of a summer palace of sixteenth-century Dubrovnik shipowner Vice Stjepović Skočibuha. Running round the side of the palace, the village's main alleyway ascends towards a blockhouse-shaped fortified church; bearing right here will take you into one of the most attractive corners of the island, with dense maquis broken up by agaves, olive groves and pines. The similarly fortified **St Mary's Church** (Crkva svete Marije), 2km northeast of Suđurađ in the hamlet of Pakljena, is hardly ever open – but the sight of its crenellated sixteenth-century tower peeking above the greenery provides a convenient excuse to wander this far.

Mljet

The westernmost of the islands accessible by local ferry from Dubrovnik is **MLJET**, a thin strip of land some 32km long and never more than 3km wide, running roughly parallel to the Pelješac peninsula. The most visited part of the island is the green and unspoilt west, where untouched Mediterranean forest and two saltwater lakes provide the focus of the **Mljet National Park**, an area of arcadian beauty within which lie the villages of **Polače** and **Pomena**. Despite a nascent package-holiday industry in the village of Pomena, the region remains invitingly quiet and there are few shopping or nightlife opportunities.

According to legend, Odysseus holed up here for some time with the nymph Calypso, and Mljet also has fair claim to being the island of Melita, where St Paul ran aground on his way to Italy and was bitten by a viper before he set sail again (Mljet's snake problem was once so bad that a colony of mongooses had to be imported from India to get rid of them, and the fat-tailed creatures are still very much in evidence in the National Park). The Romans used the island as a place of exile, and it was briefly owned by the kings of Bosnia, who sold it to the Dubrovnik in 1333. The republic sent an emissary on May 1 every year to rule the island for a year, and many of Dubrovnik's admirals built summer houses here.

Coming **from Dubrovnik**, there are two ways of getting to the island. The easiest option is the passenger-only *Nona Maria* catamaran (May–Sept; information and tickets from Atlantagent, Obala Stjepana Radića 26; ☏020/419-044) which sails daily to Polače in the morning, and leaves you with several hours to look round the park before returning to Dubrovnik in the evening. The year-round Jadrolinija car ferry sails to Sobra in the eastern part of the island (it's a good 20km short of the park; Sobra–Polače–Pomena buses await incoming ferries), and doesn't return to Dubrovnik until early the following morning, making an overnight stay on the island unavoidable. If you come here by car, be sure to fill your tank before you cross the water – there's nowhere to get petrol on the island. Approaching **from Korčula** or **Orebić**, you can reach Mljet on the regular hydrofoil excursions (arriving at either Polače or Pomena) run by local travel agents – expect to pay 220–250Kn per person, including the park entrance fee.

Sobra to Pomena

Jadrolinija ferries from Dubrovnik dock 3km south of **SOBRA**, an insignificant settlement roughly halfway along the island. After winding its way over to the west the road descends to **POLAČE**, little more than a row of houses stretched along a small harbour – whose waters are clean enough to swim in. The harbour is bordered to the north by the impressively lofty walls of a fourth-century AD **Roman palace**, the inner courtyard of which is now home to a couple of lemon trees. A small white house on the harbour contains a **tourist office** (mid-June to mid-Sept Mon–Sat 8am–noon & 4–7pm; mid-Sept to mid-June Mon–Fri 8am–1pm; ☏020/745-125) which can point you in the direction of locals offering **rooms** (**❶**). For **food and drink**, there are a couple of café-restaurants along the front, and a small provisions store open mornings and evenings.

Sheltering in a bay at the western tip of Mljet, **POMENA** is a seaside hamlet similar to Polače – save for the presence of a large modern hotel and a harbour which is becoming increasingly popular with touring yachtspeople. The

Odisej **hotel** (☎020/744-022, ⓦwww.hotelodisej.hr; ❻) is a prim collection of whitewashed modern blocks and has **exchange** facilities. Room quality varies from one part of the complex to the other – insist on a room with air conditioning and TV. Next door, the family-run, seven-room *Pansion Pomena* (☎020/744-075; ❷) presents a more down-to-earth alternative, with plain rooms and shared facilities. For **food**, the restaurant of the *Odisej* is respectable, and the *Pansion Pomena* offers excellent-value set lunches and a more elaborate range of pricey seafood in the evening. There are regular taxi boats (check the lobby of the *Odisej* for details) to the naturist islet of **Pomeštak**, just offshore.

The Mljet National Park

There's no official entrance point to the **Mljet National Park** (ⓦwww.np -mljet.hr) as such, and by the time you arrive in Polače or Pomena you're already well inside it. However, you're expected to buy a ticket (50Kn) from one of the kiosks in Pomena, Polače or just outside Goveđari once you've settled in, and certainly before you start exploring. The kiosks also have park information and **maps** (50Kn).

The park's main attractions are its two forest-shrouded "lakes" (actually inlets connected to the sea by narrow channels), **Malo jezero** ("Small Lake") and **Veliko jezero** ("Big Lake"), which together form a stretch of water some 4km long. Both are encircled by foot- and cycle paths, and the clear, blue-green waters are perfect for bathing. If you're staying in Polače, it's possible to walk over to the lakes by road or by well-signed forest path (via the 253-metre Montokuc hill) in about 45 minutes. From Pomena, Malo jezero is ten minutes' walk south, by way of a stone-paved footpath that heads over a wooded ridge just up from the port. Once you hit the shore of Malo jezero, it's another ten-minute walk to **Mali most** ("Little Bridge"), spanning the channel feeding into Veliko jezero, edged by magnificently soothing, tree-shaded pathways.

Mali most is the departure point for an hourly boat service (vouchers for the trip are included with the entrance ticket) down Veliko jezero to **St Mary's Island** (Otok svete Marije), where the Benedictines established a monastery in the twelfth century. Overlooked by a sturdy defensive tower, the monastery church features unusually chunky altarpieces carved from local stone and exuberantly coloured. The central dome is enclosed in a squat quadrangular tower, whose dog-tooth-patterned exterior can be admired from the neighbouring courtyard. There's a **café-restaurant** in the monastery grounds.

Bikes are a handy way to get around the lakes: they can be rented from Mali most, the National Park kiosk in Polače, or in front of the *Odisej* hotel in Pomena (30Kn per hour, 90Kn per day). **Kayaks** (same price) can also be rented at Mali most.

Travel details

Buses

Dubrovnik to: Cavtat (hourly; 40min); Korčula (1 daily; 4hr); Orebić (2 daily; 3hr); Ploče (hourly; 2hr); Pula (1 daily; 16hr); Rijeka (3 daily; 13hr); Šibenik (9 daily; 6hr 30min); Split (13 daily; 5hr); Ston (3 daily; 1hr 30min); Trsteno (hourly; 40min); Vela Luka (1 daily; 5hr); Zagreb (4 daily; 11hr).

Šipanska Luka to: Suđurađ (Mon–Fri 5 daily, Sat 2 daily, 15min).
Sobra to: Pomena (2 daily; 1hr 10min).

Ferries

Dubrovnik to: Koločep (1–4 daily; 30min); Lopud (1–4 daily; 50min); Polače (1 daily; 1hr 40min);

Rijeka (summer 1 daily, winter 4 weekly; 22hr);
Sobra (1–2 daily; 2hr 15min); Šipanska Luka
(1–4 daily; 1hr 45min); Suđurađ (1–4 daily;
1hr).

Domestic flights

Dubrovnik to: Zagreb (2–3 daily; 1hr).

International buses

Dubrovnik to: Mostar (2 daily; 5hr); Sarajevo (2
daily; 7hr); Trieste (1 daily; 20hr).

International ferries

Dubrovnik to: Ancona (weekly; 15hr); Bari (5
weekly; 8hr); Corfu (2 weekly; 25hr).

Contexts

Contexts

A brief history of Croatia..403–428

Croatian folk music 429–434

Books 435–438

A brief history of Croatia

History is a serious business in a country which has spent so much of its past under the sway of foreign powers. It's also exceedingly complicated, as the history of Croatia is interlinked, for lengthy periods, with the histories of Hungary, Austria and Venice, not to mention that of the former Yugoslavia.

Croatia before the Croatians

Our knowledge of the first humans to inhabit Croatia is patchy, although a form of Neanderthal – named **Krapina Man** after the town in which remains have been found (see p.106) – is known to have roamed the hills north of Zagreb some thirty millennia ago. By about the seventh millennium BC, Neolithic farmers had spread out along the Adriatic coast, and were increasingly using the islands as stepping stones to cross the Adriatic. Advanced Neolithic cultures certainly existed on Hvar, where 5000-year-old painted pottery offers evidence of the so-called Hvar Culture, and beside the River Danube in eastern Slavonia, where similarly rich ceramics have been unearthed at Vučedol near Vukovar.

By the first millennium BC the indigenous peoples of the region now covered by Croatia, Bosnia, Albania and Serbia had begun to coalesce into a group of tribes subsequently known as the **Illyrians**. Although they were united by common styles of fortress-building and burial-mound construction, it's not clear whether the Illyrians ever existed as a culturally homogenous group, and they were never politically united. They did, however, produce some powerful tribal states: the Histri in Istria and the Liburnians in the Kvarner and northern Dalmatia were minor maritime powers, building towns whose names – in modified, Slavonic form – still survive, like Aenona (Nin) and Jadera (Zadar).

Greeks, Romans and Byzantines

Greek city-states, led by Syracuse in Sicily, began dispatching trade missions and settlers to the Adriatic coast from the fourth century BC onwards, founding colonies such as Issa (on present-day Vis) and Paros (on Hvar). There were various attempts by the Illyrians to drive the new colonists out, the most serious coming from King Agron and his queen and successor Teuta, whose territory stretched from present-day Zadar in the north to what is now Albania in the south.

In 229 BC the Greeks asked for Roman help against Teuta, beginning a period of **Roman expansion** that continued until 9 AD, when the eastern Adriatic and its hinterland were annexed by the future emperor Tiberius. The seaboard was reorganized into the Roman province of Dalmatia, while northern and eastern Croatia were divided between the provinces of Noricum (which covered much of present-day Austria) and Pannonia (which stretched into modern Hungary). The older Greek settlements continued to flourish, but were outshone as political and cultural centres by new Roman cities, often founded on or near sites that had previously served as power bases for the Illyrian tribes. The main Roman centres were Salona (Solin, near Split) and

Jadera (Zadar), although the vast amphitheatre at Pula attests to the prosperity of Istria during this period. The Illyrians were either Romanized or absorbed by later immigrants like the Slavs.

Roman power in the Adriatic ended temporarily in 493, when the region fell to King Teodoric of the Ostrogoths, although Justinian, emperor of the eastern half of the Roman Empire, whose capital was at **Byzantium**, reconquered the area in 544. Inland, things were more chaotic: the **Avars**, a warlike central Asian people, briefly forged a central European empire at the beginning of the seventh century, and even reached the coast, sacking Salona and Epidaurum in 614. Refugees from these cities went on to found Split and Dubrovnik.

The arrival of the Croats

Precisely when the **Croats** – a Slav tribe who came to southeastern Europe from an area north of the Carpathians – arrived in the territories they now inhabit is a bit of a mystery, although the Byzantine emperor Constantine Porphyrogenitus (writing three hundred years after the event) stated that they were invited by one of his predecessors, Heraclius, in the early seventh century in order to serve as a counterweight to the Avars.

One problem in tracking the movement of the Croats before their arrival in southeast Europe is that the name "Croat" (Hrvat) is thought to be of Persian rather than Slav origin, suggesting that the Croats were subject to Persian-speaking tribes before moving towards southeastern Europe, or even that the Croats were themselves of Iranian origin and picked up the Slav tongue from neighbours as they migrated. The latter theory has always been popular among Croatian nationalists keen to emphasize the uniqueness of their people, athough it's disputed by more mainstream scholars.

The Croats probably migrated to southeastern Europe at the same time as the **Serbs**, who settled in the middle of the Balkan peninsula. The fact that the groups share a common language suggests that they originated in the same area, and Serbs and Croats – along with other tribes speaking similar Slav dialects such as the Slovenes, Bulgarians and Macedonians – were subsequently to be known collectively as the **South Slavs**.

The medieval Croatian state

The Croats who settled along the Dalmatian seaboard established a tribal state ruled by a **knez** (prince or duke), who assumed leadership of other Slav tribes already settled in the region, as well as of sundry Avars and surviving remnants of the Illyrian and Roman populations. Inland areas to the north, such as present-day Slavonia, fell under independent chieftains loosely allied to the Croats on the Adriatic. The existence of two Croatian heartlands – a southern one oriented towards the Mediterranean and a northern one looking towards central Europe – has had a profound effect on Croatian culture ever since.

Both areas maintained a tenuous independence until squeezed by powerful neighbouring empires: the Byzantines, who still held several Adriatic towns and islands, and the Carolingian Empire of the Franks, which was expanding into central Europe by the late 700s. Croat leaders boosted their legitimacy in the eyes of their more advanced western neighbours by accepting **Christianity**, and although the northern Croatian state became subject to the Franks in the 790s, the southern state played one predator off against another and prospered. Ruling from their citadel at Klis (see p.313), princes such as Mislav (ruled 835–845), Trpimir (845–864) and Domagoj (864–876) paid homage to either Byzantines or Franks as necessary, while preserving *de facto* independence and simultaneously beating off two newcomers to the Adriatic: the Venetians and the Arabs.

With the Croatian state growing stronger militarily, Branimir (879–892) threw off Byzantine vassalage once and for all, and was recognized by Pope John VIII as an independent ruler, definitively tying Croatia to the Roman rather than the Byzantine Church. His successor-but-one, **Tomislav** (910–928), pushed things further, defeating the Hungarians to gain control of northern Croatia and battling the Bulgarians to win northwestern Bosnia. Eager to secure an alliance with Tomislav, the Byzantines ceded sovereignty over Split, Trogir, Osor, Rab and Krk. Declaring himself king in 925 (previous Croatian leaders had kept to the title "knez"), Tomislav reorganized the Croatian Church, placing all his lands under the control of a Croatian archbishop at Split, thereby lessening papal influence without actually questioning his ultimate loyalty to the pope.

For the seventy years following Tomislav's death Croatia was financially, militarily and dynastically stable, until a succession crisis in the early eleventh century allowed both Venice and Byzantium to regain footholds on the Adriatic coast, while northern Croatia was lost to the Hungarians. **Petar Krešimir IV** (1058–75) presided over a revival of fortunes, and reunion with northern Croatia was achieved by weaning the ruler of Slavonia, **Dimitr Zvonimir**, away from Hungary and appointing him co-ruler (though Zvonimir's marriage to Princess Jelena of Hungary would later complicate the dynastic picture). Petar Krešimir died childless, and power passed to Zvonimir (1075–89), though he too died without issue, leaving the nobles to chose Stjepan II (1089–91), who also failed to produce an heir.

The kingdom began to disintegrate, leaving Zvonimir's brother-in-law, King Ladislas of Hungary, free to secure control of the north, while a group of nobles in the south regrouped under King Petar (1093–97). Independent Croatia's last monarch was defeated by a Hungarian army under Ladislas's successor Koloman at **Gvozd** (subsequently named Petrova gora or Peter's Mountain), the highland region south of Zagreb.

Hungarian control of Croatia was confirmed by the **Pacta Conventa** of 1102, according to the terms of which Croatia and Hungary remained separate states united by the same royal family. Croatia retained its own institutions – a **Ban** (governor) appointed by the king, and the **Sabor** (parliament) representing the nobility – but, despite these provisions, the Hungarian crown steadily reduced the power of the Croatian aristocracy in the years that followed, speeding Croatia's demise as a united and distinct state.

Croatia under the Hungarians

Life in what became known as the **Hungaro-Croatian kingdom** was characterized by a strengthening of the feudal order, with the landed nobility growing stronger at the expense of a rural population overloaded with feudal obligations. Town life, especially in northern Croatia, underwent rapid development as

Varaždin, Vukovar, Samobor.and Zagreb were earmarked as centres of trade.

The Croatian lands were overrun by the **Tatars** in 1242, but King Bela IV managed to keep royal authority alive by moving from one coastal stronghold to the next (innumerable Adriatic towns were subsequently given special privileges for assisting Bela in his flight). The material damage was enormous, however, and much medieval Croatian architecture was lost. The Hungarian monarchy was strengthened under **Charles Robert of Anjou** (1301–42), who further weakened the remaining independence of the south Croatian nobles. Hungarian control of the Adriatic seaboard – slowly eroded by Venetian penetration during the previous century – was reasserted by Charles Robert and his son **Louis of Anjou** (1342–82), who threw the Venetians out of Dalmatia in 1358. Louis died without a male heir, and his inheritance was disputed by Sigismund of Luxembourg (Louis's son-in-law) and Charles III of Naples. The nobles of southern Croatia appointed Charles's son, **Ladislas of Naples**, king of Croatia in 1403, but his armies were no match for those of Sigismund. In 1409, Ladislas fled, selling his rights over Dalmatia to the Venetians for the sum of 100,000 ducats.

Venice was now in command of almost all of Istria and Dalmatia apart from a few Habsburg territories and **Dubrovnik**, an independent city-state owing nominal allegiance to the Hungarian crown. The Venetians were to stay for over 350 years, flooding the Adriatic seaboard with Italianate art and architecture, but taking away the traditional autonomy of the towns at the same time.

Cut off from the Adriatic, the Croatian lands in the Dalmatian hinterland and the north were also being squeezed from another direction. Croatia's immediate neighbour to the southeast was **Bosnia**, a mountainous inland region which had long been a buffer zone between Croatia, the Byzantine Empire and, more recently, Serbia, which had emerged as a unified and independent state at the end of the twelfth century. The inhabitants of Bosnia were the ethnic kin of the Serbs and Croats, and both the Croatian and Serbian churches had made inroads into the region. Large parts of Bosnia – especially the north and west – had long been in the Hungaro-Croatian sphere of influence, and from 1138 Bosnia had been a vassal of Hungary ruled by its own Ban. Powerful and resourceful rulers like Kulin (1180–1204), Stjepan II Kotromanić (1322–53) and Tvrtko I (1353–91) were nevertheless able to expand their territory at the expense of the south Croatian aristocracy, though by the fifteenth century the northward expansion of the **Ottoman Turks** had begun to threaten Bosnia, something which would have grave consequences for the Croats.

The Ottoman threat

From their heartland in Anatolia, the Ottoman Turks had gained a foothold in southeastern Europe in the early 1300s and soon expanded their territory, fatally weakening Byzantium, swallowing Bulgaria and reducing Serbia to vassal status within a century. Staving off the Ottoman advance was a major preoccupation of Sigismund and his successors, although the mid-fifteenth-century victories of Transylvanian warlord **János Hunyadi** initially made it look as if central Europe might be saved from the Turks. However, the conquest of Bosnia by the Ottomans in the 1460s and 1470s left Croatia in an extremely vulnerable position.

In 1493, a large Hungarian-Croatian force assembled at **Krbavsko polje** (in the Lika, just south of Plitvice) was decisively beaten by the Turks, leaving the

Adriatic open to Ottoman raids. In 1517, Pope Leo X called Croatia *antemurale christianitatis* ("the ramparts of Christendom") in recognition of its frontline status. To the east, the defeat of Hungary at the **Battle of Mohács** in 1526 left the Turks in command of much of Pannonia, with Slavonia and north-western Croatia at their mercy.

The Hungarian King Louis II had died childless at Mohács, leaving the throne to his designated successor, the Austrian **Ferdinand I of Habsburg**. The Hungarian state was thus absorbed into the growing Habsburg Empire, taking Croatia with it. Despite the resources of his vast central European empire, however, Ferdinand could do little to stem the Ottoman advance. Klis, the last Croatian fortress in middle Dalmatia, fell in 1537, and by the 1540s the Turks had overrun the whole of Slavonia as far as Sisak, only 50km south of Zagreb. By the end of the century Croatia had been reduced by the Turks and Venetians to a belt of territory running from the Kvarner Gulf in the south-west to the Međimurje in the northeast, with Zagreb at its centre. The Venetians continued to hold Istria and the Dalmatian coastal strip, and the city-state of Dubrovnik further south retained its independence by paying tribute to the Ottoman Empire. The rest of Croatia was occupied by the Ottomans.

The expansion of Turkish power had also set in train a sequence of population movements, with refugees fleeing to areas that were still under the control of Christian powers. Areas depopulated by war and migration were often filled by itinerant stockbreeders, or **Vlachs**, many of whom were descended from the romanized inhabitants of ancient Illyria and still spoke a dialect of Latin akin to modern Romanian. A mixture of Catholic and Orthodox Christians, the Vlachs fell under the influence of the Croatian and Serbian churches, and were soon slavicized, coming to identify themselves as Croats or Serbs as time went on.

Vlach tribes had already served both Ottoman and Christian rulers as border guards, experience which was put to good use by the Habsburgs. The Vlachs were settled in a belt running along Croatia's borders with Ottoman territory and given lands in return for military service. This belt became known as the **Military Frontier** (Vojna krajina), a defensive cordon ruled directly from either Graz or Vienna. It was to remain in existence until the mid-nineteenth century, by which time the Ottoman threat had long receded.

The seventeenth and eighteenth centuries

Habsburg forces – with many Croats in their ranks – scored an important victory over the Turks at the **Battle of Sisak** in 1593, ending the myth of Ottoman invincibility and stabilizing the Habsburg–Ottoman frontier. A further Ottoman attack on Vienna in 1683 was thrown back by a combined force of Austrians, Germans and Poles. In the decades that followed, Habsburg armies led by **Prince Eugene of Savoy** gradually drove the Ottomans out of central Europe. The Venetians, who had often avoided all-out war with the Turks owing to the precariousness of their position in Dalmatia, exploited Austrian gains by winning back parts of the Dalmatian hinterland. By the time of the **Peace of Passarowitz** in 1718, the Habsburgs had won back the whole of Slavonia, while the Venetians gained control of a belt of highland territory running from Knin to Imotski. Significantly, the Turks retained Bosnia and Hercegovina (the latter a belt of territory along southwest Bosnia), and the frontiers agreed at Passarowitz are very close to those still dividing Bosnia-Hercegovina from Croatia today.

Despite the removal of immediate Turkish danger, the eighteenth century was largely one of stagnation. Because the Habsburg lands were made up of a multitude of states – its rulers were simultaneously Duke of Austria, Holy Roman Emperor and King of Hungary – political authority within the empire was often confused. In Croatia, the Military Frontier (considerably enlarged after the capture of Slavonia) was still under the direct control of Vienna, while the nobles in the rest of Croatia enjoyed a semblance of autonomy through the Croatian Sabor, which met in Zagreb and (briefly) in Varaždin. However Croatia still nominally belonged to the Hungarian Crown, making the Hungarian parliament in Buda the real focus of political power and intrigue. The Croatian aristocracy had been progressively Hungarianized from the late seventeenth century on (when its last great magnates, **Petar Zrinski** and **Fran Krsto Frankopan**, were executed for treason; see box on p.113), and took little interest in the Croatian language or culture.

Agriculturally rich areas of northwestern Croatia and Slavonia were reasonably prosperous in the eighteenth century, but little was done to develop town life, trade or industry. Most official deliberations took part in either German or Latin (the official language of Hungary) rather than Croat, and few of society's leading figures took an interest in promoting indigenous culture. Venetian-controlled Dalmatia was increasingly impoverished due to a fall-off in trade, and Dubrovnik had been in slow decline since suffering a catastrophic earthquake in 1667.

The nineteenth century

In 1797 the Venetian Republic was dissolved by **Napoleon**. Its possessions in Istria and Dalmatia were initially awarded to the Habsburgs in compensation for territories they had lost to the French in northern Italy, but after another bout of fighting between 1806 and 1808, Napoleon gained control of the whole of the eastern Adriatic seaboard. Stretching from Villach in Austria to the Bay of Kotor (now part of Montenegro) in southern Dalmatia, this new French protectorate was named the **Illyrian Provinces** and placed under a French governor, Marshal Marmont. He set about building roads, developing the education system and promoting Slav-language publishing, although the provinces were soon abandoned to the Austrians in 1813 following Napoleon's defeat at the hands of the Russians.

Habsburg dominance of Dalmatia was confirmed by the **Treaty of Vienna** in 1815, and the economic fortunes of the Adriatic began to revive under Austrian stewardship. The main language of the Adriatic sea trade, however, was Italian, and economic development went hand-in-hand with the italianization of maritime Croatia, disappointing many who had seen the return of Austrian power as an opportunity to renew links between the Croats of Dalmatia and the Croats of the north.

The Croatian national revival

One of Napoleon's aims in the creation of the Illyrian Provinces had been to encourage the growth of South Slav consciousness, in the hope that Croats, Slovenes and Serbs could be weaned away from other great powers that might pose as their protectors, notably Austria and Russia. For the Croatian elite, the example of Serbia itself was increasingly important. Subject to the Ottoman Empire since the fifteenth century, the Serbs had risen up against the Turks in 1804 and 1815, and the emergence of an **autonomous Serbian principality** in 1830 was greeted by many Croat intellectuals as an example of what South Slavs could achieve. Apart from an undercurrent of distrust between the Catholic and Orthodox churches, the Serbs had never been regarded as historic enemies, and the development of common links between Serbs and Croats became a popular intellectual theme.

The closeness of the Croat and Serb languages sparked a renewed interest in the orally transmitted folk poems – often speaking of heroic resistance to the Turks or some other common foe – that characterized both Serbian and Croatian popular culture, especially in mountainous areas like the Dalmatian hinterland, where the two communities lived side by side. The interest in folk poems led to a new awareness of the languages themselves: a literary form of written Serbian was established by Vuk Stefanović Karadžić, whose example was followed by the Croatian writer **Ljudevit Gaj** (1809–72). Gaj set about developing a form of literary Croatian close enough to Serbian for the two to be mutually intelligible, basing it on the Štokavski dialect used by Croats in Slavonia, Hercegovina and Dubrovnik. *Danica*, the cultural supplement of his own newspaper, *Novine Hrvatske*, changed over to the new, Štokavski-based written language in 1835.

The movement which grew out of Gaj's reforming zeal was known as **Illyrianism** (*Ilirizam*) – a name which harked back to the ancient Roman province of Illyria and therefore avoided too close an identification with any single ethnic group. Illyrianism contributed enormously to the flowering of Croatian language and culture in the mid-nineteenth century known as the **Croatian National Revival**. Although the movement was originally intended to provide a bridge between Croats and Serbs, it remained a purely Croatian affair: the fact that the Croats used the Roman alphabet and the Serbs wrote in Cyrillic characters made it unlikely that the two languages and cultures would ever be harmonized. The infant Serbian state was in any case much more interested in expansion than in co-operation with its Slav neighbours.

Vienna initially tolerated Illyrianism as a politically useful counterweight against the boisterous nationalism of the Hungarians, but eventually took fright and came down heavily, banning any mention of the word "Illyria" in 1843. The movement lived on, however, with the formation of the Narodna stranka – the "National Party", whose members were known as the **Narodnjaci** – which from now on was to be the country's main pro-Croat, anti-Hungarian force.

1848 and after

With the outbreak of **revolution in Paris** in February 1848, a wave of reforming fervour spread through Europe. In Hungary, the fiery Lajos Kossuth agitated for the introduction of a constitutional monarchy, while mobs on the streets of Vienna demanded democratic reforms. The fall of the Austrian chancellor Metternich, who had been right-hand man to a succession of emperors for nearly forty years, produced a power vacuum throughout the Habsburg Empire which new organizations and personalities rushed to fill. Croatian opinion saw the 1848 revolution as a means of winning autonomy from the Hungarians and forging a new Croatian or South Slav unit within the Austrian Empire. This conflict of national interests pitched Croatian radicals against the Hungarian radicals under Kossuth who, despite their liberal credentials, continued to regard Croatia as a junior partner in a reinvigorated Hungary.

Fast losing control of a complex situation, the Habsburg court had no choice but to tolerate the emergence of Croatian national sentiment, in the hope that it would serve to counterbalance the Hungarians. Vienna succumbed to popular pressure and elevated Colonel **Josip Jelačić**, a popular garrison commander in the Military Frontier and a well-known supporter of the Narodnjaci, to the position of Ban of Croatia. Jelačić immediately called elections to the Croatian Sabor in order to provide himself with a popular mandate. The Narodnjaci won a sweeping victory and, armed with the Sabor's support, Jelačić first broke off relations with the Hungarians, then declared war on them. Ultimately, however, he became a pawn in a wider game: after relying on his support to crush the revolutionaries in Hungary and Austria, reactionaries at the Viennese court gradually forgot about Croatian demands for autonomy and reintroduced centralized rule.

The late nineteenth century

Revolution was followed by the era of **Bach's Absolutism**, named after the Austrian interior minister, Alexander Bach. Under Bach's stewardship, the Habsburg Empire, headed by arch-conservative **Franz Josef I** (1848–1916), attempted to reorganize itself as a centralized state in which all regionalist aspirations were suppressed in favour of loyalty to the Habsburg dynasty. Bach was dispensed with in 1860, but continuing tension between Vienna and Budapest forced another reorganization of the empire in 1867. According to the terms of the **Ausgleich** ("Compromise"), the Habsburg state became the **Dual Monarchy of Austria-Hungary**. Franz Josef was to be emperor of Austria and king of Hungary simultaneously, and Vienna was to retain overall control of defence and foreign policy, but in all other respects the Austrian and Hungarian halves of the empire were to run their own affairs. This had serious consequences for the Croats: while Dalmatia was to remain in the Austrian half, the bulk of Croatia found itself in a semi-independent Hungary, thereby preventing the emergence of a unified Croatian national movement with clear goals.

Political life in **Dalmatia** after the Ausgleich was characterized by a struggle between the local branch of the Narodnjaci, who promoted Croat rights and called for the unification of Dalmatia and the rest of Croatia, and the pro-Italian Autonomaši, who argued that Dalmatia was not wholly Croat and had a distinct Latin–Slav identity of its own. The Serbs of the Dalmatian hinterland sided with the Autonomaši after the 1870s to prevent the Narodnjaci from gaining the upper hand, but by the end of the century fear of Italian designs on Dalmatia was beginning to unite Serbs and Croats of all political persuasions.

In the territories ruled by the Hungarians, there were two strands to Croatian nationalism in the second half of the nineteenth century: one emphasized the cultural similarities between all South Slavs, while the other had a more exclusively Croat perspective. The principal representative of the former strand was **Juraj Strossmayer** (1815–1905), Bishop of Đakovo and leader of the Narodnjaci, who thought that Croats and Serbs within the Habsburg Empire could unite to form a South Slav state within a federal Austria-Hungary. Strossmayer also seriously considered the possibility of Austria-Hungary's collapse, concluding that an independent Yugoslav (which literally means "South Slav" in Croatian and Serbian) state, including all Croats and Serbs and supported by Russia, would be the best solution. Strossmayer used the income from his episcopal estates to fund cultural projects, founding the Yugoslav Academy of Science and Arts in Zagreb in 1867. Opposition to Strossmayer's nascent Yugoslavism was supplied by **Ante Starčević** (1823–96), who formed the

Croatian Party of Rights in 1861. Starčević favoured the formation of an independent Croatian state under Habsburg auspices and was suspicious of any deal with the Serbs, believing that they would never treat the Croats as equals.

Party politics in Croatia after 1867 were largely manipulated by the Ban, who was responsible to the Hungarian government in Budapest. The worst offender in this regard was Ban **Károly Khuen-Héderváry** (1883–1903), who promoted Hungarian language and culture at the expense of Croatian, and indulged in electoral gerrymandering to secure a docile Sabor. Héderváry was especially adept at playing off Croats against Serbs. Austria-Hungary had occupied the Ottoman province of Bosnia-Hercegovina in 1878, thereby ending the *raison d'être* of the Military Frontier, which was abolished in 1881 and absorbed into Croatia, thereby increasing the number of Orthodox Serbs in the country. The majority of these Serbs had been living peacefully with Catholic Croats for centuries, but the existence of a youthful and expanding Serbian state to the southeast gave the Serbs of Croatia a new focus of loyalty, and they increasingly turned to political parties of their own. The Héderváry administration supported the publication of a Serb newspaper, *Srbobran*, which in 1901 ran an article which claimed that neither the Croat nation nor language really existed, and that the Serb national agenda was the only one with any future. Although by no means a reflection of what most Serbs felt, it led to anti-Serb riots in Zagreb.

A wave of anti-Hungarian protests in northern Croatia in 1903 provoked the breakdown of the Héderváry regime, creating new political opportunities. The first sign of the so-called **New Course** in Croatian politics came with 1905's **Rijeka Resolution**, when Croatian deputies joined with the Hungarian opposition in calling for democratic reforms and the unification of Dalmatia with the rest of Croatia. Almost immediately, Serb politicians from northern Croatia and Dalmatia followed with the **Zadar Resolution**, which promised support for the aims of the Rijeka Resolution providing that the equality of Serbs in Croatia could be guaranteed. The two sides came together to form the **Croat–Serb Coalition**, which scored a resounding success in the 1906 elections to the Croatian Sabor. Faced by a hostile Sabor, successive Bans found it difficult to form a workable government. Vienna's attempts to split the Croat–Serb Coalition by accusing 53 Croatian Serbs of working secretly for the creation of a Greater Serbia merely produced the opposite effect, and became the subject of international outrage. Croatia rapidly became ungovernable after Ban Nikola Tomašić's failed attempts to manage the elections of 1911, and the Sabor was suspended later that year by his successor, Slavko Cuvaj.

World War I and the creation of Yugoslavia

After forty years of occupation, Austria-Hungary formally annexed Bosnia-Hercegovina in 1908, assuming responsibility for its mixed population of Catholic Croats, Orthodox Serbs and Muslim Slavs of both Serbian and Croatian stock. The annexation went down badly in Serbia, which viewed Bosnia-Hercegovina as a potential area for Serbian expansion. The ultimate goal of Serbian foreign policy – to forge a state which would include all Serbs wherever they lived, was a serious challenge to Austria-Hungary, which had a large Serbian population within its own borders. Serbian successes in the **Balkan**

Wars of 1912–13, when Ottoman forces were driven out of Macedonia, increased Serbian prestige, especially among those Croats who saw Serbia as the potential nucleus of a future South Slav state.

Tension between Austria-Hungary and Serbia was therefore high when Franz Josef's nephew and heir **Archduke Franz Ferdinand** was assassinated in the Bosnian capital Sarajevo on June 28, 1914, by **Gavrilo Princip**, a young Bosnian Serb who had been supplied with weapons by Serbia's chief of military intelligence. The anti-Serbian mood in Viennese court circles had achieved critical mass, and Austria-Hungary declared war on Serbia on July 28. Germany was pulled in on the Austrian side, making a response from the anti-German alliance of Russia, France and Great Britain inevitable, and **World War I** was under way.

Initially Croats fought loyally on the Habsburg side, but the longer the war went on, the clearer it became that Austria-Hungary might not survive. Faced by the possibility of a future without the Habsburgs, few Croatian politicians considered it practical to work for the establishment of an independent Croatia – such a state would be vulnerable to predatory Hungarian, Italian and Serbian neighbours. Instead they increasingly embraced the idea of **Yugoslavia** – a South Slav state which would include Serbs, Croats and Slovenes and be strong enough to stand up to outside powers. With Italy joining the Entente in the hope of gaining a foothold in Dalmatia, the need to promote the Yugoslav ideal was paramount.

In 1915, veteran Dalmatian politicians Frano Supilo and Ante Trumbić, joined by sculptor Ivan Meštrović and other exiles, formed the **Yugoslav Committee** in Paris in order to lobby foreign governments and make contacts with Serbian leaders. The Serbs were initially unwilling to treat the committee as an equal partner, but negotiations culminated in the signing of the **Corfu Declaration** of July 1917, in which both sides agreed that any future South Slav state would be a constitutional monarchy in which Serbs, Croats and Slovenes would enjoy equal rights, but which would be headed by Serbia's Karađorđević dynasty. In October 1918 the political leaders of Austria-Hungary's Serbs, Croats and Slovenes formed the **National Council** in Zagreb and declared their independence from Budapest and Vienna.

Austria-Hungary collapsed on November 3, and Italian troops landed in Dalmatia ready to stake a claim to the parts they coveted. The territory ruled by the National Council was in chaos: they had no army, bands of deserting soldiers were roaming the countryside, and fear of social revolution was rife. Desperate to restore order and keep the Italians out, the National Council rushed to declare union with Serbia on the basis of the Corfu Declaration, and the Serbian Prince Aleksandar Karađorđević declared the creation of the **Kingdom of Serbs, Croats and Slovenes** on December 1, 1918. The name "Yugoslavia" had been quietly dropped because Belgrade didn't think it sounded Serbian enough. The other areas incorporated into the new state were the Principality of Montenegro (Crna gora), which had strong ties to Serbia, and Macedonia, which had been conquered by Serbia during the Balkan Wars.

The first Yugoslavia

Many Croats entered the new state on the assumption that it would have a federal constitution which would guarantee each of its constituent peoples a degree of autonomy. Unfortunately, the leading Serb politicians of the time had other ideas. Nikola Pašić (Serbia's wartime prime minister) and Svetozar Pribićević (leader of those Serbs who had hitherto lived in Habsburg territory) were both keen to draw Croats and Slovenes into a state controlled by Serbian politicians, arguing that because large numbers of Serbs were scattered throughout Croatia and Bosnia, only a unitary state could protect their interests.

The Croats were against the idea of a unitary state because they feared that they would always be outvoted by the numerically superior Serbs, and they gravitated towards the **Croatian Republican Peasant Party (HRSS)**, a republican movement that backed the interests of farmers against the urban bourgeoisie and which was also suspicious of Serbian centralism. When elections to the new kingdom's constituent assembly took place on November 28, 1920, the HRSS won 50 of the 93 seats allocated to Croatia. HRSS leader **Stjepan Radić** claimed that the party's victory had given him a mandate to declare Croatia an independent republic, and spoke enthusiastically of replacing the Kingdom of Serbs, Croats and Slovenes with a Balkan peasant federation comprising Slovenia, Croatia, Serbia and Bulgaria (where a democratically elected pro-peasant government under Alexander Stamboliiski was already in power). Belgrade kept a lid on the situation by packing Radić off to prison and sending in the troops, but the HRSS's reputation as the main defender of Croat interests was secured.

Croatian deputies were unable to prevent the Constituent Assembly from passing the 1921 **Vidovdan Constitution**, which declared the new kingdom a unitary state and convinced many Croats that their new homeland was merely Greater Serbia under a different name. Radić immediately withdrew the HRSS from parliament and tried to raise support for the Croatian cause abroad, although Great Britain, France and the US were far too committed to the idea of a strong Yugoslavia to aid those hostile to the central government in Belgrade.

By the mid-1920s the complete freeze in relations between Belgrade and the Croatian political elite had persuaded Radić to change tack. He dropped the "R" for "Republican" from the party's name, ended the boycott of parliament and began working for Croatian autonomy rather than outright independence. He briefly served as a government minister before joining his old adversary, the Serbian Svetozar Pribićević, in forming a new opposition bloc, the **Peasant–Democratic Coalition**. The Radić–Pribićević alliance was a serious threat to the Belgrade establishment, and passions were already running high when Stjepan Radić was shot in the parliamentary chamber by the pro-Belgrade Montenegrin deputy Puniša Račić on June 20, 1928. Radić died two months later; his funeral in Zagreb was attended by 100,000 people. Fearful of further inter-ethnic violence, King Aleksandar suspended parliament and launched the **Sixth of January Dictatorship** at the beginning of 1929. The name of the state was changed to **Yugoslavia** later the same year, in the hope that an appeal to South Slav idealism might help paper over the country's cracks.

The 1930s

Radić was succeeded as leader of the HSS by **Vlatko Maček**, who broadened the party's appeal to make it a national movement representing all classes of Croats. Banned from political activity, the HSS sponsored various front organizations such as the Peasant Accord, which supported cultural activities in rural areas, and the Croatian Peasant Defence Force, a paramilitary organization which was tolerated by the government because it occasionally beat up socialists.

One other organization that opposed the unitary nature of the Yugoslav state was the **Communist Party of Yugoslavia** (**KPJ**), which despite being banned in 1920 continued to exert a strong influence over the intelligentsia. Initially the KPJ had envisaged Croatia as part of either a federal Yugoslavia or a wider Balkan confederation. In the mid-1920s it became communist policy to encourage the break-up of Yugoslavia into independent states, but by the mid-1930s the Comintern had ordered a return to the idea of a federal Yugoslavia as a potential bulwark against the rise of Nazism. It was this concept that was inherited by **Josip Broz Tito**, whom Moscow appointed leader of the KPJ in December 1937.

Diametrically opposed to communism was the **Ustaše** – a right-wing Croatian separatist organization inspired by Italian fascism and dedicated to the violent overthrow of the Yugoslav state – which had been founded by **Ante Pavelić** in 1929. Together with the similarly inclined Internal Macedonian Revolutionary Organization (IMRO), the Ustaše orchestrated the assassination of the Yugoslav King Aleksandar in Marseilles in October 1934.

Fearful that the Croat question would tear Yugoslavia apart, Prime Minister Milan Stojadinović tried to reach an accommodation with the HSS, relaxing the ban on its activities. Maček, however, turned to the Serbian opposition instead, joining up with the Serbian Radical and Peasant parties to put together the **Alliance for National Agreement**, which won 37.5 percent of the vote in the government-manipulated elections of 1935, rising to 44.9 percent in 1938. New Yugoslav Prime Minister Dragiša Cvetković was charged with the task of making a deal with the Croats amid a worsening international situation and the fear that Yugoslavia's internal weaknesses could be exploited by predatory neighbours. The result was the Cvetković–Maček Agreement, or **Sporazum**, signed on August 26, 1939, according to which an autonomous Croatian territory, the **Banovina**, was created within the borders of Yugoslavia, including all of present-day Croatia as well as those portions of western Bosnia inhabited by large numbers of Croats. Maček became deputy prime minister in the Yugoslav government, while fellow HSS leader **Ivan Šubašić** became Ban of Croatia. Inside the Banovina the HSS became the party of government, although they were supported by the Serbian Democratic Party (SDS), which represented Serbs in Croatia.

World War II

Yugoslavia initially opted for a policy of neutrality when **World War II** broke out in September 1939, although German pressure eventually forced Cvetković to sign up to the Tripartite Pact (the alliance forged by Germany, Italy and Japan) on March 25, 1941. Pro-British officers in the Yugoslav Army launched a successful coup on March 27 and denounced the pact, but most of the leading figures in the coup were Serbs, and the new regime didn't enjoy the loyalty of Croats. When the Germans declared war on Yugoslavia on April 6, resistance quickly melted away.

German troops entered Zagreb on April 10, 1941, and quickly established a puppet government, with the Ustaše declaring the formation of the **Independent State of Croatia** (**NDH**). Ustaše exiles returned home to usher in a new order on the Nazi model, with Ante Pavelić styling himself the "Poglavnik" (a Croatian rendering of "Führer") in imitation of Hitler. The rest of Yugoslavia was carved up between Germany and her allies, although a rump of Serbia was allowed to survive under German occupation. Bosnia was awarded to the NDH, although large chunks of northern and middle Dalmatia, together with the islands, were given to Italy, something for which many Croats never forgave the Ustaše. Even the NDH's own territory was split into German and Italian spheres of influence, and NDH military commanders were under the supervision of their German and Italian colleagues.

As a result of the inclusion of Bosnia, the NDH now included large numbers of Serbs and Bosnian Muslims. The Muslims were regarded as allies (some Croat historians have always regarded the Bosnian Muslims as ethnic Croats who abandoned the Catholic faith in the sixteenth century), while the Serbs were regarded as a potentially traitorous element which had from be eliminated. It soon became clear that the Ustaše's attitude to Serbs was little different from the Nazi Party's attitude to Jews. The NDH immediately embarked on three main **anti-Serbian policies**: the deportation of Croatian and Bosnian Serbs to Serbia proper, their mass conversion to Catholicism or their mass murder. It's estimated that one in six Croatian Serbs died between 1941 and 1945, many of them killed in concentration camps like Jasenovac (see p.120), where Jews, Gypsies and anti-fascist Croats were also murdered.

The sheer ferocity of the Ustaše campaign against the Serbs led to an immediate increase in guerrilla activity. The most important group early on were the **Četniks**, Serbs loyal to the Yugoslav government in exile, who often carried out vicious revenge attacks upon Croats and Muslims, but they were soon eclipsed by Tito's communist **Partisans**, who played down ethnic differences in order to forge a popular anti-fascist movement that drew support from all races and areas of society. The collapse of Italy in September 1943 allowed the Partisans to capture weaponry and take command of large chunks of territory in Istria and Dalmatia, although they were soon chased out by the Germans. In 1944 the Partisans were recognized by the British, who withdrew all remaining support from the Četniks and persuaded the Yugoslav government in exile in London to sign an agreement recognizing Tito's authority.

The Partisans entered Zagreb on May 8, 1945. Thousands of Croatian **Domobrani** (home guardsmen), the majority of whom were no great supporters of the Ustaše, had been mobilized by Pavelić in the preceding weeks and ordered to retreat to Austria – in the hope that they could surrender to the Allies and preserve themselves as the nucleus of some future anti-communist force. The British unit that received them at the town of Bleiburg shipped them back across the border to the waiting Partisans. As many as fifty thousand of these Croatian prisoners were murdered in the weeks that followed: some were shot immediately and thrown into mass graves; others were marched to internment camps in the deep south of Yugoslavia – a journey subsequently dubbed the *Križni put* or Way of the Cross. Pavelić himself escaped to South America, then Spain, where he died in 1959.

Tito's Yugoslavia

The British had hoped that Tito's agreement with the Yugoslav government in exile would help preserve a degree of democracy in Yugoslavia after the war, but Tito acted swiftly to quash dissent. As the country moved towards democratic elections, most of the country's political parties were encouraged to join the **People's Front**, an organization dominated by the communists; those that declined were effectively prevented from campaigning. Although the ballot was nominally secret, anyone voting against the People's Front had to place their ballot papers in a separate box – sufficiently intimidating to ensure that few people took the risk. Packed with the communists and their supporters, the resulting National Assembly voted unanimously to declare Yugoslavia a republic on November 29, 1945. A new Soviet-inspired constitution was adopted, creating a federation of six national republics – Slovenia, Croatia, Bosnia-Hercegovina, Serbia, Montenegro and Macedonia. The rigid discipline of the Communist Party was to hold the whole structure together.

In Croatia, the communists' elimination of political opponents went hand in hand with an attack on the **Catholic Church**. Some members of the Church hierarchy had been enthusiastic supporters of the NDH, and it wasn't difficult to discredit the whole organization using the charge of collaboration. Archbishop Stepinac (see p.70) was offered a role in the new order if he broke off links with the Vatican – and was rewarded with a sixteen-year prison sentence when he refused.

The birth of Yugoslav socialism

The Yugoslav economy was in a state of ruin in 1945, and the new government used the need for speedy reconstruction as an excuse to rush ahead with wholesale revolutionary change. Large estates were confiscated, businesses were nationalized, and a five-year plan, with the emphasis on heavy industry, was instituted. Yugoslavia's efforts to ape the USSR made it look like the model pupil, but in June 1948 Soviet leader **Josef Stalin** denounced the Yugoslav party for indulging in ideological deviations, expecting the Yugoslavs to ditch Tito and appoint a more pliant leader. With cold-war tensions rising in Europe, it's likely that Stalin wanted to enforce unity among the communist states of Eastern Europe by making an example of Tito, the only Eastern European leader who had risen to power more or less independently of the Red Army. Yugoslavia was expelled from the Cominform, the Soviet-controlled organization of European communist countries, and the Soviets made an unsuccessful appeal to Yugoslav communists to overthrow Tito.

A period of acute tension between the two countries followed, with a very real threat of Soviet invasion. Tito responded to the crisis by protesting his loyalty to the Soviet Union, while at the same time purging members of his circle whom he suspected of being Soviet agents. On the whole, however, Tito's wartime Partisan colleagues stood by their leader, and Yugoslavia's resistance to Soviet pressure won Tito new levels of popularity both at home and abroad. Party members who sided with Stalin were dubbed "Cominformists" and shipped off to endure years of harsh treatment on the infamous Goli otok, or "Bare Island" (see box on p.239).

Stalin's economic blockade, coupled with a string of bad harvests brought about by bungled attempts at collectivization, led Yugoslavia to the brink of economic collapse. Aid from the capitalist West was gratefully received, and a drastic rethink of the country's political objectives followed. The support of industrial workers was cultivated by introducing a system of **workers' self-management**, in which all enterprises would be controlled not by the state but by the people who worked in them – on the surface, a decisive move away from Stalinism. The Communist Party itself was renamed the **Yugoslav League of Communists**, in a (largely cosmetic) attempt to suggest that it would play a less overbearing role in the country's future. The League of Communists in each republic was allowed increasing autonomy, with the personal authority of Tito and his wartime comrades holding the whole thing together. Meanwhile, Tito joined Nehru and Nasser to form the **Non-Aligned Movement** in 1961 and, although the movement itself was largely ineffective, Tito's delicate balancing act between East and West gained Yugoslavia international credibility far in excess of its size or power.

The liberalization of Yugoslav communism had its limits, however. The Montenegrin **Milovan Đilas**, federal vice-president and one of Tito's closest Partisan colleagues, was forced out of office in 1954 for suggesting that the introduction of self-management should be followed by a gradual abdication of the entire communist bureaucracy. He remained Yugoslavia's most notorious dissident – whenever Tito felt the need to improve relations with the USSR, he packed Đilas off to jail as a sign of Yugoslavia's continuing communist orthodoxy.

Throughout this period **Croatia** was in the firm grip of Tito's trusted side-kick Vladimir Bakarić, who did his best to protect Croatian interests in the Yugoslav federation without going too far. Above all, the break with the Soviet Union removed the Stalinist straitjacket, allowing Croatia to renew its spiritual and cultural links with the West. As one of the more developed republics in the federation Croatia was well placed to profit from the economic boom of the 1960s, a decade which saw real wages almost double. The relaxation of visa requirements for visitors from capitalist countries led to a **tourist explosion** on the Adriatic – although the role of Belgrade-based travel companies in creaming off the profits was always resented.

The Croatian spring

During the 1960s the quickening pace of economic liberalization created a rift between the conservative communists and their more reform-minded colleagues. Tito initially sided with the reformists, moving in 1966 to oust another of his wartime comrades, the Serb **Aleksandar Ranković**, the feared head of the secret police. Ranković was in favour of a unitary state in which the autonomy enjoyed by the republics would be strictly limited, and most non-Serb Yugoslavs were pleased to see him go. However, the expected democratization never really materialized, petering out in a morass of inter-republican disputes. The phenomenal economic growth of the 1960s also created tensions within the federation, with the developed northern republics of Slovenia and Croatia anxious to exploit their prosperity without the interference of central government.

In Croatia, growing national sentiment first expressed itself in the cultural sphere. In 1967, 130 writers and intellectuals, worried by attempts to create a single Serbo-Croatian literary language, issued a declaration – supported by the country's leading cultural organization, the **Matica Hrvatska** – stating the unique nature of the Croatian tongue. A group of Serbian intellectuals responded by saying that, if that was the case, then the Serbian minority in Croatia had the right to use their own language together with the Cyrillic script. Official bodies denounced the two declarations as being provocative, and the leaders of the Matica Hrvatska were forced to resign.

By the beginning of the 1970s, the leaders of the **Croatian League of Communists** (the Yugoslav League of Communists was divided into six republican parties) were increasingly keen to play the nationalist card, hoping to gain domestic support in bargaining with central institutions for more republican autonomy. The Matica Hrvatska itself re-emerged as a mouthpiece of nationalist opinion in 1971, drawing on the support of thousands of ordinary Croats, and when nationalists won control of the Zagreb university students' union in April 1971 the republican authorities pointedly failed to take action against them. Mixing demands for economic liberalization with calls for more republican autonomy, the ferment of ideas and debate that characterized Croatia throughout 1971 came to be dubbed the "**Croatian Spring**". In November 1971 Zagreb students went on strike, calling for opponents of reform to be sacked from the party, but Tito was by this time seriously worried that things were getting out of hand, and in December accused the Croatian leadership of not taking effective steps against nationalism and chauvinism. The leaders of the Croatian League of Communists were forced to resign, Matica Hrvatska leaders were put on trial, and the short-lived Spring was at an end.

The 1970s

The crackdown on the Croats sounded the death-knell for liberalization all over Yugoslavia. The silencing of reformists in Serbia soon followed, and Yugoslav socialism entered a period of ideological stagnation from which it never really recovered. Tito's personal authority kept the lid on any further outbreaks of inter-republican animosity; in Croatia itself, nationalism was once more a taboo subject, while a disproportionate number of Serbs were appointed to top posts, storing up more resentment for the future. The Croatian patriotic song *Ljepa naša domovino* (Our Beautiful Homeland) was made the official hymn of the republic in 1972, but could only be performed in certain circumstances, and was never allowed to take precedence over the Yugoslav national anthem, *Hej slaveni*. Unofficial performances of the song were rewarded with a prison sentence of sixty days. Outside the country, Croatian exiles assassinated the Yugoslav ambassador to Sweden in 1971 and hijacked a TWA airliner in 1976, giving Western observers the impression that Croatian nationalism was a volatile and dangerous political force which was not to be encouraged. The Yugoslav secret services responded by sending hit squads abroad to silence the state's critics.

The 1980s

Tito died on May 4, 1980, leaving the country without an effective leader. He was replaced by an eight-man presidency in which each republic took turns to supply a head of state. The federal government was relatively weak compared with those of the individual republics, making it difficult to adopt nationwide policies capable of dealing with Yugoslavia's worsening economic problems. The economic boom of the 1960s had been financed by Western loans, but the oil-crisis-ridden 1970s had seen a drying-up of credit, leaving Yugoslavia with crippling foreign debt, galloping inflation and high unemployment.

Problems began in Kosovo, a province of southwestern Serbia which had been given autonomous status because the majority of its inhabitants were ethnic Albanians. In 1981, Albanian demonstrations in Kosovo demanding that the province be upgraded to a full republic had been put down by the army. In 1986, the Serbian Academy of Sciences issued a **Memorandum** which stated that the Serbian minority in Kosovo was under threat from Albanian nationalists, adding (without much supporting evidence) that the Serbian community in Croatia was also under pressure from Croatian cultural hegemony. The Memorandum was eagerly seized upon by Serbian intellectuals who argued that the constitution of Yugoslavia should be re-centralized in order to give the Serbs (numerically superior to the other nations) more power.

The Serbian League of Communists, loyal to the federalist ideal, was initially against the Memorandum. Then, on April 24, 1987, **Slobodan Milošević**, a little-known apparatchik recently installed as Serbian party chairman, visited the town of Kosovo Polje to meet leaders of the Serbian minority in Kosovo. When local police started jostling Serb demonstrators, Milošević intervened with the now famous words "Niko ne sme da vas bije!" ("Nobody has the right to beat you!"). Propelled to national prominence as a defender of Serbian rights, Milošević realized that nationalism was the tool with which he could remould Yugoslav communism in his own image. Using support for the Serbs in Kosovo as the issue on which all other politicians should be judged, he soon drove liberal communists out of the Serbian League of Communists, purged the Serbian media and overthrew the leadership of Vojvodina, the other province of Serbia that had been given autonomy in 1974.

Many of the Serbs who joined the mass meetings in support of Milošević mistakenly thought that they were taking part in some kind of democratic revolution: in fact, they were accessories to a neo-Stalinist putsch. In March 1989 a new Serbian constitution ended the autonomy of Kosovo and Vojvodina, while shortly afterwards Milošević supporters succeeded in winning control of the leadership of another republic, Montenegro; he also found allies in the Macedonian and Bosnian parties. Milošević hoped that this growing bloc of support would be sufficient to outvote his remaining opponents in federal institutions, thereby making it possible to recast Yugoslavia in new and more centralized form.

In November 1989 the Berlin Wall came down. As the rest of Eastern Europe prepared for multi-party rule, the biggest republic in Yugoslavia was reverting to hard-line communism. The Slovenes and Croats had to assert themselves before it was too late.

The break-up of Yugoslavia

By 1989, Slovenia, the most westernized and liberal of Yugoslavia's republics, was moving inexorably towards multi-party elections. Croatia was initially slow to follow this lead, and by the late 1980s the phrase **Hrvatska šutnja** ("Croatian silence") had been coined to describe the unwillingness of the republic's politicians to discuss the future of Yugoslavia or to champion Croatian interests. The crunch came when the Slovenes insisted on changes to the Yugoslav constitution which would guarantee the autonomy of individual republics: the Croats had to choose between supporting Slovenia or being left to the mercy of Milošević. At the last-ever congress of the Yugoslav League of Communists in January 1990, the Slovenes called for complete independence for each of the republican communist parties, a move rejected by the Serbs and their allies. The Slovene delegates walked out of the congress, followed by the Croats, who were now led by the reform-oriented **Ivica Račan**, effectively burying the Yugoslav League of Communists for good.

Democratization was moving at different speeds in different republics, however, making a smooth, pan-Yugoslav transition to non-communist rule impossible. May 1989 saw the creation of Croatia's first non-communist political organizations, among them the Croatian Democratic Union, or **HDZ**, led by former army general and dissident historian **Franjo Tuđman**. The HDZ held their first congress in February 1990, calling for Croatia's right to secede from

Yugoslavia and for a reduction in the number of Serbs in Croatia's police force and state bureaucracy. This anti-Yugoslav tone caught the mood of a country increasingly frustrated by the state's failure to offer any resistance to Milošević, and the HDZ easily won Croatian **elections** in April 1990. On May 13, a football match between Dinamo Zagreb and Red Star Belgrade was abandoned on account of a three-way fight between the two sets of fans and the Serb-dominated police, worsening relations between Croatia and Serbia still further. When the Sabor met on May 30, Tuđman was sworn in as president, and Croatian "statehood" (a potential step to full independence) was declared. The HDZ's **Stipe Mešić** became Croatia's first post-communist prime minister. The Sabor immediately began work on a new **constitution**, which contained one highly controversial passage: the Serbs who lived in Croatia were no longer to be classified as one of the constituent nations of the republic, but as a national minority – a form of words which caused understandable anxiety among the Serbs themselves.

The rebellion of Croatia's Serbs

Ever since Milošević's rise to power, the Serbs of Croatia (numbering 580,000 according to the 1991 census, most living in the arc of territory which ran alongside Croatia's border with Bosnia-Hercegovina) had been subjected to a Belgrade media campaign designed to make them feel endangered by their Croatian neighbours. In February 1990, the Serbian Democratic Party, or **SDS**, was formed in the largely Serbian town of Knin, just inland from Šibenik, and they soon assumed leadership of a community fearful of what might happen to them in a Croatia increasingly independent of Belgrade. On June 2 the SDS organized a referendum on autonomy for Serbs living in Croatia. The Croatian authorities banned the referendum, but weren't able to prevent it. Not surprisingly, the vote was massively in favour of autonomy.

Throughout the spring and summer of 1990 the Knin Serbs had been arming themselves with the connivance of the intelligence services in Serbia proper, aided by pro-Serb officers in the Yugoslav People's Army, the **JNA**. In July of that year the SDS declared the autonomy of the Knin region, creating the so-called **Kninska Krajina**. Barricades went up on the roads around the town, policed by paramilitary units organized by Milan Martić, the Knin police chief. Croatian authorities sent police helicopters to restore order, but they were forced back to Zagreb by Yugoslav airforce MIGs. The Krajina declared its independence from Croatia in February 1991, seeking union with Serbia. The rebellion now spread to other areas of the republic: in March, the Serb-dominated town council of Pakrac in Slavonia stated that it no longer recognized the Croatian authorities, provoking the latter to send in the police to re-establish control of the town. The JNA moved in to keep the peace. The resulting stand-off didn't produce any casualties, but Belgrade Radio reported 11 Serb deaths all the same.

The drift to war

Despite the installation of democratically elected governments in Croatia and Slovenia, the state of Yugoslavia still existed at the end of 1990, and many feared that the JNA – possibly with the connivance of Milošević – would launch a military coup to prevent its break-up. However the JNA surprised everyone by failing to act, despite numerous promptings from the Serbian leader. Sensing that the break-up of Yugoslavia was now inevitable, Milošević began instead to plan for the next best thing: the creation of a **Greater Serbia** which would include all the parts of Croatia and Bosnia-Hercegovina where Serbs lived.

Belgrade subsequently stepped up aid and encouragement to the Knin Serbs, and in March 1991 Knin paramilitaries took control of the Plitvice National Park. Croatian police units were dispatched to arrest them, and the resulting shoot-out produced the first casualties of the Serb–Croat conflict, with two Serbs and one Croat killed. The JNA moved in, ostensibly to keep the two factions apart, but in reality sealing off the area from Croatian civilian control, a pattern to be repeated elsewhere as the spring and summer progressed. On April 29 the Croat village of Kijevo near Knin was surrounded by Serb irregulars and its inhabitants were either forced to leave or shot – the first step in a campaign to **ethnically cleanse** the Serb-held parts of Croatia of any remaining Croats.

At the beginning of May, twelve Croatian policemen were massacred in Borovo Selo, a predominantly Serbian suburb of Vukovar. On May 6 a big anti-JNA demonstration in Split ended in tragedy when one soldier was killed – a conscript from Macedonia. On May 17 the head of Yugoslavia's presidency, the Serb Borislav Jović, came to the end of his one-year term. The next incumbent was due to be Croatia's delegate, Stipe Mesić. Other members of the presidency were split on whether to endorse his accession: four members voted for Mesić and four against, leaving Yugoslavia without a head of state.

The Slovenes had voted for full independence from Yugoslavia in a referendum in December 1990; on May 19, 1991, the Croats followed suit. Co-ordinating their actions, both Slovenia and Croatia declared their **independence** on June 26. Yugoslav Prime Minister Ante Marković, still believing that the federation could be saved, ordered the JNA to secure the country's borders, but Slovene territorial units quickly surrounded and neutralized JNA columns, and the "war" came to an end ten days later with the EU offering to mediate. The Slovenes and Croats agreed to place a three-month moratorium on independence, while the JNA withdrew from Slovenia, and the Serbs and their allies agreed to recognize Stipe Mesić as Yugoslav president. In terms of injecting new life into Yugoslavia the agreement was meaningless – Slovenia had won *de facto* independence if not outright recognition, while the fate of Croatia was left to be fought over.

The war in Croatia

The withdrawal of the JNA from Slovenia meant that military strength could now be concentrated in the Serb-inhabited areas of Croatia, where low-level conflict – largely waged by Serbian irregulars against the Croatian police – dragged on through the summer. In late August the JNA and Serb irregulars launched a major offensive to gain control of eastern Slavonia, beginning with air bombardments of Vukovar and Vinkovci. In response, the newly formed Croatian National Guard began a blockade of all JNA barracks in Croatia. Areas under firm JNA and Serb control – a chain running from Knin in the southwest through the Plitvice area, Slunj, Glina and Petrinja to the environs of Pakrac in the west – were organized into the **Republic of the Serbian Krajina (RSK)**, and Croats who lived in the region were expelled, creating almost half a million refugees. An attempt was made to cut northern Croatia off from

Dalmatia by advancing towards the ports of Zadar and Šibenik, but neither city fell. In October, JNA and Montenegrin forces began the siege of **Dubrovnik**, an operation designed to weaken Croatian morale and reward Montenegro for its support of the Serbs with opportunities for territorial aggrandizement and plunder.

The Serb advance in eastern Slavonia was held up by the defenders of **Vukovar**, who displayed incredible heroism against vastly superior odds. Many believe that Zagreb could have done more to aid Vukovar's defenders, but saw a prolonged siege as a useful way of gaining international sympathy for the Croatian cause. Vukovar fell on November 18, after which the Serb–JNA forces began the bombardment of the next big city to the north, **Osijek**.

The defence of Croatia had initially been a hastily improvised affair, but as fighting continued, the Croats gradually assembled a highly motivated military force armed with weapons captured from JNA barracks. Serb advances were halted, while a counteroffensive won back portions of western Slavonia in December. Some Croatian paramilitaries committed acts of revenge: the murder of civilians, torture of prisoners and dynamiting of Serb-owned houses was widespread throughout Croatia.

The EU made consistent attempts to bring the two warring sides to the table, however, and agreement became possible once it became clear that the Serb–JNA offensive had been stalled by tenacious Croatian defence. The **Geneva Agreement** brokered a ceasefire: the Croats agreed to end the siege of all remaining JNA barracks, and the JNA agreed to withdraw from Croatia. At the same time, a UN peace mission headed by Cyrus Vance secured the deployment of an international peacekeeping force, UNPROFOR, to police the ceasefire line. The Serbs were happy to accept this because it froze the front line at its current position, apparently confirming their territorial gains. The peacekeepers were deployed in March 1992 and the JNA departed as agreed, but gave most of its weaponry to the forces of the RSK.

Meanwhile, Croatia was emerging from its diplomatic isolation. The Germans believed that EU recognition of Slovenia and Croatia would dissuade the JNA from further aggression, and despite initial opposition from the French and British, **Croatian statehood** was recognized by all the EU countries on January 15, 1992.

The ceasefire wasn't perfect, and shells continued to fall on Osijek, Dubrovnik and other Croatian towns. Summer 1992 saw a Croatian counter-attack break the siege of Dubrovnik, and in January 1993 the Croats recaptured the area around Maslenica in northern Dalmatia, taking the pressure off Zadar. When the Croats took the Medak Pocket (Medački džep) near Gospić in September, irregular troops allegedly murdered over 100 Serb civilians and prisoners. The international community protested at Croatia's breaches of the truce, but was too preoccupied with events in neighbouring **Bosnia** to take action.

The war in Bosnia

The ethnic balance in **Bosnia-Hercegovina** was more delicate than that of any other Yugoslav republic, with a three-way split between Serbs, Croats and Muslims. The Croats, who made up about twenty percent of the population, lived in western Hercegovina near the border with Dalmatia, where they were in the majority, and scattered among Serbs and Muslims throughout central Bosnia.

Bosnia-Hercegovina had received international recognition as an independent state at the same time as Croatia in the hope that it would discourage any attempts to partition it. In fact it had the opposite effect, and a Serbian community which wanted no part in an independent Bosnia gradually moved towards armed rebellion in spring 1992. A familiar pattern of events ensued: Serbian irregulars aided by the JNA quickly gained control of areas where Serbs lived, together with any strategic towns that potentially stood in their way, ejecting or murdering a large portion of the non-Serb population.

Initially, Bosnian Croats and Bosnian Muslims cooperated in the struggle against the Serbs, although the highly organized Bosnian–Croat army – the Croatian Defence Council or **HVO** – remained independent of the largely Muslim army of the Bosnian government in Sarajevo. With Croats and Muslims in central Bosnia increasingly squeezed by Serbian successes, the two sides started fighting each other for territory, beginning a vicious Croat–Bosnian war which began in spring 1993 and continued sporadically for a year. The conflict was disastrous for the Croats of central Bosnia, who were forced to flee towards Hercegovina or Croatia proper. It was also disastrous for the international reputation of the Croatian state, whose support for the HVO in Bosnia led to accusations that Tuđman was as cynical as Milošević in his attempts to destroy multinational Bosnia by carving it up into ethnically pure units. Indeed, Tuđman and Milošević had discussed the possibility of dividing up Bosnia between them as early as spring 1991, and it seemed that the Croatian president – in league with the hardline Croats of Hercegovina – was prepared to sacrifice the Croats of central Bosnia in order to achieve his goal. Croatian atrocities in Bosnia – the massacre of at least 104 Muslim civilians in the village of Ahmići, the internment of Muslim men in Dretelj concentration camp and the destruction of the 500-year-old Turkish bridge at Mostar – were propaganda disasters for the Croatian cause.

The road to Dayton

In the end the Croat–Muslim conflict was brought to an end by the US, which had adopted a harder line against the Serbs since the election of President Clinton in 1992. US sympathies were primarily with the Bosnian Muslims and their besieged capital of Sarajevo, but it was widely recognized that Croat military power would have to play a part in any solution. The US-sponsored **Washington Agreement** of March 1994 created a federation of Croats and Muslims in Bosnia-Hercegovina, and an alliance between this Croat–Muslim Federation and the state of Croatia. The Croats of western Hercegovina continued to run their territory (so-called "**Herceg-Bosna**") as if it was an independent statelet, although this was overlooked in the interests of unity.

Changes on the battlefield pushed all sides nearer to a settlement in 1995. In Croatia proper, the Croats overran the remaining portions of western Slavonia in the operation known as **Blijesak** ("Flash") on May 1–2, allowing the Croatian army to liberate Serb-held parts of Bosnia near the Croatian border. On August 4, the **Oluja** ("Storm") offensive was launched with an artillery bombardment of Knin, and the Serbian Krajina collapsed within three days. Fearing reprisals, the Serbian population fled through Serb-controlled Bosnian territory into Serbia proper. Oluja was followed by successful Croat–Muslim operations in Bosnia which, combined with NATO air strikes in September, persuaded both the Bosnian Serbs and their masters in Belgrade to seek a negotiated peace.

The war in Croatia had virtually ended with the Oluja campaign, although the Serbs remained in control of eastern Slavonia. According to the US-sponsored **Erdut Agreement**, eastern Slavonia would be governed by the UN for a transitional period before being returned to Croatia in January 1998. The war in Bosnia was formally brought to an end by the **Dayton Accords** of November 10, 1995, which created a unified Bosnian state comprising two so-called "entities": one Serbian and one Croat–Muslim. On paper, Dayton brought an end to the existence of Herceg-Bosna, but in practice it continued to lead a life quite separate from the rest of Bosnia-Hercegovina, flying Croatian flags from its public buildings and using the Croatian currency as legal tender.

Croatia after the war

The HDZ which had come to power in 1990 was a broad movement which aimed to unify all Croats in the face of an outside menace. If it had any ideology it all, it was right-of-centre, preaching traditional family values, respect for the Catholic Church and national solidarity. The movement's creator, and Croatia's first president, **Franjo Tuđman**, was not a great admirer of Western democracy and did not want to be constrained by a strong parliament. From the start, the advisory bodies assembled by the president had more power than the Sabor or the prime minister, and policy was usually decided by Tuđman's inner circle of confidants.

The HDZ's authoritarian streak was seen as a necessary evil while the nation was fighting for its survival in 1991, but began to look increasingly anachronistic as the years progressed, while the government's actions at home and in Bosnia helped significantly to tarnish the reputation of the new nation. After 1995, Croatia dragged its feet in helping Serbs who had fled the country to return and, worse still, seemed to be providing the Croats of Hercegovina with moral support in their attempts to frustrate full implementation of the Dayton Accords, something which led the West to believe that Tuđman was still secretly working for the partition of Bosnia-Hercegovina. Croatia was threatened with UN sanctions in 1996 and again in 1999 following her refusal to extradite suspects to the Hague war crimes tribunal, while the country's unsatisfactory state of democracy – with free and fair elections rendered impossible by the fact that the state-owned TV network was a blatant government mouthpiece – ensured that Croatia was held at arm's length by the EU. Croatia was also excluded from the aid programmes made available to other former communist states, and was placed behind less developed countries like Romania and Bulgaria in the queue for EU membership.

With the war over, political dissatisfaction within the country slowly made itself felt. In early 1997 a coalition of opposition parties won a majority in Zagreb's municipal elections, but the HDZ – still the largest single party in the council chamber – refused to cede control. Tuđman himself blocked the appointment of an opposition mayor, and fringe members of the opposition coalition were gradually bought off with promises of political promotion, taking the sting out of the HDZ's defeat.

Franjo Tuđman

Franjo Tuđman was born on May 14, 1922, to a peasant family in the Zagorje village of Veliko Trgovišće, only 15km south of Kumrovec, birthplace of Tito. His father was local leader of the Croatian Peasant Party (HSS), and Franjo involved himself in left-wing politics from an early age before joining the Partisans in 1941, rising to become a political commissar in liberated territories in eastern Croatia.

After the war, Tuđman went to the Yugoslav Defence Ministry in Belgrade, working his way through the ranks before being elevated to the rank of **general** – the youngest in the army – in 1960. He also began to make his name as a **historian**, graduating in 1957 and publishing the first of his theoretical works, *Rat protiv rata* (War Against War). Resigning from the army in 1961 to concentrate on academic research, Tuđman was appointed to head the Institute for the History of the Workers' Movement. His thoughts were moving away from party orthodoxy, however, and while researching into Ustaše war crimes he became convinced that the numbers of their victims had been deliberately inflated by a regime eager to discredit Croatian nationalism.

Expelled from the Yugoslav League of Communists Central Committee and forced to leave the Institute on account of his work and views, Tuđman began to establish a reputation as a prominent **dissident** which would make him ideally placed to take advantage of the communist system's decline in the late 1980s. He was briefly imprisoned following the collapse of the Croatian Spring, and again in 1981 after giving an interview to French radio in which he spoke of Yugoslavia's need to move towards political pluralism.

Tuđman emerged from nowhere to become the leader of Croatia's anti-communist opposition in 1989. His big idea was the **Pomirba** (best translated as a "setting aside of old scores"), which emphasized the coming together of all strands of Croatian opinion – from Partisan to Ustaše – to build a new patriotic consensus that could stand up to Belgrade. In part this was a pragmatic move which allowed Tuđman to tap the financial resources of right-wing exiles, but it also reflected his own personal journey from left-wing idealist to **social conservative**. An over-readiness to accommodate the far right was a weakness of the Tuđman regime from beginning to end. At the HDZ's first congress in 1990 Tuđman described the NDH (the fascist puppet regime which ruled Croatia during World War II), as an authentic expression of Croatia's yearning for independent statehood, and during the 1990 election campaign notoriously stated "Thank God my wife is neither a Serb nor a Jew", an opinion he never retracted.

Tuđman's other major hobby horse was the unviability of Bosnia-Hercegovina as an independent state. He had always regarded the **division of Bosnia** between himself and Milošević as a potential way of settling Serbian and Croatian differences, and even had negotiations with the Serb leader to this effect in March 1991. Many people in Croatia proper opposed Tuđman's support for the Hercegovinian Croats in the Bosnian Croat–Muslim war of 1993–94, and Croats from Hercegovina – where Croatian nationalism was traditionally purer than anywhere else – rose to positions of prominence and power under Tuđman far out of proportion with their actual numbers.

Tuđman demanded deference from his subjects, donning a red, white and blue sash whenever attending official functions, and appearing in a white uniform to receive the salute at military parades – prompting criticisms that he was becoming another Tito. Debate about whether members of his family personally profited from the kind of dodgy business deals that characterized the Croatian economy in the 1990s still continues.

When Tuđman **died**, however, thousands of ordinary Croats headed for the presidential palace to file past the coffin. He was still seen as the man who had stiffened Croatian resolve during the dark days of 1991–92, winning the country international recognition as an independent state for the first time since the Middle Ages. The final, damning verdict on the political system he had built was delivered at the general election barely one month later.

The brazen way in which the HDZ exercised power was an increasing source of resentment, and the public grew increasingly critical of the new breed of tycoons who had taken control of big enterprises with HDZ support, only to siphon off the profits and drive their companies to bankruptcy. Like the communist party before it, the HDZ began to extend its influence into all spheres of life, controlling cultural appointments and even trying to subvert the football league. It was revealed in June 1999 that secret-service operatives had been trailing referees in an attempt to ascertain which officials were the most corruptible – in the hope of securing victories for Croatia Zagreb, the president's favourite team.

In the meantime, daily life for many Croats was becoming increasingly hard. The country ended the decade with twenty percent unemployment, an average wage of around $400 a month and many companies unable to pay salaries with any regularity.

The end of the Tuđman era

It had been an open secret that Tuđman had been ill with cancer ever since 1996, but he had chosen not to designate a successor, preferring to remain in sole charge until the end. The HDZ – by now lacking any coherent political ideology – began to resemble a collection of warring factions rather than a party. The opposition parties on the other hand were beginning to unite around the need to defeat the HDZ at the next elections, which were scheduled for December 1999. By the autumn of that year, an anti-HDZ grouping led by the SDP (former communists who had re-branded themselves as Social Democrats) and the HSLS (right-of-centre liberals) had banded together to form a coalition.

Tuđman entered hospital at the beginning of November 1999, and died on December 10. A genuine outpouring of popular grief ensued, but the HDZ had lost the one talismanic figure who could persuade Croats, out of a sense of loyalty if nothing else, to keep the party in power. The elections were put off until January 4, 2000, in the hope that the festive season would knock the wind out of the opposition's sails, with Croatian national television unleashing hitherto unseen levels of pro-HDZ bias. It was all to no avail however, as the SDP–HSLS coalition won a staggering 52 percent of the vote, against the HDZ's 24 percent. The SDP's **Ivica Račan**, the calm and capable technocrat who had previously served as reformist head of the Croatian League of Communists, became prime minister, while HSLS leader **Dražen Budiša** (student leader during the Croatian Spring; see p.417) set his sights on the presidential elections due in three weeks' time. In the event he was surprisingly beaten by another centrist candidate **Stipe Mesić**, the jocular charmer who had once served as the unenthusiastic president of a dying Yugoslavia. A former HDZ leader who had split with Tuđman over the latter's policies in Bosnia-Hercegovina, Mesić had spent the intervening years amassing solid liberal-democratic credentials. His election was received with glee by an international community eager for proof that Croatia was moving in a decidedly pro-western direction.

Croatia's diplomatic position began to improve almost overnight. The HDZ defeat seemed to mark the end of the Croatian government's support for the hardline nationalists of Hercegovina, and also held out the possibility of a more conciliatory attitude towards Croatia's Serbs. Mesić seemed keen to strip himself of some of the presidential trappings adopted by Tuđman, giving the Sabor and the prime minister more real power.

The present

The incoming administration was cautious about its ability to significantly improve the Croatian economy in the short term, and with good reason. Croatia's improved standing abroad has brought about a gradual increase in foreign investment, but this has been slow to manifest itself in the shape of more jobs or higher wages. Although certain sectors of the Croatian economy – such as tourism and the service industries – are booming, the number of people drawing significant profits from these activities is small indeed. Agriculture and heavy industry are still struggling to pay their way, and will find the going even tougher as Croatia is opened up more and more to outside competition.

The most troublesome aspect of government policy has been the question of cooperation with the **International War Crimes Tribunal** in the Hague. Such cooperation is necessary if Croatia is going to be taken seriously as a potential member of the EU and NATO, and is broadly supported by those Croats who want their country to be accepted as an equal member of the international community. The fact that individual Croats committed atrocities during the 1991–95 war is broadly accepted in Croatia, although most people would prefer to see them tried in Croatia rather than abroad. It was in any case largely assumed that the Hague Tribunal would be mostly concerned with hunting down high-ranking Serbian perpetrators rather than Croats – and the Hague's determination to pursue prominent Croatian generals has come as a shock to many.

The first signs of a crisis came in February 2001, when international warrants were issued for the arrest of General **Mirko Norac**, suspected of overseeing the murder of Serbs in Gospić in 1991. The government's eagerness to extradite Norac (who initially evaded arrest by going into hiding) split Croatian society down the middle, with some arguing that the honour of the country would be best served by complying with international demands, others claiming that the memory of Croatia's wartime struggle would be irreparably tarnished by subjecting decorated officers to the jurisdiction of foreign courts. The affair played into the hands of the HDZ, who denounced Mesić and Račan as traitors, and presented themselves as the true guardians of patriotic values. There were mass demonstrations in Norac's support, and posters announcing "Svi smo mi Mirko Norac" ("We are all Mirko Norac") are still visible in areas where memories of the war – and the often heroic resistance put up by Croatia's defenders – are still strong. Things got worse in July of that year, when the Hague put the dashing general **Ante Gotovina** on its wanted list – Gotovina was an officer-in-charge during the Oluja campaigns of 1995, when numerous atrocities are alleged to have taken place. Gotovina promptly went into hiding, and hasn't been seen since. Eager to dissociate themselves from unpopular policies, the HSLS left the government, leaving Račan in charge of a much weakened coalition composed of the SDP and several smaller centrist parties. By the time the Hague issued a warrant for General **Janko Bobetko** (commanding officer at the notorious Medak Pocket operation; see p.422) in September 2002, Račan had had enough. Fearful of further defections from his government, he decided not to extradite Bobetko – the fact that the aging Bobetko was in any case too ill to travel prevented this from escalating into a major international incident. President Mesić handled the awkward task of reassuring the international community that Croatia's long-term cooperation with the Tribunal was not in doubt, and popped over to the Hague himself in October 2002 to testify against his erstwhile adversary Slobodan Milošević.

The main beneficiary of the Norac, Gotovina and Bobetko controversies has been a political Right eager to demonstrate that, January 2000 notwithstanding, it's still a major player on the Croatian scene. The idea that a proud, nationalist Croatia is preferable to a fully Europeanized Croatia which kowtows to international organizations still enjoys enormous popular appeal, and dovetails neatly with the attitudes of large sections of the Croatian Catholic church – for whom decadent western liberalism has always been rather suspect. However a return to outright Tuđmanism is not on the cards: the HDZ is currently shedding itself of right-wing radicals in an attempt to turn itself into a modern conservative party, aware that the silent majority in Croatia is more interested in managerial competence than ideological extremes. With the popularity of the main parties more balanced than at any time since independence, the consensus politics of the post-Tuđman era look as if they're here to stay. The main planks of Croatian policy – integration with international organizations such as the EU and NATO, and economic reform at home – are unlikely to be disrupted by any future change of government.

Croatian folk music

Croatian folk music (*narodna glazba* or *narodna muzika*) is as diverse as you would expect from a country poised between the cultural worlds of the Mediterranean, central Europe and the Balkans. Traditional music still forms a part of everyday life in many towns and villages, with local folklore societies preserving knowledge of songs and dances long associated with weddings, feasts and seasonal merrymaking. The state has often been an enthusiastic supporter of folk culture: communist Yugoslavia encouraged the activities of folklore groups as a way of emphasizing the shared cultural roots linking Yugoslavia's many nationalities, while post-independence Croatia (taking a slightly different view of the genre) has stressed the importance of folklore as a way of promoting Croatia's unique identity. A good deal of folk culture has filtered through into the commercial mainstream, producing a style of pop in some ways similar to country and western in the US – many of the tunes hark back to traditional melodies, but everything else is pure showbiz.

One of the best ways to hear folk music in Croatia is to catch one of the concerts given by the various folklore societies. **Lado**, based in Zagreb, is the state's one professional troupe, performing songs and dances from all over Croatia. All the other folklore ensembles comprise amateur enthusiasts and are likely to concentrate on a more regional repertoire. The biggest of these regional ensembles, Dubrovnik's **Linđo**, has a reputation comparable with that of Lado, and often plays a part in the city's annual arts festival.

There's quite a range of folk-related festivals (see p.42), but the biggest single folk event is Zagreb's **International Folklore Festival** (Međunarodna smotra folklora; ⊛www.msf.hr), which brings together an array of performers from all over the country alongside international guests. The cultural happenings arranged in tourist resorts throughout the summer always include at least some traditional music, and package hotels often lay on performances for their guests. Otherwise, look out for Croatian **weddings**, which usually take place on Saturdays and often involve celebrants gathering in a town park or square to be serenaded by traditional musicians.

Slavonia and the tamburica

The indigenous folk music of eastern Croatia, particularly Slavonia, has grown to dominate Croatian music over the last century and a half. It's characterized by the tambura (more commonly known by its diminutive form, **tamburica**), a lute-like instrument which is plucked or strummed to produce a sound not dissimilar to that of a mandolin.

Originally of Anatolian origin, the tamburica was brought to southeastern Europe by the Ottoman Turks in the fourteenth and fifteenth centuries. The instrument was gradually taken up by the local Slav population, whose frequent migrations (often between Ottoman and Habsburg lands) helped spread it still further. By the nineteenth century, the tamburica was the most common folk instrument throughout both eastern Croatia and the northern Serb province of Vojvodina.

Because the instrument was popular with both Croats and Serbs, it was championed in the mid-nineteenth century by the Illyrian movement, a Zagreb-based group of intellectuals who aimed to promote South Slav unity. As the nineteenth century progressed, the tamburica was increasingly seen as a symbol of an indigenous culture under threat from the dominant Germanic and Hungarian influences of the Habsburg Empire. Tamburica orchestras were formed in Croatian towns and cities to play popular folk tunes, concentrating on the jolly, rhythmic melodies which often accompanied rural merrymaking. These orchestras often featured a lot of tamburica players playing in unison, creating a wall of thrumming sound which has remained a feature of tamburica music ever since; they also often provided the music for village dances at which locals performed the *kolo* – a local variant of the circle dances found throughout southeastern Europe.

In the twentieth century the Slavonian sound increasingly came to symbolize Croatia as a whole. The Croatian Peasant Party, the main voice for Croatian aspirations during the 1920s and 1930s, promoted the music as a way of renewing village cultural life, and it also grew in significance among the many Croatian emigrés in North America, for whom it was an important link with the homeland.

Remaining popular through the Yugoslav period, tamburica music was increasingly dragged into the commercial mainstream in the 1980s, when a new generation of tamburica bands began to mix folk melodies with a modern pop sound. Foremost among these were **Zlatni Dukati** (The Golden

Ducats), who mixed tamburicas with electric bass and guitar and were initially popular with Serbs in Vojvodina as well as Croats throughout Croatia. By
the end of the decade the band's output was beginning to reflect the changing mood of Croatian society, with the release of an album entitled *Hrvatska
pjesmarica* (Croatian Songbook) featuring patriotic songs which, while not
actually banned, were certainly considered subversive enough to merit
scathing criticism from communist politicians. Needless to say, the album was
a big hit in Croatia, and Zlatni Dukati went on to record more patriotic material during the 1991–95 war. Other tamburica-pop bands have followed in
Zlatni Dukati's footsteps, most notably **Gazde** (The Bosses), who ditched the
folksy costumes traditionally associated with the tamburica scene in favour of
a leather-clad rockabilly image, and developed a similarly modified, pop-rock-
influenced sound.

The need for morale-boosting popular music heavily flavoured with
indigenous folk motifs led to an explosion of tamburica music during the
early 1990s. The nation's radio and TV stations were quite deliberate in their
attempts to replace the folk-pop music of the former Yugoslavia with something more exclusively Croatian, and the tamburica sound is nowadays an
ever-present feature of the airwaves. The number of amateur and semi-

professional acts is huge, although Zlatni Dukati and Gazde are probably the only tamburica groups to make a living from concert tours and album sales alone.

Tamburica music still constitutes an important element in the diet of radio stations and TV show programmes. It also provides the *raison d'être* of at least one major festival, the **Zlatne žice Slavonije** (Golden Strings of Slavonia), which takes place every September in the provincial town of Požega. A glitzy showbiz occasion, the festival concentrates on newly composed commercial songs rather than traditional, folkloric material.

Other inland Croatian music

The ubiquity of tamburica music has tended to overshadow the other musical traditions of inland Croatia, especially in Slavonia itself, where many local instruments (such as the *gajde* and *dude*, both local types of bagpipe) have almost totally died out.

The music of the **Zagreb region** and the **Zagorje** centres on the polkas and waltzes common to central Europe. There's a strong tradition of brass-band music here too, although more common are the four- or five-piece string bands that you'll see playing at weddings or in restaurants, usually featuring double bass, a couple of violins and a guitar or tamburica.

The traditional sounds of the area **southwest of Zagreb** couldn't be more different, having more in common with the Balkan south than with any part of central Europe. Arid mountain regions like Lika and Hercegovina (the latter, although forming part of Bosnia-Hercegovina, is predominantly populated by Croats) are home to a harsh and dissonant form of polyphonic singing known as *ojkanje* (characterized by the ululating "oy" sound at the end of every line) or *gange*. Unaccompanied *gange* songs are traditionally performed at village festivities, and even now are rarely performed in concerts. As in Slavonia, the *kolo* is more popular in these highland areas than dancing in pairs. A form of *kolo* typical to the region is the *nijemo kolo*, or "dumb kolo", a dance performed without music, the only sound coming from the whirling and stamping of the dancers themselves. A particularly acrobatic form of this is the *Vrličko kolo* from Vrlika, a town inland from Šibenik, in which dancers hang onto each other by their belts and swing each other into the air.

The music of the **Međimurje**, in the far northeast of Croatia, has much in common with the music of neighbouring Hungary, with lilting melodies accompanied by a string band and occasionally a zither or a cimbalom. There's also a strong tradition of unaccompanied narrative songs sung by women, including many tales of unrequited love featuring, oddly enough, railway stations, at which village boys waved goodbye to their sweethearts before going off to serve with the Austro-Hungarian army. Many of these were rediscovered in the early twentieth century, when the folklorist Vinko Žganec started systematically transcribing them. The songbooks produced by Žganec were plundered by a new generation of folk singers in the 1980s and 1990s, although there's always been a question mark about their authenticity: Žganec asked local organist Florijan Andrašec to help him collect traditional tunes, paying him for every new song he came up with – it's believed Andrašec made up many songs himself to earn extra cash.

The coast

Traditionally, the music of rural **Dalmatia** revolved around two-part songs on heroic or tragic themes, mostly sung by women. Although these still survive in some places, the tradition was superseded in the last century by the growth of the male-voice choir, or **klapa**. Today almost every town or village has a *klapa*, which usually consists of up to ten members and performs smoothly harmonized songs of a sentimental nature. Some *klape* sound like barbershop quartets; others have a raw feeling reminiscent of male polyphonic singing from Corsica or Georgia. Many Dalmatian towns hold *klapa* festivals in the summer – the most famous is at Omiš, just south of Split, in July. Further south, towards **Dubrovnik**, a three-string fiddle known as the *lirica* provides droning accompaniment to dances such as the *linđo* (an ancient courtship dance), which you'll still see performed outside Čilipi church on Sunday mornings.

Utterly different is the startling music of the **Istrian peninsula**, which uses a distinctive local scale (the *istarska ljestvica*). A lot of Istrian songs employ two-part harmonies which sound discordant to the average non-Istrian ear, and this singing style has given rise to an entire body of instruments dedicated to reproducing such harmonies. Prominent among these are the *sopila*, a large oboe which is always played in pairs; the *šurla*, which consists of two pipes with a single mouthpiece, allowing a single musician to play two parts; and the *mijeh* (also known as *meh* or *mih*), a bagpipe made from the bladder of a young goat. Istrian styles of singing and bagpipe playing are also found on the **Kvarner Gulf** islands of Cres, Krk and Rab. The most exciting exponent of Istrian music today is the *sopila* player Dario Marušić, who brings a modern-jazz sensibility to bear on a selection of raucous, uneasy-listening traditional tunes. His albums are hard to get hold of, but he does feature on the *Ethno Ambient Live: Salona 98* CD (see p.431).

New sounds

The last decade has seen an increasing hybridization of Croatian roots music, with a string of performers attempting to breath new life into traditional forms with studio technology or new musical styles. Most of them have drawn inspiration from the fringe areas of Croatian folk (notably Međimurje and Istria), as if consciously offering an alternative to the monopoly of mainstream tamburica-pop.

First off the mark were **Vještice** (The Witches), formed in 1988 by veterans of the Zagreb New Wave scene, who created a whole new audience for traditional music by performing Međimurje folk songs in alternative rock style. This interest in the music of northeastern Croatia was picked up in the early 1990s by **Dunja Knebl** (ⓦwww.dunjaknebl.com), a Zagreb woman who didn't start singing professionally until already in her mid-40s, fired by enthusiasm for the newly fashionable Međimurje songs. Around the same time, the younger Međimurje-born singer-songwriter **Lidija Bajuk** (ⓦscena.hgu.sr/lidijabajuk) was moving in a similar direction. Both Knebl and Bajuk had grown up listening to acoustic-guitar-wielding folkies from Joan Baez onwards, and their interpretations of traditional Croatian songs have an uncomplicated accessibility – without losing too much of the other-worldly strangeness of the originals.

The mid-1990s also saw the emergence of **Legen**, an ambitious techno-folk crossover act using synthesizers and samples to soup up folk in the manner of Transglobal Underground or Loop Guru, though with less danceable results. Legen tried to put the mystery back into Croatian folk, building their repertoire around songs celebrating seasonal rites with pagan undertones – such as St George's Day fertility rituals, or the St John's Day bonfires which still take place in many parts of the country. Knebl and Bajuk collaborated with Legen on the 1995 album **Ethno Ambient Live**, an outstanding recording of (largely acoustic rather than synth-driven) performances in Zagreb's *Gjuro II* nightclub, which helped bring their work to a hip young audience. A second album, **Ethno Ambient Live: Salona 98**, came out in 1999, using a wider pool of sounds and performers, notably Dalmatian *klapa* singers.

One not-so-traditional vocalist who found her way onto *Ethno Ambient Live: Salona 98* was jazz siren **Tamara Obrovac**, who draws inspiration from Istrian melodies – lullabies and harvest-time songs rather than the ear-bending stuff – to produce an intriguing folk-jazz hybrid, featuring rolling, part-improvised songs sung in Istrian dialect. As far as dance culture is concerned, **DJ Boxer** has gone further down the ethno-techno road pioneered by Legen, although for him folk songs are useful ingredients in a wider sound collage rather than an end in themselves.

One of Croatia's more maverick groups is Pula-based **Gustafi**, who began as a new-wave rock band before metamorphosing into an accordion-driven Mexican–Istrian crossover act that defies categorization. Their irreverent, eclectic approach seems to have rubbed off on other acts such as the Zagreb group **Cinkuši**, who perform traditional north Croatian songs with a wilfully non-traditional choice of instruments, including Mediterranean mandolin and African *djembe* drums. Among the many Irish-influenced bands in Croatia, look out for the Pogues-ish **Belfast Food**, who sing a memorable version of "Dirty Old Town" (Šporki stari grad) in coastal dialect.

Gypsy singing legends **Esma Redžepova** (from Macedonia) and **Šaban Bajramović** (from Serbia) have both benefited from the upsurge in enthusiasm for roots music in Croatia. The country's biggest record company, Croatia Records (known until 1990 as Yugoton) owns the rights to many of their early recordings, and has produced a brace of astounding CD compilations (entitled *Čaje Šukarije* and *Hederlezi* respectively) that deserve to be snapped up by any self-respecting world-music fan.

Finally, one artist whose name you'll see everywhere – but whose albums you may not want to buy – is **Marko Perković Thompson**, a rabblerousing right-winger whose anthemic tunes owe a great deal – rather paradoxically given his political stance – to the Balkan-tinged folk pop that once ruled the airwaves of the former Yugoslavia. A participant in the 1991–95 war (and taking his nickname from a well-known make of machine gun), Thompson purveys a simple and at times extreme brand of nationalism – some of the fans who pack out his concerts wear black shirts in order to drive the point home. His songs are at least delivered with authentic feeling, which helps to explain why his 2002 collection *Ej moj narode!* ("Oh my people!") was one of the biggest-selling albums in Croatian history.

Books

There's a dearth of good books about Croatia in the English language. Many of the most entertaining accounts are by nineteenth-century travellers to the Adriatic though, sadly, their books are often only available from larger public libraries or specialist book dealers. The number of publications devoted to the break-up of the former Yugoslavia is considerable: we've listed the best of them, rather than trying to offer an exhaustive survey of the entire field. In the reviews that follow, "o/p" means out of print; titles marked ⚹ are especially recommended.

Travel writing

Abbé Alberto Fortis *Travels into Dalmatia* (o/p). Classic eighteenth-century travelogue written by an Italian priest and containing a mine of historical anecdote and observations. Fortis's tendency to romanticize the simple and brutish lifestyles of the locals exerted a strong influence over subsequent generations of travel writers.

T.G. Jackson *Dalmatia, the Quarnero and Istria* (o/p). First published in 1887, this is an illuminating and exhaustive three-volume guide to the architecture of the Adriatic coast, with sizeable dollops of history and reportage en route.

A.A. Paton *Highlands and Islands of the Adriatic* (o/p). Record of a journey made in 1846–47 with the usual mixture of historical anecdote and firsthand description. Very good for

local colour, and especially strong on social life in nineteenth-century Split and Dubrovnik. Paton finished his life as the British consul in Dubrovnik – his grave can still be seen in the cemetery on Liechtensteinov put.

⚹ **Rebecca West** *Black Lamb and Grey Falcon*. Classic travel book based on West's journey through Yugoslavia in the 1930s. Mixing opinionated observations with character sketches and extensive forays into history, this is definitely an acquired taste, particularly the sweeping generalizations about the Balkan Slavs, about whom West has the tendency to be over-rhapsodic. The first quarter of the book covers Croatia, after which the intrepid author moves on to Bosnia, Serbia, Macedonia and Montenegro.

History and politics

Phyllis Auty *Tito* (o/p). Originally researched when the dictator was still alive, this book is over-deferential towards its subject and offers little in the way of salacious gossip. However it's still the best available chronology of the man and his career, and works quite well as a general history of twentieth-century Yugoslavia.

Ivo Banac *The National Question in Yugoslavia*. Absorbing history of the competing currents of Croatian nationalism, Serbian nationalism and Yugoslavism, culminating with the Vidovdan Constitution of 1921.

Catherine Wendy Bracewell *The Uskoks of Senj: Piracy, Banditry and Holy War in the Sixteenth-century*

Adriatic. Definitive and scholarly account of the Uskoks, which lays to rest some of the more romantic myths surrounding their freebooting activities. It's also an excellent introduction to sixteenth-century Adriatic life in general.

Milovan Djilas *Tito: the Story from Inside* (o/p). Montenegrin communist Djilas was Tito's right-hand man in the 1940s, before falling foul of the regime and becoming Yugoslavia's most celebrated dissident. As lighthearted as it is bitter, this is an entertaining series of digressions on the nature of power rather than a straightforward biography. The same author's *Conversations with Stalin* and *The New Class* offer further insights into the workings of the communist mind.

Ivo Goldstein *Croatia*. Sober, impartial overview of Croatian history from the earliest times to the present day, written by a leading medievalist at Zagreb University.

Tim Judah *The Serbs*. Excellent analysis of the main themes in Serbian history, providing illuminating background to Serbia's central role in all the Balkan conflicts of the 1990s. The same author's *Kosovo: War and Revenge* takes the story up to NATO's campaign against Belgrade in 1999.

Bariša Krekić *Dubrovnik in the 14th and 15th Centuries: a City between East and West* (o/p). Probably the best English-language introduction to Dubrovnik's golden age, if you can find it.

★ **John R. Lampe** *Yugoslavia as History*. If a general account of Yugoslavia and its peoples is what you're looking for, then this is the best place to start – the author has carefully sifted all the existing scholarship on the subject to produce an objective, accessible history.

Michael McConville *A Small War in the Balkans* (o/p). Chapter and verse on British commando campaigns in the former Yugoslavia during World War II, written – with an eye for telling detail rather than dewy-eyed nostalgia – by one of the old soldiers themselves.

★ **Marcus Tanner** *Croatia: a Nation Forged in War*. The best general history of Croatia currently available. Balanced, thorough, and written with enthusiasm and verve by an *Independent* journalist who observed Yugoslavia's disintegration at first hand.

The break-up of Yugoslavia

Mark Almond *Europe's Backyard War*. Well-informed analysis of Yugoslavia's break-up written by an academic historian. It's broadly sympathetic to the Croatian cause, and Almond's most forceful prose is directed against the cynicism of Serbian policy and the hapless blundering of the Western powers.

Christopher Bennett *Yugoslavia's Bloody Collapse*. Scholarly and informed account from a journalist who was in Yugoslavia when war broke out. His central thesis – that Yugoslavia's break-up was far from inevitable until the rise of Serbian national communism under Milošević – is convincingly argued.

★ **Misha Glenny** *The Fall of Yugoslavia*. Vivid and often moving front-line reportage of the conflict by the BBC's former central Europe correspondent. The book is regarded by some Croat observers as being pro-Serb – a tribute to Glenny's impassioned objectivity. The same author's *The Balkans* is a compendious account of southeastern European history from the early nineteenth century onwards, in which Croatia plays a walk-on part. It's sometimes too wide ranging for its own good, but Glenny's attempt to explain the history of the Balkans

– and the outside world's meddling in Balkan affairs – is consistently readable and thought-provoking.

Brian Hall *The Impossible Country*. Hall travelled through Croatia, Serbia and other parts of Yugoslavia during the summer of 1991, just as the country was beginning to fall apart. As well as being a studiously impartial observer, he is an excellent writer, historically informed, witty and humane, and the result is one of the most compelling accounts of the last days of Yugoslavia you will find.

★ **Branka Magaš** *The Destruction of Yugoslavia: Tracking the Break-up 1980–1992* (o/p). Collection of essays and articles written by a veteran Yugoslavia-watcher. Not much on Croatia, but excellent analysis of Milošević's rise and his single-handed demolition of Yugoslav federalism.

Alec Russell *Prejudice and Plum Brandy*. Wide-ranging Balkan reportage from the Romanian revolution to the Yugoslav break-up, including a revealing eye-witness account of the siege of Dubrovnik, when the author was holed up in the *Hotel Argentina*.

Louis Sell *Slobodan Milošević and the Destruction of Yugoslavia*. Incisive biography of the man who singlehandedly destroyed the Yugoslav ideal while blithely claiming to defend it. Written by a former US diplomat who observed Milošević at close quarters.

Brendan Simms *Unfinest Hour: Britain and the Destruction of Bosnia.* Masterly dissection of the cynicism, incompetence and pure intellectual cowardice that characterized British policy towards the former Yugoslavia in the 1990s. Simms convincingly argues that British dithering was crucial in prolonging the Bosnian war (and the misery of its inhabitants), although he rejects the theory – popular among Croatian nationalists – that the British secret services deliberately stoked the conflict between the Bosnia's Croats and Muslims.

★ **Laura Silber and Alan Little** *The Death of Yugoslavia* (UK)/*Yugoslavia: Death of a Nation* (US). Combining journalistic immediacy with prodigious research, this is by far the best blow-by-blow account of the war, although it sheds little light on the long-term causes of Yugoslavia's demise. The authors had access to many of the key players in the events described, resulting in a wealth of revealing quotes.

Mark Thompson *A Paper House*. Thompson travelled throughout Yugoslavia on the eve of its break-up to produce this insightful book, part travelogue, part analysis of a fragmenting society. The same author's *Forging War: the Media in Croatia, Serbia, Bosnia and Hercegovina* examines the role of the Yugoslav press in stoking ethnic hatred.

Croatian literature

Ivo Andrić *The Bridge on the Drina*. A Croat who grew up in Bosnia and wrote in the Serbian literary language, Andrić left a vast body of work which currently lies unclaimed by any of Yugoslavia's successor states – despite the fact that he won the Nobel Prize for Literature in 1960. A complex, generation-spanning narrative set in Bosnia under the Ottoman Empire, this book is typical of Andrić's oeuvre.

Slavenka Drakulić *As If I Was Not There* (UK)/*A Novel About the Balkans* (US). Unflinching, often harrowing novel about a Bosnian woman's experience of life in a Serbian internment camp, written by one of Croatia's leading novelists. Drakulić's previous novel, *The Taste of* *a Man*, couldn't be more different, dealing with love and cannibalism in New York. Earlier works *Marble Skin* and *Holograms of Fear* are short on plot, but offer powerful meditations on sensuality and mortality respectively. Drakulić's book of essays, *Café Europa*, eloquently captures the author's dismay at the flowering of nationalism in the former Yugoslavia.

★ **Miljenko Jergović** *Sarajevo Marlboro*. A Bosnian Croat who grew up in Sarajevo and currently lives in Zagreb, Jergović is one of Croatia's most productive novelists, essayists and magazine feature-writers. This sparkling collection of short stories recounts Balkan lives, loves and tragedies with the kind of wry, self-deprecating humour that's typical of the city in the title.

★ **Miroslav Krleža** *The Return of Philip Latinowicz*. The best-known novel by Croatia's leading twentieth-century writer, in which a painter returns home to a provincial Slavonian town sometime in the 1920s and embarks on an affair which ends in tragedy. Intended as a

dissection of Croatia's directionless upper classes in the wake of World War I, it's not as powerful as his *On the Edge of Reason*, set in the same period, which convincingly preaches the message that bourgeois society is a form of self-deluding madness, but to rebel against it drives you insane.

Slobodan Novak *Gold, Frankincense and Myrrh* (o/p). A difficult but rewarding read, this sombre, meditative study of a man looking after his sick and elderly mother one winter on the island of Rab was highly regarded in Yugoslavia when it was first published in the 1970s.

Dubravka Ugrešić *The Museum of Unconditional Surrender*. Dismayed by Croatia's descent into right-wing authoritarianism, Ugrešić spent most of the 1990s living outside Croatia, and this largely autobiographical novel is a powerful meditation on memory and exile. By the same author, the heavyweight collection of essays *Culture of Lies* is an essential read for anyone interested in the negative side of Croatian culture and nationalism in the 1990s.

Language

Language

Grammar and pronunciation 441

Useful words and phrases..442

Food and drink..445

Glossary 449

Croatian

C **roatian** is a difficult language to learn, and the locals rarely expect anyone to bother, making them all the more pleasantly surprised if you make the effort to learn a few phrases. The vast majority of Croatians speak at least one foreign language: most people – especially the young – understand some English, while German and Italian are also widely spoken on the coast.

Croats, Serbs and Bosnians can understand one another perfectly well, despite developing separate literary languages at different times in their history; Croatian, Serbian and Bosnian are usually regarded as dialects of a single Slavonic language described by linguists as **Croato–Serbian** or **Serbo–Croat** (although native speakers hardly ever use either description themselves). That said, each community has preserved its own linguistic idiosyncrasies, even in areas where they have lived side by side for generations.

You'll find variations in **dialect** all over Croatia itself, the principal ones being named after the three different ways of saying "what?" – *kaj?*, *ča?* and *što?* In Zagreb and the Zagorje people speak *kajkavski*, because of their use of the word *kaj* for "what", while on the Adriatic coast people speak *čakavski*, and in Hercegovina and Slavonia *štokavski*. The literary language is based on *štokavski*, and although the other dialects are heard on the streets, they don't feature on the radio, TV or in newspapers – except in a humorous context.

The best of the **self-study courses** available are *Colloquial Croatian and Serbian* by Celia Hawkesworth (Routledge), closely followed by *Teach Yourself Serbo-Croat* by David Norris (Hodder Headline). Both books concentrate on the Croatian variant of the language, although Serbian reading passages are also included.

Grammar and pronunciation

There are three **genders** in Croatian – masculine, feminine and neuter. Masculine nouns usually end with a consonant, feminine nouns with a *-a*, neuter nouns with *-o* or *-e*. Plurals are usually formed by adding *-i*, *-ovi* or *-evi* to masculine nouns (*autobus*, bus, becomes *autobusi*, buses; *vlak*, train, becomes *vlakovi*, trains); *-e* to feminine nouns (*plaža*, beach, becomes *plaže*, beaches); and *-a* to neuter nouns (*auto*, car, becomes *auta*, cars) – although there are plenty of irregular nouns which don't follow these rules exactly. It's also worth bearing in mind that there are six noun **cases** in Croatian, ensuring that each noun (and any adjectives qualifying it) changes its ending according to what part of the sentence it occupies. Travelling around the coast, for example, you'll notice that "*u Dubrovnik*" means "to Dubrovnik", "*u Dubrovniku*" means "in Dubrovnik", and "*od Dubrovnika*" means "from Dubrovnik". Similarly, look out for *u Pulu* (to Pula), *u Puli* (in Pula), and *od Pule* (from Pula).

Pronunciation is not as difficult as it first appears. Every word is spoken exactly as it's written, and each letter represents an individual sound. The only letters you're likely to have problems with are the following consonants, which differ from their English equivalents.

c	"ts" as in cats	g	always hard, as in get
č	"ch" as in church	j	"y" as in youth
b	a softer version of č; similar to the "t" in future	r	always rolled; fulfils the function of a vowel in words like Hrvatska ("Croatia")
đ	somewhere between the "d" in endure and the "j" in jam	š	"sh" as in shoe
		ž	"s" as in pleasure

There are no hard-and-fast rules governing **stress** in Croatian, save to say that it hardly ever falls on the last syllable of a word, and quite frequently falls on the first.

Useful words and phrases

Greetings and civilities

hello/good day	**dobar dan**	good morning	**dobro jutro**
hi!/bye!	**bog!**	good evening	**dobra večer**
how are you? (polite)	**kako ste?**	good night	**laku noć**
how are you? (informal)	**kako si?**	goodbye	**do viđenja**
fine, thanks	**dobro, hvala**	please	**molim**
whassup?/where have you been?	**gdje si? (literally: "where are you?")**	thank you (very much)	**hvala (lijepo)**
		excuse me	**izvinite**
what have you been up to?/what's new?	**što radiš? (literally: "what are you doing?")**	sorry	**oprostite** or **sorry**
		here you are	**izvolite**
		let's go!	**hajdemo!**

Basic terms and phrases

yes	**da**	I don't understand	**ne razumijem**
no	**ne**	I don't know	**ne znam**
when?	**kada?**	what is this called in Croatian?	**kako se zove ovo na hrvatskom?**
where?	**gdje?**		
why?	**zašto?**	Croatia	**Hrvatska**
how much?	**koliko?**	Croatian person (m)	**Hrvat**
large	**veliko**	Croatian person (f)	**Hrvatica**
small	**malo**	Croatian language	**Hrvatski**
more	**više**	where are you from (polite)?	**odakle ste?**
less	**manje**		
good	**dobro**	where are you from (familiar)?	**odakle si?**
bad	**loše**		
cheap	**jeftino**	I am from . . .	**Ja sam iz . . .**
expensive	**skupo**	Australia	**Australije**
open	**otvoreno**	Canada	**Kanade**
closed	**zatvoreno**	Great Britain	**Velike Britanije**
hot	**toplo**	Ireland	**Irske**
cold	**hladno**	New Zealand	**Nove Zelandije**
with/without	**sa/bez**	the US	**Amerike**
do you speak English?	**govorite li engleski?**		

Directions and getting around

where to?	**kamo?/kuda?**	the nearest hotel	**najbliži hotel**
where is . . . ?	**gdje je?/gdje se nalazi . . . ?**	here	**ovdje**
		there	**tamo**
the nearest bank	**najbliža banka**	left	**lijevo**

right	**desno**	bus/ferry/train leave for . . . ?	**sljedeći autobus/ trajekt/vlak za ...?**
straight on	**pravo**		
backwards	**natrag**	is it running late?	**ima li zakašnenja?**
above; upstairs	**gore**	a ticket for . . . please	**jednu kartu za ... molim**
below; downstairs	**dolje**		
north	**sjever**	single	**u jednom pravcu**
south	**jug**	return	**povratnu kartu**
east	**istok**	can I reserve a seat?	**mogu li rezervirati sjedište?**
west	**zapad**		
I'm lost (m)	**Izgubio sam se**	no smoking	**zabranjeno pušenje**
I'm lost (f)	**Igubila sam se**	entrance	**ulaz**
is it nearby?	**je li to blizu?**	exit	**izlaz**
how far is it?	**koliko je daleko?**	beach	**plaža**
airport	**zračna luka**	car park	**parkiralište**
(bus/train) station	**(autobusni/ ž eljeznički) kolodvor**	cinema	**kino**
		embassy	**veleposlanstvo**
		gallery	**galerija**
platform	**kolosijek**	hospital	**bolnica**
bus stop	**stajalište autobusa**	market	**tržnica**
		museum	**muzej**
tram stop	**tramvajsko stajalište**	optician	**optičar**
		petrol station/gas station	**benzinska stanica**
port	**luka**	pharmacy	**ljekarna**
ferry terminal	**trajektna luka**	police station	**policijska stanica**
pier	**gat**	post office	**pošta**
mooring	**vez**	shop	**dućan**
left-luggage office	**garderoba**	stadium	**stadion**
arrival	**polazak**	supermarket	**samoposluga**
departure	**odlazak**	swimming pool	**bazen**
what time does the train/bus/ferry leave?	**u koliko sati polazi vlak/autobus/ trajekt?**	theatre	**kazalište**
		tourist office	**turistički ured** or **turistički informativni centar**
when does the next	**kada polazi**		

Accommodation

do you have . . .	**imate li . . .**	full board/half board	**pansion/polupansion**
a (single/double) room?	**(jednokrevetnu/ dvokrevetnu) sobu?**	I have a reservation	**imam rezervaciju**
		can I book a room?	**mogu li rezervirati sobu?**
an apartment	**apartman**		
a private room	**privatnu sobu**	the tap/light/telephone/ TV/air conditioning doesn't work	**slavina/svijetlo/ telefon/televizor/ klimatizacija ne radi**
with . . .	**sa . . .**		
a double bed	**francuskim ležajem**		
a shower/bath	**tušem/banjom**	key	**ključ**
a sea view	**pogledom na more**	where's the nearest campsite?	**gdje je najbliži autokamp?**
can I see the room?	**mogu li pogledati sobu?**		
		tent	**šator**
do you have anything cheaper?	**imate li nešto jeftinije?**	caravan	**prikolica**
		sleeping bag	**vreća za spavanje**
bed and breakfast	**noćenje i doručak**		

Shopping

where can I buy . . . ?	**gdje mogu kupiti . . . ?**	postcards	**razglednice**
bathing costume	**kupaći kostim**	soap	**sapun**
batteries	**baterije**	toilet paper	**toaletni papir**
cigarettes	**cigarete**	toothpaste	**pastu za zube**
cigarette lighter	**upaljač**	towel	**ručnik**
corkscrew	**vadičep**	washing powder	**prašak za pranje**
food	**hranu**	how much does it cost?	**koliko stoji/koliko**
matches	**šibice**		**košta?**
phonecard	**telekartu**	that's expensive	**to je skupo**
postage stamps	**poštanske marke**		

Numbers

1	**jedan**	17	**sedamnaest**
2	**dva**	18	**osamnaest**
3	**tri**	19	**devetnaest**
4	**četiri**	20	**dvadeset**
5	**pet**	21	**dvadeset i jedan**
6	**šest**	30	**trideset**
7	**sedam**	40	**četrdeset**
8	**osam**	50	**pedeset**
9	**devet**	60	**šezdeset**
10	**deset**	70	**sedamdeset**
11	**jedanaest**	80	**osamdeset**
12	**dvanaest**	90	**devedeset**
13	**trinaest**	100	**sto**
14	**četrnaest**	200	**dvjesta**
15	**petnaest**	300	**trista**
16	**šesnaest**	1000	**tisuća**

Times and dates

day	**dan**	Tuesday	**utorak**
week	**tjedan**	Wednesday	**srijeda**
month	**mjesec**	Thursday	**četvrtak**
year	**godina**	Friday	**petak**
today	**danas**	Saturday	**subota**
tomorrow	**sutra**	Sunday	**nedjelja**
yesterday	**jučer**	holiday	**praznik**
the day after tomorrow	**prekosutra**	church holiday, saint's day	**blagdan**
the day before yesterday	**prekjučer**	January	**siječanj**
in the morning	**ujutro**	February	**veljača**
in the afternoon	**popodne**	March	**ožujak**
in the evening	**uvečer**	April	**travanj**
early	**rano**	May	**svibanj**
late	**kasno**	June	**lipanj**
what time is it?	**koliko je sati?**	July	**srpanj**
hour	**sat**	August	**kolovoz**
minute	**minuta**	September	**rujan**
10 o'clock	**deset sati**	October	**listopad**
10.15	**deset i petnaest**	November	**studeni**
10.30	**deset i trideset** *or*	December	**prosinac**
	pola jedanaest	spring	**proljeće**
10.45	**petnaest do**	summer	**ljeto**
	jedanaest	autumn	**jesen**
Monday	**ponedjeljak**	winter	**zima**

Food and drink

Basic terms

čaša	glass	nož	knife
dobar tek!	bon appetit!	pečeno *or* u pećnici	baked
doručak	breakfast		
gableci	brunch	pekarna or pekarnica	bakery
hrana	food	pladanj	platter
ispod peke *or* pod pekom	baked under a lid covered with hot embers	pohani	fried in breadcrumbs
		prženo	fried
		račun	bill
jelovnik	menu	ručak	lunch
konoba	inn, tavern, folksy restaurant	slastičarnica	patisserie
		šolja	cup
kuhano	boiled	tanjur	plate
marenda	brunch	večera	dinner
lešo	boiled	viljuška	fork
na ražnju	spit roasted	zajutrak	breakfast
na roštilju/na žaru	grilled	živjeli!	cheers!
nazdravje!	cheers!	žlica	spoon

Basic foods

burek	greasy pastry, usually filled with cheese	omlet	omelette
		papar	pepper
jaje	egg	pašteta	paté
jogurt	yogurt	pekmez	jam
kifla	breakfast pastry, croissant	riža	rice
		salata	salad
kruh	bread	salsa	tomato sauce
maslac	butter	šećer	sugar
masline	olives	sir	cheese
maslinovo ulje	olive oil	sol	salt
med	honey	umak	sauce
mlijeko	milk	vrhnje	cream
ocat	vinegar		

Soups (*juhe*) and starters (*predjela*)

fažol	bean soup from Istria	paški sir	hard piquant cheese from the island of Pag
grah	soup made from haricot beans		
		pršut	home-cured ham similar to Italian prosciutto
jota	bean-and-sauerkraut soup		
		sir iz ulja	hard yellow cheese with piquant rind, kept under vegetable or olive oil
kobasica	sausage		
kozji sir	goat's cheese		
kulen	spicy paprika-flavoured pork and beef salami from Slavonia		
		sir s vrhnjem	cream cheese
		škripavac	mild hard cheese from Lika
maneštra	bean-and-vegetable soup from Istria		
		šunka	ham
punjene paprike	stuffed peppers	vrat	cured pork neck
ovčji sir	sheep's cheese		

Vegetables (*povrće*) and pasta (*tjestenine*)

ajvar	spicy relish made from puréed aubergines and peppers	krastavac	cucumber, gherkin
		krumpir	potato
		kukuruz	corn on the cob
bijeli luk	garlic	kupus	cabbage
blitva	spinach-like leaves of mangelwurzel (eaten with fish)	luk	onion
		mlinci	ragged sheets of baked pasta dough
češnjak	garlic	mrkva	carrot
đuveč *or* đuveđ	ratatouille-style mixture of vegetables and rice, heavily flavoured with paprika	njoki	gnocchi
		paprika	pepper, paprika
		paradajz, pomadora *or* rajčica	tomato
fuži	pasta twirls	patlidžan	aubergine
gljiva	mushroom	repa	turnip
grah	beans; also bean soup	šampinjoni	champignon mushrooms
grašak	peas		
hren	horseradish	šparoga	asparagus
kapulica	spring onion	šurlice	pasta twirls
kiseli kupus	sauerkraut	tartufi	truffle

Fish (*riba*)

bakalar	cod (often dried)	mušule	mussels
barbun	mullet	orada	gilthead sea bream
brancin	sea bass	oslić	hake
brodet	fish stew	ostrige	oysters
cipal	golden grey mullet	pastrva	trout
crni rižot	squid risotto	rak	crab
dagnje	mussels	ribice	whitebait, sprats
girice	small fish like whitebait, usually deep fried whole	riblja salata	literally "fish salad", usually octopus
		šaran	carp
hobotnica	octopus	sipa	cuttlefish
iglica	garfish	škampi	scampi
jakopove kapice	scallops	školjke	mussels
jastog	lobster	škrpan/škrpina	groper, sea scorpion
jegulja	eel	skuša	mackerel
kalamari	squid	smuđ	pike-perch
kamenice	oysters	som	catfish
kapica	clam	srdele	anchovies
kovač	John Dory	štuka	pike
lignje	squid	trilja	striped or red mullet
list	sole	žablji kraci	frogs' legs
lubin	sea perch	zubatac	dentex

Meat (*meso*) and poultry (*perjad*)

arambašica	cabbage leaves stuffed with meat and rice	ombolo	Istrian pork chop
		panceta	bacon
bečki odrezak	Wiener schnitzel	pašticada	beef cooked in wine, vinegar and prunes
bubrezi	kidneys		
buncek	pork hock	patka	duck
ćevapčići *or* ćevapi	grilled mincemeat rissoles	piletina	chicken
		pljeskavica	hamburger-style minced-meat patty
čobanec	paprika-flavoured meat stew		
govedina	beef	pulić	donkey
gulaš	goulash	purica	turkey
guska	goose	ražnjići	pieces of pork grilled on a skewer; kebab
janjetina	lamb		
jetra	liver	sarma	cabbage leaves stuffed with rice
koljenica	pork knuckle		
kotlet	cutlet, chop	slanina	bacon
kunić	rabbit	srnetina	venison
lungić	lean, boneless and tender pork chop	svinjetina	pork
		teletina	veal
mućkalica	paprika-flavoured meat stew	tuka	turkey
		zagrebački odrezak	schnitzel stuffed with ham and cheese and fried in breadcrumbs
nogice	pigs' trotters		
odrezak	escalope of veal or pork		

Desserts (*deserti*)

fritule *or* uštipci	deep-fried dough balls dusted with icing sugar	orehnjača	walnut cake
		palačinke	pancakes
kolač	cake	rožata	creme-caramel-style custard from Dubrovnik
kremšnita	cream cake or custard slice		
		savijača *or* štrudla	strudel
krofna	doughnut	štrukli	dough blobs stuffed with cheese
kroštule	deep-fried twists of pastry		
		sladoled	ice cream
makovnjača	poppy seed cake	torta	gateau

Fruit (*voće*)

ananas	pineapple	kruška	pear
banana	banana	limun	lemon
breskva	peach	lubenica	watermelon
dinja	melon	naranča	orange
grožđe	grapes	šljiva	plum
jabuka	apple	smokva	fig
jagoda	strawberry	trešnja	cherry
kajsija	apricot	višnja	sour cherry

Drinks (*pića*)

bambus	red wine and cola	pelinkovac	bitter juniper-based aperitif
bevanda	wine mixed with water		
bijelo vino	white wine	penjušac	sparkling wine
biska	mistletoe-flavoured brandy	pivo	beer
borovnica	bilberry juice	rakija	brandy
čaj	tea	šljivovica	plum brandy
crno vino	red wine	sok	juice
crveno vino	rosé wine	špricer	white wine and soda
džus *or* đus	juice	svjetlo pivo	light, lager-style beer
gemišt	white wine and mineral water	topla čokolada	hot chocolate
		travarica	herb-based spirit similar to Italian *grappa*
kava	coffee		
limunada	lemonade	viljamovka	pear brandy
loza/lozovača	grape brandy	voda	water
medenica/ medovina	honey-flavoured brandy	vodka	vodka
		led	ice
mineralna voda	mineral water	s ledom	with ice
orahovača	walnut-flavoured brandy	bez leda	without ice

Glossary

General terms

Autocesta Motorway.
Beč Vienna.
Beograd Belgrade.
Brdo/Brijeg Hill.
Buk Waterfall.
Bura Strong wind which often blows in northern Adriatic.
Centar Centre.
Cesta Road.
Crkva Church.
Dolac Dell (in karst areas, a small cultivable area enclosed by wall).
Dolina Valley.
Donji grad Lower town.
Draga Vale, bay.
Dvor Palace, court, courtyard.
Dvorac Castle.
Dvorište Yard, courtyard.
Fortica Fortress.
Gaj Grove.
Gat Quay.
Gornji grad Upper town.
Grad Town.
Gradska vijećnica Town hall.
Groblje Graveyard.
Hram Temple, church.
Jadran Adriatic Sea.
Jama Pit, cave.
Jezero Lake.
Kamenjar Stony, infertile land; used to describe the arid areas of Hercegovina and inland Dalmatia.
Kaštel Castle, fortress.
Kavana Café.
Kolo Folk dance.
Kolodvor Station.
Konoba Inn, tavern, folksy restaurant.
Korzo Evening promenade.
Krčma Inn, tavern.
Kuća House.
Lučka kapetanija Harbourmaster's office.
Luka Port.
Lungomare Shoreline road or promenade.
Maestral North wind.
Magistrala Highway running the length of the Adriatic coast.

Mandrać Inner harbour for small boats.
Mleci Venice.
More Sea.
Most Bridge.
Obala Shore, quayside.
Oluja Storm.
Otok Island.
Palača Palace.
Park prirode Nature park, nature reserve.
Perivoj Park, public garden.
Plaža Beach.
Poljana/Polje Field, square.
Poluotok Peninsula.
Put Road, way.
Rat/Rt Cape.
Rijeka River.
Riva Seafront.
Riznica Treasury.
Samostan Monastery.
Selo Village.
Stajalište Bus stop.
Stari grad (i) Old town; (ii) Castle.
Staza Path.
Šetalište Walkway, promenade.
Školj Small island.
Škor/Škver Shipyard or part of fishing village where boats are repaired.
Špilja Cave.
Šuma Forest, wood.
Toranj Tower.
Trg Square.
Tržnica Market.
Tvrđava Fortress.
Ulica Street.
Uvala Bay.
Varoš Central residential quarter of an old town.
Vijećnica Council chamber, town hall.
Vikendica Holiday house or cottage.
Vodopad Waterfall.
Vrata Gate, door.
Vrh Peak.
Vrt Garden.
Žal Beach.
Zaljev Bay, gulf.
Zdenac Well.

Ždrilo Gorge.
Zidine Walls.

Županija County.
Zvonik Bell-tower, campanile.

Artistic and architectural terms

Apse Semicircular recess at the altar (usually eastern) end of a church.

Baldachin Canopy, often resting on columns, above main altar.

Cardo Principal north–south street in a Roman town.

Caryatid Pillars in the form of women, often decorating the facade of a building.

Ciborium See "Baldachin".

Decumanus Principal east–west street in a Roman town.

Incunabula Books printed before 1500.

Lapidarium Collection of sculpture.

Loggia Arcaded porch – often in front of the town hall – intended to provide Renaissance citizenry with a place to meet and talk.

Lunette Semicircular niche above a doorway or portal.

Peristyle Colonnade surrounding a courtyard or building.

Plutej Pleatwork design characteristic of early medieval Croatian stone carving.

Polyptych Painting on several joined wooden panels.

Revelin Bastion; defensive tower.

Secession Movement of artists who split from Vienna's Academy of Arts in 1897. Also used more generally as a term roughly synonymous with Art Nouveau.

Political and historical terms

Austria-Hungary Official name adopted by the Habsburg Empire in 1867, designed to make the Hungarians feel that they were equal partners with the Austrians in the imperial enterprise.

AVNOJ Literally "anti-fascist council of national liberation of Yugoslavia", a provisional parliament established by the Partisans during World War II, first convened in Jajce, Bosnia-Hercegovina, in 1943.

Ban Governor or viceroy. Title given to rulers of Croatia appointed by Hungarian (later Austrian) monarchs.

Blijesak "Flash". Name given to the Croatian Army offensive which drove Serbian forces out of western Slavonia in 1995.

Bošnjak Bosnian Muslim.

Četnik Serbian irregular fighter. The term was first coined during the anti-Turkish struggles of the nineteenth century and subsequently used to describe nationalist anti-communists in World War II, then Serbian forces active in Croatia and Bosnia in 1991–95.

Domovinski rat "Homeland War". Official Croatian name for the 1991–95 conflict.

Dragovoljac Croatian volunteer in the Domovinski rat (see above).

Frankopans Aristocratic family long associated with the island of Krk.

Glagolitic The script used by the Croatian Church in the early Middle Ages. Survived in some areas of Istria and the Kvarner region until the early nineteenth century, when it was replaced by the Latin script.

Habsburg Empire The central European state ruled by the Habsburg family, who first gained control of parts of Austria in the early thirteenth century, and went on to control an empire comprising – among others – Germans, Italians, Czechs, Slovaks, Hungarians, Slovenes and Croats. The empire was broken up in 1918.

Hajduk Brigand. Romantically associated with popular struggles against the Turks, the term has positive connotations for Croats, Serbs, Bulgarians and other southeast European peoples.

HDZ Croatian Democratic Union. Right-of-centre pro-independence political movement formed in 1989 and led by Franjo Tuđman. The governing party in Croatia from 1990 to 2000.

HRT Croatian Radio and Television. The main state-owned broadcasting network.

Hrvatski narodni preporod Croatian National Renaissance. Name given to the the mid-nineteenth-century upsurge in Croatian culture, language and consciousness.

HSLS Croatian Social Liberal Party. Croatia's main centre party; in opposition 1991–2000, briefly shared power with the SDP (see below) 2000–02.

HVO Croatian Defence Council. Formed by Croats in Bosnia-Hercegovina to organize themselves militarily against the Serbs (and subsequently Muslims) in the Bosnian war of 1992–95.

Illyria Roman name for the territories which are nowadays roughly covered by the states of Croatia, Bosnia-Hercegovina, Serbia and Albania. The term was resurrected by Napoleon in 1805 with the creation of the Illyrian Provinces, which stretched from Villach in southern Austria to Dubrovnik in Dalmatia. Some Western writers continued to use the term "Illyria" to describe the South Slav lands throughout the nineteenth century.

Illyrianism Early nineteenth-century Croatian cultural movement which stressed the linguistic affinities of Croats and Serbs.

JNA Yugoslav People's Army. Official title of Yugoslavia's army from 1945 to 1991. Generally sided with the Serbs during the 1991–92 conflict.

Knez Prince, duke or (in Dubrovnik and other Dalmatian towns) city governor or rector.

Kralj King.

Military frontier (Vojna krajina in Croatian; Militärgrenze in German). Belt of territory running along Croatia's border with Ottoman-controlled Bosnia-Hercegovina, created in the early sixteenth century and finally dismantled in the mid-nineteenth. Designed to prevent Ottoman expansion, it was under the direct rule of Habsburg military bodies in Graz or Vienna.

NDH Puppet Croatian state established under Nazi auspices 1941–45.

Non-Aligned Movement Created by Tito, Nehru and Nasser to give a voice to countries which existed outside the East–West divisions of the Cold War.

Oluja "Storm". The Croatian offensive of August 1995 which finally defeated secessionist Serb forces and brought an end to the war in Croatia.

Partisan Anti-fascist fighter in World War II.

Ragusa Old name for Dubrovnik.

RS Serbian Republic. Name adopted by Serbian-controlled areas of Bosnia after 1992.

RSK Republic of the Serbian Krajina. Serbian name for the territories controlled by Serbian secessionists in Croatia 1991–95.

Sabor Assembly, parliament.

SDP Social Democratic Party. Successor to the SKH. Principal opposition party from 1990 to 2000, and leading partner in the coalition elected to power in January 2000.

Developed in the 1950s to distinguish Yugoslav communism from the Soviet model.

SKH Croatian League of Communists.

SKJ Yugoslav League of Communists.

Uskok Sixteenth-century freebooters operating out of the port of Senj; see p.227.

Ustaša (plural Ustaše). Croatian nazi movement formed by Ante Pavelić which came to power with German help in 1941, forming the NDH.

Index

+ small print

Index

Map entries are in **colour**

A

accommodation 31–34
Adam, Robert 300, 305
Adriatic Gulag 239
airlines
  in Australia and
    New Zealand 16
  in Britain...............................11
  in Ireland 11
  in North America................14
d'Annunzio,
  Gabriele 195, 196
apartments......................32
Autocesta......................124

B

Bad Blue Boys..........59, 90
Bakar.............................225
Bale................................167
Ban Jelačić *see* Jelačić,
  Josip
banks...............................26
Bapska...........................134
Baranja..........................129
Barban 186
Baška 222
Baška Voda....................356
Batomalj.........................223
Belec..............................102
Beli 210
Beram 178
Bijele stijene..................143
Bilje 129
Biograd-na-moru 270
Biokovo..........................359
Biserujka Cave...............225
Biševo 339
Bjelolasica......................143
Blaca Hermitage 322
Blato...............................347
Blue Cave, The 339
Bol 320–322
Bollé, Hermann
  ....59, 69, 75, 80, 101
books 435–438
Boraja.............................284
Bosnia-Hercegovina,
  onward travel into 361
Božava...........................269
Brač 316–322
Brač 317

Brbinj.............................269
Brela..............................356
Brestova.........................189
Brijuni............................163
Brodarica 279
Broz, Josip *see* Tito
Buje...............................182
Bukovac,
  Vlaho...........76, 386, 393
Bura, The 225
buses
  in Croatia......................27–28
  to Croatia 20
Buševec 117
Buzet..............................183

C

Čakovec.........................112
campsites...................33–34
car rental 29–30
Cavtat 392
Cetina Gorge.................354
cigarettes 50
Čigoć 120
Čilipi 394
cinema 50
consulates......................21
costs 25
credit cards.....................26
Cres 208–212
Cres and Lošinj 208
Cres Town......................209
Crikvenica 226
Crna Mlaka 137
Crni lug 144
Čunkova Draga..............141
currency 25

D

Đakovo...........................131
Dalmatia 243–363
Dalmatia 246–247
Dalmatinac, Juraj..234, 240,
  278, 303, 369, 376, 380
d'Annunzio,
  Gabriele 195, 196
Delnice 144
Dinamo Zagreb..44, 59, 90
Diocletian.....292, 294, 312,
  319

directory 50
disabled travellers 49–50
diving 46
Dobrinj 224
Dominis,
  Markantun..........227, 235
Donja Kupčina 138
Donja Zdenčina.............138
Donje Čelo 395
Draguć 186
drinks 37–38
driving
  in Croatia......................29–30
  to Croatia 18–19
Drniš..............................283
Drvenik..........................360
Držić, Marin 309, 320
DUBROVNIK 367–391
Dubrovnik 377
Dubrovnik and the
  south.........................368
greater Dubrovnik..372–373
  accommodation 372
  arrival and information 371
  cathedral 381
  City Museum......................380
  city walls 376
  Dominican monastery.......383
  eating and drinking...........388
  festivals 390
  Franciscan monastery 378
  Gruž 387
  history 369
  Lokrum..............................386
  Lovrijenac..........................387
  Luža Square......................379
  Museum of Modern
    Art.................................386
  nightlife and
    entertainment 390
  Rector's Palace.................380
  Rijeka Dubrovačka............387
  Srđ 387
  St Blaise's Church 379
  Stradun 376
  synagogue 378
  the siege of 371
Dugi otok 268–270
Dugopolje......................314
Dužica 117
Dvigrad 179

E

Elaphite Islands ...394–396
embassies......................21

F

ferries
  in Croatia 28
  to Croatia 19
festivals 41–44
Fetivi, Boduli and Vlaji ..293
Firentinac,
  Nikola..277, 287, 289, 304
flights
  in Croatia 29
  to Croatia from Britain 10
  to Croatia from Ireland........10
  to Croatia from North
    America....................14–15
folk music..............429–434
food...........................34–37
football 44–45
Fortis, Abbé Alberto.....212,
  222, 250–251, 435
Frankopan family..113, 139,
  142, 217, 218, 222, 225,
  408
Fruška Gora 134

G

gays and lesbians in
  Croatia 50
Generalić, Ivan........72, 115
getting around Croatia
  by air...................................29
  by bus 27–28
  by car 29–30
  by ferry...............................28
  by train 27
getting to Croatia
  from Australia and New
    Zealand.....................15–16
  from Britain 9–13
  from Ireland........................10
  from North America 14–15
Glagolitic script.............222
glossary.................449–451
Goli otok 239
Gornja Stubica.............100
Gornje Čelo..................395
Gorski kotar 142–144
Gospić 229
Gračišće........................179
Grgur............................239
griffon vultures 211
Grožnjan.......................181
Gubec, Matija 72, 100

H

Hajduk Split 44, 295, 306
health 25

Hegedušić,
  Krsto .....72, 76 , 115, 180
Hektorović,
  Petar 324, 330, 331
hiking........................45–46
history of Croatia....403–428
Hlebine..........................115
Hlebine School 115
hostels 33
hotels 31
Hum 184
Hungary, onward travel
  to.......................112, 126
Hvar 322–333
Hvar 323
Hvar Town 324–330
Hvar Town 325

I

Ilok 135
Imotski 355
inland Croatia.................98
insurance 24
Internet..........................38
Istarske Toplice.............182
Istria 149–190
Istria............................152
Ivanić,
  Matija..........248, 324, 331
Iž...................................268

J

Jablanac 229
Jasenovac....................120
Jelačić,
  Josip 67, 143, 195, 410
Jelisavac 125
Jelsa............................332
Joyce, James........158, 163
Jurandvor.....................223
Jurjev, Blaž ...277, 288, 328,
  344, 345

K

Kali 266
Kampor 238
Kanfanar 179
Karlobag 229
Karlovac 138
Kaštel Gomilica.............291
Kaštel Kambelovac.......291
Kaštel Lukšić 291
Kaštel Novi....................291

Kaštel Štafilić 291
Kaštel Stari 291
Kaštel Sućurac.............291
Kaštela 290
Kastav 202
Klek (near Ogulin) 143
Klek (Dalmatia).............361
Klis 313
Knin......................118, 283
Koločep........................394
Komiža..........................336
Kopačevo......................130
Kopački Rit 129
Koprivnica.....................114
Korčula..................339–347
Korčula and the Pelješac
  Peninsula..................340
Korčula Town.......340–346
Korčula Town 341
Kornati archipelago.......271
Kotli..............................185
Koversada......................172
Krajina, the...118, 119, 283,
  421–422, 424
Kraljevica 225
Krapanj........................279
Krapina.........................106
Krapinske Toplice 106
Krapje...........................120
Krašić 141
Krk 216–225
Krk 217
Krk Town 218–220
Krka National Park........281
Kučište 351
Kukljica 267
Kula 125
Kumrovec......................102
Kvarner Gulf 191–242
Kvarner Gulf 194

L

Labin 187
land mines......................47
language 441–451
Lastovo 347–349
Lastovo Town................348
laundry 51
Lepoglava 107
Lika 144–146
Limski kanal 171
Lonja 120
Lonjsko polje................117
Lopar............................238
Lopud............................395
Lošinj....................213–216
Lovran 205

Ložišća..........................319
Lubenice 212
Lumbarda.....................346

M

Makarska 357
**Makarska Riviera,
  the**......................356–360
Mali Drvenik 290
Mali Lošinj....................213
Mali Ston.....................352
map outlets....................23
Marija Bistrica 101
Martinišćica..................212
Marulić,
  Marko..........79, 248, 304
Maslenica bridge 252
Maslinica......................316
media 39–40
Medveja 207
Meštrović, Ivan...70, 74, 77,
  109, 283, 288, 304,
  307–308, 318, 320, 392
Military
  Frontier.........59, 118, 407
Miljana..........................103
Milna 319
mines, unexploded 47
Mljet.....................397–398
Mljet National Park 398
mobile phones 39
money 25
Moreška, the...43, 341, 343
Morlachs,
  the 249, 250–251
Mošćenička Draga........208
Motovun.......................180
Mraclin 117
Muline 267
Murter 271
Mužilovčica 120

N

Naive art 72, 115
Našice 125
Naturist holidays..12–13, 51
NDH (Nezavisna država
  hrvatska or Independent
  State of Croatia)
  ....70, 118, 414
Nečujam........................316
Neum 361
newspapers and
  magazines 39–40

Nin..............................253
northern Dalmatia..252–291
Novalja 241
Novi Vinodolski 226
Novigrad (Istria)............175
Novigrad (Dalmatia) 252

O

Ogulin...........................142
Oluja (Operation Storm)
  ....119, 283, 423, 451
Omiš............................353
Opatija 202
opening hours................40
Oprtalj 181
Orebić 349
Osijek 126–129
Osijek...........................127
Osor 212
Otavice.........................283
Ozalj............................140

P

package holidays to
  Croatia
  from Britain 12–13
  from North America 14–15
Pag 239–242
Pag Town 240
Paklenica National
  Park....................229–231
Pakoštane.....................271
Papuk...........................125
Pašman.........................267
Pašman village..............267
Pasadur........................348
Pavelić, Ante...70, 308, 414
Pazin 177
**Pelješac
  peninsula**..........349–352
Pisko Bausfeld..............479
Plisko polje 339
Plitvice Lakes 144–147
Plitvice Lakes..............145
Ploče............................360
Plomin..........................189
Podgora 360
Poklad, The.....42, 347, 348
Polače 397
police 47
Pomena........................397
Poreč 172–175
Poreč 173
post offices 38
Požega..........................124

Pregrada 106
Preko...........................266
Pribić...........................141
Primošten.....................284
private rooms..................32
Privić Luka 281
Prizna...........................229
pršut ix
public holidays...............41
PULA 154–162
Pula.............................157
around Pula..................155
  accommodation...............155
  Amphitheatre 156
  arrival and information......154
  beaches 160
  eating, drinking and
    entertainment 161
  Forum.................................159
  Temple of Augustus..........159
Punat...........................221

R

Rab 231–238
Rab 231
Rab Town 232–238
Rab Town 233
Rabac...........................188
radio..............................40
rafting............................46
rail passes.......................17
Raša............................187
Rendić, Ivan...80, 317, 318,
  335, 382
RIJEKA 194–201
Rijeka...........................197
  accommodation...............197
  arrival and information......196
  carnival.............................201
  eating, drinking and
    entertainment 200
  history 194
  Old Town...........................198
  Trsat 199
Risnjak 144
Roč 184
Rogač 316
Rovinj 167–171
Rovinj...........................168
rural homestays 33

S

sailing 13
Sali 269
Salona..........................312
Samobor 135–137

Samobor hills 136
San Marino 238
Šarengrad 134
Savudrija 176
scuba diving 46
Seline 230
Senj 226
Šepurine 281
Šibenik 274–279
Šibenik 275
Silba 265
Šilo 224
Sinj 314
Šipan 396
Šipanska luka 396
Sisak 118
skiing 46
Skradin 282
Škrip 319
Slavonia 123–135
Slavonski Brod 130
Slunj 144
Sobra 397
Šolta 316
Sošice 141
southern
   Dalmatia 292–362
Sovinjak 186
SPLIT 292–311
Diocletian's Palace 301
Split 296–297
   accommodation 297
   Archeological Museum 305
   arrival and information 295
   Bačvice beach 309
   cathedral 302
   city transport 296
   Diocletian's Palace 300
   Diocletian's Palace 301
   drinking 310
   eating 309
   entertainment 310
   festivals 311
   history 293
   Kaštelet 307
   Marjan peninsula 306
   Meštrović Gallery 307
   Museum of Croatian
      Archeological
      Monuments 307
   nightlife 310
sport 44–45
Stara Baška 221
Stari Grad 330
Starigrad–Paklenica 229
Stari Limburg 499
Stepinac, Alojzije 69, 70,
   107, 122, 141, 416
Ston 351
Strossmayer,
   Josip Juraj ...76, 131, 410

Stubičke Toplice 100
studying in Croatia 48
Suđurađ 396
Supetar 317
Susak 216
Sutivan 319
Svetvinčenat 179

T

Telašćica Bay 270
telephones 38–39
television 40
tipping 51
Tito, Josip Broz 70, 103,
   104–105, 107, 136, 142,
   163, 164, 239, 334, 338,
   414–418
Tkon 268
toilets 51
tourist offices 22
trains
   in Croatia 27
   to Croatia 17
Trakošćan 107
travel agents and tour
   operators
   in Australia and
      New Zealand 16
   in Britain 11–13
   in Ireland 12
   in North America 14–15
traveller's cheques 26
Trilj 355
Trogir 285–290
Trogir 285
Trpanj 351
Trstenik 351
Trsteno 392
truffles 183
Tučepi 360
Tuđman, Franjo 59, 60,
   107, 104, 122, 284, 419,
   424–425
Turpolje 116

U

Ubli 348
Učka 206
Ugljan 265–267
Ugljan village 267
Uluz Ali 324, 327, 331,
   332, 340, 344
Umag 176
Uskoks, the 227

V

Valun 212
vampires 347
Varaždin 108–112
Varaždin 110
vegetarians 36
Vela Luka 347
Velebit 228–231
Veli Drvenik 290
Veli Lošinj 215
Velika Gorica 117
Velika Mlaka 117
Veliki Tabor 103
Veneziano,
   Paolo 165, 236, 259
Viganj 351
Vinkovci 132
Vis 333–339
Vis 334
Vis Town 334
visas 21
Vlachs ...118, 249, 293, 407
Vladovići 314
Vodice 273
Vodnjan 165
Volosko 204
Vrančić, Faust 280
Vranjača Cave 314
Vrbnik 224
Vrboska 332
Vrsar 171
Vukovar 132–134

W

Waugh, Evelyn 338
websites 22
West,
   Rebecca 251, 370, 435
windsurfing 46
wiring money 26
women in Croatia 47
working in Croatia 48

Y

yachting 13

Z

ZADAR 255–264
Borik area 259
central Zadar 257
   accommodation 256

Archeological Museum 258
arrival and information 256
cathedral 260
eating, drinking and
    entertainment 262
Exhibition of Church Art ...259
Forum................................258
St Donat's Church 258
St Simeon's Church.........261
Zadvarje 355
ZAGREB 56–92
around Zagreb 58
Kaptol and Gradec 68
Zagreb 62–63
    accommodation..................64
    Archeological Museum 75
    arrival 60
    cathedral.............................69
    Donji grad 75

drinking 85
eating 83
entertainment......................88
Ethnographic Museum 78
festivals..............................88
Gallery of Naive Art............72
Gradec 71
history 58
information..........................60
Internet cafés.....................87
Jarun..................................81
Kaptol 69
Maksimir park 80
Medvedgrad.......................83
Meštrović Atelier................74
Mimara Museum.................77
Mirogoj cemetery...............80
Mount Medvednica 82
Museum of Arts and
    Crafts..............................77

Museum of Zagreb 74
nightlife 87
Novi Zagreb 81
public transport 61
shopping 91
Sljeme 82
sport...................................91
St Mark's Church 72
Technical Museum..............79
Trg bana Jelačića...............67
Zagorje 99–108
Zagorje 100
Zaklopatica 349
Zaostrog.........................360
Zlarin 280
Zlatar.............................102
Zrinski family........112, 113,
    225, 408
Žumberak............140–142

Twenty Years of Rough Guides

In the summer of 1981, Mark Ellingham, Rough Guides' founder, knocked out the first guide on a typewriter, with a group of friends. Mark had been travelling in Greece after university, and couldn't find a guidebook that really answered his needs.There were heavyweight cultural guides on the one hand – good on museums and classical sites but not on beaches and tavernas – and on the other hand student manuals that were so caught up with how to save money that they lost sight of the country's significance beyond its role as a place for a cool vacation. None of the guides began to address Greece as a country, with its natural and human environment, its politics and its contemporary life.

Having no urgent reason to return home, Mark decided to write his own guide. It was a guide to Greece that tried to combine some erudition and insight with a thoroughly practical approach to travellers' needs. Scrupulously researched listings of places to stay, eat and drink were matched by careful attention to detail on everything from Homer to Greek music, from classical sites to national parks and from nude beaches to monasteries. Back in London, Mark and his friends got their Rough Guide accepted by a farsighted commissioning editor at the publisher Routledge and it came out in 1982.

The Rough Guide to Greece was a student scheme that became a publishing phenomenon. The immediate success of the book – shortlisted for the Thomas Cook award – spawned a series that rapidly covered dozens of countries. The Rough Guides found a ready market among backpackers and budget travellers, but soon acquired a much broader readership that included older and less impecunious visitors. Readers relished the guides' wit and inquisitiveness as much as the enthusiastic, critical approach that acknowledges everyone wants value for money – but not at any price.

Rough Guides soon began supplementing the "rougher" information – the hostel and low-budget listings – with the kind of detail that independent-minded travellers on any budget might expect. These days, the guides – distributed worldwide by the Penguin group – include recommendations spanning the range from shoestring to luxury, and cover more than 200 destinations around the globe. Our growing team of authors, many of whom come to Rough Guides initially as outstandingly good letter-writers telling us about their travels, are spread all over the world, particularly in Europe, the USA and Australia. As well as the travel guides, Rough Guides publishes a series of dictionary phrasebooks covering two dozen major languages, an acclaimed series of music guides running the gamut from Classical to World Music, a series of music CDs in association with World Music Network, and a range of reference books on topics as diverse as the Internet, Pregnancy and Unexplained Phenomena. Visit **www.roughguides.com** to see what's cooking.

SMALL PRINT

Rough Guide credits

Text editor: Richard Lim
Series editor: Mark Ellingham
Editorial: Martin Dunford, Jonathan Buckley,
Kate Berens, Ann-Marie Shaw, Helena Smith,
Olivia Swift, Ruth Blackmore, Geoff Howard,
Claire Saunders, Gavin Thomas, Alexander
Mark Rogers, Polly Thomas, Joe Staines,
Duncan Clark, Peter Buckley, Lucy Ratcliffe,
Clifton Wilkinson, Alison Murchie, Matthew
Teller, Andrew Dickson, Fran Sandham,
Sally Schafer (UK); Andrew Rosenberg,
Yuki Takagaki, Richard Koss, Hunter Slaton
(US)
Cover art direction: Louise Boulton
Picture research: Sharon Martins,
Mark Thomas

Production: Link Hall, Helen Prior,
Julia Bovis, Katie Pringle, Rachel Holmes,
Andy Turner, Dan May
Cartography: Maxine Repath, Ed Wright,
Katie Lloyd-Jones
Online: Kelly Martinez, Anja Mutic-Blessing,
Jennifer Gold, Audra Epstein,
Suzanne Welles, Cree Lawson (US)
Finance: John Fisher, Gary Singh,
Edward Downey, Mark Hall, Tim Bill
Marketing & Publicity: Richard Trillo,
Niki Smith, David Wearn, Chloë Roberts,
Demelza Dallow, Claire Southern (UK);
David Wechsler, Megan Kennedy (US)
Administration: Julie Sanderson,
Karoline Densley

Publishing information

This second edition published June 2003 by
Rough Guides Ltd,
80 Strand, London WC2R 0RL.
345 Hudson St, 4th Floor,
New York, NY 10014, USA.
Distributed by the Penguin Group
Penguin Books Ltd,
80 Strand, London WC2R 0RL
Penguin Putnam, Inc.
375 Hudson Street, New York, NY 10014, USA
Penguin Books Australia Ltd,
487 Maroondah Highway, PO Box 257,
Ringwood, Victoria 3134, Australia
Penguin Books Canada Ltd,
10 Alcorn Avenue, Toronto, Ontario,
Canada M4V 1E4
Penguin Books (NZ) Ltd,
182–190 Wairau Road, Auckland 10,
New Zealand
Typeset in Bembo and Helvetica to an
original design by Henry Iles.

Printed in Italy by LegoPrint S.p.A

480pp includes index
A catalogue record for this book is available
from the British Library

ISBN 1-84353-084-8

The publishers and authors have done their
best to ensure the accuracy and currency of
all the information in **The Rough Guide to
Croatia**, however, they can accept no
responsibility for any loss, injury, or
inconvenience sustained by any traveller as a
result of information or advice contained in
the guide.

Help us update

We've gone to a lot of effort to ensure that
the second edition of **The Rough Guide to
Croatia** is accurate and up to date. However,
things change – places get "discovered",
opening hours are notoriously fickle,
restaurants and rooms raise prices or lower
standards. If you feel we've got it wrong or
left something out, we'd like to know, and if
you can remember the address, the price, the
time, the phone number, so much the better.

We'll credit all contributions, and send a
copy of the next edition (or any other Rough

Guide if you prefer) for the best letters.
Everyone who writes to us and isn't already a
subscriber will receive a copy of our full-
colour thrice-yearly newsletter. Please mark
letters: **"Rough Guide Croatia Update"** and
send to: Rough Guides, 80 Strand, London
WC2R 0RL, or Rough Guides, 4th Floor, 345
Hudson St, New York, NY 10014. Or send an
email to **mail@roughguides.com**

Have your questions answered and tell
others about your trip at
www.roughguides.atinfopop.com

Acknowledgements

Jonathan Bousfield would like to thank Reneta Deželjin, Željka Dubravica and everyone at the Hrvatska turistička zajednica. Thanks also go to Joshua Amidon, Višnja Arambašić, Robert Bacać, Vinko Bakija, Martina Csiffary, Mirjana Darrer, Nevenka Fuchs, Stanka Kraljević, Tonći Lalić, Marin Matošić, Maja Milovčić, Lidija Mišćin, Gordana Perić, Igor Prikaski, Nada Prodan-Mraković, Vesna from Pula and Elida Ravnić. Thanks are also due to Martin Dunford, Jack Holland and Kate Berens for getting the project underway, to Richard Lim for patient editing, Link Hall for layout, Sharon Martins for picture research, Katie Lloyd-Jones for cartography and Susannah Wight for proofreading.

Readers' letters

Thanks to the following readers who took the trouble to write in with their comments and suggestions (and apologies to anyone whose name we've misspelt or omitted).

Ray Ballantyne, Frank Bonner, Bruno van den Broecke, Licia Corbolante, Philip Fogarty and Anna Lardi, Mark Greaves, Kitty Gunsing, Jennifer A. Heindl, Jenny Hoggar, Neil Hunter, Judy Jennings, David Mediavilla, Robert and Sabine Monro, Alex Needham, Tony Nichols and Yves Jatteau, B.W. Roberts, Henry Sayers, Eithne Staunton,

SMALL PRINT

Photo Credits

Cover Credits

Main front picture Dalmatian Coast © Robert Harding

Small front top picture Arts & Crafts Museum, Zagreb © Robert Harding

Small front lower picture Pula © Getty

Back top picture Korita © Robert Harding

Back lower picture St Mark's Church, Zagreb © Robert Harding

Colour introduction section

Sunset over Vis © Croatia Tourist Board

Crashing waves at Brela © Croatia Tourist Board

Traditional fabric, Konavle © Croatia Tourist Board

Windsurfing, Bol © Jon Bousfield

Tower, Korčula © Croatia Tourist Board

Passengers sitting out on ferry deck © M. Barlow/TRIP

Sculpture, Mestrović Gallery grounds, Split © Jonathan Blair/CORBIS

Pršut © Croatia Tourist Board

Good Friday Procession © Hans Georg Roth/CORBIS

Ruins, Rab © Croatia Tourist Board

Opatija at dusk © Croatia Tourist Board

Ice cream parlour © Jon Bousfield

River rafting, Cetina © Croatia Tourist Board

Cooking meat *ispod peke* © Croatia Tourist Board

Zrmanja © Croatia Tourist Board

Things not to miss

1. Veliki Tabor © Croatia Tourist Board
2. Small bay, Komiza © Croatia Tourist Board
3. Rovinj street © Grahma Pritchard/TRIP
4. Outdoor café © Richard Bickell/CORBIS
5. Scuba diver and anemone © Reinhard Dirscherl/Alamy
6. Neptune fountain, Botanical gardens, Trsteno © Croatia Tourist Board
7. Painting of St Blaise, Dubrovnik Dominican monastery © Croatia Tourist Board
8. White stork © Chris Hellier/CORBIS
9. Farmhouse © Croatia Tourist Board
10. Motovun © Roy Westlake/Travel Ink

11. Men in traditional costume, Zagreb Folk Festival © M. Barlow/TRIP
12. Dugi otok © Croatia Tourist Board
13. St Donat's church, Zadar © K. Gilllham/ Robert Harding
14. Hvar Town and harbour © M. Barlow/TRIP
15. Dubrovnik's walls © Richard Bickel/CORBIS
16. Grah © Croatia Tourist Board
17. Diocletian's palace, Split © M. Wilson/ TRIP
18. Windsurfing © Jonathan Blair/CORBIS
19. Baroque buildings, Varazdin © Jon Bousfield
20. Paklenica © Croatia Tourist Board
21. Women on boat, Komiza, Vis © M. Wilson/ TRIP
22. Trogir cathedral, the west portal © Croatia Tourist Board
23. Church of St Mark, Zagreb © M. Barlow/ TRIP
24. Amphitheatre, Pula © Jon Bousfield
25. Kornati islands © Croatia Tourist Board
26. Truffle omelette © Jon Bousfield
27. Swimming at Skradinski buk © Jon Bousfield
28. Dubrovnik festival crowds © Jonathan Blair/ CORBIS
29. Plitvice Lakes © Docevoc Velimir/TRIP
30. Grilled fish © Croatia Tourist Board

Black and white images

Tram, Josep Jalacica © Phil Robinson/ Travel Ink

Funicular railway © Phil Robinson/ Travel Ink

Rural scene with church, Zagorje © K. Gillham/ Robert Harding

War damage, Vukovar © Jon Bousfield

Church, Vodnjan © TH-Foto-Werbung/TRIP

Window arches, Poreč © Croatia Tourist Board

Opatija © Croatia Tourist Board

Well head, Komiza © Jon Bousfield

Šibenik Cathedral © Croatia Tourist Board

Rector's Palace, Dubrovnik © Croatia Tourist Board

Franciscan church © Jon Bousfield

stay in touch

roughnews

● TRAVEL ● MUSIC ● REFERENCE ● PHRASEBOOKS

Rough Guides travel

Europe
Algarve
Amsterdam
Andalucia
Austria
Barcelona
Belgium
 & Luxembourg
Berlin
Britain
Brittany
 & Normandy
Bruges & Ghent
Brussels
Budapest
Bulgaria
Copenhagen
Corsica
Costa Brava
Crete
Croatia
Cyprus
Czech & Slovak
 Republics
Devon & Cornwall
Dodecanese
 & East Aegean
Dordogne
 & the Lot
Dublin
Edinburgh
England
Europe
First-Time Europe
Florence
France
French Hotels
 & Restaurants
Germany
Greece
Greek Islands
Holland
Hungary
Ibiza
 & Formentera
Iceland
Ionian Islands
Ireland
Italy
Lake District

Languedoc
 & Roussillon
Lisbon
London
London Mini Guide
London
 Restaurants
Madeira
Madrid
Mallorca
Malta & Gozo
Menorca
Moscow
Norway
Paris
Paris Mini Guide
Poland
Portugal
Prague
Provence & the
 Côte d'Azur
Pyrenees
Romania
Rome
Sardinia
Scandinavia
Scotland
Scottish Highlands
 & Islands
Sicily
Spain
St Petersburg
Sweden
Switzerland
Tenerife & La
 Gomera
Turkey
Tuscany & Umbria
Venice
 & The Veneto
Vienna
Wales

Asia

Bali & Lombok
Bangkok
Beijing
Cambodia
China

First-Time Asia
Goa
Hong Kong
 & Macau
India
Indonesia
Japan
Laos
Malaysia,
 Singapore
 & Brunei
Nepal
Singapore
South India
Southeast Asia
Thailand
Thailand Beaches
 & Islands
Tokyo
Vietnam

Australasia

Australia
Gay & Lesbian
 Australia
Melbourne
New Zealand
Sydney

**North
America**

Alaska
Big Island of
 Hawaii
Boston
California
Canada
Florida
Hawaii
Honolulu
Las Vegas
Los Angeles
Maui
Miami & the
 Florida Keys
Montréal
New England
New Orleans
New York City

New York City
 Mini Guide
New York
 Restaurants
Pacific Northwest
Rocky Mountains
San Francisco
San Francisco
 Restaurants
Seattle
Southwest USA
Toronto
USA
Vancouver
Washington DC
Yosemite

**Caribbean
& Latin
America**

Antigua & Barbuda
Argentina
Bahamas
Barbados
Belize
Bolivia
Brazil
Caribbean
Central America
Chile
Costa Rica
Cuba
Dominican
 Republic
Ecuador
Guatemala
Jamaica
Maya World
Mexico
Peru
St Lucia
Trinidad & Tobago

**Africa &
Middle East**

Cape Town
Egypt
Israel & Palestinian
 Territories

Jerusalem
Jordan
Kenya
Morocco
South Africa,
 Lesotho
 & Swaziland
Syria
Tanzania
Tunisia
West Africa
Zanzibar
Zimbabwe

**Dictionary
Phrase-
books**

Czech
Dutch
European
 Languages
French
German
Greek
Hungarian
Italian
Polish
Portuguese
Russian
Spanish
Turkish
Hindi & Urdu
Indonesian
Japanese
Mandarin Chi
Thai
Vietnamese
Mexican Spar
Egyptian Arab
Swahili

Maps
Amsterdam
Dublin
London
Paris
San Francisco
Venice

Rough Guides publishes new books every month

Music

Acoustic Guitar
Blues: 100 Essential CDs
Cello
Clarinet
Classical Music
Classical Music: 100 Essential CDs
Country Music
Country: 100 Essential CDs
Cuban Music
Drum'n'bass
Drums
Electric Guitar & Bass Guitar
Flute
Hip-Hop
House
Irish Music
Jazz
Jazz: 100 Essential CDs
Keyboards & Digital Piano
Latin: 100 Essential CDs
Music USA: a Coast-To-Coast Tour
Opera
Opera: 100 Essential CDs
Piano
Reading Music
Reggae
Reggae: 100 Essential CDs
Rock
Rock: 100 Essential CDs
Saxophone
Soul: 100 Essential CDs
Techno
Trumpet & Trombone
Violin & Viola
World Music: 100 Essential CDs

World Music Vol1
World Music Vol2

Reference

Children's Books, 0–5
Children's Books, 5–11
China Chronicle
Cult Movies
Cult TV
Elvis
England Chronicle
France Chronicle
India Chronicle
The Internet
Internet Radio
James Bond
Liverpool FC
Man Utd
Money Online
Personal Computers
Pregnancy & Birth
Shopping Online
Travel Health
Travel Online
Unexplained Phenomena
Videogaming
Weather
Website Directory
Women Travel

Music CDs

Africa
Afrocuba
Afro-Peru
Ali Hussan Kuban
The Alps
Americana
The Andes
The Appalachians
Arabesque
Asian Underground
Australian Aboriginal Music
Bellydance
Bhangra
Bluegrass

Bollywood
Boogaloo
Brazil
Cajun
Cajun and Zydeco
Calypso and Soca
Cape Verde
Central America
Classic Jazz
Congolese Soukous
Cuba
Cuban Music Story
Cuban Son
Cumbia
Delta Blues
Eastern Europe
English Roots Music
Flamenco
Franco
Gospel
Global Dance
Greece
The Gypsies
Haiti
Hawaii
The Himalayas
Hip Hop
Hungary
India
India and Pakistan
Indian Ocean
Indonesia
Irish Folk
Irish Music
Italy
Jamaica
Japan
Kenya and Tanzania
Klezmer
Louisiana
Lucky Dube
Mali and Guinea
Marrabenta Mozambique
Merengue & Bachata
Mexico
Native American Music
Nigeria and Ghana
North Africa

Nusrat Fateh Ali Khan
Okinawa
Paris Café Music
Portugal
Rai
Reggae
Salsa
Salsa Dance
Samba
Scandinavia
Scottish Folk
Scottish Music
Senegal & The Gambia
Ska
Soul Brothers
South Africa
South African Gospel
South African Jazz
Spain
Sufi Music
Tango
Thailand
Tex-Mex
Wales
West African Music
World Music Vol 1: Africa, Europe and the Middle East
World Music Vol 2: Latin & North America, Caribbean, India, Asia and Pacific
World Roots
Youssou N'Dour & Etoile de Dakar
Zimbabwe

Rough Guides music, reference & CDs

Visit us online
roughguides.com

Information on over 25,000 destinations around the world

- **Read** Rough Guides' trusted travel info
- **Share** journals, photos and travel advice with other readers
- Get exclusive Rough Guide **discounts** and travel **deals**
- Earn membership points every time you contribute to the Rough Guide **community** and get **free** books, flights and trips
- Browse thousands of CD reviews and artists in our **music** are

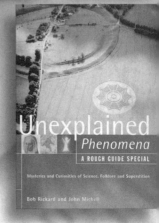

The ideas expressed in this code were developed by and for independent travellers.

Learn About The Country You're Visiting

Start enjoying your travels before you leave by tapping into as ma sources of information as you can.

The Cost Of Your Holiday

Think about where your money goes - be fair and realistic about h cheaply you travel. Try and put money into local peoples' hands; drink local beer or fruit juice rather than imported brands and stay locally owned accommodation. Haggle with humour and not aggressively. Pay what something is worth to you and remember h wealthy you are compared to local people.

Embrace The Local Culture

Open your mind to new cultures and traditions - it will transform y experience. Think carefully about what's appropriate in terms of y clothes and the way you behave. You'll earn respect and be more readily welcomed by local people. Respect local laws and attitude towards drugs and alcohol that vary in different countries and communities. Think about the impact you could have on them.

Exploring The World – The Travellers' Coc

Being sensitive to these ideas means getting more out of your travels - and giving more back to the people you meet and the places you visit.

Minimise Your Environmental Impact

Think about what happens to your rubbish - take biodegradable products and a water filter bottle. Be sensitive to limited resource like water, fuel and electricity. Help preserve local wildlife and habitats by respecting local rules and regulations, such as stickin footpaths and not standing on coral.

Don't Rely On Guidebooks

Use your guidebook as a starting point, not the only source of information. Talk to local people, then discover your own adventu

Be Discreet With Photography

Don't treat people as part of the landscape, they may not want the picture taken. Ask first and respect their wishes.

We work with people the world over to promote tourism that benefits their communities, but we can only carry on our work v the support of people like you. For membership details or to fine out how to make your travels work for local people and the environment, visit our website.

www.tourismconcern.org.uk